CW00741469

STRE...

Edinburgh

and East Central Scotland

First published in 1995 by

Philip's, a division of
Octopus Publishing Group Ltd
2-4 Heron Quays, London E14 4JP

Third colour edition 2006
First impression 2006
EDICA

ISBN-10 0-540-08839-0 (pocket)
ISBN-13 978-0-540-08839-3 (pocket)

© Philip's 2006

This product includes mapping data licensed from
Ordnance Survey® with the permission of the
Controller of Her Majesty's Stationery Office.
© Crown copyright 2006. All rights reserved.
Licence number 100011710.

Printed by Toppan, China

Contents

II **Administrative and Postcode boundaries**

III **Key to map symbols**

IV **Key to map pages**

VI **Route planning**

1 **Street maps** at 2⅔ inches to 1 mile

218 **Street maps** at 1⅓ inches to 1 mile

228 **Street map of Edinburgh city centre** at 5⅓ inches to 1 mile

230 **Index** of towns and villages

231 **Index** of streets, hospitals, industrial estates, railway stations, schools, shopping centres, universities and places of interest

Digital Data

The exceptionally high-quality mapping found in this atlas is available as digital data in TIFF format, which is easily convertible to other bitmapped (raster) image formats.

The index is also available in digital form as a standard database table. It contains all the details found in the printed index together with the National Grid reference for the map square in which each entry is named.

For further information and to discuss your requirements, please contact Philip's on 020 7644 6932 or james.mann@philips-maps.co.uk

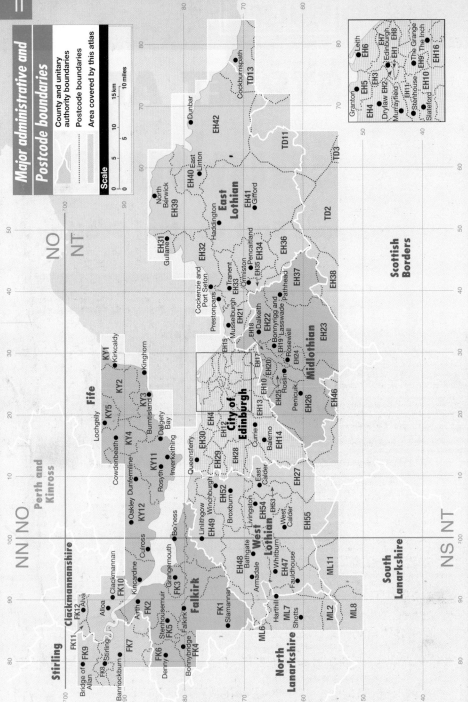

Major administrative and Postcode boundaries

County and unitary authority boundaries
Postcode boundaries
Area covered by this atlas

Scale

0   5   10   15km
0   5   10 miles

Stirling

Clackmannanshire

Perth and Kinross

Fife

Falkirk

West Lothian

City of Edinburgh

East Lothian

Midlothian

Scottish Borders

North Lanarkshire

South Lanarkshire

NN | NO
NO
NT
NS | NT

FK11
FK12
Bridge of Allan
Alva
FK9
Stirling
FK8
Bannockburn
FK7
Denny
FK6
FK5
Stenhousemuir
Airth
FK2
Kincardine
Clackmannan
FK10
Alloa
FK3
Grangemouth
Falkirk
FK4
Bonnybridge
FK1
Slamannan
Culross
Bo'ness
Linlithgow
EH49
Winchburgh
Broxburn
EH52
EH48
Bathgate
Armadale
EH47
Whitburn
Faulhouse
Harthill
Shotts
ML7
ML6
ML2
ML8
ML11
EH55
West Calder
EH54
Livingston
EH53
East Calder
EH27
Currie
Balerno
EH14
EH28
EH29
EH30
EH4
EH11
EH12
EH13
EH10
EH25
Roslin
Penicuik
EH26
EH46
EH24
Roslin
Rosewell
EH19 Lasswade
EH20
EH23
Bonnyrigg and Lasswade
EH22
EH17
EH18
EH16
Dalkeith
EH21
EH15
Musselburgh
Prestonpans
Cockenzie and Port Seton
EH32
EH33
Tranent
Ormiston
EH35 EH34
Pencaitland
EH36
EH37
Pathhead
EH38
TD2
TD3
TD11
EH42
Dunbar
Cockburnspath
TD13
EH40
East Linton
EH41
Gifford
Haddington
EH31
Gullane
North Berwick
EH39

Queensferry
Inverkeithing
Rosyth
KY11
Dunfermline
KY12
Oakley
Cowdenbeath
KY4
Lochgelly
KY5
KY2
KY3
Burntisland
Dalgety Bay
Kinghorn
KY1
Kirkcaldy

Inset (Edinburgh):
Granton
Leith
EH6
EH5
EH7
EH8
EH4
EH3
Drylaw EH2
Murrayfield
Edinburgh
EH1
EH11
EH9
Stenhouse
EH10
Slateford
EH16
Slateford
The Grange
The Inch

Motorway with junction number		◆	**Ambulance station**
Primary route – dual/single carriageway		◆	**Coastguard station**
A road – dual/single carriageway		◆	**Fire station**
B road – dual/single carriageway		◆	**Police station**
Minor road – dual/single carriageway		✚	**Accident and Emergency entrance to hospital**
Other minor road – dual/single carriageway		Ⓗ	**Hospital**
Road under construction		✛	**Place of worship**
Tunnel, covered road		🄸	**Information Centre** (open all year)
Rural track, private road or narrow road in urban area		🛒	**Shopping Centre**
Gate or obstruction to traffic (restrictions may not apply at all times or to all vehicles)		**P** **P&R**	**Parking, Park and Ride**
Path, bridleway, byway open to all traffic, road used as a public path		**PO**	**Post Office**
		⋏ 🚐	**Camping site, caravan site**
Pedestrianised area		► ✕	**Golf course, picnic site**
DY7 **Postcode boundaries**		Prim Sch	**Important buildings, schools, colleges, universities and hospitals**
County and unitary authority boundaries			**Built up area**
Railway, tunnel, railway under construction			**Woods**
Tramway, tramway under construction		River Medway	**Water name**
Miniature railway			**River, weir, stream**
Railway station Walsall			**Canal, lock, tunnel**
Private railway station			**Water**
Metro station South Shields			**Tidal water**
Tram stop, tram stop under construction		Church	**Non-Roman antiquity**
Bus, coach station		ROMAN FORT	**Roman antiquity**

Acad	**Academy**	Inst	**Institute**	Recn Gd	**Recreation Ground**			
Allot Gdns	**Allotments**	Ct	**Law Court**					
Cemy	**Cemetery**	L Ctr	**Leisure Centre**	Resr	**Reservoir**			
C Ctr	**Civic Centre**	LC	**Level Crossing**	Ret Pk	**Retail Park**			
CH	**Club House**	Liby	**Library**	Sch	**School**			
Coll	**College**	Mkt	**Market**	Sh Ctr	**Shopping Centre**			
Crem	**Crematorium**	Meml	**Memorial**	TH	**Town Hall/House**			
Ent	**Enterprise**	Mon	**Monument**	Trad Est	**Trading Estate**			
Ex H	**Exhibition Hall**	Mus	**Museum**	Univ	**University**			
Ind Est	**Industrial Estate**	Obsy	**Observatory**	W Twr	**Water Tower**			
IRB Sta	**Inshore Rescue Boat Station**	Pal	**Royal Palace**	Wks	**Works**			
	Boat Station	PH	**Public House**	YH	**Youth Hostel**			

◄ **87** **Adjoining page indicators and overlap bands**
The colour of the arrow and the band indicates the scale of the adjoining or overlapping page (see scales below)

▼ **237**

■ The small numbers around the edges of the maps identify the 1 kilometre National Grid lines
■ The dark grey border on the inside edge of some pages indicates that the mapping does not continue onto the adjacent page

	Railway or bus station building
	Place of interest
	Parkland

The scale of the maps on the pages numbered in blue is 4.2 cm to 1 km • 2⅔ inches to 1 mile • 1: 23810	0 ¼ ½ ¾ 1 mile 0 250m 500m 750m 1 kilometre
The scale of the maps on pages numbered in green is 2.1 cm to 1 km • 1⅓ inches to 1 mile • 1: 47620	0 ¼ ½ ¾ 1 mile 0 250m 500m 750m 1 kilometre
The scale of the maps on pages numbered in red is 8.4 cm to 1 km • 5⅓ inches to 1 mile • 1: 11900	0 220 yards 440 yards 660 yards ½ mile 0 125m 250m 375m ½ kilometre

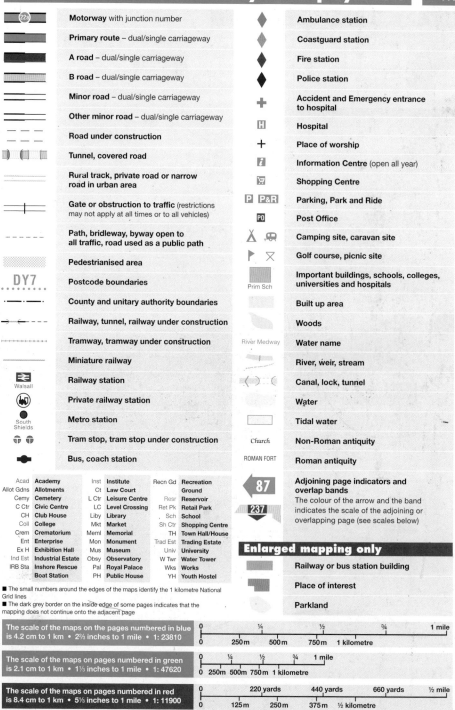

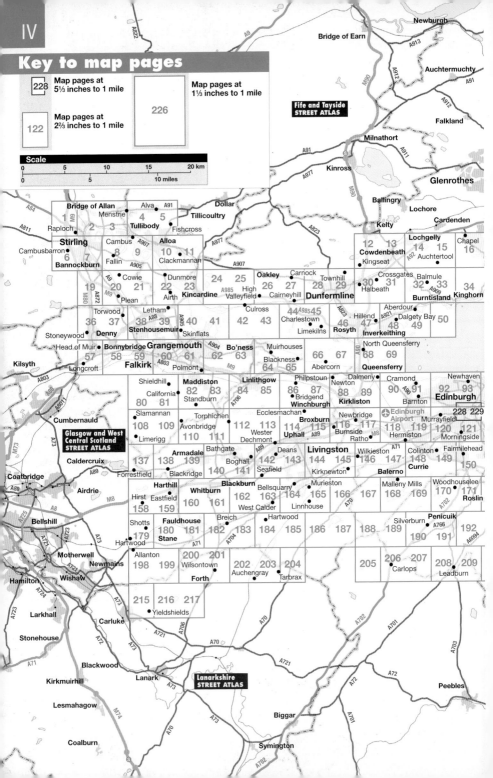

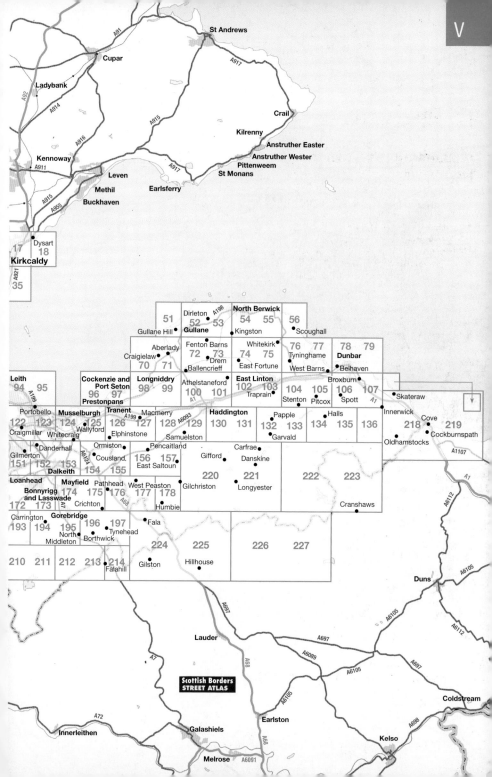

St Andrews
Cupar
Ladybank
Kennoway
Leven
Methil
Buckhaven
Earlsferry
St Monans
Pittenweem
Anstruther Wester
Anstruther Easter
Kilrenny
Crail

Dysart
17 18
Kirkcaldy
35

51
Dirleton
52 53
Gullane
Gullane Hill
Aberlady
Craigielaw
70 71
North Berwick
54 55 56
Kingston
Scoughall
Fenton Barns
72 73
Drem
Ballencrieff
East Fortune
Whitekirk
74 75
Tyninghame
76 77
West Barns
Dunbar
78 79
Belhaven

Leith
94 95
Portobello
Cockenzie and
Port Seton
96 97
Prestonpans
Longniddry
98 99
Athelstaneford
100 101
Traprain
East Linton
102 103
Stenton
104 105
Pitcox
Broxburn
106 107
Spott
Skateraw

Craigmillar
122 123
Whitecraig
Musselburgh
124 25
Wallyford
Tranent
126 127
Elphinstone
Macmerry
128 129
Samuelston
Haddington
130 131
Papple
132 133
Garvald
Halls
134 135 136
Innerwick
218 219
Cove
Cockburnspath
Oldhamstocks

Gilmerton
151 152 153
Dalkeith
Danderhall
Ormiston
154 155
Cousland
East Saltoun
156 157
Pencaitland
Gifford
Carfrae
Danskine
220 221
Longyester
222 223
Cranshaws

Loanhead
Bonnyrigg
and Lasswade
172 173
Mayfield
174 175
Crichton
Pathead
176 177 178
West Peaston
Humbie
Gilchriston

Carrington
193 194
Gorebridge
195 196 197
North
Middleton
Borthwick
Tynehead
Fala
224 225 226 227
Duns

210 211 212 213 214
Falahill
Gilston
Hillhouse

Scottish Borders
STREET ATLAS

Lauder
A697
A6089
A6105
A6697

Innerleithen
Galashiels
Earlston
Kelso
Coldstream

Melrose

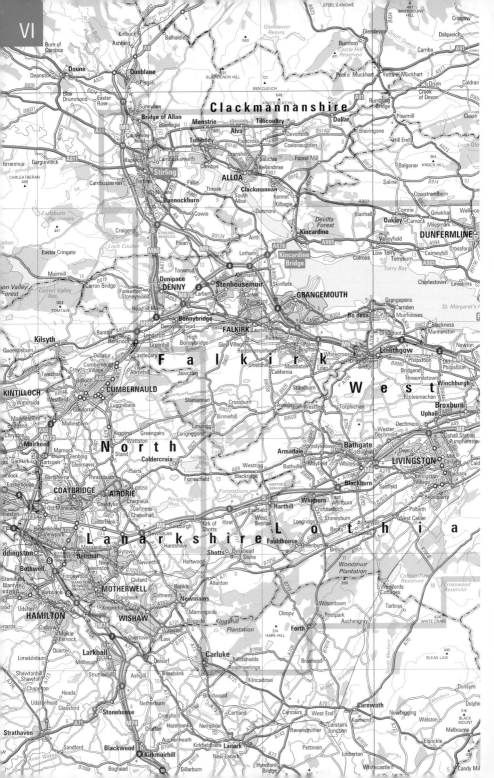

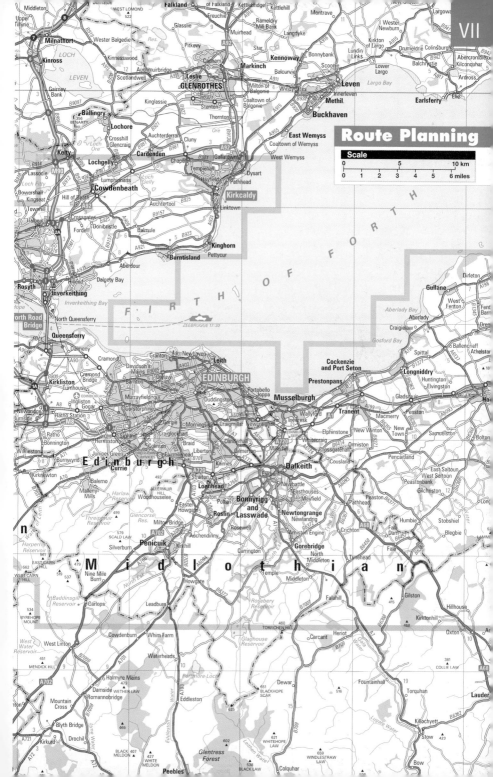

Route Planning

Scale

| 0 | | | | 5 | | | 10 km |
| 0 | 1 | 2 | 3 | 4 | 5 | 6 miles | |

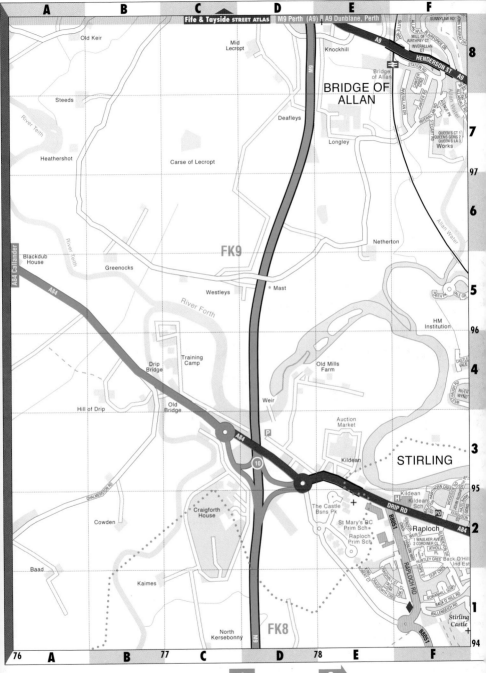

Fife & Tayside STREET ATLAS M9 Perth (A9) ⬆ A9 Dunblane, Perth

Old Keir

Mid Lecropt

Knockhill

Sunnylaw Rd

Mill of Airthrey Ct
Inverallan Ct

A9

HENDERSON ST

Station Rd

8

Steeds

Bridge of Allan

BRIDGE OF
ALLAN

Deafleys

Longley

Works

Queen's Ct 1
Queen's Gdns 2
Queen's La 3

7

Heathershot

Carse of Lecropt

97

6

Blackdub House

A84 Callander

A84

River Teith

River Teith

Greenocks

Westleys

Mast

FK9

Netherton

Allan Water

Perth Pk · Vale Dr

5

River Forth

HM Institution

96

Castle Vale

Drip Bridge

Training Camp

Weir

Old Mills Farm

River Wynd

4

Hill of Drip

Old Bridge

P

A84

10

Auction Market

Kildean

STIRLING

3

Chalmerston Rd

Craigforth House

The Castle Bsns Pk

St Mary's RC Prim Sch

Raploch Prim Sch

Kildean

Kildean Sch

DRIP RD

H

PO

Raploch

A84

95

Cowden

Huntley Cres

Weir St

1 Waulker Ave
2 Cordiner Cl
Atholl Pl

Back O'Hill
Ind Est

2

Baad

Kaimes

Raploch Rd

B8051

Gowanhill Gdns

Back O'Hill Rd

Ballengeich Rd

Stirling Castle

B8051

1

North Kersebonny

FK8

M9

94

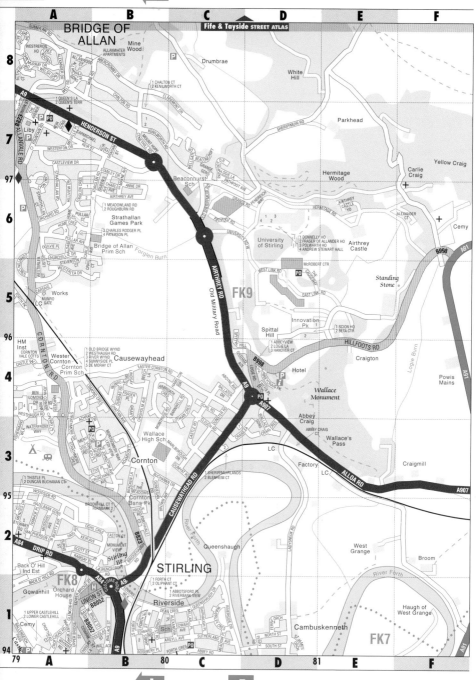

Fife & Tayside STREET ATLAS

Fife & Tayside STREET ATLAS

Dumyat

Castle Law

Ewe Lairs

The Kips

Craig Gullies

The Blair

Dumyat Farm

OCHIL RD

Hotel

Hillfoots Rd

Cotkerse

Menstrie

CASTLE RD 1
CASTLE CT 2
MENSTRIE PL 3
MILLBROOK PL 4
CRAIGOMUS CRES 5

Bsns Ctr

Menstrie Castle

FK11

Blairlogie

Logie Villa

Blair Mains

FK9

Gogar Mains

Gogar House

Girnal

Menstrie Burn

Powis Burn

Powis House

Manor

West Gogar

East Gogar

River Devon

Manor Powis

Alloa Rd

A907

Blackgrange Rd8t

Manornuek

Manor Powis Cotts

Manor Steps

LC

Blackgrange Crossing

LC

FK10

River Forth

Bonded Warehouses

FK7

Lower Taylorton

Poultry Farm

Garvel

Midtown

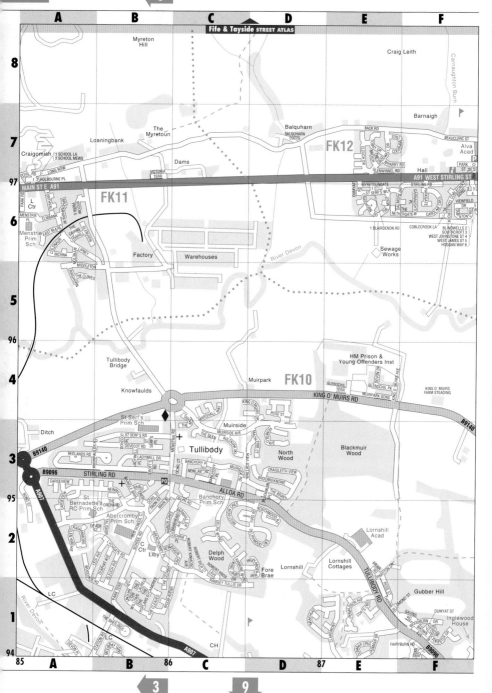

Fife & Tayside STREET ATLAS

FK12

FK11

FK10

Myreton Hill

Craig Leith

Barnaigh

The Myretoun

Balquharn

BALQUHARN COTTS

BACK RD

BEAUCLERC ST

Alva Acad

Loaningbank

Craigomish
1 SCHOOL LA
2 SCHOOL MEWS
1 HOLBOURNE PL

LONG ROW

Dams

VICTORIA TERR

Hall

PARK ST

MAIN ST E A91

A91 WEST STIRLING ST

STIRLING RD

L Ctr

MYRETOUNGATE

VIEWFIELD DR

Menstrie Prim Sch

THE NETHERGATE

1 BLAIRDENON RD

COBLECROOK LA

1 BLINDWELLS 2
SOUTHCROFT 3
WEST JOHNSTONE ST 4
WEST JAMES ST 5
HOGAN WAY 6

Factory

Warehouses

River Devon

Sewage Works

HM Prison & Young Offenders Inst

Tullibody Bridge

Muirpark

GLENOCHIL TERR

GLENOCHIL PK

MUIRPARK GDNS

KING O' MUIRS FARM STEADING

Knowfaulds

KING O' MUIRS RD

B9140

St Serf's Prim Sch

Muirside

MARSHALL WAY

ROSE AVE

MUIRSIDE AVE

THE GLEN

Ditch

ST SERF'S RD

Tullibody

North Wood

Blackmuir Wood

B9140

REDLANDS RD

DOVECOT RD

LADYWELL DR

BANCHORY TERR

CRAIGLEITH VIEW

BROOMIEKNOWE

STIRLING RD

NEWLANDS

THE BRAES

PO

St Bernadette's RC Prim Sch

THE ORCHARD

Banchory Prim Sch

ALLOA RD

CARSEVIEW

Abercromby Prim Sch

Lornshill Acad

CARSEVIEW

Ctr

Liby

Delph Wood

Lornshill Cottages

Lornshill

TULLIBODY RD

Gubber Hill

A907

LC

Fore Brae

DUMYAT ST

Inglewood House

River Devon

LC

THE SHIELINGS

CH

A907

FAIRYBURN RD

B9096

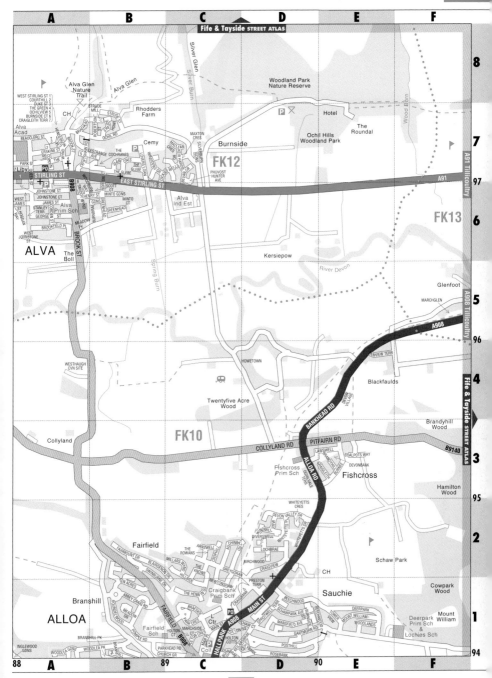

Fife & Tayside STREET ATLAS

8

7

97

6

5

96

4

3

95

2

1

94

A91 Tillicoultry

A908 Tillicoultry

Fife & Tayside STREET ATLAS

Woodland Park
Nature Reserve

Alva Glen
Nature
Trail

Alva Glen

Rhodders
Farm

Hotel

The
Roundal

Ochil Hills
Woodland Park

Burnside

FK12

FK13

WEST STIRLING ST 1
COURTHILL 2
DUKE ST 3
THE GREEN 4
OCHILVIEW 5
BURNSIDE CT 6
CRAIGLEITH TERR 7

Alva
Acad

Cemy

CH

STRUDE
MILL

MAXTON
CRES

PHUVOST
HUNTER
AVE

STIRLING ST

EAST STIRLING ST

A91

PARK ST
Libry
PO

JOHNSTONE CT
JOHNSTONE CT

WEST
JAMES
ST

STANLEY
TERR
GEORGE
ST

JAMES ST

Alva
Prim Sch

MEADOW
PK

BROOKFIELD PL

WEST
JOHNSTONE

MINTO GDNS

MINTO
CT

GREENHEAD

Alva
Ind Est

ALVA

The
Boll

BROOK ST

B908

Spring Burn

Kersiepow

River Devon

Glenfoot

MARCHGLEN

A908

HOWETOWN

WESTHAUGH
CVN SITE

BAVIEW TERR

Blackfaulds

FK10

Twentyfive Acre
Wood

BANKHEAD RD

Brandyhill
Wood

Collyland

COLLYLAND RD

PITFAIRN RD

B9140

LAWSWELL

COALPOTS WAY

DEVONBANK

Fishcross
Prim Sch

ALLOA RD

Fishcross

Hamilton
Wood

WHITEYETTS
CRES

DEVON VALLEY DR

RIVERSWELL

Fairfield

The
ROWANS

ARASWELL

The
KNOWE

LOCHBRAE

BIRCHWOOD

CRAIGVIEW

Schaw
Park

Cowpark
Wood

TOURMOUNT DR

BLAIRLOGIE DR

MILLARS WYND

SKIRSLING LN

NEWTONSHAW

PRESTON
TERR

CH

Sauchie

Mount
William

Deerpark
Prim Sch
&
Lochies Sch

DEERPARK

MOUNT
WILLIAM

WOODLANDS

BEECHWOOD

Branshill

TEN ACRES

MEADOW
GR

ABBEY CRAIG RD

JOHNSRIE RD

SPRINGSIDE

Craigbank
Prim Sch

FAIRFIELD

HOLTON

MARCHSIDE

HALLPARK

B908

MAIN ST

A908

SCHAWPARK AVE

MANSFIELD AVE

GARTMORN RD

ALLOA

BRANSHILL PK

INGLEWOOD
GDNS

WOODLEA GDNS

WOODLEA PK

Fairfield
Sch

Ctr

PARKHEAD RD

CHURCH RD

POSTHILL

ROSEBANK

88   **89**   **90**   **94**

A   B   C   D   E   F

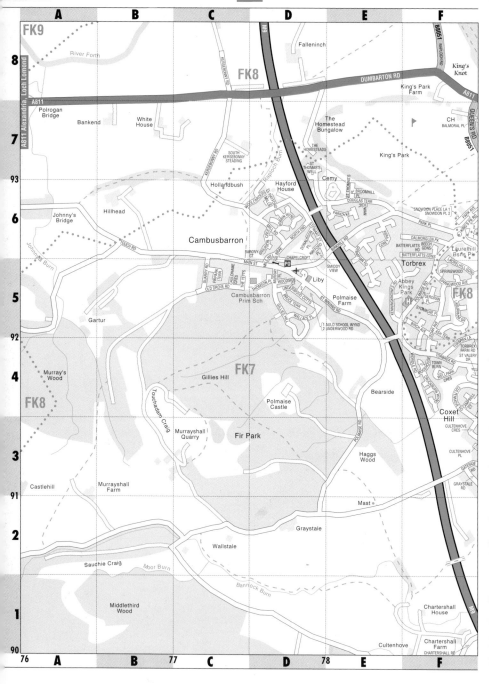

FK9

8

River Forth

Falleninch

DUMBARTON RD

King's Knot

King's Park Farm

FK8

93

A811 Alexandria, Loch Lomond

A811

Polrogan Bridge

Bankend

White House

Hollandbush

South Kersebonny Steading

Hayford House

The Homestead Bungalow

THE HOMESTEADS

ST THOMAS'S WELL

Cemy

King's Park

CH BALMORAL PL 1

QUEEN'S RD

B8051

7

KERSEBONNY RD

KERSEBONNY RD

WOOLENDERS GT

Raploch Burn

BROOMHILL PL

DOUGLAS TERR

SNOWDON PLACE LA 1

PINE AVE

FINK AVE

6

Johnny's Bridge

Hillhead

Cambusbarron

MILL END

NORTH END

DONNARULLIE GT

SCHOOL GT

PARKVIEW

BIRKHILL RD

CAREY

PARK PL

SNOWDON PL 2

GLEN TERR'S RD

DALMORGLEN PK

BEECH HO GDNS

BATTERFLATTS GDNS

Laurelhill Bsns Pk

LAURELHILL GDNS

Torbrex

SPRINGWOOD

SPRINGWOOD AVE

FK8

TOUCH RD

Johnny's Burn

BARONY CT

CHAPELCROFT

Liby

SMIDDY VIEW

Abbey Kings Park

H

SYCAMORE PL

DEROBAN

5

QUARRY RD

PIRNHALL TERR

GILLANDER PL

GILLANS BRAE

MAIN ST

THE GLEBE

THOMSON PL

MURRAY PL

WOODSIDE

UNDERWOOD COTTS

ST NINIANS RD

Cambusbarron Prim Sch

BRUCE TERR

WALLACE PL

GILLIES RD

Polmaise Farm

1 AULD SCHOOL WYND

2 UNDERWOOD RD

KENNINGKNOWES RD

BIRCH AVE

OAK AVE

ASH TERR

TORBREX FARM RD

ST VALERY DR

TOWN BURN

WELLPARK CRES

92

Gartur

OLD DROVE RD

FK7

Gillies Hill

Polmaise Castle

Bearside

WHITTET RD

GATESIDE LA

Coxet Hill

CULTENHOVE CRES

4

Murray's Wood

Touchadam Craig

Murrayshall Quarry

Fir Park

Haggs Wood

POLMAISE RD

CULTENHOVE PL

FK8

3

Castlehill

Murrayshall Farm

GRAYSTALE RD

91

Mast

Graystale

2

Wallstale

Sauchie Craig

Moor Burn

Bannock Burn

Chartershall House

1

Middlethird Wood

Cultenhove

Chartershall Farm

CHARTERSHALL RD

A9

90

76 A   B   77   C   D   78   E   F

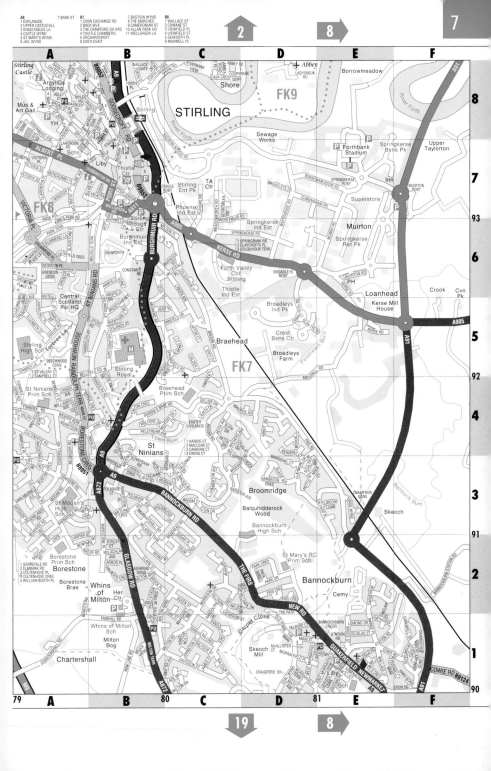

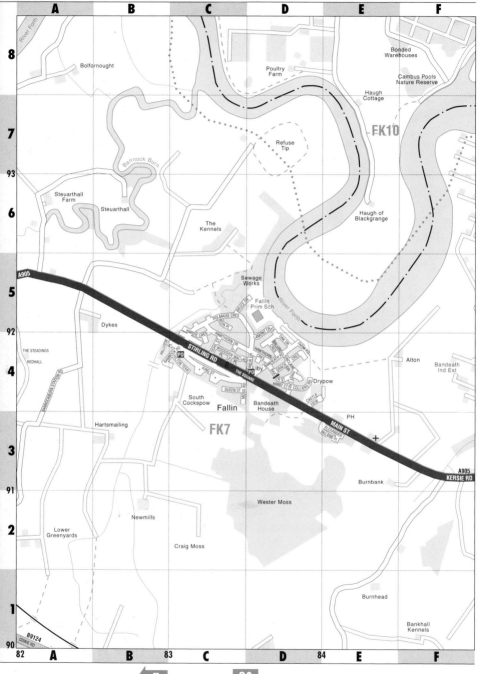

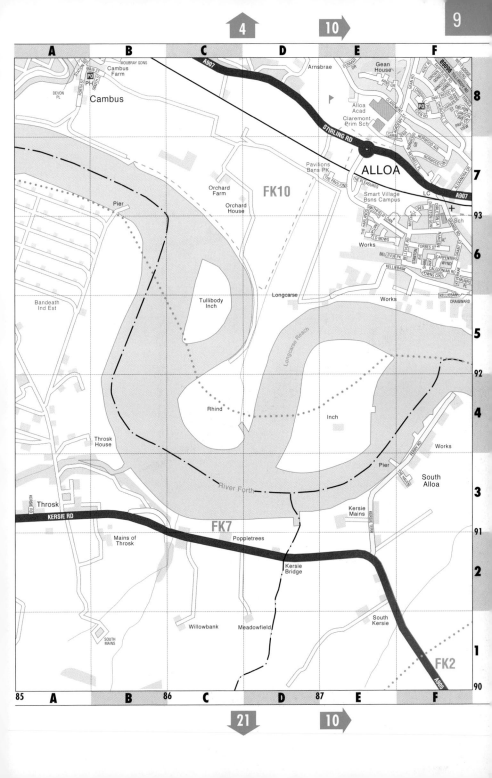

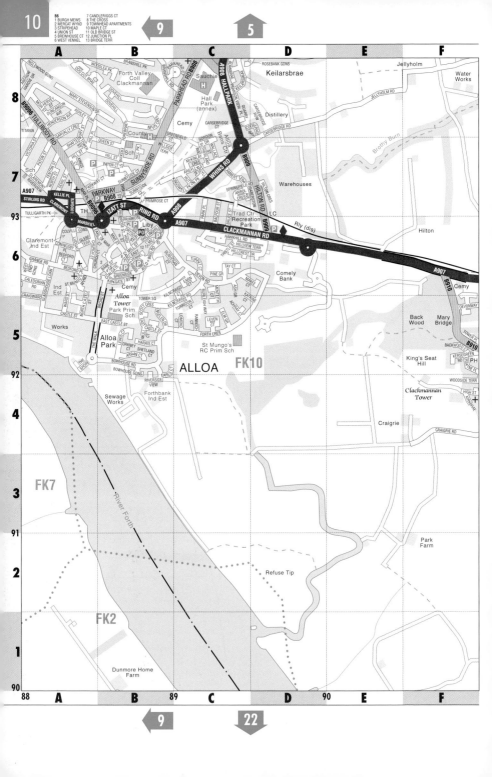

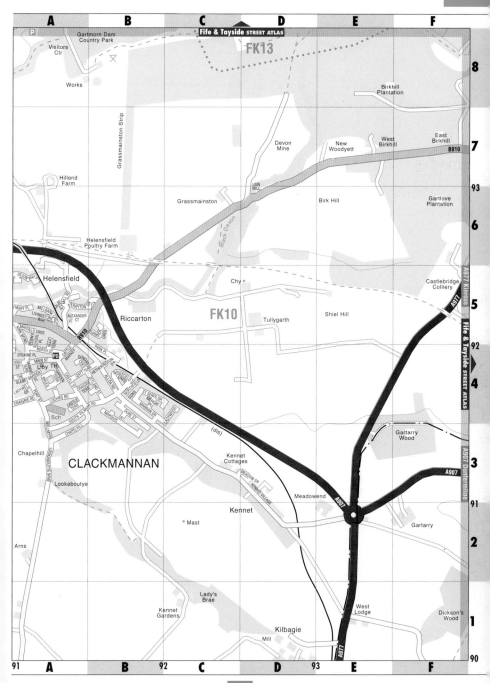

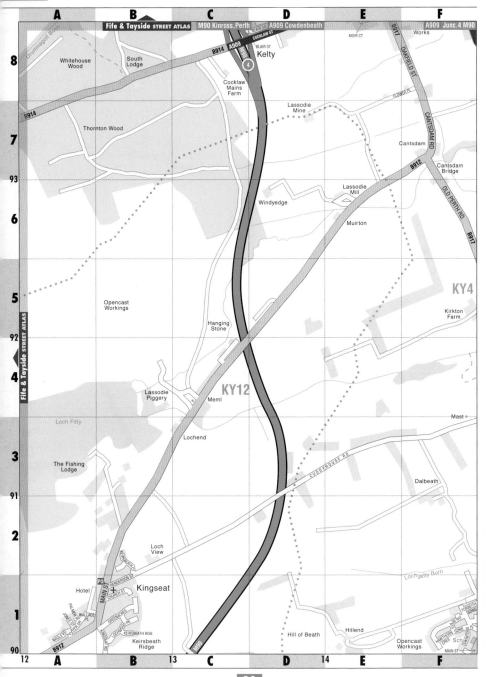

Whitehouse Wood

South Lodge

Cocklaw Mains Farm

Kelty

MOIR CT

Works

BLAIR ST

COCKLAW ST

Lassodie Mine

Thornton Wood

Cantsdam

Cantsdam Bridge

Lassodie Mill

Windyedge

Muirton

Opencast Workings

KY4

Kirkton Farm

Hanging Stone

KY12

Lassodie Piggery

Meml

Loch Fitty

Lochend

Mast

The Fishing Lodge

CUDYHOUSE RD

Dalbeath

Loch View

Lochgelly Burn

Hotel

Kingseat

Keirsbeath Ridge

Hill of Beath

Hillend

Opencast Workings

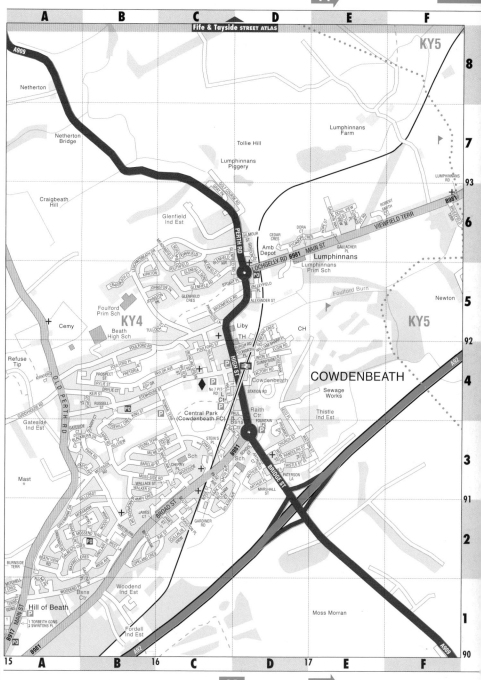

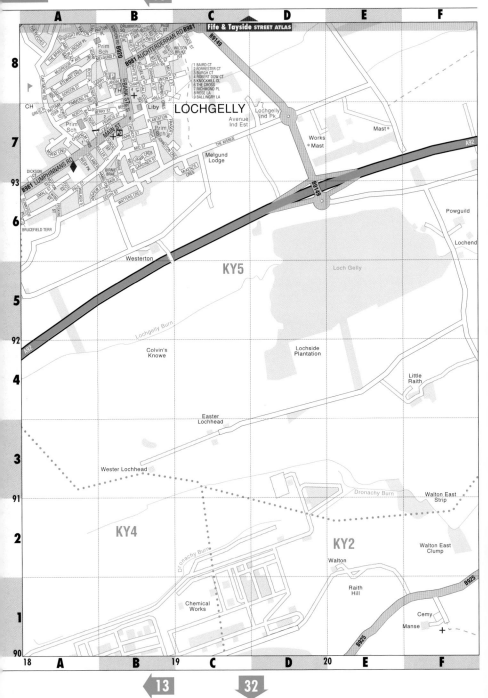

Fife & Tayside STREET ATLAS

1 BAIRD CT
2 FORRESTER CT
3 BURGH CT
4 ROBERT DOW CT
5 KNOCKHILL CL
6 THE CROSS
7 RICHMOND PL
8 ROSE LA
9 BALLINGRY LA

LOCHGELLY

Lochgelly Ind Pk

Avenue Ind Est

Mast

Works
Mast

Melgund Lodge

Powguild

Lochend

Bruecfield Terr

Westerton

KY5

Loch Gelly

Colvin's Knowe

Lochside Plantation

Little Raith

Easter Lochhead

Wester Lochhead

Dronachy Burn

Walton East Strip

KY4

KY2

Walton East Clump

Walton

Raith Hill

Chemical Works

Cemy

Manse

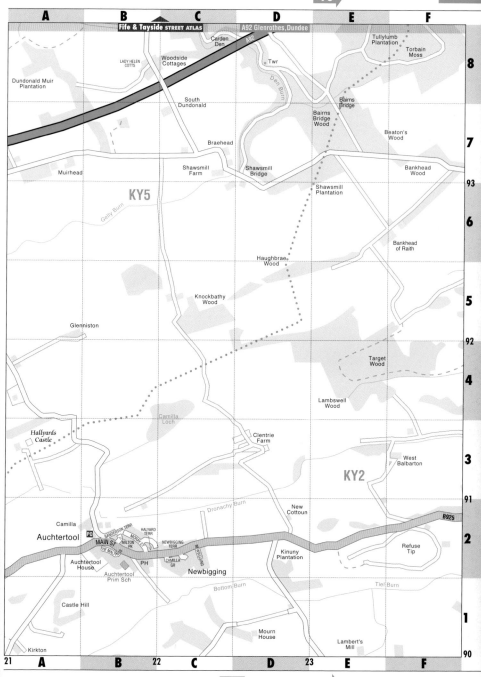

A B C D E F

Fife & Tayside STREET ATLAS   A92 Glenrothes, Dundee

8

Dundonald Muir
Plantation

LADY HELEN
COTTS

Woodside
Cottages

Carden
Den

A92

Twr

Tullylumb
Plantation

Torbain
Moss

South
Dundonald

Den Burn

Bairns
Bridge

Bairns
Bridge
Wood

Beaton's
Wood

7

Braehead

Muirhead

Shawsmill
Farm

Shawsmill
Bridge

Bankhead
Wood

KY5

93

Gelly Burn

Shawsmill
Plantation

6

Bankhead
of Raith

Haughbrae
Wood

Glenniston

Knockbathy
Wood

5

92

Target
Wood

4

Lambswell
Wood

Hallyards
Castle

Camilla
Loch

Clentrie
Farm

West
Balbarton

3

KY2

91

Dronachy Burn

New
Cottoun

B925

Camilla

Auchtertool

PO

SANDERSON TERR

HALYARD
TERR

McKAY
PK

NEWBIGGING
TERR

NEWBIGGING

Kinuny
Plantation

Refuse
Tip

2

MAIN ST

THE MALT'GS

MILTON
PK

Auchtertool
House

PH

CAMILLA
GR

Newbigging

Auchtertool
Prim Sch

Bottom Burn

Tiel Burn

1

Castle Hill

Mourn
House

Kirkton

Lambert's
Mill

90

21 A B 22 C D 23 E F

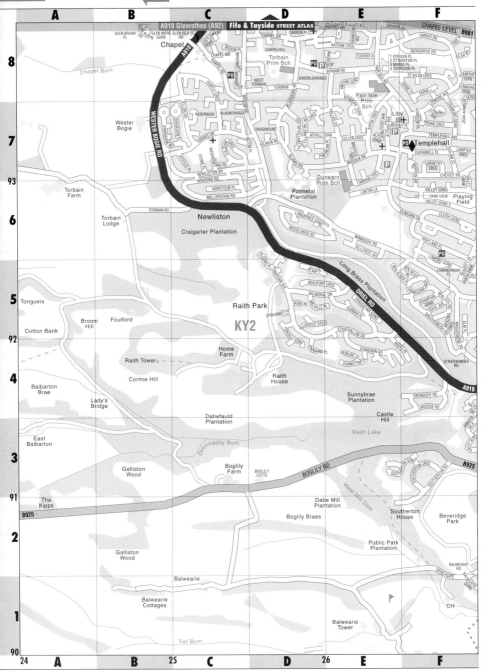

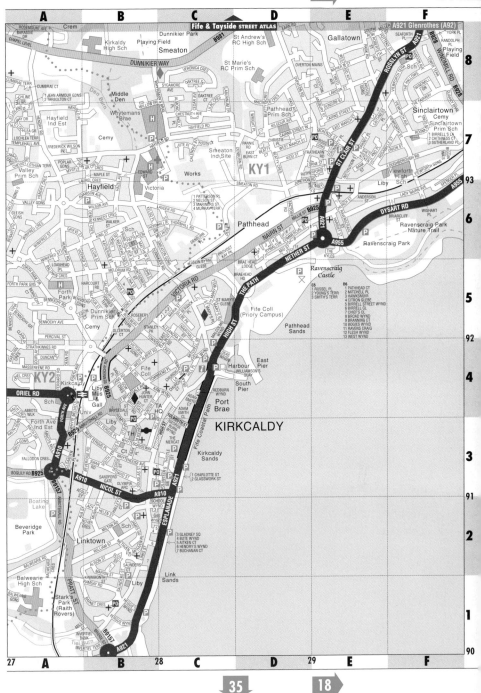

A955 Leven

B929

A955

Frances
Ind Pk

KY1

BORELAND
RD

Randolph
Ind Est

Blair
Point

NORMAND RD

FRASER

STEWART ST

Sch

Fife Coastal Path

Dysart
1 LOUGHBOROUGH RD
2 WEST PORT
3 ST SARF'S PL
4 WEST QUALITY ST
5 EAST QUALITY ST
6 ORCHARD PL
7 ORCHARD LA
8 FITZROY ST
9 McDOUALL STUART PL
10 VICTORIA ST

B929

TH

PO

DYSART

A955

Mus.

Panhall

Ravenscraig
Park

RECTORY LA

PAN HA

SHORE RD

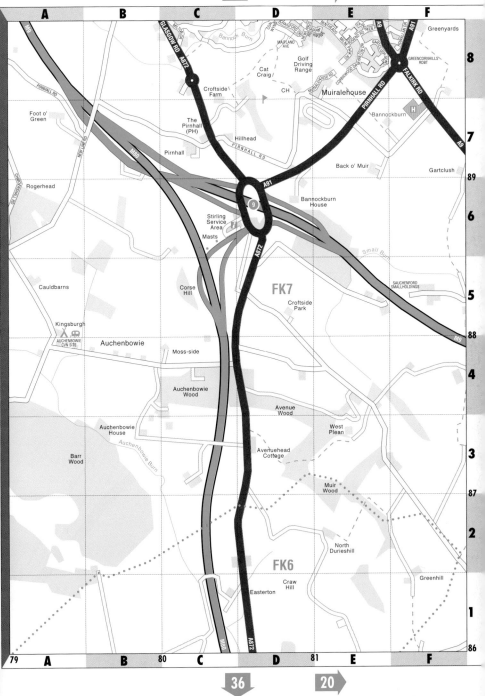

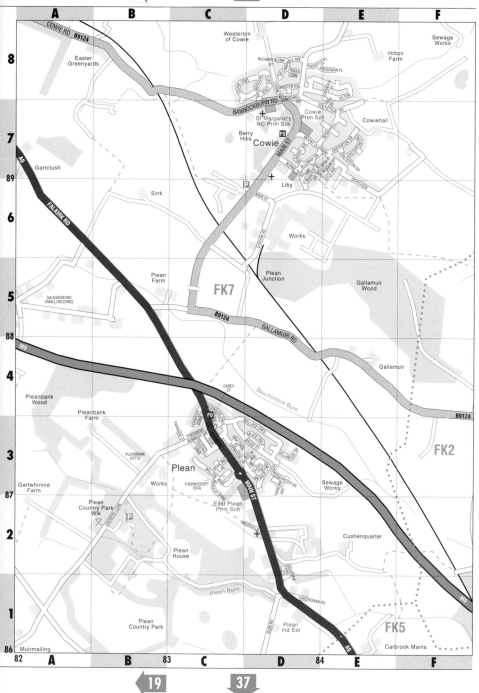

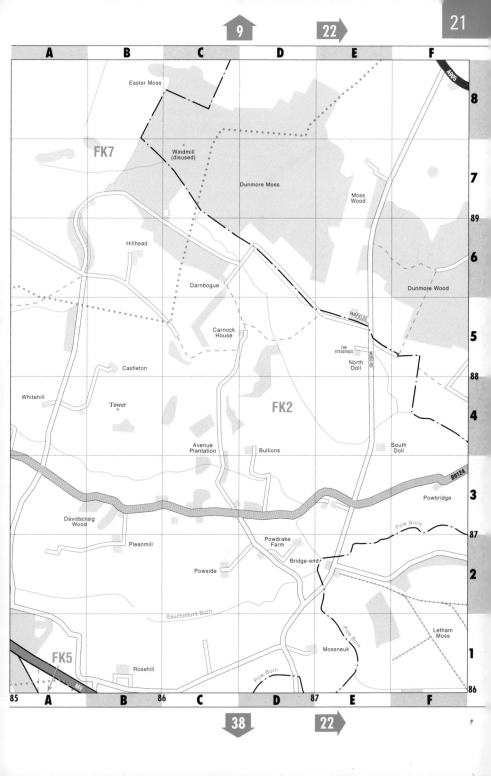

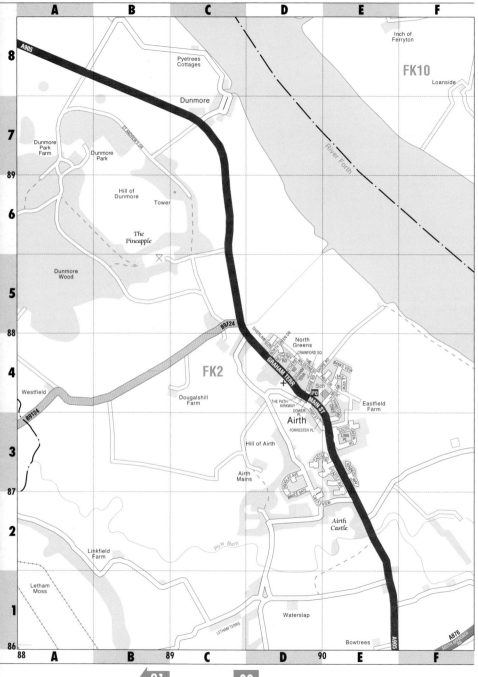

A | B | C | D | E | F

8

A905

Inch of Ferryton

FK10

Loanside

Pyetrees Cottages

7

ST ANDREWS DR

Dunmore

89

Dunmore Park Farm

Dunmore Park

River Forth

Hill of Dunmore

Tower

6

The Pineapple

Dunmore Wood

5

B9124

88

North Greens

FK2

SHIERLAW GDNS

NORTH GREEN DR

CRAWFORD SQ

4

Westfield

B9124

Dougalshill Farm

GRAHAM TERR

THE WYND

ELPHINSTONE ST

SHORE RD

BANKS VIEW

Sch

GREEN RD

PO

Eastfield Farm

THE PATH

KIRKWAY

DOWER PL

SOUTH GREEN RD

Airth

FORRESTER PL

SOUTH LINN PL

3

Hill of Airth

MAIN ST

DOUGLAS AVE

CASTLE

KINGSPARK RD

87

Airth Mains

BRUCE GATE

CASTLE AVE

CASTLE VIEW

2

Airth Castle

Pow Burn

Linkfield Farm

1

Letham Moss

LETHAM TERRS

Waterslap

A905

A876

SOUTH ALLOA RD

86

Bowtrees

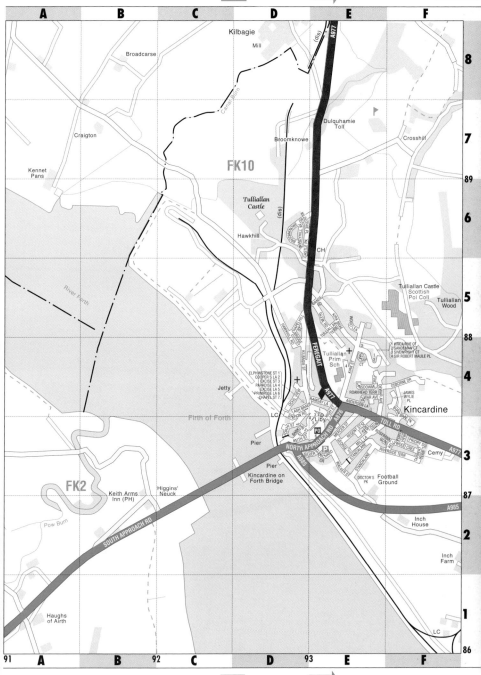

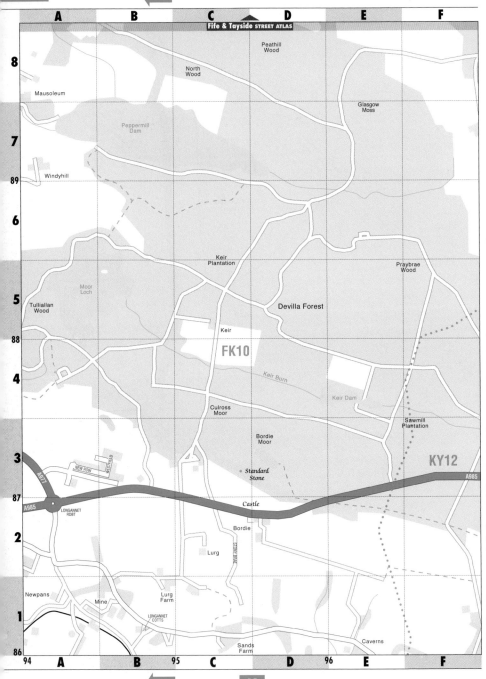

Fife & Tayside STREET ATLAS

Peathill
Wood

North
Wood

Glasgow
Moss

Mausoleum

Peppermill
Dam

Windyhill

Keir
Plantation

Praybrae
Wood

Moor
Loch

Tulliallan
Wood

Devilla Forest

Keir

FK10

Keir Burn

Keir Dam

Culross
Moor

Bordie
Moor

Sawmill
Plantation

KY12

NEW ROW

WESTFIELD

A977

Standard
Stone

A985

A985

LONGANNET
RDBT

Castle

Bordie

Lurg

STONEYBRAE

Newpans

Mine

Lurg
Farm

LONGANNET
COTTS

Caverns

Sands
Farm

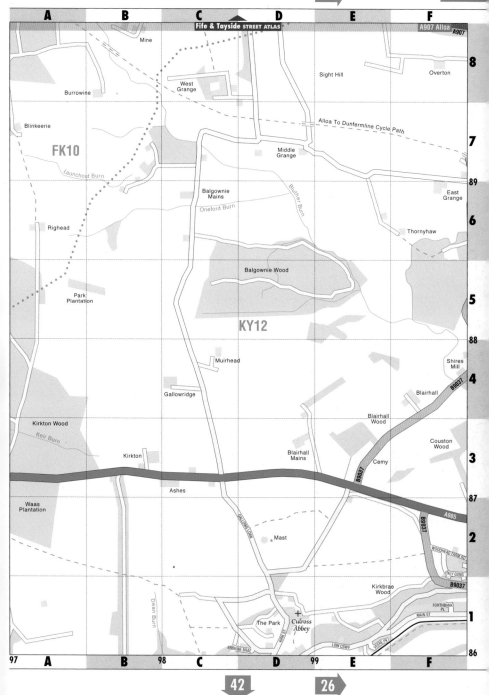

Fife & Tayside STREET ATLAS

A907 Alloa
A907

A B C D E F

8

Mine

West Grange

Sight Hill

Overton

Burrowine

Blinkeerie

7

FK10

Alloa To Dunfermline Cycle Path

Middle Grange

89

Launchcot Burn

Balgownie Mains

Oneford Burn

Bluther Burn

East Grange

6

Righead

Thornyhaw

Balgownie Wood

5

Park Plantation

KY12

88

Muirhead

Shires Mill

4

Gallowridge

B9037

Blairhall

Kirkton Wood

Blairhall Wood

Couston Wood

Keir Burn

Kirkton

Blairhall Mains

3

Ashes

Cemy

B9037

87

Waas Plantation

A985

B9037

2

Mast

WOODHEAD FARM RD

DALY GDNS

B9037

Kirkbrae Wood

FORTHBANK PL

MAIN ST

Dean Burn

The Park

Culross Abbey

1

ERSKINE BRAE

KIRK ST

LOW CSWY

86

97 A B 98 C D 99 E F

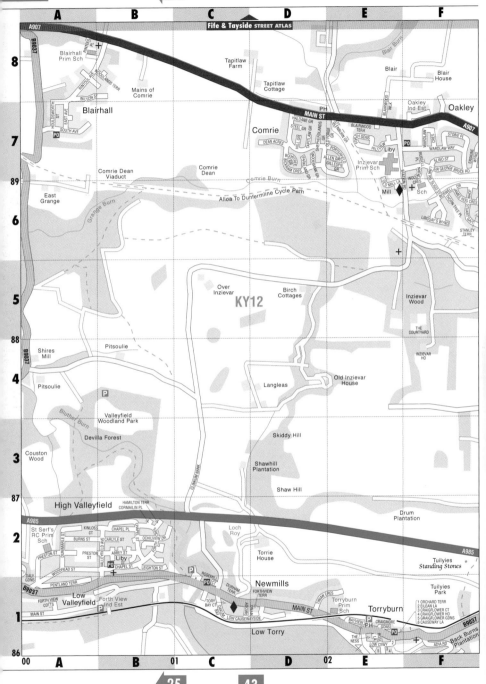

Fife & Tayside STREET ATLAS

A907

B9037

8

Blairhall

Blairhall Prim Sch

Mains of Comrie

WOODLANDS TERR

RINTOUL

BINTOUL

WILSON ST

HOLLSWORTH

EAST AVE

SOUTH AVE

P

7

Tapitlaw Farm

Tapitlaw Cottage

Comrie

DEAN ACRES

HALDANE GR

STEEL GR

BOUD RIGG

BLOSSOM GR

PITLAW GR

RANKIN GR

WOODHEAD GR

PONTEFRET GR

SHEPHERDLANDS GR

ELIZABETH GR

CLUB RIGG

ALLEN GR

GILLESPIE GR

ELIZABETH GR

MAIN ST

PH

BLACKWOOD

WALKY

BLAIRWOOD TERR

HILLVIEW

ROW GDNS

STOBIE PL

SLIGO ST

WARDLAW WAY

RUSSELL PL

SIR GEORGE BRUCE RD

ROSWELL DR

UNION TREE PL

STUART ST

Blair

Blair House

Oakley

Oakley Ind Est

PO

Liby

Inzievar Prim Sch

Mill

Sch

89

Comrie Dean Viaduct

Comrie Dean

Comrie Burn

Alloa To Dunfermline Cycle Path

East Grange

Grange Burn

LINDSAY'S WYND

STANLEY TERR

6

5

Over Inzievar

Birch Cottages

KY12

Inzievar Wood

THE COURTYARD

INZIEVAR HO

88

Shires Mill

Pitsoulie

B9037

4

Pitsoulie

P

Valleyfield Woodland Park

Devilla Forest

Bluther Burn

Langleas

Old Inzievar House

3

Couston Wood

CLINKUM MARK

Skiddy Hill

Shawhill Plantation

Shaw Hill

Drum Plantation

87

High Valleyfield

HAMILTON TERR

CORMAILIN PL

A985

2

St Serf's RC Prim Sch

KINLOSS CT

CHAPEL PL

BURNS ST

CARLYLE ST

CHAPEL PL

OCHILVIEW DR

ABBEY ST

Liby

PO

CHAPEL ST

LEIGHTON ST

DUNVARLIE ST

VALLEYFIELD AVE

PRESTON ST

WOODHEAD ST

PRESTON ST

DALY GDNS

PENTLAND TERR

Loch Roy

Torrie House

ROSEGATE

PO

DURHAM TERR

FORTHVIEW TERR

TORY BAY CT

DALCOW

LOW CAUSEWAYSIDE

TINGAL CRES

MAIN ST

Newmills

Torryburn Prim Sch

Tuilyies Standing Stones

Tuilyies Park

A985

1 ORCHARD TERR
2 EILEAN LA
3 CRAIGFLOWER CT
4 CRAIGFLOWER HO
5 GRAIGFLOWER GDNS
6 CAUSEWAY LA

B9037

1

Low Valleyfield

FORTH VIEW COTTS

MAIN ST

Forth View Ind Est

P

Torryburn

BAYVIEW

PH

CRAIGMORE GDNS

PO

THE NESS

LOW CSWY

ADVA RD

Back Burns Plantation

Low Torry

86

00

A

B

01

C

D

02

E

F

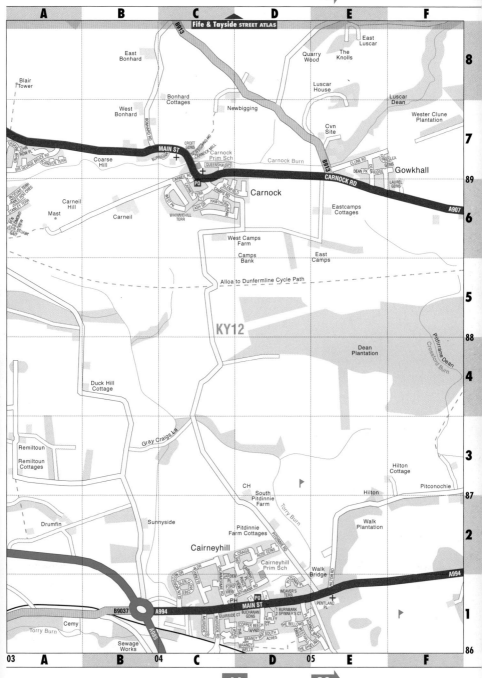

Fife & Tayside STREET ATLAS

8

East Luscar

East Bonhard

Quarry Wood

The Knolls

Blair Tower

Luscar House

Bonhard Cottages

Newbigging

Luscar Dean

Wester Clune Plantation

7

West Bonhard

MAIN ST

CROFT GDNS

Coarse Hill

Carnock Prim Sch

Carnock Burn

CLUNE RD

DEAN PK

Gowkhall

QUEENSHAUGH

89

CARNOCK RD

Carnock

LAUREL GDNS

A907

Carneil Hill

Mast

Carneil

WHINNIEHILL TERR

Eastcamps Cottages

6

West Camps Farm

Camps Bank

East Camps

Alloa to Dunfermline Cycle Path

5

KY12

88

Dean Plantation

Pittirrane Dean

Crossford Burn

4

Duck Hill Cottage

Gray Craigs La

Remiltoun

Remiltoun Cottages

Hilton Cottage

3

Pitconochie

CH

South Pitdinnie Farm

Hilton

87

Drumfin

Sunnyside

Pitdinnie Farm Cottages

Torry Burn

Walk Plantation

2

Cairneyhill

Cairneyhill Prim Sch

Walk Bridge

HILTON RD

A994

MAIN ST

Torry Burn

B9037

A994

Cemy

PH

PO

Weaver's Terr

PENTLAND PL

1

Torry Burn

Sewage Works

1 BURNBANK
2 SPINNER'S CT

COPPER BEECH

THE WILLOWS

SOUTH LOCHES

BRANDY WELLS

86

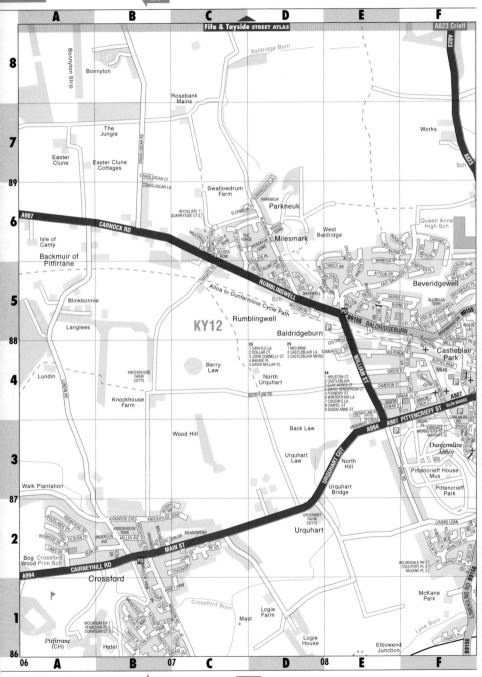

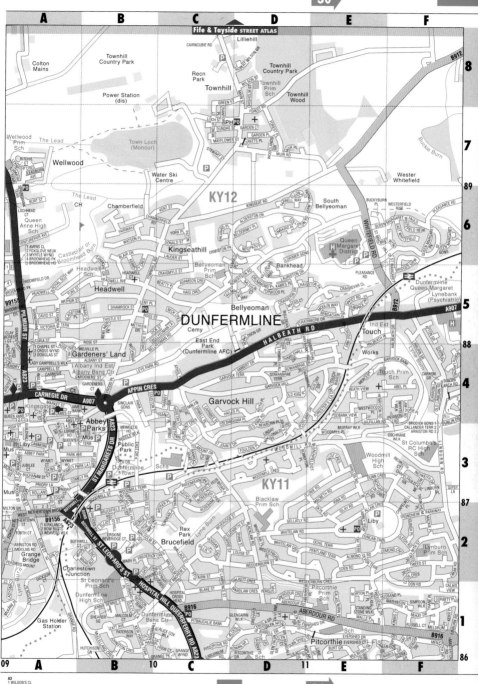

Fife & Tayside STREET ATLAS

A3
1 WILSON'S CL
2 MUSIC HALL LA
3 MAYGATE
4 COMMERCIAL SCHOOL LA

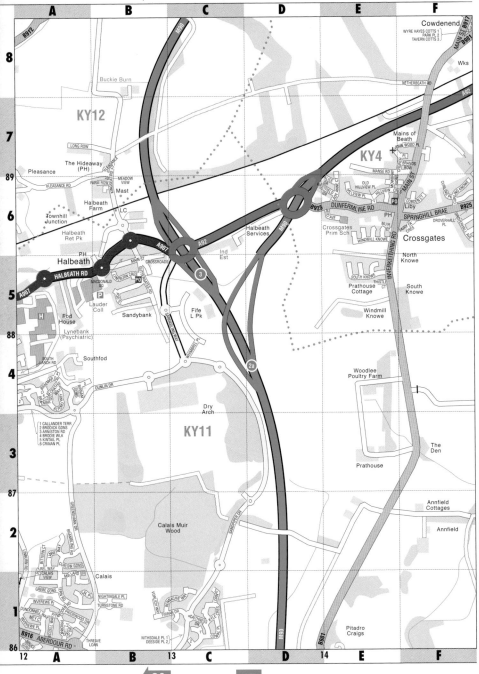

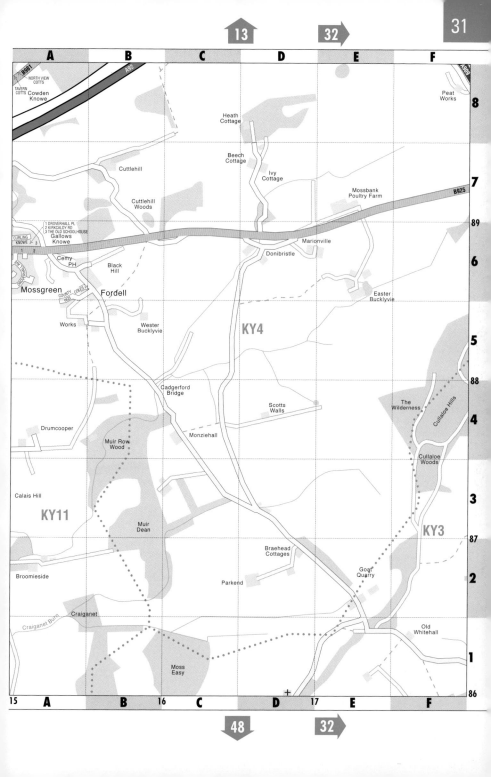

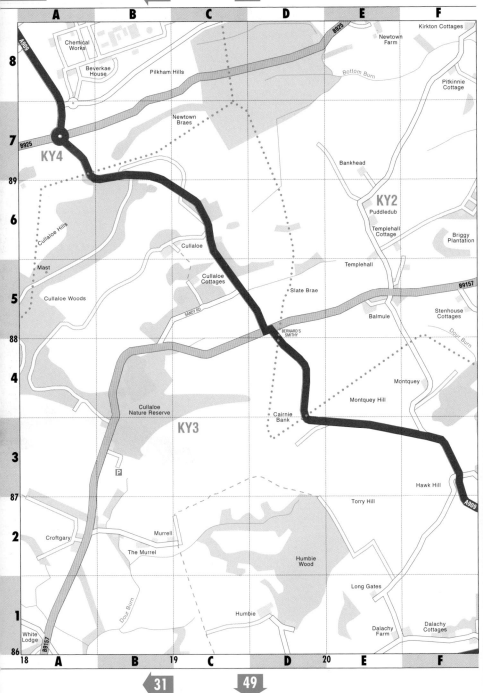

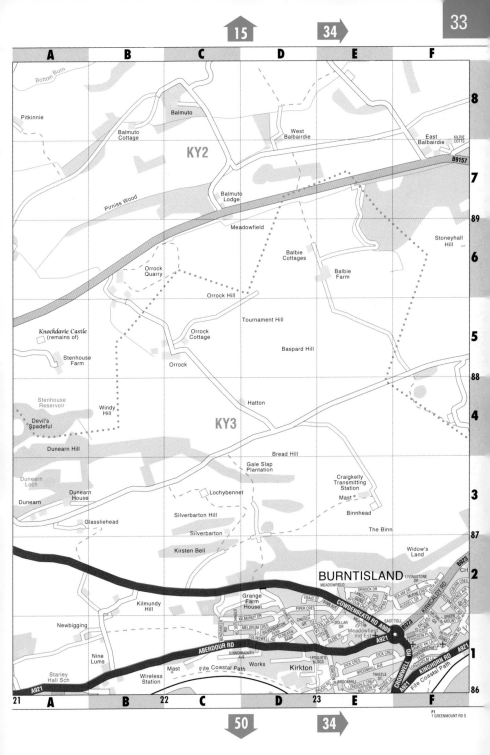

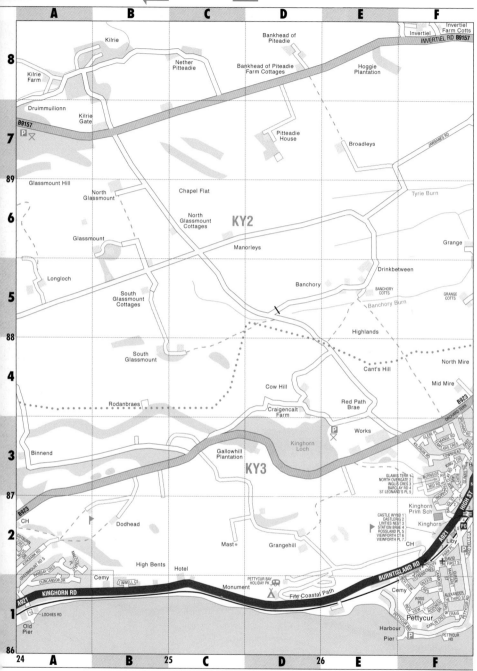

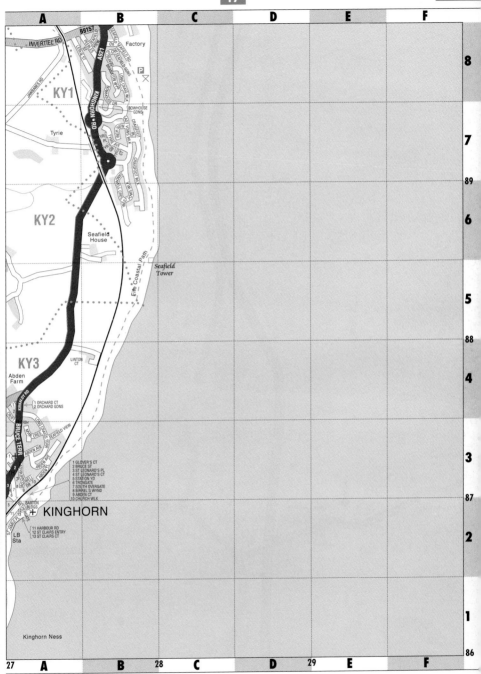

KINGHORN

Kinghorn Ness

1 GLOVER'S CT
2 BRUCE ST
3 ST LEONARD'S PL
4 ST LEONARD'S CT
5 STATION YD
6 TRONGATE
7 SOUTH OVERGATE
8 BIRREL S WYND
9 ABDEN CT
10 CHURCH WLK
11 HARBOUR RD
12 ST CLAIRS ENTRY
13 ST CLAIRS CT

1 ORCHARD CT
2 ORCHARD GDNS

KY1
KY2
KY3

Tyrie
Seafield House
Seafield Tower
Abden Farm
LINTON CT
BRUCE TERR
LB Sta
BARTON BLDGS

Factory
INVERTIEL RD
B9157
A921
KINGHORN RD
Fife Coastal Path

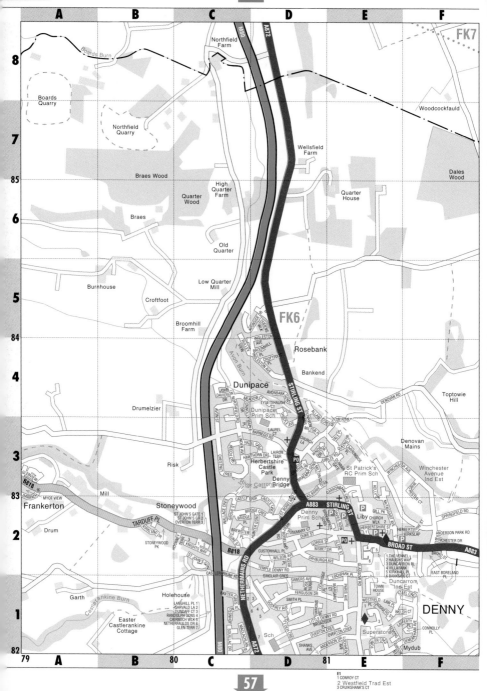

E1
1 CONROY CT
2 Westfield Trad Est
3 CRUIKSHANK'S CT

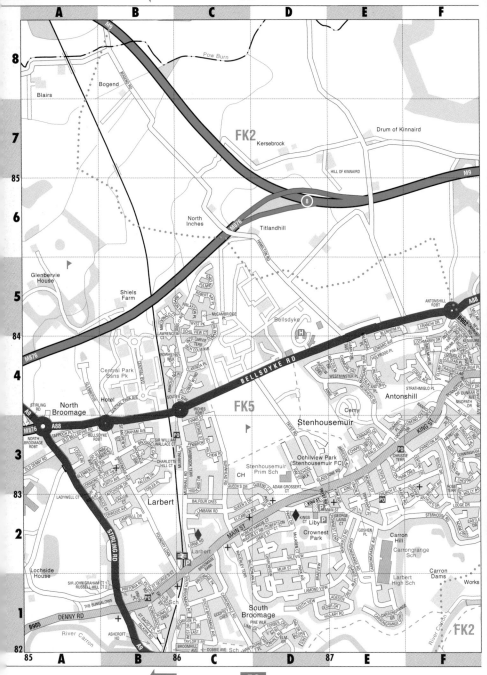

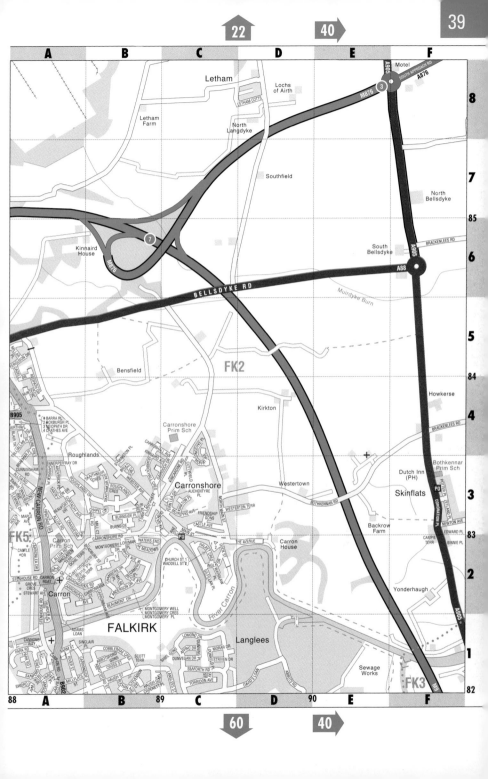

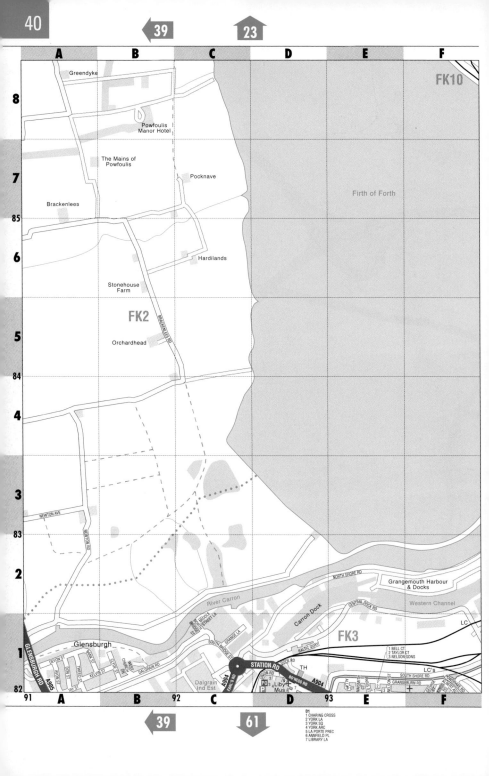

A   **B**   **C**   **D**   **E**   **F**

FK10

8

Greendyke

Powfoulis
Manor Hotel

The Mains of
Powfoulis

7

Pocknave

Firth of Forth

Brackenlees

85

6

Hardilands

Stonehouse
Farm

FK2

5

Orchardhead

84

4

3

NEWTON AVE

83

NEWTON RD

2

NORTH SHORE RD

Grangemouth Harbour
& Docks

River Carron

Carron Dock

Western Channel

CENTRAL DOCK RD

FK3

LC

1

Glensburgh

GLENSBURGH RD

A905

DEVON ST

DON ST

TWEED ST

TAY ST

KELVIN ST

CLYDE DR

MOSS CHURCH DR

DALGRAIN RD

SOUTH BRIDGE ST

GRANGE LA

A904

ANN'S RD

STATION RD

BO'NESS RD

TH

A904

1 BELL CT
2 TAYLOR CT
3 NELSON/GDNS

LC's

SOUTH SHORE RD

GRANGEBURN RD

82

Dalgrain
Ind Est

PO
P

Liby
Mus

91   **A**   **B**   **92**   **C**   **D**   **93**   **E**   **F**

D1
1 CHARING CROSS
2 YORK LA
3 YORK SQ
4 YORK ARC
5 LA PORTE PREC
6 ANNFIELD PL
7 LIBRARY LA

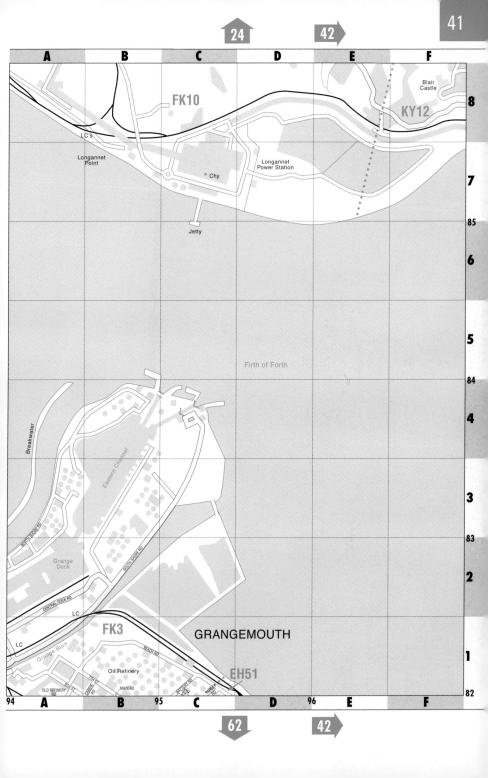

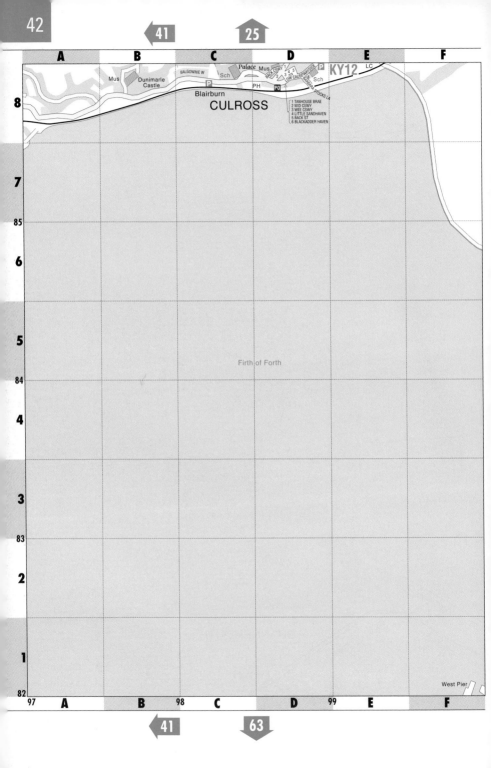

41
25

A **B** **C** **D** **E** **F**

Mus
Dunimarle
Castle
BALGOWNIE W
Sch
Palace Mus
P
Sch
P KY12 LG
8
Blairburn
PH
PO
CULROSS
1 TANHOUSE BRAE
2 MID CSWY
3 WEE CSWY
4 LITTLE SANDHAVEN
5 BACK ST
6 BLACKADDER HAVEN

7

85

6

5

Firth of Forth

84

4

3

83

2

1

82
West Pier

97 **A** **B** 98 **C** **D** 99 **E** **F**

41
63

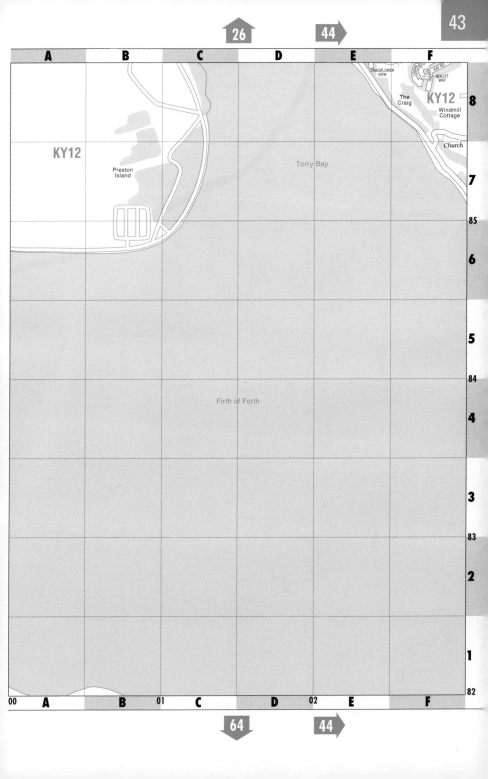

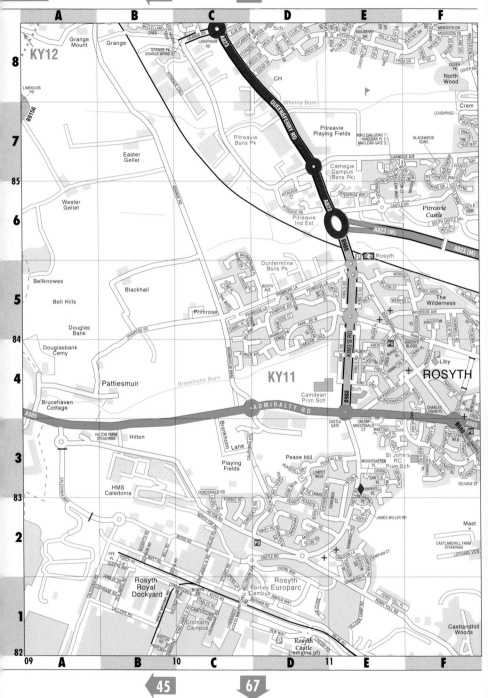

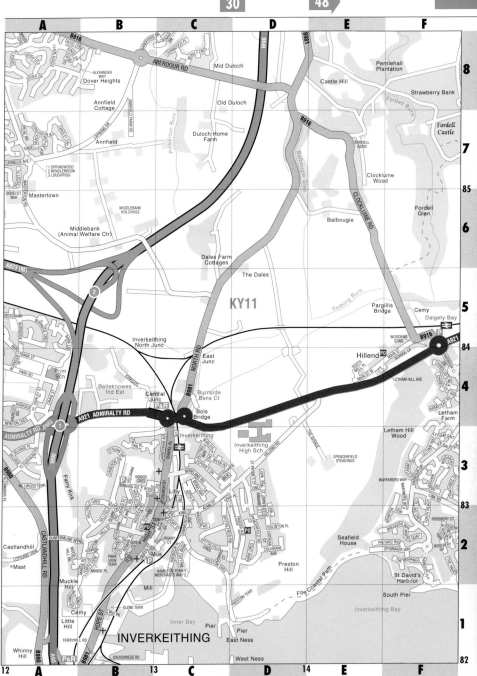

INVERKEITHING

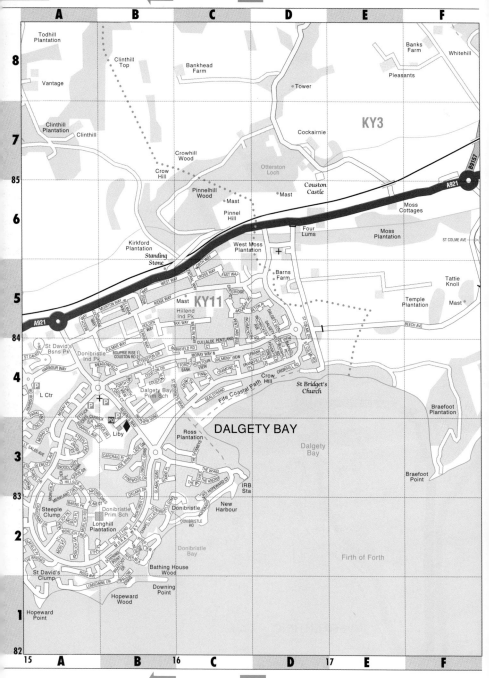

DALGETY BAY

KY3

KY11

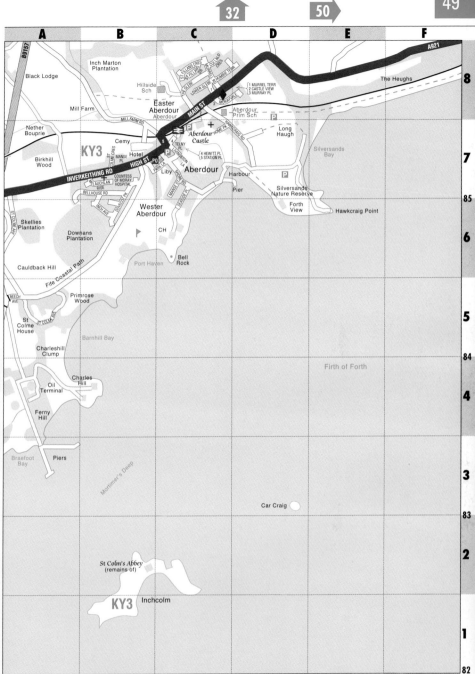

B9157
Black Lodge
Inch Marton Plantation
Hillside Sch
Mill Farm
Easter Aberdour
MILL FARM RD
MAIN ST
Nether Bouprie
Cemy
KY3
Hotel
HIGH ST
Birkhill Wood
INVERKEITHING RD
COUNTESS OF MORAY HOSPITAL
BELLHOUSE RD
ST CLAIR CRES
MANSE PL
ST AUCHLAN RISE
INGLIS AVE
Aberdour Castle
TELNY
LIVINGSTONE
Liby
PRIN LA
PO
Aberdour
MANSE ST
SEASIDE LA
The Heughs
A921
1 MURREL TERR
2 CASTLE VIEW
3 MURRAY PL
SHUMBLE TERR
ST LLANS CRES
GLEBE
FILLANS
CULLALO DRES
LOWER GLEBE
Aberdour Prim Sch
4 HEWITT PL
5 STATION PL
Long Haugh
Silversands Bay
Harbour
Pier
Silversands Nature Reserve
Forth View
Hawkcraig Point

Skellies Plantation
Downans Plantation
Cauldback Hill
Fife Coastal Path
Primrose Wood
BEECH AVE
St Colme House
JT COLME AVE
Charleshill Clump
Charles Hill
Oil Terminal
Ferny Hill
Braefoot Bay
Piers
Wester Aberdour
CH
Port Haven
Bell Rock
Barnhill Bay
Mortimer's Deep
Firth of Forth
Car Craig
St Colm's Abbey (remains of)
KY3
Inchcolm

8
7
85
6
5
84
4
3
83
2
1
82

A   B   C   D   E   F
18   19   20

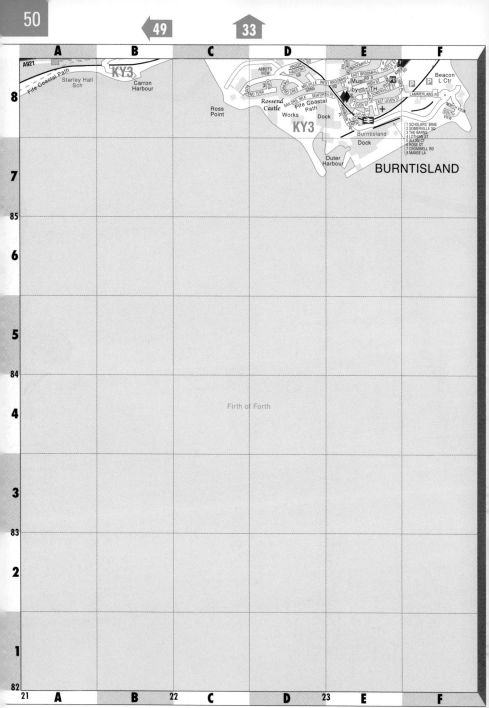

BURNTISLAND

Firth of Forth

Gullane Bay

Gullane Bents

Gullane Point

Maggie's Loop

The Old Man

Jophies Neuk

Gullane Hill

SANDY LA

HILL RD

WARREN HILL

NISBET RD

MARINE TERR

BLEACHFIELD

WHIM RD

WEST LINKS RD

EH31

Gullane Links

A198

51

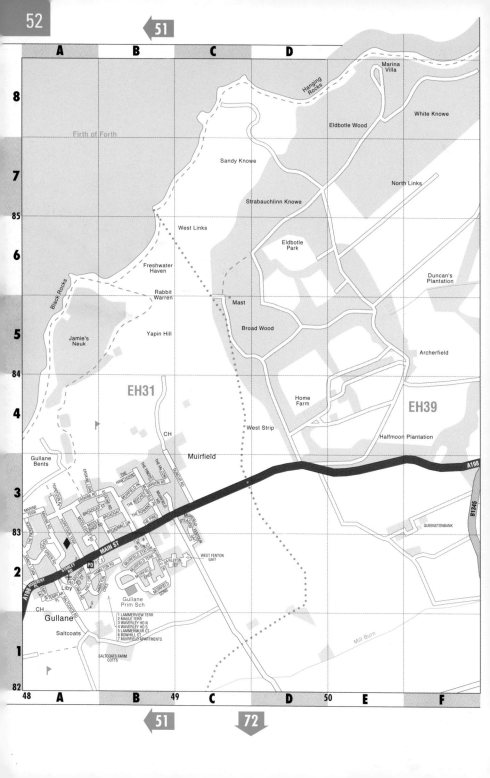

A   B   C   D

8

7

85

Firth of Forth

Hanging Rocks

Marina Villa

Eldbotle Wood

White Knowe

Sandy Knowe

North Links

Strabauchlinn Knowe

West Links

6

Eldbotle Park

Freshwater Haven

Duncan's Plantation

Rabbit Warren

Mast

Black Rocks

5

Jamie's Neuk

Yapin Hill

Broad Wood

Archerfield

84

EH31

Home Farm

EH39

4

CH

West Strip

Halfmoor Plantation

Muirfield

Gullane Bents

3

THE HAWTHORNS
ERSKINE LOAN
ERSKINE RD
MUIRFIELD'S
THE REECHES
HANDON RD
MUIRFIELD
DUNCAN RD

A198

B1345

MARINE TERR
BROADGAIT CT
THE BOWLING
THE PINES

QUEENSTONBANK

83

THE PADDOCK
BROADGAIT
BROADGAIT LN

MAIN ST

MUIRFIELD STATION

MUIRFIELD GARDENS

WEST FENTON GAIT

2

HAMILTON RD
PO
MUIRFIELD TERR
MUIRFIELD CRES
CARLETON CT

MUIRFIELD GDNS

Liby

Gullane Prim Sch

CH

Gullane

Saltcoats

1 LAMMERVIEW TERR
2 MAULE TERR
3 WAVERLEY HO N
4 WAVERLEY HO S
5 LAMMERMUIR CT
6 BOWHILL CT
7 MUIRFIELD APARTMENTS

Mill Burn

1

SALTCOATS FARM COTTS

82

48   A   B   49   C   D   50   E   F

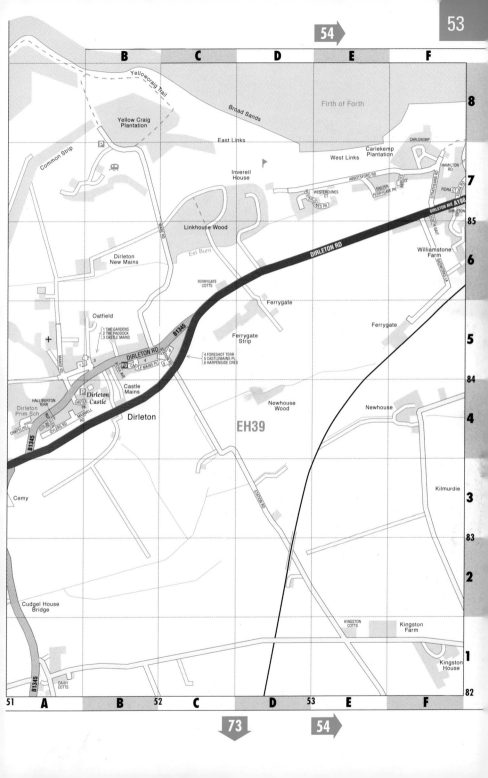

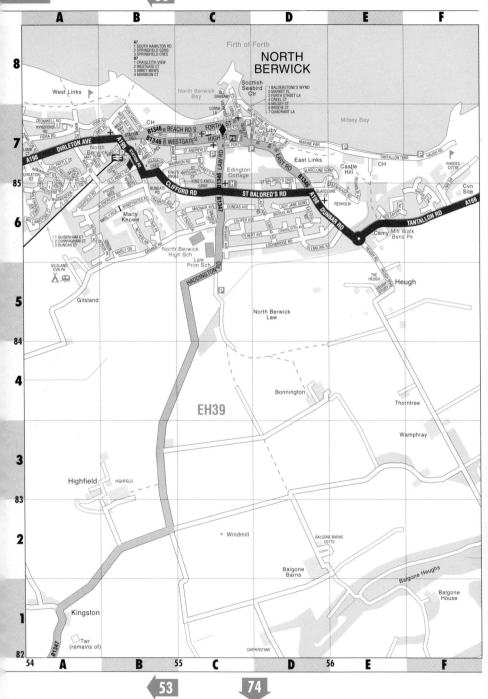

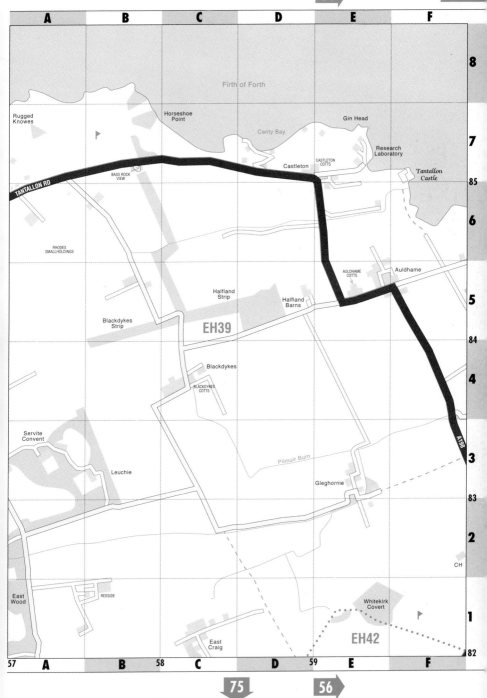

Firth of Forth

Rugged Knowes

Horseshoe Point

Canty Bay

Gin Head

Research Laboratory

Castleton

CASTLETON COTTS

Tantallon Castle

TANTALLON RD

BASS ROCK VIEW

RHODES SMALLHOLDINGS

AULDHAME COTTS

Auldhame

Halfland Strip

Halfland Barns

Blackdykes Strip

EH39

Blackdykes

BLACKDYKES COTTS

Servite Convent

Pilmuir Burn

Leuchie

Gleghornie

A198

CH

East Wood

REDSIDE

Whitekirk Covert

EH42

East Craig

55

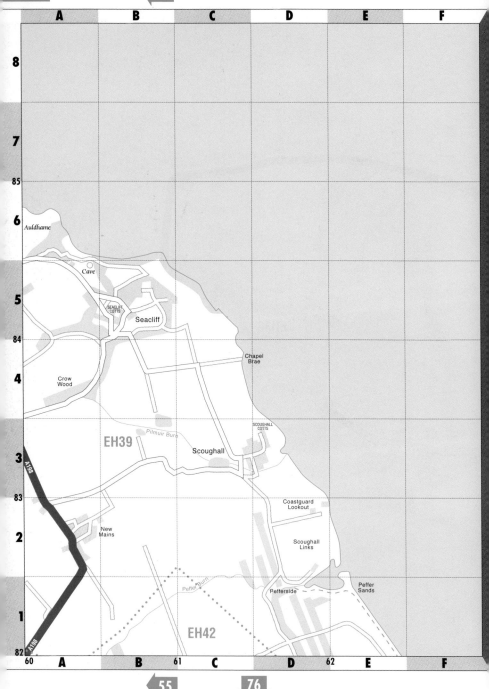

Auldhame

Cave

SEACLIFF COTTS

Seacliff

Chapel Brae

Crow Wood

EH39

Pilmuir Burn

SCOUGHALL COTTS

Scoughall

A198

Coastguard Lookout

New Mains

Scoughall Links

Peffer Burn

Pefferside

Peffer Sands

EH42

A198

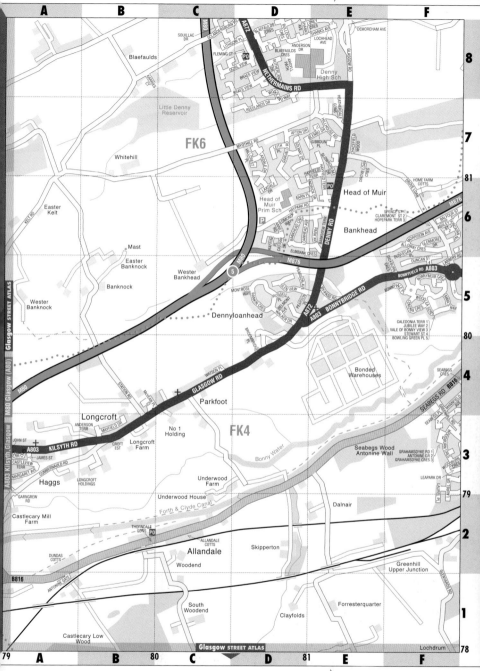

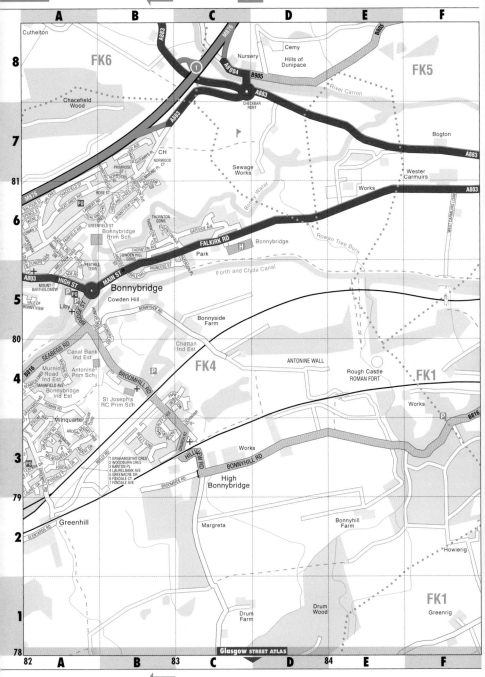

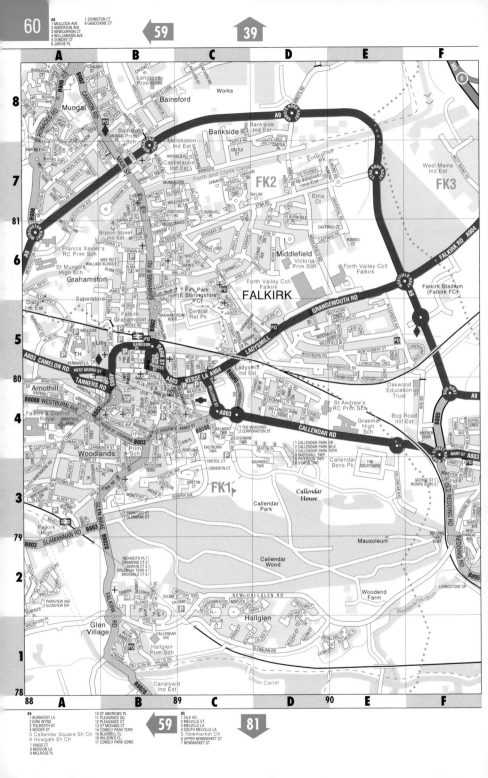

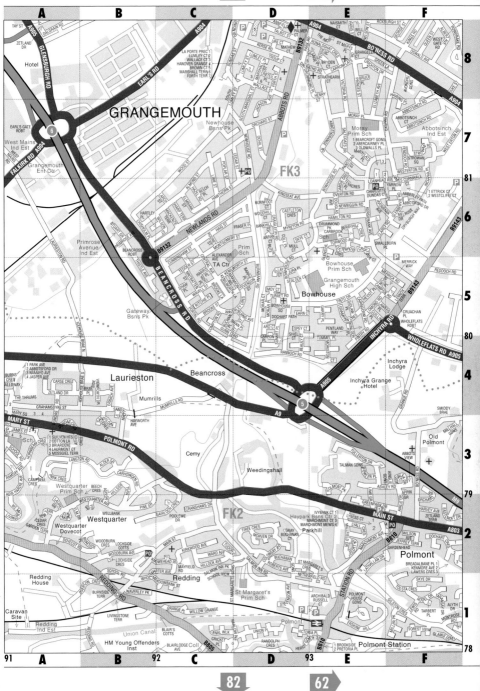

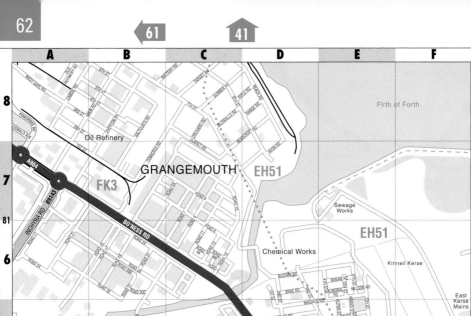
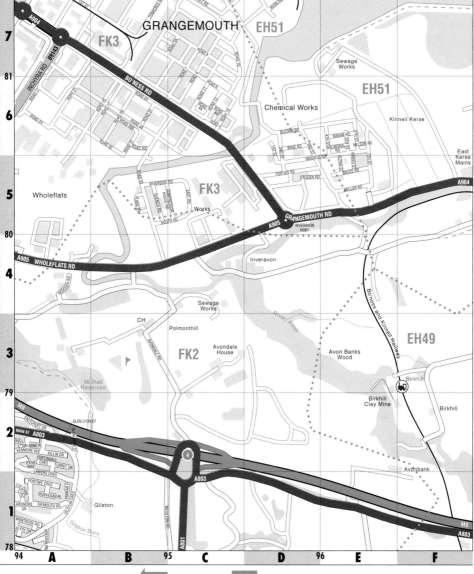

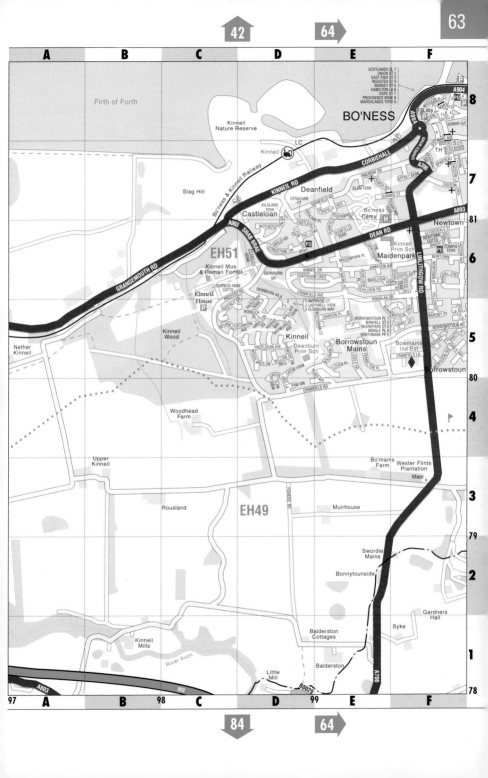

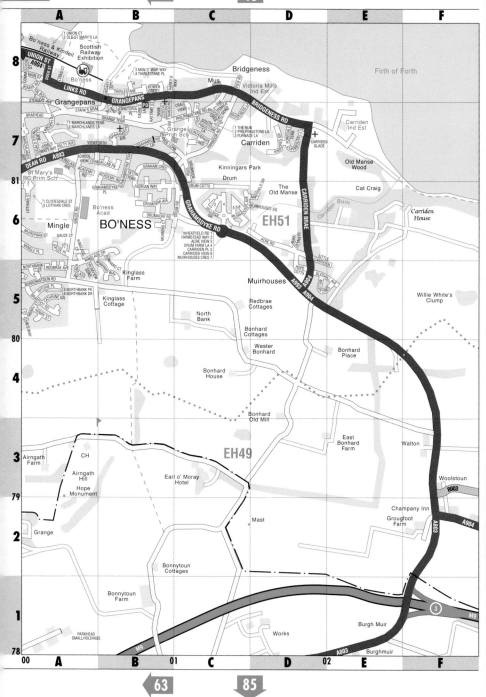

A   B   C   D   E   F

Firth of Forth

1 UNION CT
2 OLD ST MARY'S LA

Bo'ness & Kinneil
Railway

Scottish
Railway
Exhibition

UNION ST
A904

8

DOCK RD

Bo'ness

3 MAN O' WAR WAY
4 THIRLESTANE PL

Bridgeness

LINKS RD

Grangepans

Mus

Victoria Mills
Ind Est

GRANGEPANS

BRIDGENESS RD

Carriden
Ind Est

Grange
Prim Sch

1 THE RUN
2 PHILPINGSTONE LA
3 FURNACE LA

Carriden
Glade

7

DEAN RD
A993

Carriden

Old Manse
Wood

St Mary's
RC Prim Sch

81

Kinningars Park

Drum

The
Old Manse

CARRIDEN BRAE

Cat Craig

Carriden
House

1 CLYDESDALE ST
2 LOTHIAN CRES

Bo'ness
Acad

MUIRHOUSES SQ

EH51

6

Mingle

BO'NESS

GRAHAMSDYKE RD

5 6

MUIR

WHEATFIELD RD 1
FARMSTEAD WAY 2
ACRE VIEW 3
DRUM FARM LA 4
CARRIDEN PL 5
CARRIDEN VIEW 6
MUIRHOUSES CRES 7

ACRE RD

Little
Carriden

Muirhouses

HOPE
COTTS

A993 A904

Willie White's
Clump

5

Kinglass
Farm

Redbrae
Cottages

Kinglass
Cottage

North
Bank

Bonhard
Cottages

80

Wester
Bonhard

Bonhard
Place

4

Bonhard
House

Bonhard
Old Mill

East
Bonhard
Farm

Walton

3

Airngath
Farm

CH

EH49

Earl o' Moray
Hotel

Woolstoun

A903

Airngath
Hill

Hope
Monument

79

Champany Inn

Groufoot
Farm

A803

A904

2

Grange

Mast

Bonnytoun
Cottages

1

Bonnytoun
Farm

3

M9

Burgh Muir

PARKHEAD
SMALLHOLDINGS

Works

A803

Burghmuir

78

00   A   B   01   C   D   02   E   F

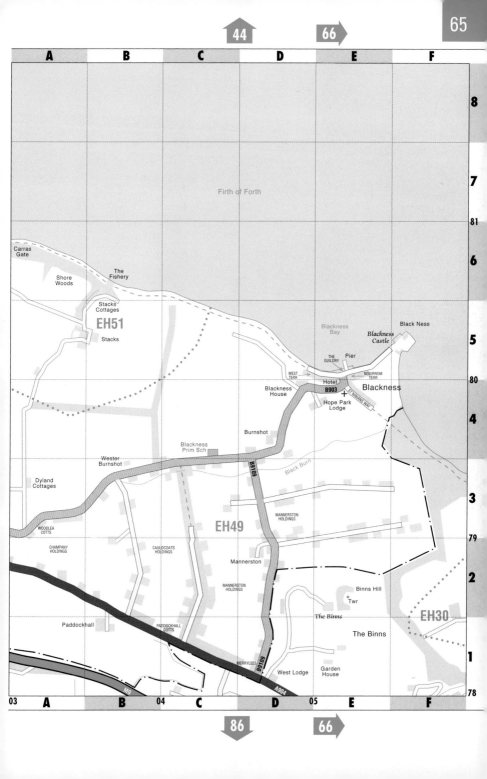

	A	B	C	D	E	F

Firth of Forth

Carras Gate

Shore Woods

The Fishery

Stacks Cottages

EH51

Stacks

Blackness Bay

Black Ness

Blackness Castle

THE GUILDRY

Pier

WEST TERR

Hotel

NOSIRROM TERR

Blackness House

B903

ST NINIANS WAY

Blackness

Hope Park Lodge

Burnshot

Blackness Prim Sch

Wester Burnshot

Black Burn

Dyland Cottages

EH49

MANNERSTON HOLDINGS

WOODLEA COTTS

CHAMPANY HOLDINGS

CAULDCOATS HOLDINGS

Mannerston

MANNERSTON HOLDINGS

Binns Hill

Twr

The Binns

EH30

The Binns

Paddockhall

PADDOCKHALL COTTS

MERRYLEES

West Lodge

Garden House

M9

A904

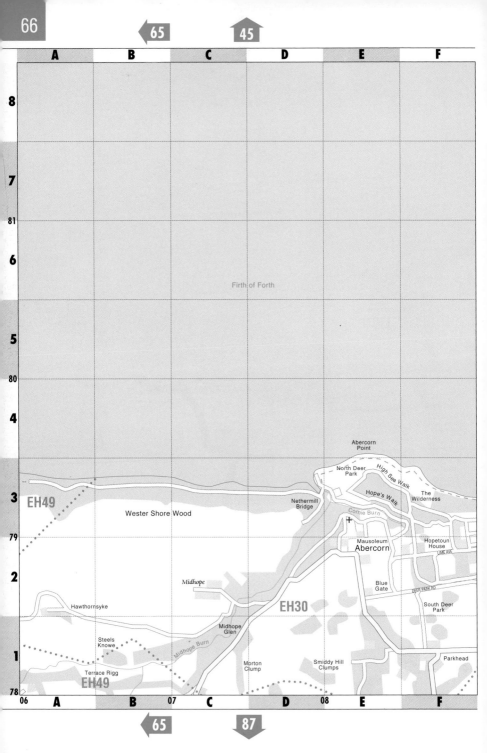

8

7

81

6

5

80

4

Firth of Forth

Abercorn
Point

North Deer
Park

High Sea Walk

3

EH49

Wester Shore Wood

Nethermill
Bridge

Hope's Walk

The
Wilderness

Cornie Burn

79

Mausoleum
Abercorn

Hopetoun
House

LIME AVE.

2

Midhope

Blue
Gate

DEER PARK RD.

South Deer
Park

EH30

Hawthornsyke

Midhope
Glen

Steels
Knowe

Midhope Burn

Morton
Clump

Smiddy Hill
Clumps

Parkhead

1

Terrace Rigg

EH49

78

06 A B 07 C D 08 E F

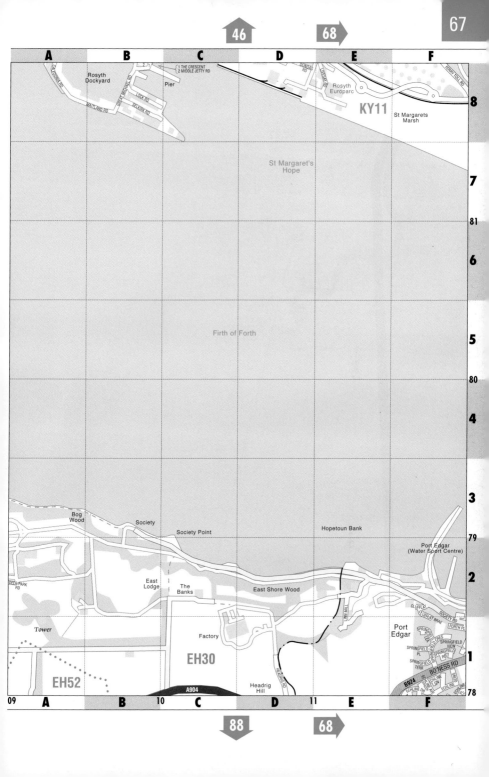

A **B** **C** **D** **E** **F**

CALEDONIA RD

Rosyth
Dockyard

Pier

1 THE CRESCENT
2 MIDDLE JETTY RD

ROBERT MAITCHEL RD

LOCH RD

SELKIRK RD

MAITLAND RD

DUNDAS
RD

OVEMS RD

Rosyth
Europarc

KY11

St Margarets
Marsh

FERRY TOLL RD

8

St Margaret's
Hope

7

81

6

Firth of Forth

5

80

4

3

Bog
Wood

Society

Society Point

Hopetoun Bank

Port Edgar
(Water Sport Centre)

79

DEER PARK
RD

East
Lodge

The
Banks

East Shore Wood

LINN MILL

CLUFFLAT

CLUFFLAT BRAE

SOCIETY RD

2

Tower

Factory

Port
Edgar

SPRINGFIELD

FORTH PL

CRES

SPRINGFIELD
VIEW

SPRINGFIELD
PL

SPRINGFIELD
RD

SPRINGFIELD
TERR

EH30

SPRINGFIELD
LGN

BO NESS RD

1

EH52

A904

Headrig
Hill

HEADRIG RD

ECHLINE

ECHLINE DR

B924

78

09 **A** **B** 10 **C** **D** 11 **E** **F**

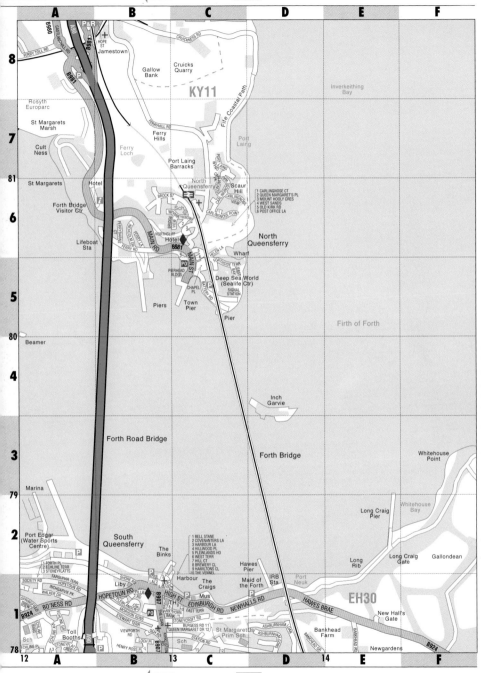

Firth of Forth

Tanker
Berths

Hound
Point

Peldraught
Bay

The
Warrens

Fishery
Cottage

EH30

Leuchold

Leuchold Wood

Castle Craig
Clump

Castle
Craig

Midlothian
Clump

Crow
Thickets

Barnbougle
Castle

Mons Hill

New England

Dalmeny Park

Peacock Ride

Livingston
Clump

Dalmeny
House

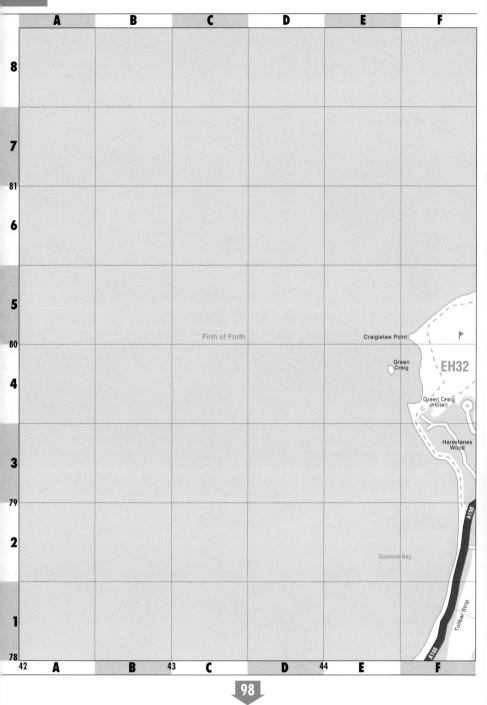

Firth of Forth

Craigielaw Point

Green Craig

EH32

Green Craig
(Hotel)

Harestanes
Wood

A198

Gosford Bay

Tollbar Strip

A198

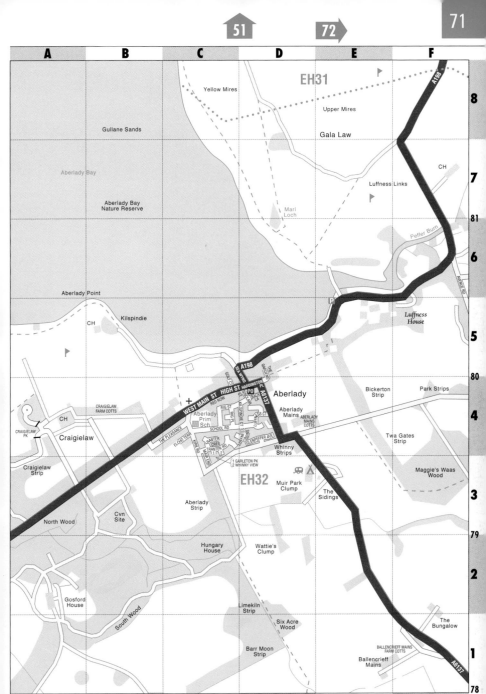

EH31

Yellow Mires

Upper Mires

Gala Law

Gullane Sands

A198

CH

Luffness Links

Aberlady Bay

Aberlady Bay
Nature Reserve

Marl
Loch

Peffer Burn

81

Aberlady Point

AVENUE RD

6

Kilspindie

CH

Luffness
House

5

80

A198

WEST MAIN ST   HIGH ST

HADDINGTON

Aberlady

Bickerton
Strip

Park Strips

CRAIGIELAW
FARM COTTS

CH

RED ROW

RIG ST

A6137

Aberlady
Mains

ABERLADY
MAINS
COTTS

CRAIGIELAW
PK

Craigielaw

Aberlady Prim
Sch

SCHOOL RD

Twa Gates
Strip

4

THE PLEASANCE

ELCHO TERR

HANTER
CRES

HANTER
RD

GLENPEFFER AVE

Maggie's Waas
Wood

Craigielaw
Strip

1 GARLETON PK
2 WHINNY VIEW

Whinny
Strips

EH32

Muir Park
Clump

The
Sidings

3

North Wood

Cvn
Site

Aberlady
Strip

79

Gosford
House

Hungary
House

Wattie's
Clump

2

South Wood

Limekiln
Strip

Six Acre
Wood

The
Bungalow

BALLENCRIEFF MAINS
FARM COTTS

Barr Moon
Strip

Ballencrieff
Mains

A6137

1

78

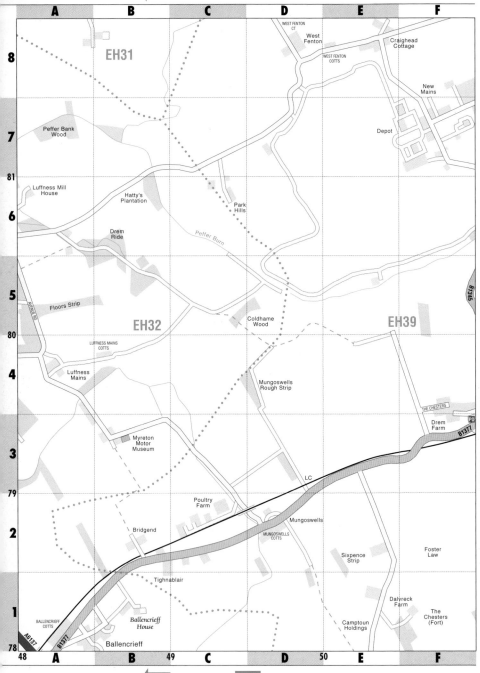

EH31

Craighead
Cottage

WEST FENTON
CT

West
Fenton

WEST FENTON
COTTS

New
Mains

8

Peffer Bank
Wood

Depot

7

81

Luffness Mill
House

Hatty's
Plantation

Park
Hills

6

Drem
Ride

Peffer Burn

5

Floors Strip

Coldhame
Wood

EH32

EH39

B1345

80

LUFFNESS MAINS
COTTS

4

Luffness
Mains

Mungoswells
Rough Strip

THE CHESTERS

Drem
Farm

PO

3

Myreton
Motor
Museum

LC

B1377

79

Poultry
Farm

Mungoswells

2

Bridgend

MUNGOSWELLS
COTTS

Sixpence
Strip

Foster
Law

Tighnablair

Dalvreck
Farm

The
Chesters
(Fort)

1

BALLENCRIEFF
COTTS

Ballencrieff
House

Camptoun
Holdings

A6137

B1377

78

Ballencrieff

48   A   B   49   C   D   50   E   F

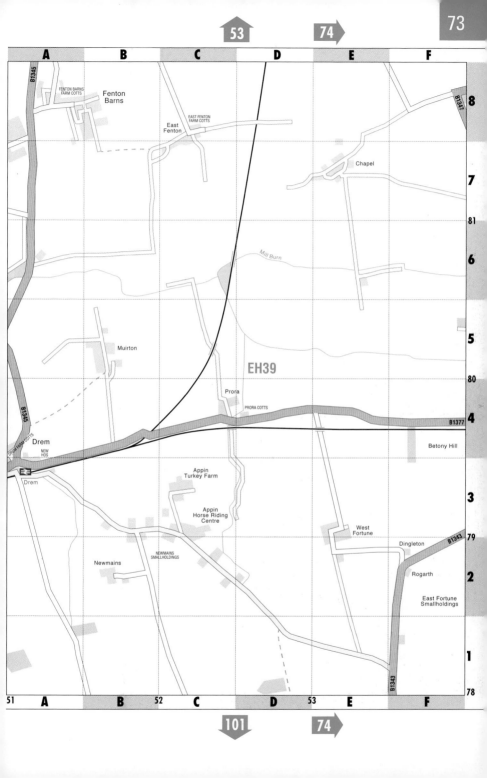

73
54

| | A | B | C | D | E | F |

8

B1347

Sydserf

SHERRIFF HALL COTTS

Rockville

Sherriff Hall

The Bratt

7

Rockville Heights

Craigmoor Wood

Congalton Cottages

81

Waughton Castle

6

CONGALTON MAINS COTTS

Congalton Mains

Congalton Mains

Rockville Gardens

Brownrigg

BROWNRIGG FARM COTTS

WAUGHTON STEADING

5

Congalton Gardens

Peffer Burn

EH39

WAUGHTON COTTS

EH40

80

Cowr Cottage

4

B1377

Betony Bridge

East Fortune Smallholdings

B1377

NEW ROW

East Fortune

2

Sewage Works

East Fortune House

NEW HOS 1 ORLIT COTTS 2

Merryhatton Nurseries

3

Betony Hill

B1377

Fortoun Bank

B1343

79

SMITHY ROW

Greenburn

Nursery

Airfield (dis)

2

Crauchie

National Museum of Flight

Depot

1

Cemy

Athelmead

B1347

Sunnyside Strip

Peffer Burn

78

Acres Plantation

Big Wood

| 54 | A | B | 55 | C | D | 56 | E | F |

73
102

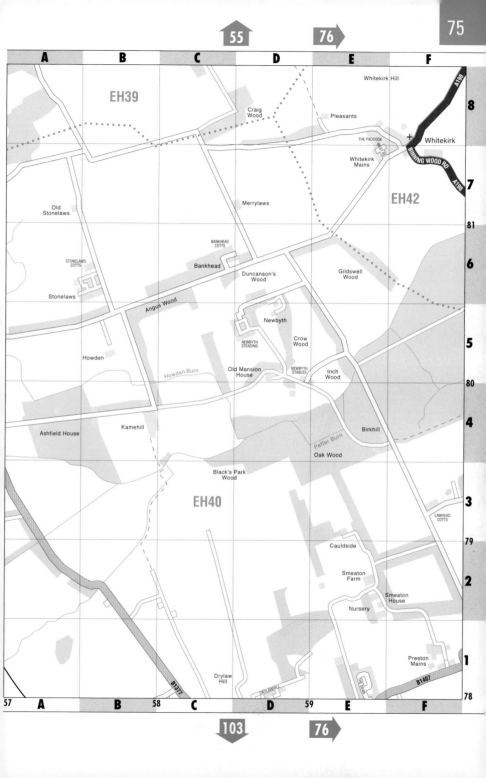

75
56

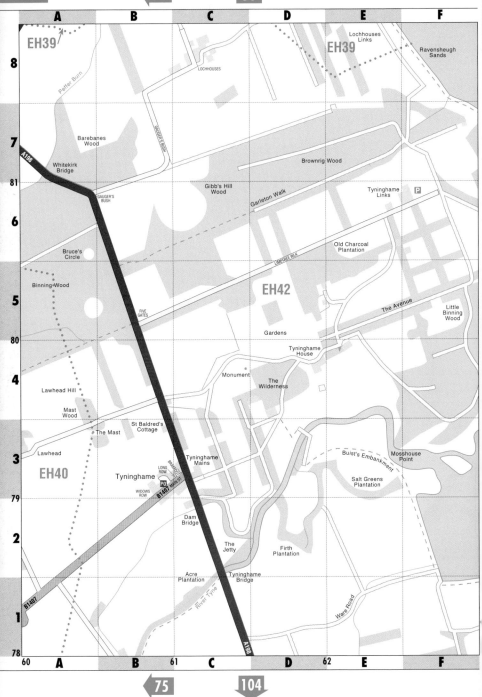

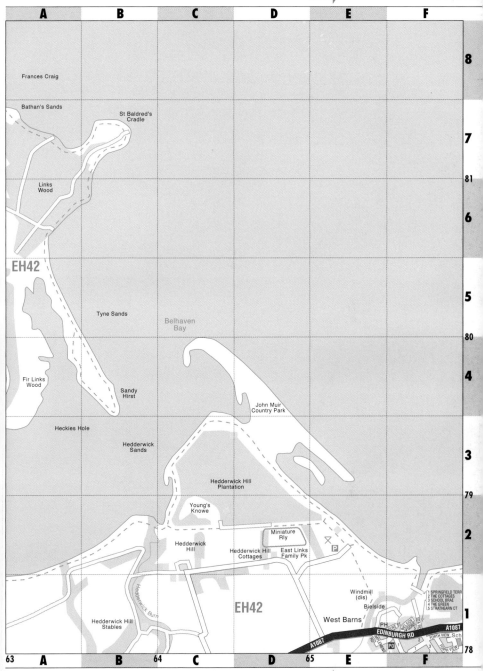

8

Frances Craig

Bathan's Sands

St Baldred's Cradle

7

81

Links Wood

6

EH42

5

Tyne Sands

Belhaven Bay

80

Fir Links Wood

4

Sandy Hirst

Heckies Hole

Hedderwick Sands

3

Hedderwick Hill Plantation

79

Young's Knowe

John Muir Country Park

Miniature Rly

2

Hedderwick Hill

Hedderwick Hill Cottages

East Links Family Pk

P

Hedderwick Burn

Windmill (dis)

Bielside

EH42

West Barns

1 SPRINGFIELD TERR
2 THE COTTAGES
3 SCHOOL BRAE
4 THE GREEN
5 STRATHEARN CT

Hedderwick Hill Stables

PH

EDINBURGH RD

A1087

FORTH VIEW Sch

A1087

PO

1

78

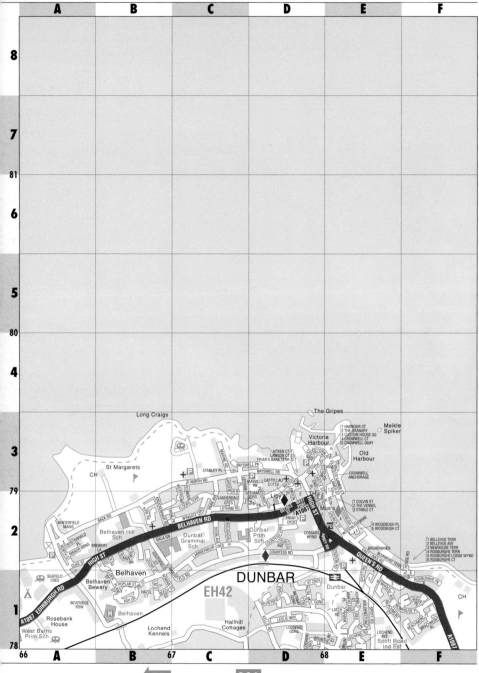

	A	B	C	D	E	F

8

7

81

6

5

80

4

Long Craigs

The Gripes

3

St Margarets

Victoria Harbour

Meikle Spiker

1 HARBOUR CT
2 THE GRANARY
3 CUSTOM HOUSE SQ
4 CROMWELL CT
5 CROMWELL QUAY

Old Harbour

AITKEN CT 1
LAWSON CT 2
FRIAR'S BANK TERR 3

STANLEY PL

BAYSWELL RD

CROMWELL ANCHORAGE

CH

NORTH RD

MAYVILLE
PK

CASTELLAU
COTTS

79

LAUDERDALE CRES

Lib

1 COLVIN ST
2 THE VENNEL
3 STABLE CT

LETHAM
GDNS

LETHAM TERR

Mus's

4 WOODBUSH PL
5 WOODBUSH CT

2

WINTERFIELD
MAINS

BELHAVEN RD

Belhaven Hill Sch

GALA GRN

FRIAR'S CROFT

COSSARS WYND

BROADHAVEN

1 BELLEVUE TERR
2 BELLEVUE AVE
3 NEWHOUSE TERR
4 ROXBURGHE TERR
5 ROXBURGHE LODGE WYND
6 ROXBURGHE CT

WINTERFIELD
PL

MANOR GDNS

BREWERY
LA

HIGH ST

Dunbar Grammar Sch

LAMMERMUIR CRES

Dunbar Prim Sch

COUNTESS RD

QUEEN'S RD

ROXBURGHE PK

SEAFIELD
CRES

Belhaven Brewery

Belhaven

POPLAR ST

HAZEL
CT

OLD RD

DOUNTESS RD

DUNBAR

Dunbar

CH

1

A1087 EDINBURGH RD

Rosebank
House

BEVERIDGE
ROW

H Belhaven

EH42

Hallhill
Cottages

LESLIE WAY

AT CRES

LATCH

SPOTT RD

LOCHEND

Spott Road
Ind Est

A1087

West Barns
Prim Sch

78

Lochend
Kennels

LOCHEND
GDNS

	A	B	C	D	E	F	
							8
							7
							81
							6
							5
							80
							4
							3
							79
							2
							1

Lawrie's Den

The Vaults

West Links

EH42

Vaults Wood

Mill Stone Neuk

Sports & Social Centre

Fluke Dub

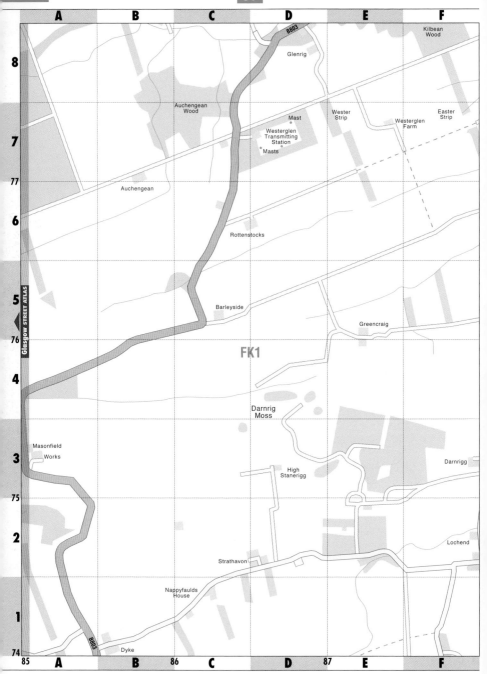

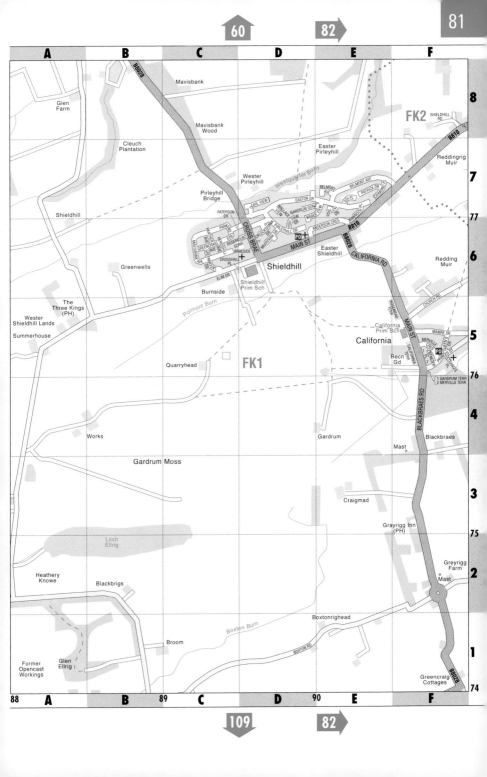

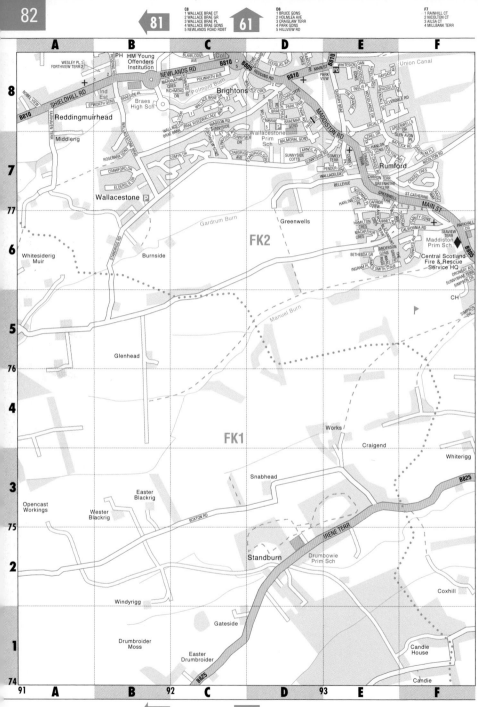

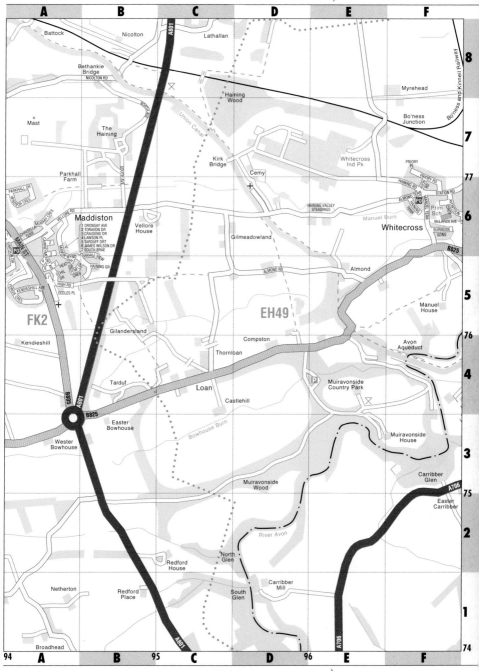

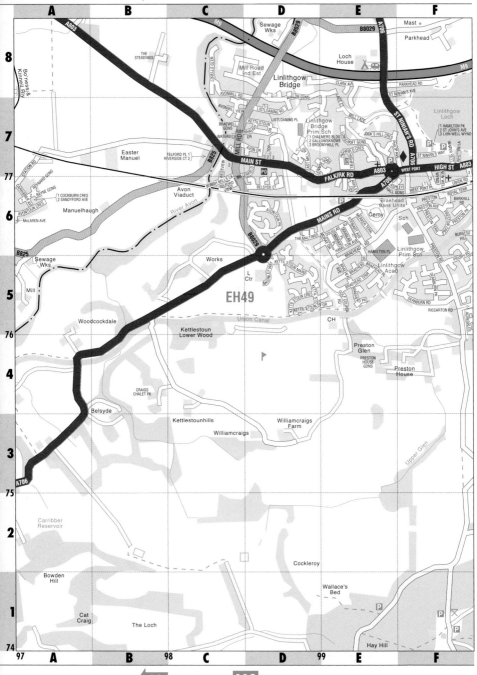

EH49

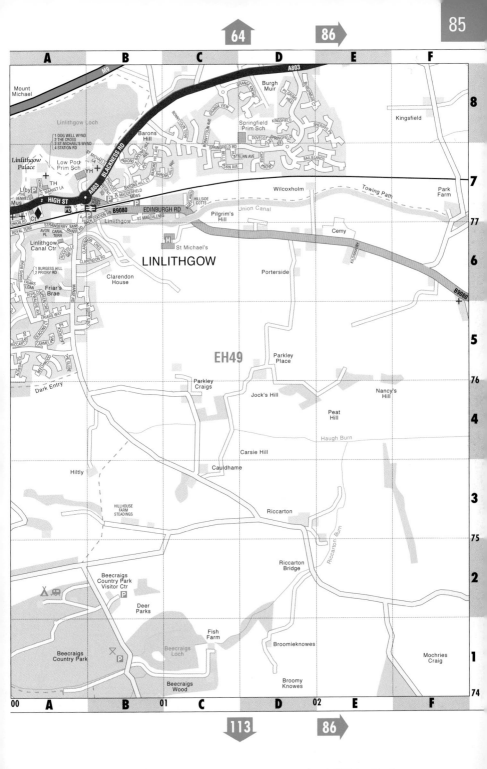

85
65

A B C D E F

8

Works

Errick Burn

M9

A904

A904

B8046

②

M9

7

Pardovan
House

PARDOVAN
HOLDINGS

Philpstoun

Old
Philpstoun

Pardovan Burn

WYNDFORD
BRAE

THE
AVENUE

PARDOVAN
CRES

B8046

77

MAIN ST

CAMERON KNOWE

PO

MANSE
VIEW

CHURCH

Union Canal

6

Champfleurie
House

CHAMPFLEURIE
STABLES

Fairniehill

Spoil
Heap

B8046

B9080

CHAMPFLEURIE
COTTS

EH49

5

Kingscavil

Bridgend
Farm

Haugh Burn

Cameron
Knowe

CHAMPFLEURIE
MEWS

76

AULDHILL CT

Sewage
Works

AULDHILL
COTTS

Gateside

BURNSIDE
COTTS

Threemiletown

ST JAMES
PL

ROSEBANK

B9080

4

NILDHILL DR

WILDINGCAN

AULDHILL

TERR

AULDHILL

AULDHILL
ENTRY

AULDHILL

PO

B8046

CH

AULDHILL ORCH

AULDHILL PK

Bridgend

WOODSIDE
TERR

THE
COTTAGES

REDHOUSE
COTTS

Bridgend
Prim Sch

3

75

2

Wester
Ochiltree

Little
Ochiltree

Waterstone

EH52

1

Ecclesmachan Burn

B8046

74

03 A B 04 C D 05 E F

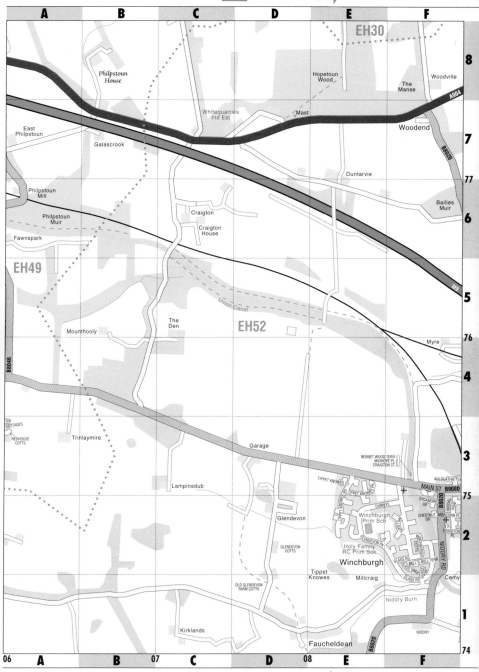

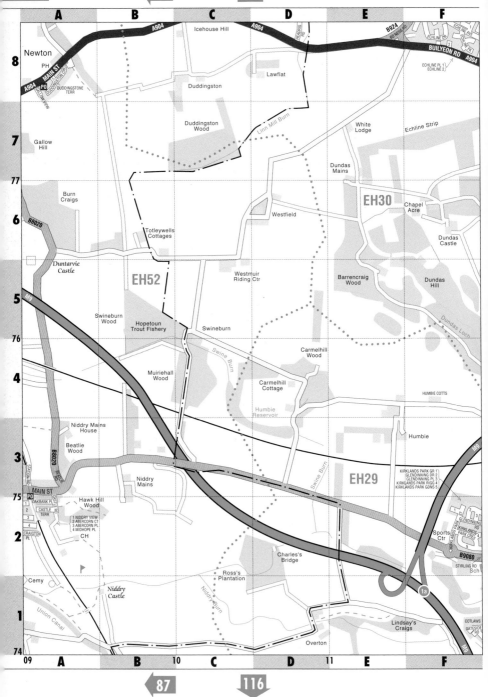

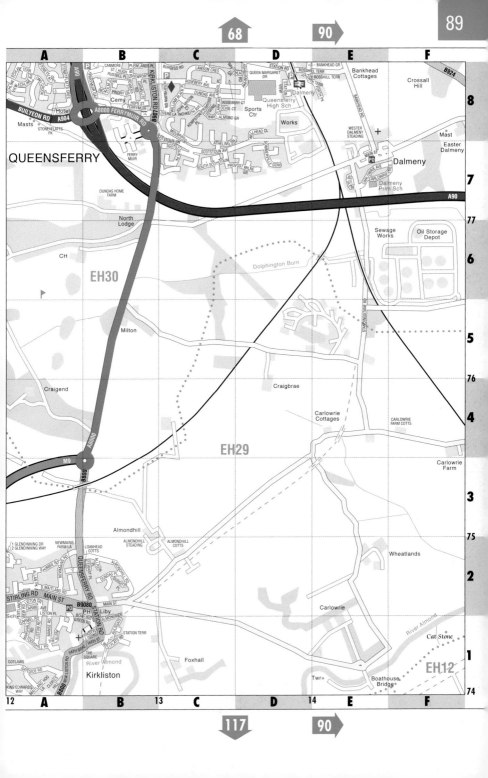

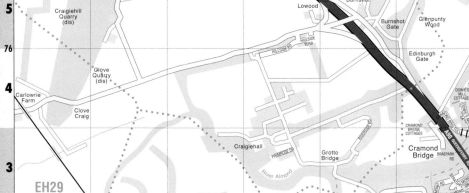

A B C D E F

8

Shepherds Bog

B924

Chapel Gate

Dunter Hill

Chapel Coppice

Mouse Wood

Royal Clump

P

Easter Dalmeny

Mansion Hill

Dalmeny Park

Long Green Wood

Long Green

7

Barnbougle Gate

Mansion Hill Wood

Home Farm

A90

B924

Dolphington Burn

BARNBOUGLE RIDE

Cockle Burn

HOME FARM COTTS

77

Dolphington House

Burnshot Wood

6

Dolphington

Dolphington Cottages

EH30

EH4

Craigie Hill

West Craigie Farm

New Burnshot

East Craigie

5

Craigiehill Quarry (dis)

Lowood

Burnshot Gate

Glenpunty Wood

76

Glove Quarry (dis)

HILLSIDE RD

HILLSIDE TERR

Edinburgh Gate

4

Carlowrie Farm

Clove Craig

DOWIE'S MILL COTTAGES

DOWIE'S MILL LA

A90 QUEENSFERRY RD

CRAMOND BRIDGE COTTAGES

EH29

Craigiehall

PRIMROSE DR

River Almond

Grotto Bridge

BRAEPARK RD

Cramond Bridge

RIVERSIDE DR

3

Nether Lennie

EH12

Craigiehall Temple

CAMMO RD

Cammo Home Farm

STRATHALMOND RD

STRATHALMOND RD

STRATHALMOND PK

STRATHALMOND GN

CAMMO DR

75

Lennie Gate

Cammo

2

Edinburgh Airport

Lennie Mains

Lennie Hill

CAMMO WK

Bughtlin Burn

1

LENNYMUIR

Turnhouse

Tower

CAMMO DR

74

MAYFIELD WAY

TURNHOUSE RD

TURNHOUSE FARM RD

A B C D E F

15   16   17

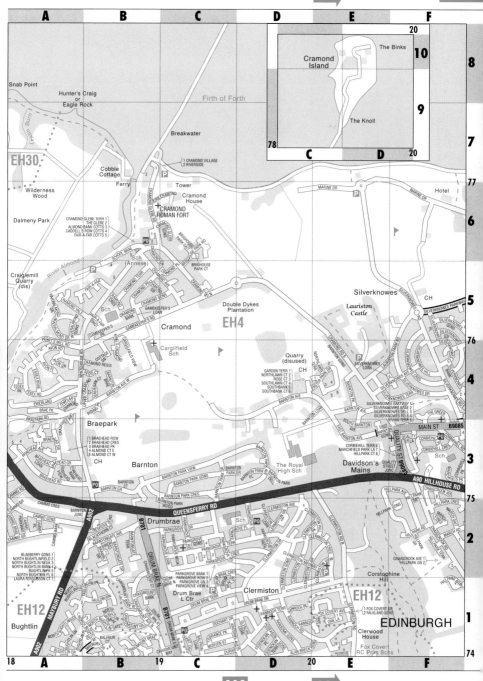

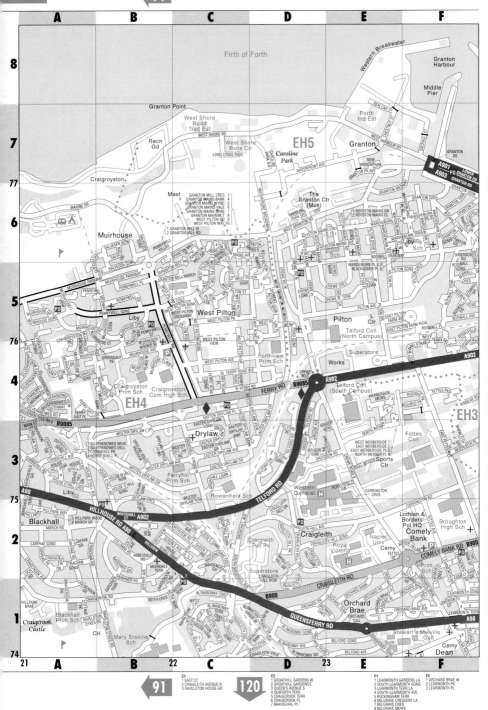

91

120

C1
1 EAST CT
2 CRAIGLEITH AVENUE N
3 RAVELSTON HOUSE GR

C2
1 GROATHILL GARDENS W
2 GROATHILL GARDENS E
3 QUEEN'S AVENUE S
4 SEAFORTH TERR
5 CRAIGCROOK TERR
6 CRAIGCROOK PL
7 MARISCHAL PL

F1
1 LEARMONTH GARDENS LA
2 SOUTH LEARMONTH GDNS
3 LEARMONTH TERR LA
4 SOUTH LEARMONTH AVE
5 BUCKINGHAM TERR
6 BELGRAVE CRESCENT LA
7 BELGRAVE CRES
8 BELGRAVE MEWS
9 BACK DEAN

F2
1 ORCHARD BRAE LA
2 LEARMONTH PK
3 LEARMONTH PL

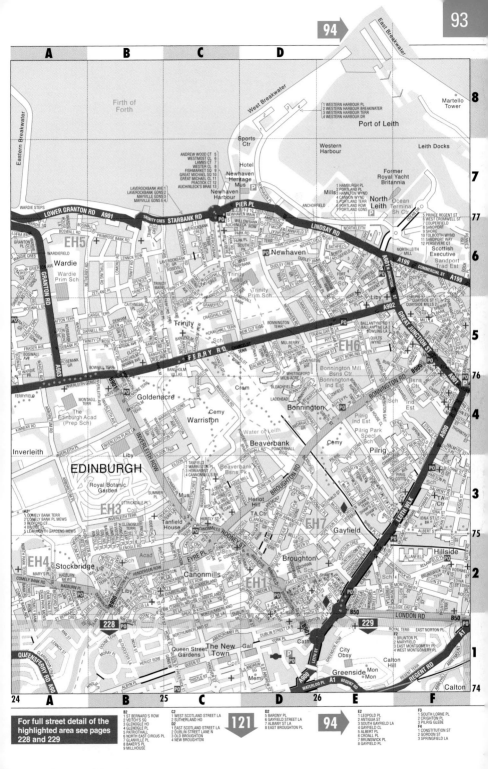

Firth of Forth

East Breakwater

Eastern Breakwater

West Breakwater

1 WESTERN HARBOUR PL
2 WESTERN HARBOUR BREAKWATER
3 WESTERN HARBOUR TERR
4 WESTERN HARBOUR DR

Martello Tower

Port of Leith

Sports Ctr

Western Harbour

Leith Docks

ANDREW WOOD CT 5
WESTMOST CL 6
LAMBS CT 7
WESTER CL 8
FISHMARKET SQ 9
GREAT MICHAEL SQ 10
GREAT MICHAEL CL 11
PEACOCK CT 12
AUCHINLECK'S BRAE 13

Hotel
Newhaven Heritage Mus

Former Royal Yacht Britannia

Ocean Terminal Sh Ctr

LAVEROCKBANK AVE 1
LAVEROCKBANK GDNS 2
MAYVILLE GDNS 3
MAYVILLE GDNS E 4

Newhaven Harbour

Mills

North Leith

ANCHORFIELD

1 HAMBURGH PL
2 PORTLAND PL
3 HAMILTON WYND
4 CANNON WYND
5 PORTLAND TERR
6 PORTLAND ROW
7 PORTLAND GDNS

Scottish Executive

5 PRINCE REGENT ST
6 WEST CROMWELL ST
7 COUPERFIELD
8 SANDPORT
9 TOLBOOTH WYND
10 SANDPORT WAY
11 SANDPORT ST
12 PERSEVER CT

Sandport Trad Est

WARDIE STEPS

LOWER GRANTON RD A901 TRINITY CRES STARBANK RD

PIER PL

LINDSAY RD

A901 JUNCTION RD

A199

NORTH LEITH

COMMERCIAL ST A199

EH5

Wardie
Wardie Prim Sch

GRANTON RD
A903

PRIMROSE BANK RD

1 WILLOWBANK ROW
Newhaven

Newhaven

Trinity Acad

Trinity Prim Sch

DUDLEY CRES

FORTH

A902

GREAT JUNCTION ST

A901

Quilts Wynd

QUAYSIDE ST 1
QUAYSIDE MILLS 2

Trinity

CRAIGHALL GDNS

NEW CUT RIGG

BONNINGTON TERR

TRAFALGAR

Mulberry

EH6

BOWLING GREEN ST 2

BANGOR
BALLANTYNE PL
BALLANTYNE LA 1
BOWLING LA 2

FERRY RD

DALMENY RD

WHITINGFORD
MILN-ACRE

BANGHOLM VILLAS

Cream

BLEACHFIELD

Bonnington Mill Bsns Ctr
Bonnington Ind Est

LADEHEAD

BONNINGTON RD B900

Bsns Ctr

Ind Est

FERRYFIELD

MONTAGU TERR

Goldenacre

Warriston

Cemy

Water of Leith

Beaverbank

POWDERHALL

Bonnington

Pilrig Ind Est

Pilrig Park Specl Sch

A900

Inverleith

The Edinburgh Acad (Prep Sch)

Liby

INVERLEITH ROW

Cemy

LEITH WALK

Pilrig

EDINBURGH

Royal Botanic Garden

1 TANFIELD
2 WARRISTON PL
3 HOWARD PL
4 CANNONMILLS RD

Beaverbank Bsns Pk

Loug Mill

BROUGHTON RD

Sch

EH3

Coll

Heriot Hill
TA Ctr

EH7

Gayfield

A920
1 COMELY BANK TERR
2 COMELY BANK PL MEWS
3 BEDFORD CT
4 BRIDGE PL
5 LEARMONTH GARDENS MEWS

Tanfield House

CANONMILLS

HUNTLY ST

RODNEY ST

Sch

Broughton

Allanfield

Hillside

EH4

Stockbridge

Canonmills

EYRE PL

EH1

BRUNTON PL

EAST MONTGOMERY ST

Comely Bank Rd

HENDERSON ROW

CUMBERLAND ST

Liby

LONDON RD

B50

228 PO

Queensferry Rd A90

QUEEN STREET GARDENS

The New Town

Gall

DUBLIN STREET LA

229

Royal Terr EAST NORTON LA

F2
1 MAYFIELD
2 MARYFIELD
3 EAST MONTGOMERY ST
4 WEST MONTGOMERY PL

MORAY PL

HERIOT ROW

Queen Street Gardens

Coll

ST ANDREW SQ

City Obsy

Calton Hill

REGENT RD A1

QUEENSFERRY RD A90

THISTLE ST

WATERLOO PL A1 REGENT RD

Greenside

Mon Mon

Calton

74

77

7

6

5

4

3

2

1

8

121   94

B2
1 ST BERNARD'S ROW
2 VEITCH'S SQ
3 GLENOGLE HO
4 GLENOGLE PL
5 PATRIOTHALL
6 NORTH EAST CIRCUS PL
7 GLANVILLE PL
8 BAKER'S PL
9 MILLHOUSE

C2
1 WEST SCOTLAND STREET LA
2 SUTHERLAND HO

D2
1 EAST SCOTLAND STREET LA
2 DUBLIN STREET LANE N
3 OLD BROUGHTON
4 NEW BROUGHTON

D2
5 BARONY PL
6 GAYFIELD STREET LA
7 ALBANY ST LA
8 EAST BROUGHTON PL

E2
1 LEOPOLD PL
2 ANTIGUA ST
3 SOUTH GAYFIELD LA
4 GAYFIELD CL
5 ALBERT PL
6 CROALL PL
7 BRUNSWICK ST
8 GAYFIELD PL

F3
1 SOUTH LORNE PL
2 CRIGHTON PL
3 PILRIG GLEBE

F4
1 CONSTITUTION ST
2 GORDON ST
3 SPRINGFIELD LA

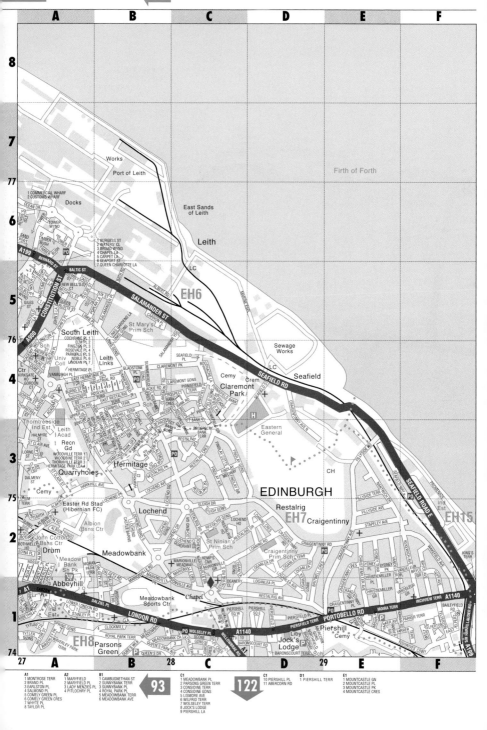

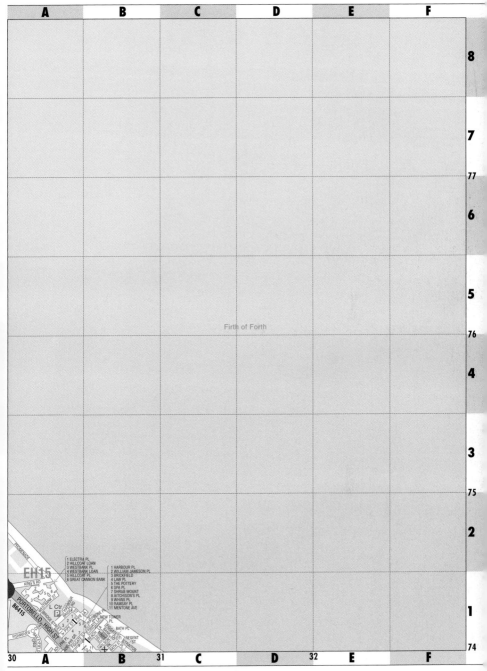

Firth of Forth

EH15

1 ELECTRA PL
2 HILLCOAT LOAN
3 WESTBANK PL
4 WESTBANK LOAN
5 HILLCOAT PL
6 GREAT CANNON BANK

1 HARBOUR PL
2 WILLIAM JAMESON PL
3 BRICKFIELD
4 LAW PL
5 THE POTTERY
6 SPA PL
7 SHRUB MOUNT
8 AITCHISON'S PL
9 WHINS PL
10 RAMSAY PL
11 MENTONE AVE

PROMENADE
KING'S RD
PORTOBELLO HIGH ST
B6415
FISHWIVES' CAUSEWAY
L Ctr
P
NEW TOWER PL
BATH PL
SCH
REGENT ST
STATION

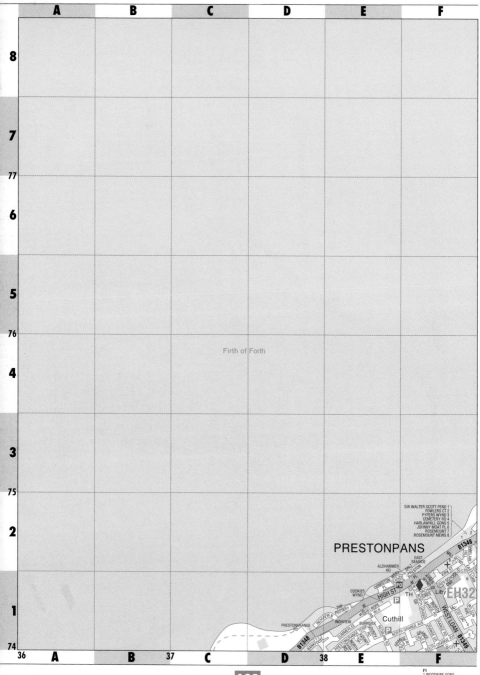

Firth of Forth

SIR WALTER SCOTT PEND 1
FOWLERS CT 2
PYPERS WYND 3
CEMETERY RD 4
HARLAWHILL GDNS 5
JOHNNY MOAT PL 6
ROSEMOUNT 7
ROSEMOUNT MEWS 8

PRESTONPANS

EAST
SEASIDE

ALDHAMMER
HO

COOKIES
WYND

HIGH ST

TH

Liby

EH32

THE
POTTERY

PRESTONGRANGE
RD

INCHVIEW

Cuthill

NORTH GRANGE AVE

WEST LOAN

B1348

B1348

BANKFOOT

SOUTH GRANGE

Sch

F1
1 WOODBINE GDNS
2 NORTHFIELD CT
3 PRESTON TOWER
4 GLEBE GDNS
5 LABURNUM ARCH CT

Firth of Forth

**COCKENZIE AND
PORT SETON**

Port Seton
Harbour

Pier

Cockenzie
Harbour

HAWTHORN
BANK

Power
Station

Whin Park
Ind Est

Cockenzie
Prim Sch

Liby

EH32

Seton Chapel
(formerly
Collegiate Church)

Seton
House

Coal Store

ROWANHILL
CL

Seton
East

Seton

EH33

Seton West Mains

Opencast
Workings

Cemy

Preston

Preston Lodge
High Sch

Meadowmill

Preston Tower
Preston Cross
L Ctr

LINKS RD

B1348

SETON SANDS
CVN PK

A198

B1361

A198

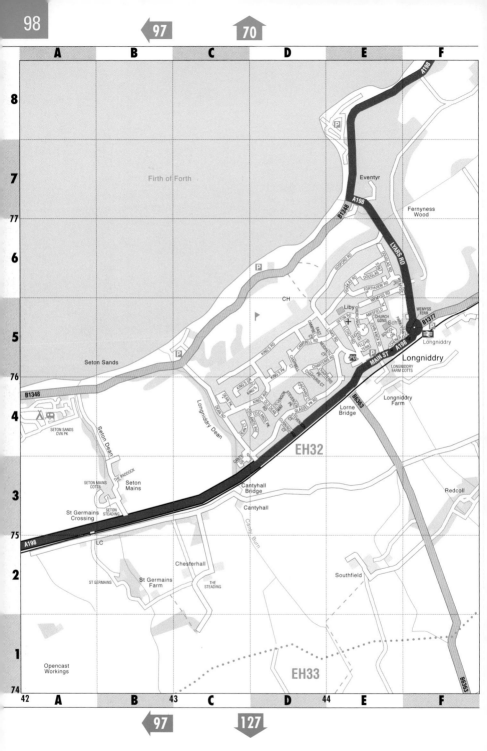

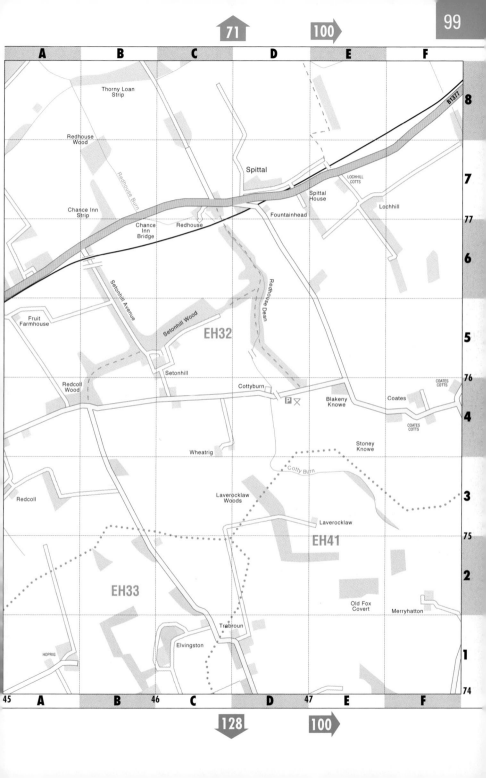

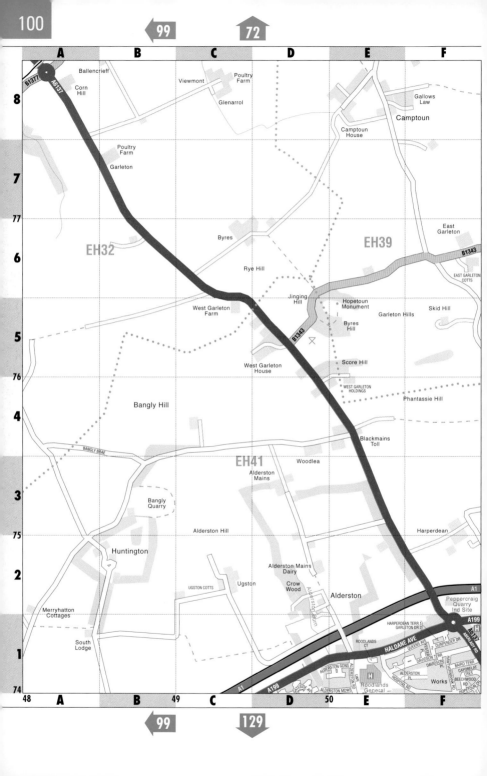

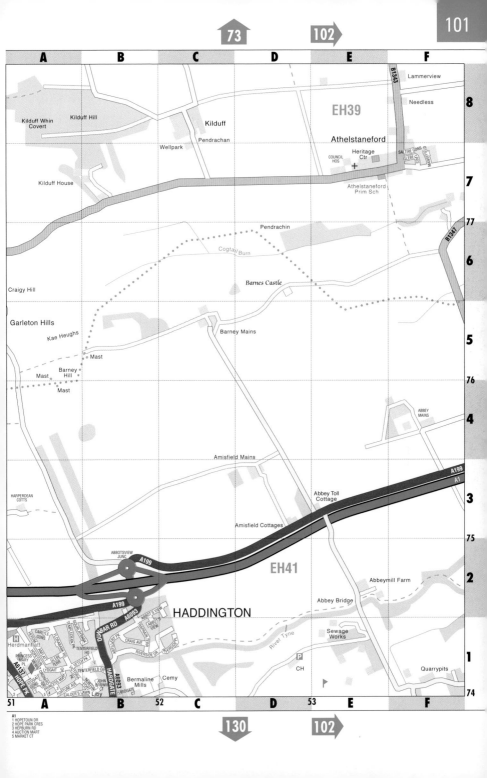

102

A **B** **C** **D** **E** **F**

Lammerview

EH39

Needless

Kilduff Whin Covert

Kilduff Hill

Kilduff

Kilduff

Pendrachan

Wellpark

Athelstaneford

COUNCIL HOS

Heritage Ctr

SALTIRE GDNS

GLEBE CRES

Kilduff House

Athelstaneford Prim Sch

B1343

B1347

Pendrachin

Cogtail Burn

Craigy Hill

Barnes Castle

Garleton Hills

Kae Heughs

Barney Mains

Mast

Mast

Barney Hill

Mast

Mast

ABBEY MAINS

HARPERDEAN COTTS

Amisfield Mains

A199

A1

Abbey Toll Cottage

Amisfield Cottages

Abbeymill Farm

ABBOTSVIEW JUNC

A199

EH41

Abbey Bridge

A199

A6093

HADDINGTON

Sewage Works

River Tyne

DUNBAR RD

CARLYLE

Herdmanflat

HARDGATE

H

Bermaline Mills

Cemy

P

CH

Quarrypits

Liby

HOPE PK

A6137

PRINCESS MARY

A **B** 52 **C** 53 **D** **E** **F**

8

7

77

6

5

76

4

3

75

2

1

74

51

102

A1
1 HOPETOUN DR
2 HOPE PARK CRES
3 HEPBURN RD
4 AUCTION MART
5 MARKET CT

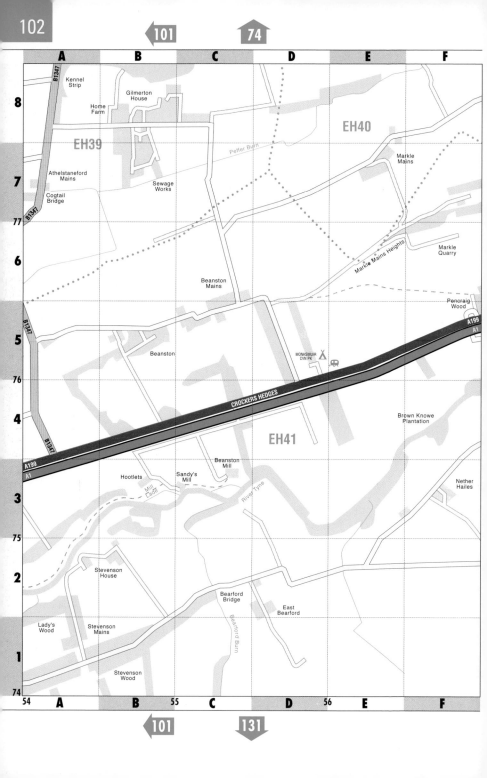

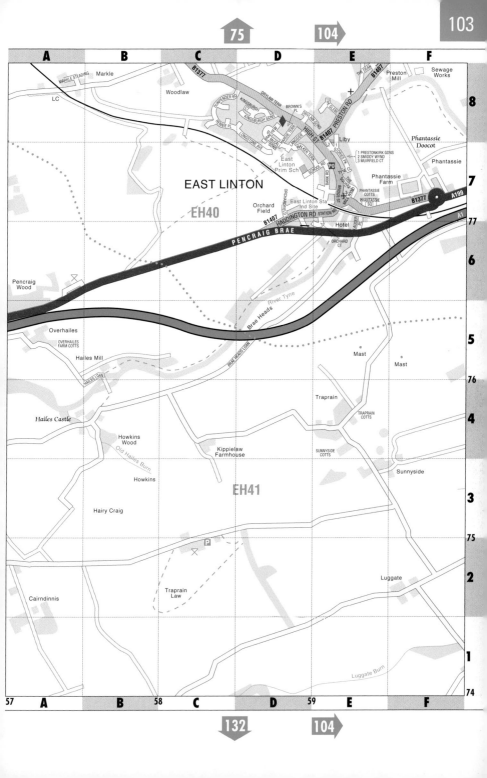

103
76

A **B** **C** **D** **E** **F**

8

Knowes
Mill
Ford
Knowes
Kirklandhill
Tynefield
A1168
Kirklandhill
Cottages
North
Lodge
A199
Standing
Stone

EH40

7
A199
Ninewar
A1168
Ninewar Wood
A1

77
A1

Howmuir

6

EH42
Pudlum

5

Beesknowe

76
West
Lodge

4
Biel Water
Bielmill
Grangelea
Biel Park
Cottage
BIELGRANGE
COTTS
Bielgrange

3
Grangemuir
Whittingehame Water

75
Ginglet
House
East
Lodge
Ginglet
Hill

2
Newbarns
B6370
MILL LA
Quarry
Hill
Luggate Burn
Saucott Water
ROOD WELL COTTS

1
EASTFIELD
COTTS
EH41
Eastfield
Ruchlaw
Mains
THE CROFTS
Luggate Burn
Whittingehame Water
Stenton
B6370

74
Redcliff
Ruchlaw
Stenton
House
Loanhead
Stenton
Prim Sch
STENTON LOAN

60 **A** **B** 61 **C** **D** 62 **E** **F**

103
133

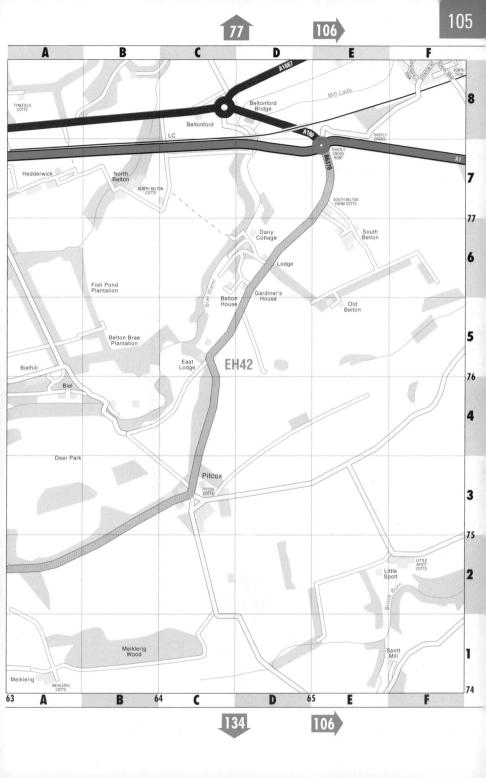

105
78

A	B	C	D	E	F

8

Lochend Wood

HALLHILL

 Eweford

LOCHEND CRES
BRUNT CR
BRUNT PL
KELLIE RD

Trad Est

Newtonlees Mast

MURRAY CRES

JOHN MUIR PL 1
JOHN MUIR RD 2

EWEFORD COTTS

READING CRES

BRODIE RD

JOHN MUIR CRES

JOHN MUIR GDNS

MURR

MUIR

A1087

Newtonlees Cotts

7

A1

Myreside

EASTER BROOMHOUSE COTTS

A1

77

6

Lodge

Easter Broomhouse

Bowerhouse

Oswald Dean

5

Hurkletillane

Resr

EH42

WESTER BROOMHOUSE COTTS

Wester Broomhouse

Doon

76

Spott Burn

Doon Bridge

4

Pleasants

Ivy Bank

CANONGATE

Easter Spott +

Doon Hill

Doon Hill Hall

Spott

THE SQUARE

ST JOHN PL

HIGH RD

SPOTT LOAN

The Dean

SPOTT AVE

3

Spott Farm

Washing Green

Spott House

Skaw Plantation

Home Farm

Daniel's Side Brae

Pond Strip

75

Spott Cottage

Horsepark

Ward's Wood

2

Hardhead Plantation

West Mains Wood

Spott West Mains

Mast

Brunt Hill Strips

Spott Dod

Brunt Hill

1

East Kirkshotts Plantation

Henchie Cleugh Plantation

74

66	A	B	67	C	D	68	E	F

105
135

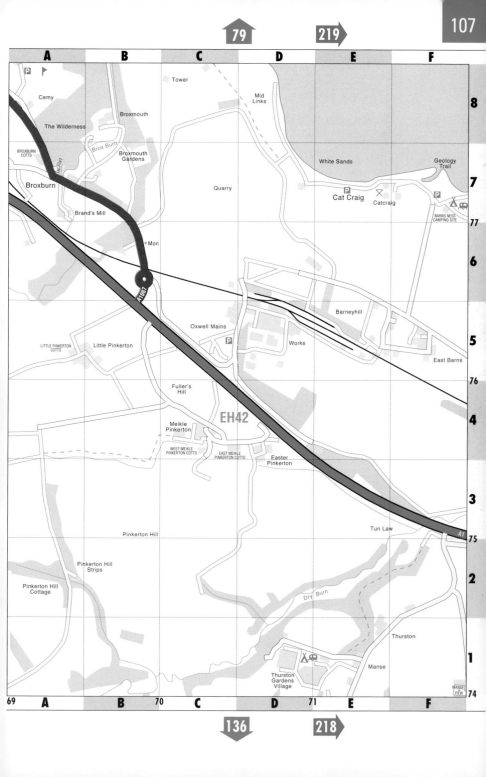

79
219
136
218

A **B** **C** **D** **E** **F**

8

Cemy

Tower

Mid Links

Broxmouth

The Wilderness

BROXBURN COTTS

Brox Burn

Broxmouth Gardens

White Sands

Geology Trail

7

Broxburn

Quarry

Cat Craig

Catcraig

BARNS NESS CAMPING SITE

Brand's Mill

77

Mon

A1087

6

Oxwell Mains

Barneyhill

LITTLE PINKERTON COTTS

Little Pinkerton

Works

5

East Barns

76

Fuller's Hill

EH42

4

Meikle Pinkerton

WEST MEIKLE PINKERTON COTTS

EAST MEIKLE PINKERTON COTTS

Easter Pinkerton

3

Tun Law

A1

75

Pinkerton Hill

2

Pinkerton Hill Strips

Pinkerton Hill Cottage

Dry Burn

Thurston

1

Manse

Thurston Gardens Village

MANSEL VIEW

74

69 **A** **B** 70 **C** **D** 71 **E** **F**

80

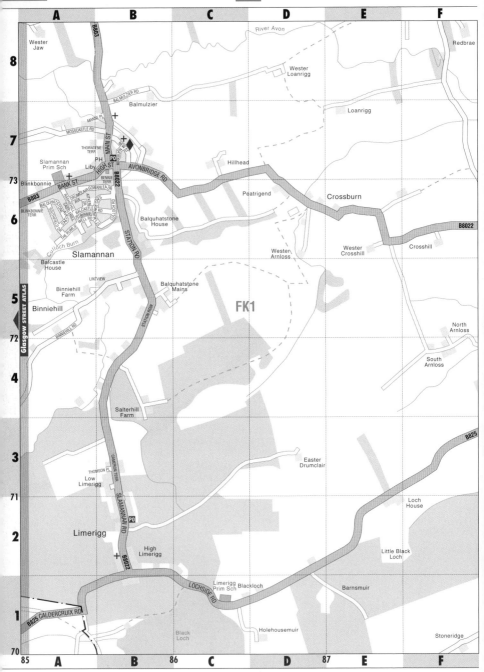

137

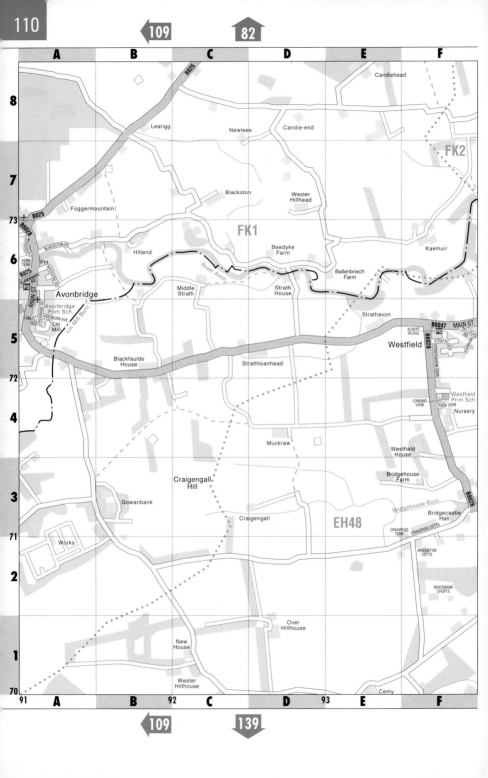

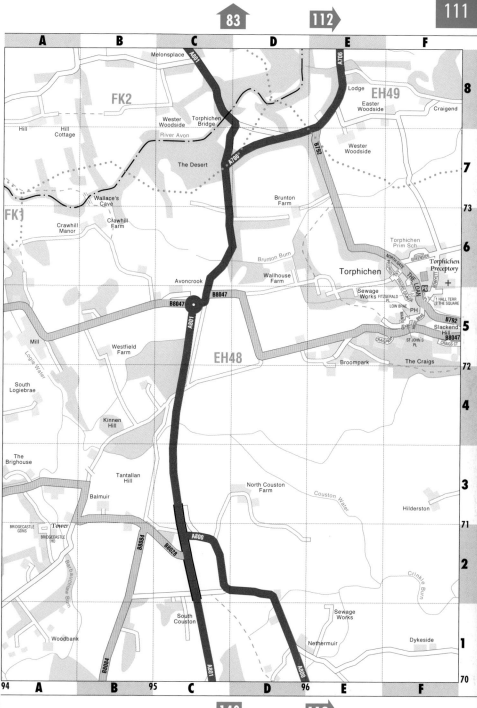

111
84

A B C D E F

8

Cow Hill

EH49

Tower

Lochcote Resr

Kipps
(remains of)

Kipps Hill

Kipps
Farm

Beecraigs Wood

EH49

Beecraigs
Country Park

7

Refuge
Stone

Wairdlaw

73

Gormyre

Witch Craig
Wood

6

Gormyre
Hill

The Scottish Korean
War Memorial

Hanging Rock
Plantation

Torpichen
Hills

Cathlaw
House

Craigmailing

Stoney Manuel
Plantation

5

B792
B8047
CRAIGS
CT

MALLEN'S BRAE

CATHLAW LA

Slackend

Cathlawhill

EH48

North Mine
Plantation

72

Bishopbrae
Strips

4

Cairnpapple
Hill

Cairnpapple
Henge & Cairn

Mast

P

The Glebe

Hilderston
Hills

3

Bishopbrae

Knock

P   The
Knock

71

Crinkle Burn

Resr

2

Crinkle
Bridge

Ballencrieff
Mains

Sheddon Braes

Raven Craig
Wood

1

Bathgate
Hills

B792

BALLENCRIEFF
TOLL

BATHGATE RD

Resr

Galabraes

Wester
Drumcross

70

97   A   B   98   C   D   99   E   F

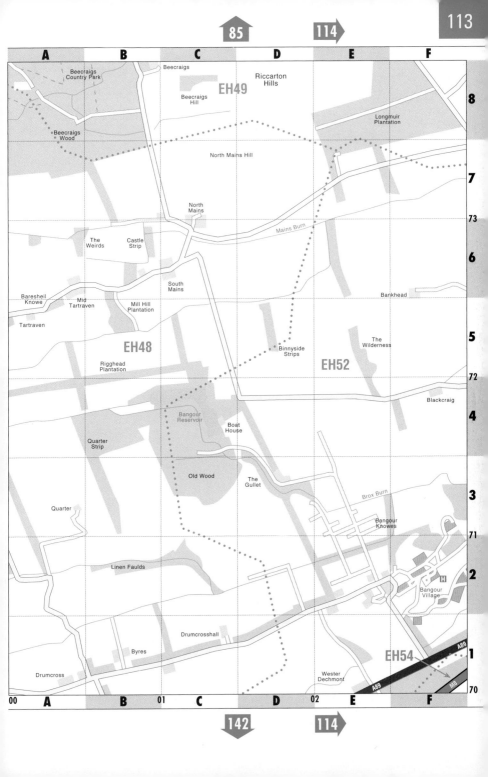

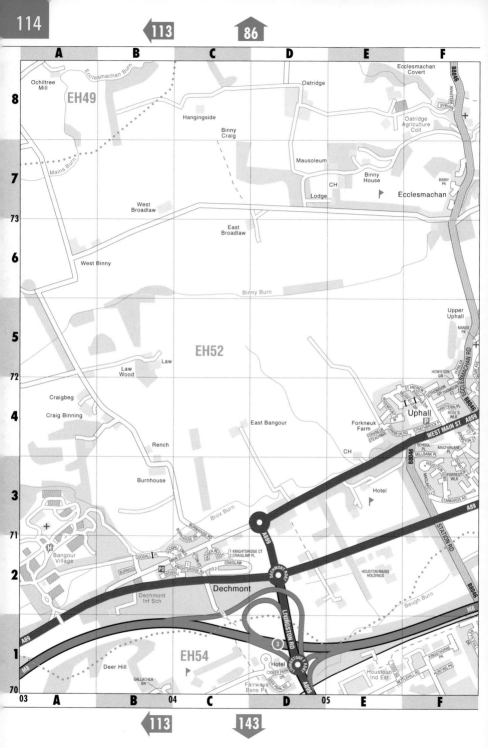

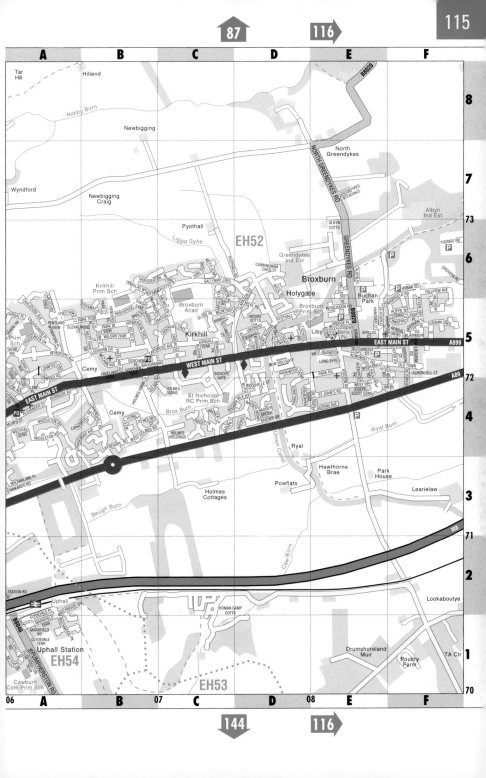

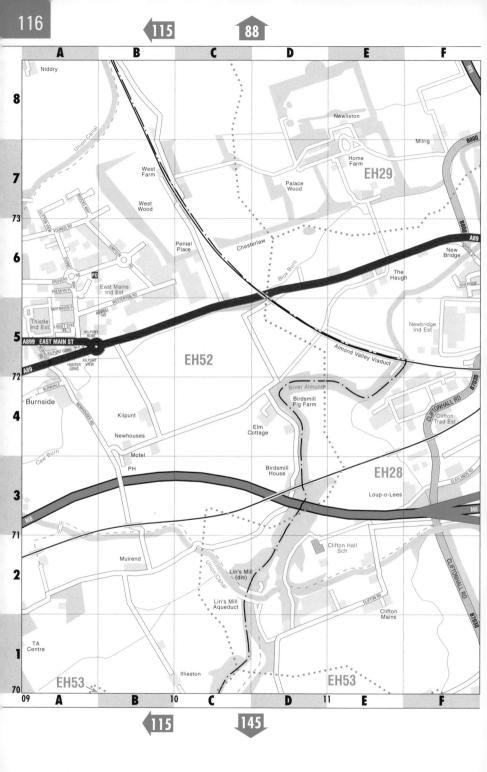

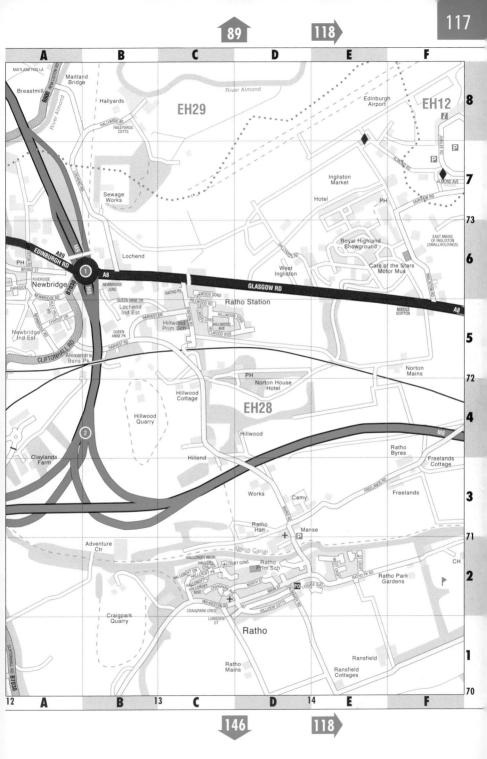

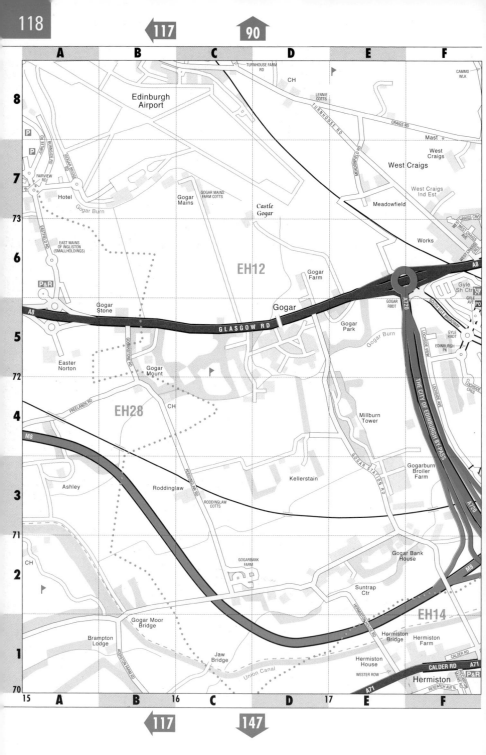

117
90
117
147

Edinburgh Airport

TURNHOUSE FARM RD

CH

LENNIE COTTS

CAMMO WLK

West Craigs

West Craigs

Mast

West Craigs Ind Est

Meadowfield

Works

Gogar Mains

GOGAR MAINS FARM COTTS

Castle Gogar

Hotel

Gogar Burn

EH12

FAIRVIEW RD

EAST MAINS OF INGLISTON (SMALLHOLDINGS)

Gogar Farm

Gogar RBDT

A720

Gyle Sh Ctr

GYLE AVE

P&R

Gogar Stone

GLASGOW RD

Gogar

Gogar Park

Gogar Burn

SOUTH GYLE BROADWAY

GYLE RBDT

Edinburgh Pk

A8

Easter Norton

Gogar Mount

CH

EH28

Millburn Tower

THE CITY OF EDINBURGH BY-PASS

LOCHSIDE VIEW

A720

LOCHSIDE AVE

LOCHSIDE CRES

M8

FREELANDS RD

GOGAR STATION RD

Ashley

Roddinglaw

RODDINGLAW COTTS

Kellerstain

Gogarburn Broiler Farm

M8

CH

GOGARBANK FARM

Gogar Bank House

Suntrap Ctr

EH14

Gogar Moor Bridge

Brampton Lodge

Jaw Bridge

Union Canal

Hermiston Bridge

Hermiston House

WESTER ROW

Hermiston Farm

CALDER RD

CALDER RD

A71

P&R

A71

Hermiston

RESEARCH AVE N

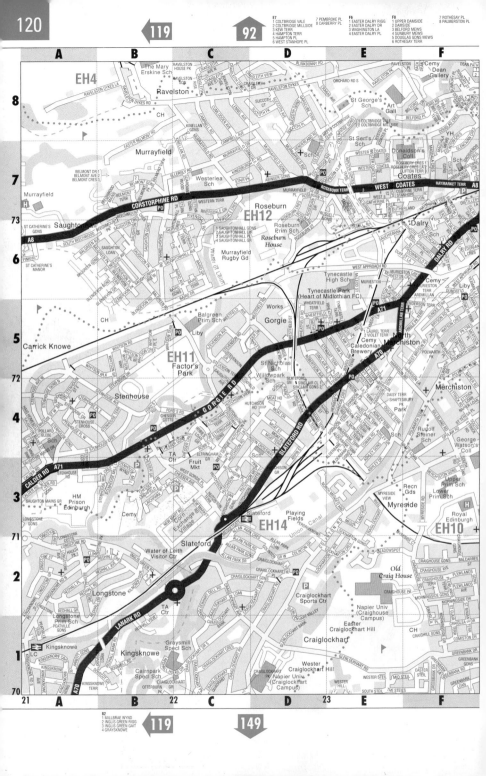

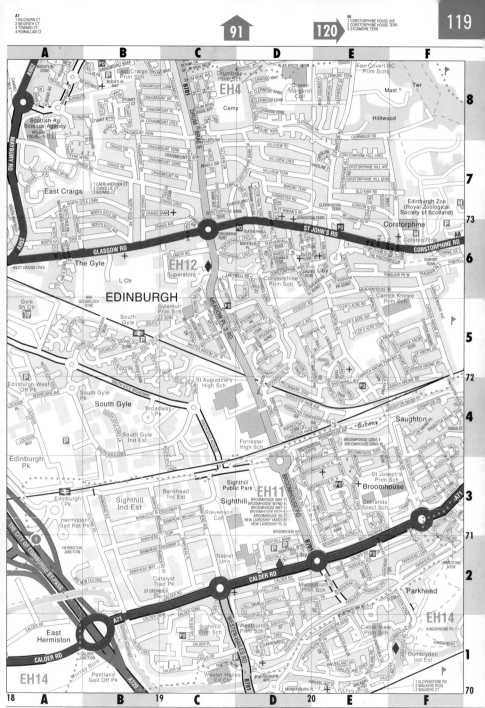

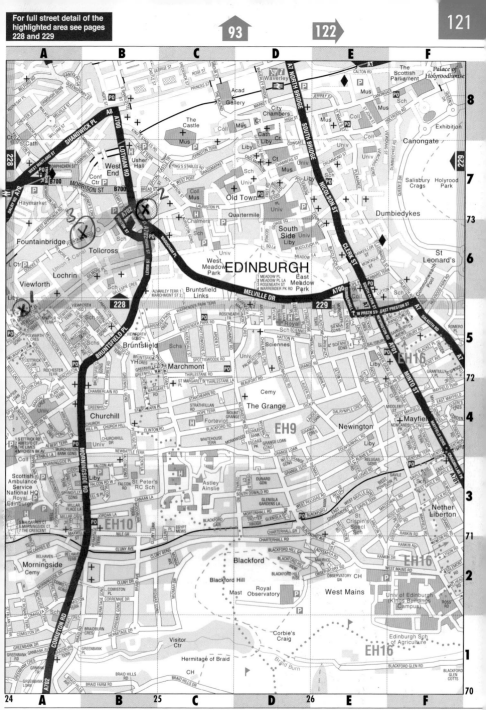

E5
5 SCIENNES PL
2 EAST SCIENNES ST
3 SCIENNES HOUSE PL
4 SCIENNES HILL PL
5 GRANGE CT
6 EAST PRESTON STREET LA
7 WEST NEWINGTON PL

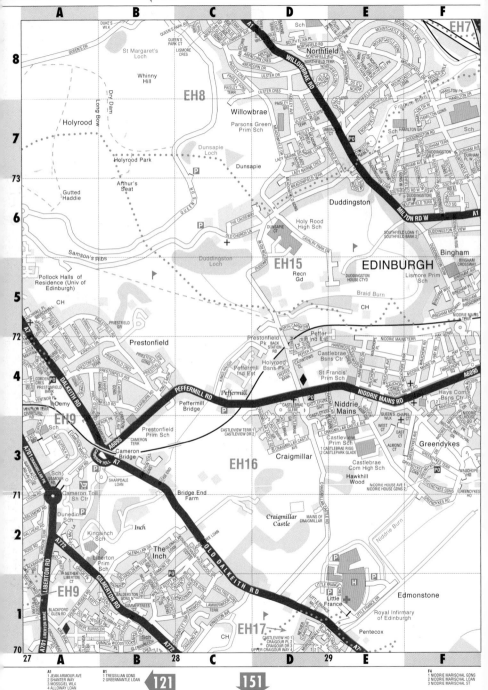

A1
1 JEAN ARMOUR AVE
2 SHANTER WAY
3 MOSSGIEL WLK
4 ALLOWAY LOAN

B1
1 TRESSILIAN GDNS
2 GREENMANTLE LOAN

F4
1 NIDDRIE MARISCHAL GDNS
2 NIDDRIE MARISCHAL LOAN
3 NIDDRIE MARISCHAL ST

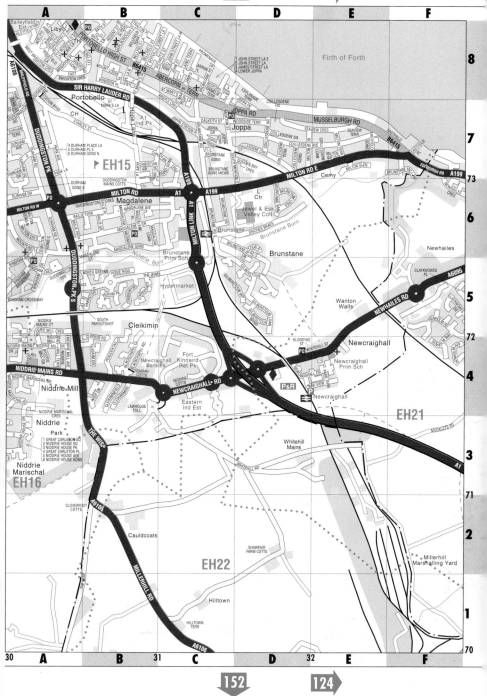

A8
1 ADELPHI GR
2 WILLIAMFIELD SQ
3 BEACH LA

123

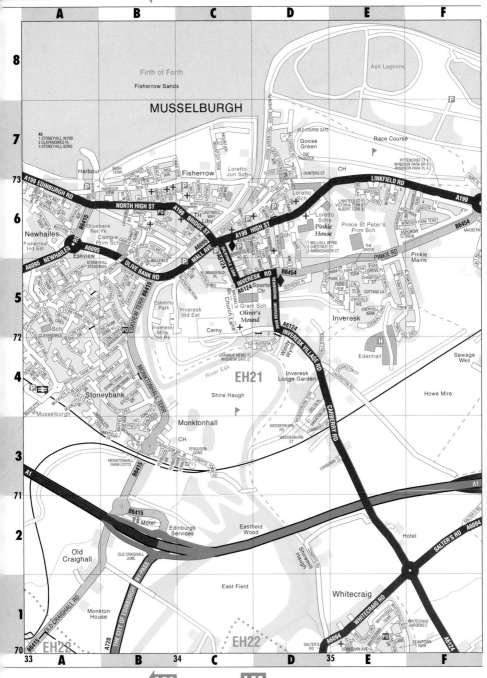

MUSSELBURGH

Firth of Forth

Fisherrow Sands

Ash Lagoons

Race Course

Goose Green

Fisherrow

EH21

Inveresk

Stoneybank

Monktonhall

Old Craighall

Whitecraig

East Field

Eastfield Wood

Howe Mire

Sewage Wks

Edenhall

EH22

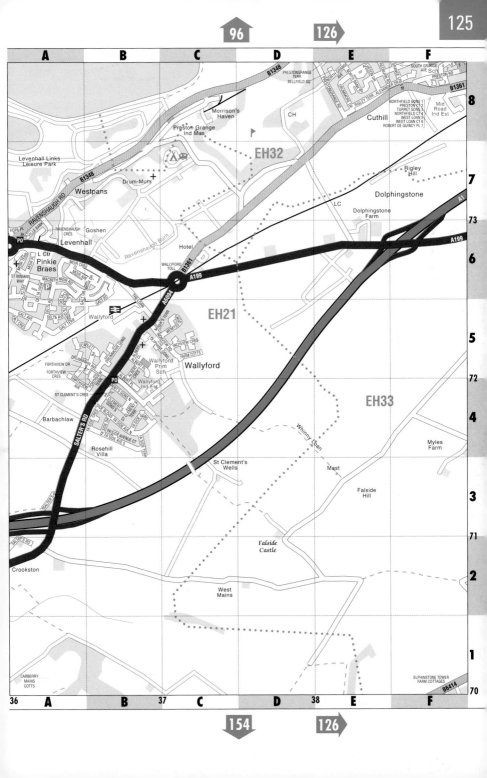

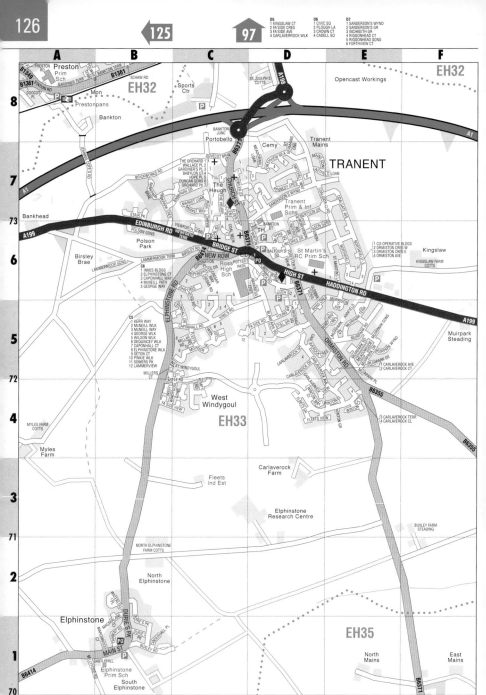

D5
1 KINGSLAW CT
2 FA'SIDE CRES
3 FA'SIDE AVE
4 CARLAVEROCK WLK

D6
1 CIVIC SQ
2 PLOUGH LA
3 CROWN CT
4 CADELL SQ

D7
1 SANDERSON'S WYND
2 SANDERSON'S GR
3 INCHKEITH GR
4 RIGGONHEAD CT
5 RIGGONHEAD GDNS
6 FORTHVIEW CT

EH32

Opencast Workings

EH32

Preston
Prim
Sch

Prestonpans

Bankton

SCHAW RD
EH32

Sports
Ctr

St JOSEPH'S
COTTS

BANKTON
JUNC
Portobello

Cemy

Tranent
Mains

TRANENT

The Heugh

Tranent
Prim & Inf
Schs

Bankhead

EDINBURGH RD
A199

Polson
Park

Birsley
Brae

BRIDGE ST

NEW ROW

Ross
High
Sch

St Martin's
RC Prim Sch

HIGH ST

HADDINGTON RD

Kingslaw

KINGSLAW FARM
COTTS

1 CO-OPERATIVE BLDGS
2 ORMISTON CRES W
3 ORMISTON CRES E
4 ORMISTON AVE

C6
1 INNES BLDGS
2 ELPHINSTONE CT
3 CAPONHALL WAY
4 McNEILL PATH
5 GEORGE WAY

C5
1 KERR WAY
2 McNEILL WLK
3 McNEILL WAY
4 GEORGE WLK
5 WILSON WLK
6 DEQUINCEY WLK
7 CAPONHALL CT
8 ELPHINSTONE WLK
9 SETON CT
10 PINKIE WLK
11 SOMERS PK
12 LAMMERVIEW

ORMISTON RD

Muirpark
Steading

1 CARLAVEROCK AVE
2 CARLAVEROCK CT

West
Windygoul

EH33

3 CARLAVEROCK TERR
4 CARLAVEROCK CL

B6355

MYLES FARM
COTTS

Myles
Farm

Carlaverock
Farm

Fleets
Ind Est

Elphinstone
Research Centre

BUXLEY FARM
STEADING

NORTH ELPHINSTONE
FARM COTTS

North
Elphinstone

EH35

Elphinstone

DURIE'S PK

MAIN ST

Elphinstone
Prim Sch

South
Elphinstone

North
Mains

East
Mains

B6371

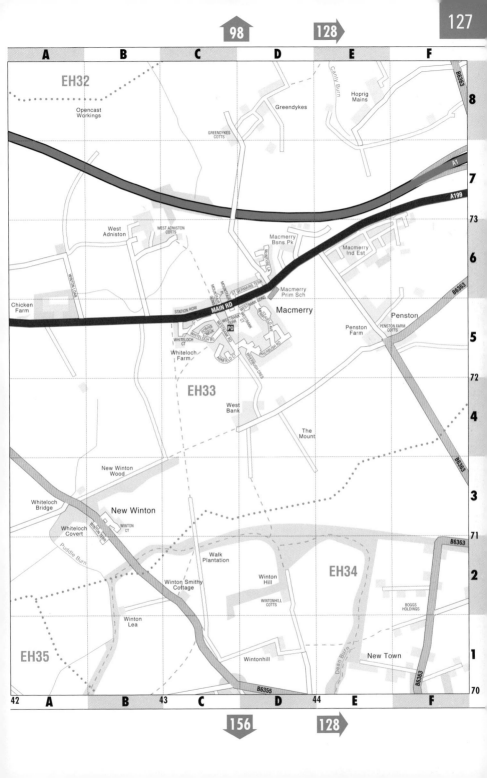

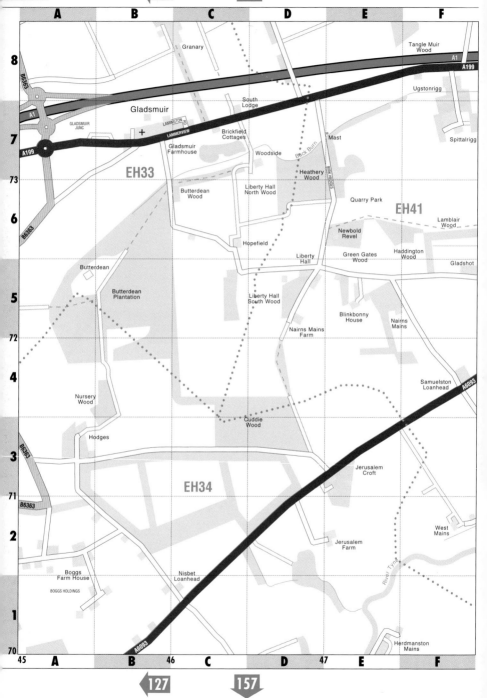

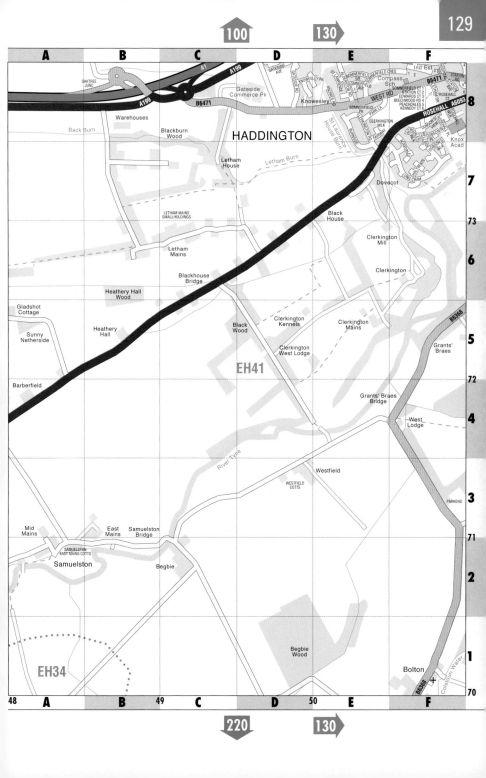

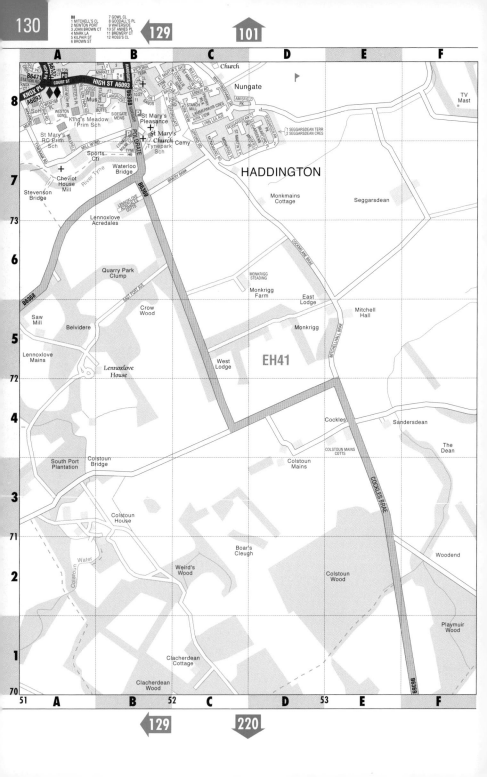

88
1 MITCHELL'S CL
2 NEWTON PORT
3 JOHN BROWN CT
4 MARK LA
5 KILPAIR ST
6 BROWN ST
7 GOWL CL
8 GOODALL'S PL
9 WATERSIDE
10 ST ANNES PL
11 BREWERY CT
12 ROSS'S CL

129
101
129
220

HADDINGTON

Nungate

Church

EH41

TV Mast

1 SEGGARSDEAN TERR
2 SEGGARSDEAN CRES

Monkmains Cottage

Seggarsdean

Monkrigg Steading

Monkrigg Farm

East Lodge

Mitchell Hall

Monkrigg

West Lodge

Cockles

Sandersdean

The Dean

Colstoun Mains Cotts

Colstoun Mains

Colstoun Wood

Woodend

Colstoun Bridge

South Port Plantation

Colstoun House

Boar's Cleugh

Weird's Wood

Playmuir Wood

Clacherdean Cottage

Clacherdean Wood

Lennoxlove Acredales

Quarry Park Clump

Crow Wood

Saw Mill

Belvidere

Lennoxlove Mains

Lennoxlove House

Stevenson Bridge

Cheviot House Mill

Waterloo Bridge

Sports Ctr

King's Meadow Prim Sch

St Mary's RC Prim Sch

St Mary's Pleasance

St Mary's Church

Tynepark Sch

Cemy

River Tyne

HIGH ST A6093

KNOX PL

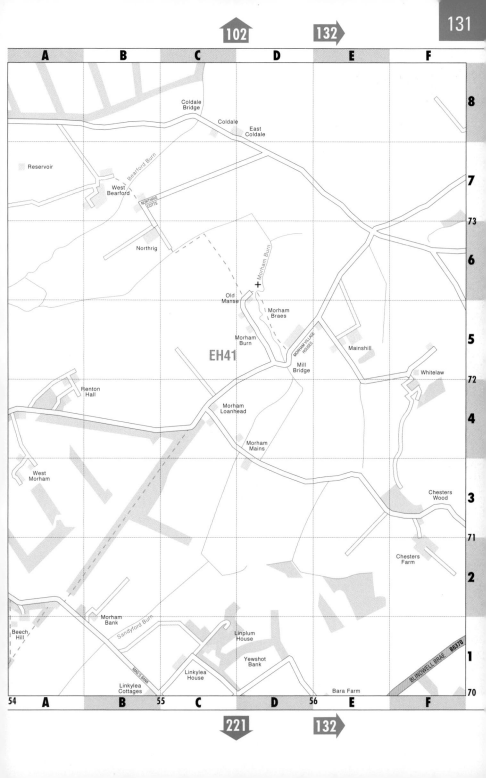

102 132

A B C D E F

8

Coldale
Bridge

Coldale

East
Coldale

7

Reservoir

Bearford Burn

West
Bearford

NORTHRIG
COTTS

73

Northrig

6

Morham Burn

Old
Manse

Morham
Braes

5

Morham
Burn

EH41

MORHAM VILLAGE
HOUSES

Mainshill

Mill
Bridge

Whitelaw

72

Renton
Hall

Morham
Loanhead

4

Morham
Mains

West
Morham

Chesters
Wood

3

71

Chesters
Farm

2

Morham
Bank

Sandyford Burn

Linplum
House

Beech
Hill

Yewshot
Bank

BLINDWELL BRAE B6370

1

BA'S BANK

Linkylea
House

Linkylea
Cottages

Bara Farm

70

54 A B 55 C D 56 E F

221 132

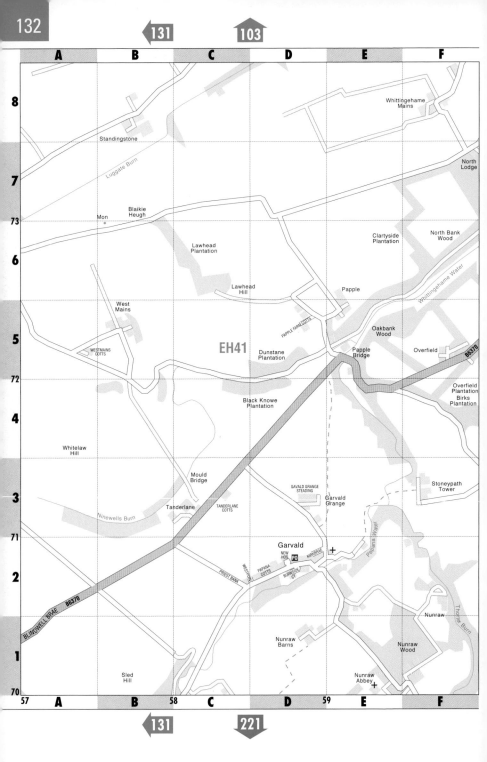

A **B** **C** **D** **E** **F**

8

Whittingehame
Mains

Standingstone

North
Lodge

7

Luggate Burn

73

Blaikie
Mon   Heugh

Clartyside
Plantation

North Bank
Wood

6

Lawhead
Plantation

Whittinghame Water

Lawhead
Hill

Papple

West
Mains

Oakbank
Wood

5

WESTMAINS
COTTS

EH41

Dunstane
Plantation

PAPPLE FARM COTTS

Papple
Bridge

Overfield

B6370

72

Overfield
Plantation
Birks
Plantation

Black Knowe
Plantation

4

Whitelaw
Hill

Mould
Bridge

Stoneypath
Tower

3

GAVALD GRANGE
STEADING

Garvald
Grange

Ninewells Burn

Tanderlane

TANDERLANE
COTTS

71

Papana Water

Garvald

NEW
HOS.
PO

KIRK BRAE

2

PRIEST BANK

WESTPORT

PAPANA
COTTS

BURNSIDE
CT.

Nunraw

Thorter Burn

BLINKBONNY BRAE   B6370

1

Sled
Hill

Nunraw
Barns

Nunraw
Wood

Nunraw
Abbey

70

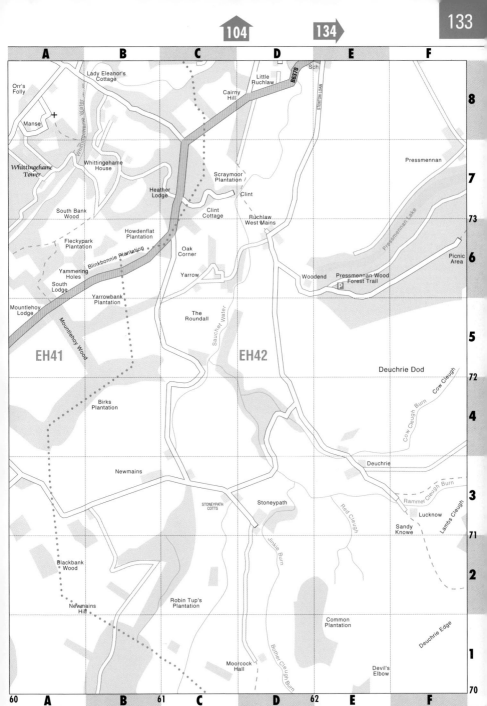

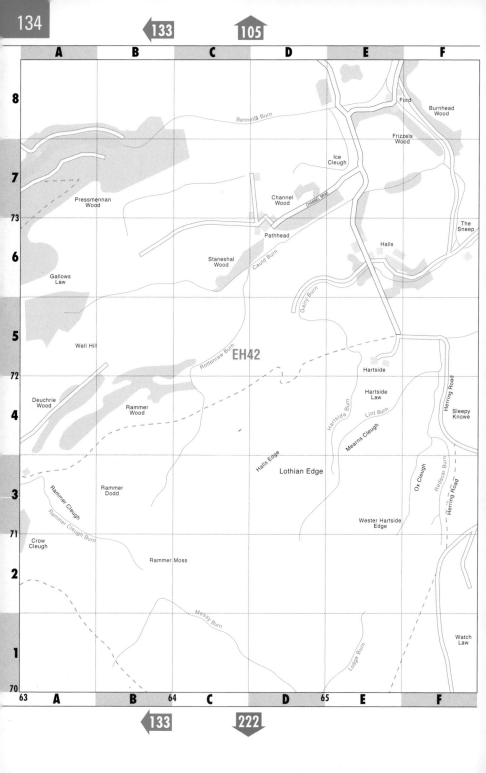

133
105

A B C D E F

8

Bennet@ Burn

Ford

Burnhead
Wood

Frizzels
Wood

7

Ice
Cleugh

The
Sneep

Pressmennan
Wood

73

Channel
Wood

CHANNEL BRAE

Pathhead

Halls

6

Staneshal
Wood

Cauld Burn

Gallows
Law

Gairy Burn

5

Well Hill

Rottenraw Burn

EH42

Hartside

72

Deuchrie
Wood

Rammer
Wood

Hartside
Law

Hartside Burn

Lint Burn

Herring Road

Sleepy
Knowe

4

Halls Edge

Lothian Edge

Mearns Cleugh

Ox Cleugh

Redscar Burn

Herring Road

3

Rammer Cleugh

Rammer
Dodd

Rammer Cleugh Burn

Wester Hartside
Edge

Crow
Cleugh

71

Rammer Moss

2

Mossy Burn

Lodge Burn

Watch
Law

1

70

63 **A** **B** 64 **C** **D** 65 **E** **F**

133
222

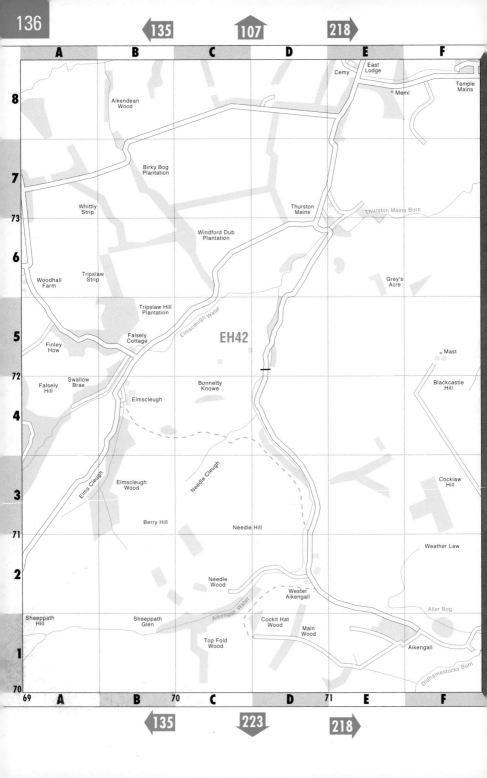

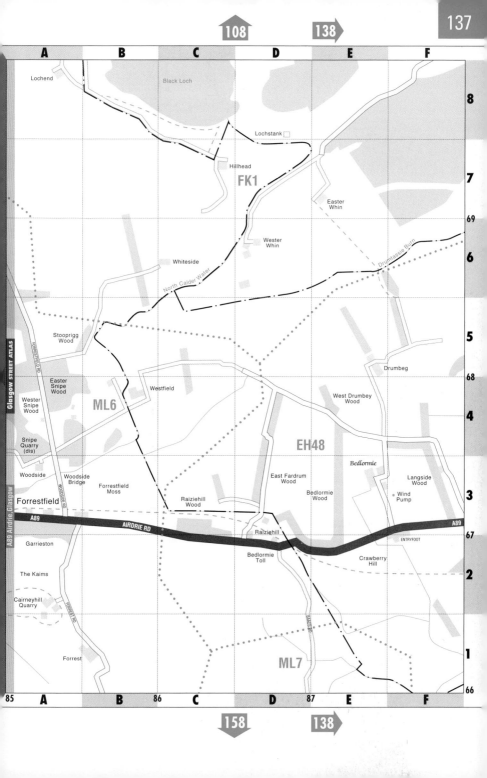

A B C D E F

8

7

69

6

5

68

4

3

67

2

1

66

85 A B 86 C D 87 E F

Glasgow STREET ATLAS

A89 Airdrie, Glasgow

Lochend

Black Loch

Lochstank

Hillhead

FK1

Easter Whin

Wester Whin

Whiteside

North Calder Water

Drumtassie Burn

Stooprigg Wood

Drumbeg

Easter Snipe Wood

Wester Snipe Wood

Westfield

West Drumbey Wood

ML6

Snipe Quarry (dis)

EH48

Bedlormie

Woodside

Woodside Bridge

Forrestfield Moss

East Fardrum Wood

Bedlormie Wood

Langside Wood

Wind Pump

Forrestfield

Raiziehill Wood

A89

AIRDRIE RD

A89

Garrieston

Raiziehill

ENTRYFOOT

Bedlormie Toll

Crawberry Hill

The Kaims

Cairneyhill Quarry

FORREST RD

WOODSIDE RD

MAIN RD

Forrest

ML7

A B C D E F

8

Burnhead
Moss

Burnhead

Drum Park
Plantation

Croft
Plantation

Wester Burnhead
Wood

Drumtassie Burn

FK1

Heights

7

Tawnycraw
Hill

West Rhodens
Plantation

69

Drumelzie

6

East Backmuir
Wood

Reservoir

Blawhorn Moss

Eastcraigs
Hill

5

68

Crowns
Hill

4

Blawhorn
Wood

EH48

Craigs

1 CRAIGHILL VIEW
2 BLACKHILL RD
3 SUNNYDALE RD

Barn
Wood

Westcraigs
Hill

GREENHILL RD

PARK RD

SUNNYDALE DR

A89

Heatherhouse
Wood

Wester
Redburn

Easter
Redburn

MATTHEWS
CROFTS

Blackridge

Blackridge
Community
Mus

CRAIG ST

Westrigg

3

Bedlormie
House

FARQUHAR
SQ

Blackridge
Prim Sch

DRUMMOND

Liby

MACLEAN TERR

CRAIGINN TERR

PH

MAIN ST

HILLSIDE DR

CRAIGIEA CT

CRAIGINN
CT

A89

67

QUARRY
COTTS

WESTCRAIGS
PK

LOUBURN

BEDLORMIE DR

OGILFACE
CRES

REDBURN RD

PO

B718

WESTCRAIGS RD

Mosshouse

Standhill
Farm

STATION
RD

2

HARTHILL RD

WHITELAW ST

1

B718

Torrance
Farm

66

Bogend
Farm

ML7

ML7

88 A 89 B C 89 D 90 E F

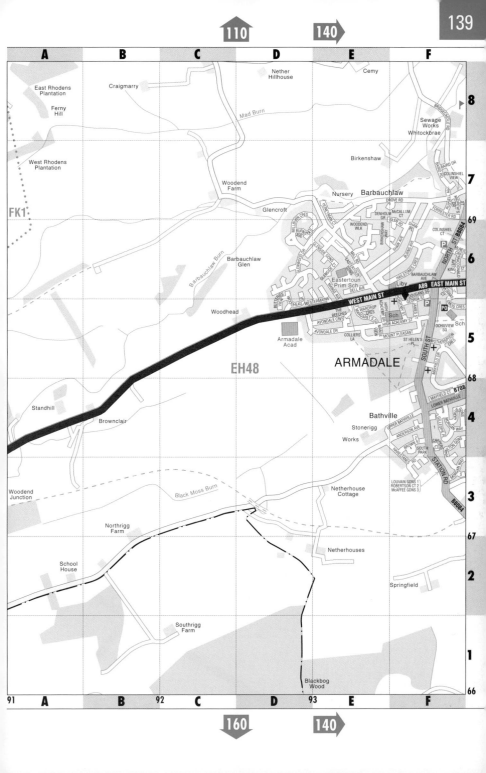

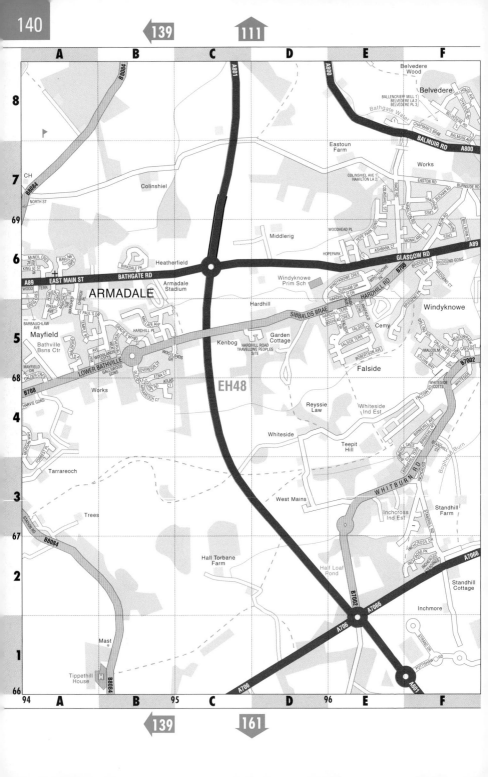

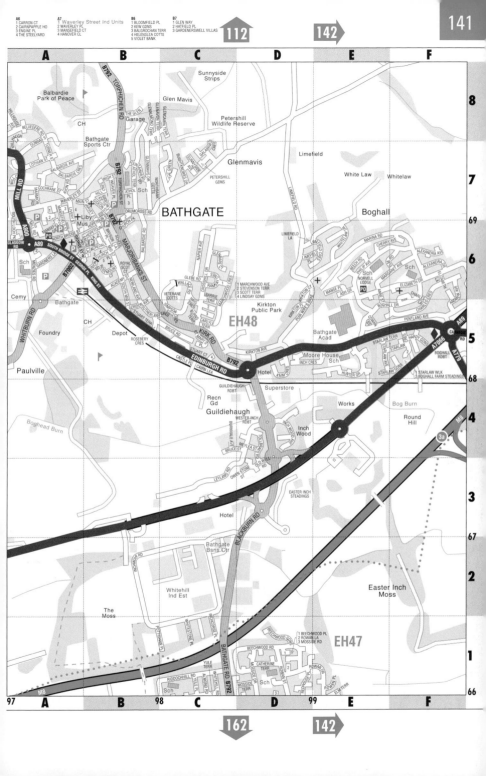

A6
1 CARRON CT
2 CAIRNPAPPLE HO
3 ENGINE PL
4 THE STEELYARD

A7 Waverley Street Ind Units
1 WAVERLEY PL
2 MANSEFIELD CT
4 HANOVER CL

B6
1 BLOOMFIELD PL
2 KEW GDNS
3 BALGROCHAN TERR
4 HELENGLEA COTTS
5 VIOLET BANK

B7
1 GLEN WAY
2 HATFIELD PL
3 GARDENERSWELL VILLAS

Sunnyside Strips

Balbardie Park of Peace

Glen Mavis

Petershill Wildlife Reserve

Limefield

Glenmavis

White Law
Whitelaw

Bathgate Sports Ctr

BATHGATE

Boghall

PETERSHILL GDNS

Limefield La

1 MARCHWOOD AVE
2 STEVENSON TERR
3 SCOTT TERR
4 LINDSAY GDNS

Norvell Lodge

Kirkton Public Park

EH48

Bathgate Acad

Moore House Sch

1 STARLAW WLK
2 BOGHALL FARM STEADINGS

Cemy

Bathgate

Foundry

CH

Depot

ROSEBERY CRES

Paulville

Boghead Burn

Hotel

Superstore

Recn Gd

Guildiehaugh

Inch Wood

Works

Bog Burn

Round Hill

3a

Boghead Burn

Easter Inch Steadings

Hotel

Bathgate Bsns Ctr

Easter Inch Moss

Whitehill Ind Est

The Moss

Whitehill Ind Est

1 BEECHWOOD PL
2 ROWAN LA
3 MOSSIDE RD

EH47

Yule Terr

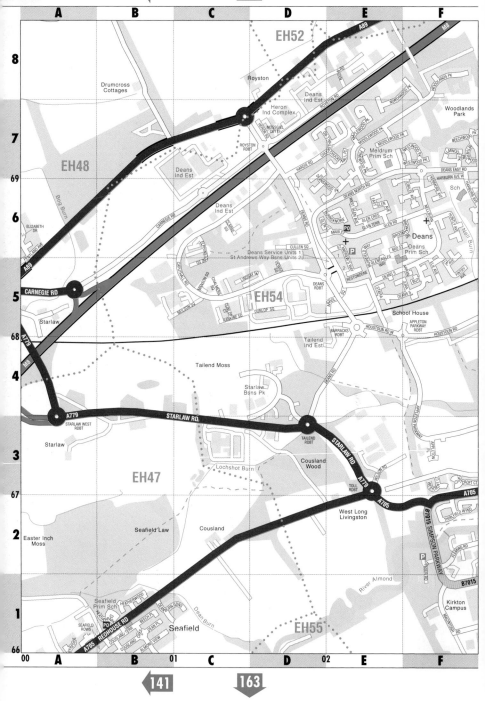

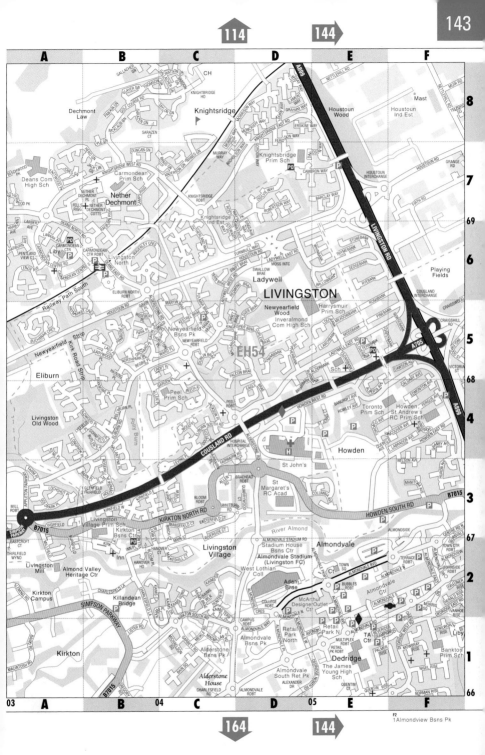

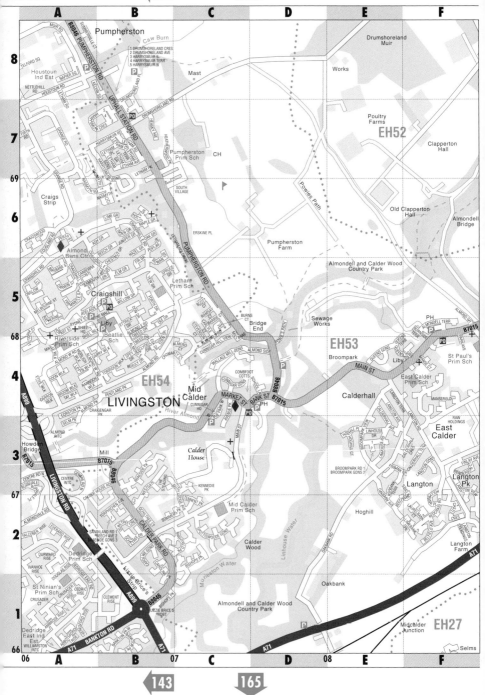

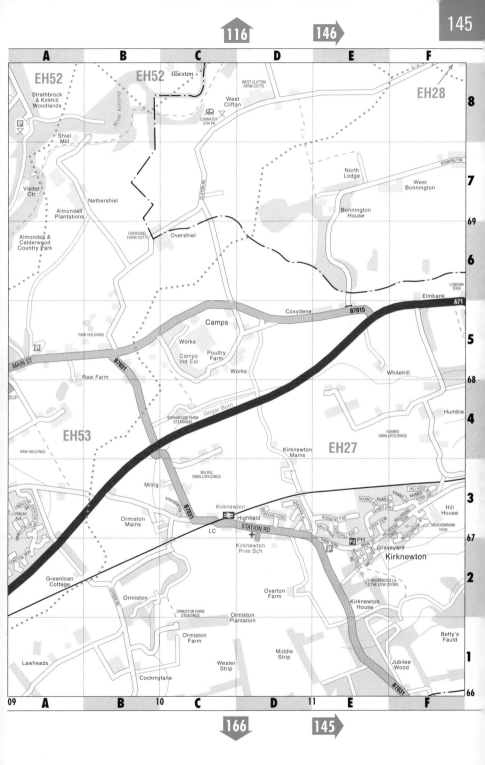

145
117

	A	B	C	D	E	F

8

EH28

Tormain

Cup & Ring
marked Rocks

B7030
CLIFTONHALL RD

BONNINGTON

7

Bonnington
Mains

Craw
Hill

Ratho Park
Hotel

St
Mary's
Hall

A71

BONNINGTON RD

69

Entry +
Head

Dalmahoy
Stables

Hatton
Bridge

Hatton
Mains

Hillview

BRIDGE END
COTTS

6

Hatton
House

Hatton
Sports Club

Dalmahoy
Country Club

Wilkieston

Orchardfield

Hatton

CH

B7030

Burnwynd

ORCHARDFIELD
TERR

A71 P0

LINBURN RD

5

Linburn

EH27

LINBURN RD

Spittalton
Wood

68

Kinrura

4

Waterloo
Tower

Haggs
Farm

Long
Dalmahoy

Dalmahoy
Mains

Ravelrig
Junction

LONG DALMAHOY RD

3

Dalmahoy Hill
Plantation

Green Burn

Easter
Newton

Ravelrig
Quarries
(dis)

67

Dalmahoy
Hill

2

The
Dean

A70

Kaimes
Hill

1

Kaimes

Kaimes
Quarry

EH14

A70

Burial
Ground
Wood

Kaimes
Wood

GLENBROOK RD

66

| 12 | A | | B | 13 | C | | D | 14 | E | | F |

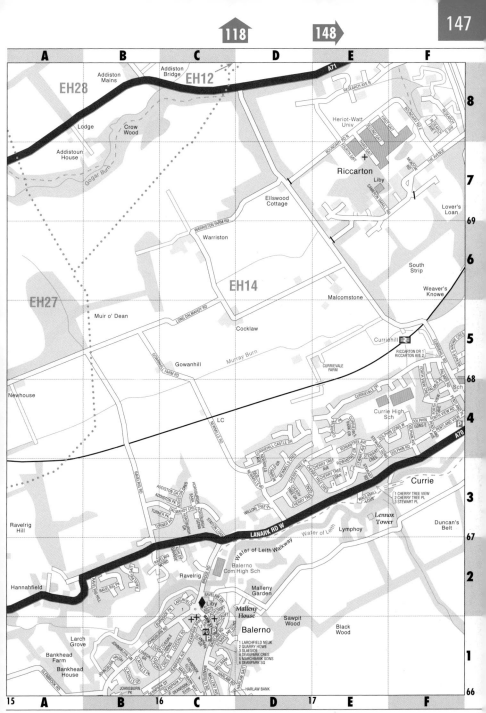

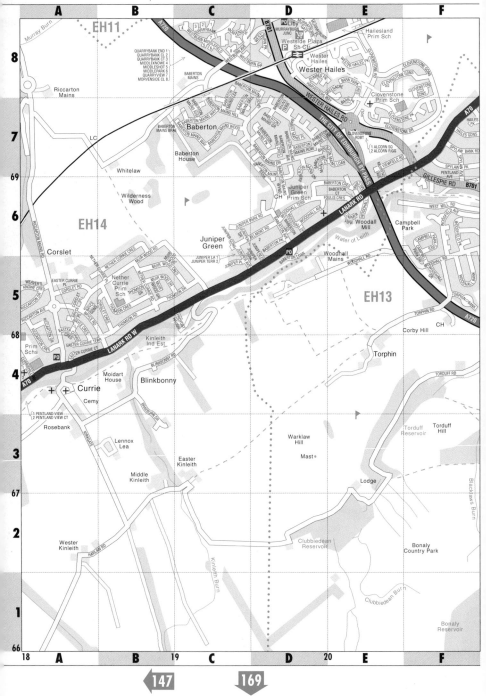

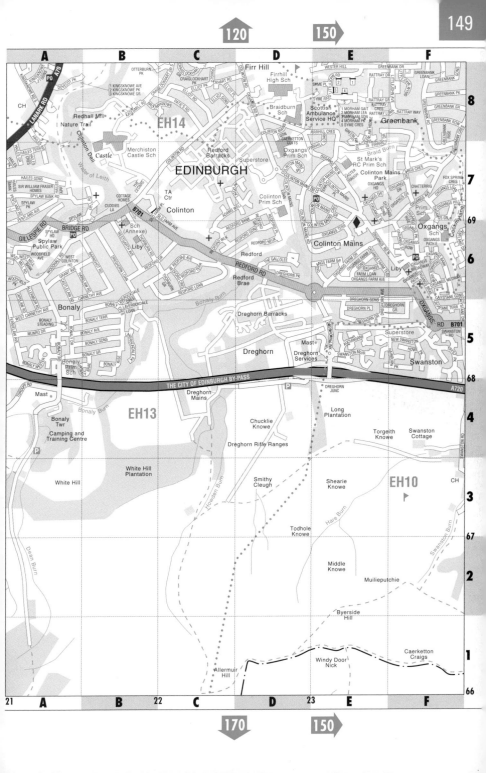

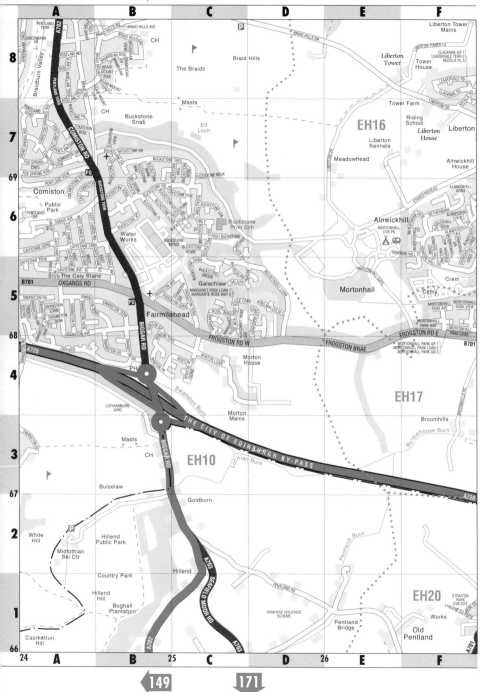

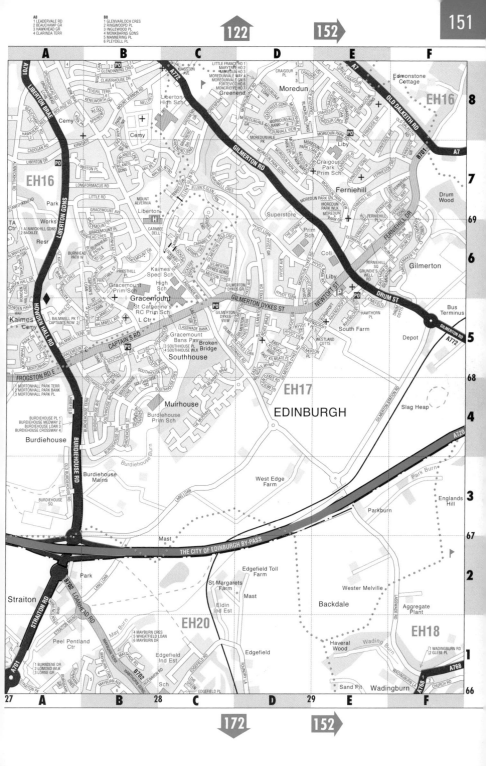

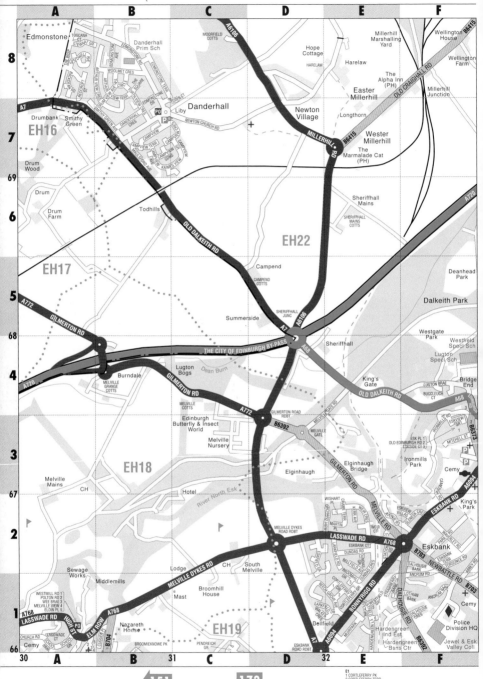

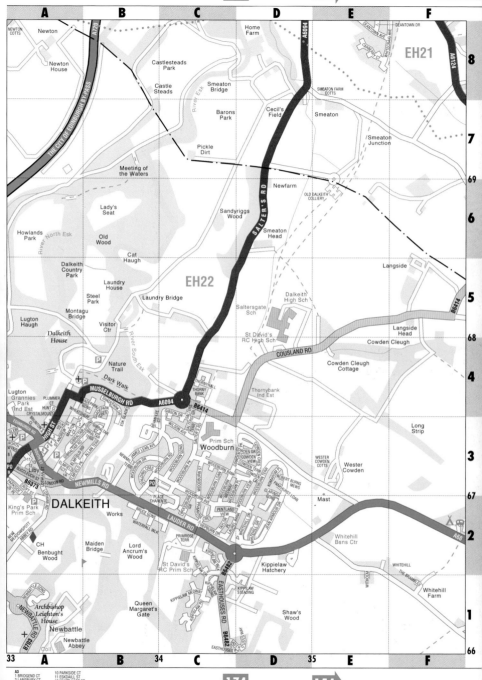

EH21

EH22

EH22

DALKEITH

A3
1 BRIDGEND CT
2 LANSBURY CT
3 TAIT ST
4 ROBERTSON'S CL
5 WHITE'S CL
6 PETTIGREW'S CL
7 JARNAC CT
8 OLD EDINBURGH RD
9 ESBANK RD
10 PARKSIDE CT
11 ESKDAILL ST
12 WHITE HART ST
13 ESKDAILL CT
14 LAUDER LODGE

153
125

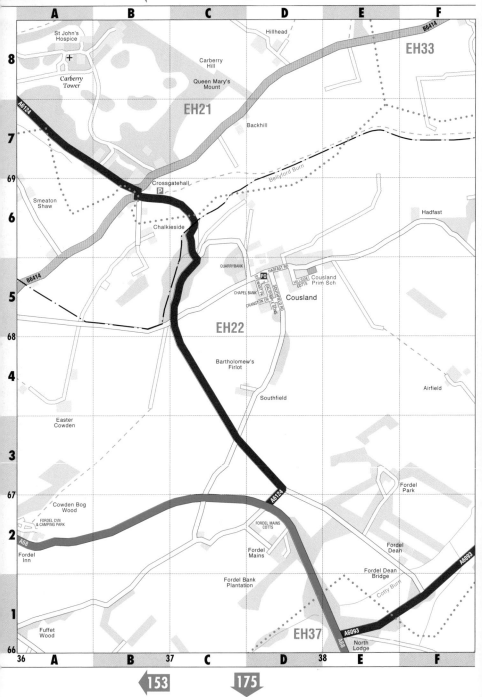

153
175

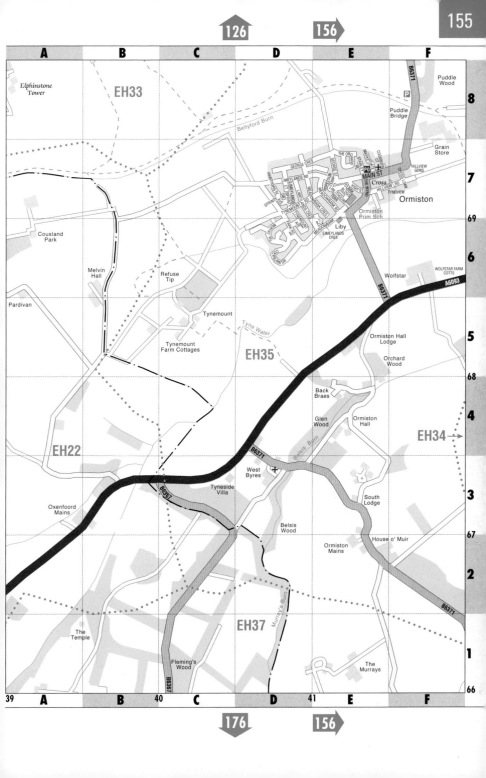

A B C D E F

126
156

Elphinstone Tower

EH33

Puddle Wood

P

Puddle Bridge

Bellyford Burn

Grain Store

THE ORCHARD
GEORGE CRES
HAWTHORN ST
LIMEYLANDS RD
SPRINGFIELD
LIMEYLANDS CT
MEADOWBANK CRES
HIGH ST
VICTORIA ST
CROSS ST
GOSFORD
HILLVIEW GDNS
TYNEVIEW
HILLVIEW RD

MAIN ST
Cross
Ormiston

SPRING
TYNEMOUNT AVE
TYNEMOUNT RD
RD
LENNOX DR
MEADOWBANK
PO

Liby
LIMEYLANDS CRES

Ormiston Prim Sch

8

7

69

6

Cousland Park

Melvin Hall

Refuse Tip

Tynemount

Tynemount Farm Cottages

EH35

Tyne Water

Wolfstar

WOLFSTAR FARM COTTS

A6093

B6371

Ormiston Hall Lodge

Orchard Wood

5

68

4

Pardivan

EH22

Back Braes

Glen Wood

Ormiston Hall

EH34 →

Belsis Burn

B6371

West Byres

Tyneside Villa

B6367

South Lodge

Oxenfoord Mains

Belsis Wood

Ormiston Mains

House o' Muir

3

67

2

The Temple

EH37

Fleming's Wood

Murray's Burn

The Murrays

B6367

B6371

1

66

39 A B 40 C D 41 E F

176
156

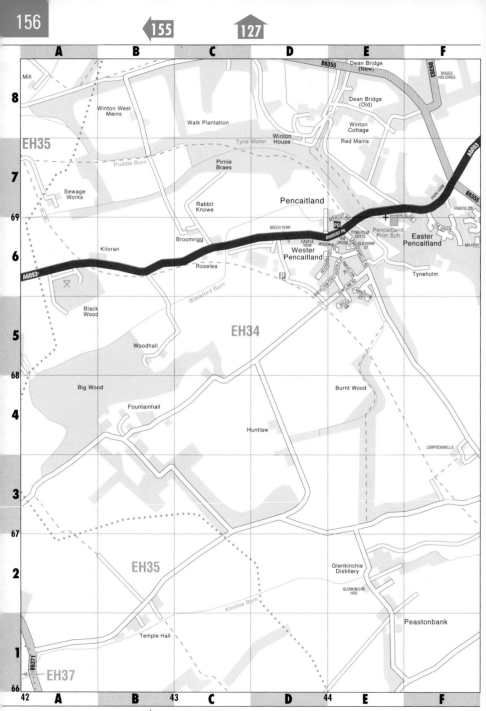

155
127

Mill

Winton West
Mains

Walk Plantation

Dean Bridge
(New)

B6355

B6363

BOGGS
HOLDINGS

Dean Bridge
(Old)

EH35

Tyne Water

Winton
House

Winton
Cottage

Red Mains

A6093

B6355

Puddle Burn

Pirnie
Braes

PARK VIEW

VINEFIELDS

Sewage
Works

Rabbit
Knowe

Pencaitland

THE GLEB

DOVECOT WY

THE GREEN

Broomrigg

BEECH TERR

PO

DOVECOT PK

Pencaitland
Prim Sch

Easter
Pencaitland

Kiloran

CASTLE
VIEW

TYNEHOLM
COTTS

WOODHALL CROSS

OLD FARM
CT

MILLWAY

Roselea

Wester
Pencaitland

WOODHALL
PL

PRIESTLAW

Tyneholm

A6093

Blackford Burn

P

WOODHALL
DR

THE STEILS

BRUCE
GR

Black
Wood

EH34

HAREWELLS RD

PRIESTLAW RD

DUMPLAW RD

LAMBERTON
CT

Woodhall

Big Wood

Burnt Wood

Fountainhall

Huntlaw

LEMPOCKWELLS

Glenkinchie
Distillery

EH35

GLENKINCHIE
HOS

Kinchie Burn

Peastonbank

Temple Hall

B6371

155

EH37

155
177

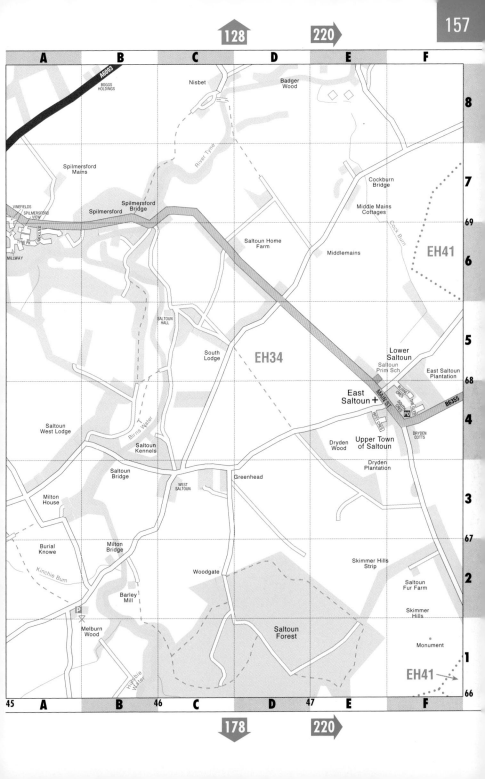

128
220

A B C D E F

8

BOGGS
HOLDINGS

A6093

Nisbet

Badger
Wood

River Tyne

Spilmersford
Mains

7

Cockburn
Bridge

Middle Mains
Cottages

Spilmersford
Bridge

Spilmersford

VINEFIELDS
SPILMERSFORD
VIEW

Saltoun Home
Farm

Middlemains

69

Cock Burn

EH41

6

TYNE PK
TOCKLINS

MILLWAY

SALTOUN
HALL

South
Lodge

EH34

Lower
Saltoun

5

Saltoun
Prim Sch

East Saltoun
Plantation

68

East
Saltoun

MAIN ST

BLINKB
ONNIE
CRES

THE GLEBE

East Saltoun

B6355

Saltoun
West Lodge

Birns Water

Upper Town
of Saltoun

WEST MEA

SOUTH
CROFT
PO

DRYDEN
COTTS

4

Saltoun
Kennels

Dryden
Wood

Dryden
Plantation

Saltoun
Bridge

WEST
SALTOUN

Greenhead

Milton
House

3

67

Burial
Knowe

Milton
Bridge

Skimmer Hills
Strip

Kinchie Burn

Woodgate

Saltoun
Fur Farm

2

Barley
Mill

Skimmer
Hills

P

Melburn
Wood

Saltoun
Forest

Monument

1

EH41

Humbie Water

66

45 A B 46 C D 47 E F

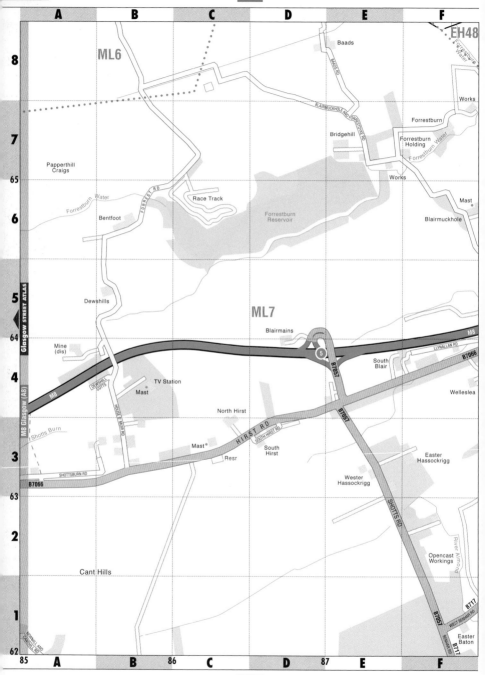

ML6

8

Baads

EH48

Works

BLAIRMUCKHOLE AND FORRESTIVE RD

Forrestburn

BAADS RD

Bridgehill

Forrestburn
Holding

7

Papperthill
Craigs

65

Forrestburn Water

FORREST RD

Works

Mast

Bentfoot

Race Track

Forrestburn
Reservoir

Blairmuckhole

6

Dewshills

5

ML7

Blairmains

M8

64

Mine
(dis)

LLYNALLAN RD

B7066

M8 Glasgow (A8)

M8

DEWSHILLS COTTS

TV Station

South
Blair

B7057

Welleslea

4

Mast

North Hirst

HOUSE O' MUIR RD

HIRST RD

SOUTH HIRST RD

B7057

Shotts Burn

Mast

Resr

South
Hirst

Easter
Hassockrigg

3

SHOTTSBURN RD

Wester
Hassockrigg

63

B7066

SHOTTS RD

River Almond

2

Cant Hills

Opencast
Workings

B717

1

B7057

WEST BENHAR RD

B717

62

NEWMILL AND CANT HILL RD

Easter
Baton

BENHAR RD

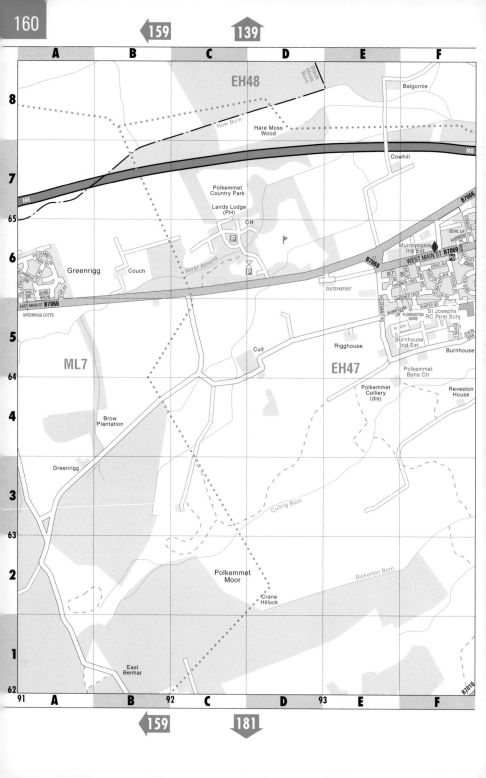

159 139

A   B   C   D   E   F

EH48

Black Moss Burn

8

Balgornie

How Burn

Hare Moss
Wood

M8

Cowhill

7

Polkemmet
Country Park

B7066

65

Lairds Lodge
(PH)

CH

P

OCHIL LA
FAIRMONT
PK
STEWART RD

6

Murraysgate
Ind Est

B7069   PO

WEST MAIN ST

Greenrigg

Couch

River Almond

B7069

CRAIG AVE
GATESIDE CRES

P

ALLAN RD
WOOD RD

POLKEMMET
TAGGS RD

BURNHOUSE RD
DYKE RD
DYKE CT

CULTSYKEFOOT

GARDNER CRES
GARDNER
GDNS

TAYLOR RD
HUNTER GR

STANLEY
DR   DYKE
BRO   BROB

BURNHOUSE
DR   FLEMINGTON
GDNS

St Josephs
RC Prim Schl

DIXON
TERR

EAST MAIN ST   B7066

Burnhouse
Ind Est

POLKEMMET RD

GREENRIGG COTTS

DIXON
TERR

5

Cult

Rigghouse

Burnhouse

ML7

64

EH47

Polkemmet
Bsns Ctr

Polkemmet
Colliery
(dis)

Reveston
House

4

Brow
Plantation

3

Greenrigg

Cultrig Burn

63

2

Polkemmet
Moor

Bickerton Burn

Crane
Hillock

1

East
Benhar

B7010

62

91   A   B   92   C   D   93   E   F

159 181

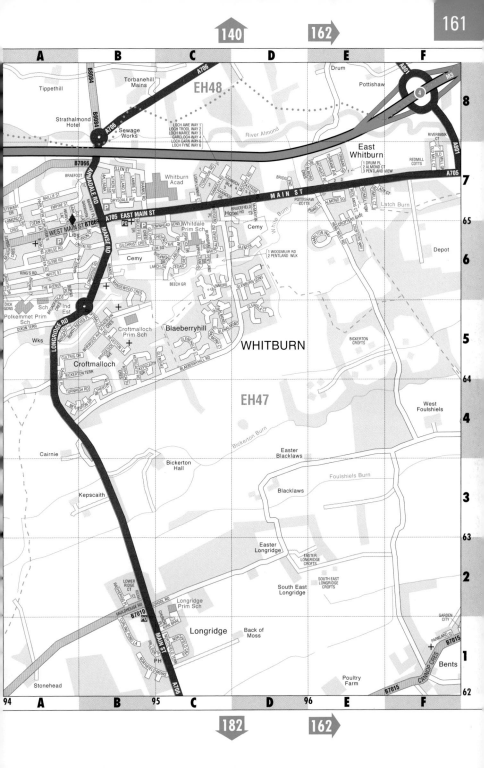

140
162

A **B** **C** **D** **E** **F**

Tippethill

Torbanehill
Mains

EH48

Drum

Pottishaw

8

Strathalmond
Hotel

Sewage
Works

B8084

A706

LOCH AWE WAY 1
LOCH TROOL WAY 2
LOCH MAREE WAY 3
GARELOCH WAY 4
LOCH EARN WAY 5
LOCH FYNE WAY 6

River Almond

East
Whitburn

RIVERBANK
CT

REDMILL
COTTS

OLD
MILL CT

A801

A705

4

B7066

Braefoot

Whitburn
Acad

BRIDGE

Pottishaw
Cotts

ALMOND SQ

Latch Burn

7

Ellen St

EAST MAIN ST

MAIN ST

65

ARMADALE RD

WEST MAIN ST

Lib

P

A705

B7066

MANSE RD

Whitdale
Prim Sch

Bruecefield
Hotel

Cemy

White Burn

Depot

PO

Cemy

GILCHRIST CRES

1 WOODMUIR RD
2 PENTLAND WLK

6

Sch
Ind
Est

BEECH GR

LARCH DR

Blaeberryhill

WHITBURN

BICKERTON
CROFTS

5

Polkemmet Prim
Sch

DIXON TERR

Wks

Croftmalloch
Prim Sch

64

Cairnie

BICKERTON TERR

TURNHIGH RD

LONGRIDGE RD

Croftmalloch

EH47

West
Foulshiels

4

Bickerton
Burn

Easter
Blacklaws

Bickerton
Hall

Foulshiels Burn

Kepscaith

Blacklaws

3

63

Easter
Longridge

EASTER
LONGRIDGE
CROFTS

SOUTH EAST
LONGRIDGE
CROFTS

2

LOWER
RIDGE
CT

South East
Longridge

GARDEN
CITY

B7015

Longridge
Prim Sch

PARKLAND ST

CANNOP CRES

B7010

FAULDHOUSE RD

SCHOOL RD

MAIN ST

PO

Longridge

Back of
Moss

Bents

1

PH

A705

Poultry
Farm

Stonehead

B7015

62

A 94 **B** 95 **C** **D** 96 **E** **F**

182
162

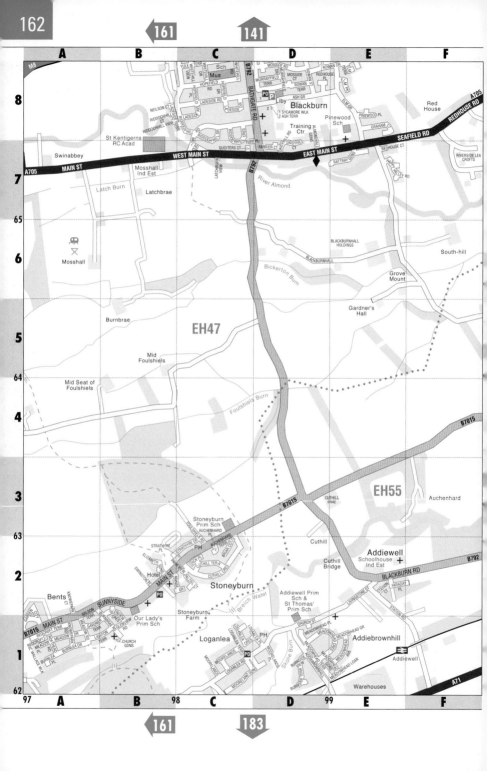

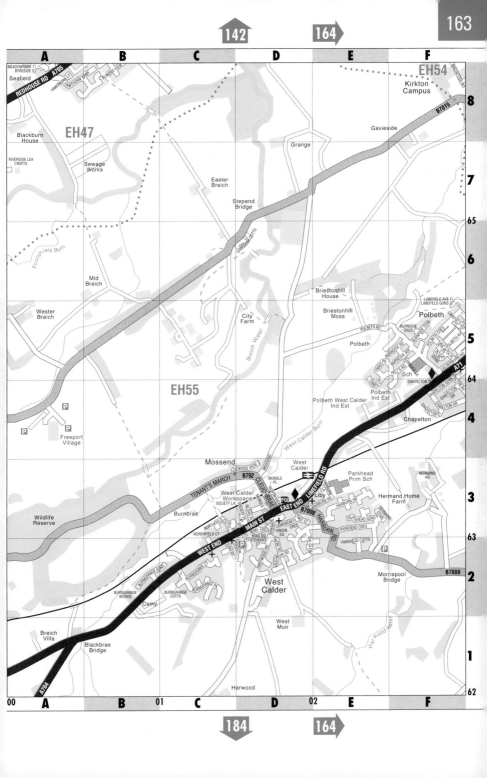

A B C D E F

MEADOWPARK 1
BYRESIDE 2
Seafield
REDHOUSE RD A705
HAWTHORN CT
HAWTHORN BANK
ALMOND VIEW

EH54

Kirkton
Campus
B7015

8

EH47

Blackburn
House

RIVERSIDE LEA
CROFTS

Sewage
Works

Gavieside

Grange

Easter
Breich

Stepend
Bridge

7

65

Foulshiels Burn

Mid
Breich

City
Farm

Briestonhill
House

Briestonhill
Moss

6

Wester
Breich

Breich Water

POLBETH RD

Polbeth

LIMEFIELD AVE f
LIMEFIELD GDNS 2

Polbeth

BURNSIDE
CRES

Sch

5

EH55

Polbeth West Calder
Ind Est

Polbeth
Ind Est

A71
CALDERHALL AVE

CHAPELTON TER

CHAPELTON GDNS
CHAPELTON
GR
CHAPELTON DR

Chapelton

64

P

P

P

Freeport
Village

West Calder Burn

West Calder Burn

4

Mossend

NWOOD VIEW

B792

MUNGLE
PL

West
Calder

LIMEFIELD RD

Parkhead
Prim Sch

HERMAND
HO

TENANT'S MARCH

CLEUKBRAE

West Calder
Workspace
SOCIETY LA

MAIN ST
UNION
SQ

POS
EAST END

HARBURN RD

HARBURN DR

PARKHEAD GDNS

Hermand Home
Farm

3

Burnbrae

NORTHFIELD CT

B7008

KING SQ
STEWART

YARMONTH ST

CRES

PARKHEAD CRES

PARKHEAD COTTS

63

Wildlife
Reserve

WEST END

P

MUIR

CALDER RD

P

Morrispool
Bridge

B7008

2

BURNGRANGE GDNS
BURNGRANGE PK
BURNGRANGE CT

BURNGRANGE
WORKS

Cemy

BURNGRANGE
COTTS

West Calder

West
Muir

Har Wood Water

Breich
Villa

Blackbrae
Bridge

Harwood

1

62

A704

00 A B 01 C D 02 E F

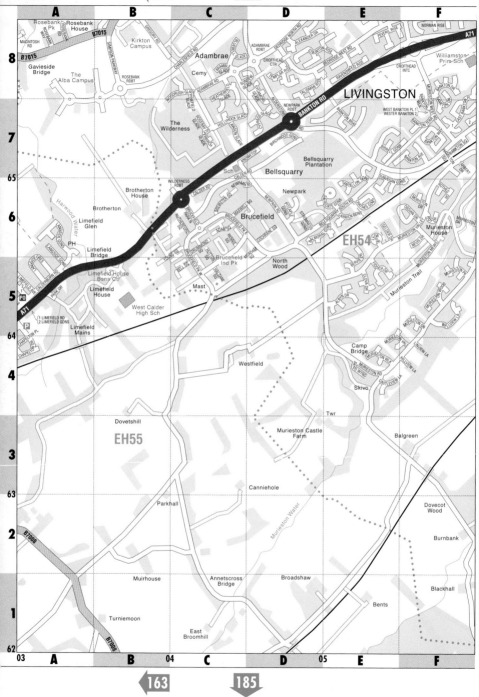

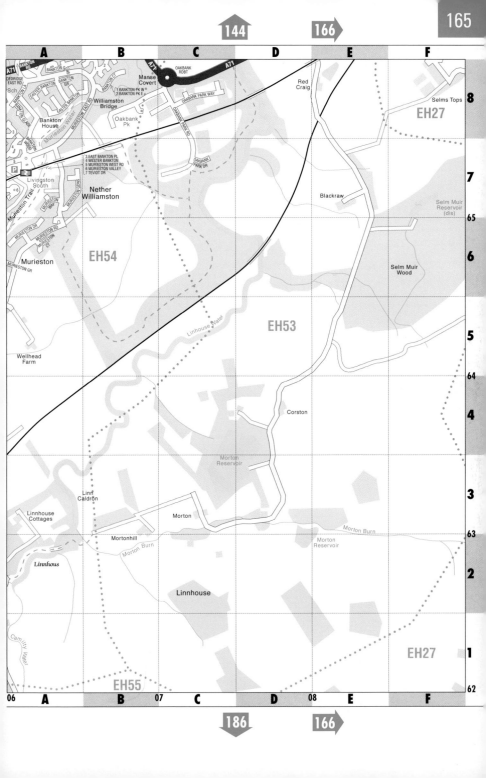

144
166
186
166

A **B** **C** **D** **E** **F**

8
7
65
6
5
64
4
3
63
2
1
62

Selms Tops

EH27

Red Craig

Oakbank Park Way
OAKBANK PARK RD
OAKBANK PARK DR

Manse
Covert

OAKBANK
RDBT

A71

Williamston
Bridge

Oakbank
Pk

Bankton
House

Easter Bankton

Muirston Water

1 BANKTON PK W
2 BANKTON PK E
3 EAST BANKTON PL
4 WESTER BANKTON
5 MURIESTON WEST RD
6 MURIESTON VALLEY
7 TEVIOT DR

Livingston
South

Nether
Williamston

Blackraw

Selm Muir
Reservoir
(dis)

Selm Muir
Wood

EH54

Muirston

Muirston Trail

Wellhead
Farm

Linhouse Water

EH53

Corston

Morton
Reservoir

Linn
Caldron

Linnhouse
Cottages

Morton

Mortonhill

Morton Burn

Morton Burn

Morton
Reservoir

Linnhous

Linnhouse

EH27

Camilty Water

EH55

06   07   08

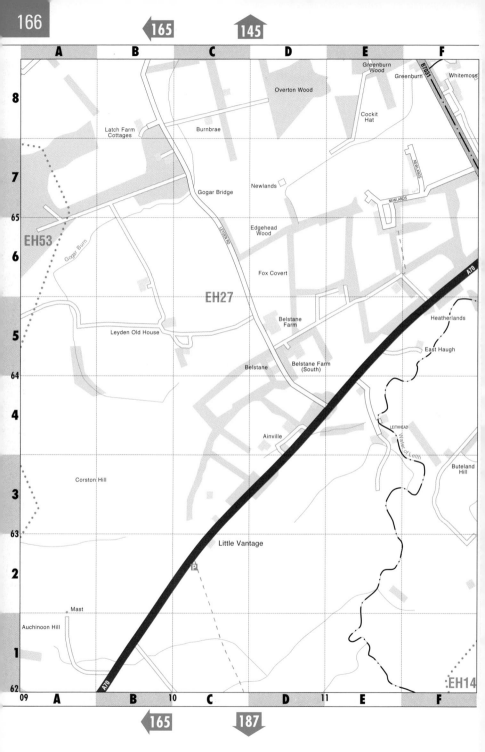

A B C D E F

8

Greenburn
Wood

Greenburn

Whitemoss

B7031

Overton Wood

Cockit
Hat

Latch Farm
Cottages

Burnbrae

7

NEWLANDS

Gogar Bridge

Newlands

NEWLANDS

65

Edgehead
Wood

EH53

6

Gogar Burn

LEYDEN RD

Fox Covert

A70

EH27

Belstane
Farm

Heatherlands

5

Leyden Old House

East Haugh

64

Belstane

Belstane Farm
(South)

4

Ainville

LEITHHEAD

Water of Leith

Buteland
Hill

3

Corston Hill

63

Little Vantage

2

P

Mast

1

Auchinoon Hill

A70

EH14

62

09 A B 10 C D 11 E F

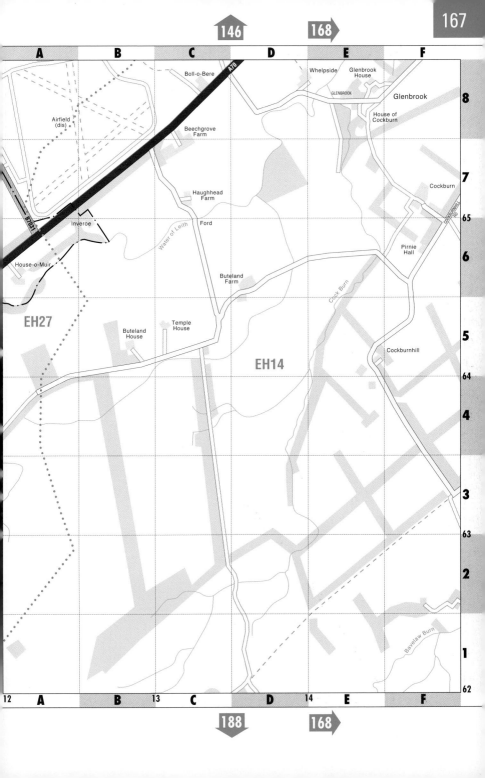

146 168

A B C D E F

Boll-o-Bere

Whelpside Glenbrook House

GLENBROOK Glenbrook

8

Airfield (dis)

Beechgrove Farm

House of Cockburn

Cockburn

7

Haughhead Farm

Inveroe

Ford

65

House-o-Muir

Water of Leith

Pirnie Hall

6

Buteland Farm

Cloak Burn

EH27

Buteland House

Temple House

EH14

Cockburnhill

5

64

4

3

63

2

Bavelaw Burn

1

62

12 A B 13 C D 14 E F

188 168

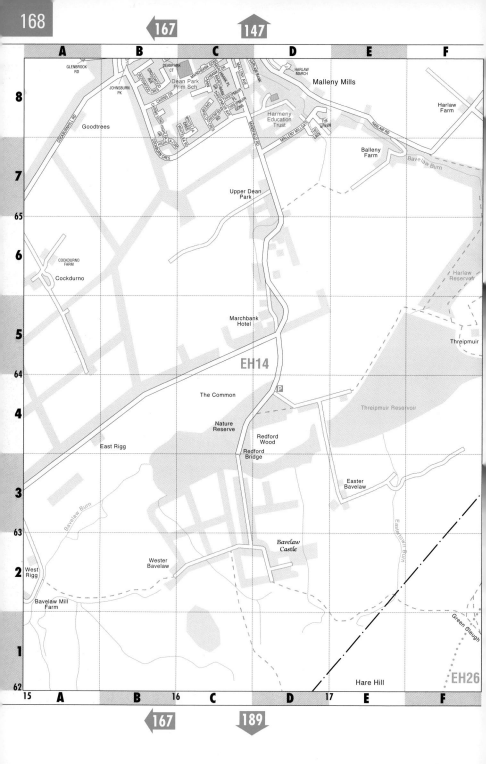

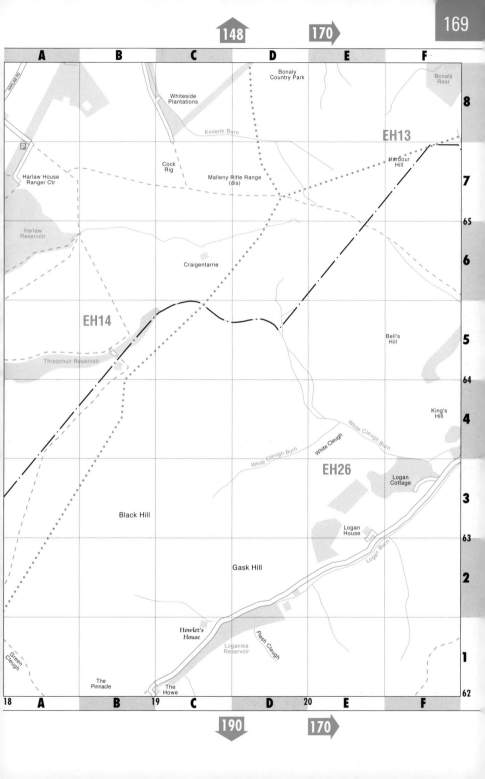

A B C D E F

8

Bonaly
Country Park

Bonaly
Resr

Whiteside
Plantations

Kinleith Burn

EH13

Cock
Rig

Harbour
Hill

7

Harlaw House
Ranger Ctr

Malleny Rifle Range
(dis)

Harlaw
Reservoir

65

Craigentarrie

6

EH14

Bell's
Hill

5

Threipmuir Reservoir

64

King's
Hill

4

White Cleugh Burn

White Cleugh

White Cleugh Burn

EH26

Logan
Cottage

3

Black Hill

Logan
House

63

Gask Hill

Logan Burn

2

Howlet's
House

Green Cleugh

Loganlea
Reservoir

Flesh Cleugh

1

The Pinnacle

The
Howe

62

18 A B 19 C D 20 E F

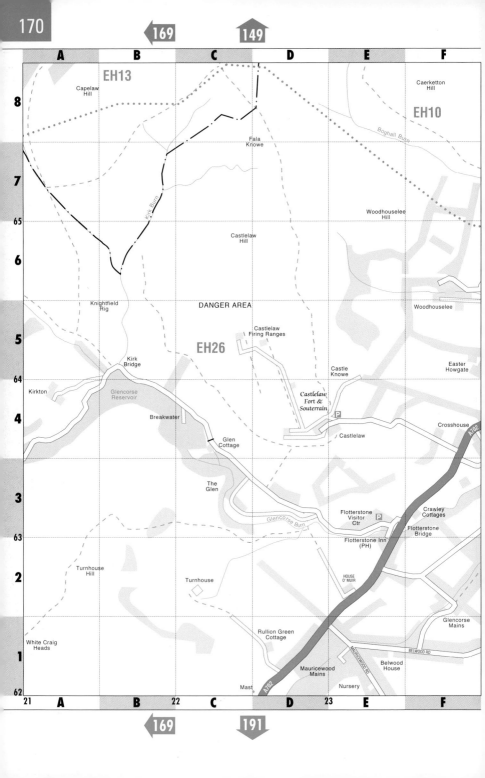

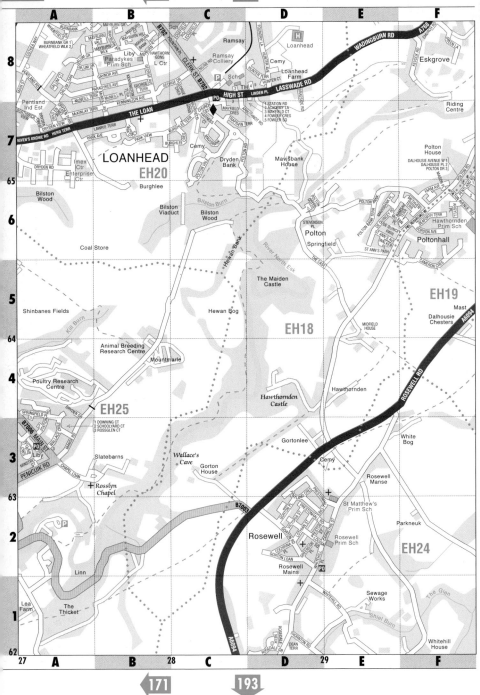

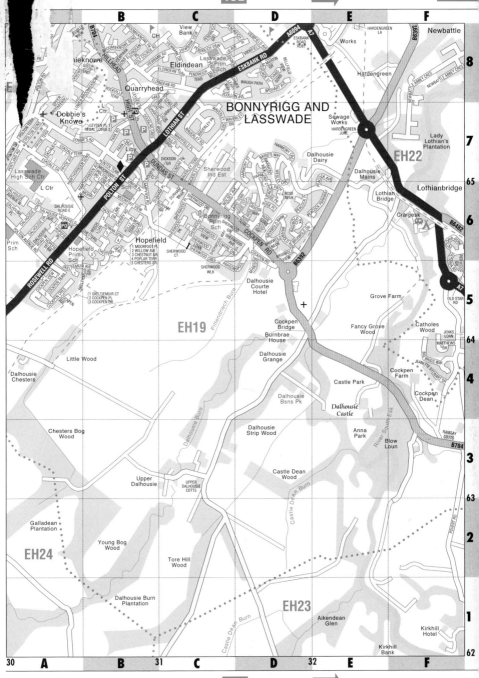

BONNYRIGG AND LASSWADE

EH22

EH19

EH24

EH23

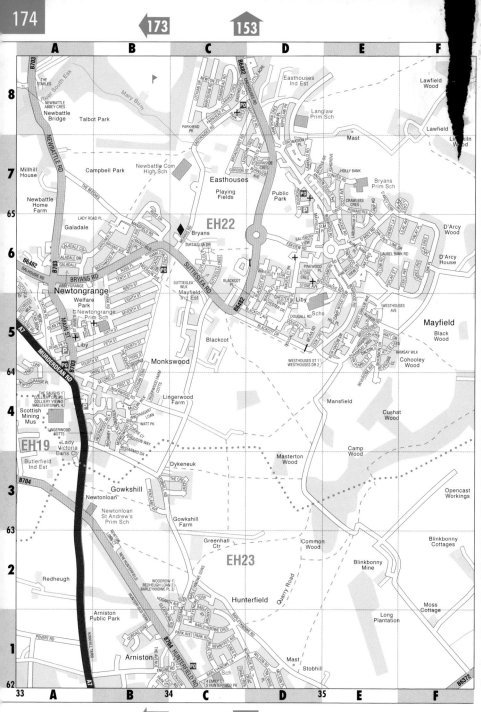

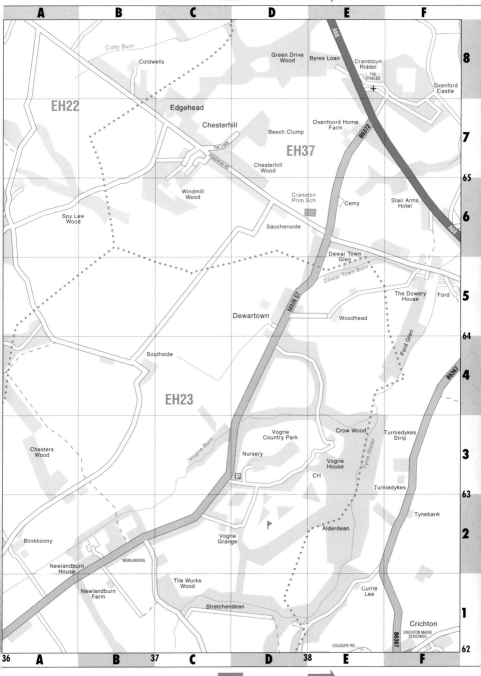

154 176

196 176

EH22

EH37

EH23

Cotty Burn
Coldwells
Green Drive Wood
Byres Loan
Cranstoun Riddel
THE STABLES
Oxenford Castle

Edgehead
Chesterhill
Beech Clump
Oxenfoord Home Farm

THE LOAN
FUSHIEHEAD RD
Chesterhill Wood
Cranston Prim Sch
Cemy
Stair Arms Hotel

Windmill Wood
Sauchenside

Spy Law Wood
Dewar Town Glen
Dewar Town Burn

The Dowery House
Ford

Dewartown
MAIN ST
Woodhead
Ford Glen

Southside
B6367

Chesters Wood
Vogrie Country Park
Crow Wood
Turniedykes Strip

Vogrie Burn
Nursery
Vogrie House
Turniedykes

Blinkbonny
P
CH
Alderdean
Tynebank

Newlandburn House
NEWLANDRIG
Vogrie Grange
Tyne Water

Newlandburn Farm
Tile Works Wood
Currie Lee

Stretcherdean
Crichton
B6367
CRICHTON MAINS STEEDINGS
COLEGATE RD

A68
B6372
A68

8
7
65
6
5
64
4
3
63
2
1
62

36 A B 37 C D 38 E F

A B C D E F

8

Preston
Hall

Jeffrey's
Wood

B6367

RED
ROW

Rose
Mains

Preston
Toll

Preston
Cottage

Preston
Dene

Preston
Mains

7

Tyne Water

Lion's
Lodge

Remote

Dodridge
Farm

65

6

Depot

A68

Lothian
Bridge

HILL RD

B6367

ORMISTON RD

CRICHTON RD

Pathhead

FOUNTAIN PL

Loanhead

5

Drippy Burn

CHAPEL PL

CRICHTON DR

CRICHTON AVE

OXENFOORD DR

OXENFOORD RD

1 COCKBURN SQ
2 FARMER'S BLDGS

ROMAN CAMP RD

MAIN ST

CALDER WY

EH37

MOOR RD

64

B6367

PRESTON PL

CHAPEL CT

PO

Pathhead
Prim Sch

Whippielaw

Whitburgh
Mains

WHITBURGH
MAINS COTTS.

4

New
Wood

LAIRD'S ENTRY

3

SALTERS RD

63

Burnside

Reservoir

Hope

Magazine
Wood

2

Kirk
Hill

Crichton
House

Marl Law
Wood

Crow
Law

Marldene

Salter's Burn

A68

1

Longfaugh Farm
Cottages

62

39 A B 40 C D 41 E F

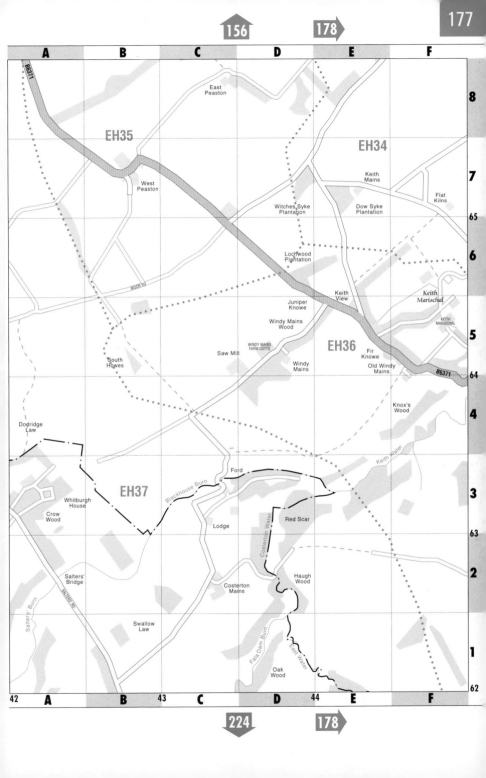

A B C D E F

8

EH35

7

East Peaston

West Peaston

65

EH34

Keith Mains

Flat Kilns

Witches Syke Plantation

Dow Syke Plantation

6

Lochwood Plantation

MOOR RD

Keith View

Keith Marischal

KEITH MARISCHAL

Juniper Knowe

Windy Mains Wood

5

EH36

South Howes

Saw Mill

WINDY MAINS FARM COTTS

Fir Knowe

Windy Mains

Old Windy Mains

B6371

64

Knox's Wood

4

Dodridge Law

Keith Water

EH37

Ford

Blackhouse Burn

3

Whitburgh House

Crow Wood

Lodge

Costerton Water

Red Scar

63

Salters' Bridge

SALTERS RD

Haugh Wood

2

Salters' Burn

Costerton Mains

Swallow Law

Fala Dam Burn

East Water

1

Oak Wood

62

42 A B 43 C D 44 E F

B6371

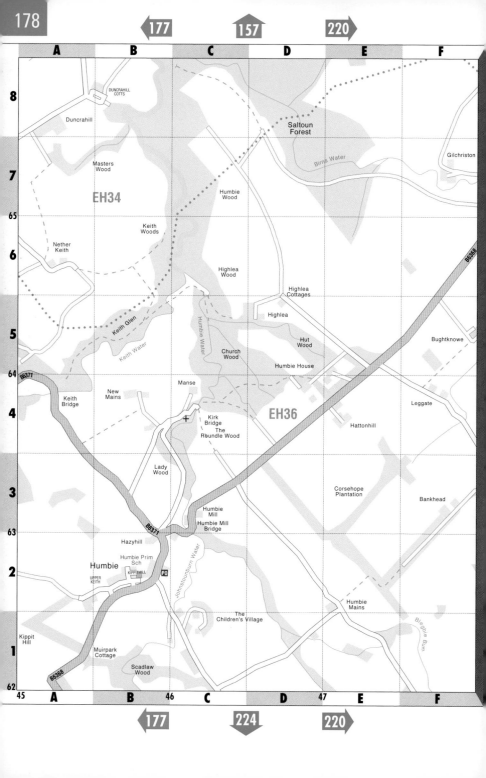

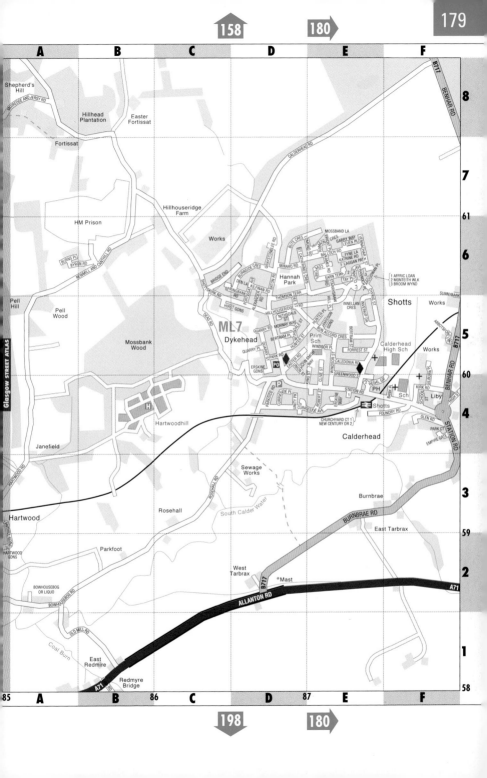

ML7

EH47

BENHAR RD
B717
B717

CH

Starryshaw Farm

South Calder Water

Stanebent

Spoil Heap

Cairneyhead

Stane

Stane Prim Sch

Torbothie

Stane GN

Cemy

Stane

SANDVALE PL

MAIN ST
B7010
PO

Springhill

SPRINGHILL RD
B7010

Springhill

Works

Springhill

SPRINGHILL AND LEADLOCH RD

Knowton Farm

B715
HEADLESSCROSS RD
B7010

A71

Works

Lingore Linn

A71

1 ETIVE WLK
2 JIG WAY
3 CAIN WYND
4 BOWMORE WLK
5 TORRIN LOAN
6 SPRINGHILL VIEW
7 DORINE WYND
8 MORAR WAY
9 CORIE LOAN
10 SUNA PATH
11 SALEN LOAN

CEMETERY RD

TULLOCH RD

LAGGAN AVE

LANSDOWNE CRES

BELMONT DRIVE

LARCHFIELD PATH

NORTHFIELD AVE

ELMWOOD RD

BLINNY CT 1
TARBRAX PATH 2

GARTEN DR

NEVIS PL

LOCHURD CRES

APPIN TERR

CHARLOTTE ST

MANSE RD

BRIDGE PL

KNOLL COTTS

STANE RD

88   89   90
58 59 60 61 1 2 3 4 5 6 7 8
A B C D E F

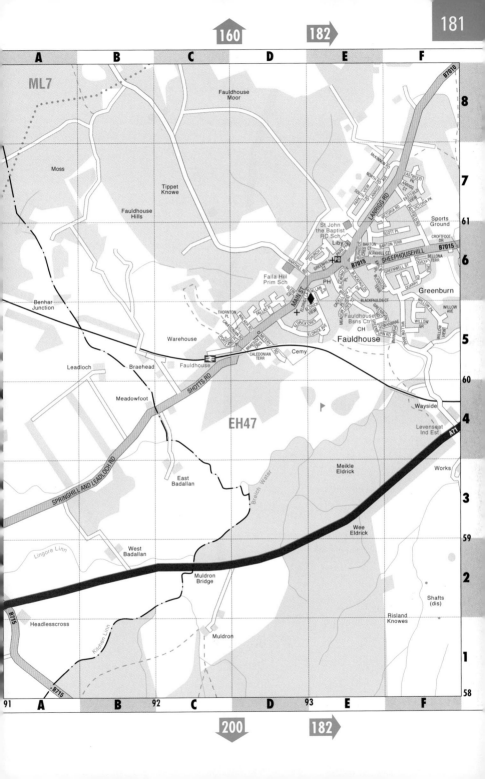

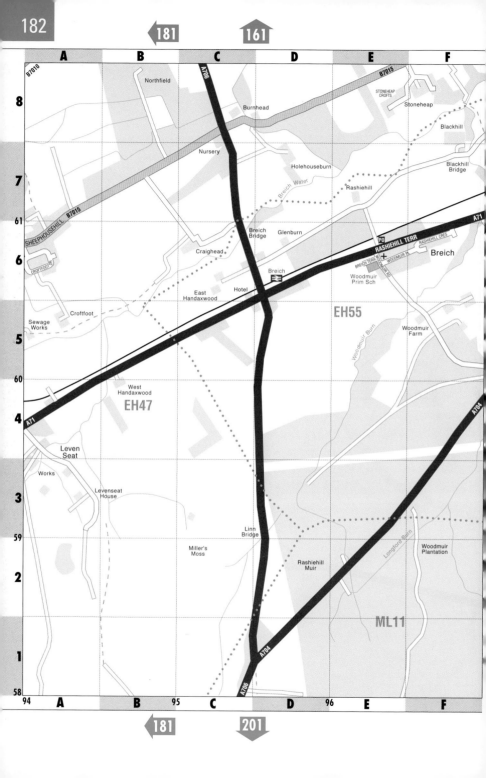

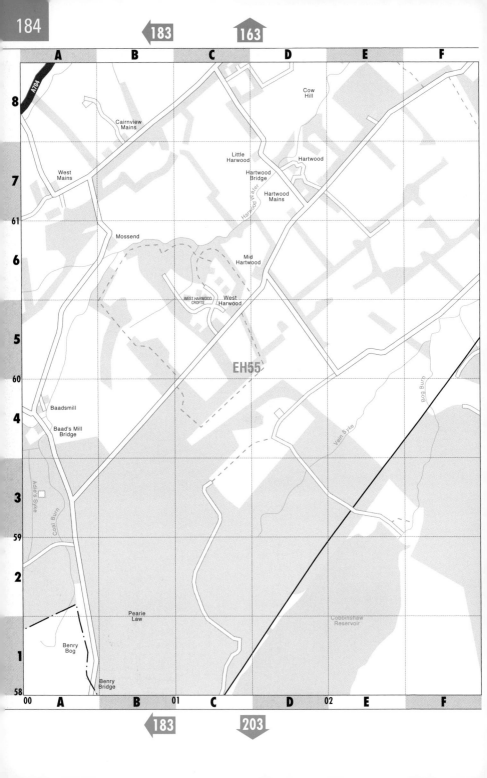

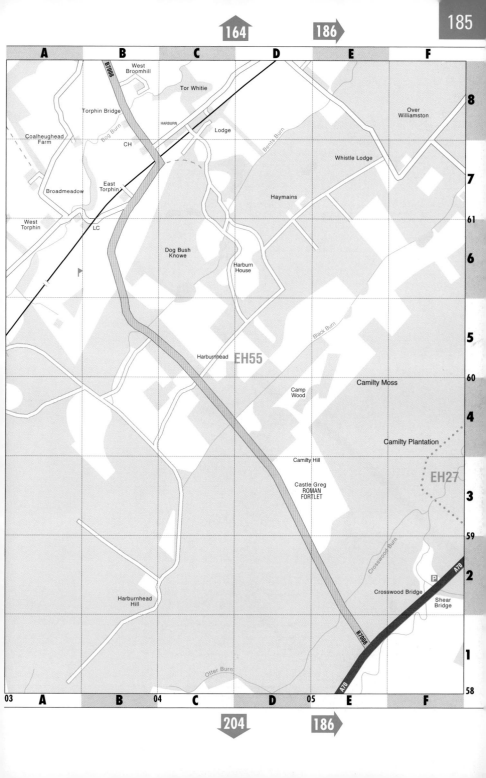

164
186

A   B   C   D   E   F

8

West
Broomhill

Tor Whitie

Torphin Bridge

HARBURN

Lodge

Over
Williamston

Coalheughead
Farm

CH

Whistle Lodge

7

Bog Burn

Bents Burn

Broadmeadow

East
Torphin

Haymains

61

West
Torphin

LC

6

Dog Bush
Knowe

Harburn
House

5

Black Burn

Harburnhead

EH55

60

Camp
Wood

Camilty Moss

4

Camilty Plantation

Camilty Hill

EH27

Castle Greg
ROMAN
FORTLET

3

59

Crosswood Burn

2

Harburnhead
Hill

Crosswood Bridge

Shear
Bridge

1

58

Otter Burn

03   A   B   04   C   D   05   E   F

204
186

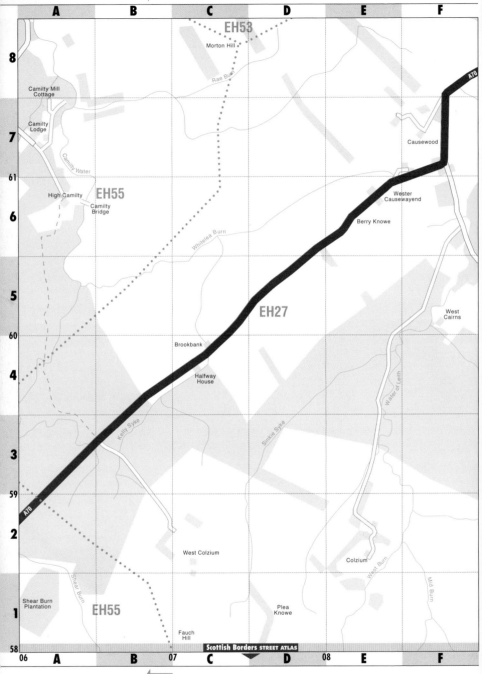

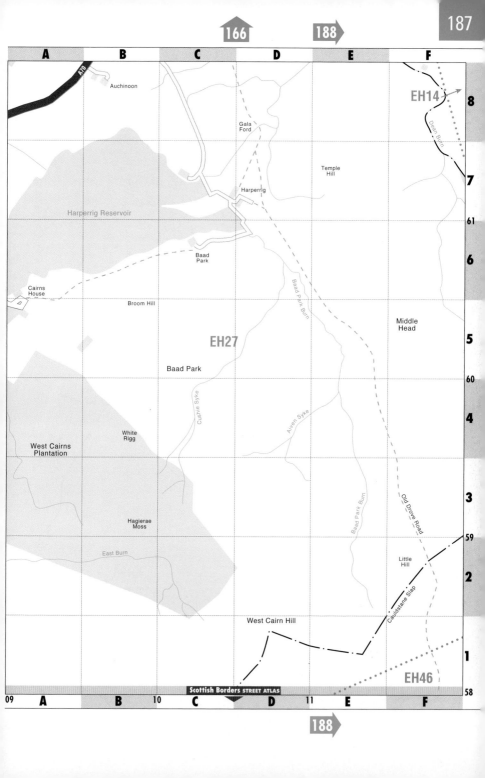

A   B   C   D   E   F

Auchinoon

A70

EH14

8

Gala
Ford

Temple
Hill

7

Dean Burn

Harperrig

61

Harperrig Reservoir

Baad
Park

6

Cairns
House

Broom Hill

Baad Park Burn

Middle
Head

5

EH27

Baad Park

60

Cushie Syke

Alven Syke

White
Rigg

4

West Cairns
Plantation

Baad Park Burn

Old Drove Road

3

Hagierae
Moss

59

East Burn

Little
Hill

2

Cauldstane Slap

West Cairn Hill

EH46

1

58

09 A   B   10   C   D   11   E   F

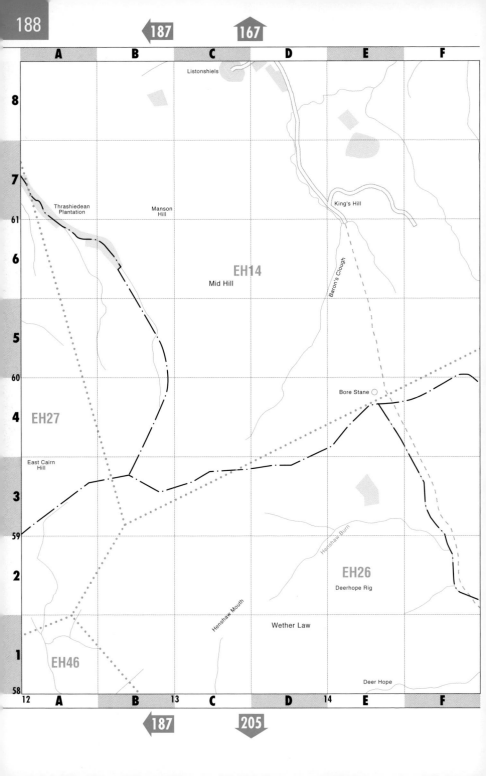

187
167

A **B** **C** **D** **E** **F**

8

7

61

Thrashiedean
Plantation

Manson
Hill

King's Hill

6

EH14

Mid Hill

Baron's Clough

5

60

Bore Stane ○

4

EH27

East Cairn
Hill

3

59

2

EH26

Deerhope Rig

Henshaw Burn

1

EH46

Henshaw Mouth

Wether Law

58

Deer Hope

187
205

Listonshiels

168
190

A B C D E F

8

EH14 Pentland Hills Regional Park

7

Logan Burn

61

6

West Kip

Kitchen Moss

5

Eastside Burn

60

Cap Law

4

Green Law

EH26

Font Stone

3

Cock Rig

Gutterford Burn

59

Monks Burn

2

Spittal Hill

Greystone Head

Scroggy Hill

1

North Esk Reservoir

58

15 A B 16 C D 17 E F

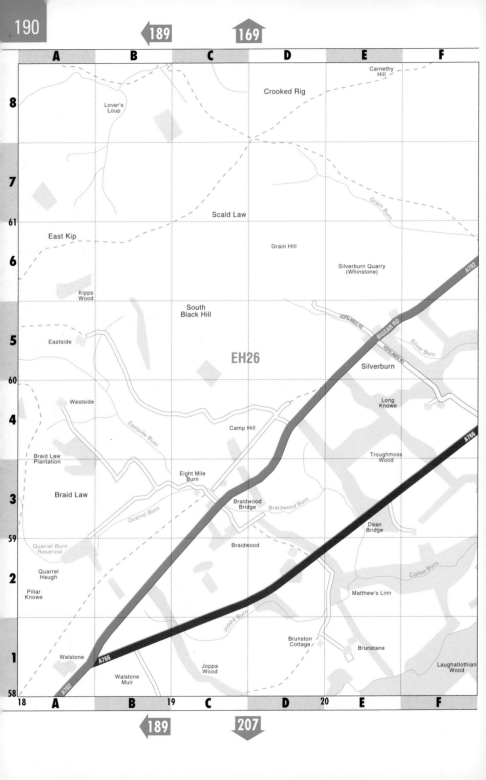

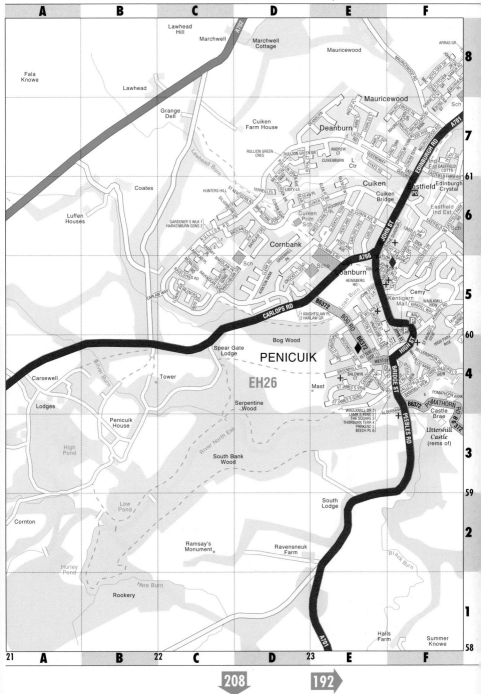

170
192
208
192

PENICUIK

EH26

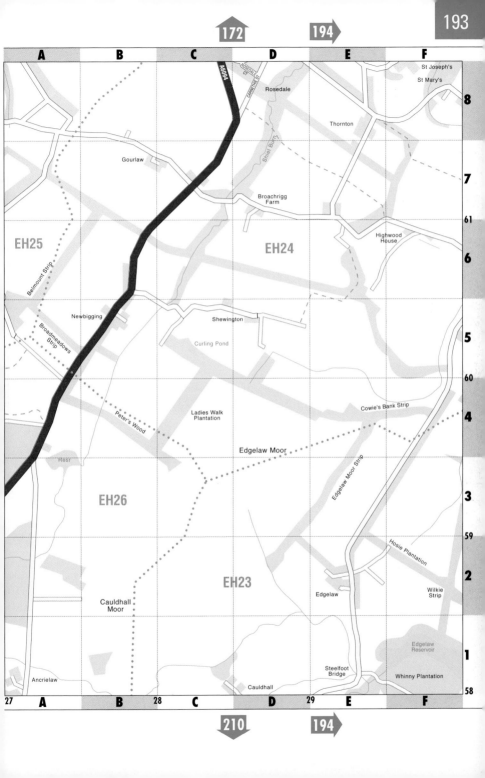

A B C D E F

8

St Joseph's
St Mary's

Rosedale

Thornton

7

Gourlaw

Broachrigg
Farm

61

EH25

EH24

Highwood
House

6

Belmount Strip

Newbigging

Shewington

Broadmeadows
Strip

Curling Pond

5

60

Cowie's Bank Strip

Ladies Walk
Plantation

Peter's Wood

4

Edgelaw Moor

Edgelaw Moor Strip

Resr

EH26

3

59

Hosie Plantation

EH23

Wilkie
Strip

2

Edgelaw

Cauldhall
Moor

Edgelaw
Reservoir

1

Ancrielaw

Steelfoot
Bridge

Whinny Plantation

Cauldhall

58

27 A B 28 C D 29 E F

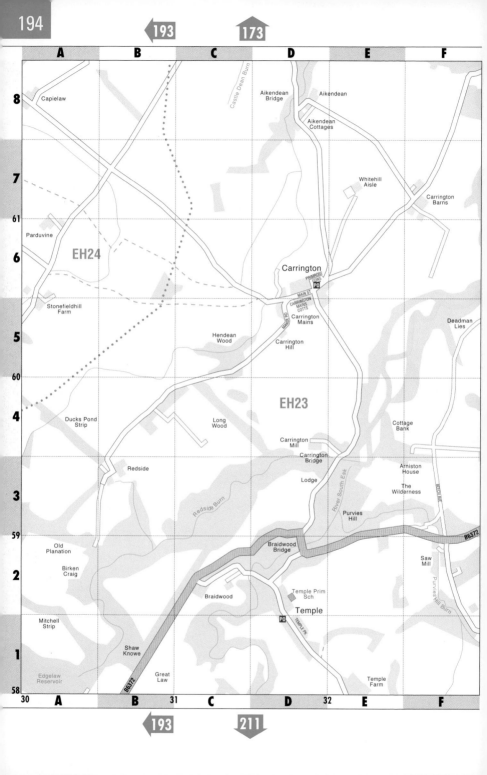

A **B** **C** **D** **E** **F**

8 Capielaw

Castle Dean Burn

Aikendean
Bridge
Aikendean

Aikendean
Cottages

7

Whitehill
Aisle

Carrington
Barns

61

Parduvine

EH24

6

Carrington

PRIMROSE
PARK
PO

MAIN ST

Stonefieldhill
Farm

CARRINGTON
MAINS
COTTS

Carrington
Mains

Deadman
Lies

5

Hendean
Wood

Carrington
Hill

MAIN RD

60

EH23

4

Ducks Pond
Strip

Long
Wood

Carrington
Mill

Cottage
Bank

Carrington
Bridge

Arniston
House

Redside

Lodge

River South Esk

The
Wilderness

BEECH AVE

3

Redside Burn

Purvies
Hill

59

Old
Planation

Braidwood
Bridge

B6372

Saw
Mill

2

Birken
Craig

Braidwood

Temple Prim
Sch

Purvies Hill Burn

Mitchell
Strip

PO

Temple

TEMPLE PK

1

Shaw
Knowe

Edgelaw
Reservoir

B6372

Great
Law

Temple
Farm

58
30 **A** **B** **31** **C** **D** **32** **E** **F**

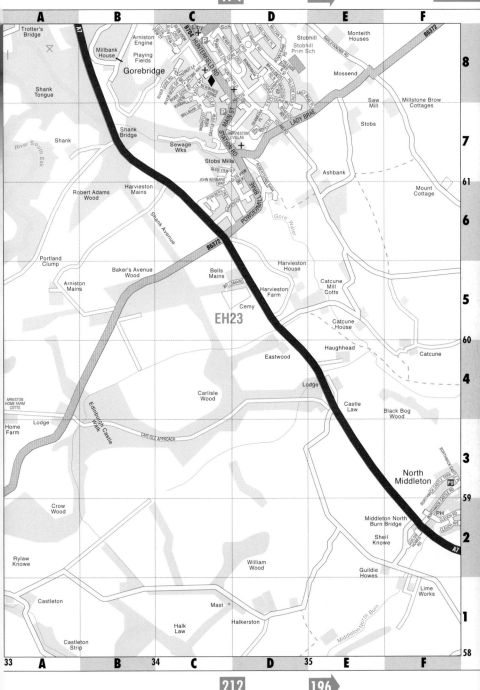

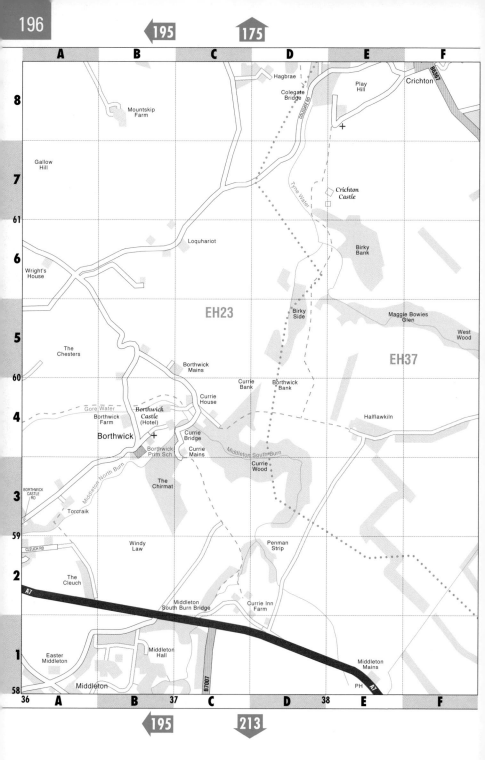

195
175

8

7

61

6

5

60

4

3

59

2

1

58

A B C D E F

Mountskip
Farm

Gallow
Hill

Wright's
House

The
Chesters

Loquhariot

EH23

Borthwick
Mains

Currie
House

Currie
Bank

Borthwick
Bank

Birky
Side

Hagbrae

Colegate
Bridge

Crichton
Castle

Play
Hill

Crichton

Birky
Bank

Maggie Bowies
Glen

West
Wood

EH37

Halflawkiln

Gore Water

Borthwick
Farm

Borthwick
Castle
(Hotel)

Borthwick

Currie
Bridge

Currie
Mains

Borthwick
Prm Sch

The
Chirmat

Middleton South Burn

Currie
Wood

BORTHWICK
CASTLE
RD

Torcraik

CLEUCH RD

Windy
Law

Penman
Strip

Middleton North Burn

The
Cleuch

A7

Middleton
South Burn Bridge

Currie Inn
Farm

Easter
Middleton

Middleton
Hall

Middleton

Middleton
Mains

PH

A7

B7007

Tyne Water

COLEGATE RD

B6367

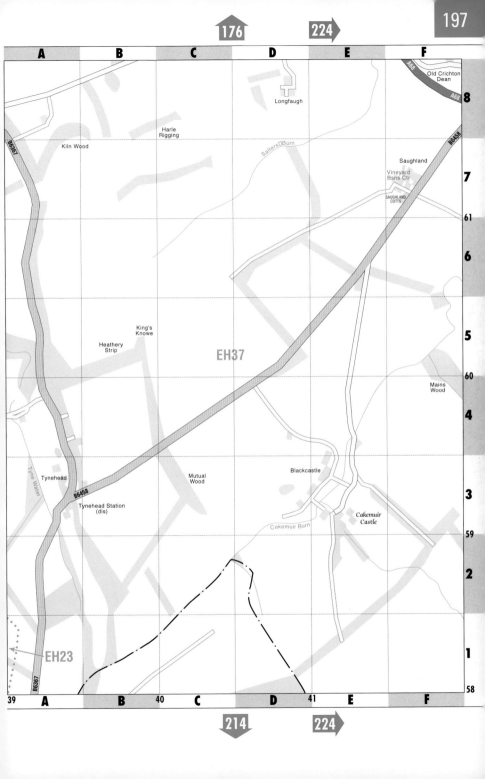

A B C D E F

Old Crichton
Dean
A68
A68
8

Longfaugh

Harle
Rigging

Kiln Wood

Salters Burn

Saughland

B6367

B6458

Vineyard
Bsns Ctr

7

SAUGHLAND
COTTS

61

6

King's
Knowe

5

Heathery
Strip

EH37

60

Mains
Wood

4

Tyne Water

Tynehead

B6458

Mutual
Wood

Blackcastle

3

Tynehead Station
(dis)

Cakemuir Burn

Cakemuir
Castle

59

2

EH23

1

B6367

58

39   A   B   40   C   D   41   E   F

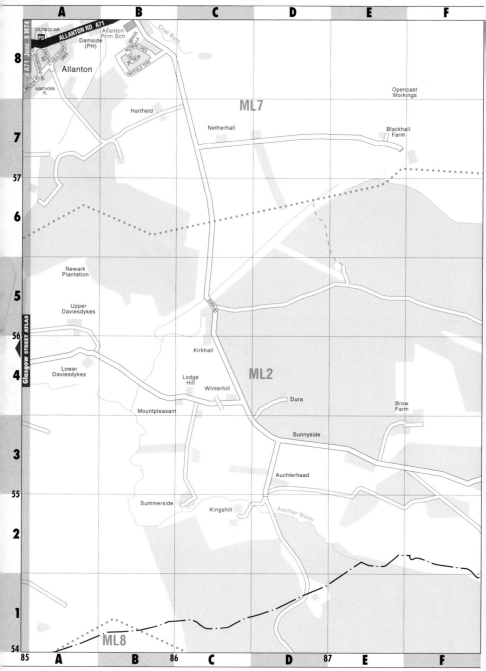

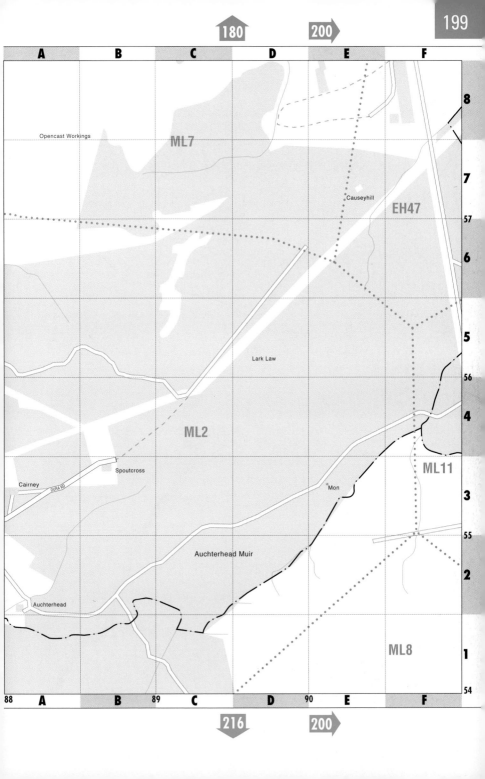

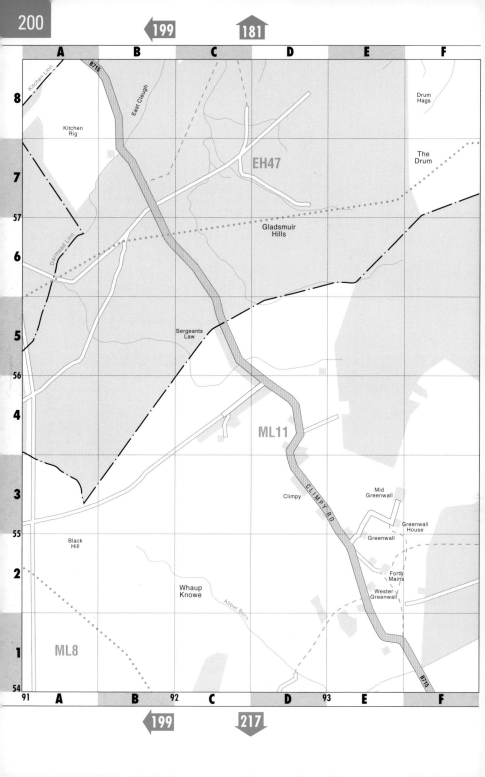

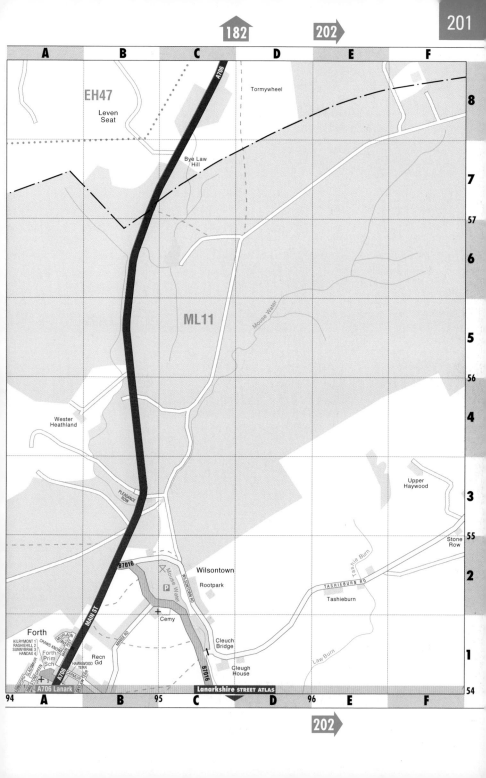

EH47

Leven
Seat

Tormywheel

Bye Law
Hill

ML11

Mouse Water

Wester
Heathland

Upper
Haywood

PLEASANCE
ROW

Stone
Row

B7016

Wilsontown

Rootpark

Tashie Burn

TASHIEBURN RD

Tashieburn

Cemy

MAIN ST

Mouse Water

WILSONTOWN RD

MANSE RD

Cleuch
Bridge

Law Burn

Forth

KILRYMONT 1
RASHIEHILL 2
SUNNYBRAE 3
HANDAX 4

CRAWS KNOWE
BURNLAW

Forth
Prim
Sch

HAWKWOOD
TERR

Recn
Gd

B7016

Cleugh
House

LONGFORD
WELLSHOLM

PLEASMUIR
MAIN ST

CAIRNBRAE
A706

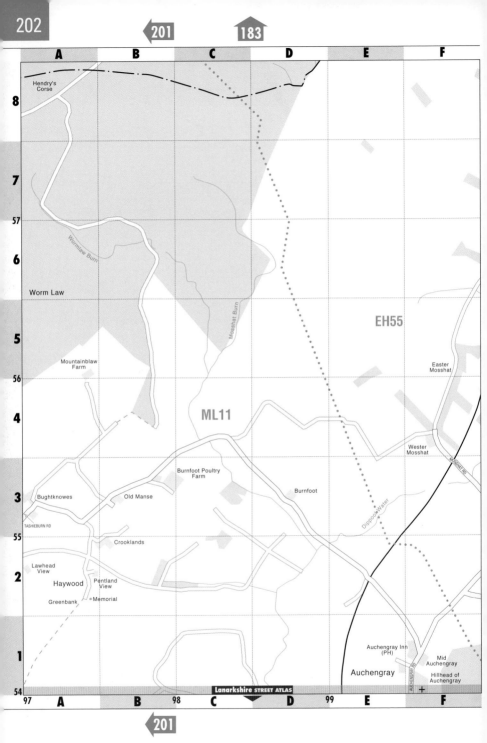

A B C D E F

8

7

57

6

Worm Law

5

EH55

56

4

ML11

3

55

2

Haywood

1

54

Hendry's
Corse

Wormlaw Burn

Mosshat Burn

Mountainblaw
Farm

Easter
Mosshat

Wester
Mosshat

MOSSHAT RD

Burnfoot Poultry
Farm

Burnfoot

Dippool Water

Bughtknowes

Old Manse

TASHIEBURN RD

Crooklands

Lawhead
View

Pentland
View

Greenbank

Memorial

Auchengray Inn
(PH)

AUCHENGRAY RD

Mid
Auchengray

Auchengray

Hillhead of
Auchengray

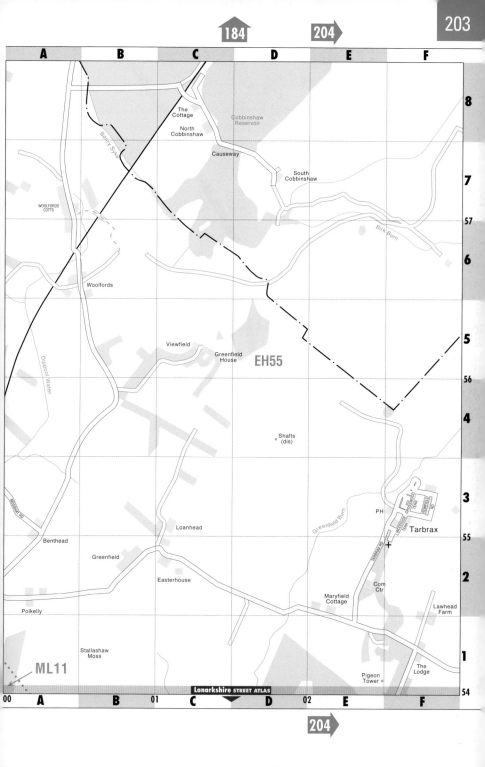

A B C D E F

8

The
Cottage

Cobbinshaw
Reservoir

North
Cobbinshaw

Causeway

7

South
Cobbinshaw

WOOLFORDS
COTTS

57

Birk Burn

Barty Syke

6

Woolfords

Dippool Water

Viewfield

5

Greenfield
House

EH55

56

4

Shafts
(dis)

Greenfield Burn

3

PH

CROSSWOOD
TERR

VIEWFIELD
RD

WINDSOR
CRES

Tarbrax

TARBRAX RD

Loanhead

55

Benthead

Greenfield

2

Easterhouse

Maryfield
Cottage

Com
Ctr

Lawhead
Farm

Polkelly

MOSSAT RD

Stallashaw
Moss

Pigeon
Tower

The
Lodge

1

ML11

54

00 A 01 B C 01 C 02 D E 02 F

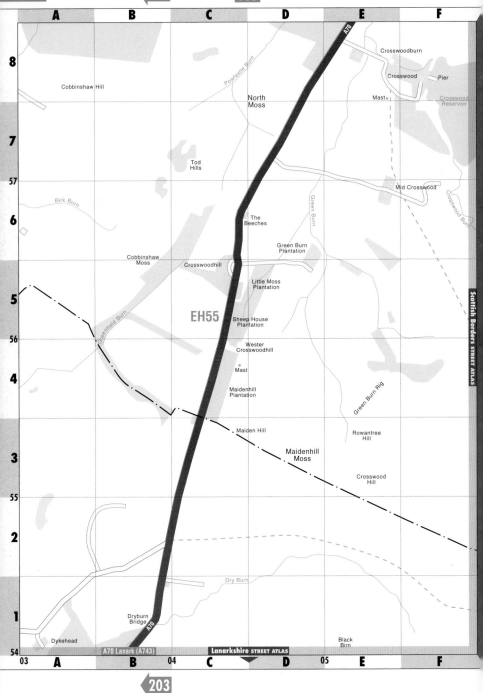

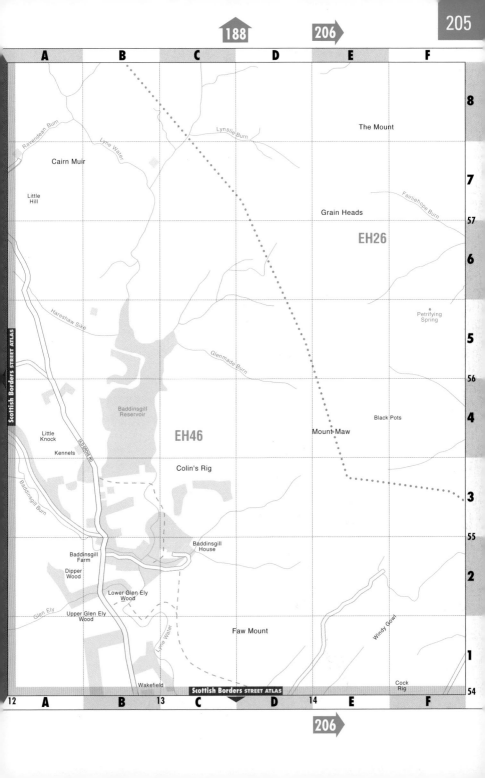

A   **B**   **C**   **D**   **E**   **F**

8

The Mount

Cairn Muir

7

Little
Hill

Lynslie Burn

Grain Heads

Fairliehope Burn

57

EH26

6

Ravendean Burn

Lyne Water

Hareshaw Sike

5

Petrifying
Spring

Glenmade Burn

56

Baddinsgill
Reservoir

EH46

4

Black Pots

Mount Maw

Little
Knock

Kennels

Colin's Rig

Baddinsgill Burn

OLD DROVE RD

3

55

Baddinsgill
House

Baddinsgill
Farm

2

Dipper
Wood

Lower Glen Ely
Wood

Glen Ely

Upper Glen Ely
Wood

Lyne Water

Faw Mount

Windy Gowl

1

Wakefield

Cock
Rig

54

12   **A**   **B**   13   **C**   **D**   14   **E**   **F**

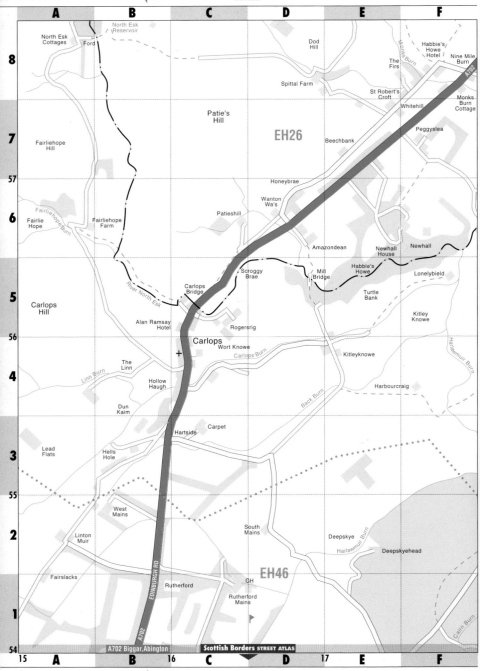

North Esk
Cottages

Ford

North Esk
Reservoir

Dod
Hill

Habbie's
Howe
Hotel

Nine Mile
Burn

The Firs

Spittal Farm

St Robert's
Croft

Monks
Burn
Cottage

Whitehill

Patie's
Hill

EH26

Peggyslea

Fairliehope
Hill

Beechbank

Honeybrae

Fairlie
Hope

Fairliehope
Burn

Fairliehope
Farm

Patieshill

Wanton
Wa's

Amazondean

Newhall
House

Newhall

Scroggy
Brae

Mill
Bridge

Habbie's
Howe

Lonelybield

River North Esk

Carlops
Bridge

Turtle
Bank

Kitley
Knowe

Carlops
Hill

Alan Ramsay
Hotel

Rogersrig

Wort Knowe

Carlops Burn

Kitleyknowe

Harlawmuir Burn

Carlops

The Linn

Linn Burn

Hollow
Haugh

Back Burn

Harbourcraig

Dun
Kaim

Lead
Flats

Hells
Hole

Hartside

Carpet

West
Mains

South
Mains

Deepskye

Harlawmuir Burn

Deepskyehead

Linton
Muir

EDINBURGH RD

Fairslacks

Rutherford

CH

Rutherford
Mains

EH46

Cairn Burn

Scottish Borders STREET ATLAS

A702

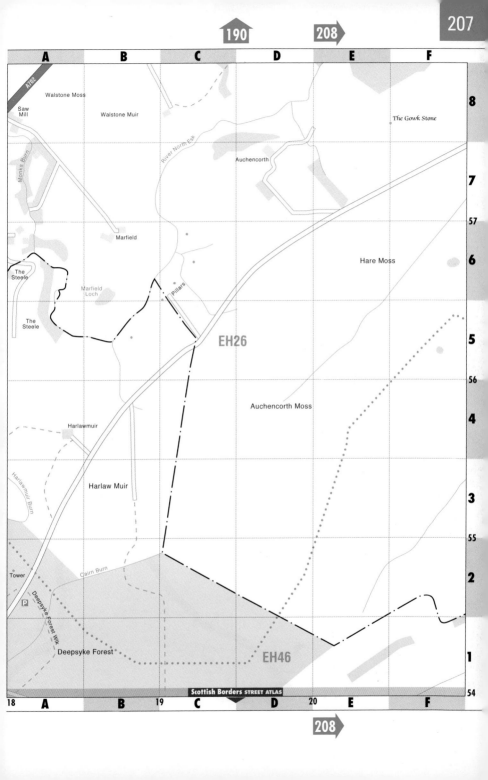

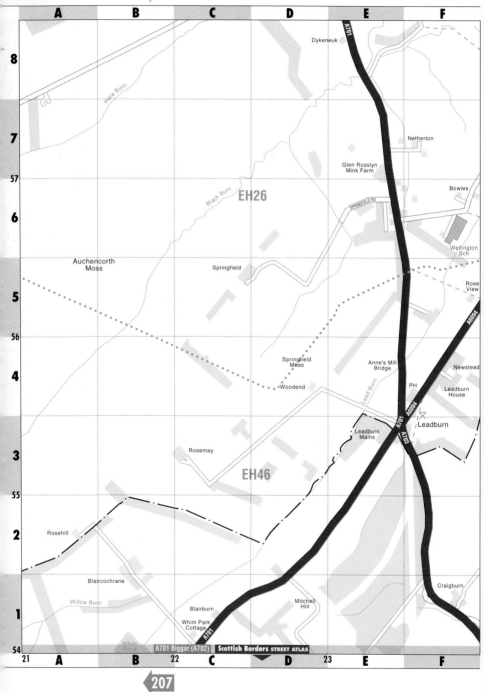

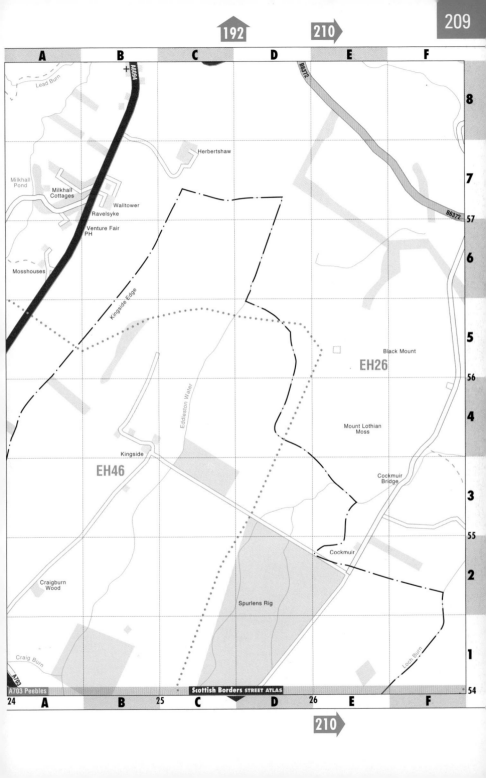

A B C D E F

8

7

Herbertshaw

57

6

Milkhall
Pond

Milkhall
Cottages

Walltower

Ravelsyke

Venture Fair
PH

Mosshouses

Kingside Edge

Black Mount

5

EH26

56

Eddleston Water

4

Mount Lothian
Moss

Kingside

EH46

Cockmuir
Bridge

3

55

Cockmuir

2

Craigburn
Wood

Spurlens Rig

Loch Burn

1

Craig Burn

A703 Peebles

54

24 A B 25 C D 26 E F

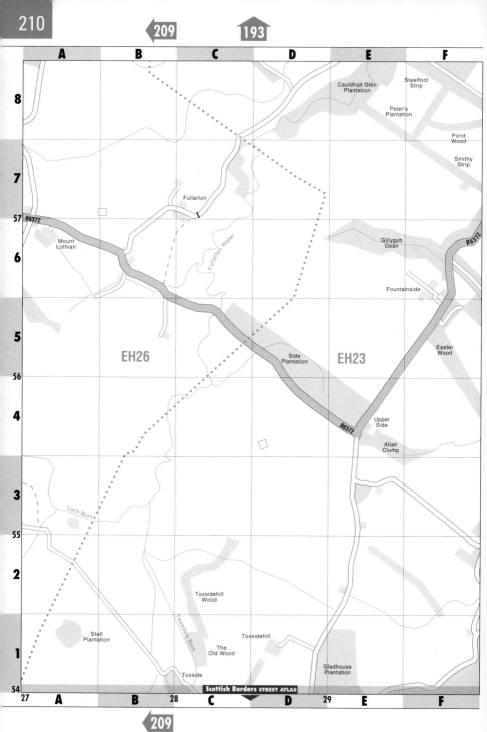

A B C D E F

8

7

57 B6372

6

5

56

4

3

55

2

1

54

27 A B 28 C D 29 E F

EH26

EH23

Mount
Lothian

Fullarton

Fullarton Water

Side
Plantation

Cauldhall Glen
Plantation

Steelfoot
Strip

Peter's
Plantation

Pond
Wood

Smithy
Strip

Gillygub
Dean

Fountainside

B6372

Easter
Wood

B6372

Upper
Side

Allan
Clump

Loch Burn

Toxsidehill
Wood

Stell
Plantation

Tweedale Burn

The
Old Wood

Toxsidehill

Toxside

Gladhouse
Plantation

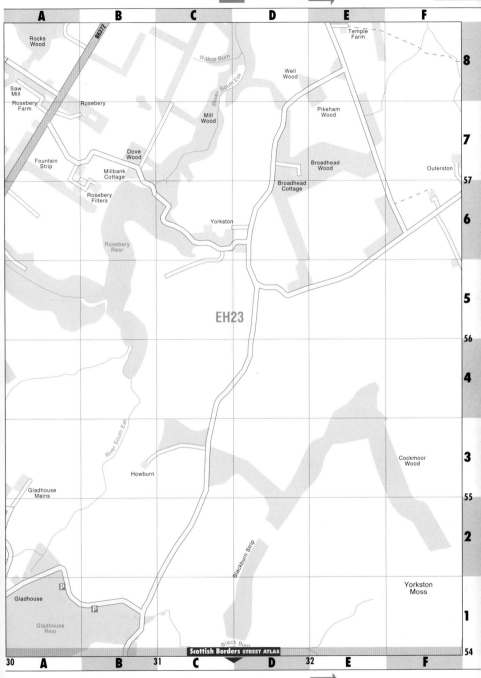

Rocks
Wood

Saw
Mill

Rosebery
Farm

Rosebery

Walcot Burn

River South Esk

Temple
Farm

Well
Wood

Mill
Wood

Pikeham
Wood

Outerston

Fountain
Strip

Dove
Wood

Broadhead
Wood

Millbank
Cottage

Broadhead
Cottage

Rosebery
Filters

Yorkston

Rosebery
Resr

EH23

River South Esk

Cockmoor
Wood

Howburn

Gladhouse
Mains

Blackburn Strip

Gladhouse

P

P

Yorkston
Moss

Gladhouse
Resr

Black Burn

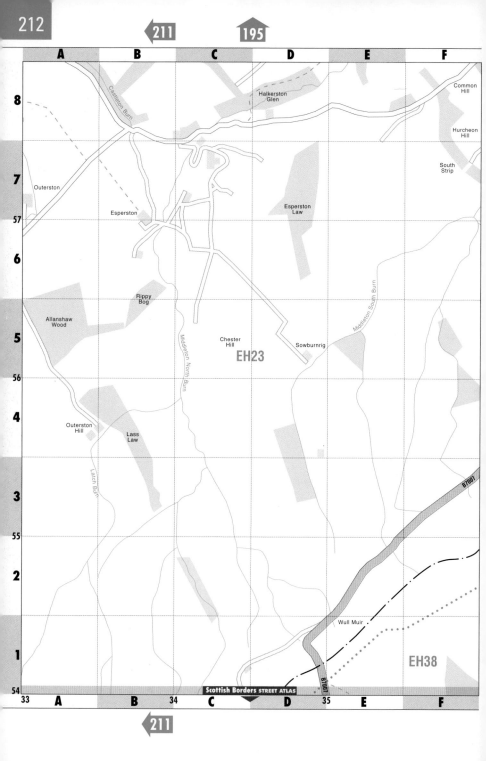

A **B** **C** **D** **E** **F**

8

Common
Hill

Halkerston
Glen

Hurcheon
Hill

7

Outerston

South
Strip

57

Esperston

Esperston
Law

Castleton Burn

6

Rippy
Bog

Middleton South Burn

Allanshaw
Wood

5

Chester
Hill

Sowburnrig

EH23

56

Middleton North Burn

4

Outerston
Hill

Lass
Law

3

Latch Burn

B7007

55

2

Wull Muir

EH38

1

B7007

54

33 **A** **B** 34 **C** **D** 35 **E** **F**

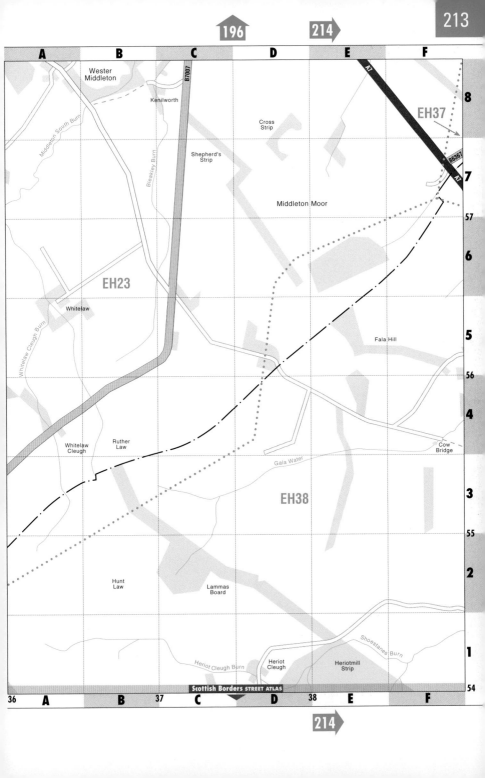

214

Wester
Middleton

Kenilworth

Cross
Strip

EH37

Shepherd's
Strip

Middleton Moor

EH23

Whitelaw

Fala Hill

Whitelaw
Cleugh

Ruther
Law

Cow
Bridge

Gala Water

EH38

Hunt
Law

Lammas
Board

Heriot Cleugh Burn

Heriot
Cleugh

Heriotmill
Strip

Shoestanes Burn

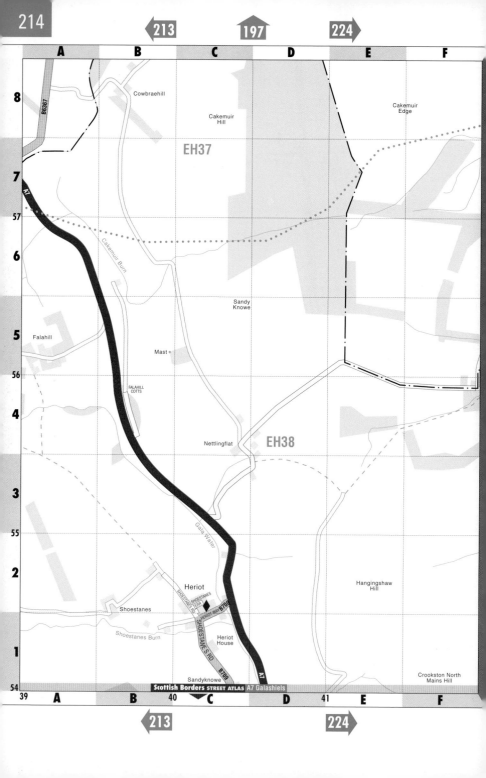

8

Cowbraehill

Cakemuir
Hill

Cakemuir
Edge

EH37

7

57

Cakemuir Burn

6

Falahill

5

Sandy
Knowe

Mast

56

FALAHILL
COTTS

4

Nettlingflat

EH38

3

Gala Water

55

2

Hangingshaw
Hill

Heriot

Shoestanes

SHOESTANES RD

SHOESTANES TERR

HERIOT MAIN

B709

Heriot
House

SHOESTANES RD

B709

1

Shoestanes Burn

Sandyknowe

A7

Crookston North
Mains Hill

54

B6367

A7

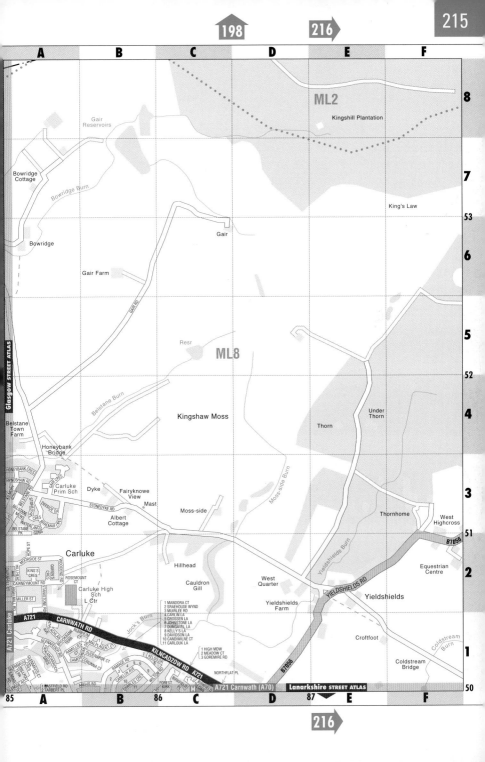

ML2

Kingshill Plantation

Gair
Reservoirs

Bowridge
Cottage

King's Law

53

Bowridge Burn

Bowridge

Gair

7

Gair Farm

6

Resr

ML8

5

52

Belstane Burn

Under
Thorn

Kingshaw Moss

Thorn

4

Belstane
Town
Farm

Moss-side Burn

Honeybank
Bridge

HONEYBANK CRES

Carluke
Prim Sch

Dyke

Fairyknowe
View

Mast

Moss-side

Thornhome

West
Highcross

3

Albert
Cottage

Yieldshields Burn

51

B7056

Carluke

Hillhead

Cauldron
Gill

West
Quarter

Equestrian
Centre

2

Carluke High
Sch
L Ctr

1 MANDORA CT
2 SRAEHOUSE WYND
3 MUIRLEE RD
4 CARLIN LA
5 CROSSEN LA
6 JOHNSTONE LA
7 DUNGAVEL LA
8 KELLY'S LA
9 DAVIDSON LA
10 CANDIMILNE CT
11 CARLOUK LA

YIELDSHIELDS RD

Yieldshields

Yieldshields
Farm

A721 Carluke

CARNWATH RD

Jock's Burn

KILNCADZOW RD

1 HIGH MDW
2 MEADOW CT
3 GOREMIRE RD

A721

Croftoot

Coldstream Burn

1

B7056

NORTHFLAT PL

Coldstream
Bridge

A721 Carnwath (A70)

Lanarkshire STREET ATLAS

50

85   A   B   86   C   D   87   E   F

Glasgow STREET ATLAS

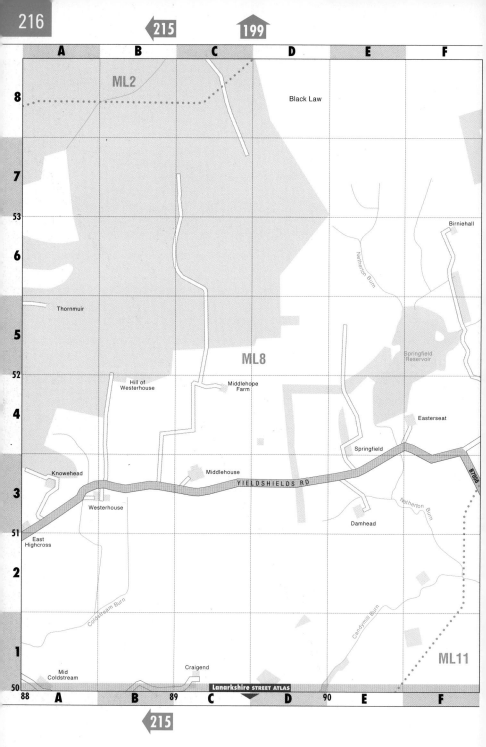

ML2

Black Law

8

7

53

Birniehall

6

Thornmuir

Netherton Burn

5

Springfield
Reservoir

ML8

52

Hill of
Westerhouse

Middlehope
Farm

4

Easterseat

Springfield

Knowehead

Middlehouse

YIELDSHIELDS RD

B7056

3

Westerhouse

Netherton Burn

Damhead

East
Highcross

51

2

Coldstream Burn

Candymill Burn

ML11

1

Mid
Coldstream

Craigend

50

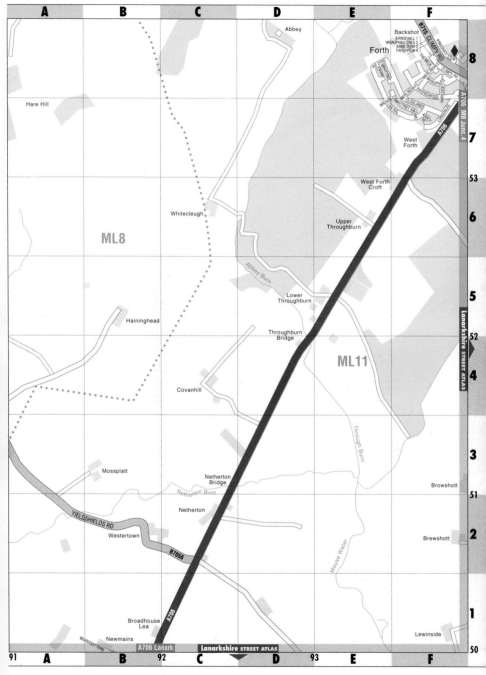

200

A B C D E F

Forth

Abbey

Backshot

BIRNIEHALL 1
WHAUPHILL CRES 2
BANK TERR 3
TINTO VIEW 4

West
Forth

West Forth
Croft

Hare Hill

ML8

Whitecleugh

Upper
Throughburn

Abbey Burn

Lower
Throughburn

Haininghead

Throughburn
Bridge

ML11

Covanhill

Through Burn

Mossplatt

Netherton
Bridge

Browshott

YIELDSHIELDS RD

Netherton Burn

Netherton

Brewshott

Westertown

B7056

Mouse Water

Broadhouse
Lea

Newmains

MURDCOT TERR

A706 Lanark

Lewinside

Lanarkshire STREET ATLAS

8
7
53
6
5
52
4
3
51
2
1
50

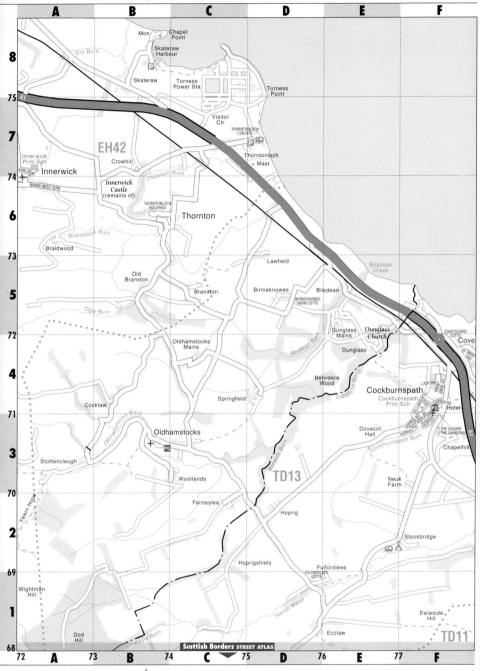

Scale: 1⅓ inches to 1 mile

0   ¼   ½ mile
0   250m   500m   750m   1 km

A   **B**   **C**   **D**   **E**   **F**

Dry Burn

Mon
Chapel Point
Skateraw
Harbour
Skateraw
Torness
Power Sta
Torness
Point

Visitor
Ctr

Thorntonloch
CVN Site
Thorntonloch
Mast

EH42
Crowhill

Innerwick
Prim Sch
Innerwick
KIRK PK
BARNS NESS TERR

Thornton Burn

Innerwick
Castle
(remains of)
THORNTONLOCH
HOLDINGS

Thornton

Braidwood Burn
Braidwood

Lawfield

Old
Branxton

Branxton
Birnieknowes
Bilsdean

Bilsdean
Creek

BIRNIEKNOWES
FARM COTTS

Ogle Burn

Oldhamstocks
Mains

Dunglass
Mains
Dunglass
Church
COASTGUARD
COTTS

Bilsdean Burn

Dunglass
Cove
WEST
END

Belvidere
Wood

Dunglass Burn

Cockburnspath
Cockburnspath
Prim Sch
Hotel

Cocklaw

Oldhamstocks Burn

Springfield

Oldhamstocks

Dovecot
Hall

Cockburnspath Burn

Neuk
Farm

LADY HALL RD
TOLL RD
NEW RD
SPRING RD
HOMES H
PROPT
SQUARE THE

1 THE SQUARE
2 THE CAUSEWAY

Chapelhill

Stottencleugh

Woollands

TD13

Branxt Burn

Ferneylea

Hoprig

Stockbridge

Yearn Hope

Hoprigshiels

Fulfordlees
FULFORDLEES
COTTS

Wightman
Hill

Dod
Hill

Kallis Burn

Henol Water

Ecclaw

Ewieside
Hill

TD11

A   73   **B**   74   **C**   75   **D**   76   **E**   77   **F**

Scale: 1½ inches to 1 mile

0   ¼   ½ mile

0   250m   500m   750m   1 km

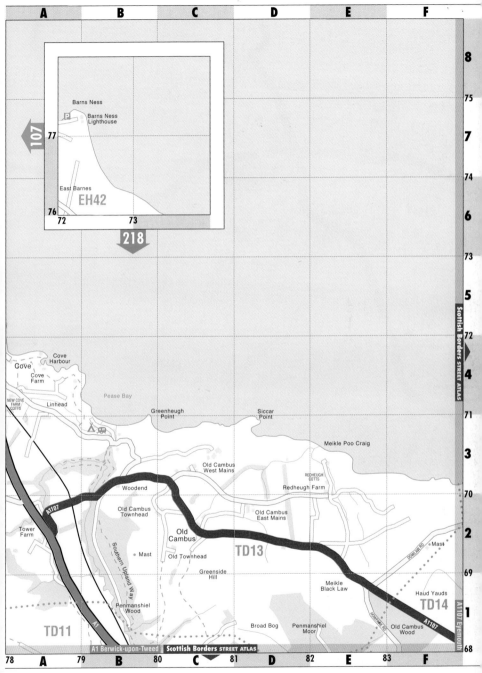

| | A | B | C | D | E | F |

107

218

Barns Ness

P

Barns Ness
Lighthouse

77

East Barnes

EH42

76

72   73

8

75

7

74

6

73

5

72

4

71

3

70

2

69

1

68

Scottish Borders STREET ATLAS

Cove
Harbour

Cove

Cove
Farm

NEW COVE
FARM
COTTS

Linhead

Pease Bay

Greenheugh
Point

Siccar
Point

Meikle Poo Craig

Old Cambus
West Mains

REDHEUGH
COTTS

Woodend

Redheugh Farm

Old Cambus
Townhead

Old Cambus
East Mains

Tower
Farm

A1107

Old
Cambus

TD13

Southern Upland Way

Mast

Old Townhead

Greenside
Hill

Meikle
Black Law

DOW LAW RD

Mast

Haud Yauds

TD14

A1107 Eyemouth

Penmanshiel
Wood

A1

Broad Bog

Penmanshiel
Moor

Old Cambus
Wood

DOWLAW RD

A1107

TD11

A1 Berwick-upon-Tweed

Scottish Borders STREET ATLAS

78   A   79   B   80   C   81   D   82   E   83   F

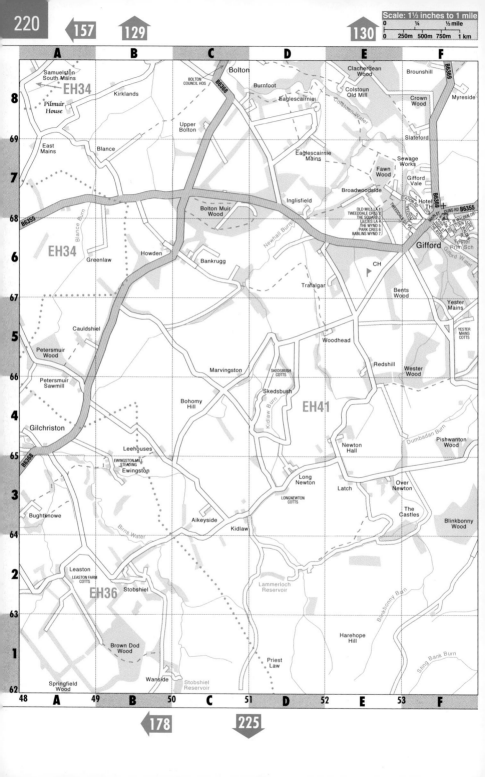

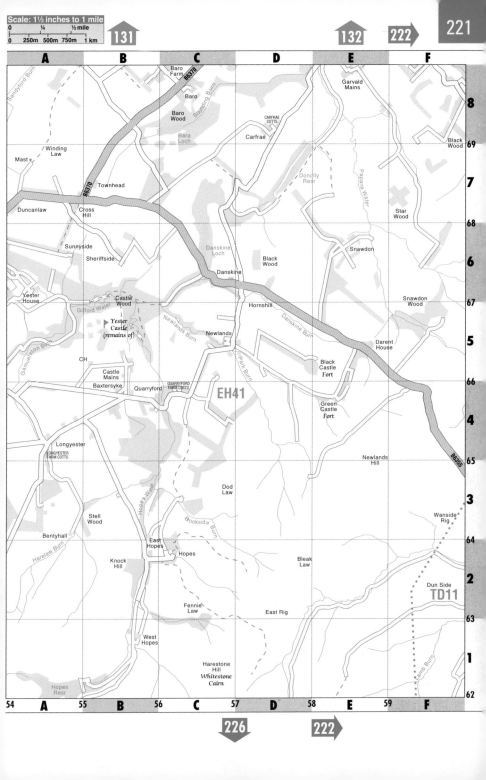

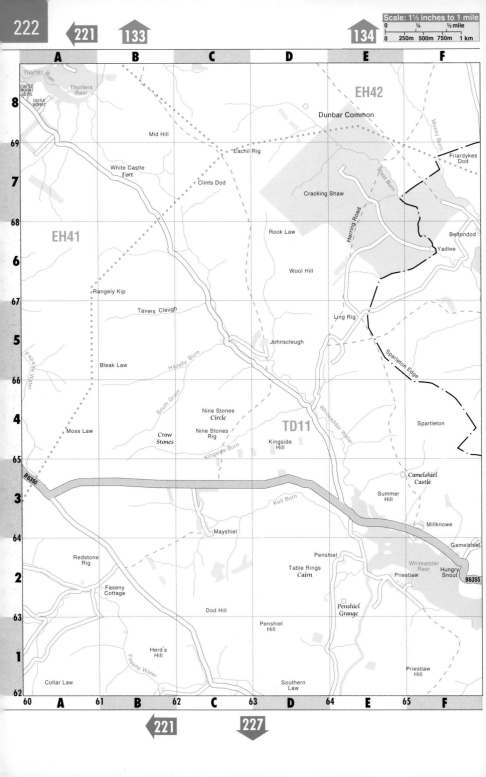

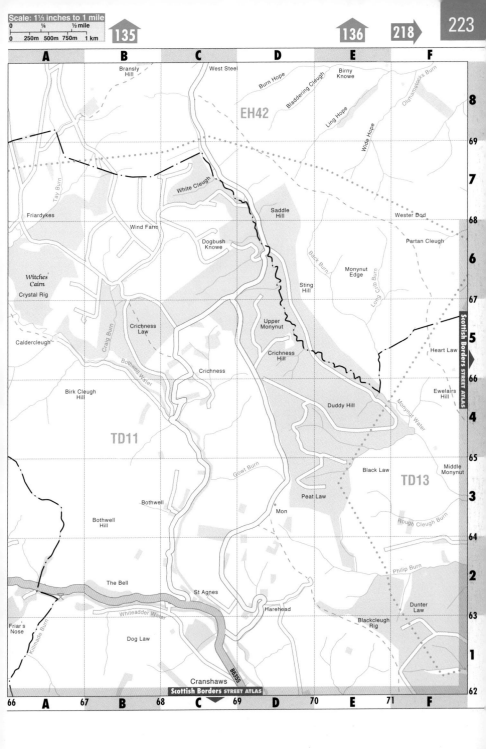

Scale: 1⅓ inches to 1 mile

0   ¼   ½ mile

0   250m 500m 750m 1 km

135

136

218

223

A   B   C   D   E   F

8

Bransly
Hill

West Steel

Burn Hope

Bladdering Cleugh

Birny
Knowe

Oldhamstocks Burn

69

EH42

Ling Hope

Wide Hope

Wester Dod

7

White Cleugh

Saddle
Hill

68

Friardykes

Wind Farm

Dogbush
Knowe

Back Burn

Partan Cleugh

Long Crib Burn

6

Monynut
Edge

Witches'
Cairn

Sting
Hill

67

Crystal Rig

Craig Burn

Crichness
Law

Upper
Monynut

Heart Law

5

Caldercleugh

Bothwell Water

Crichness

Crichness
Hill

66

Birk Cleugh
Hill

Ewelairs
Hill

Duddy Hill

Monynut Water

4

TD11

Gowl Burn

Black Law

Middle
Monynut

65

TD13

Bothwell

Peat Law

Mon

Rough Cleugh Burn

3

Bothwell
Hill

64

The Bell

Philip Burn

2

Friar's
Nose

Killmade Burn

Whiteadder Water

St Agnes

Harehead

Dunter
Law

63

Blackcleugh
Rig

Dog Law

Cranshaws

B6355

1

62

66   A   67   B   68   C   69   D   70   E   71   F

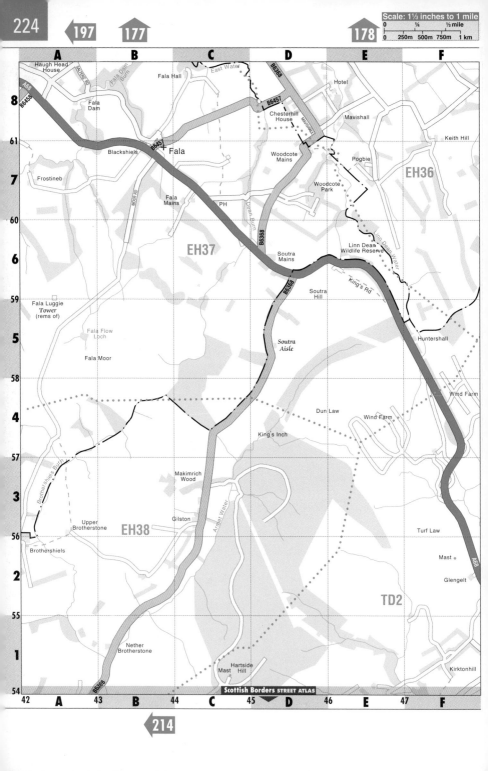

A   B   C   D   E   F

8   Haugh Head House
A68   B6458
SCLEISS RD
Fala Dam Burn
Fala Hall
East Water
B6368
B6457
Chesterhill House
Hotel
Mavishall

61   Blackshiels   B6457   + Fala
Fala Dam
Keith Hill

7   Frostineb
MOOR RD
Fala Mains
PH
Deen Burn
Woodcote Mains
Woodcote Park
Pogbie
EH36

60   B6368

6   EH37
Soutra Mains
Linn Dean Wildlife Reserve
King's Rd
Linn Dean Water
Huntershall

59   Fala Luggie Tower (rems of)
B6368
Soutra Hill

5   Fala Flow Loch
Fala Moor
Soutra Aisle

58   Wind Farm

4   Brothershiels Burn
Dun Law
Wind Farm
King's Inch
Wind Farm

57   Makimrich Wood
King's Inch

3   Upper Brotherstone
EH38
Gilston
Ankel Water
Turf Law

56   Brothershiels

2   Nether Brotherstone
Mast
Glengelt
A68

55   TD2

1   B6368
Mast
Hartside Hill
Kirktonhill

54   Scottish Borders STREET ATLAS

42   A   43   B   44   C   45   D   46   E   47   F

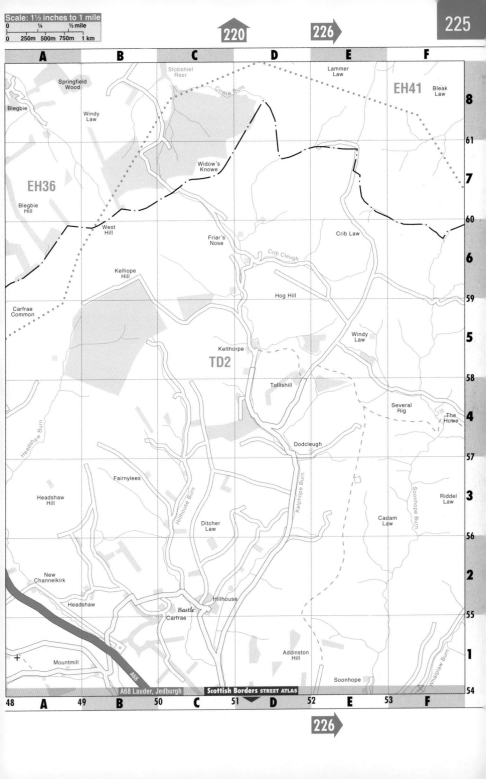

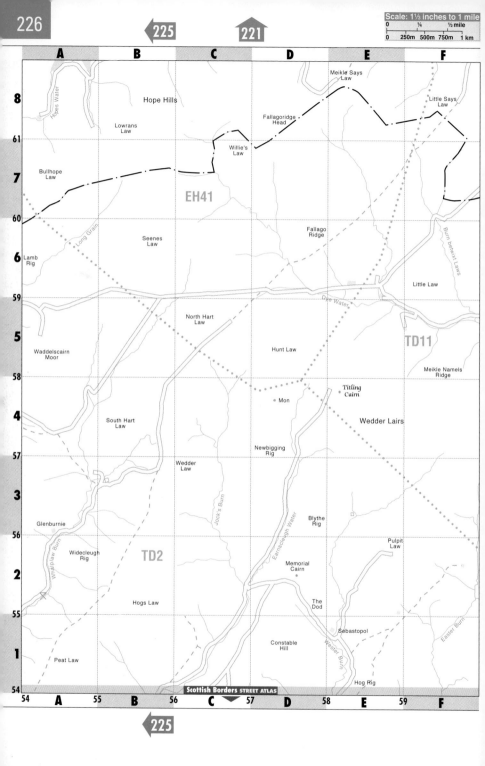

Scale: 1½ inches to 1 mile

0   ¼   ½ mile

0   250m   500m   750m   1 km

A   **B**   **C**   **D**   **E**   **F**

Hopes Water

Hope Hills

8

Lowrans Law

Meikle Says Law

Little Says Law

Fallagoridge Head

61

Willie's Law

EH41

Bullhope Law

7

Long Grain

Seenes Law

Fallago Ridge

60

Lamb Rig

6

Little Law

Dye Water

59

North Hart Law

Burn betwixt Laws

Waddelscairn Moor

5

Hunt Law

TD11

Meikle Namels Ridge

58

Titling Cairn

Mon

4

South Hart Law

Wedder Lairs

57

Newbigging Rig

Wedder Law

3

Jock's Burn

Blythe Rig

Glenburnie

56

Pulpit Law

Whalplaw Burn

Widecleugh Rig

TD2

2

Earnscleugh Water

Memorial Cairn

Hogs Law

The Dod

55

Sebastopol

Wester Burn

Easter Burn

Constable Hill

1

Peat Law

Hog Rig

54

Scottish Borders STREET ATLAS

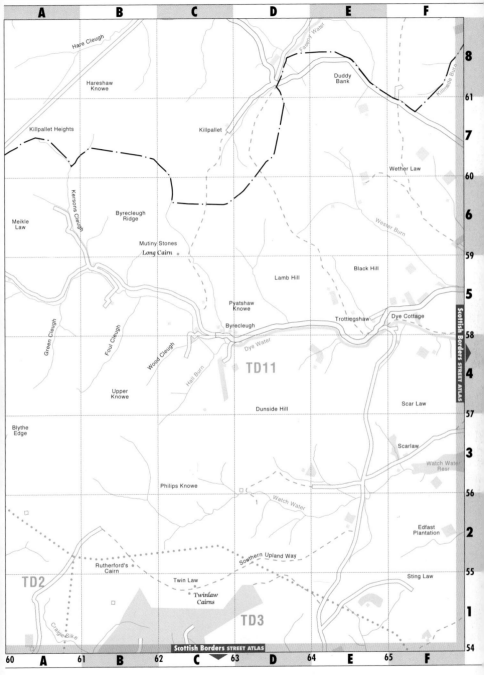

Hare Cleugh

Hareshaw Knowe

Fasidly Water

Duddy Bank

Killmade Burn

Killpallet Heights

Killpallet

Wether Law

Kersons Cleugh

Byrecleugh Ridge

Meikle Law

Wester Burn

Mutiny Stones
Long Cairn

Lamb Hill

Black Hill

Green Cleugh

Foul Cleugh

Wood Cleugh

Pyatshaw Knowe

Byrecleugh

Trottingshaw

Dye Cottage

Hall Burn

Dye Water

TD11

Upper Knowe

Dunside Hill

Scar Law

Blythe Edge

Scarlaw

Watch Water Resr

Philips Knowe

Watch Water

Edfast Plantation

TD2

Rutherford's Cairn

Southern Upland Way

Sting Law

Twin Law

Twinlaw Cairns

TD3

Craigie Sike

Scottish Borders STREET ATLAS

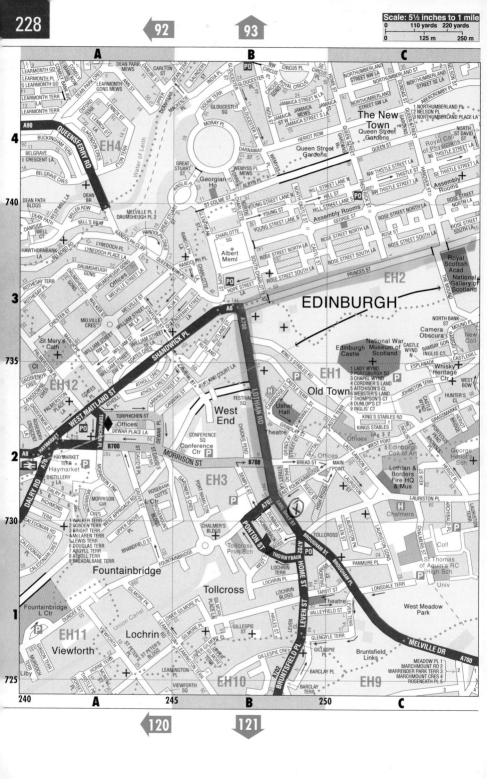

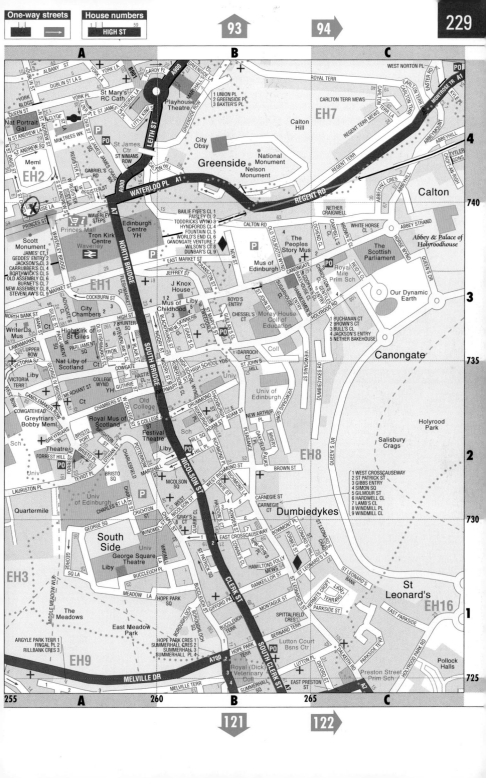

Index

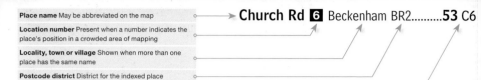

Place name May be abbreviated on the map

Location number Present when a number indicates the place's position in a crowded area of mapping

Locality, town or village Shown when more than one place has the same name

Postcode district District for the indexed place

Page and grid square Page number and grid reference for the standard mapping

Church Rd **6** Beckenham BR2..........**53** C6

Public and commercial buildings are highlighted in magenta   Places of interest are highlighted in blue with a star *

Abbreviations used in the index

Acad	**Academy**	Comm	**Common**	Gd	**Ground**	L	**Leisure**	Prom	**Promenade**
App	**Approach**	Cott	**Cottage**	Gdn	**Garden**	La	**Lane**	Rd	**Road**
Arc	**Arcade**	Cres	**Crescent**	Gn	**Green**	Liby	**Library**	Recn	**Recreation**
Ave	**Avenue**	Cswy	**Causeway**	Gr	**Grove**	Mdw	**Meadow**	Ret	**Retail**
Bglw	**Bungalow**	Ct	**Court**	H	**Hall**	Meml	**Memorial**	Sh	**Shopping**
Bldg	**Building**	Ctr	**Centre**	Ho	**House**	Mkt	**Market**	Sq	**Square**
Bsns, Bus	**Business**	Ctry	**Country**	Hospl	**Hospital**	Mus	**Museum**	St	**Street**
Bvd	**Boulevard**	Cty	**County**	HQ	**Headquarters**	Orch	**Orchard**	Sta	**Station**
Cath	**Cathedral**	Dr	**Drive**	Hts	**Heights**	Pal	**Palace**	Terr	**Terrace**
Cir	**Circus**	Dro	**Drove**	Ind	**Industrial**	Par	**Parade**	TH	**Town Hall**
Cl	**Close**	Ed	**Education**	Inst	**Institute**	Pas	**Passage**	Univ	**University**
Cnr	**Corner**	Emb	**Embankment**	Int	**International**	Pk	**Park**	Wk, Wlk	**Walk**
Coll	**College**	Est	**Estate**	Intc	**Interchange**	Pl	**Place**	Wr	**Water**
Com	**Community**	Ex	**Exhibition**	Junc	**Junction**	Prec	**Precinct**	Yd	**Yard**

Index of localities, towns and villages

Abbeyhill 94 A1
Abbey Parks 29 B3
Abercorn 49 E2
Aberdour 49 C7
Aberlady 71 D4
Adambrae 164 C8
Addiebrownhill 162 E1
Addiewell 162 E2
Airth 22 D3
Alderston 100 E2
Allandale 57 C2
Allanton 198 A8
Alloa 10 C5
Alloa Park 10 B5
Almondvale 143 E2
Alnwickhill 150 E6
Alva 5 A6
Antonshill 38 E4
Armadale 139 E5
Arniston 174 B1
Arnothill 60 A4
Athelstaneford 101 E8
Auchenbowie 19 B4
Auchendinny 171 D1
Auchengray 202 E1
Auchtertool 15 A2
Avonbridge 110 A6
Baberton 148 C7
Backdale 151 E2
Backmuir of Pitfirrane . .28 A6
Bainsford 60 B8
Baldridgeburn 28 D5
Balerno 147 D1
Ballencrieff 72 B1
Bangly Hill 100 B4
Bankhead 57 E6
Bankside 60 C8
Bannockburn 5 C7
Bantaskin 59 F4
Barnton 91 B3
Bathgate 141 C7
Beancross 61 C4
Beaverbank 93 D4
Beeslack 192 A7
Belhaven 78 B1
Bellsquarry 164 D7
Bellyeoman 29 C5
Belvedere 140 F8
Bents 162 A2
Beveridgewell 28 F5
Bilston 171 E5
Bingham 122 F6
Binniehill 108 A5
Blackburn 162 D8
Blackhall 92 A2
Blackness 65 E4
Blackridge 138 C3
Blaeberryhill 161 C5

Blairburn 42 C8
Blairhall 26 A7
Blairlogie 3 B6
Blinkbonny 148 B4
Boghall 141 E7
Bolton 129 F1
Bonaly 149 A5
Bo'ness 63 E8
Bonnington 93 D4
Bonnybridge 58 B5
Bonnyrigg and
  Lasswade 173 D7
Borestone 7 A2
Borrowstoun 63 F5
Borrowstoun Mains . . .63 E5
Borthwick 196 B4
Bowhouse 61 C5
Braehead 7 C5
Braepark 91 B3
Branshill 5 A1
Breich 182 F6
Bridgend 86 C4
Bridgeness 64 C8
Bridge of Allan 2 A8
Brightons 82 C8
Broomhouse 119 E3
Broomieknowe 173 A8
Broughton 93 D3
Broxburn Dunbar 107 A7
  Livingston 115 E6
Brucefield Dunfermline . .29 C2
  Livingston 164 D6
Brunstane 123 D6
Bruntsfield 121 B5
Bughtlin 91 A1
Burdiehouse 151 A4
Burnside 5 C7
Burntisland 33 E2
Burnwynd 146 C5
Bush 171 B3
Cairneyhill 27 C4
Calderhall 144 E4
Calderhead 179 E4
California 81 E5
Calton 229 C4
Cambus 9 B8
Cambusbarron 6 C6
Cambuskenneth 2 D1
Camelon 59 C5
Cammo 90 F2
Camptoun 100 F8
Canongate 229 C3
Canonmills 93 C2
Carlops 206 C4
Carluke 215 A2
Carmuirs 59 B5
Carnock 27 D6

Carriden 64 C7
Carrington 194 D6
Carron 39 A2
Carronshore 39 C3
Castleblair Park 28 F4
Castleloan 63 D7
Cat Craig 107 E7
Causewayhead 2 B4
Chapel 16 C8
Charlestown 45 B4
Chartershall 7 A1
Chesterhill 175 C7
Churchill 121 B4
Clackmannan 11 B3
Claremont Park 94 C4
Cleikimin 123 B5
Clermiston 91 D1
Coates 120 F7
Cockburnspath 218 E4
Cockenzie & Port Seton . .97 B5
Colinton 149 C7
Colinton Mains 149 E6
Comely Bank 92 F2
Comiston 150 A6
Comrie 26 D7
Cornbank 191 D6
Cornton 2 B3
Corslet 148 A6
Corstorphine 119 F6
Cousland 154 D5
Cowie 20 D7
Coxet Hill 6 C4
Craigentinny 94 E2
Craigielaw 71 A4
Craigleith 92 E3
Craiglockhart 120 D1
Craigmillar 122 D3
Craigshill 144 B5
Cramond 91 C5
Cramond Bridge 90 F3
Cranshaws 223 C1
Crichton 196 F8
Croftmalloch 161 B5
Crombie 44 C4
Crossford 28 B1
Crosshore 108 E6
Crossford 28 B1
Crossgates 30 F6
Cuiken 191 E6
Culross 42 C8
Currie 147 F3
Cuthill 96 E1
Dalgety Bay 48 C3
Dalkeith 156 E7
Dalmeny 89 F7
Dalry 120 F6
Danderhall 152 C7

Davidsons Mains 91 E3
Dean 92 F1
Deanburn 191 E7
Deanfield 63 D7
Deans 142 F6
Dechmont 114 C2
Dedridge 143 E1
Denny 36 F1
Dennyloanhead 57 D5
Dewartown 175 D5
Dirleton 53 B4
Dobbie's Knowe 173 A7
Dolphingstone 125 F7
Dreghorn 149 D5
Drem 73 A4
Drum 94 A2
Drumbrae 91 C2
Drylaw 92 C3
Duddingston 122 E6
Dumbiedykes 229 B2
Dunbar 78 D1
Dunfermline 29 A3
Dunipace 36 D4
Dunmore 22 C7
Dykehead 179 D5
Dysart 18 B7
East Calder 144 F3
East Craigs 119 A7
Easter Aberdour 49 C8
Easter Howgate 171 A5
Easter Millerhill 152 E8
Easter Pencaitland . . .156 F6
Eastfield Penicuik 191 F6
  Whitburn 159 C4
East Fortune 74 B3
East Hermiston 119 A1
Easthouses 174 C7
East Linton 103 C7
East Saltoun 157 E4
East Whitburn 160 C7
Ecclesmachan 114 F7
Edgehead 175 C7
Edinburgh 228 C3
Edmonstone 152 A8
Eldindean 173 C8
Elphinstone 126 A5
Elphinstone 126 A5
Entry Head 146 E7
Eskbank 156 D7
Eskgrove 172 F8
Factor's Park 120 C5
Fairfield 5 B2
Fairmilehead 150 B5
Fala 224 C7
Falkirk 60 D6
Fallin 21 B8
Falside 140 E5
Faucheldean 87 F1

Fauldhouse 181 A6
Fenton Barns 73 B4
Ferniehill 151 E7
Firr Hill 149 D8
Fishcross 5 E3
Fisherrow 124 C7
Fordell 31 B6
Forrestfield 137 A3
Forth 201 A1
Fountainbridge 228 A1
Frankerton 36 A2
Garbethill 17 E8
Gardeners' Land 29 B4
Garleton Hills 101 A5
Garvald 132 D2
Garvock Hill 29 C4
Gayfield 93 E3
Gifford 220 F6
Gilchriston 220 A4
Gilmerton 151 F6
Gladsmuir 128 B7
Glenmavis 141 D7
Glensburgh 40 A1
Glen Village 60 B1
Gogar 118 D5
Goldenacre 93 B4
Gorebridge 195 B8
Gorgie 120 D5
Gowkhall 27 E7
Gowkshill 174 B3
Gracemount 151 B5
Grahamston 60 A6
Grangemouth 61 B7
Grangepans 64 A7
Granton 92 E7
Greenbank Edinburgh . .149 E8
  Falkirk 59 C3
Greenburn 181 A8
Greendykes 122 F3
Greenhill 58 A2
Greenlaw Mains 192 A8
Greenside 229 B4
Guildiehaugh 141 C4
Gullane 52 A1
Gullane Hill 51 E2
Haddington 130 D7
Haggs 57 A3
Halbeath 30 A5
Hallglen 60 D1
Harburn 185 C8
Harthill 159 F5
Hartwood 179 A3
Hayfield 17 B6
Haywood 202 A2
Head of Muir 57 A3
Headwell 29 B5
Helensfield 11 A5
Heriot 214 C2

Hermiston 118 F1
Hermitage 94 B3
Heugh 54 F5
High Bonnybridge 58 C3
High Valleyfield 26 A2
Hillend 47 E4
Hill Of Beath 13 A1
Hillside 93 F2
Holygate 115 D6
Holyrood 122 A7
Hopefield 173 B6
Howden 143 E4
Howgate 192 B1
Humbie 178 B2
Hunterfield 174 D2
Huntington 100 B1
Inch The 122 B2
Innerwick 218 A7
Inveresk 124 E5
Inverkeithing 47 B1
Inverleith 93 A4
Jock's Lodge 94 D1
Joppa 123 D7
Juniper Green 148 C6
Kaimes 151 A5
Keilarsbrae 10 D8
Kelty 12 D8
Kennet 11 C2
Kilbagie 11 D1
Kilduff 101 C8
Kincardine 23 F4
Kinghorn 35 A2
Kingseat 12 B1
Kingseathill 29 C6
Kingsknowe 120 B1
Kingston 54 A1
Kinneil 63 D5
Kirkcaldy 17 C3
Kirkhill Broxburn 115 C5
Penicuik 192 A5
Kirkliston 89 B1
Kirknewton 145 F2
Kirkton Burntisland 33 D1
Livingston 143 A1
Kirkton Campus 163 F8
Kingshridge 143 C8
Ladywell 143 D6
Ladywood 192 A6
Langlees 39 D1
Langton 144 F3
Langton Pk 144 F3
Larbert 38 B2
Laurieston 61 B4
Leadburn 208 F3
Leith 94 A2
Letham 39 C8
Levenhall 125 A6
Leven Seat 182 A4
Liberton 150 F7
Limekilns 45 E3
Limerigg 108 B2
Linktown 17 B2
Linlithgow 85 C6
Linlithgow Bridge 84 D8
Livingston 143 D6

Livingston Village 143 C2
Loan 83 C4
Loanburn 191 E5
Loanhead Edinburgh 172 B7
Stirling 7 E6
Loanstone 192 B5
Lochend 94 B2
Lochgelly 14 C7
Lochrin 228 A1
Loganlea 162 C1
Longcroft 57 B3
Long Dalmahoy 146 E4
Longniddry 98 F5
Longridge 161 C1
Longstone 120 B2
Lothianbridge 173 F6
Lower Saltoun 157 F5
Low Torry 26 D1
Low Valleyfield 26 A1
Lumphinnans 13 E6
Macmerry 127 D5
Maddiston 83 B6
Magdalene 123 B6
Maidenpark 63 E6
Manor Powis 3 A3
Marchmont 121 C5
Mauricewood 191 E7
Mayfield Armadale 140 A5
Dalkeith 174 F5
Edinburgh 121 F4
Meadowbank 94 B2
Menstrie 3 E6
Merchiston 120 F4
Mid Calder 144 C4
Middlefield 60 D6
Middleton 196 A1
Milesmark 28 D6
Milton Bridge 171 B2
Mingle 64 A6
Monkswood 174 B5
Monktonhall 124 C3
Moredun 151 D8
Morningside 121 A2
Mortonhall 150 E5
Mossend 163 C3
Mossgreen 31 A6
Muiralehouse 19 E8
Muirfield 52 C3
Muirhouse 92 B6
Muirhouses 64 D5
Muirton 7 E6
Mungal 60 A8
Murrayfield 120 B7
Musselburgh 124 C7
Myreside 120 E3
Nether Dechmont 143 B7
Nether Liberton 121 F3
Newbattle 153 A1
Newbigging 15 C2
Newbridge 117 A6
Newcraighall 123 E4
Newhailes 124 A6
Newhaven 93 D6
Newington 121 E4
Newlchirn 16 C6

Newmills 26 D1
New Pentland 171 F7
Newton 88 A8
Newtongrange 174 A6
Newton Village 152 D7
Newtown 63 F6
New Town 127 E1
New Winton 127 B3
Niddrie 123 A3
Niddrie Mains 122 E4
Niddrie Marischal 123 A3
Niddrie Mill 123 A4
North Berwick 54 D8
North Broomage 38 A4
Northfield 122 D8
North Leith 93 E7
North Merchiston 120 E5
North Middleton 195 F3
North Queensferry 68 D6
Nungate 130 C8
Oakley 26 F7
Old Cambus 219 C2
Old Craighall 124 A2
Oldhamstocks 218 C3
Old Pentland 150 F1
Old Philpstoun 86 F7
Old Town 228 B2
Orchard Brae 92 E1
Ormiston 155 F7
Oxgangs 149 F6
Panhall 18 A6
Parkfoot 57 C4
Parkhead 119 F2
Parkneuk 28 D6
Parsons Green 94 B1
Pathhead Dalkeith 176 B5
Kirkcaldy 17 D6
Pattiesmuir 46 B4
Paulville 141 A5
Peastonbank 156 F1
Pencaitland 156 D7
Penicuik 191 D4
Penston 127 F5
Pettycur 34 F1
Philpstoun 86 D7
Piershill 94 E1
Pirleg 93 E4
Pilton 92 E5
Pinkie Braes 125 A6
Pitcorthie 29 E1
Pitcox 105 C3
Plean 20 C3
Polbeth 163 F5
Polmont 61 E1
Polmont Station 61 E1
Polton 172 D6
Poltonhall 172 F6
Port Brae 17 C4
Port Edgar 45 A3
Portobello 123 B8
Port of Leith 93 E8
Preston 97 A2
Prestonfield 122 B4
Prestonpans 96 E2
Pumpherston 144 B8

Quarryhead 173 B8
Quarryholes 94 A3
Queensferry 89 A7
Raith Park 16 C5
Raploch 2 A4
Ratho 117 D1
Ratho Station 117 D5
Ravelston 120 B8
Redding 61 C1
Reddingmuirhead 82 A8
Restalrig 94 D2
Riccarton Clackmannan 3 A1
Currie 147 E7
Riverside 2 B1
Rosebank 36 C4
Roseburn 120 E7
Rosewell 172 D2
Roslin 171 F3
Rosyth 46 F4
Rumblingwell 28 C5
Rumford 82 E7
St Leonard's 229 C1
St Ninians 7 B4
Samuelston 129 A2
Sauchie 5 E1
Saughtonhall 120 A6
Scoughall 56 C3
Seacliff 56 B5
Seafield Blackburn 142 C1
Edinburgh 94 D4
Loanhead 171 D6
Seton 97 E2
Shieldhill 81 D6
Shore 7 C8
Shotts 179 F5
Sighthill 119 D3
Silverburn 190 E5
Silverknowes 91 E5
Sinclairtown 17 F7
Skinflats 39 F3
Slamannan 108 A6
Slateford 120 C2
Smeaton 17 C8
South Alloa 9 F3
South Broomage 38 D1
South Gyle 119 B4
Southhouse 151 C5
South Leith 94 A5
South Queensferry 68 B2
South Side 229 A1
Spittal 99 D7
Spott 106 C4
Springhill 180 B2
Stanburn 82 D2
Stane 180 A3
Stenhouse 120 B4
Stenhousemuir 38 D3
Stenton 104 E1
Stirling 7 C8
Stockbridge 93 A2
Stoneybank 124 B4
Stoneyburn 162 C2
Stoneywood 36 C2
Straiton 151 A2
Summerford 59 D4

Swanston 149 F5
Tamfourhill 59 C4
Tarbrax 203 F3
Temple 194 D2
Templehall 16 F7
The Gyle 119 B6
The New Town 228 C4
Thornton 218 C6
Threemiletown 86 F4
Throsk 9 A3
Tollcross 228 B1
Torbothie 180 B4
Torbrex 6 C3
Torphichen 111 E6
Torphin 148 E4
Torryburn 26 E1
Torwood 37 E6
Touch 29 E5
Townhill 29 C8
Tranent 126 E7
Trinity 93 C5
Tullibody 4 C3
Tyninghame 76 B3
Uphall 114 F4
Uphall Station 115 A1
Upper Town of Saltoun .157 E4
Urquhart 28 D2
Viewforth 228 A1
Wadingburn 151 F1
Wallacestone 82 B7
Wallyford 125 C5
Wardie 93 A6
Warriston 93 C4
Wellwood 29 A7
West Barns 77 E1
West Benhar 159 B4
West Calder 163 D2
West Craigs 118 E7
West End 228 B2
Wester Aberdour 49 B6
Wester Hailes 148 D8
Wester Millerhill 152 E7
Wester Pencaitland 156 D6
Westfield 110 F5
West Mains 121 E2
Westpans 125 E1
West Pilton 92 C5
Westquarter 61 B2
Westrigg 138 F3
West Saltoun 157 C3
West Windygoul 126 C4
Whins of Milton 7 B2
Whitburn 161 D5
Whitecraig 124 E1
Whitecross 83 F6
Whitekirk 75 F8
Wilkieston 146 A6
Willowbrae 122 D7
Wilsontown 201 C2
Winchburgh 87 E2
Windyknowe 140 F5
Woodburn 153 C3
Woodend 87 F7
Woodlands 60 B4
Yieldshields 215 E2

Index of streets, hospitals, industrial estates, railway stations, schools, shopping centres, universities and places of interest

1st St
  Grangemouth,Chemical Works
  FK3 ....62 D6
  Grangemouth,Oil Refinery
  FK3 ....62 A7
2nd St
  Grangemouth,Chemical Works
  FK3 ....62 D6
  Grangemouth,Oil Refinery
  FK3 ....62 A8
3rd St
  Grangemouth,Chemical Works
  EH51 ....62 D6
  Grangemouth,Oil Refinery
  FK3 ....62 A8
4th St
  Grangemouth,Chemical Works
  EH51 ....62 E6
  Grangemouth,Oil Refinery
  FK3 ....62 B8
5th St
  Grangemouth,Chemical Works
  EH51 ....62 E6
  Grangemouth,Oil Refinery
  FK3 ....62 B8
6th St
  Grangemouth,Chemical Works
  EH51 ....62 E6
  Grangemouth,Oil Refinery
  FK3 ....62 B8
7th St
  Grangemouth,Chemical Works
  EH51 ....62 E5
  Grangemouth,Oil Refinery
  FK3 ....62 C8
8th St FK3,EH51 ....62 C8

A
A1 Ind Pk EH15 ....123 B7
Abbey Craig Ct FK9 ....2 D3
Abbeycraig Pk FK9 ....2 D3
Abbey Craig Rd FK10 ....5 B1
Abbey Cres EH39 ....54 B7
Abbey Ct EH39 ....54 B7

Abbeyfield Ho EH4 ....92 B2
Abbeygrange EH22 ....174 A6
Abbeyhill EH8 ....229 C4
Abbeyhill Cres EH8 ....229 C4
Abbeyhill Ind Est EH8 ....94 A1
Abbeyhill Prim Sch EH7 ....94 A1
Abbey Kings Park Hospl
  FK 6 F5
Abbey La EH8 ....94 A1
Abbey Mains EH41 ....101 F4
Abbey Mews 3 EH39 ....54 B7
Abbey Mill EH6 ....7 C8
Abbeymount EH8 ....229 C4
Abbey & Palace of
  Holyroodhouse EH8 ....229 C3
Abbey Park Pl EH39 ....29 A3
Abbey Pl ML11 ....217 F7
Abbey Rd Dalkeith EH22 ....153 A2
  Dunbar EH42 ....78 D2
  North Berwick EH39 ....54 B7
  Stirling FK8 ....2 C1
Abbey Road Pl FK8 ....7 C8
Abbey St Edinburgh EH7 ....94 A1
  High Valleyfield KY12 ....26 B2
Abbey Strand EH8 ....229 C3
Abbeyview EH9 ....2 D4
Abbey View
  Crossford KY12 ....28 C1
  Dunfermline KY12 ....29 E2
Abbot's View EH41 ....101 B2
Abbots Cl EH39 ....53 F7
Abbots Ct FK2 ....60 D7
Abbotsford Cres
  Grangemouth FK3 ....61 F6
  Laurieston FK2 ....61 A4
Abbotsford Gdns FK2 ....39 B1
Abbotsford Pk EH10 ....121 A4
Abbotsford Pl FK8 ....2 C1
Abbotsford Rd EH39 ....53 E7
Abbotsford Rise EH54 ....144 A1
Abbotsford St FK2 ....60 B8

Abbotshall Rd
  Kirkcaldy KY1,KY2 ....17 B3
  Kirkcaldy,Linktown KY1,KY2 .17 A2
Abbotsinch Ct FK3 ....61 F7
Abbotsinch Ind Est FK3 ....61 F7
Abbotsinch Rd FK3 ....61 F7
Abbots Mill KY2 ....17 A3
Abbots Moss Dr FK1 ....59 F1
Abbots Rd
  Falkirk,Bankside FK2 ....60 D8
  Falkirk,Middlefield FK2 ....60 D7
  Grangemouth FK3 ....61 D7
Abbots Road Rdbt FK2 ....60 D8
Abbot St KY12 ....29 A3
Abbots View KY2 ....61 F3
Abbot's View KY1 ....59 D8
Abbotsview Junc EH41 ....101 B2
Abbots Wlk KY7 ....16 F3
Abbott Rd KY12 ....29 A3
Abden Ave KY3 ....35 A3
Abden Ct KY3 ....35 A3
Abden Pl KY3 ....35 A3
Abel Pl KY11 ....29 F4
Abercairny Cres FK2 ....82 E6
Abercairney Pl FK3 ....61 E7
Abercorn Ave EH8 ....122 D8
Abercorn Cres EH8 ....122 D8
Abercorn Ct
  Edinburgh EH8 ....122 D7
  Winchburgh EH52 ....88 A2
Abercorn Dr EH8 ....122 D8
Abercorn Gdns EH8 ....122 D8
Abercorn Gr EH8 ....122 C8
Abercorn Rd EH8 ....122 C8
Abercorn Terr EH15 ....123 C8
Abercrombie Pl FK1 ....59 E6
Abercromby Dr FK9 ....2 B8
Abercromby Pl
  Edinburgh EH3 ....228 C4
  Stirling FK8 ....2 A1
  Tullibody FK10 ....4 B2
Abercromby Prim Sch
  FK10 ....4 B2

Aberdour Castle KY3 ....49 C7
Aberdour Cres KY11 ....29 D1
Aberdour Pl KY11 ....29 D1
Aberdour Prim Sch KY3 .49 C8
Aberdour Rd
  Burntisland KY3 ....33 C1
  Dunfermline KY11 ....30 A1
Aberdour Sta KY3 ....49 C7
Aberdour Bay Nature Reserve
  EH32 ....71 B7
Aberlady Mains Cotts
  EH32 ....71 D4
Aberlady Prim Sch EH32 .71 C4
Aberlady Rd EH41 ....100 F1
Aberlour St KY11 ....46 E4
Abinger Gdns EH12 ....120 D7
Abinger Rd KY12 ....28 F2
Aboyne Ave FK9 ....2 C4
Aboyne Gdns KY2 ....16 E8
Academy La EH20 ....172 C8
Academy Pk EH6 ....94 A4
Academy Pl KY7 ....7 E1
  Stirling FK8 ....7 A8
Academy Rd Bo'ness EH51 .64 A7
Academy Sq KY11 ....47 A3
Academy St Alloa FK10 ....9 F8
  Armadale EH48 ....139 F5
  Bathgate EH48 ....141 B6
  Edinburgh EH6 ....94 A4
Acheson Dr EH32 ....125 E8
Achray Ct FK10 ....10 C5
Achray Dr FK9 ....2 A4
Acklam Path EH20 ....171 F7
Acorn Cres FK5 ....38 D1
Acredale EH48 ....141 B6
Acredales
  Haddington EH41 ....129 F7
  Linlithgow EH49 ....85 A5
Acre Rd EH41 ....64 B6
Acre View EH41 ....64 C6
Acre Valley Rd EH32 ....64 C6
Adambrae Rdbt EH54 .164 C8
Adambrae Rdbt EH54 .164 D8
Adam Cres FK5 ....38 D1
Adam Grossett Ct FK5 .38 D3
Adam Pl KY5 ....14 A8

1st–Ain

Adams Loan FK2 ....39 A1
Adam Smith Cl KY1 ....17 C4
Adam Smith St KY1 ....17 C4
Adamson Ave KY2 ....17 B6
Adamson Cres KY12 ....29 C5
Adamson Pl KY11 ....47 B3
Adam Sq EH54 ....164 C6
Adam St EH8 ....60 D6
Adams Well EH13 ....149 C7
Addiebrownhill EH55 ....162 D1
Addiewell Prim Sch & St
  Thomas' Prim Sch
  EH55 ....162 D1
Addiewell Sta EH55 ....162 E1
Addiston Cres EH14 ....147 C3
Addiston Farm Rd EH28 .118 B1
Addiston Gr EH14 ....147 C3
Addiston Pk EH14 ....147 C3
Adelaide St EH54 ....144 A5
Adelphi Gr 1 EH15 ....123 A8
Adelphi Pl EH15 ....123 A8
Adia Rd KY12 ....26 F1
Admiral Terr EH10 ....121 B5
Admiralty Rd
  Inverkeithing KY11 ....47 B4
  Rosyth KY11 ....46 D4
Admiralty St EH6 ....93 F6
Advocate's Cl EH1 ....229 A3
Affleck Ct EH12 ....119 A8
Affric Dr FK2 ....39 C1
Affric Loan ML7 ....179 E6
Affric Way KY12 ....28 B1
Afton Ct Dechmont EH52 .114 C2
  Stirling FK7 ....7 C5
Afton Dr FK6 ....57 D7
Afton Gr KY11 ....29 C5
Afton Pl EH5 ....93 A5
Afton Terr EH5 ....93 A5
Agnew Terr EH6 ....93 D5
Ailsa Cl 3 EH22 ....82 F7
Ailsa Gr KY2 ....16 E8
Ainslie Gdns FK2 ....61 F3

Ainslie Pl EH3 . . . . **228** B4
Airdrie Rd EH48,ML6. . . . . **137** B3
Airlie Dr FK2 . . . .**61** F2
Airlie Pl EH3 . . . .**93** C2
Airth Dr FK7 . . . .**7** C4
Airth Prim Sch FK2 . . . .**22** E4
Airthrey Ave FK9. . . . .**2** B6
Airthrey Castle Yd FK9 . . . . .**2** E6
Airthrey Dr FK5. . . . .**38** F4
Airthrey Rd FK9 . . . .**2** C5
Aitchison's Cl EH1. . . . .**228** C2
Aitchison Dr FK5. . . . .**38** B3
Aitchison Pl FK1. . . . .**60** B3
Aitchison's Pl EH15 . . . .**95** A1
Aitken Cres FK7 . . . .**7** B2
Aitken Ct Dunbar EH42 . . . . .**78** D3
Kirkcaldy KY1 . . . .**17** B2
Aitken Dr Slamannan FK1 . .**108** A6
Whitburn EH47 . . . .**161** B7
Aitken Gdns FK1. . . . .**59** E6
Aitken Orr Dr EH52 . . . .**115** F5
Aitken Rd FK1. . . . .**59** D6
Aitken St KY1. . . . .**17** A3
Aitken Terr FK1 . . . .**59** D6
Akarit Rd FK5 . . . .**38** E2
Alan Breck Gdns EH4 . . . . . .**91** D1
Alba Campus The EH54. . . . .**164** A8
Albany Bsns Ctr KY12 . . . . . .**29** B4
Albany Ind Est KY12 . . . .**29** B4
Albany St Dunfermline KY12 .**29** B4
Edinburgh EH1. . . . .**229** A4
Albany Street La **7** EH3 . . . .**93** D2
Alberta Ave EH54 . . . .**143** E4
Albert Ave FK3 . . . .**61** F8
Albert Bldgs EH8 . . . .**110** F5
Albert Cl EH21. . . . .**125** B5
Albert Cres EH21 . . . .**125** B5
Albert Pl **5** Edinburgh EH7 .**93** E2
Stirling FK8 . . . .**7** A7
Wallyford EH21. . . . .**125** E6
Albert Rd Edinburgh EH6 . . .**94** B5
Falkirk FK1. . . . .**60** A3
Harthill ML7 . . . .**159** E5
Albert St Edinburgh EH7 . . . .**93** F3
Rosyth KY11 . . . .**46** E4
Albert Terr
Edinburgh EH10. . . . .**121** A4
Musselburgh EH21 . . . .**124** E6
Albion Bsns Ctr EH7 . . . .**94** A2
Albion Gdns EH7. . . . .**94** A2
Albion Pl EH7 . . . .**94** A2
Albion Rd EH7 . . . .**94** A2
Albion Terr EH7 . . . .**94** A2
Albyn Cotts EH52 . . . .**115** E6
Albyn Dr EH54 . . . .**164** E5
Albyn Ind Est EH52 . . . .**115** F7
Albyn Pl Broxburn EH52 . . . .**115** E6
Edinburgh EH2. . . . .**228** B4
Albyn Terr EH52. . . . .**115** F5
Alcorn Rigg EH14. . . . .**148** E7
Alcorn Sq EH14. . . . .**148** E7
Alderbank
Livingston EH54. . . . .**143** E5
Penicuik EH26 . . . .**191** F4
Alderbank Gdns EH11. . . . . .**120** E4
Alderbank Pl EH11. . . . .**120** E4
Alderbank Terr EH11. . . . . . .**120** E4
Alder Gr Dunfermline KY11. . .**29** D1
Westquarter FK2. . . . .**61** B3
Alder Rd EH22 . . . .**97** D3
Alderston Dr KY12 . . . .**29** D6
Alderstone Bsns Pk
EH54 . . . .**143** C1
Alderstone Rd
Livingston, Adambrae
EH54. . . . .**164** D7
Livingston, Howden EH54 . .**143** D4
Alderston Gdns EH41. . . . . .**100** E1
Alderston Mdws EH41. . . . . .**100** E1
Alderston Pl EH41. . . . .**100** E1
Alderston Rd EH41. . . . .**129** E8
Aldhammer Ho EH32. . . . .**96** F1
Alemoor Cres EH7 . . . .**94** B3
Alemoor Pk EH7 . . . .**94** B3
Alexander Ave Falkirk FK2. . .**60** E5
Grangemouth FK3 . . . .**61** C5
Alexander Ct
Clackmannan FK10 . . . .**11** A5
Stirling FK9. . . . .**2** F6
Alexander Dr
Bridge of A FK9 . . . .**2** A8
Edinburgh EH11. . . . .**120** D5
Livingston EH54 . . . .**164** D8
Prestonpans EH32. . . . .**125** F8
Alexander McLeod Pl FK7. .**8** E3
Alexander Pk EH52. . . . .**115** E4
Alexander Pl KY11. . . . .**46** F3
Alexander Rd ML7 . . . .**179** D5
Alexander St
Cowdenbeath KY4 . . . .**13** D5
Dysart KY1. . . . .**18** A8
Uphall EH52. . . . .**115** A4
Alexander The Third St
KY3. . . . .**34** F1
Alexander Way KY11. . . . .**47** B8
Alexandra Ave EH41. . . . . . .**141** F6
Alexandra Bsns Pk EH28 . .**117** A5
Alexandra Dr Alloa FK10 . . . . .**9** F7
Bathgate EH48. . . . .**141** F6
Alexandra Pl FK8 . . . .**2** C1
Alexandra St
Dunfermline KY12. . . . .**29** A5
Kirkcaldy KY1 . . . .**17** C5

Alford Ave KY2 . . . .**16** E7
Alford Gdns KY2 . . . .**16** E7
Alford Way KY11. . . . .**30** A4
Alfred Pl EH9. . . . .**121** F4
Alice Cox Wlk KY11 . . . .**29** C1
Alice Gr KY4. . . . .**30** E6
Aline Ct KY11. . . . .**48** A2
Alison Gr KY12 . . . .**28** B2
Alison St KY1. . . . .**17** B2
Allan's Prim Sch FK8 . . . .**7** A7
Allanbank Rd FK5. . . . .**38** C2
Allan Barr Ct FK1. . . . .**60** B1
Allan Cres Denny FK6. . . . .**36** D3
Dunfermline KY11 . . . .**29** B4
Allan Ct Burntisland KY3. . . . .**50** E8
Grangemouth FK3 . . . .**40** E1
Allandale Cotts FK4. . . . .**57** C2
Allanfield EH7 . . . .**93** F2
Allanfield Pl EH7 . . . .**93** F2
Allanlea Terr KY12 . . . .**28** E5
Allan Park Cres EH14 . . . . . .**120** C2
Allan Park Dr EH14 . . . .**120** C2
Allan Park Gdns EH14 . . . . .**120** C2
Allan Park Ho **10** FK8 . . . .**7** B7
Allan Park Loan EH14. . . . . .**120** C2
Allan Park Rd EH14 . . . .**120** C2
Allan Pk Cowdenbeath KY4. .**13** A1
Kirkliston EH29 . . . .**89** A2
Stirling FK8. . . . .**7** A7
Allan Rd EH47. . . . .**160** E6
Allan St EH4. . . . .**93** A2
Allan Terr EH22 . . . .**153** B3
Allanton Prim Sch ML7 . . . .**198** B8
Allanton Rd ML7 . . . .**179** D2
Allanvale Rd FK9 . . . .**1** F7
Allanwater Apartments
FK9. . . . .**2** A8
Allanwater Gdns FK9. . . . .**2** A8
Allan Wlk FK9 . . . .**1** F8
Allanwood Ct FK9. . . . .**2** A8
Allardice Cres KY2. . . . .**16** D5
Allen Gr KY12 . . . .**26** E7
Allen Rd EH54 . . . .**143** C3
Allermuir Ave EH25 . . . .**171** E5
Allermuir Rd EH13 . . . .**149** A6
Aller Pl EH54 . . . .**143** B4
Allison Pl EH29 . . . .**89** B2
Alloa Acad FK10 . . . .**9** E8
Alloa Bsns Ctr FK10. . . . .**10** C7
Alloa Rd Clackmannan FK10 .**11** B4
Fishcross FK10 . . . .**5** E1
Menstrie FK5 . . . .**3** B3
Stenhousemuir FK5. . . . .**38** F4
Tullibody FK10 . . . .**2** E3
Tullibody FK10. . . . .**4** C3
Alloa Tower FK10 . . . .**10** B5
Alloa Trad Ctr FK10 . . . .**10** C7
Alloway Dr KY12 . . . .**28** B2
Alloway Cres FK4. . . . .**57** F6
Alloway Dr Cowie FK7 . . . .**7** F6
Kirkcaldy KY2. . . . .**16** C7
Alloway Loan **4** EH16. . . . .**122** A1
Alloway Wynd FK5 . . . .**38** C4
Alma La FK2. . . . .**60** B6
Alma St Falkirk FK2. . . . .**60** B6
Inverkeithing KY11 . . . .**47** C3
Alma Terr FK2 . . . .**60** B6
Almond Ave EH52 . . . .**139** F4
Almond Bank Cotts EH4. . . .**91** B5
Almondbank Terr EH11. . . . .**120** E4
Almond Ct Burntisland KY3. . .**50** E8
Almond Court E EH4. . . . .**91** A3
Almond Court W EH4 . . . .**91** A3
Almond Cres EH49 . . . .**173** B6
Almond Ct
East Whitburn EH47. . . . . . .**161** E7
Edinburgh EH16. . . . .**122** E3
Falkirk FK2. . . . .**60** E7
Livingston EH54. . . . .**144** C4
Stirling FK7 . . . .**7** C5
Almond E EH54 . . . .**144** B4
Almondell & Calder Wood
Ctry Pk EH53. . . . .**144** E5
Almondell Ct EH52. . . . .**115** E5
Almondell Rd EH52 . . . .**115** E5
Almondell Terr EH53 . . . . . .**144** E5
Almond E Rd EH54. . . . .**144** B5
Almond Gn EH12. . . . .**119** A8
Almond Gr
East Calder EH53. . . . .**144** F5
Queensferry EH30 . . . .**89** B2
Almondhill Cotts EH29 . . . . .**89** C2
Almondhill Rd EH29. . . . .**89** B2
Almondhill Steading
EH29 . . . .**89** B2
Almond Intc EH54. . . . .**144** A4
Almond Pk EH54 . . . .**144** A4
Almond Pl KY11 . . . .**47** C7
Almond Rd
Blackburn EH47 . . . .**141** C1
Dunfermline KY11 . . . .**29** E2
Falkirk FK2 . . . .**60** E7
Livingston EH54 . . . .**144** B4
Ratho Station EH12,EH28 . .**117** F7
Whitecross EH49 . . . .**83** F5
Almond Side EH53 . . . .**144** D4
Almond Sq
East Whitburn EH47. . . . . . .**161** E7
Edinburgh EH12. . . . .**119** A8
Almond S Rd EH53. . . . .**144** C4
Almond St EH7 . . . .**94** A3
Almond Terr Harthill ML7 . .**159** C5
Whitecross EH49 . . . .**83** F6
Almondvale Ave EH54. . . . . .**143** E2
Almondvale Bsns Pk
EH54 . . . .**143** D1

Almondvale Bvd EH54. . . . .**143** E2
Almondvale Cres EH54. . . . .**143** D2
Almondvale Cres EH54 . . . .**143** C2
Almondvale Ctr EH54 . . . . . .**143** E2
Almondvale Dr EH54 . . . . . .**143** E2
Almondvale East Rd
EH54 . . . .**143** F2
Almondvale Gdns EH47 . . . .**162** D7
Almondvale N
Livingston EH54. . . . .**143** D2
Livingston EH54. . . . .**143** E2
Almondvale Parkway
EH54 . . . .**143** E2
Almondvale Pl EH54 . . . .**143** D1
Almondvale Rd EH54. . . . . . .**143** E1
Almondvale Rdbt EH54 . . . .**143** C1
Almondvale S
Livingston EH54. . . . .**143** D1
Livingston EH54. . . . .**143** D1
Almondvale South Ret Pk
EH54 . . . .**143** D1
Almondvale Stadium
(Livingston FC) EH54. . . .**143** D2
Almondvale Stadium Rd
EH54 . . . .**143** D2
Almondvale W EH54 . . . .**143** D1
Almondvale Way EH54 . . . . .**143** D1
Almond Valley Heritage Ctr
EH54 . . . .**143** A2
Almondview EH54 . . . .**143** F2
Almond View EH47 . . . .**142** B1
Almondview Bsns Pk **1**
EH54 . . . .**143** F2
Almond W Rd EH54 . . . .**144** A4
Alness St EH2 . . . .**28** F2
Alnwickhill Cres EH16. . . . . .**150** E4
Alnwickhill Ct EH16. . . . .**150** E4
Alnwickhill Dr EH16. . . . .**150** E4
Alnwickhill Gdns EH16. . . . .**150** E4
Alnwickhill Loan EH16. . . . .**150** E4
Alnwickhill Loan EH16. . . . .**150** E4
Alnwickhill Pk EH16. . . . .**151** A6
Alnwickhill Rd EH16 . . . .**151** A7
Alnwickhill Terr EH16 . . . . . .**150** F4
Alnwickhill View EH16. . . . . .**150** F6
Alpha St EH15 . . . .**62** E5
Alva Acad FK12. . . . .**5** C3
Alva Glen Nature Trail
FK12 . . . .**5** A8
Alva Ind Est FK12 . . . .**5** C6
Alvanley Terr EH9 . . . .**121** B5
Alva Pl EH7. . . . .**94** A2
Alva Prim Sch FK12. . . . .**5** A6
Alva St EH2. . . . .**228** A3
Alyth Dr FK2. . . . .**22** A1
Ambassador Ct EH21 . . . . . .**124** D6
Amberley Path **61** F6
Ambrose Rise EH54 . . . .**144** A1
Amisfield Pk EH41 . . . .**130** C8
Amisfield Pl
Haddington EH41. . . . .**130** D7
Longniddry EH32 . . . .**98** E5
Amos Path EH20 . . . .**171** F7
Amulree Pl EH51. . . . .**63** F7
Anchorfield EH6 . . . .**93** D6
Ancroft EH42 . . . .**107** A7
Ancrum Bank EH22 . . . .**152** F1
Ancrum Rd EH22 . . . .**152** F1
Anderson Ave
Armadale EH48. . . . .**139** F4
Denny FK6. . . . .**36** E1
Falkirk FK2. . . . .**39** B2
Anderson Gdns FK2. . . . .**82** E6
Anderson Gn EH54. . . . .**143** C7
Anderson La
Kincardine FK10. . . . .**23** E4
Rosyth KY11 . . . .**46** E3
Anderson Park Rd FK6. . . . . .**36** F2
Anderson Pl Edinburgh EH6 .**93** E5
Stirling FK7 . . . .**7** A4
Anderson St
Bonnybridge FK4. . . . .**58** B5
Dysart KY1. . . . .**18** A7
Kirkcaldy KY1. . . . .**17** E6
Anderson Terr FK4. . . . .**57** B3
Andrew Ave EH48 . . . .**141** F6
Andrew Carnegie Birthplace
Mus KY12 . . . .**29** A3
Andrew Cres FK5. . . . .**38** D4
Andrew Ct EH26. . . . .**191** E7
Andrew Dodd's Ave
EH22. . . . .**174** E7
Andrew Hardie Dr FK10. . . . .**10** A8
Andrew St KY5 . . . .**14** A6
Andrew Stewart Hall FK9 . .**2** D6
Andrew Wood Ct FK6. . . . .**93** C6
Angle Park Terr EH11 . . . . . .**120** F5
Angres Ct EH22. . . . .**152** C7
Angus Rd Bo'ness EH51. . . . . .**63** D6
Carluke ML8 . . . .**215** B1
Annabel Ct KY11 . . . .**47** C6
Annan Ct FK1. . . . .**60** C1
Annandale St EH7 . . . .**93** E2
Annandale Street La EH7. . .**93** E2
Anne Dr Bridge of A FK9. . . . . .**2** A8
Stenhousemuir FK5. . . . .**38** E4
Anne St Alloa FK10 . . . .**9** F8
Bathgate EH48. . . . .**141** E6
Penicuik EH26 . . . .**191** E7
Annet Rd FK6 . . . .**57** D6
Annfield Edinburgh EH6. . . . . .**93** D6
Tranent EH33. . . . .**126** C5
Annfield Ct EH33 . . . .**127** C5

Annfield Farm Rd KY11 . . . . .**47** B7
Annfield Gdns FK8 . . . .**7** B6
Annfield Pl FK3. . . . .**61** D8
Annfield St EH6. . . . .**93** D6
Ann St EH4. . . . .**228** A4
Anson Ave FK1. . . . .**59** E4
Antigua St **2** EH1 . . . .**93** E2
Antonine Cl EH54 . . . .**163** D5
Antonine Gate FK4. . . . .**57** B3
Antonine Gdns FK4. . . . .**59** C5
Antonine Pr FK4. . . . .**57** F3
Antonine Prim Sch FK4 . . . . .**58** A4
Antonine St FK1. . . . .**59** C5
Antonine Wall FK4. . . . .**58** D4
Antonshill Rdbt FK5 . . . .**38** F5
Appin Cres
Dunfermline KY12. . . . .**29** B4
Kirkcaldy KY2. . . . .**16** E7
Appin Dr EH32. . . . .**97** A2
Appin Gr FK2 . . . .**61** F3
Appin St EH14 . . . .**120** D4
Appin Terr
Edinburgh EH14. . . . .**120** D4
Shotts ML7 . . . .**180** B3
Appleton Parkway FK4.**142** F3
Appleton Parkway Rdbt
EH54 . . . .**142** F5
Appleton Pl FK4 . . . .**142** F3
Arboretum Ave EH3. . . . .**93** A2
Arboretum Pl EH3 . . . .**93** A3
Arboretum Rd EH3. . . . .**93** A4
Arbroath Cres FK9 . . . .**2** B4
Arbuthnot Rd EH20 . . . .**172** C7
Arbuthnot St FK1. . . . .**59** E6
Archers Ave FK7 . . . .**7** C4
Archers Ct EH41 . . . .**52** A2
Archibald Pl EH3 . . . .**228** C2
Archibald Russell Ct FK2. . .**61** E1
Ard Ct FK3. . . . .**61** D5
Ardeer Pl KY11 . . . .**29** C2
Arden St EH9 . . . .**121** C5
Ardgay Cres FK4. . . . .**58** A3
Ardgay Dr FK4. . . . .**58** A3
Ardgay Rd FK4 . . . .**58** A3
Ardgay Terr FK4 . . . .**58** A3
Ardgowan Pl Cowie FK7. . . . .**20** E8
Shotts ML7 . . . .**179** E6
Ardmillan Pl EH11. . . . .**120** F5
Ardmillan Terr EH11. . . . . . .**120** E5
Ardmore Dr FK2. . . . .**62** A1
Ardshiel Ave EH4 . . . .**91** C2
Ardvreck Pl FK2 . . . .**39** A3
Argyle Cres EH15 . . . .**123** C7
Argyle Park Terr EH9 . . . . . .**229** A1
Argyle Pl EH9 . . . .**121** D5
Argyle St EH6 . . . .**93** E6
Argyll Ave Falkirk FK2. . . . . . .**60** C6
Argyll Cres
Stirling FK8 . . . .**2** A1
Argyll Ct ML7. . . . .**159** F5
Argyll Path FK6. . . . .**57** D8
Argyll Pl Alloa FK10. . . . .**10** C7
Bonnyrigg and Lasswade
EH19 . . . .**172** F6
Argyll's Lodging FK8. . . . .**7** A8
Argyll St FK10 . . . .**10** C7
Argyll Terr EH11 . . . .**228** A2
Arkaig Dr KY12 . . . .**28** C1
Arkwright Ct EH39. . . . .**54** A7
Armadale Acad EH48. . . . . . .**139** F5
Armadale Prim Sch
EH48. . . . .**139** F5
Armadale Rd EH47. . . . .**161** B7
Armine Pl EH26. . . . .**192** B7
Armour Ave FK7. . . . .**20** D7
Armour Mews FK5. . . . .**38** B4
Arneil Pl FK2 . . . .**22** A2
Arniston Home Farm Cotts
EH23 . . . .**195** A4
Arniston House EH23 . . . . . .**194** F3
Arniston Pl FK10. . . . .**30** A4
Arnot Gn EH54. . . . .**60** A4
Arnothill Bank FK1. . . . .**60** A4
Arnothill Ct FK1. . . . .**59** F5
Arnothill Gdns FK1 . . . .**60** A4
Arnothill La FK1 . . . .**59** F4
Arnothill Mews FK1. . . . .**60** A4
Arnot St FK1 . . . .**60** C4
Arnott Gdns EH14. . . . .**120** A1
Arnprior Rd EH23 . . . .**195** D8
Arns Gr FK10 . . . .**9** E8
Arnswell FK10 . . . .**5** C2
Arran Cres EH54. . . . .**142** F5
Arran Cres KY2 . . . .**16** F7
Arran Ct Alloa FK10 . . . .**10** B5
Grangemouth FK3 . . . .**61** D6
Arran Pl EH15 . . . .**123** C8
Arran Terr FK1. . . . .**59** C4
Arras Gr EH26 . . . .**192** A8
Arrol Cres FK10 . . . .**10** C7
Arrol Pl EH30 . . . .**89** C8
Arrol Sq EH54 . . . .**142** E5
Arthur's Dr FK5 . . . .**38** E2
Arthur Ct KY4 . . . .**13** D3
Arthur Pl EH30 . . . .**89** C8
Arthur St Cowdenbeath KY4 .**13** D3
Dunfermline KY12 . . . .**29** B5
Edinburgh EH6. . . . .**93** F3
Whitburn EH47 . . . .**161** A6
Arthur View Cres EH22. . . . .**152** B8
Arthur View Terr EH22. . . . .**152** B8
Artillery Pk EH41 . . . .**101** B1
Ashbank Ct EH48 . . . .**140** E6
Ashbank Terr EH53. . . . .**144** E3
Ashbrae Gdns FK7. . . . .**7** B2
Ash Braes FK10 . . . .**23** D4

Ashburnham Gdns EH30. . . .**68** D1
Ashburnham Loan EH30. . . . .**68** D2
Ashburnham Rd EH30. . . . . . .**89** D8
Ashcroft Ho FK5. . . . .**38** B1
Ashfield Ct EH42. . . . .**78** E1
Ashfield Pl EH42. . . . .**78** E1
Ash Gr Alloa FK10 . . . .**10** C6
Bathgate EH48. . . . .**141** E6
Blackburn EH47. . . . .**162** D8
Carnock KY12 . . . .**27** F4
Cowdenbeath KY4. . . . .**13** B4
Dunbar EH42. . . . .**78** D2
Dunfermline KY11 . . . .**46** D8
Livingston EH54. . . . .**144** B6
Stenhousemuir FK5. . . . .**38** F2
Westquarter FK2 . . . .**61** B2
Ashgrove
Mayfield EH22. . . . .**174** E7
Musselburgh EH21 . . . .**124** E6
Ashgrove Pl EH21 . . . .**124** F6
Ashgrove View EH21 . . . . . .**124** F6
Ash La EH20 . . . .**171** F7
Ashley Ct EH49 . . . .**84** E6
Ashley Dr EH12. . . . .**120** E3
Ashley Gdns EH11 . . . .**120** E4
Ashley Gr EH11. . . . .**120** E4
Ashley Grange EH14 . . . . . .**147** C2
Ashley Hall Gdns EH49 . . . . .**84** E6
Ashley Pl EH6 . . . .**93** E5
Ashley Rd FK2. . . . .**61** F3
Ashley St EH4. . . . .**57** F6
Ashley Terr Alloa FK10 . . . .**9** E8
Edinburgh EH11. . . . .**120** E4
Ash Terr Blackburn EH47. . .**162** D8
Stirling FK6 . . . .**6** F5
Ashton Gr EH16. . . . .**122** B1
Ashville Terr EH6 . . . .**94** B3
Asquith St KY1. . . . .**17** B3
Assembly St EH6 . . . .**94** A5
Assynt Bank EH26 . . . .**192** A6
Astley Ainslie Hospl EH9 . .**121** C3
Atheling Gr EH30. . . . .**89** C7
Athelstaneford Prim Sch
EH39 . . . .**101** E7
Athol Cres FK2. . . . .**61** A3
Atholl Cres EH3. . . . .**228** A2
Atholl Crescent La EH3 . . .**228** A2
Atholl Pl Edinburgh EH3 . . .**228** A2
Falkirk FK2. . . . .**60** F2
Stirling FK8 . . . .**1** F2
Atholl Terr
Edinburgh EH11. . . . .**228** A2
Kirkcaldy KY2. . . . .**16** D7
Atholl View EH32. . . . .**97** A2
Atholl Terr EH48. . . . .**141** B7
Dunfermline KY12. . . . .**29** C4
Atholl Terr EH48. . . . .**141** B7
Atlas St FK3 . . . .**140** B4
Atrium Way FK4 . . . .**58** A3
Attlee Cres EH22 . . . .**174** E5
Auchenbowie Cvn Site
FK7. . . . .**19** A4
Auchengray Rd ML11. . . . . .**202** F1
Auchenhard Pl EH47 . . . . . .**162** C2
Auchenhard Terr EH47. . . . .**162** C2
Auchentyre Pl FK2. . . . .**39** C3
Auchinbaird FK10. . . . .**5** C2
Auchincruive EH10. . . . .**149** E5
Auchinleck's Brae EH6. . . . . .**93** C6
Auchinleck Ct EH6. . . . .**93** C6
Auchterderran Rd KY5 . . . . .**14** B8
Auchtertool Prim Sch
KY2. . . . .**15** B2
Auction Mart **4** EH41. . . . .**101** A1
Auld Brig Rd EH10 . . . .**10** B6
Auldcathie Pl EH52 . . . .**87** F3
Auldgate EH30 . . . .**89** B3
Auldhame Cotts EH39 . . . . . .**55** F5
Auldhill Ave EH49 . . . .**86** C4
Auldhill Cotts EH49. . . . .**86** C3
Auldhill Cres EH49 . . . .**86** C3
Auldhill Dr EH49. . . . .**86** C3
Auldhill Entry EH49. . . . .**86** C4
Auldhill Pl EH49. . . . .**86** C4
Auldhill Rd EH49 . . . .**86** C4
Auldhill Terr EH49. . . . .**86** C4
Auldkirk Rd FK10 . . . .**4** C3
Auld School Wynd FK7. . . . .**6** D5
Avalon Gdns EH49. . . . .**84** F6
Ava St KY1 . . . .**17** A2
Aven Dr FK2. . . . .**60** F3
Avens Rd FK10. . . . .**23** D4
Avenue Ind Est KY5. . . . .**14** C7
Avenue Park W EH53. . . . . .**144** C4
Avenue Pk Bridge of A FK9 . . . .**2** A7
Mid Calder EH53. . . . .**144** C4
Avenue Rd Aberlady EH32. . .**72** A5
Cockenzie & Port Seton
EH32. . . . .**97** C3
Dalkeith EH22 . . . .**152** E2
Avenue The Bridge of A FK9. .**2** A7
Falkirk FK2. . . . .**39** D2
Gifford EH41. . . . .**220** F6
Gorebridge EH23. . . . .**174** B1
Inverkeithing KY11. . . . .**47** E3
Lochgelly KY5 . . . .**14** C7
Philpstoun EH49. . . . .**86** D7
Riccarton EH14. . . . .**147** F4
Whitburn EH47 . . . .**161** A6
Avenue Villas EH4. . . . .**92** F2
Averton ML11 . . . .**201** A1
Avenuehead Rd FK4 . . . .**59** C6
Avonbank Gdns FK6. . . . .**36** D4
Avonbridge Prim Sch
FK1. . . . .**110** A5
Avonbridge Rd EH48. . . . . . .**108** B7
Avon Ct FK1 . . . .**60** D3

Avondale Cres EH48 . . . . .139 E5
Avondale Dr EH48 . . . . . .139 E5
Avondale Dr EH3 . . . . .93 B2
Avondale Rd FK2 . . . . .62 B3
Avondhu Gdns FK3 . . . . . .61 F8
Avon Dr EH49 . . . . .84 D7
Avon Gr Edinburgh EH4 . . . .91 A4
  Penicuik EH26 . . . . . . .192 A6
Avonlea Dr FK2 . . . . .61 F3
Avonmill Rd EH49 . . . . . . .84 C8
Avonmill View EH49 . . . . . .84 C7
Avonpark FK1 . . . . .109 F6
Avon Pl Bo'ness EH51 . . . . .63 F8
  Edinburgh EH4 . . . . . . .91 A4
  Linlithgow EH49 . . . . . . .85 A6
Avon Rd Bathgate EH48 . . .141 A7
  Edinburgh EH4 . . . . . . .91 A4
  Grangemouth FK3 . . . . . .62 D7
  Whitecross EH49 . . . . . .83 F6
Avonside Dr FK6 . . . . .36 D5
Avon St Denny FK6 . . . . . .36 C4
Avontoun Pk EH49 . . . . . . .84 D6
Axwell Ho FK2 . . . . .116 B5
Ayres Wynd EH32 . . . . . . .96 F1
Aytoun Grs KY3 . . . . .33 E2
Aytoun Gr KY12 . . . . .28 E5

B

Baads Rd
  Blackridge EH48,ML7 . . . .137 D1
  Harthill ML7 . . . . .158 E8
Baberton Cres EH14 . . . . .148 C6
Baberton Ct EH14 . . . . . . .148 E6
Baberton Loan EH14 . . . . .148 C6
Baberton Mains EH14 . . . .148 C8
Baberton Mains Ave
  EH14 . . . . .148 D7
Baberton Mains Bank
  EH14 . . . . .148 D7
Baberton Mains Brae
  EH14 . . . . .148 C7
Baberton Mains Cres
  EH14 . . . . .148 D7
Baberton Mains Ct EH14 . .148 D7
Baberton Mains Dell
  EH14 . . . . .148 C7
Baberton Mains Dr
  EH14 . . . . .148 D7
Baberton Mains Gdns
  EH14 . . . . .148 D7
Baberton Mains Gn
  EH14 . . . . .148 D7
Baberton Mains Gr EH14 . .148 D7
Baberton Mains Hill
  EH14 . . . . .148 C7
Baberton Mains Lea
  EH14 . . . . .148 C7
Baberton Mains Loan
  EH14 . . . . .148 D7
Baberton Mains Pk
  EH14 . . . . .148 D7
Baberton Mains Rise
  EH14 . . . . .148 C7
Baberton Mains Row
  EH14 . . . . .148 D7
Baberton Mains Terr
  EH14 . . . . .148 D7
Baberton Mains View
  EH14 . . . . .148 D7
Baberton Mains Way
  EH14 . . . . .148 D7
Baberton Mains Wood
  EH14 . . . . .148 D7
Baberton Mains Wynd
  EH14 . . . . .148 D7
Baberton Pk EH14 . . . . . .148 D6
Baberton Sq EH14 . . . . . .148 D6
Bablins Wynd EH41 . . . . .220 F6
Babylon Ct EH33 . . . . . . .126 C7
Back Cswy KY12 . . . . .42 D8
Back Dean EH4 . . . . .120 F8
Backdean Rd EH22 . . . . . .152 A8
Back La EH32 . . . . .71 D4
Backlee EH16 . . . . .151 A6
Backmarch Cres KY11 . . . . .46 E4
Back O' Hill Ind Est FK8 . . . .2 A2
Back O' Hill Rd FK8 . . . . . . .1 F1
Back O' Yds KY11 . . . . . . .47 B2
Back St KY12 . . . . .42 D8
Back Station Rd
  Edinburgh EH16 . . . . . .122 D4
  Linlithgow EH49 . . . . . . .85 B7
Backwell Ct KY12 . . . . . . .28 D5
Back Wlk **2** FK8 . . . . .7 B7
Backwood Ct FK10 . . . . . . .10 F5
Badallan Pl EH47 . . . . . . .181 E6
Badger Brook EH52 . . . . .115 D4
Badger Ct EH52 . . . . . . .115 C4
Badger Gr EH52 . . . . . . .115 D4
Badger La EH52 . . . . . . .115 C4
Badger Mdws EH52 . . . . .115 C4
Badger Pk EH52 . . . . . . .115 C4
Badger Pl EH52 . . . . . . .115 C4
Badger Wlk EH52 . . . . . .115 D4
Badger Wood EH52 . . . . .114 C2
Baileyfield Cres EH15 . . . .123 A8
Baileyfield Rd EH15 . . . . .123 A8
Baileyfield Rd
  Edinburgh,Northfield EH15 . .94 F1

Baileyfield Rd continued
  Edinburgh,Portobello
  EH15 . . . . .123 A8
Bailie Fyfe's Cl EH1 . . . . .229 B3
Bailie Gr EH15 . . . . .123 B6
Bailielands EH49 . . . . .85 D7
Bailie Path EH15 . . . . . . .123 A6
Bailie Pl EH15 . . . . .123 B6
Bailie Terr EH15 . . . . . . .123 B6
Baillie Ave ML7 . . . . . . .159 F5
Baillie St EH47 . . . . .161 A4
Baillie Waugh Rd KY7 . . . . .7 C3
Baingle Brae FK10 . . . . . . .4 B3
Baingle Cres FK10 . . . . . . .4 B3
Bainsford Phen Sch FK2 . . .60 B8
Bain Sq EH54 . . . . .143 C1
Bain St KY5 . . . . .14 B7
Baird Ave EH12 . . . . . . .120 C6
Baird Ct KY5 . . . . .14 A7
Baird Dr Armadaie EH48 . .139 F7
  Edinburgh EH12 . . . . . .120 C6
Baird Gdns EH12 . . . . . .120 C6
Baird Gr EH12 . . . . .120 C6
Baird Rd Armadale EH48 . .139 F7
  Livingston EH54 . . . . . .143 A1
  Ratho EH28 . . . . .117 D3
Baird St FK1 . . . . .59 D5
Baird's Way EH19 . . . . . .173 D7
Baird Terr
  Edinburgh EH12 . . . . . .120 C6
  Haddington EH41 . . . . .100 F1
  Harthill ML7 . . . . .159 C5
Bairns Ford Ave FK2 . . . . .60 A7
Bairns Ford Ct FK2 . . . . . .60 A7
Bairns Ford Dr FK2 . . . . . .60 A7
Bakehouse Cl EH8 . . . . . .229 B3
Baker's Pl **8** EH3 . . . . . . .93 B2
Baker St Bo'ness EH51 . . . .63 F6
  Stirling FK8 . . . . .7 A8
Balbakie Rd ML7 . . . . . . .159 E5
Balbardie Ave EH48 . . . . .141 A7
Balbardie Cres EH48 . . . .141 A7
Balbardie Prim Sch
  EH48 . . . . .141 B8
Balbardie Rd EH48 . . . . .141 B6
Balbirnie Pl EH12 . . . . . .120 E7
Balcarres Ct EH10 . . . . . .121 A2
Balcarres Pl EH21 . . . . . .124 D7
Balcarres Rd EH21 . . . . . .124 D7
Balcarres St EH10 . . . . . .121 A2
Balcastle Rd FK1 . . . . . . .108 A6
Balderstone's Wynd EH39 . .54 C7
Balderston Gdns EH16 . . . .122 B1
Balderston Gdns N EH16 . .122 B1
Baldridgeburn KY12 . . . . . .28 E5
Baldwin Cres KY12 . . . . . .17 A5
Baldwin Ct EH26 . . . . . . .191 E4
Balerno Com High Sch
  EH14 . . . . .147 C2
Balfour Cres Plean FK7 . . . .20 D3
  Stenhousemuir FK5 . . . . .38 C2
Balfour Ct
  Dunfermline KY12 . . . . . .29 D5
  Edinburgh EH12 . . . . . .91 B1
  Plean FK7 . . . . .20 D3
Balfour Dr EH6 . . . . .93 F4
Balfour St Alloa FK10 . . . . .10 C7
  Bannockburn FK7 . . . . . . .7 C1
  Bonnybridge FK4 . . . . . .57 F6
  Edinburgh EH6 . . . . . . .93 F3
  Kirkcaldy KY2 . . . . .17 B5
  North Berwick EH39 . . . . .54 D7
Balfour Terr EH26 . . . . . .171 B1
Balfron Loan EH4 . . . . . . .91 C1
Balgone Barns Cotts
  EH39 . . . . .54 D2
Balgownie W KY12 . . . . . .42 C8
Balgreen Ave EH12 . . . . .120 A6
Balgreen Gdns EH12 . . . .120 A6
Balgreen Pk EH12 . . . . . .120 B6
Balgreen Prim Sch EH11 . .120 C5
Balgreen Rd EH11 . . . . . .120 B5
Balgrochan Terr **3**
  EH48 . . . . .141 B6
Baliol St KY3 . . . . .34 F2
Ballantyne La EH6 . . . . . . .93 F5
Ballantyne Pl EH54 . . . . .143 B4
Ballantyne Rd EH6 . . . . . .93 F5
Ballast Bank KY11 . . . . . . .47 C2
Ballater Dr FK9 . . . . .2 C4
Ballencrieff Cotts EH32 . . . .72 A1
Ballencrieff Mains Farm
  Cotts EH32 . . . . .71 F1
Ballencrieff Mill EH48 . . . .140 E8
Ballencrieff Toll EH48 . . . .112 B1
Ballengeich Pass FK8 . . . . .2 A1
Ballengeich Rd FK8 . . . . . . .1 F1
Ballingry La KY5 . . . . .14 A7
Ballingry St KY5 . . . . .14 A7
Balloch Rd KY2 . . . . .179 E6
Balmoral Dr Falkirk FK1 . . . .59 E3
  Kirkcaldy KY2 . . . . .16 D5
Balmoral Gdns
  Grangemouth FK2 . . . . . .82 D7
  Livingston EH54 . . . . . .164 D6
Balmoral Pl Edinburgh EH3 . .93 B2
  Stenhousemuir FK5 . . . . .38 E4
  Stirling FK8 . . . . .2 B3
Balmoral Rd EH51 . . . . . . .62 E6
Balmoral St FK1 . . . . .59 E3
Balmuir Ave EH48 . . . . . .140 F8
Balmuir Rd EH48 . . . . . . .140 F7
Balmulzier Rd FK1 . . . . . .108 B8
Balmwell Ave EH16 . . . . .151 B5
Balmwell Gr EH16 . . . . . .151 B5
Balmwell Pk EH16 . . . . . .151 B5

Balmwell Terr EH16 . . . . .151 A5
Balnacraig KY12 . . . . .28 B1
Balquharn Cotts FK12 . . . . .4 D7
Balquhatstone Cres FK1 . .108 A6
Balquhidderock FK7 . . . . . .7 C4
Balsasney Rd KY2 . . . . . . .17 B5
Baltic Ave KY2 . . . . .17 B5
Baltic Quay FK3 . . . . .40 D1
Baltic St EH6 . . . . .94 A5
Balure Cres FK7 . . . . .8 D4
Balvaird Pl KY12 . . . . .29 C6
Balwearie Cres KY2 . . . . . .17 A2
Balwearie Gdns KY2 . . . . . .16 F1
Balwearie High Sch KY2 . . .17 A1
Balwearie Rd KY2 . . . . . . .17 A2
Banchory Cotts KY2 . . . . . .34 E5
Banchory Pl KY10 . . . . .4 C3
Banchory Prim Sch FK10 . . .4 C3
Bancroft Ave EH54 . . . . . .143 E4
Bandeath Ind Est FK7 . . . . .9 A5
Bandeath Rd FK7 . . . . .8 D4
Bandon Ave KY1 . . . . .17 F8
Bangholm Ave EH5 . . . . . .93 B5
Bangholm Bower Ave
  EH5 . . . . .93 B5
Bangholm Gr EH5 . . . . . . .93 C5
Bangholm Loan EH5 . . . . .93 C5
Bangholm Pk EH5 . . . . . . .93 B5
Bangholm Pl EH5 . . . . . . .93 B5
Bangholm Rd EH5 . . . . . . .93 B5
Bangholm Terr EH3 . . . . . .93 B4
Bangholm View EH5 . . . . . .93 C5
Bangholm Villas EH5 . . . . .93 C5
Bangly Brae FK12 . . . . . . .100 A4
Bangor Rd EH6 . . . . .93 F5
Bangour Village Hospl
  EH52 . . . . .114 A2
Bankfoot EH32 . . . . .96 D1
Bankhead Ave EH11 . . . . .119 C3
Bankhead Broadway
  EH11 . . . . .119 B3
Bankhead Cotts EH40 . . . . .75 C6
Bankhead Cres FK4 . . . . . .57 D6
Bankhead Crossway N
  EH11 . . . . .119 B3
Bankhead Crossway S
  EH11 . . . . .119 C2
Bankhead Dr EH11 . . . . . .119 B3
Bankhead Gr EH30 . . . . . . .68 D1
Bankhead Ind Est EH11 . . .119 C3
Bankhead Medway EH11 . .119 C3
Bankhead Pl EH11 . . . . . .119 C2
Bankhead Rd
  Fischcross FK10 . . . . . . .5 D3
  Queensferry EH30 . . . . . .89 E8
Bankhead St EH11 . . . . . .119 C2
Bankhead Terr EH11 . . . . .119 C2
Bankhead Way EH11 . . . . .119 B2
Bankhill Crt FK4 . . . . .61 A8
Bankmill View EH26 . . . . .191 F4
Bankpark Brae EH33 . . . . .126 B7
Bankpark Cres EH33 . . . . .126 B7
Bankpark Gr EH33 . . . . . .126 C7
Bank Pl ML7 . . . . .179 F4
Bank Rd East Linton EH40 . .103 E7
  Harthill ML7 . . . . .159 E5
Bankside EH52 . . . . .60 C7
Bankside Ct FK6 . . . . .36 E2
Bankside Ind Est FK2 . . . . .60 D8
Bank St Alloa FK10 . . . . . .10 B6
  Edinburgh EH1 . . . . . . .229 A3
  Falkirk FK1 . . . . .60 B5
  Grangemouth FK3 . . . . . .40 A1
  Inverkeithing KY11 . . . . . .47 C2
  Kincardine FK10 . . . . . . .23 D3
  Kirkcaldy KY1 . . . . .17 E7
  Lochgelly KY5 . . . . .14 B8
  Mid Calder EH53 . . . . . .144 D7
  North Berwick EH39 . . . . .54 B7
  Penicuik EH26 . . . . . . .191 E4
  Slamannan FK1 . . . . . . .108 A4
  7 Stirling FK8 . . . . .7 A7
  Whitburn EH47 . . . . . . .161 A7
Banks View EH47 . . . . . . .22 E4
Bank Terr ML11 . . . . .217 F8
Bankton Ave EH54 . . . . . .164 E7
Bankton Ct
  Livingston EH54 . . . . . .165 B8
  Tranent EH33 . . . . .126 C6
Bankton Dr EH54 . . . . . . .164 F8
Bankton Gdns EH54 . . . . .165 A8
Bankton Glade EH54 . . . . .165 A8
Bankton Gn EH54 . . . . . .165 A8
Bankton Gr EH54 . . . . . . .165 A8
Bankton Junc EH54 . . . . .165 A8
Bankton La EH54 . . . . . . .165 A8
Bankton Pk E EH54 . . . . . .144 B1
Bankton Pk W EH54 . . . . .144 B1
Bankton Prim Sch EH54 . .143 F1
Bankton Rd EH54 . . . . . . .164 D8
Bankton Terr
  Livingston EH54 . . . . . .164 F7
  Prestonpans EH32 . . . . . .97 B1
  Tranent EH32 . . . . .126 B8
Bankton Wlk EH54 . . . . . .164 F7
Bankton Wood EH54 . . . . .144 B1
Bankview Terr EH14 . . . . . .57 E6
Bannerman Ave KY11 . . . . .47 C3
Bannerman St KY12 . . . . . .29 A5
Bannoch Brae KY12 . . . . . .29 C3
Bannockburn Heritage Ctr
  FK7 . . . . .7 E1
Bannockburn High Sch
  FK7 . . . . .7 D2
Bannockburn Hospl FK7 . . .19 F7

Bannockburn Prim Sch
  FK7 . . . . .7 E1
Bannockburn Rd
  Cowie FK7 . . . . .20 C8
  Stirling FK7 . . . . .7 C3
Bannockburn Station Rd
  FK7 . . . . .8 A4
Bannock Rd EH7 . . . . .8 C4
Bantaskine Dr FK1 . . . . . .59 E4
Bantaskine Gdns FK1 . . . . .59 E3
Bantaskine Prim Sch FK1 . .59 E4
Bantaskine St FK1 . . . . . . .59 E3
Banton Pl EH4 . . . . .58 A3
Baptie Pl EH51 . . . . .63 E5
Barassie Dr KY12 . . . . . . .17 A8
Barbara Stocks La KY12 . . .42 D8
Barbauchlaw Ave EH48 . . .139 F6
Barbour Ave FK7 . . . . .7 D4
Barbour Gr KY12 . . . . .28 E5
Barclay Pl EH10 . . . . .228 B1
Barclay Rd KY3 . . . . .34 F3
Barclay St KY4 . . . . .13 B3
Barclay Terr EH10 . . . . . . .228 B1
Barclay Way EH54 . . . . . . .143 E7
Barham Rd KY11 . . . . .46 D1
Barkhill Rd EH49 . . . . .84 F6
Barkin Ct FK1 . . . . .60 B2
Barlaw Gdns EH48 . . . . . .140 A6
Barleyhill FK4 . . . . .58 B5
Barleyknowe Cres EH23 . . .174 C1
Barleyknowe Gdns EH23 . .174 C1
Barleyknowe La EH23 . . . .174 C1
Barleyknowe Pl EH23 . . . .174 C1
Barleyknowe Rd EH23 . . . .174 C1
Barleyknowe St EH23 . . . .174 C1
Barleyknowe Terr EH23 . . .174 C1
Barnbougle Ride EH30 . . . . .90 C2
Barnego Rd FK6 . . . . .36 D3
Barnes Gn EH54 . . . . . . .143 C7
Barnet Cres KY11 . . . . . . .17 B1
Barnhill Dr FK10 . . . . .4 C2
Barnhill Pl KY11 . . . . .48 D4
Barnhill Rd KY11 . . . . .48 D4
Barn Park EH14 . . . . .148 E6
Barn Park Cres EH14 . . . . .148 E7
Barn Pl EH54 . . . . .143 B3
Barn Rd FK8 . . . . .7 A6
Barns Ct EH4 . . . . .161 E7
Barnsdale Rd FK7 . . . . .7 A3
Barnshot Rd EH13 . . . . . .149 B6
Barns Ness Camping Site
  EH42 . . . . .107 F2
Barns Ness Terr EH42 . . . .218 A6
Barns Pk KY11 . . . . .48 A2
Barns The KY3 . . . . .50 E8
Barnton Ave EH4 . . . . .91 B4
Barnton Ave W EH4 . . . . . .91 A4
Barnton Brae EH4 . . . . . . .91 A4
Barnton Ct EH4 . . . . .91 B4
Barnton Gdns EH4 . . . . . . .91 A4
Barnton Gr EH4 . . . . .91 A4
Barntongate Ave EH4 . . . . .91 A4
Barntongate Dr EH4 . . . . . .91 A4
Barntongate Terr EH4 . . . . .91 A4
Barnton Gdns EH4 . . . . . . .91 A4
Barnton Gr EH4 . . . . .91 A3
Barnton Junc EH4 . . . . . . .91 B4
Barnton Loan EH4 . . . . . . .91 E4
Barnton Park Ave EH4 . . . . .91 D3
Barnton Park Cres EH4 . . . .91 D3
Barnton Park Dell EH4 . . . . .91 D3
Barnton Park Dr EH4 . . . . . .91 C3
Barnton Park Gdns EH4 . . . .91 C3
Barnton Park Gr EH4 . . . . . .91 D3
Barnton Park View EH4 . . . .91 D3
Barnton Park Wood EH4 . . . .91 C2
Barnton Pk EH4 . . . . .91 E4
Barnton Rd FK8 . . . . .7 B8
Barnwell Rd FK9 . . . . .2 C4
Baronscourt Terr EH8 . . . .122 D8
Barons Hill Ave EH49 . . . . .85 B7
Barons Hill Ct EH49 . . . . . .85 B7
Barony Ct Bo'ness EH51 . . . .63 F5
Barony Pl **5** EH3 . . . . .93 D2
Barony St EH3 . . . . .93 D2
Barony Terr EH12 . . . . . . .119 D7
Barracks Rdbt EH54 . . . . .142 E5
Barracks St EH32 . . . . . . .97 D4
Barra Pl FK5 . . . . .39 A4
Barr Cres KY12 . . . . .47 D2
Barrie Ct EH54 . . . . .144 C5
Barrie Ho
  4 Dunfermline KY12 . . . . .28 E5
  Grangemouth FK3 . . . . . .61 D5
Barrie Pl FK5 . . . . .38 F3
Barrie St KY12 . . . . .28 E5
Barr Rd FK7 . . . . .7 A3
Barrie Terr EH48 . . . . . . .141 C5
Barton Bldgs KY3 . . . . . . .35 A2
Barton Ct EH47 . . . . .181 B1
Barton Terr EH47 . . . . . . .181 F6
Bass Rock View EH39 . . . . .55 B7
Bastion Wynd **7** FK8 . . . . . .7 B7
Bathfield EH6 . . . . .93 E6
Bathgate Acad EH48 . . . . .141 E5
Bathgate Bsns Ctr EH48 . .141 C2
Bathgate Rd
  Armadale EH48 . . . . . . .140 B6
  Blackburn EH47 . . . . . . .162 C8
  East Whitburn EH48 . . . .161 E7
Bathgate Sta EH48 . . . . . .141 B4
Bath Pl EH15 . . . . .95 B1
Bath Rd EH6 . . . . .94 B5
Bath St EH15 . . . . .123 B8
Bath Street La EH15 . . . . .123 B8

Bathville Bsns Ctr EH48 . . .140 A5
Baton Rd ML7 . . . . .179 D6
Batterflatts Gdns FK7 . . . . . .6 F6
Batterflatts Ho FK7 . . . . . . .6 F6
Battery Rd
  Grangemouth FK3 . . . . . .62 C8
  North Queensferry KY11 . . .68 C5
Battock Rd FK2 . . . . .82 F7
Bavelaw Cres EH26 . . . . . .191 D6
Bavelaw Gdns EH14 . . . . .147 C1
Bavelaw Gn EH14 . . . . . . .147 C1
Bavelaw Rd EH14 . . . . . . .147 C1
Baxter's Wynd FK1 . . . . . . .60 B4
Baxter Cres FK6 . . . . .36 C1
Baxter's Pl EH1 . . . . .229 B4
Baxter St FK7 . . . . .8 D4
Bayne Gdns EH49 . . . . . . .84 A6
Bayne St FK8 . . . . .2 A1
Bayswell Pk EH42 . . . . . . .78 D3
Bayswell Rd EH42 . . . . . . .78 D3
Bay View EH32 . . . . .97 C4
Beach La Edinburgh EH15 . . .95 B1
  Musselburgh EH21 . . . . .124 B7
Beachmont Ct EH42 . . . . . .78 E1
Beachmont Pl EH42 . . . . . .78 E1
Beach Rd Grangemouth FK3 . 41 B3
  North Berwick EH39 . . . . .54 B7
Beaconcroft FK3 . . . . .2 C7
Beaconhurst Sch FK9 . . . . .2 C6
Beancross Prim Sch FK3 . . .61 C5
Beancross Rd FK3 . . . . . . .61 B6
Bean Row 60 B4
Bearcroft Gdns FK3 . . . . . .61 E7
Bearford Pl EH41 . . . . . . .130 D8
Bearside Rd FK7 . . . . .7 A3
Beath High Sch KY4 . . . . . .13 A2
Beath View Rd KY4 . . . . . .13 A2
Beatlie Rd EH52 . . . . .88 A3
Beatlie Sch EH54 . . . . . . .144 B5
Beaton Ave FK7 . . . . .7 C1
Beatty Ave FK8 . . . . .2 A2
Beatty Cres KY1 . . . . .17 D7
Beatty Ct KY12 . . . . .29 C5
Beauchamp Gr **2** EH16 . . .151 A8
Beauchamp Rd EH16 . . . . .151 A8
Beauclerc St EH7 . . . . .5 A7
Beaufort Cres KY2 . . . . . . .16 F1
Beaufort Dr FK2 . . . . .39 A3
Beaufort Rd EH9 . . . . . . .121 D4
Beauly Cres Falkirk FK1 . . . .60 C1
  Grangemouth FK3 . . . . . .61 F8
Beauly Dr KY2 . . . . .16 F7
Beaumont Dr FK2 . . . . . . .39 B2
Beaverbank Bsns Pk EH7 . .93 C3
Beaverbank Pl EH7 . . . . . .93 D3
Beaverhall Rd EH7 . . . . . . .93 D3
Beck Cres KY12 . . . . .29 C5
Beda Pl FK7 . . . . .8 C5
Bedford Ct Alloa FK10 . . . . .10 A6
  3 Edinburgh EH4 . . . . . .93 A2
Bedford Pl FK10 . . . . .10 A6
Bedford St EH4 . . . . .93 A2
Bedford Terr EH15 . . . . . .123 C8
Bedlam Theatre EH1 . . . . .229 A2
Bedlormie Dr EH48 . . . . . .138 C2
Beech Ave
  Carrington EH23 . . . . . .194 F3
  Dalgety Bay KY3,KY11 . . . .48 F5
  Mid Calder EH53 . . . . . .144 B2
  Plean FK7 . . . . .20 C3
Beechbank Cres EH54 . . . .144 E2
Beech Cres Denny FK6 . . . .36 E2
  Larbert FK5 . . . . .59 C8
  Westquarter FK2 . . . . . . .61 B3
Beech Gdns EH42 . . . . . . .78 B1
Beech Gr Dunfermline KY12 . .28 C3
  Livingston EH54 . . . . . .144 B6
Beech Grove Ave EH22 . . .152 E1
Beech La FK9 . . . . .2 A3
Beech Loan EH19 . . . . . . .173 B6
Beechmount Cres EH12 . . .120 B7
Beechmount Pk ML7 . . . . .180 B2
Beechmount Pk EH42 . . . . .120 B6
Beech Pl Grangemouth FK3 . .13 A4
  Livingston EH54 . . . . . .143 C4
  Penicuik EH26 . . . . . . .191 F4
  Seafield EH47 . . . . .142 B1
Beech Rd EH48 . . . . .141 E6
Beech St EH42 . . . . .78 B1
Beech Way KY11 . . . . .48 A5
Beechwood Alloa FK10 . . . . .5 E1
  Crossford KY12 . . . . . . .22 B2
  Linlithgow EH49 . . . . . . .85 A5
  Sauchie EH50 . . . . .5 D1
Beechwood Gdns
  Blackburn EH47 . . . . . . .141 D1
  Stirling FK8 . . . . .7 A5
Beechwood Gr EH54 . . . . .115 A2
Beechwood Mains EH12 . . .120 B7

Beechwood Pk
Livingston EH54. . . . . .142 F7
Newtongrange EH22 . . . . .174 B6
Uphall Station EH54. . . . . . .115 A1
Beechwood Rd FK7 . . . . .141 D1
Beechwood Rd
Blackburn EH47. . . . . .141 D1
Haddington EH41. . . . . . . .129 F8
Beechwood Terr EH6 . . . . .94 B3
Beecraigs Ctry Pk Visitor Ctr
EH49. . . . . .85 B2
Beeslack Com High Sch
EH26 . . . . .192 A7
Begbie Pl EH54 . . . . .143 B5
Begg Ave FK1 . . . . .59 E4
Beldorney Rd KY12 . . . . . . .29 D6
Belfield Ave EH53. . . . . . . .144 F2
Belford Ave EH4 . . . . .92 E1
Belford Gdns EH4 . . . . .92 E1
Belford Mews 3 EH4. . . . .120 F8
Belford Pk EH4 . . . . .120 F8
Belford Pl EH4 . . . . .120 F8
Belford Rd EH4. . . . . .120 F8
Belford Terr EH4 . . . . .120 F8
Belgrave Cres EH4 . . . . . . .228 A4
Belgrave Crescent La
EH4 . . . . .228 A4
Belgrave Gdns EH12 . . . . . .119 E7
Belgrave Mews 8 EH4. . . . .92 F1
Belgrave Pl EH4 . . . . .92 F1
Belgrave Rd EH12. . . . . .119 E6
Belhaven Bevery EH42. . . . . .78 B1
Belhaven Hill Sch EH42 . . . .78 B2
Belhaven Hospl EH42 . . . . . .78 B1
Belhaven Pl EH10 . . . . .121 A2
Belhaven Rd EH42 . . . . .78 C2
Bell Pl EH3 . . . . .93 D3
Bell's Brae EH4 . . . . .228 A3
Bell's Mills EH4. . . . . .120 F8
Bell's Wynd FK1 . . . . .60 B4
Bellamond Cres EH47 . . . . .161 E7
Bell Ct Falkirk FK2 . . . . .60 C7
Grangemouth FK3 . . . . .40 E1
Belleknowes Ind Est KY11 .47 B4
Bellenden Gdns EH16 . . . . .122 C1
Bellerophon Dr EH26 . . . . .191 F4
Grangemouth FK2 . . . . .40 E1
Bellevue Edinburgh EH3 . . . .93 D2
Grangemouth FK2 . . . . .82 E7
Bellevue Ave EH42 . . . . .78 E1
Bellevue Cres EH3 . . . . .93 D3
Bellevue Gdns EH7 . . . . .93 D3
Bellevue Gr EH7 . . . . .93 D2
Bellevue Pk FK10 . . . . .9 E6
Bellevue Pl EH7. . . . . .93 D2
Bellevue Rd Alloa FK10 . . . . . .9 F6
Edinburgh EH7. . . . . .93 D2
Falkirk FK1. . . . . .60 C4
Bellevue Terr Dunbar EH42 .78 E1
Edinburgh EH7. . . . . .93 D2
Bellfield Ave
Dalkeith EH22 . . . . .152 E2
Musselburgh EH21 . . . . . . .124 B5
Bellfield Cres KY11 . . . . . . .18 A8
Bellfield St EH15. . . . . .123 B8
Bellfield Terr EH15 . . . . . . .123 B8
Bellfield View EH19 . . . . . . .173 D8
Bellhouse Rd KY3. . . . . .49 B7
Bellman's Rd FK26 . . . . . . .191 E6
Bellman Way KY11. . . . . . . .48 B5
Bellona Terr EH47. . . . . . . .181 F6
Bell Pl EH3 . . . . .93 B2
Bell Rd KY11 . . . . .46 B2
Bells Burn Ave EH49 . . . . . . .35 C7
Bellsdyke Hospl FK5 . . . . . . .38 D3
Bellsdyke Rd Falkirk FK2 . . . .37 C6
Stenhousemuir FK5. . . . . . . .38 D4
Bellsdyke Rdbt FK5 . . . . .38 B3
Bellsmains EH23 . . . . .195 D5
Bellsmeadow Rd FK1 . . . . . . .60 C4
Bell's Mill Terr EH52 . . . . . . .87 F2
Bell Sq EH54 . . . . .164 C5
Bellsquarry Prim Sch
EH54 . . . . .164 C7
Bellsquarry South Rd
EH54 . . . . .164 G6
Bell Stane EH30 . . . . .68 B1
Bellyeoman La KY12 . . . . . . .29 C5
Bellyeoman Prim Sch
KY12. . . . . .29 C5
Bellyeoman Rd KY12 . . . . . . .29 C5
Bellyford Rd EH33 . . . . .126 A1
Belmont Ave
Bonnybridge FK4 . . . . .57 D5
Edinburgh EH12. . . . . .120 B7
Shieldhill FK1. . . . . .81 E7
Belmont Cres EH12. . . . . . .120 B7
Belmont Dr
Edinburgh EH12. . . . . .120 B7
Shotts ML7 . . . . .180 B2
Belmont Gdns EH12. . . . . . .120 B7
Belmont Pk EH12 . . . . .120 B7
Belmont Rd EH14 . . . . .148 D6
Belmont St EH11. . . . . .60 C4
Belmont Terr EH12. . . . . . . .120 B7
Belmont View EH12 . . . . . . .120 B7
Belstane Mews ML8. . . . . . .215 A3
Belstane Rd ML8. . . . . .215 A3

Belstane Rd ML8. . . . . .215 A3
Belsyde Ct EH49 . . . . .84 D6
Belvedere La EH48 . . . . .140 F8
Belvedere Pk EH6 . . . . .93 C6
Belvedere Pl EH48 . . . . .140 F8
Belvedere Rd EH48 . . . . .140 F8
Belwood Cres EH26 . . . . . . .171 B1
Belwood Rd EH26. . . . . .170 F1
Ben Alder Pl KY2 . . . . .16 E5
Benarty St KY2 . . . . .16 F5
Bendachin Dr KY12 . . . . .29 E5
Bendameer Rd KY3 . . . . .33 C1
Benhar Rd ML7 . . . . .180 A6
Benjamin Dr EH51 . . . . .63 E5
Ben Ledi Rd KY2 . . . . .16 F5
Ben Lomond Dr FK9 . . . . .2 A4
Ben Lomond View KY12 . . . . .27 A6
Bennachie Way KY11. . . . . . .30 B1
Bennet Wood Terr EH52 . . . .87 F3
Ben Nevis Pl KY2 . . . . .16 F5
Bennie Mus EH48 . . . . .141 A6
Bennie Terr FK1 . . . . .108 B7
Bennochy Ave KY2 . . . . .17 A5
Bennochy Ct KY2 . . . . .17 A5
Bennochy Gdns KY2 . . . . . . .17 A5
Bennochy Gr KY2 . . . . .17 A5
Bennochy Rd Kirkcaldy KY1 .17 B4
Kirkcaldy,Templehall KY2. . . .16 F5
Bennochy View KY2. . . . . . . .17 A5
Bentheads FK7 . . . . .19 E8
Benview FK7 . . . . .7 C2
Benview Terr FK10 . . . . .5 E4
Benview Ave EH5. . . . . .93 C5
Beresford Gdns EH5 . . . . . . .93 C5
Beresford Pl EH5 . . . . .93 B5
Beresford Rise EH54 . . . . . .144 A1
Beresford Terr EH5. . . . . .93 C6
Berkeley St FK7 . . . . .7 A4
Bernard's Smithy KY3 . . . . . .28 D5
Bernard Shaw St KY12 . . . . .28 D5
Bernard St EH6 . . . . .94 A5
Bernard Terr EH8 . . . . .229 B1
Berryhill FK7 . . . . .20 E7
Berryhill Cres EH5 . . . . .61 E6
Berryhill Pl ML7. . . . . .180 B2
Berrylaw Pl KY12 . . . . .28 E4
Berrylaw Rd KY12. . . . . .28 D4
Berry St KY5. . . . . .14 B7
Bertram St Harthill ML7 . . . .179 D5
Shotts ML7 . . . . .179 E5
Bervie Dr EH54. . . . . .164 E5
Berwick Pl Dysart KY1 . . . . . .18 A8
Kirkcaldy KY1. . . . . .17 C5
Beta Ctr FK9 . . . . .2 D5
Bethesda Gr FK2. . . . . .82 E6
Beulah EH12. . . . . .124 E6
Bevan Dr FK12. . . . . .5 C7
Bevan-Lee Ct EH22 . . . . . . .153 B3
Bevan Pl KY11 . . . . .46 E3
Bevan Rd EH22 . . . . .174 D5
Beveridge Ave EH22 . . . . . . .174 E5
Beveridge Cl EH22 . . . . .174 E5
Beveridge Rd KY1 . . . . .17 B3
Beveridge Row EH42 . . . . . . .78 A1
Beveridge Sq EH54 . . . . . . .143 E1
Beveridge St KY11. . . . . .29 C2
Bickerton Crofts EH47 . . . . .161 E5
Bickerton Terr EH47 . . . . . . .161 A5
Bickram Cres KY12 . . . . .26 D7
Bielgrange Cotts EH42 . . . .104 D4
Bielside Gdns EH42 . . . . .77 F1
Big Brigs Way EH22. . . . . . .173 D4
Biggar Rd Edinburgh EH10 .170 A3
Silverburn EH26. . . . . .190 C5
Bigjin Wa's KY1. . . . . .17 F7
Bingham Ave EH15. . . . . . . .123 A5
Bingham Broadway
EH15. . . . . .123 A5
Bingham Cres EH15 . . . . . . .123 A5
Bingham Crossway
EH15. . . . . .123 A5
Bingham Dr EH15. . . . . .123 A5
Bingham Medway EH15 . . . .122 F5
Bingham Pl EH15. . . . . .122 F5
Bingham Way EH15. . . . . . . .122 F5
Binn Ave KY3 . . . . .33 E2
Binney Wells KY1 . . . . .17 E6
Binniehill Rd KY1. . . . . .108 A5
Binnie Pl FK2. . . . . .39 F2
Binning Rd KY11. . . . . .47 B3
Binning Wood Rd EH42 . . . . .75 F7
Binns The EH49 . . . . .65 F5
Binny Pk EH52 . . . . .114 F7
Birch Ave FK8 . . . . .6 F5
Birchbank KY4 . . . . .13 B2
Birch Cres EH20 . . . . .171 F7
Birch Ct Edinburgh EH4. . . . . .91 B2
Livingston EH54. . . . . .143 C2
Birch Gr KY11 . . . . .46 D8
Birchwood FK10 . . . . .5 D7
Birchwood Gdns EH54 . . . . .164 D7
Birkdale Dr EH52 . . . . .114 F4
Birkdale Pk EH48 . . . . .140 B6
Birkenshaw Way EH48 . . . . .139 E4
Birkenside EH23 . . . . .195 C6
Birkfield Loan ML8 . . . . .215 C1
Birkfield Pl ML8 . . . . .215 C1
Birk Hedges EH41 . . . . .128 E6
Birkhill Clay Mine EH49. . . .62 E2
Birkhill Cres EH51. . . . . .63 F6
Birkhill Rd FK7. . . . . .6 B8
Birkhill St EH51. . . . . .63 F6
Birkhill St EH4 . . . . .62 F3
Birnam Gdns KY11. . . . . .30 A4
Birnam Pl KY12 . . . . .29 F6
Birnam Rd KY2 . . . . .16 E8

Birnie Brae KY5. . . . . .14 B7
Birniehall ML11. . . . . .217 F8
Birniehill Ave EH48 . . . . . . .140 F4
Birniehill Cres EH48 . . . . . .140 F4
Birniehill Ind Est EH48 . . . .140 F4
Birniehill Rd EH48 . . . . .140 F4
Birniehill Terr EH48 . . . . . . .140 F4
Birnieknowes Farm Cotts
TD13 . . . . .218 D5
Birnie St KY5. . . . . .14 B7
Birnie Well Rd FK1. . . . . . . .108 A6
Birrel's Wynd KY3 . . . . .35 A3
Birrell's La KY1. . . . . .17 E7
Birrell Cl 6 KY1. . . . . .17 D6
Birrell Dr KY11 . . . . .29 D1
Birrell Street Wynd 5
KY1. . . . . .17 D6
Birsley Rd EH33. . . . . .126 C6
Bishops Gate EH52. . . . . . . .115 C5
Bishops Pk
Livingston EH54. . . . . .144 B1
Mid Calder EH53 . . . . .144 C2
Bittern Ct KY11. . . . . .30 A2
Blackadder Haven KY12 . . . .42 D8
Blackadder Pl EH5. . . . . .92 E6
Blackarony Rd EH16 . . . . . . .122 C8
Blackbraes Rd FK1. . . . . .81 F4
Blackburn Ave KY12 . . . . . . .28 D6
Blackburn Crag EH17 . . . . . .151 D8
Blackburn Dr KY4. . . . . .13 A3
Blackburn Rd EH47 . . . . . . .162 D6
Blackburn Prim Sch
EH47 . . . . .141 C1
Blackburn Rd
Addiewell EH55. . . . . .162 E2
Blackburn EH48 . . . . .141 D3
Blackchapel Cl EH15. . . . . .123 B4
Blackchapel Rd EH15. . . . . .123 B4
Blackcot Ave EH22. . . . . . . .174 D5
Blackcot Dr EH22 . . . . .174 D5
Blackcot Pl EH22 . . . . .174 D5
Blackcot Rd EH22. . . . . .174 D6
Blackdykes Cotts EH39 . . . . .55 C4
Blacket Ave EH9. . . . . .121 F5
Blacket Pl EH9. . . . . .121 F5
Blackfaulds Ct EH47 . . . . . .181 E6
Blackfaulds Dr EH47 . . . . . .181 E6
Blackfaulds Pl EH47 . . . . . . .181 E6
Blackford Ave EH9 . . . . .121 D3
Blackford Bank EH9 . . . . . . .121 E3
Blackford Gate EH9. . . . . . . .121 C3
Blackford Glen Cotts
EH16. . . . . .121 F1
Blackford Glen Rd EH16. . . .121 F1
Blackford Hill Gr EH9 . . . . . .121 D2
Blackford Hill Rise EH9 . . . .121 D2
Blackford Hill View EH9 . . . .121 D2
Blackford Rd EH9 . . . . .121 C4
Blackfriars St EH1 . . . . .229 B3
Blackgrange Rdbt FK9 . . . . . . .3 D3
Blackhall Prim Sch EH4. . . . .92 A1
Blackhall St ML7. . . . . .180 B3
Blackhill Rd EH48 . . . . .138 F3
Blackie Rd EH6 . . . . .94 B4
Blacklaw Rd KY11. . . . . .29 D2
Blackmill Cres FK2 . . . . .39 B3
Blackmount Terr FK2. . . . . . .82 E6
Blackmuir Pl FK10 . . . . .4 D3
Blackness Castle EH49. . . .65 F5
Blackness Prim Sch EH49 .65 C4
Blackness Rd EH49. . . . . .85 B7
Blackraigs KY2 . . . . .16 C7
Blackridge Prim Sch
EH48 . . . . .138 D3
Blackston Rd FK1. . . . . .110 A6
Blackthorn Ct EH4. . . . . .91 B2
Blackwood Cres EH9. . . . . . .121 E5
Blackwood Ct KY11 . . . . .46 F7
Blackwood Gdns KY11 . . . . . .46 F7
Blackwood Gn KY11. . . . . . . .46 F6
Blackwood Way KY11. . . . . . .46 F7
Blaeberry Rd EH4 . . . . .91 B2
Blaeberryhill Rd EH47. . . . .161 C5
Blaefaulds Cres FK6 . . . . . . .57 D8
Blair's Cotts FK2. . . . . .61 C1
Blair Ave EH51. . . . . .63 E5
Blairdenon Cres FK6. . . . . . .59 F3
Blairdenon Dr FK10. . . . . .5 B2
Blairdenon Rd FK12. . . . . .4 E6
Blair Dr Dunfermline KY12 . . .29 B6
Kelty KY4 . . . . .12 D8
Blair Terr KY5. . . . . .39 A4
Blairwood Terr KY12 . . . . . . .28 E3
Blairwood WIk KY12. . . . . . . .28 E3
Blake St KY1. . . . . .29 C1
Blamey Cres KY4 . . . . .13 B2
Blandfield EH7 . . . . .93 D3
Blantyre Terr EH10 . . . . .121 A4
Blawearie Rd EH33 . . . . . . .126 D5
Bleachfield Edinburgh EH6. .93 D4
Falkirk FK2. . . . . .60 A5
Bleachfield Ct FK1 . . . . .60 A5
Blenheim Ct Carluke ML8 .215 B1

Blenheim Ct continued
Penicuik EH26 . . . . .192 A8
Stirling FK9 . . . . .2 C3
Blenheim Pl FK5. . . . . .38 E5
Blindwells FK12 . . . . .4 F8
Blindwell Brae EH41 . . . . . .131 F1
Blinkbonny Ave EH4 . . . . .92 D1
Blinkbonny Cres EH4 . . . . . . .92 C1
Blinkbonny Gdns EH4 . . . . . . .92 D1
Blinkbonny Gr EH4 . . . . .92 D1
Blinkbonny Gr W EH4 . . . . . . .92 D1
Blinkbonny Rd
Currie EH14. . . . . .148 B4
Edinburgh EH4 . . . . .120 D8
Falkirk FK1. . . . . .59 E4
Blinkbonny Terr EH4 . . . . . . .92 C1
Blinny Ct ML7 . . . . .180 A3
Bloom Ct EH54 . . . . .143 B3
Bloomfield Pl 1 EH48 . . . . .141 B6
Bloom Pl EH54 . . . . .143 B2
Bloom Rdbt EH54 . . . . .143 C3
Bluebell Cl 15 KY11 . . . . . . .60 B4
Bluebell Glade EH54 . . . . . .164 C8
Blyth Rd EH52 . . . . .115 D4
Blyth St KY1. . . . . .17 E8
Bo'mains Rd EH51 . . . . .63 E6
Bo'ness Acad EH51 . . . . .64 A6
Bo'ness Hospl EH51. . . . . . . .63 E7
Bo'ness & Kinneil Rly
EH51 . . . . .63 C7
Bo'ness Public Sch (Prim)
EH51 . . . . .63 F7
Bo'ness Rd
Grangemouth FK3 . . . . .62 B6
Polmont FK2 . . . . .61 F3
Queensferry EH30. . . . . .67 F1
Boat Gn EH3. . . . . .93 C3
Bobbin Wynd FK7. . . . . .6 D6
Bogend Rd
Bannockburn FK7 . . . . .19 E8
Larbert FK2 . . . . .38 B8
Torwood FK5. . . . . .37 F8
Boggs Holdings EH34 . . . . .128 A1
Boghall Dr EH48 . . . . .141 E5
Boghall Farm Cotts
EH10 . . . . .171 B6
Boghall Farm Steadings
EH48 . . . . .141 F5
Boghall Prim Sch EH48 .141 F6
Boghall Rdbt EH48 . . . . .141 F5
Boghead Cres EH48. . . . . . . .140 E5
Bogies Wynd 10 KY1 . . . . . . .17 D6
Boglily Cotts KY2 . . . . .16 D3
Boglily Rd KY2. . . . . .16 D3
Bogpark Rd EH21. . . . . .124 A6
Bog Rd Laurieston FK2 . . . . . .60 F4
Penicuik EH26 . . . . .191 E5
Whitburn EH47 . . . . .161 A7
Bog Rdbt FK2. . . . . .60 F4
Bog Road Ind Est FK2. . . . . . .60 F4
Bogsmill Rd EH14. . . . . .120 B1
Bog The EH51 . . . . .64 A8
Bogwood Ct EH22. . . . . .174 D7
Bogwood Dr KY12 . . . . .28 A2
Bogwood Rd EH22 . . . . .174 D7
Bog Wynd FK7 . . . . .7 D4
Bolam Dr KY3. . . . . .33 F2
Bolton Council Hos
EH41 . . . . .220 C8
Bomar Ave EH51. . . . . .64 A8
Bon Accord Cres ML7 . . . . . .179 E5
Bonaly Ave EH13. . . . . .149 B5
Bonaly Brae EH13. . . . . .149 B5
Bonaly Cres EH13. . . . . .149 B5
Bonaly Ctry Pk EH13. . . . .148 F2
Bonaly Dr EH13 . . . . .149 A5
Bonaly Gdns EH13 . . . . .149 A5
Bonaly Prim Sch EH13 .149 A5
Bonaly Prim Sch (Annexe)
EH13. . . . . .149 B6
Bonaly Rd EH13 . . . . .149 A4
Bonaly Rise EH13 . . . . .149 B5
Bonaly Steading EH13. . . . .149 A5
Bonaly Terr EH13 . . . . .149 A5
Bonaly Wester EH13 . . . . . . .149 A5
Bonar Pl EH6 . . . . .93 D5
Bond St FK10 . . . . .4 A3
Bo'ness Sta EH51 . . . . . . .64 A8
Bonhard Ct EH51 . . . . .64 A8
Bonhard Rd KY12 . . . . .22 B7
Bonnar St EH6 . . . . .64 B5
Bonnar St KY12. . . . . .29 A4
Bonnington EH27 . . . . .146 A7
Bonnington Ave EH6 . . . . . . .93 D5
Bonnington Bsns Ctr EH6 .93 E4
Bonnington Gait EH6. . . . . . .93 D5
Bonnington Gr EH6 . . . . .93 D5
Bonnington Ind Est EH6 . . . .93 E4
Bonnington Mill Bsns Ctr
EH6 . . . . .93 E5
Bonnington Prim Sch
EH6 . . . . .93 D4
Bonnington Rd
Edinburgh EH6 . . . . .93 D5
Wilkieston EH27 . . . . .146 A6
Bonnington Rd La EH6 . . . . . .93 E4
Bonnington Terr EH6 . . . . . . .93 D5
Bonnybank Ct EH23 . . . . . . .195 D8
Bonnybank Rd EH23. . . . . . .195 D8
Bonnybridge Hospl FK4 . . . . .58 C6
Bonnybridge Ind Est FK4 . . .58 A4
Bonnybridge Prim Sch
FK4. . . . . .58 B6
Bonnybridge Rd FK4 . . . . .57 E5
Bonnyfield Rd FK4 . . . . .57 F5
Bonnyhaugh EH6 . . . . .93 D4

Bonnyhaugh La EH6 . . . . . . .93 D4
Bonnyhill Rd
Bonnybridge FK4 . . . . .58 D3
Falkirk FK1. . . . . .59 A4
Bonnymuir Cres FK4 . . . . . . .57 F5
Bonnyrigg Prim Sch
EH19 . . . . .173 C6
Bonnyrigg Rd EH22 . . . . . . .152 E1
Bonnyside Rd FK4 . . . . .58 B5
Bonnyton Pl KY11. . . . . .29 D3
Bonnytoun Ave EH49. . . . . . .85 C8
Bonnytoun Terr EH49. . . . . . .85 C8
Bonnyvale Pl FK4 . . . . .57 F5
Bonnyview Gdns FK4. . . . . . . .58 B6
Bonnywood Ave FK4 . . . . .58 B7
Boothacre La EH6 . . . . .94 C4
Booth Ave KY11. . . . . .46 D5
Booth Pl FK1. . . . . .60 B4
Boreland Pk KY11. . . . . .47 C3
Boreland Rd Dysart KY1 . . . .18 A8
Inverkeithing KY11 . . . . .47 C3
Borestone Cres FK7. . . . . .7 A4
Borestone Ct FK7 . . . . .7 A2
Borestone Pl FK7 . . . . .7 A2
Borestone Prim Sch FK7 . . . .7 A2
Boroughdales EH42 . . . . .78 C2
Boroughloch EH8. . . . . .229 B1
Boroughloch Sq EH8. . . . . . .229 B1
Boroughmuir High Sch
EH10 . . . . .121 A5
Boroughmuir High Sch
Annexe EH10. . . . . .121 A5
Borrowlea Rd FK7 . . . . .7 C7
Borrowmeadow Rd FK7 . . . . . .7 E7
Borrowstoun Cres EH51. . . . .63 F5
Borrowstoun Pl EH51 . . . . . .63 F5
Borrowstoun Rd EH51. . . . . . .64 A5
Borthwick's Cl EH1 . . . . .229 A3
Borthwick Castle Pl
EH23 . . . . .195 F3
Borthwick Castle Rd
EH23 . . . . .195 F2
Borthwick Castle Terr
EH23 . . . . .195 F3
Borthwick Pl EH12. . . . . . . .120 E7
Borthwick Prim Sch
EH23 . . . . .196 A4
Borthwick View EH20 . . . . . .172 A7
Boswall Ave EH5. . . . . .92 F5
Boswall Cres EH5. . . . . .92 F5
Boswall Dr EH5 . . . . .93 A5
Boswall Gdns EH5. . . . . .92 F5
Boswall Gn EH5 . . . . .93 A5
Boswall Gr EH5 . . . . .93 A5
Boswall Loan EH5 . . . . .92 F5
Boswall Parkway EH5 . . . . . .92 F5
Boswall Quadrant EH5 . . . . .92 F5
Boswall Rd EH5 . . . . .93 A6
Boswall Sq EH5 . . . . .92 F5
Boswall Terr EH5 . . . . .92 F5
Boswell Dr Kinghorn KY3 . . . .35 A3
Oakley KY12. . . . . .26 F6
Boswell Rd KY5. . . . . .14 B8
Bothkennar Prim Sch FK2 .39 F3
Bothkennar Rd FK2 . . . . .39 E3
Bothwell Ct KY11 . . . . .29 A2
Bothwell Gdns
Dunbar EH41. . . . . .78 D1
Dunfermline KY11,KY12 . . . .29 A2
Bothwell Ho FK7. . . . . .94 A2
Bothwell St
Dunfermline KY11. . . . . .29 B2
Edinburgh EH7. . . . . .94 A2
Boundary Rd E EH14 . . . . . .147 E8
Boundary Rd N EH14. . . . . . .147 E7
Boundary St EH51 . . . . .64 A8
Bouprie Rise KY11. . . . . .48 B4
Bourtree Gr KY12 . . . . .26 D7
Bow Butts KY12 . . . . .29 A2
Bowhill Ct EH31. . . . . .52 B2
Bowhill Terr EH5. . . . . .93 B5
Bowhousebog or Liquo
ML7 . . . . .179 A2
Bowhousebog Rd ML7 . . . . . .179 A2
Bowhouse Dr KY11. . . . . .35 B8
Bowhouse Gdns
Alloa FK10 . . . . .10 B5
Kirkcaldy KY1. . . . . .35 B7
Bowhouse Prim Sch FK1 . . .61 C5
Bowhouse Rd Alloa FK10. . . .10 B5
Grangemouth FK3 . . . . .61 D5
Bowhouse Sq FK3 . . . . .61 D5
Bowling Green Pl
Kirkliston EH29 . . . . .89 B1
Whitburn EH47 . . . . .161 A4
Bowling Green Rd KY4 . . . . .13 C4
Bowling Green The EH6 . . . . .93 F5
Bowling La EH6. . . . . .93 F5
Bowmans Ind Est EH6. . . . . .63 F5
Bowmont Pl EH8 . . . . .229 B1
Bowmont Terr EH42. . . . . . . .78 E2
Bow St ML7 . . . . .180 A3
Bow St EH6 . . . . .7 A8
Bowyett EH41. . . . . .111 F6
Boxton Rd California FK1. . . . .81 D1
Standburn FK1. . . . . .82 C3
Boyd's Entry EH1 . . . . .229 B3
Boyd La FK2 . . . . .61 C2
Boyd-Orr Dr EH26 . . . . .191 F8
Boyd Pl KY5 . . . . .14 A8
Boyd St Falkirk FK2 . . . . .60 A5
Laurieston FK2 . . . . .61 A3
Bracken La FK9. . . . . .7 F7
Brackenlees Rd FK2 . . . . .40 B5
Brackensbrae EH52 . . . . . . .115 B5
Bracklinn Brae KY12 . . . . . . .28 E5

Bradbury St FK2 . . . . .39 B2
Braeburn Dr FK14 . . . . .148 B4
Braefoot Tyninghame EH42 . .76 C3
Whitburn EH47 . . . . .161 B7
Braefoot Gr KY11 . . . . .48 B2
Braefoot Rd EH51 . . . . .64 A5
Braefoot Terr EH16 . . . . . .122 A1
Braehead Alloa FK10 . . . . . . .4 D1
Alva FK10 . . . . .5 A7
Bo'ness EH51 . . . . .63 F7
Braehead Ave
Edinburgh EH4 . . . . .91 A3
Linlithgow EH49 . . . . .84 E5
Tullibody FK10 . . . . .4 C2
Braehead Bank EH4 . . . . . .91 A3
Braehead Bsns Units
EH49 . . . . .84 E6
Braehead Cres EH4 . . . . . .91 A3
Braehead Dr
Edinburgh EH4 . . . . .91 A3
Linlithgow EH49 . . . . .84 E5
Braehead Ho KY1 . . . . .17 D5
Braehead Loan EH4 . . . . . .91 A3
Brae Head Lodge KY1 . . . .17 D5
Braehead Pk
Edinburgh EH4 . . . . .91 A3
Linlithgow EH49 . . . . .84 E6
Braehead Pl EH49 . . . . .84 E5
Braehead Prim Sch FK7 . . . .7 C4
Braehead Rd
Edinburgh EH4 . . . . .91 A3
Linlithgow EH49 . . . . .84 E6
Stirling FK7 . . . . .7 C4
Braehead Rdbt EH54 . . . . .143 D3
Braehead Row EH4 . . . . . . .91 A3
Brae Heads Loan HE41 . .103 D5
Braehead Terr EH49 . . . . . .84 E5
Braehead View EH4 . . . . . .91 A3
Braekirk Ave EH27 . . . . . .145 D3
Braekirk Gdns EH27 . . . . .145 D3
Braemar Cres
Carluke ML8 . . . . .215 A3
Falkirk FK2 . . . . .60 C6
Braemar Dr Falkirk FK2 . . .60 C6
Halbeath KY11 . . . . .30 A4
Braemar Gdns Denny FK6 . .36 C2
Grangemouth FK2 . . . . . .82 D8
Braemar Pl FK5 . . . . .39 A4
Braehead View EH4 . . . . . .91 A3
Braemount KY4 . . . . .13 A2
Braepark Rd EH4 . . . . .91 A4
Brae Pk EH4 . . . . .91 A4
Brae Rd FK3,EH51 . . . . . . .62 D6
Braes High Sch FK2 . . . . . .82 B8
Braeside Alloa FK10 . . . . . . .5 C1
Shieldhill FK1 . . . . .81 D6
Braeside Cres EH47 . . . . .161 D5
Braeside Gdns EH53 . . . . .144 B2
Braeside Pk EH53 . . . . . . .144 B3
Braeside Pl
Grangemouth FK2 . . . . . .82 B8
Laurieston FK2 . . . . .61 B4
Westquarter FK2 . . . . .61 B2
Braeside Rd
Gorebridge EH23 . . . . . .195 D4
Loanhead EH20 . . . . .172 D8
Braeside Rd N EH23 . . . . .195 D8
Braeside Rd S EH23 . . . . .195 D7
Braes The Lochgelly KY5 . .14 A8
Tullibody FK10 . . . . .4 B2
Braes View Denny FK6 . . . .57 D8
Shieldhill FK1 . . . . .81 E7
Brae The Bannockburn FK7 . .7 D1
Cambusbarron FK7 . . . . . .6 D6
Penicuik EH26 . . . . .171 C4
Braeview
East Linton EH40 . . . . . . .103 D8
Laurieston FK2 . . . . .60 F3
Stenhousemuir FK5 . . . . . .38 D2
Braewell Gdns EH49 . . . . . .84 C7
Braid Ave EH10 . . . . .121 A5
Braidburn Cres EH10 . . . .121 A1
Braidburn Sch EH14 . . . . .149 D8
Braid Cres EH10 . . . . .121 A1
Braidburn Terr EH10 . . . . .121 A1
Braid Farm Rd EH10 . . . . .121 B1
Braid Gn EH54 . . . . .143 C7
Braid Hills App EH10 . . . . .150 B8
Braid Hills Cres EH10 . . . .150 A6
Braid Hills Dr EH10 . . . . . .150 C6
Braid Hills Dr EH10 . . . . . .150 D8
Braid Hills Rd EH10 . . . . . .150 B8
Braidlaw Pk EH26 . . . . . . .191 C5
Braid Mount EH10 . . . . . . .150 B8
Braid Mount Cres EH10 . .150 B8
Braid Mount Rise EH10 . . .150 B8
Braid Mount View EH10 . . .150 B8
Braid Rd EH10 . . . . .150 B8
Braigh Gdns KY12 . . . . . . .28 D6
Bramble Dr EH4 . . . . .91 B2
Bramble Glade EH54 . . . . .164 C8
Brambles The EH22 . . . . . .153 F1
Brambling Rd KY11 . . . . . .30 A2
Bramdean Gr EH10 . . . . . .150 B8
Bramdean Pl EH10 . . . . . . .150 B8
Bramdean Rise EH10 . . . . .150 B8
Bramdean View EH10 . . . .150 B8
Brand Dr EH15 . . . . .123 B7
Brandfield St EH3 . . . . . . .228 A1
Brand Gdns EH15 . . . . . . .123 C7
Brandon St EH3 . . . . .93 C2
Brandon Terr EH3 . . . . .93 C3
Brand Pl 🄳 EH7 . . . . .94 A1
Brands Row KY4 . . . . .30 F7
Brandyhill EH10 . . . . .5 E3
Brandy Riggs KY12 . . . . . . .27 D1

Brandy Wells KY12 . . . . . . .27 D1
Brankholm Brae KY11 . . . .46 C4
Brankholm Cres KY11 . . . .46 D5
Brankholm La KY11 . . . . . .46 D2
Branning Ct 🄹 KY1 . . . . . .17 D6
Bransfield Pk Alloa FK10 . .10 B8
Sauchie FK10 . . . . .5 B1
Branshill Rd FK10 . . . . . . .10 B8
Branxton Wynd KY1 . . . . . .35 B8
Bravo St EH51 . . . . .62 E5
Breadalbane Pl FK2 . . . . . .62 A2
Breadalbane St EH6 . . . . . .93 E4
Breadalbane Terr EH1 . . . .228 A2
Bread St EH3 . . . . .228 B2
Bread Street La EH3 . . . . .228 B2
Breakers Way KY11 . . . . . .47 F2
Brechin Dr FK2 . . . . .62 A1
Breck Terr EH26 . . . . .192 A8
Breich Sta EH55 . . . . .182 D6
Breich Terr EH55 . . . . . . .182 E6
Brentham Ave FK8 . . . . .7 B5
Brentham Cres FK8 . . . . . . .7 B5
Breslin Terr ML7 . . . . .159 C5
Breton Ct FK1 . . . . .60 C3
Brewery Cl EH30 . . . . .68 B1
Brewery Ct 🄳 EH41 . . . . . .130 B8
Brewery La EH42 . . . . .78 B2
Brewery Pk EH41 . . . . . . .130 A8
Brewhouse Ct 🄳 FK10 . . .10 B6
Brewlands Ave EH14 . . . . .63 D5
Brewster Pl FK6 . . . . .36 C2
Brewster Sq EH54 . . . . . .146 C6
Briarbank EH54 . . . . .143 D4
Briarbank Terr EH11 . . . . .120 E4
Briar Brae FK2 . . . . .82 D8
Briarcliff St KY1 . . . . .17 F6
Briar Cotts EH47 . . . . .162 C2
Briardene FK2 . . . . .61 A3
Briarhill Ave KY11 . . . . . . .48 A3
Briar Pl KY11 . . . . .29 C3
Briar Rd FK10 . . . . .4 C1
Brickfield EH15 . . . . .95 A1
Brickworks Rd EH33 . . . . .126 B7
Bridgecastle Gdns EH48 . .111 A2
Bridgecastle Rd EH48 . . . .111 A2
Bridgecastle Rd EH48 . . . .139 F8
Bridge Cres FK6 . . . . .36 D2
Bridge End
East Whitburn EH47 . . . . .161 D7
Edinburgh EH16 . . . . .122 B3
Shotts ML7 . . . . .179 C6
Bridge End Cotts EH47 . . .146 D6
Bridgehaugh Rd FK9 . . . . . .2 B2
Bridgehill FK1 . . . . .110 A6
Bridgend Ct
Bathgate EH48 . . . . .140 F6
🄳 Dalkeith EH22 . . . . . . .153 A3
Bridgend Gdns EH48 . . . .140 F6
Bridgend Pk EH48 . . . . . .140 F5
Bridgend Pl
Bathgate EH48 . . . . .140 F6
Whitburn EH47 . . . . .161 C7
Bridgend Prim Sch EH48 . .86 C3
Bridge Pl Broxburn EH52 . .115 E5
Denny FK6 . . . . .36 C2
🄳 Edinburgh EH3 . . . . . . .93 A2
Shotts ML7 . . . . .180 A3
Bridge Rd Balerno EH14 . . .147 C2
Edinburgh EH13 . . . . . . .149 A6
Bridgeside Ave EH47 . . . . .161 B5
Bridge St Bonnybridge FK4 .58 A5
Cowdenbeath KY4 . . . . . .13 D3
Dunfermline KY12 . . . . . . .28 F3
East Linton EH40 . . . . . . .103 E7
Edinburgh EH15 . . . . .95 A1
Fauldhouse EH47 . . . . . . .181 E6
Haddington EH41 . . . . . . .130 B8
Kincardine FK10 . . . . .23 D4
Kirkcaldy KY1 . . . . .17 B1
Musselburgh EH21 . . . . . .124 C6
Newbridge EH28 . . . . .117 A6
Penicuik EH26 . . . . .191 F4
Tranent EH33 . . . . .126 C6
Bridges The KY11 . . . . .48 A2
Bridge Street La EH15 . . . . .95 A1
Bridges View KY12 . . . . . . .29 F6
Bridge Terr 🄳 FK10 . . . . . .10 B6
Bridgeton Cotts EH48 . . . .110 F2
Bridge View KY11 . . . . .68 C6
Brierbush Cres EH33 . . . . .127 D5
Brierbush Rd EH33 . . . . . .127 D5
Briery Bank EH41 . . . . . . .130 C7
Briery Bauks EH8 . . . . . . .229 B2
Brighouse Park Ct EH4 . . . .91 C6
Brighouse Park Gait EH4 . . .91 C6
Brighouse Park Rd EH4 . . . .91 C6
Bright's Cres EH9 . . . . . . .121 F4
Brighton Pl EH15 . . . . . . .123 A8
Brighton St EH1 . . . . .229 A2
Bright Terr EH11 . . . . .228 A2
Brig-O-Doon Gr FK7 . . . . .20 E7
Brisbane St EH54 . . . . . . .144 A5
Bristo Pl EH1 . . . . .229 A2
Bristo Port EH1 . . . . .229 A2
Bristo Sq EH8 . . . . .229 A2
Britwell Cres EH7 . . . . .94 D2
Brixwood Bank EH19 . . . . .173 D6
Brixwood Dr EH19 . . . . . . .173 D6
Brixwood Neuk EH19 . . . . .173 D6
Brixwood Pk EH19 . . . . . . .173 D6
Brixwood Rise EH19 . . . . .173 D6

Brixwood View EH19 . . . . .173 D6
Broadfaulds Cres EH47 . . .161 A5
Broadgait EH31 . . . . .52 B3
Broadgait Ct EH31 . . . . . . .52 A3
Broadgait Gn EH31 . . . . . . .52 B3
Broadhaven EH47 . . . . . . .174 C2
Broadhurst Rd EH22 . . . . .174 C7
Broadleys Ind Pk FK7 . . . . .7 D5
Broadleys Rd FK7 . . . . .7 D7
Broadleys Rdbt FK7 . . . . . . .7 D6
Broadside Pl FK6 . . . . .36 D1
Broad St Alloa FK10 . . . . . .10 B5
Cowdenbeath KY4 . . . . . .13 C2
Denny FK6 . . . . .36 F2
Stirling FK8 . . . . .7 C4
Broad Wynd Edinburgh EH6 .94 A5
🄳 Kirkcaldy KY1 . . . . .17 D6
Brock Pl FK7 . . . . .7 B2
Brock St KY11 . . . . .68 B6
Brocks Way EH52 . . . . . . .116 A7
Brockwood Ave EH26 . . . .191 D6
Brodick Gdns KY11 . . . . . .30 A4
Brodick Pl FK1 . . . . .59 C4
Brodick Rd KY2 . . . . .16 E7
Brodie Ave EH39 . . . . .54 D6
Brodie Ct EH39 . . . . .54 D7
Brodie Rd EH42 . . . . .106 D8
Brodie St FK2 . . . . .60 B8
Brodie Wlk KY11 . . . . .30 A4
Broich The FK12 . . . . .4 E7
Bronte Pl FK5 . . . . .38 C3
Brookbank Terr ML8 . . . . .215 A1
Brooke La FK3 . . . . .61 C5
Brooke St FK3 . . . . .61 C5
Brookfield Pl FK2 . . . . .5 A6
Brookfield Terr EH25 . . . . .171 E6
Brookside EH11 . . . . .61 E1
Brook St Alva FK12 . . . . .5 A6
Alva FK12 . . . . .5 A7
Menstrie FK11 . . . . .3 F6
Broomage Ave FK5 . . . . . . .38 B3
Broomage Bank FK5 . . . . .38 C2
Broomage Cres FK5 . . . . . .38 B3
Broomage Dr FK5 . . . . .38 B3
Broomage Pk FK5 . . . . . . .38 B3
Broomage Rd FK5 . . . . . . .38 C1
Broombank Terr EH12 . . . .119 D5
Broomburn Gr EH12 . . . . .119 E4
Broom Ct FK7 . . . . .7 C3
Broomfield Cres EH11 . . . .119 E3
Broomfield Dr KY12 . . . . . .29 A5
Broomfield Rd KY4 . . . . . . .13 C5
Broom Gr KY11 . . . . .46 F8
Broomhall Ave EH12 . . . . .119 D5
Broomhall Bank EH12 . . . .119 D5
Broomhall Cres EH12 . . . .119 D5
Broomhall Dr EH12 . . . . . .119 C5
Broomhall Gdns EH12 . . . .119 D5
Broomhall Loan EH12 . . . .119 D5
Broomhall Pk EH12 . . . . . .119 D5
Broomhall Pl EH12 . . . . . .119 D5
Broomhall Rd EH12 . . . . . .119 D5
Broomhall Terr EH12 . . . . .119 D5
Broomhead Dr EH12 . . . . . .28 F5
Broomhead Ho KY12 . . . . .29 A5
Broomhead Pk KY12 . . . . .29 A5
Broomhill Ave
Burntisland KY3 . . . . .33 E1
Larbert FK5 . . . . .59 C8
Penicuik EH26 . . . . .191 E4
Broomhill Ct FK6 . . . . .2 B3
Broomhill Dr EH22 . . . . . .152 E1
Broomhill Pk 🄳 EH22 . . . .152 E1
Broomhill Pl Denny FK6 . . . .36 D4
Stirling FK7 . . . . .6 E6
Broomhill Rd
Bonnybridge FK4 . . . . . . .58 B4
Penicuik EH26 . . . . .191 E4
Broomhills Rd EH17 . . . . . .150 F6
Broomhill St ML7 . . . . .159 C5
Broomhouse Ave EH11 . . .119 D3
Broomhouse Bank EH11 . .119 E3
Broomhouse Cotts EH11 . .119 E3
Broomhouse Ct EH11 . . . .119 E3
Broomhouse Dr EH11 . . . .119 D3
Broomhouse Gdns E
EH11 . . . . .119 E4
Broomhouse Gdns W
EH11 . . . . .119 D4
Broomhouse Gr EH11 . . . .119 E3
Broomhouse Loan EH11 . .119 E3
Broomhouse Medway
EH11 . . . . .119 E4
Broomhouse Mkt EH11 . . .119 E3
Broomhouse Path EH11 . .119 D3
Broomhouse Pl N EH11 . . .119 D3
Broomhouse Pl S EH11 . . .119 D3
Broomhouse Rd EH12 . . . .119 D3
Broomhouse Row EH11 . . .119 E3
Broomhouse Sq EH11 . . . .119 E3
Broomhouse St N EH11 . . .119 E3
Broomhouse St S EH11 . . .119 E3
Broomhouse Terr EH11 . . .119 E4
Broomhouse Way EH11 . . .119 E3
Broomhouse Wlk EH11 . . .119 E3
Broomhouse Wynd EH11 . .119 E3
Broomieknowe
Bonnyrigg and Lasswade
EH18 . . . . .173 A8
Dunfermline KY11 . . . . . . .29 C3
Tullibody KY9 . . . . .4 D3
Broomieknowe Gdns
EH19 . . . . .173 B8
Broomieknowe Pk EH19 . .173 B8
Broomknow Dr FK10 . . . . .23 D6
Broomlea Cres EH12 . . . . .119 D5

Broompark E FK11 . . . . . . .4 A6
Broompark Gdns
Denny FK6 . . . . .36 E2
East Calder EH53 . . . . . . .144 E3
Broompark Rd
East Calder EH53 . . . . . . .144 E3
Edinburgh EH12 . . . . .119 E5
Broompark View EH53 . . . .144 E3
Broompark W FK11 . . . . . . .4 A6
Broom Pl KY2 . . . . .16 C8
Broom Rd Kirkcaldy KY2 . . .16 C7
Stirling FK7 . . . . .7 C4
Broomridge Pl FK4 . . . . . . .57 D4
Broomridge Rd FK7 . . . . . . .7 B3
Broomside Gr EH12 . . . . . .16 C8
Broomside Pl FK5 . . . . .38 C1
Broomside Rd FK4 . . . . . . .58 B3
Broomside Terr EH12 . . . . .119 E3
Broomview Ho EH11 . . . . .119 D2
Broom Wlk EH54 . . . . .144 A4
Broom Wynd ML7 . . . . . . .179 E6
Broomyhill Pl EH49 . . . . . .84 D7
Broomyknowe EH54 . . . . .149 B8
Broomyknowe Dr EH54 . . .142 E6
Brora P
Brosdale Ct FK2 . . . . .60 B2
Brougham Pl EH3 . . . . . . .228 C1
Brougham St EH3 . . . . . . .228 B1
Broughton High Sch EH4 . .92 F2
Broughton Market EH3 . . . .93 D3
Broughton Pl EH1 . . . . .93 D2
Broughton Place La EH1 . . .93 D2
Broughton Prim Sch EH7 . .93 D3
Broughton Rd EH7 . . . . . . .93 D3
Broughton St EH1 . . . . .93 D2
Brown's Cl EH8 . . . . .229 C3
Brown's Ct EH1 . . . . .229 C3
Brown's Pl EH1 . . . . .228 C2
Brown Ave Alloa FK10 . . . . .4 F1
Stirling FK9 . . . . .2 B2
Brown Ct FK2 . . . . .61 D8
Brown St EH8 . . . . .229 C3
Brownrigg Farm Cotts
EH39 . . . . .74 C6
Brown's Rd KY12 . . . . .59 F8
Brown St Armadale EH48 . .139 F4
Edinburgh EH8 . . . . .229 B2
Falkirk FK1 . . . . .59 D5
🄳 Haddington EH41 . . . . .130 B8
Shotts ML7 . . . . .180 B3
Whitburn EH47 . . . . .161 A6
Broxburn Acad EH52 . . . . .115 E5
Broxburn Cotts EH42 . . . . .107 A7
Broxburn Prim Sch EH52 . .115 E5
Bruart Ave FK5 . . . . .38 F3
Bruce Cres Falkirk FK2 . . . .39 B3
Plean FK7 . . . . .20 D3
Bruce Dr Fallin FK7 . . . . . . .8 C5
Stenhousemuir FK5 . . . . . .38 F3
Brucefield Ave KY11 . . . . . .29 E2
Brucefield Cres FK10 . . . . .11 A8
Brucefield Dr EH47 . . . . . .161 B6
Brucefield Feus KY11 . . . . .29 C2
Brucefield Ind Pk EH54 . . .164 C6
Brucefield Pk E EH54 . . . .164 C6
Brucefield Pk N EH54 . . . .164 C6
Brucefield Pk W EH54 . . . .164 C6
Brucefield Terr KY4 . . . . . . .13 F6
Bruce Gate FK2 . . . . .82 D8
Bruce Haven Cres EH54 . . .156 C5
Bruce Rd Bathgate EH48 . .141 C6
Grangemouth FK3 . . . . . . .61 E8
Bruce St Alloa FK10 . . . . . .10 C7
Bannockburn FK7 . . . . .7 E1
Bathgate EH48 . . . . .141 C4
Clackmannan FK10 . . . . . .11 A4
Dunfermline KY12 . . . . . . .28 E4
Edinburgh EH12 . . . . .121 A2
Falkirk FK2 . . . . .60 C6
Kinghorn KY3 . . . . .35 A3
Plean FK7 . . . . .20 D3
Stirling FK8 . . . . .2 B1
Bruce Terr
Cambusbarron FK7 . . . . . .6 D5
Kinghorn KY3 . . . . .35 A3
Stirling FK7 . . . . .7 B1
Bruculay Bank EH15 . . . . .123 C6
Brunstane Cres EH15 . . . .123 C6
Brunstane Dr EH15 . . . . . .123 C6
Brunstane Gdns
Edinburgh EH15 . . . . .123 C7
Penicuik EH26 . . . . .191 D6
Brunstane Gdns Mews
EH15 . . . . .123 C7
Brunstane Mill Rd EH15 . .123 F7
Brunstane Prim Sch
EH15 . . . . .123 C6
Brunstane Rd EH15 . . . . . .123 C7
Brunstane Rd N EH15 . . . .123 C6
Brunstane Rd S EH15 . . . .123 C6
Brunstane Sta EH15 . . . . .123 C6
Brunswick Pl 🄳 EH7 . . . . . .93 E2
Brunswick Rd EH7 . . . . . . .93 F2
Brunswick St EH7 . . . . .93 E2
Brunswick Street La EH7 . .93 E2
Brunswick Terr EH7 . . . . . .93 E2
Brunt Ct EH42 . . . . .106 E8
Brunt Gr EH42 . . . . .106 D8
Brunt La EH42 . . . . .78 D1
Brunton's Cl EH22 . . . . . . .153 A3
Brunton Pl 🄳 EH7 . . . . .93 E2

Brunton Terr EH7 . . . . .93 F2
Brunt Pl EH42 . . . . .106 E8
Bruntsfield Ave EH10 . . . .121 B5
Bruntsfield Cres
Dunbar EH42 . . . . .78 D1
Edinburgh EH10 . . . . .121 B5
Bruntsfield Gdns EH10 . . .121 B5
Bruntsfield Pl EH10 . . . . . .121 B5
Bruntsfield Prim Sch
EH10 . . . . .121 A5
Bruntsfield Terr EH10 . . . .121 B5
Bryans Ave EH22 . . . . .174 B6
Bryans Prim Sch EH22 . . .174 B7
Bryans Rd EH22 . . . . .174 A6
Bryce Ave Edinburgh EH7 . .94 F2
Falkirk FK2 . . . . .39 B2
Bryce Cres EH14 . . . . .148 A5
Bryce Gdns EH14 . . . . . . .148 A5
Bryce Gr EH7 . . . . .94 F2
Bryce Pl EH14 . . . . .148 A5
Bryce Rd EH14 . . . . .148 A5
Bryden Ct FK3 . . . . .61 E8
Bryony The FK10 . . . . .4 E8
Bryson St Bathgate EH48 . .141 B6
Stenhousemuir FK5 . . . . . .38 C5
Bryson Rd EH11 . . . . .120 F5
Bryson St FK2 . . . . .60 B6
Bryson Street Ind Est FK2 .60 B6
Bubbles Rdbt 143 E2
Buccleuch Ct EH22 . . . . . .152 F4
Buccleuch Pl EH8 . . . . . . .229 A1
Buccleuch St
Dalkeith EH22 . . . . .153 A3
Edinburgh EH8 . . . . .229 B1
Buccleuch Terr EH8 . . . . . .229 B1
Buchanan Cres EH54 . . . . .143 A5
Buchanan Ct Bo'ness EH51 .63 E5
Edinburgh EH1 . . . . .229 C3
Falkirk FK2 . . . . .60 A8
Kirkcaldy KY1 . . . . .17 B2
Buchanan Dr FK9 . . . . .2 B3
Buchanan Gdns
Cairneyhill KY12 . . . . .27 D1
Polmont FK2 . . . . .61 D2
Buchanan St
Dunfermline KY12 . . . . . . .29 A3
Edinburgh EH6 . . . . .93 B1
Buchan Ave FK2 . . . . .39 B1
Buchan Ct FK12 . . . . .115 D5
Buchan La EH52 . . . . .115 E5
Buchan Pl FK3 . . . . .61 D1
Buchan Rd Bathgate EH48 .140 F7
Broxburn FK52 . . . . .115 C5
Grangemouth FK3,EH51 . .62 D8
Buckie Rd EH22 . . . . .174 E6
Buckingham Terr EH4 . . . .228 A4
Buckstane Pk EH10 . . . . . .150 A7
Buckstone Ave EH10 . . . . .150 B6
Buckstone Bank EH10 . . . .150 C6
Buckstone Circ EH10 . . . . .150 C6
Buckstone Cres EH10 . . . .150 C7
Buckstone Crook EH10 . . .150 C5
Buckstone Ct EH10 . . . . . .150 B6
Buckstone Dell EH10 . . . . .150 B7
Buckstone Dr EH10 . . . . . .150 B7
Buckstone Gardens EH10 . .150 B6
Buckstone Gate EH10 . . . .150 C6
Buckstone Gn EH10 . . . . . .150 C6
Buckstone Gr EH10 . . . . . .150 B7
Buckstone Hill EH10 . . . . .150 C7
Buckstone Howe EH10 . . .150 C6
Buckstone Lea EH10 . . . . .150 C6
Buckstone Loan EH10 . . . .150 C6
Buckstone Loan E EH10 . .150 C6
Buckstone Neuk EH10 . . . .150 C7
Buckstone Pl EH10 . . . . . .150 B6
Buckstone Prim Sch
EH10 . . . . .150 C6
Buckstone Rd EH10 . . . . . .150 B6
Buckstone Rise EH10 . . . .150 C6
Buckstone Row EH10 . . . .150 C7
Buckstone Shaw EH10 . . .150 C5
Buckstone Terr EH10 . . . . .150 B6
Buckstone View EH10 . . . .150 B7
Buckstone Wood EH10 . . .150 B6
Buckstone Way EH10 . . . .150 C6
Buckstone Wynd EH10 . . .150 C6
Buckyburn Pl KY12 . . . . . .29 E6
Buffies Brae KY12 . . . . .28 F4
Bughtknowe EH48 . . . . . . .141 C7
Bughtlin Dr EH12 . . . . .91 A1
Bughtlin Gdns EH12 . . . . . .91 A1
Bughtlin Gn EH12 . . . . .91 A1
Bughtlin Loan EH12 . . . . . .119 B8
Bughtlin Mkt EH12 . . . . . .119 B8
Bughtlin Pl EH12 . . . . .91 A1
Bughtlin Rd EH30 . . . . .89 F4
Bull's Cl EH1 . . . . .229 C3
Buller St KY5 . . . . .14 B7
Bullet Loan EH41 . . . . .130 C8
Bulloch Cres FK6 . . . . .36 D1
Bungalows The FK5 . . . . . .38 B1
Buntine Cres FK7 . . . . .7 A3
Burder Pk FK2 . . . . .39 A2
Burdiehouse Ave EH17 . . .151 B4
Burdiehouse Cres EH17 . .151 B4
Burdiehouse Crossway
EH17 . . . . .151 B4
Burdiehouse Dr EH17 . . . .151 B4
Burdiehouse Loan EH17 . .151 B4
Burdiehouse Medway
EH17 . . . . .151 B4
Burdiehouse Pl EH17 . . . .151 B4

Burdiehouse Prim Sch
EH17 . . . . .151 B4
Burdiehouse Rd EH17 . . .151 A3
Burdiehouse Sq EH17 . . .151 A3
Burdiehouse St EH17 . . . .151 B4
Burdiehouse Terr EH17 . .151 B4
Burgess Hill EH49 . . . . .85 A6
Burgess Rd EH30 . . . . .68 C1
Burgess St EH6 . . . . .94 A5
Burgess Terr EH9 . . . . . . .122 A4
Burgh Ct KY5 . . . . .14 A7
Burghlee Cres EH20 . . . . .172 C7
Burghlee Terr EH20 . . . . .172 C7
Burgh Mews **1** FK10 . . . .10 B6
Burgh Mills La EH49 . . . . . .84 C6
Burghmuir Ct EH49 . . . . . . .85 D8
Burghmuir Ind Est FK8 . . . .7 B6
Burghmuir Rd FK7 . . . . .7 B6
Burgh Rd EH4 . . . . .13 D4
Burghtoft EH17 . . . . .151 E5
Burleigh Cres KY11 . . . . . . .47 C3
Burleigh Way FK10 . . . . . . .10 C6
Burlington St EH6 . . . . .93 F5
Burnbank Cairneyhill KY12 . .27 D1
  Carnock KY12 . . . . .27 C7
  Livingston EH54 . . . . .143 D5
  Loanhead EH20 . . . . .172 A4
Burnbank Cres EH20 . . . . .151 A1
Burnbank Gr EH20 . . . . . . .151 A1
Burnbank Rd Falkirk FK2 . .60 B7
  Grangemouth FK3 . . . . .61 D5
Burnbank Terr EH5 . . . . . .171 E6
Burnbrae Alloa FK10 . . . . . .10 C8
  Edinburgh EH12 . . . . .119 A8
  Fauldhouse EH47 . . . . . . .181 F5
  Sauchie FK10 . . . . .5 C1
Burnbrae Gdns Alva FK12 . .5 B6
  Falkirk FK1 . . . . .60 A5
Burn Brae Pk FK10 . . . . .23 F4
Burnbrae Rd Falkirk FK1 . .60 A5
  Harthill ML7 . . . . .160 A6
  Shotts ML7 . . . . .179 E3
  Stoneyburn EH47 . . . . . . .162 B1
Burnbrae Terr FK7 . . . . . .161 C6
Burndene Dr EH20 . . . . . .151 A1
Burn Dr FK7 . . . . .7 C4
Burnee FK10 . . . . .9 E3
Burnet's Ct EH1 . . . . .229 A3
Burney Pl KY11 . . . . .46 E4
Burnfield EH54 . . . . .143 A2
Burnfield Pl FK2 . . . . .60 D7
Burnfoot Ct FK3 . . . . .61 D6
Burnfoot La **1** FK1 . . . . . . .60 B4
Burngrange Cotts EH55 . .163 C2
Burngrange Ct EH55 . . . . .163 C2
Burngrange Gdns EH55 . .163 B2
Burngrange Pk EH55 . . . . .163 C2
Burngrange Works EH55 .163 B2
Burnhead Cres EH16 . . . . .151 B6
Burnhead Gr EH16 . . . . . . .151 B6
Burnhead La FK1 . . . . .60 C4
Burnhead Loan EH16 . . . .151 B6
Burnhead Path E EH16 . . .151 B6
Burnhead Path W EH16 . .151 B6
Burnhead Rd FK5 . . . . .38 C3
Burnhouse Dr
  Dechmont EH52 . . . . .114 C2
  Whitburn EH47 . . . . .160 E5
Burnhouse Farm Steadings
  EH27 . . . . .145 C4
Burnhouse Ind Est EH47 .160 F5
Burnhouse Rd EH52 . . . . .114 C3
Burnhouse Sch EH47 . . . .161 A5
Burnlea Dr EH47 . . . . .162 A1
Burnlea Pl EH47 . . . . .162 A1
Burns Ave Armadale EH48 .139 F6
  Grangemouth FK3 . . . . .61 D5
  Stenhousemuir FK5 . . . . . .38 C5
Burns Cres Harthill ML7 . .159 F6
  Laurieston FK2 . . . . .60 C7
  Whitburn EH47 . . . . .161 A6
Burns Ct EH54 . . . . .144 C5
Burnside Dechmont EH52 .114 B2
  Edinburgh EH12 . . . . .119 A8
  Haddington EH41 . . . . . . .129 E8
  Prestonpans EH32 . . . . .96 E1
Burnside Ave
  Armadale EH48 . . . . .139 D6
  Easthouses EH22 . . . . . . .174 D7
  Kinghorn KY3 . . . . .34 F3
  Polbeth EH55 . . . . .163 F5
  Burnside Bsns Ct EH11 . . .47 C4
Burnside Cotts EH49 . . . . . .86 E4
Burnside Cres
  Clackmannan FK10 . . . . . . .11 B5
  Easthouses EH22 . . . . . . .174 D7
  Fauldhouse EH47 . . . . . . .181 E6
  Plean FK7 . . . . .20 C4
  Polbeth EH55 . . . . .163 F5
  Rosyth KY11 . . . . .47 A5
  Shotts ML7 . . . . .179 D6
Burnside Ct Alva FK12 . . . . .5 A7
  Falkirk,Camelon FK1 . . . . .59 E5
  Garvald EH41 . . . . .132 D2
Burnside Gdns EH49 . . . . . .83 F6
Burnside La EH55 . . . . . . .163 F5
Burnside Pk EH14 . . . . . . .146 C7
Burnside Pl Falkirk FK2 . . . .39 B3
  Rosyth KY11 . . . . .47 A7
Burnside Rd
  Bathgate EH48 . . . . .140 F7
  Gorebridge EH23 . . . . . . .174 D1
  Menstrie FK11 . . . . .3 F6
  Polbeth EH55 . . . . .163 F5
  Ratho Station EH12 . . . . .118 A7

Burnside Rd continued
  Uphall EH52 . . . . .115 A4
Burnside Rdbt EH54 . . . . .143 F2
Burnside St Alloa FK10 . . . . .5 D1
  Rosyth KY11 . . . . .47 A5
  Stirling FK7 . . . . .7 C6
Burnside Terr
  Addiewell EH55 . . . . .162 D1
  Cowdenbeath KY4 . . . . .13 A2
  East Calder EH53 . . . . . . .144 F5
  Falkirk FK1 . . . . .59 E5
  Fauldhouse EH47 . . . . . . .181 E6
  Oakley KY12 . . . . .27 A7
  Polbeth EH55 . . . . .163 F5
  Redding FK2 . . . . .61 B1
Burnside View EH55 . . . . .162 D1
Burnsknowe EH14 . . . . . . .142 G6
Burns Pl ML7 . . . . .179 A6
Burns St Dunfermline KY12 .28 C5
  Edinburgh EH6 . . . . .94 A4
  High Valleyfield KY12 . . . . .26 A2
  Stirling FK8 . . . . .2 A2
Burns Terr Bathgate EH48 .141 C5
  Cowie FK7 . . . . .20 D7
Burntisland Mus KY3 . . . . .50 E8
Burntisland Prim Sch KY3 .33 F1
Burntisland Rd KY3 . . . . . . .34 F2
Burntisland Sta KY3 . . . . . .50 E8
Burnvale Broxburn EH52 . .116 A4
  Livingston EH54 . . . . .143 F3
Burnvale Ave EH48 . . . . . .141 C4
Burnvale Pl EH54 . . . . .143 F3
Burr Ave KY3 . . . . .34 F2
Burt Gr KY11 . . . . .29 E1
Burt St KY12 . . . . .29 A6
Bush St EH11 . . . . .124 B6
Bush Terr EH21 . . . . .124 B6
Bute EH54 . . . . .142 F5
Bute Cres
  Dunfermline KY11 . . . . .29 E3
  Shotts ML7 . . . . .179 D6
Bute Pl KY3 . . . . .61 D6
Bute St FK2 . . . . .60 B6
Bute Wynd KY1 . . . . .17 B2
Butler's Pl EH54 . . . . .143 B4
Butlerfield Ind Est EH22 .174 A3
Butterdean Wood EH33 .128 C6
Butteries View EH48 . . . . .139 D5
Butts The EH41 . . . . .130 B8
Buxley Farm Steading
  EH33 . . . . .126 F3
Buxley Rd EH33 . . . . .126 B1
Byburn EH52 . . . . .114 F8
By-Pass Rd FK4 . . . . .57 E5
Byrehope Rd EH52 . . . . . .115 B4
Byreside EH47 . . . . .142 A1
Byres The KY11 . . . . .46 C5
Byron Rd ML7 . . . . .179 B6

C

Cables Wynd EH6 . . . . .93 F5
Cables Wynd Ho EH6 . . . . .93 F5
Caddell's Row Cotts EH4 . .91 B5
Cadell Dr
  Cockenzie & Port Seton
  EH32 . . . . .97 C4
  Fauldhouse EH47 . . . . . . .181 E6
Cadell Reach KY11 . . . . .47 A7
Cadell Sq **4** EH33 . . . . . .126 D6
Cadgers Loan FK7 . . . . .20 B2
Cadiz St EH6 . . . . .94 A5
Cadogan Rd EH16 . . . . . . .151 A4
Cadzow Ave EH51 . . . . .63 F6
Cadzow Cres EH51 . . . . . . .63 F7
Cadzow La EH51 . . . . .63 F7
Cadzow Pl EH7 . . . . .94 A1
Caerketton Ave EH25 . . . .171 E6
Caerketton Cotts EH14 . .149 D8
Caerlaverock Ct EH12 . . . .119 B7
Caesar Rd EH33 . . . . .126 C6
Caesar Way EH33 . . . . .126 C6
Cairn Ave EH21 . . . . .124 B7
Cairn's La EH51 . . . . .64 A8
Cairnbank Gdns EH26 . . . .191 E4
Cairnbank Rd EH26 . . . . . .191 E4
Cairncubie Rd KY12 . . . . . .29 C8
Cairneyhill Prim Sch
  KY12 . . . . .27 D1
Cairneyhill Rd KY12 . . . . . .28 B2
Cairneymount Ave FK2 . . .83 A6
Cairneymount Rd ML8 . . .215 A2
Cairngorm Cres KY2 . . . . . .16 F5
Cairngorm Rd FK3 . . . . .61 E5
Cairn Gr KY12 . . . . .28 C2
Cairnhill Ct ML8 . . . . .215 A2
Cairnie Pl EH47 . . . . .161 A5
Cairn Lea EH48 . . . . .141 C4
Cairnmuir Rd EH12 . . . . . .119 C8
Cairnoch Way FK7 . . . . .7 F1
Cairnoch Wlk FK7 . . . . .36 D1
Cairnpapple Henge & Cairn
  EH48 . . . . .112 D4
Cairngorm Ho **2** EH48 .141 A6
Cairnpark Sch EH14 . . . . .120 B1
Cairns Dr EH14 . . . . .168 B8
Cairns Gdns EH14 . . . . . . .168 B8
Cairns Pl EH47 . . . . .161 A5
Cairns St W KY1 . . . . .17 E7
Cairns The
  Charlestown KY11 . . . . .45 A4
  Menstrie FK11 . . . . .4 A1
Cairntows Cl EH16 . . . . . .122 D4
Cairnwell Pl
  Cairneyhill KY12 . . . . .27 D1
  Kirkcaldy KY2 . . . . .16 F7

Caithness Ct KY1 . . . . .17 E7
Caithness Dr KY1 . . . . .30 C1
Caithness Pl
  Edinburgh EH5 . . . . .93 B5
  Kirkcaldy KY1 . . . . .17 E7
Caiyside EH10 . . . . .150 A6
Caystane Ave EH10 . . . . . .150 A5
Caystane Cres EH10 . . . . .150 A6
Caystane Dr EH10 . . . . . . .149 F5
Caystane Gdns EH10 . . . . .150 A6
Caystane Hill EH10 . . . . . .150 A5
Caystane Terr EH10 . . . . . .150 A5
Caystane View EH10 . . . . .150 A5
Calaisburn Pl KY11 . . . . . . .29 E1
Calais Ct KY11 . . . . .29 E1
Calais View KY11 . . . . .29 E1
Calder's Lawn EH41 . . . . .101 A1
Calderburn Rd EH55 . . . . .164 A5
Calder Cres
  Armadale EH48 . . . . .140 A5
  Edinburgh EH11 . . . . .119 B1
Calder Ct Edinburgh EH11 .119 C2
  Stirling FK7 . . . . .7 B6
  Shotts ML7 . . . . .180 B4
Calder Gdns EH11 . . . . . . .119 C2
Calder Gr EH11 . . . . .119 C1
Calderhall Ave EH53 . . . . .144 E3
Calderhall Cres EH53 . . . .144 F3
Calderhall Terr EH53 . . . .144 F3
Calderhead High Sch
  ML7 . . . . .179 F5
Calderhead Rd ML7 . . . . . .179 D7
Calder House Rd EH53 . . .144 B3
Calder Junc EH11 . . . . .119 B1
Calder Park Rd EH53 . . . . .144 B2
Calder Pl EH11 . . . . .119 C1
Calder Pl Dalgety Bay KY11 .48 A3
  Edinburgh EH11 . . . . .119 C1
  Falkirk FK1 . . . . .60 D1
Calder Rd
  Edinburgh,Sighthill EH11 . .119 D2
  Edinburgh,Stenhouse
  EH11 . . . . .120 A3
  Hermiston EH14 . . . . .118 F1
  Livingston EH54 . . . . .164 C7
Calder Rd Gdns EH11 . . . .120 A3
Calder View EH11 . . . . . . .119 B1
Caledonia Hts KY11 . . . . . .46 C3
Caledonian Brewery
  EH11 . . . . .120 C5
Caledonian Cres EH11 . . .228 A1
Caledonian Ct FK2 . . . . .60 C7
Caledonian Pl EH11 . . . . .228 A1
Caledonian Rd Alloa FK10 . .9 F6
  Edinburgh EH11 . . . . .228 A1
Caledonian Terr EH47 . . . .181 D5
Caledonia Rd Rosyth KY11 .46 A1
  Shotts ML7 . . . . .179 E5
Caledonia Way FK4 . . . . . . .57 F5
Caledonia Way EH11 . . . . . .46 A3
Calender Ave EH54 . . . . . . .17 C7
Calgary Ave EH54 . . . . . . .143 F4
California Prim Sch FK1 . . .81 F5
California Rd
  Maddiston FK2 . . . . .82 F6
  Shieldhill FK1 . . . . .81 E6
California Terr EH11 . . . . . .81 F5
Callander Dr FK5 . . . . .59 C8
Callander Dr TD13 . . . . . . .218 F4
Callendar Ave FK1 . . . . .60 B1
Callendar Bsns Pk FK1 . . . .60 E3
Callendar Park Dr FK1 . . . .60 D3
Callendar Park Terr FK1 . . .60 D4
Callendar Park Wlk FK1 . . .60 D4
Callendar Rd FK1 . . . . .60 C4
Callendar Riggs FK1 . . . . . .60 C4
Callendar Square Sh Ctr **5**
  FK1 . . . . .60 C4
Calliope Rd KY11 . . . . .46 B1
Calton Cres FK7 . . . . .7 B4
Caltonhill EH1 . . . . .229 B4
Calton Hill EH7 . . . . .229 B4
Calton Rd EH8 . . . . .229 B3
Caltrop Pl FK7 . . . . .7 E3

Cameron House Ave
  EH16 . . . . .122 B3
Cameronian Dr ML8 . . . . .215 B1
Cameronian St **9** FK8 . . . .7 B7
Cameron Knowe EH49 . . . .86 D6
Cameron March EH16 . . . .122 A3
Cameron Pk EH16 . . . . . . .122 B3
Cameron Pl ML7 . . . . .39 B2
Cameron Smaill Rd
  EH14 . . . . .147 E7
Cameron St KY12 . . . . .28 E4
Cameron Terr
  Edinburgh EH16 . . . . .122 B3
  Limerigg FK1 . . . . .108 B3
Cameron Toll EH16 . . . . . .122 B3
Cameron Toll Gdns
  EH16 . . . . .122 B3
Cameron Toll Sh Ctr
  EH16 . . . . .122 A3
Cameron Way
  Livingston EH54 . . . . .143 E7
  Prestonpans EH32 . . . . .97 A2
Camilla Gr KY2 . . . . .15 C2
Cammo Bank EH4 . . . . .91 A2
Cammo Brae EH4 . . . . .91 A2
Cammo Cres EH4 . . . . .91 A2
Cammo Gdns EH4 . . . . .91 A1
Cammo Gr EH4 . . . . .90 F2
Cammo Hill EH4 . . . . .90 F2
Cammo Parkway EH4 . . . . .91 A2
Cammo Pl EH4 . . . . .91 A2
Cammo Rd EH4,EH12 . . . . .90 E2
Cammo Wlk EH4,EH12 . . . .90 F1
Campbell's Cl EH8 . . . . . . .229 C3
Campbell Ave EH12 . . . . . .120 C8
Campbell Cres
  Laurieston FK2 . . . . .60 F3
  Lochgelly KY5 . . . . .14 A6
Campbell Ct
  Longniddry EH32 . . . . .98 D5
  Stirling FK7 . . . . .6 F4
Campbell Dr FK5 . . . . .38 B2
Campbell Park Cres
  EH13 . . . . .148 F6
Campbell Park Dr EH13 . .148 F6
Campbell Rd
  Edinburgh EH12 . . . . .120 C8
  Longniddry EH32 . . . . .98 D5
Campbell St KY12 . . . . .29 A4
Camperdown Rd KY11 . . . .46 C1
Campfield St FK2 . . . . .60 B7
Campie La EH21 . . . . .124 B6
Campie Gdns EH21 . . . . . .124 B6
Campie Prim Sch EH21 . .124 B6
Campie Rd EH21 . . . . .124 B6
Campie Terr EH21 . . . . .39 F2
Camp Rd Crombie KY12 . . .44 D5
  Mayfield EH22 . . . . .174 E7
Campsie Cres KY2 . . . . .16 F7
Campsie Rd FK3 . . . . .61 E5
Camps Ind Est EH27 . . . . .145 C5
Camps Rigg EH54 . . . . . . .143 B7
Campsie Rdbt EH54 . . . . .143 C5
Campview EH22 . . . . .152 B7
Campview Ave EH22 . . . . .152 C7
Campview Cres EH22 . . . .152 C7
Campview Gdns EH22 . . . .152 C7
Campview Gr EH22 . . . . . .152 C7
Campview Rd EH19 . . . . . .173 B6
Campview Terr EH22 . . . . .152 B7
Camp Wood View EH22 . .174 E5
Camus Ave EH10 . . . . .150 A6
Camus Pk EH10 . . . . .150 A6
Canaan La EH10 . . . . .121 B3
Canal Bank Ind Est FK4 . . .58 A4
Canal St
  Falkirk,Camelon FK1 . . . . .59 D5
  Falkirk FK2 . . . . .60 B7
Canal Terr EH49 . . . . .85 A6
Canal View Prim Sch
  EH14 . . . . .119 E1
Canal Wlk FK2 . . . . .61 C1
Canalyard Ind Est FK1 . . . .60 B1
Canavan Ct Falkirk FK2 . . . .60 C7
  Stirling FK7 . . . . .7 C3
Canavan Pk FK2 . . . . .60 C7
Canberra St EH54 . . . . . . .144 A5
Candie Cres EH51 . . . . .61 E6
Candie Rd FK3 . . . . .62 A8
Candimilne Ct ML8 . . . . . .215 B1
Candlemaker's Cres
  EH17 . . . . .151 F6
Candlemaker's Pk EH17 . .151 F6
Candlemaker Row EH1 . .229 A2
Candleriggs FK10 . . . . .10 B6
Candleriggs Ct **7** FK10 . .10 B6
Caneluk Ave ML8 . . . . .215 B1
Canmore Dr FK5 . . . . .38 E4
Canmore Gr KY12 . . . . .29 B5
Canmore Prim Sch KY11 . .29 C5
Canmore St
  Dunfermline KY12 . . . . .29 A3
  Kinghorn KY3 . . . . .34 F1
  Queensferry EH30 . . . . .89 B8
Canmore Terr KY12 . . . . . . .29 A3
Canning St EH3 . . . . .228 B2
Canning Street La EH3 . . .228 A2
Cannonball Ho EH1 . . . . . .229 A1
Cannonmills Br EH3 . . . . . .93 C3
Cannons Way FK2 . . . . .39 A1
Cannon Wynd EH6 . . . . . . .93 E6
Cannop Cres EH47 . . . . . . .161 F1
Canon Byrne Glebe KY11 . .45 A5
Canongate Edinburgh EH8 .229 B3
  Spott EH42 . . . . .106 D4
Canongate Venture EH1 . .229 B3

Canon La EH3 . . . . .93 C2
Canon Lynch Ct KY12 . . . . .28 F4
Canonmills EH3 . . . . .93 C3
Canon St EH3 . . . . .93 C2
Canthill Gdns ML7 . . . . . . .179 A3
Cantly Ct KY4 . . . . .46 E3
Cantsdam Rd KY4 . . . . .12 F7
Canty Gr EH32 . . . . .98 C3
Capelaw Rd EH13 . . . . .149 A5
Caplaw Way EH26 . . . . . . .191 C5
Caponflat Cres EH41 . . . . .100 F1
Caponhall Ct **7** EH33 . . .126 C5
Caponhall Dr EH33 . . . . . .126 C5
Caponhall Rd EH33 . . . . . .126 C5
Caponhall Way **8** EH33 .126 C5
Cappers Ct EH46 . . . . .139 F4
Captain's Dr EH16 . . . . . . .151 B3
Captain's Loan EH16 . . . . .151 B6
Captain's Rd EH16,EH17 . .151 B6
Captain's Row EH11 . . . . .151 B6
Caputhall Rd EH54 . . . . . .142 C5
Carberry Ct EH21 . . . . .124 E3
Carberry Cr EH21 . . . . .153 E8
Carberry Gr EH21 . . . . . . .124 E3
Carberry Mains Cotts
  EH21 . . . . .125 A1
Carberry Pl **8** EH21 . . . .120 E7
Carberry Rd EH21 . . . . . . .124 E3
Carbrook Dr FK7 . . . . .20 C3
Carbrook Pl FK3 . . . . .61 A3
Carbrook Terr FK5 . . . . .38 C3
Carcraig Pl KY11 . . . . .48 B3
Cardross Ave EH52 . . . . . .115 B5
Cardross Cres EH52 . . . . . .115 C5
Cardross Rd EH52 . . . . . . .115 C5
Cardrowan Rd FK7 . . . . .20 D1
Carey Ct FK7 . . . . .20 C4
Carfrae Cotts EH41 . . . . . .221 D8
Carfrae Gdns EH4 . . . . .92 A2
Carfrae Gr EH4 . . . . .92 A2
Carfrae Pk EH4 . . . . .92 A2
Carfrae Rd EH4 . . . . .92 A2
Cargilfield Sch EH4 . . . . . . .91 B4
Cargilfield View EH4 . . . . . .91 B4
Cargil Terr EH5 . . . . .93 B5
Carhowden Rd FK2 . . . . . . .61 B3
Carlaverock Ave EH33 . . . .126 C5
Carlaverock Cl EH33 . . . . .126 C4
Carlaverock Cres EH33 . . .126 C5
Carlaverock Dr EH33 . . . . .126 C5
Carlaverock Gr EH33 . . . . .126 C5
Carlaverock Terr EH33 . . .126 C4
Carlaverock View EH33 . . .126 C4
Carlaverock Wlk **4**
  EH33 . . . . .126 D5
Carledubs Ave EH52 . . . . .115 C5
Carledubs Cres EH52 . . . .115 A6
Carlekemp EH39 . . . . .53 F8
Carlie Ave FK2 . . . . .61 B3
Carlin Craig KY3 . . . . .34 F1
Carlin Cres KY3 . . . . .34 F1
Carlingnose Ct KY11 . . . . . .68 C6
Carlingnose Pk KY11 . . . . . .68 C6
Carlingnose Point KY11 . . .68 C6
Carlingnose View KY11 . . . .68 C6
Carlingnose Way KY11 . . . .68 C6
Carlin La ML8 . . . . .215 B1
Carlisle App EH33 . . . . . . .195 C5
Carlops Ave EH26 . . . . .191 E6
Carlops Cres EH26 . . . . . . .191 E6
Carlops Rd EH26 . . . . .191 D5
Carlouk La ML8 . . . . .215 B1
Carlowrie Ave EH30 . . . . . .89 E7
Carlowrie Cres EH30 . . . . . .89 E7
Carlowrie Farm Cotts
  EH29 . . . . .89 F4
Carlton Terr EH7 . . . . .229 C4
Carlton Terrace Brae
  EH7 . . . . .229 C4
Carlton Terrace La EH7 . . .229 C4
Carlton Terrace Mews
  EH7 . . . . .229 C4
Carluke High Sch ML8 . . .215 A2
Carluke Prim Sch ML8 . . .215 A3
Carlyle Ct
  Haddington EH41 . . . . . . .130 B8
  Livingston EH54 . . . . .144 C5
Carlyle Gdns EH41 . . . . . . .101 A1
Carlyle La **1** KY12 . . . . . .28 E5
Carlyle Pl Edinburgh EH7 . . .94 A2
  Musselburgh EH21 . . . . . .124 C6
Carlyle Rd KY12 . . . . .17 B4
Carlyle St KY12 . . . . .29 A2
Carlyle Terr EH48 . . . . .141 C5
Carmel Ave EH29 . . . . .89 A2
Carmelaws EH49 . . . . .85 A5
Carmelite Rd EH30 . . . . . . .89 B8
Carmel Rd EH29 . . . . .89 A1
Carmichael Cl FK9 . . . . .2 A7
Carmondean Centre Rd
  EH54 . . . . .143 A6
Carmondean Centre Rdbt
  EH54 . . . . .143 B5
Carmondean Ctr EH54 . . .143 A6
Carmondean Ctr S EH54 .143 A6
Carmondean Prim Sch
  EH54 . . . . .143 B6
Carmuir ML11 . . . . .201 A1
Carmuirs Ave FK1 . . . . .59 B6
Carmuirs Dr FK1 . . . . .59 B6
Carmuirs Prim Sch FK1 . . .59 C5
Carmuirs St FK1 . . . . .59 C5
Carnaughton Pl FK12 . . . . . .4 F6
Carnbee Ave EH16 . . . . . . .151 C6
Carnbee Cres EH16 . . . . . .151 C6
Carnbee Dell EH16 . . . . . .151 C6

Carnbee End EH16...... 151 C6
Carnbee Pk EH16...... 151 C6
Carnbee Pl KY12........29 C4
Carnegie Ave KY11......46 E7
Carnegie Campus (Bsns Pk)
KY11......................46 E7
Carnegie Ct
Dunfermline KY12.......29 A4
Edinburgh EH8.........229 B2
Carnegie Dr
Dunfermline KY12.......29 A4
Falkirk FK1.............59 D6
Carnegie Rd ML8......142 B6
Carnegie St EH8......229 B2
Carneil Rd KY12.......27 C7
Carneil Terr KY12.......27 C6
Carnethie St
Rosewell EH24.........172 E2
Rosewell EH24.........193 D8
Carnethy Ave
Edinburgh EH13......149 B6
Penicuik EH26........191 F6
Carnethy Cres KY2......
Carnock Mill KY12......27 C7
Carnock Prim Sch KY12..27 C7
Carnock Rd KY12.......27 E7
Carnock St FK7.........20 E8
Carnwath Rd ML8......215 A1
Caroline Cres FK12......4 F6
Caroline Gdns
Edinburgh EH12.......119 E7
Mid Calder EH53......144 B2
Caroline Park Ave EH5..92 D7
Caroline Park Gr EH5....92 D6
Caroline Pk EH53.......144 B2
Caroline Pl EH12.......119 E7
Caroline Terr EH12....119 D8
Carpenters Wynd FK10....9 F6
Carperstane EH39.......54 D1
Carpet La EH6..........94 A5
Carradale Ave FK1......59 C4
Carribber Ave EH49.....84 A6
Carrick Cres EH22.....174 C8
Carrick Ct FK7..........7 C5
Carrick Dr KY11........48 A3
Carrick Gdns EH54....164 E6
Carrick Gr KY11........48 A3
Carrick Knowe Ave
EH12................119 F5
Carrick Knowe Gr EH12.119 F5
Carrick Knowe Hill EH12.119 F5
Carrick Knowe Loan
EH12................119 F5
Carrick Knowe Parkway
EH12................119 F5
Carrick Knowe Pl EH12..119 F5
Carrick Knowe Prim Sch
EH12................119 F5
Carrick Knowe Rd EH12.119 F4
Carrick Knowe Terr
EH12................119 F5
Carrick Pl EH39........39 A3
Falkirk,Tamfourhill FK1..59 C4
Carriden Brae EH51.....64 D6
Carriden Glade EH51....64 C7
Carriden Ind Est EH51...64 C7
Carriden Pl EH51........64 C6
Carriden View EH51......64 C6
Carrington Cres EH44....92 E3
Carrington Mains Cotts
EH23................194 D5
Carronbank Ave FK2.....39 B2
Carronbank Cres FK6....36 E3
Carronbank Ct FK2......39 B2
Carron Ct **1** EH48....141 A6
Carronflats Rd FK3......61 E8
Carron Gr KY2..........
Carrongrange Ave FK5...38 E2
Carrongrange Gdns FK5..38 E1
Carrongrange Gr FK5.....38 E2
Carrongrange Rd FK5....38 E2
Carrongrange Sch FK5...38 E2
Carrongrove Ave FK2....39 A2
Carrongrove Bsns Pk FK2.39 A2
Carrongrove Rd FK2.....39 A2
Carronhall Ave FK2......39 C4
Carron La KY11.........29 F4
Carronlea Dr FK2........39 A2
Carron Pl Edinburgh EH6.94 B5
Grangemouth FK3.......61 D4
Kirkcaldy KY2..........16 D8
Stirling FK7............7 A3
Carron Prim Sch FK2....39 A1
Carron Rd Falkirk FK2....39 A1
Falkirk FK2.............60 A8
Carron Rdbt FK2........39 A2
Carronshore Prim Sch
FK2..................39 C4
Carronshore Rd FK2....39 B2
Carronside Pl FK6.......36 E3
Carronside St FK2.......60 B8
Carron Terr FK2.........82 E7
Carronvale Ave FK5.....38 D1
Carronvale Rd Larbert FK5.59 D8
Stenhousemuir FK5......38 D2
Carron View FK2........82 E7
Carron Wlk EH54.......144 A4
Carrubber's Cl EH1.....229 B3
Carsaig Ct FK9..........2 A5
Carsebridge Ct FK10....10 D3
Carsebridge Rd FK10....10 D3
Carsebridge Row FK10...10 D8
Carse Cres FK2.........61 A4

Carse Knowe EH49......85 D7
Carse Terr FK10.........9 F8
Carseview Bannockburn FK7..7 E2
Tullibody FK10...........4 A3
Carse View Airth FK2....22 E4
Bo'ness EH51............63 D5
Cars of the Stars Motor Mus
EH28................117 F6
Carson Pl KY11.........46 C5
Carswell Pl KY12.......28 F6
Cartmore Rd KY5.......14 A8
Cask Cres FK8...........7 C8
Cassel's La EH6........93 F4
Casselbank St EH6......93 F4
Castellau Cotts EH42....78 E7
Castings Ave FK2.......60 B7
Castings Ct Falkirk FK2..60 B7
Castings Dr FK2........60 C6
Castings Ho FK2........60 B6
Castings Rd FK2........60 C6
Castings The KY12......28 D6
Castlandhill Farm Steadings
KY11.................
Castle Ave Airth FK2....22 E3
Cockenzie & Port Seton
EH32................97 E4
Falkirk EH2............39 C3
Gorebridge EH23......195 C8
Castleblair **2** EH12....28 F4
Castleblair La **2** KY12..28 F5
Castleblair Mews **3** KY12.28 F5
Castleblair Pk KY12.....28 F5
Castle Brae KY11.......46 F6
Castlebrae Bsns Ctr
EH16................122 C4
Castlebrae Com High Sch
EH16................122 E3
Castlebrae Glebe EH16..122 D4
Castlebrae Gr EH16.....122 D3
Castlebrae Pl EH16.....122 D3
Castlebrae Rigg EH16...122 D3
Castlebrae Wynd EH16..122 C4
Castlegait **6** EH8......7 B7
Castle Gate Dunbar EH42.78 D3
Rosyth KY11............46 E3
Castle Gogar Rd EH12..118 D7
Castlehill Bo'ness EH51...63 D6
Edinburgh EH1........228 C3
Elphinstone EH33......126 B1
Castlehill Ave EH11....108 A6
Castlelaurie Ind Est FK2..60 C7
Castlelaurie St FK2.....60 C7
Castle Cres EH22.......33 B3
Dunfermline KY11......46 F6
Stenhousemuir FK5......38 D1
Castlegate **6** EH8......7 B7
Castle Gate Dunbar EH42.78 D3
Castlelaw Ct EH26......191 F6
Castlelaw Fort & Souterrain
EH26................170 D4
Castlelaw Rd EH13.....149 A6
Castle Mains EH39......53 B5
Castlemains Pl EH39....53 C5
Castle Mains Pl EH39....53 B5
Castle Moffat EH14.....222 A8
Castle Moffat Cotts
EH14................222 A8
Castlepark Gait EH16...122 D4
Castlepark Glade EH16..122 D4
Castlepark Gn EH16....122 D4
Castle Pk Dirleton EH39..53 C5
Kincardine FK10........23 D6
Castle Rd Bathgate EH48.141 C5
Falkirk EH42...........78 D3
Gorebridge EH23......195 C8
Castlerankine Rd FK6...36 C2
Castle Rd
Cockenzie & Port Seton
EH32................97 E4
Falkirk FK2............60 C8
Menstrie FK11...........3 F6
Rosyth KY11............46 E2
Stirling FK9.............2 C3
Tranent EH33..........126 A4
Winchburgh EH52.......88 A2
Castlerig KY3...........34 F2
Castle Row KY12........28 E6
Castle St Alloa FK10.....10 A5
Clackmannan FK10.....11 A4
Dunbar EH42...........78 D3
Edinburgh EH2........228 B3
Castle Terr
Clackmannan FK10.....11 A4
Cockenzie & Port Seton
EH32................97 E4
Denny FK6.............36 C2
Edinburgh EH1........228 B2
Winchburgh EH52......88 A2
Castleton Cres EH39....55 E7
Castleton Cres FK3.....61 D6
Castle Vale FK9.........2 A2
Castle View Aberdour KY3.49 C8
Airth FK2..............22 D2

Castle View continued
Cockenzie & Port Seton
EH32................97 E4
Dunfermline KY11......46 F6
Fallin FK7..............52 B7
Gorebridge EH23......195 C7
Pencaitland EH34......156 D6
Castleview Dr
Bridge of A FK9........2 D5
Edinburgh EH16......122 D1
Castleview Gr EH16....122 D1
Castleview Ho EH17....122 D1
Castleview La EH54....164 E4
Castleview Prim Sch
EH16................122 E3
Castleview Terr
Edinburgh EH16......122 D4
Longcroft FK4...........57 A3
Castle Wlk EH32........97 E4
Castle Wynd Kinghorn KY3..34 F2
4 Stirling FK8.........7 A8
Castle Wynd N EH1....228 C2
Castle Wynd S EH1....228 C2
Cast The EH43.........172 D5
Catalyst Trad Pk EH11...119 C2
Cathcart Pl EH11......120 F6
Cathedral La EH1......229 A4
Catherine St FK7........7 C1
Catherine Terr EH47....141 F1
Cathlaw La EH48.......112 A5
Cathrine Gr EH51.......64 A5
Cathie Terr EH26......171 B1
Cattle Market EH10.....81 A4
Cauldcoats Holdings
EH49.................65 B2
Cauldhame Cres FK7....6 C5
Causewayhead Rd FK9....2 C3
Causeway La KY12......26 E5
Causewayside EH9.....121 E5
Causeway The
Bridge of A FK9.........2 D5
Cockburnspath TD13...218 F4
Edinburgh EH16......122 C6
Cavalry Park Dr EH15...122 D6
Cawburn Com Prim Sch
EH54................115 A1
Cawder Gdns FK9.......1 F8
Cawder Rd FK9.........1 F8
Cawdor Cres KY2.......16 B6
Cecil St FK7............7 B6
Cedar Ave Kirkcaldy KY1..17 C8
Stirling FK8.............6 F5
Cedarbank EH54.......143 E5
Cedarbank Sch EH54...143 E5
Cedar Cres
Cowdenbeath KY4......13 D6
Westquarter FK2........61 A2
Whitburn EH47.........161 C6
Cedar Dr EH22..........97 C3
Cedar Gr Dunfermline KY11.46 D8
Stenhousemuir FK5......38 D1
Cedar Rd EH20........171 F7
Cedar St Dunbar EH42...78 B2
Grangemouth FK3......61 D7
Cedars The
Edinburgh EH13......149 B7
Tullibody FK10...........4 B2
Cedar Wynd ML7.......180 B4
Cedric Rise EH13......144 A1
Cemetery Rd
Dalkeith EH22.........152 F2
Fauldhouse EH47......181 D5
Prestonpans EH32......96 F2
Shotts ML7............180 B4
Central Ave FK6.........61 C5
Central Bvd FK5.........38 B4
Central Dock Rd FK3....40 E2
Central Dr FK5..........38 B3
Central Park Ave FK5...38 B4
Central Park Bsns Pk FK5.38 B4
Central Pk (Cowdenbeath
FC) KY4..............13 C4
Central Rd KY4.........13 C4
Central Ret Pk FK1......60 C5
Central Way KY11.......48 C5
Centre Intc EH54......144 A3
Centre Rd N EH53,EH54..144 A3
Centurion Way FK7.....59 D6
Chacefield St FK4......58 A6
Chacefield Wood FK6...57 E7
Chalmers Bldg EH49....84 E3
Chalmer's Bldgs EH22..228 B1
Chalmers Cres EH9....121 D5
Chalmers Ho EH11......28 F3
Chalmers Hospl EH3...228 C2
Chalmers Sq EH54.....142 C5
Chalmers St
Dunfermline KY12......28 F4
Edinburgh EH3........228 C1
Chalmerston Rd FK9......1 B2
Chalton Ct FK9..........1 B7
Chalton Rd FK9..........2 B7
Chalybeate EH41......129 F7
Chamberfield Rd KY12...29 C6
Chamberlain Rd EH10...121 B4
Chambers Dr FK2.......39 B2
Chambers St EH1......229 A2
Chamfron Gdns FK7......7 A8
Champany Holdings EH49.65 A2
Champfleurie Cotts EH49.86 A5
Champfleurie Mews EH49.86 A5
Champfleurie Stables
EH49.................86 B6
Champigny Ct EH21....124 E5
Chancelot Cres EH6.....93 C5
Chancelot Gr EH5.......93 C5
Chancelot Terr EH6.....93 C5
Chandler's Rise KY11...47 F4

Chandlers Rise KY11.....47 F4
Chandlers Wlk KY11.....47 F4
Channel Brae EH42.....134 D7
Chapel Bank EH22.....154 D5
Chapel Cres FK2........39 B3
Chapelcroft FK7........6 D6
Chapel Ct EH16.......122 F3
Chapel Dr FK5..........38 E3
Chapelfauld Gn KY11...29 F3
Chapel Gr KY2..........16 C8
Chapelhill
Clackmannan FK10.....11 A3
Dirleton EH39..........53 A4
Kirkcaldy KY2..........16 D8
Chapelhill St EH39......23 D5
Chapel La Edinburgh EH6.94 B5
Falkirk FK1............60 B5
Chapel Level KY2.......16 F8
Chapel Loan EH25.....172 A3
Chapel Pl
High Valleyfield KY12...26 B2
Inverkeithing KY11......29 C1
North Queensferry KY11.68 C5
Pathhead EH37.........66 C1
Chapel Rd KY2..........16 C8
Chapel St
Cowdenbeath KY4......13 C3
8 Dunfermline KY12..28 F4
Edinburgh EH8........229 B1
Kincardine FK10........23 E3
Lochgelly KY5..........14 B8
Chapelton Ave EH55...163 F4
Chapelton Dr EH55....163 F4
Chapelton Gdns EH55..164 A4
Chapelton Gr EH55....164 A4
Chapelton Pl EH55....163 F4
Chapelton Rd EH55...164 A4
Chapelton Terr EH55..163 F5
Chapel Villas KY11.....48 B2
Chapelwell Pl KY11.....29 F3
Chapel Wynd EH1.....228 C2
Chapman's Brae EH48..140 F8
Charing Cross FK3......40 D1
Chariot Dr EH28........117 A5
Charles Ave FK9.........2 A3
Charles Cres
Bathgate EH48........141 F5
Carluke ML8...........215 B1
Charles Dr KY11........45 F3
Charles St KY11.........59 C8
Charlesfield EH8......229 A2
Charlesfield La EH8....229 A2
Charlesfield Rd EH54...164 C8
Charles La EH48........141 F5
Charles Logan Pl KY11..46 F4
Charles Rodger Pl FK9...2 A6
Charles St Alloa FK10.....9 F8
Dunfermline KY11......29 B2
Edinburgh EH8........229 A2
Penicuik EH26........191 E7
Shotts ML7............180 B4
Stirling FK8.............7 A5
Charles Street La EH8..229 A2
Charles Way KY11......45 E3
Charles Way S KY11.....45 E3
Charlotte Dundas Ct FK3.61 E6
Charlotte Hill Ct FK5....38 B3
Charlotte La EH2.......228 B3
Charlotte Sq EH2......228 B3
Charlotte St
Grangemouth FK2.......82 D8
Kirkcaldy KY1..........17 B3
Shotts ML7............180 B4
Charlton Gr EH25......171 F3
Charrier The KY11......29 B1
Charterhall Gr EH9....121 D3
Charterhall Rd EH9....121 D3
Charteris Ct EH32......98 D5
Charteris Pk EH32......98 D5
Chartershall Rd
Bannockburn FK7.......19 A6
Stirling FK7.............7 A1
Charter St KY7..........7 A3
Chattan Ave FK9.........2 B4
Chattan Ind Est FK4....58 C4
Chatterrig EH13........149 F7
Checkbar Rdbt FK5......58 C7
Cherry Ave EH48.......141 E6
Cherrybank KY12.......29 C5
Cherry La EH22.........154 D4
Cherry Rd KY11........29 F3
Cherry Rd EH19........173 B6
Cherryton EH FK10......11 A5
Cherry Tree Ave EH14..147 E3
Cherry Tree Cres EH14..147 E3
Cherry Tree Gdns EH14.147 E3
Cherry Tree Gr EH14...147 E3
Cherry Tree Loan EH14.147 E3
Cherry Tree Pk EH14...147 E3
Cherry Tree View EH14..147 E3
Chessel's Ct EH8......229 B3
Chesser Ave EH11.....120 C4
Chesser Cotts EH11....120 D4
Chesser Cres EH14....120 C4
Chesser Gdns EH11....120 C4
Chesser Gr EH14......120 C4
Chesser Loan EH14....120 C4
Chester Dr EH22.......174 C5
Chesters Ct EH19......173 B6
Chesters Gr EH19.....173 B6
Chesters The EH39.....72 F4
Chesters View EH19...173 B6
Chester View EH22.....174 D5

Chestnut Ave
Kirkcaldy KY1..........17 C7
Whitburn EH47........161 C6
Chestnut Cres FK6......36 C3
Chestnut Ct EH21.....124 D6
Chestnut Gr Bo'ness EH51.63 C5
Bonnyrigg and Lasswade
EH19................173 B6
Cockenzie & Port Seton
EH32................97 D3
Dunfermline KY11......46 E8
Livingston EH54......144 B5
Stenhousemuir FK5......38 F3
Winchburgh EH52......87 F2
Chestnut St EH5........92 E7
Cheviot Pl FK3.........61 E5
Cheviot Rd KY2........16 F7
Cheyne St EH4.........93 A2
Chief's Cl **7** KY1.......17 C7
Chisholm Ave KY5......2 B4
Chisholm Cres KY5.....14 A7
Chisholm Pl FK3.......61 B6
Chisholm St KY12.......29 D8
Chisholm Terr EH26...191 F7
Chrichton's Cl EH8.....229 A3
Chrisella Terr FK2.......83 A6
Christian Cres EH15...123 E7
Christian Gr EH15.....123 B7
Christianmiller Ave EH7.94 E1
Christianmiller Gr EH7..94 E1
Christianmiller Pl EH7..94 E2
Christie Pl KY1.........17 C7
Christie St KY12........29 B5
Christie Terr FK5.......38 E3
Chuckethall Rd EH54..142 E7
Chuckethall Rd EH54..142 E7
Chuckie Pend EH3.....228 B2
Church Ct Alloa FK10....10 A6
Kirkcaldy KY1..........17 C4
Philipstoun EH49.......86 D6
Church Gdns
Longniddry EH32.......98 E5
Stoneyburn EH47......162 B1
Church Gr Alloa FK10....10 A5
Burntisland KY3........33 D1
Church Hill EH10......121 B4
Churchhill Dr EH10....121 B4
Church Hill Pl EH10....121 B4
Churchill Dr FK9.........2 A6
Churchill Pl Falkirk FK2..60 C7
Rosyth KY11............46 F3
Churchill St FK10.......9 F8
Church La Denny FK6...36 C2
Kirkcaldy KY1..........17 C4
Limekilns KY11.........45 D3
Plean FK7.............20 D2
Church Pk EH48.......141 B6
Bathgate EH48........141 B6
Crossgates KY4.........30 F7
Faulds Ho KY12.........7 B4
Fauldhouse EH47......181 E6
Longridge EH47........161 C6
Church Rd Bo'ness EH51..63 E7
Bonnyrigg and Lasswade
EH18................151 F1
California FK1...........81 F5
North Berwick EH39....54 C7
Church St Addiewell EH55.162 D1
Alloa FK10.............10 A6
Bonnybridge FK4.......58 C3
Broxburn EH52.........115 C5
Burntisland KY3........33 D1
Cowdenbeath KY4......13 D3
Dunbar EH42...........78 E2
Falkirk FK1............39 C2
Haddington EH41......130 B8
Harthill ML7...........159 C5
Inverkeithing KY11......29 C1
Kingseat KY12..........12 B1
Kirkcaldy KY1..........17 C4
Loanhead EH20........172 C7
Lochgelly KY5..........14 B7
Stenhousemuir FK5......38 E3
Tranent EH33..........126 C7
Churchway KY11.......29 E5
Church Wlk Denny FK6...36 C2
Kinghorn KY3..........34 E2
Church Wynd EH51.....63 F7
Churchyard ML7......179 E4
Cinderhall Pl EH33....126 B1
Circle The EH22........152 B8
Circus Gdns EH3......228 B4
Circus La EH3.........228 B4
Circus Pl EH3.........228 B4
Citadel Pl EH6..........93 F6
Citadel St EH6..........93 F6
Citron Glebe **4** KY1...17 C6
City Obsy EH7.........229 B4
City Of Edinburgh By-Pass
The
Dalkeith EH18,EH22....152 C3
Edinburgh,Dreghorn EH10,
EH13...............149 C4
Edinburgh,East Hermiston EH11,
EH12,EH14..........119 A2
Edinburgh,Fairmilehead EH10,
EH20...............150 C3
Civic Sq **1** EH33.....126 D6
Clackmae Gr EH16....150 F8
Clackmae Rd EH16....150 F8
Clackmannan Cty Hospl
FK10.................10 B8

Clackmannan Prim Sch
FK10...............11 A4
Clackmannan Rd FK10 ...10 D6
Clackmannan Tower FK10 .10 F4
Clanranald Pl FK1 ....59 F1
Clarebank Cres EH6....94 B4
Clare Ct EH39 ....54 B7
Claremont FK10 ....9 D8
Claremont Bank EH7.....93 D3
Claremont Cres EH7.....93 D3
Claremont Ct EH7 ......93 D3
Claremont Dr FK9 ....2 C7
Claremont Gdns EH6.....94 B4
Claremont Gr EH7 ......93 D3
Claremont Ind Est FK10 ..10 A6
Claremont Pk EH6 ......94 B4
Claremont Prim Sch FK10..9 E8
Claremont Rd EH6......94 B4
Clarence St EH3 ....93 B2
Clarendon Cres
  Edinburgh EH4.........228 A4
  Linlithgow EH49........85 B6
Clarendon Pl FK8........7 A7
Clarendon Rd
  Linlithgow EH49........85 B6
  Stirling FK8............7 A7
Claret Rd
  Grangemouth,Bowhouse
  FK3.................61 E6
  Grangemouth,Oil Refinery
  FK3.................62 C7
Clarinda Ave FK1 ....59 B5
Clarinda Gdns EH22.....153 D3
Clarinda Pl FK5.........38 C4
Clarinda Terr EH10......122 A1
Clark Ave Edinburgh EH5..93 C5
  Linlithgow EH49........84 E8
Clark Bldgs EH35 ......155 E7
Clarke Sq EH54 ....142 C6
Clark Pl Edinburgh EH5....93 B5
  Kirkcaldy KY2...........17 A5
Clark Rd Edinburgh EH5..93 B5
  Inverkeithing KY11......47 B2
Clarkson Rd FK10 ......115 D5
Clark St FK7............7 B2
Claverhouse Dr EH16 ..151 B8
Clay Acres Ct KY12 .....29 A5
Claycrofts Pl FK7........7 F6
Clayhills Gr EH14......147 B1
Clayhills Pk EH14......147 B1
Clayknowes Ave EH21...124 A4
Clayknowes Cres EH21...124 A5
Clayknowes Ct EH21....124 A4
Clayknowes Dr EH21....123 F5
Clayknowes Pl ⊠ EH21 .124 A5
Clayknowes Way EH21...124 A5
Claylands Rd EH28.....116 F3
Claymore Dr FK7 ....7 D3
Clearburn Cres EH16...122 B4
Clearburn Gdns EH16...122 B4
Clearburn Rd
  Edinburgh EH16.......122 B4
  Gorebridge EH23......174 B1
Cleaves The FK10 ....4 A5
Cleekim Dr EH15 ......123 B4
Cleekim Rd EH15 ......123 B4
Cleghorn Dr EH52......115 B5
Cleikiminfield EH15.....123 B4
Cleikiminrig EH15......123 B4
Cleish Gdns KY2........16 F6
Cleish Pl KY11.........29 F2
Cleish Rd KY11.........29 F2
Cleland St EH47 ....161 B7
Clement Rise EH54 ....144 B1
Clerics Hill EH29........89 A1
Clerk Gr KY11 ....29 F1
Clerkington Rd EH41....129 E8
Clerkington Wlk EH41...129 E8
Clerk Rd EH26.........191 D5
Clerk St Edinburgh EH8..229 A2
  Loanhead EH20.......172 C8
Clermiston Ave EH4.....91 D2
Clermiston Cres EH4....91 D2
Clermiston Dr EH4......91 D2
Clermiston Gdns EH4...91 D2
Clermiston Gn EH4 .....91 D2
Clermiston Gr EH4......91 D2
Clermiston Hill EH4.....91 E2
Clermiston Loan EH4....91 D2
Clermiston Medway EH4.91 D2
Clermiston Pk EH4......91 D2
Clermiston Pl EH4......91 D2
Clermiston Prim Sch EH4 .91 C2
Clermiston Rd EH12....119 E7
Clermiston Rd N EH4....91 E2
Clermiston Terr EH12....91 E2
Clermiston View EH4....91 E2
Clerwood Bank EH12....119 D8
Clerwood Gdns EH12...119 E8
Clerwood Gr EH12.....119 E8
Clerwood Loan EH12...119 D8
Clerwood Pk EH12.....119 D8
Clerwood Pl EH12......119 E8
Clerwood Row EH12....119 D8
Clerwood Terr EH12....119 E8
Clerwood View EH12...119 E8
Clerwood Way EH12....119 D8
Cleuch Ave
  North Middleton EH23..195 F2
  Tullibody FK10..........4 B2
Cleuch Dr EH23.........4 E7
Cleuch Rd
  North Middleton EH23..195 F2

Cleuch Rd continued
  Stirling FK9............2 C3
Cleveland Dr KY11 ......47 B2
Clifford Rd
  North Berwick EH39 ....54 C6
  Stirling FK8.............7 B5
Cliffonhall Rd EH28....116 F4
Clifton Hall Sch EH28 .116 D2
Clifton Rd
  Livingston EH53.......145 C7
  Newbridge EH28.......116 E2
Clifton Terr 3 EH12.....120 F7
Clifton Trad Est EH28....116 F4
Clifton View EH52......116 A6
Climpy Rd ML11........200 D3
Clinkum Bank KY12......26 C3
Clinton Rd EH9.........121 B4
Clive St EH3............179 E4
Cloanden Pl KY2........17 A3
Clockluine Rd KY11 .....47 E6
Clockmill La EH7,EH8....94 B1
Cloglands ML11........217 F7
Close The KY11..........4 A5
Clova Dr EH54 ....164 E5
Clovenstone Dr EH14 ..148 E7
Clovenstone Gdns EH14.148 F8
Clovenstone Pk EH14 ..148 E7
Clovenstone Prim Sch
  EH14.................148 E7
Clovenstone Rd EH14 ..148 E8
Clovenstone Rdbt EH14 .148 E8
Cloverbank EH54 ......143 E5
Cloverfoot Cotts EH16..123 B2
Cloverfoot Pl EH51 .....63 E5
Cloves The FK11 ....4 A5
Cluanie Ave ML7.......179 E6
Clufflat EH30 ....67 F2
Clufflat Brae EH30 ......67 F2
Clune Rd KY12..........27 E7
Clunie Rd KY11.........29 E3
Clunivar St KY12........28 D5
Cluny Ave EH10.........121 B2
Cluny Dr Edinburgh EH10 .121 B2
  Stenhousemuir FK5......38 F4
Cluny Gdns EH10 ......121 C2
Cluny Pl EH10..........121 C3
Cluny Terr EH10........121 B2
Clyde Cres
  Dunfermline KY11.......29 F2
  Larbert FK5...........59 A4
Clyde Dr Livingston EH54 .144 B4
  Shotts ML7...........180 B4
Clydesdale St EH51......63 F6
Clyde St Falkirk FK1.....59 C5
  Grangemouth FK3.......40 B1
Clydevale Pl EH44 .....115 A2
Clydevale Terr EH54.....115 A1
Coalgate FK10 ....10 B6
Coalgate Ave EH43.....126 E7
Coalgate Rd EH33......126 D7
Coalhill EH6............93 F5
Coal Neuk EH33 ....126 C6
Coal Neuk Ct EH33.....126 C6
Coalpots Way FK10 .....5 E3
Coal Rd KY12...........36 B7
Coal Wynd Bannockburn FK7 .7 D1
  Kirkcaldy KY1..........17 C4
Coastguard Cotts TD13...18 F4
Coates Cotts EH32......99 F4
Coates Cres EH3.......228 A3
Coates Gdns EH12......120 F7
Coates Pl EH3.........228 A2
Coatfield La EH6........94 A5
Coats Cres FK10.........4 E1
Cobblebrae Cres FK2....39 B1
Cobden Cres EH9.......121 F4
Cobden Ct KY4..........30 F6
Cobden Rd EH9........121 F4
Cobden St Alva FK12......5 A6
  Alva FK12..............5 A7
Cobden Terr EH11......228 A2
Coblecrook Gdns FK12....4 F6
Coblecrook La FK12......4 F6
Coblecrook Pl FK12......4 F6
Coburg St EH6..........93 F5
Cochrane Ave Falkirk FK1 .60 B7
  Inverkeithing KY11......47 D2
Cochrane Cres FK12......4 E7
Cochrane Pl EH6........94 A4
Cochrane Rd KY11 ......46 B1
Cochrane Sq EH54.....164 D6
Cochrane St
  Bathgate EH48........141 A7
  Falkirk FK1...........60 B7
Cochranes The FK12.....5 B7
Cochrane Way KY11.....48 A5
Cochran La KY11........29 F4
Cochrie Pl FK10.........4 C2
Cochrina Pl EH24 ......172 D2
Cockburn Cres
  Balerno EH14.........168 B7
  Whitecross EH49.......84 A6
Cockburn Ct EH35 .....155 E7
Cockburn Dr EH35 .....155 D6
Cockburnhill Rd EH14..168 A8
Cockburnspath Prim Sch
  TD13.................218 F4
Cockburn Sq EH32.....176 B5
Cockburn St
  Edinburgh EH1.........229 A3
  Falkirk FK1............60 A4
Cockdurno Farm EH14 .168 A6
Cocklaw St KY4..........12 D8
Cockles Brae EH41.....130 E3
Cockmilane Brae EH41..130 D6
Cockpen Ave KY4.......173 A5
Cockpen Cres EH19....173 A5

Cockpen Dr EH19.......173 A5
Cockpen Pl EH19.......173 A5
Cockpen Rd EH19......173 D6
Cockpen Terr EH19.....173 A5
Cockpen View EH19....173 A5
Coillesdene Ave EH15...123 D7
Coillesdene Cres EH15..123 D7
Coillesdene Dr EH15....123 D7
Coillesdene Gdns EH15 .123 D7
Coillesdene Ho EH15...123 D7
Coillesdene Loan EH15..123 E7
Coire Loan ML7........180 B3
Coddingham Pl KY12....29 D4
Colegate Rd EH23,EH37 .196 D8
Coles Pl KY4............31 A6
Colinshiel Ave EH48....140 E7
Colinshiel Ct EH48.....139 F6
Colinshiel St EH48.....140 E7
Colinshiel View EH48...139 F7
Colinswell Rd KY3.......33 D1
Colinton Gr EH11......120 D2
Colinton Gr W EH11...120 D2
Colinton Mains Cres
  EH13.................149 E6
Colinton Mains Dr EH13..149 E6
Colinton Mains Gdn
  EH13.................149 D8
Colinton Mains Gn EH13 .149 D7
Colinton Mains Gr EH13 .149 E7
Colinton Mains Loan
  EH13.................149 D7
Colinton Mains Pl EH13..149 E7
Colinton Mains Rd EH13 .149 D6
Colinton Mains Terr
  EH13.................149 E7
Colinton Rd
  Edinburgh,Colinton EH13..149 C7
  Edinburgh,Firr Hill EH13..120 E3
  Edinburgh,Firr Hill EH13,
  EH14.................149 D8
Colinton Mains Gn EH13 .149 D7
Colinton Mains Rd EH13 .149 D6
Colinton Mains St EH13..149 D7
Colinton Mains Terr
  EH13.................149 E7
College Cres FK2........60 D7
College Rdbt EH54.....143 D2
College Wynd EH1......229 A2
Colliers La EH48.......139 E5
Colliers Rd FK7.........8 D4
Colliery Cres EH21......174 A4
Colliery View EH21.....174 B4
Collingwood Ct FK1.....59 E5
Collins Cres KY1........47 F2
Collins Rd FK1.........93 B2
Colliston Rd KY11.......29 D6
Coll Pl FK3.............61 D6
Collyland Rd FK10 ......5 D3
Colmestone Gate EH10..150 A6
Colonsay Ave FK2.......61 D2
Colonsay Terr FK1.......60 B2
Colquhoun St FK7.......7 C6
Colquhoun Terr FK7.....7 C6
Colsnaur FK11..........4 A6
Colstoun Mains Cotts
  EH41.................130 E4
Coltbridge Ave EH12...120 D7
Coltbridge Gdns EH12..120 D7
Coltbridge Millside ⊡
  EH12.................120 E7
Coltbridge Terr EH12...120 D7
Coltbridge Vale ⊡ EH12..120 E7
Coltness Ave ML7......198 A8
Colton Ct KY12.........28 E4
Columba Ave EH4.......92 B2
Columba Rd EH4........92 B2
Columbia Ave EH45...143 E3
Colville Gdns FK10......10 A6
Colville Pl EH3.........93 B2
Colvin St EH42.........78 E3
Combfoot Cotts EH53 .144 C4
Comely Bank EH4.......93 A2
Comely Bank Ave EH4...93 A2
Comely Bank Gr EH4....92 F2
Comely Bank Pl EH4....93 A2
Comely Bank Place Mews ⊡
  EH4..................93 A2
Comely Bank Rd EH4....93 A2
Comely Bank Row EH4...93 A2
Comely Bank St EH4....92 F2
Comely Bank Terr ⊡ EH4 .93 A2
Comely Green Cres ⊡
  EH7..................94 A1
Comely Green Pl ⊡ EH7 .94 A1
Comely Park La KY12....29 A3
Comely Park Prim Sch
  FK1..................60 B4
Comely Park Terr ⊡ FK1 .60 B4
Comely Pk
  Dunfermline KY12.......29 B3
  Grangemouth FK2.......82 E7
Comely Pl FK1..........60 B4
Comely Terr EH7........82 E7
Comiston Dr EH10 .....121 A1
Comiston Gdns EH10...121 A2
Comiston Gr EH10.....150 A7
Comiston Pl EH10......121 B2
Comiston Prim Sch
  EH13.................149 F6
Comiston Rd EH10 ....150 A7
Comiston Rise EH10....150 A7
Comiston Springs Ave
  EH10.................150 A7
Comiston Terr EH10....121 A2
Comiston View EH10...150 A7
Commando Access Way
  KY11..................46 C1
Commercial Prim Sch
  KY11..................29 C3
Commercial Rd KY11....47 C2

Commercial School La ⊠
  KY12..................29 A3
Commercial St
  Edinburgh EH6..........93 F6
  Kirkcaldy KY1..........17 D6
Commercial Wharf EH6 ..94 A6
Commissioner St EH5....64 A8
Commodores Wlk KY11..46 C1
Compass Sch The EH41..129 F8
Compressor House Rd
  FK3...................7 C8
Compton Rd FK3........61 C5
Comrie Terr EH51........63 F6
Comyn Dr FK2..........82 C7
Concorde Way KY11.....47 D3
Coneyhill Rd FK9........2 B7
Coneypark FK7..........6 E6
Conference Sq EH3....228 B2
Congalton Mains Cotts
  EH39..................74 A6
Conifer Rd EH22.......174 A7
Coningsby Pl FK10......10 A6
Connaught Pl EH6......93 D5
Conner Ave FK2.........60 A8
Connolly Dr FK6........36 C4
Connolly Pl FK6........36 E1
Conroy Ct FK6..........36 E1
Considine Gdns ⊠ EH8 .94 C1
Considine Terr ⊠ EH8 ..94 C1
Constable Dr EH6.......7 B6
Constitution St EH6....94 A5
Conway Ct FK1.........59 F4
Cook Cres EH22.......174 D5
Cookies Wynd EH32.....96 E1
Cook Pl KY1............14 B8
Cook St KY1............14 B8
Cooper's La FK10.......23 E4
Cooperage Quay FK8 ....7 C8
Cooperage Way FK10 ...10 D8
Co-operative Bldgs
  EH33.................126 E6
Cooper Bsns Pk EH52...115 E5
Cooper's Cl EH8.......229 B3
Cope La EH32...........97 C4
Copeland Cres KY4......13 B2
Copland Pl FK12.........4 F7
Copper Beech Wynd
  KY12..................27 D1
Corbett Pl KY11.........29 F1
Corbiehall EH51.........63 E7
Corbiehill Ave EH4......92 A3
Corbiehill Cres EH4.....91 F3
Corbiehill Gdns EH4....92 A3
Corbiehill Gr EH4.......92 A3
Corbiehill Pk EH4.......91 F3
Corbiehill Pl EH4.......91 F3
Corbiehill Rd EH4.......92 A3
Corbiehill Terr EH4.....91 F3
Corbieshot EH15.......123 B5
Corbiewood Dr FK7......19 E8
Corbiewynd EH15......123 B5
Cordiner's Land EH1...228 C2
Cordiner Cl FK8..........1 F2
Corentin Ct FK1.........60 A7
Cormailin Pl KY12.......26 B2
Cornbank St James' Prim
  Sch EH26.............191 D5
Corn Exchange Rd ⊡ FK8 ..7 B7
Corn Exchange Village
  EH14.................120 C3
Cornfield Rd EH54......143 B4
Cornhill Cres FK7.......7 B3
Cornhill Terr EH6........94 B4
Cornton Bsns Pk FK9 ....2 B2
Cornton Cres FK9.......2 A5
Cornton Prim Sch FK9...2 A4
Cornton Rd FK9.........2 A4
Cornton Vale Cotts FK9 ..2 A4
Cornwalls Pl EH3........93 D2
Cornwall St EH1........228 B2
Corona Cres FK4.......57 F5
Coronation Pl
  Easthouses EH22......174 D7
  Skinflats FK2...........39 F3
  Tranent EH33.........126 C6
Corpach Dr KY12........28 F2
Corporation St FK1......60 C4
Corrennie Dr EH10.....121 B2
Corrennie Gdns EH10...121 B1
Corrie Ave FK5.........38 F4
Corrie Ct EH22.........174 B4
Corrie Pl FK1..........59 D8
Corslet Cres EH14.....148 B5
Corslet Pl EH14........148 A5
Corslet Rd EH14.......148 A5
Corston Pk EH54......144 A4
Corstorphine Bank Ave
  EH12.................119 D7
Corstorphine Bank Dr
  EH12.................119 D7
Corstorphine Bank Terr
  EH12.................119 D7
Corstorphine High St
  EH12.................119 D6
Corstorphine Hill Ave
  EH12.................119 E7
Corstorphine Hill Cres
  EH12.................119 E7
Corstorphine Hill Gdns
  EH12.................119 E7
Corstorphine Hill Rd
  EH12.................119 E7
Corstorphine Hopl EH12 .119 F6
Corstorphine House Ave ⊡
  EH12.................119 E6
Corstorphine House Terr ⊡
  EH12.................119 E6

Corstorphine Park Gdns
  EH12.................119 E6
Corstorphine Prim Sch
  EH12.................119 D6
Corstorphine Rd EH12..120 B7
Cortachy Ave FK2.......39 A3
Cortleferry Dr EH22....152 E1
Cortleferry Gr EH22....152 E1
Cortleferry Pk ⊡ EH22..152 E1
Cortleferry Terr ⊠ EH22..152 E1
Corunna CH ML8.......215 B1
Corunna Pl EH6.........93 F5
Corunna Terr EH26....192 A8
Cossars Wynd EH21.....78 D2
Costkea Way EH20.....172 A8
Cotburn Cres KY3.......33 F2
Cotland Dr FK2.........59 F8
Cotlands Ave EH32......98 D4
Cotlands Pk EH32.......98 D4
Cotlaws EH29...........89 A1
Cottage Cres FK1.......59 E5
Cottage Gn EH4..........91 B4
Cottage Homes EH13...149 B7
Cottage La EH21.......124 E5
Cottage Pk EH4.........92 A1
Cottages The EH42......77 F1
Cotton La FK2..........61 A3
Cotts The EH49.........86 F3
Coulport Pl KY12........28 F2
Council Hos EH39......101 E7
Countess Ave EH42.....78 D2
Countess Cres EH42....78 D2
Countess of Moray Hospl
  KY3...................49 B7
Countess Rd EH42......78 D2
County Hos KY4.........31 A6
County Rd EH32........96 E1
County Sq EH32........96 E1
Couper Ave EH39.......54 C6
Couperfield EH6........93 F6
Couper Gr KY11........29 F3
Couper St EH6..........93 F6
Courthill FK12............5 A7
Court St EH41.........130 A8
Courtyard The Falkirk FK1 ..60 E3
  Oakley KY12............26 F5
Cousin's La ⊠ KY12.....28 F4
Cousland Cres EH47...142 B1
Cousland Intc EH54....143 F5
Cousland Prim Sch
  EH22.................154 D5
Cousland Rd
  Dalkeith EH22........153 D4
  Livingston,Craigshill EH54..144 A6
  Livingston,Livingston Village
  EH54.................143 C4
Couston Dr EH47......142 B1
Couston Pl KY11........48 B4
Couston Rd KY11.......48 B4
Couston St KY11........29 A4
Cove Cres ML7........179 E6
Covenanter Rd ML7....159 D4
Covenanters La EH30....68 B1
Covenanters Rise KY11...46 C6
Cowal Pl KY11..........30 C1
Cowan's Cl EH8.......229 B1
Cowane St FK8..........2 B1
Cowan Rd EH11.......120 E4
Cowan Terr EH26......191 F7
Cowan Rd Bathgate EH48 .141 C5
  Bonnybridge FK4........58 A6
Cowan Terr EH26......191 F7
Cowdenbeath Bsns Ctr
  KY4...................13 D3
Cowdenbeath Prim Sch
  KY4...................13 D3
Cowdenbeath Rd KY3....33 E2
Cowdenbeath Sta KY4 ..13 D3
Cowden Cres EH22.....153 D3
Cowden Gr EH22.......153 D3
Cowden Hill Gdns FK4...58 B6
Cowdenhill Rd EH51.....64 B7
Cowden La EH22.......153 D3
Cowden Pk EH22.......153 D3
Cowden Terr EH22.....153 D3
Cowden View EH22.....153 D3
Cowgate EH1..........229 A2
Cowgatehead EH1.....229 A2
Cowiehall Rd FK7.......20 D8
Cowie Prim Sch FK7....20 D7
Cowie Rd Bannockburn FK7 ..7 E1
  Cowie FK7............20 D8
Cowpits Ford Rd EH21 ..124 C3
Cowpits Rd EH21......124 D2
Cow Wynd FK1.........60 B4
Coxfield EH11.........120 C4
Coxithill Rd FK7..........7 A3
Cragganmore FK10 ......4 A2
Craigallan Rhs FK51....64 B7
Craig Ave
  Haddington EH41......101 B1
  Whitburn EH47.......160 F6
Craigbank Alloa FK10.....5 C1
  Crossford KY12.........26 D3
Craigbank Prim Sch FK10 ..5 C1
Craigbank Rd FK1......110 A5
Craigbeath Ct KY4......13 B5
Craigburn Ct ⊠ FK1.....59 F2
Craig Cres FK9..........2 D2
Craigcrook Ave EH4.....92 A2
Craigcrook Gdns EH4...92 B1
Craigcrook Pl ⊠ EH4....92 A1
Craigcrook Pl ⊠ EH4....92 C2
Craigcrook Rd
  Edinburgh EH4.........91 F3
  Edinburgh EH4.........92 A1
Craigcrook Sq EH4......92 A2

Craigcrook Terr 5 EH4 ...92 C2
Craig Ct Bridge of A FK9.....2 A5
  Burntisland KY3...............33 D2
Craigdimas KY11.......48 A2
Craigen Ave KY2........16 B7
Craigearn Pl KY2........16 C7
Craigencalt Farm KY3....34 D4
Craigend Dr FK2........83 A6
Craigend Pk EH16 ......122 C1
Craigend Rd FK7 ....7 A3
Craigengar Ave EH52....115 A4
Craigentinny Ave EH54...144 A4
Craigentinny Ave EH7...94 E2
Craigentinny Ave N EH6..94 D4
Craigentinny Cres EH7...94 E2
Craigentinny Gr EH7 ....94 E1
Craigentinny Pl EH7 ....94 E1
Craigentinny Prim Sch
  EH7.....................94 D2
Craigentinny Rd EH7....94 D2
Craigflower Ct KY12....26 E1
Craigflower Gdns KY12...26 E1
Craigflower Ho KY12.....26 E1
Craigflower View KY12...43 E8
Craigfoot Pl KY1........35 B7
Craigfoot Wlk KY1......35 B7
Craigford Dr FK7........7 D1
Craigforth Cres FK8.......1 F1
Craighall Ave EH6......93 C6
Craighall Bank EH6......93 C6
Craighall Cres EH6......93 C5
Craighall Gdns EH6......93 C5
Craighall Rd EH6........93 C6
Craighall St EH6..........1 E1
Craighall Terr
  Edinburgh EH6..........93 C5
  Musselburgh EH21......124 F6
Craighill Gdns EH10....120 F1
Craighill View EH48....138 E3
Craigholm La KY3.......33 F1
Craighorn FK11..........45 A5
Craighorn Dr FK1.......59 E2
Craighorn Rd FK12......4 E6
Craighouse Ave EH10...120 F2
Craighouse Gdns EH10...120 F2
Craighouse Pk EH10....120 F2
Craighouse Rd EH10....120 F2
Craighouse Terr EH10...120 F2
Craigiefield Cres EH26..191 E4
Craigie Ct FK5...........38 B2
Craigielaw Farm Cotts
  EH32....................71 B4
Craigielaw Pk EH32.....71 A4
Craigievar Ave FK2.....39 A3
Craigievar Cl KY12......29 E5
Craigievar Gdns KY2....16 E5
Craigievar Sq EH12 ....119 B7
Craigievar Wynd EH12 ..119 A7
Craiginn Ct EH48........138 D3
Craiginn Terr EH48......138 D3
Craiglaw EH52..........114 C2
Craiglaw Pl FK10........114 C2
Craiglaw Terr 3 FK2....82 D8
Craiglea Ct EH48........138 D3
Craiglea Dr EH10.......121 A2
Craiglea Pl EH10........120 F1
Craigleith FK10...........5 E3
Craigleith Ave Falkirk FK1...59 E2
  North Berwick EH39.....54 D6
Craigleith Ave N EH4...120 C8
Craigleith Bank EH4....92 C1
Craigleith Cres EH4.....92 C1
Craigleith Dr EH4........92 C1
Craigleith Gdns EH4....92 C1
Craigleith Gr EH4.......92 C1
Craigleith Hill EH4......92 D1
Craigleith Hill Ave EH4...92 D1
Craigleith Hill Cres EH4...92 D2
Craigleith Hill Gdns EH4...92 E2
Craigleith Hill Gn EH4...92 D2
Craigleith Hill Loan EH4...92 D2
Craigleith Hill Pk EH4...92 D2
Craigleith Hill Row EH4...92 D2
Craigleith Rd
  Edinburgh EH4..........92 E1
  Grangemouth FK3........61 D6
Craig Leith Rd FK7.......7 D6
Craigleith Retail Pk EH4...92 D2
Craigleith Rise EH4.....120 A8
Craigleith Terr FK12......5 A7
Craigleith View
  Edinburgh EH4..........120 D8
  1 North Berwick EH39...54 B7
  Tullibody KY3............4 D3
Craiglockhart Ave EH14...120 C2
Craiglockhart Bank
  EH14....................120 C1
Craiglockhart Dell Rd
  EH14....................120 C2
Craiglockhart Dr N
  EH14....................120 C2
Craiglockhart Dr S EH14...120 C1
Craiglockhart Gdns
  EH14....................120 C2
Craiglockhart Gr EH14..149 C8
Craiglockhart Loan
  EH14....................120 C2
Craiglockhart Pk EH14...120 C2
Craiglockhart Pl EH14...120 C2
Craiglockhart Prim Sch
  EH11....................120 E4
Craiglockhart Quadrant
  EH14....................120 C1

Craiglockhart Rd EH14...120 C1
Craiglockhart Rd N
  EH14....................120 D2
Craiglockhart Sports Ctr
  EH14....................120 D2
Craiglockhart Terr EH14..120 E3
Craiglockhart View
  EH14....................120 D2
Craigluscar Ct KY12....28 B7
Craigluscar La KY12.....28 A6
Craigluscar Rd KY12....28 B7
Craigmillar Castle EH16..122 D2
Craigmillar Castle Ave
  Edinburgh,Craigmillar
  EH16....................122 D3
  Edinburgh,Niddrie Mains
  EH16....................122 E3
Craigmillar Castle Gdns
  EH16....................122 D3
Craigmillar Castle Loan
  EH16....................122 E4
Craigmillar Castle Rd
  EH16....................122 A3
Craigmillar Pk EH16....122 A3
Craigmillar Pl FK5.......38 F4
Craigmore Gdns EH54...26 C1
Craigmount KY2.........16 D7
Craigmount App EH12..119 C7
Craigmount Ave EH12..119 C7
Craigmount Ave N EH4..91 B1
Craigmount Bank EH4...91 B1
Craigmount Bank W EH4..91 B1
Craigmount Brae EH12..91 A1
Craigmount Cres EH12..119 C8
Craigmount Ct EH4......91 B2
Craigmount Dr EH12....119 C8
Craigmount Gdns EH12...119 C7
Craigmount Gr EH12....119 C7
Craigmount Gr N EH12..119 B8
Craigmount Hill EH4....91 B1
Craigmount Loan EH12...119 B8
Craigmount Pk EH12....119 C7
Craigmount Pl EH12....119 C8
Craigmount Terr EH12..119 C7
Craigmount View EH12..119 B8
Craigmount Way EH12...91 C1
Craigmyle St KY12......29 D5
Craigomus Cres FK11....3 F6
Craigour Ave EH17.....151 D8
Craigour Cres EH17.....151 E8
Craigour Dr EH17.......151 E8
Craigour Gdns EH17....151 D8
Craigour Gn EH17.......151 D7
Craigour Gr EH17.......151 E8
Craigour Loan EH17.....151 E8
Craigour Park Prim Sch
  EH17....................151 E7
Craigour Pl EH17.......122 D1
Craigour Terr EH17.....151 E8
Craigpark EH48.........111 F5
Craigpark Ave EH28....117 C2
Craigpark Cres EH28....117 C2
Craigridge Rd KY11.....48 C5
Craigrie Rd FK10........11 A4
Craigrigg Cotts EH48...110 F3
Craigrigg Terr EH48....110 F3
Craigroyston Com High Sch
  EH4....................92 B4
Craigroyston Gr EH4....92 A4
Craigroyston Pl EH4....92 A5
Craigroyston Prim Sch
  EH4....................92 B4
Craigs Ave EH12.......119 C6
Craigs Bank EH12......119 B7
Craigs Chalet Pk EH49..84 B4
Craigs Cres
  Edinburgh EH12........119 C7
  Grangemouth FK3........82 F7
Craigs Ct EH48.........111 F5
Craigs Dr EH12.........119 B7
Craigsanquhar EH52....115 A6
Craigs Gdns EH12......119 B7
Craigs Gr EH12.........119 C6
Craigshill E Rd EH54...144 A5
Craigshill St EH54......144 A5
Craigs Loan EH12......119 C7
Craigs Pk EH12.........119 B7
Craigs Rd Edinburgh EH12..119 B7
  West Craigs EH12.......118 B8
Craigs Rdbt FK7.........7 B7
Craig St Blackridge EH48...138 E3
  Rosyth KY11.............47 A4
Craigs Terr FK2..........82 E7
Craigston Dr KY12......29 D5
Craigston Pk KY12......29 D5
Craigs Way FK2.........82 F7
Craigstone Cres EH54...144 A6
Craig The KY11...........46 D3
Craigton Cres FK12......4 F8
Craigton Ct EH52........87 F2
Craigton Pl
  Cowdenbeath KY4......13 C2
  Winchburgh EH52.......87 F2
Craigview Alloa FK10.....5 D2
  Bo'ness FK10............10 A6
Craigward FK10.........10 A4
Craigwell Path KY12....44 D7
Crame Terr EH22.......152 E2
Cramond Ave EH4.......91 C5
Cramond Bank EH4.....91 B5
Cramond Bridge Cotts
  EH4....................90 F3
Cramond Brig Toll EH4..90 F3
Cramond Cres EH4.....91 B5
Cramond Ct FK1.........60 B2

Cramond Gdns
  Edinburgh EH4.........91 B5
  Kirkcaldy KY2...........16 F7
Cramond Glebe Gdns EH4..91 C4
Cramond Glebe Rd EH4..91 B6
Cramond Glebe Terr EH4..91 B6
Cramond Gn EH4.......91 B5
Cramond Gr EH4........91 B5
Cramond Pk EH4........91 B5
Cramond Pl
  Dalgety Bay KY11......48 C4
  Edinburgh EH4.........91 C5
Cramond Prim Sch EH4..91 B5
Cramond Prim Sch (Annexe)
  EH4....................91 B6
Cramond Rd N EH4.....91 C5
Cramond Rd S EH4.....91 E4
Cramond Regis EH4.....91 A5
Cramond Roman Fort
  EH4....................91 C6
Cramond Terr EH4......91 B5
Cramond Vale EH4......91 A5
Cramond Village EH4....91 B7
Cranshaws Dr FK2.......61 C2
Cranston Dr EH22.......156 D5
Cranston Prim Sch EH37..175 E6
Cranston St
  Edinburgh EH8.........229 B3
  Penicuik EH26..........191 E5
Crarae Ave EH12.......120 D8
Crathes Ave FK5.........39 A4
Crathes Gdns EH54.....164 E6
Crathie Dr FK6..........36 D3
Crathie Way KY11.......30 A4
Craufurdland EH4........91 A3
Crawfield Ave EH51......63 D6
Crawfield La EH51........63 F5
Crawfield Rd EH51......63 E4
Crawford Dr FK2.........82 B7
Crawford Pl KY12.......29 C7
Crawford Sh Arc The 3
  FK8......................7 B7
Crawford Sq FK2........22 D4
Crawford Rd EH16.....122 A3
Crawlees Cres EH22....174 E6
Craws Knowe ML11....201 A1
Creel Ct EH39...........54 C7
Ceran Dr FK6............57 D6
Crescent The
  Edinburgh EH10.......121 A2
  Gorebridge EH23.......174 C3
  Rosyth KY11.............46 B1
Crest Bsns Ctr FK7.......7 D5
Creteil Ct FK1...........60 C3
Creteil Pl FK3...........61 D8
Crewe Bank EH5.........92 E5
Crewe Cres EH5........92 E5
Crewe Gr EH5..........92 E5
Crewe Loan EH5........92 D5
Crewe Pl EH5..........92 D5
Crewe Rd N EH5........92 D6
Crewe Rd S EH4........92 E3
Crewe Rd W EH5........92 D5
Crewe Road Gdns EH5..92 D5
Crewe Terr EH5.........92 E5
Crewe Toll EH4..........92 D4
Crichton Ave EH37.....176 A5
Crichton Castle EH37..196 E7
Crichton Dr
  Grangemouth FK3......61 E8
  Pathhead EH37........176 A5
Crichton Rd EH37......176 A5
Crichton St EH8.........229 A2
Crichton Terr EH37.....176 A5
Cricketfield Pl EH48....140 A5
Cricket Rd EH3..........61 C1
Crighton Pl 2 EH6......93 F3
Crimond Pl EH51........81 E7
Crinan Pl KY11..........30 A4
Cringate Gdns FK7.......7 F1
Croall St 6 EH7..........93 E2
Crockers Hedges ML11..102 C4
Crockett Gdns EH26....191 D5
Crockett Pl FK2..........60 B8
Croft's Rd FK10...........4 B3
Croft-An-Righ EH8......229 C4
Crofters Ct KY4..........35 A4
Crofters Way EH47.....161 E6
Croft Est FK4............57 B3
Croftfoot Dr EH47......182 A6
Croftfoot Pl FK6..........36 D4
Croft Gdns KY12........27 C7
Crofthead Ct FK8........2 A1
Crofthead Ctr EH54....164 D8
Crofthead Intc EH54....164 F8
Crofthead Rd Stirling FK8..2 A1
  Stoneyburn EH47.......162 A1
Crofthead St EH37......59 F8
Croftmalloch Prim Sch
  EH47....................161 B5
Croftmalloch Rd EH47..161 B5
Croft Pl EH54............143 C5
Croftsacre TD13........218 F3
Croftshaw Rd FK12......5 A7
Croftside Ct FK3..........61 E6
Crofts Rd TD13.........218 F3
Croft St Dalkeith EH22...153 A3
  Penicuik EH26..........191 E4
Crofts The EH42........104 C1
Cromar Dr KY11.........47 C8
Cromarty Campus KY11..46 C1
Cromarty Ct EH54......144 C4
Cromarty Pl KY1.........17 E7
Crombie Prim Sch KY12..47 D7

Cromwell Anchorage
  EH42....................78 E3
Cromwell Ct EH42......78 E3
Cromwell Dr FK1........60 D4
Cromwell Pl EH6........93 E6
Cromwell Quay EH42...78 E3
Cromwell Rd
  Burntisland KY3........33 F1
  Falkirk FK1..............60 D4
  North Berwick EH39....54 A7
  Rosyth KY11.............46 F5
Cromwell Rd W FK1....60 D4
Crookston Ct EH21.....124 E4
Crookston Rd EH21.....124 E4
Crophill FK10.............5 C2
Crosbies Ct FK8..........7 B7
Cross Brae FK1..........81 D6
Cross Cotts EH32........97 A1
Crossen La ML8........215 B1
Crossford Prim Sch KY12..28 A2
Crossgatehead Rd FK2..82 D8
Crossgates Prim Sch KY4...30 E6
Crossgreen Dr EH52....115 A5
Crossgreen Pl EH52....115 A5
Crosshall Pl FK1.........60 D6
Crosshill Dr
  Bathgate EH48.........141 C6
  Bo'ness EH51...........63 F5
Cross Loan EH35.......155 F7
Crossroads KY11........30 B5
Crossroads Pl KY11.....46 F4
Cross Row KY11........48 B4
Cross St Dysart KY1.....18 A2
  Falkirk FK2..............39 B1
Cross The 8 Alloa FK10..10 B6
  Linlithgow EH49........85 A7
  Lochgelly KY5...........14 B7
  Pencaitland EH34.....156 E6
Cross Way KY11........48 C5
Crosswood Ave EH14...168 B8
Crosswood Cres EH14..168 B8
Crosswood Terr EH55...203 F3
Cross Wynd KY12.......29 A4
Crowhill Rd KY11........48 D4
Crownest Loan FK5......38 D2
Crown Ct 3 EH33......126 D6
Crown Gdns FK10.......9 F8
Crown Pl EH6............93 F4
Crown St EH6............93 F4
Cruachan Ave FK9.......2 B3
Cruachan Ct Falkirk FK1...60 C2
  Penicuik EH26..........192 A6
Cruachan Pl FK3.........61 F5
Cruckburn Wynd FK7.....6 F4
Cruden Rd EH51........62 D5
Cruickness Rd KY11.....68 C8
Cruickshank Dr FK1.....81 D6
Cruikshank's Ct FK6....36 E1
Crum Cres FK7..........7 C2
Crusader Ct EH54.......144 A1
Crusader Dr EH25......171 F3
Crusader Rise EH54....144 A1
Crystalmount EH22.....153 A4
Cuddies La EH13........149 B7
Cuddyhouse Rd KY4,KY12..12 D3
Cuddy La EH10..........121 A4
Cuffabouts EH51.........64 D7
Cuguen Pl EH18........152 B1
Cuiken Ave EH26.......191 E6
Cuiken Bank EH26......191 D6
Cuikenburn EH26......191 E7
Cuiken Prim Sch EH26..191 E6
Cuiken Terr EH26.......191 E6
Cuil Gr KY12.............28 D5
Cuillin Ct FK1...........60 C1
Cuillin Pl FK3............61 F5
Culduie Circ FK2.........42 C8
Cullalo Cres KY3........49 C8
Cullaloe Ct KY11........48 C5
Cullaloe Nature Reserve
  KY3....................32 B4
Cullaloe View KY4......13 C2
Cullen Cres KY2.........16 E7
Cullen Sq EH54.........142 D6
Culloch Rd KY11........108 B6
Culmore Pl FK1..........60 E1
Culpers Prim Sch KY12..42 C8
Culrain Pl EH19.........173 A6
Culross Abbey KY12.....25 D1
Culross Palace KY12....42 C8
Culross Prim Sch KY12..42 D8
Cultenhove Cres
  Grangemouth FK3......61 E6
  Stirling FK7.............7 A3
Cultenhove Pl FK7.......7 A3
Cultenhove Rd
  Stirling,Coxet Hill FK7...7 A4
  Stirling FK7.............7 A4
Cultins Rd EH11........119 B3
Cultrig Dr EH47.........161 A5
Culvain Pl FK1..........60 C2
Culzean Cres KY2.......16 C7
Culzean Pl FK5..........38 F4
Cumberland St EH3....93 C2
Cumbrae Ct KY2........17 A8
Cumbrae Dr FK1.........59 C4
Cumbrae Pl KY2........17 A8
Cumin Pl EH9...........121 E4
Cumledon Ave EH12...120 C8
Cumnor Cres EH16.....122 A1
Cunnigar Gdns EH53...144 C4
Cunnigar View EH53...144 C4
Cunnigar Ho EH53.....144 C4
Cunningham Cres EH52..115 D6
Cunningham Ct
  North Berwick EH39....54 A6
Cunningham Dr ML7...159 D5
Cunningham Gdns FK2..60 F5

Cunningham Rd
  Rosyth KY11.............46 D2
  Stenhousemuir FK5.....39 A3
  Stirling FK7..............7 D7
Cunningham St FK1....61 C6
Curlew Brae EH54.....143 D5
Curlew Gdns KY11.....30 A2
Curling Knowe KY4....30 F6
Curling Pk KY4.........30 F6
Curling Pond La EH47..161 B1
Curran Cres EH52.....115 F5
Currie High Sch EH14...147 F4
Curriehill Castle Dr
  EH14....................147 D4
Curriehill Prim Sch
  EH14....................148 A4
Curriehill Rd EH14......147 F5
Curriehill Sta EH14.....147 F5
Currieside Ave ML7.....179 E4
Currieside Pl ML7.......179 E4
Currievale Ave EH14....147 E4
Currievale Farm EH14...147 E4
Currievale Park Gr EH14..147 E4
Currievale Pk EH14.....147 E4
Cushenquarter Dr FK7..20 D3
Custom House Sq EH42..78 E3
Customs Rdbt FK8.......2 B1
Customs Wharf EH6.....94 A6
Custonhall Pl FK6........36 D2
Cuthill Brae EH55.......162 E3
Cuthill Cres EH47.......162 C2
Cuthill Terr EH47........162 C2
Cuttyfield Pl FK2........39 C3
Cypress Glade EH54....164 D7
Cypress Gr KY11.........46 C8

D

D'arcy Cres EH22.......174 F7
D'arcy Rd EH22.........174 E6
D'arcy Terr EH22........174 E7
Daiches Braes EH15....123 D6
Daintree Terr FK1.......59 E5
Dairy Cotts EH39........53 A1
Daisyhill Ct EH47.......162 D7
Daisyhill Rd EH47......162 D6
Daisy Terr EH11.........120 E6
Dalbeath Cres KY4......13 A2
Dalbeath Gdns KY4.....12 F1
Dalcross Way KY12.....29 E5
Dalderse Ave FK2.......60 B6
Dalgety Ave EH7.........94 B6
Dalgety Bay Prim Sch
  KY11....................48 B4
Dalgety Bay Sta KY11...47 F5
Dalgety Gdns KY11.....48 C5
Dalgety House View KY11..48 D4
Dalgety Rd EH7.........94 B2
Dalgleish Ct FK8..........7 B8
Dalgrain Ind Est FK3....40 C1
Dalgrain Rd FK3.........40 C1
Dalhousie Ave EH19....173 A6
Dalhousie Ave W EH19..173 A6
Dalhousie Bank EH22...152 F2
Dalhousie Bsns Pk EH19..173 D4
Dalhousie Cres EH22...152 F1
Dalhousie Dr EH19.....173 A6
Dalhousie Gdns EH19..173 A6
Dalhousie Pl EH19......173 A6
Dalhousie Rd EH22.....152 E1
Dalhousie Rd E EH19...173 A5
Dalhousie Rd W EH19...173 A6
Dalhousie Terr EH10....121 A2
Dalkeith Ctry Pk EH22...153 D5
Dalkeith High Sch EH22..153 D5
Dalkeith Rd
  Edinburgh,Prestonfield
  EH16....................122 A4
  Edinburgh,St Leonard's
  EH16....................229 C1
Dalkeith St EH15........123 C7
Dallas Ave KY2..........33 F1
Dalling Dr EH48.........140 F5
Dalmahoy Cres EH14...147 C3
Dalmahoy Rd EH28.....117 D2
Dalmeny Prim Sch EH30..89 D7
Dalmeny Rd EH6........93 D5
Dalmeny St EH6.........93 F3
Dalmeny Sta EH30......89 D8
Dalmeny View KY11....48 C4
Dalmore Dr FK12........4 E8
Dalmorglen Pk FK7......6 F4
Dalratho Rd FK3.........61 E8
Dalry Gait EH11.........120 F7
Dalrymple Cres
  Edinburgh EH9.........121 E4
  Musselburgh EH21......124 C6
Dalrymple Gdns EH21..154 D5
Dalrymple Loan EH21..124 C5
Dalry Pl EH11...........228 A2
Dalry Prim Sch EH11...120 F6
Dalton Ct EH22.........174 E5
Dalum Ct EH20.........172 A8
Dalum Dr EH20.........172 A8
Dalum Gr EH20.........172 A8
Dalum Loan EH20.......172 A8
Daly Gdns EH20.........25 F8
Dalziel Ct EH47.........162 C2
Dalziel Pl EH7...........94 B1

Damhead Holdings Scheme
Bilston EH10 . . . . 171 C8
Edinburgh EH10 . . . . 150 D1
Damside EH4 . . . . 228 A3
Danderhall Cres EH22 . . . . 152 B7
Danderhall Prim Sch
EH22 . . . . 152 B8
Dania Ct EH11 . . . . 119 F4
Daniel Pl KY11 . . . . .46 C5
Danube St EH4 . . . . 228 A4
Dargai Pl EH52 . . . . 115 A5
Darian La EH51 . . . . .63 F7
Darmeid Pl ML7 . . . . 198 B8
Darnaway St EH3 . . . . 228 B4
Darnell Rd EH5 . . . . .93 B5
Darney Terr KY3 . . . . .34 F2
Darnley St EH8 . . . . 7 A8
Darrach Dr FK6 . . . . .36 A2
Darroch Ct EH8 . . . . 229 B3
Darwin St EH54 . . . . 144 A5
Davaar Dr KY2 . . . . .16 E8
Davaar Pl FK1 . . . . .59 C4
Davenport Pl KY11 . . . . .46 F3
David's Loan FK2 . . . . .39 D1
David Cres KY11 . . . . .47 A8
David Henderson Ct KY12 . .29 A4
David Millar Pl 5 KY12 . . . .28 E5
David Scott Ave EH22 . . . . 174 E7
Davidson's Mains Prim Sch
EH4 . . . . .91 F3
Davidson Gdns EH4 . . . . . . .92 A3
Davidson La ML8 . . . . 215 B1
Davidson Pk EH4 . . . . .92 E3
Davidson Pl EH41 . . . . 100 F1
Davidson Rd EH4 . . . . .92 E3
Davidson St FK7 . . . . .7 C1
Davidson Terr EH41 . . . . . 100 F1
Davidson Way EH54 . . . . . 143 E7
David St Dunfermline KY12 . .29 A5
  Kirkcaldy KY1 . . . . .17 B3
  Lochgelly KY5 . . . . .14 B8
David The First St KY3 . . . . .34 F2
Davies Row Denny FK6 . . . . .36 E2
  Edinburgh EH11 . . . . 119 D6
Davie St EH8 . . . . 229 B2
Daviot Rd KY12 . . . . .29 E5
Dawson Ave Alloa FK10 . . . . .9 F8
  Livingston EH54 . . . . 143 F5
Dawson Pl EH51 . . . . .63 E5
Dawson St FK2 . . . . .60 B8
Deacons Ct EH49 . . . . .85 A5
Dean Acres KY12 . . . . .26 D7
Dean Bank La EH3 . . . . .93 B2
Deanbank Pl EH23 . . . . 195 D7
Dean Br EH4 . . . . 228 A4
Deanburn EH26 . . . . 191 E7
Deanburn Gdns EH47 . . . . 142 B5
Deanburn Pk EH4 . . . . .84 F5
Deanburn Prim Sch EH51 . .63 D5
Deanburn Rd EH49 . . . . .84 F5
Deanburn Wlk EH51 . . . . . . .63 D6
Dean Cres FK8 . . . . .2 C1
Dean Ct EH32 . . . . .98 C4
Dean Dr KY12 . . . . .28 A2
Deanery Cl EH7 . . . . .94 C1
Deanfield Cres EH51 . . . . . .63 E7
Deanfield Dr EH51 . . . . .63 E6
Deanfield Pl EH51 . . . . .63 E7
Deanfield Rd EH51 . . . . .63 E6
Deanfield Terr EH51 . . . . . . .63 E7
Dean Gallery EH4 . . . . 120 F8
Deangate Gdns EH51 . . . . . .63 D6
Dean Gr KY12 . . . . .28 B2
Deanhaugh St EH3 . . . . .93 B2
Deanpark Ave EH14 . . . . . . 147 C1
Deanpark Bank EH14 . . . . 147 C1
Deanpark Brae EH14 . . . . . 147 C1
Deanpark Cres EH14 . . . . . 147 C1
Dean Park Cres EH4 . . . . . 228 A4
Deanpark Gdns EH14 . . . . . 147 C1
Deanpark Gr EH14 . . . . 147 C1
Dean Park Mews EH4 . . . . . .93 A2
Deanpark Pl EH14 . . . . 147 C1
Dean Park Pl EH22 . . . . 174 A5
Dean Park Prim Sch
EH14 . . . . 168 C8
Dean Park Prim Sch Annexe
EH14 . . . . 147 C2
Deanpark Sq EH14 . . . . 147 C1
Dean Path EH4 . . . . .92 F1
Dean Path Bldgs EH4 . . . . . .93 A2
Dean Plc Gowkhall KY12 . . . .27 E7
  Longniddry EH32 . . . . .98 C4
  Newtongrange EH22 . . . . 174 A5
Dean Pl Penicuik EH26 . . . 191 D6
  Seafield EH47 . . . . 142 B1
Dean Rd Bo'ness EH51 . . . . .63 E6
  Kirkcaldy KY2 . . . . .17 A4
  Longniddry EH32 . . . . .98 C4
  Penicuik EH26 . . . . 191 D6
Dean Ridge KY12 . . . . .27 E7
Deans Com High Sch
EH54 . . . . 143 A7
Deans East Rd
  Livingston,Deans EH54 . . 142 F7
  Livingston,Nether Dechmont
  EH54 . . . . 143 A6
Deans Ind Est EH54 . . . . . 142 C6
Deans North Rd
  Livingston, Deans EH54 . . 142 E6
  Livingston, Nether Dechmont
  EH54 . . . . 143 A6

Deans Prim Sch EH54 . . . . 142 E5
Deans Rd EH54 . . . . 142 D6
Deans Rdbt EH54 . . . . 142 D5
Deans S EH54 . . . . 142 E5
Deans Service Units
  EH54 . . . . 142 E6
Dean St Edinburgh EH4 . . . . .93 A2
  Whitburn EH47 . . . . 161 A6
Deanswood Pk EH54 . . . . . 142 E5
Dean Terr Edinburgh EH4 . . 228 A4
  Rosewell EH24 . . . . 172 D1
Dean The EH40 . . . . .75 E1
Deantown Ave EH21 . . . . . 153 E8
Deantown Dr EH21 . . . . . . 124 E1
Deantown Path EH21 . . . . 124 E1
Deas Rd Inverkeithing KY11 . .47 B2
  Shotts ML7 . . . . 179 C5
Deas Wharf KY1 . . . . .17 C8
Dechmont Inf Sch EH52 . . 114 B2
Dechmont Rd EH12 . . . . . . 119 A6
Dechmont Rdbt EH52 . . . . 114 D2
Dedridge East Ind Est
  EH54 . . . . 144 A1
Dedridge East Rd EH54 . . . 144 A1
Dedridge North Rd
  EH54 . . . . 164 D8
Dedridge Prim Sch
  EH54 . . . . 144 A2
Dedridge West Rd EH54 . . 164 E8
Dee Dr EH54 . . . . 144 A1
Dee Pl KY11 . . . . .29 F2
Deep Sea World (Sealife Ctr)
  KY11 . . . . .68 C5
Deerhill EH52 . . . . 114 C2
Deerpark FK10 . . . . .5 E1
Deer Park Dr EH54 . . . . . . 114 D1
Deerpark North Rd EH54 . . . .5 F1
Deer Park Rd
  Abercorn EH30 . . . . .66 F2
  Dechmont EH54 . . . . 114 D1
Deer Path ML7 . . . . 159 E5
Deeside Dr ML8 . . . . 215 A3
Deeside Pl KY11 . . . . .30 C1
Dee St ML7 . . . . 179 D5
Delisle St EH42 . . . . .78 D2
Dell Ave EH48 . . . . 139 E6
Dell Rd EH13 . . . . 149 B7
Delph Rd FK10 . . . . .4 C2
Delphwood Cres FK10 . . . . . .4 D2
Delph Wynd FK10 . . . . .4 C2
Delta Ave EH21 . . . . 125 A5
Delta Cres EH21 . . . . 125 A6
Delta Dr EH21 . . . . 125 A5
Delta Gdns EH21 . . . . 125 A5
Delta Pl EH21 . . . . 124 D4
Delta Rd EH21 . . . . 125 A5
Delta View EH21 . . . . 125 A6
De Moray Ct FK9 . . . . .2 A4
Demorehann Ave FK6 . . . . . .36 F1
Dempster Pl KY12 . . . . .28 F5
Denburn Pl KY1 . . . . .17 C6
Denburn Rd KY1 . . . . .17 D7
Denend Cres KY12 . . . . .27 B6
Denham Green Ave EH5 . . . .93 B5
Denham Green Pl EH5 . . . . .93 B5
Denham Green Terr EH5 . . . .93 B5
Denholm Ave EH21 . . . . . . 123 F4
Denholm Cr EH21 . . . . 124 A4
Denholm Gr EH48 . . . . 139 E7
Denholm Rd EH21 . . . . 123 F5
Denholm Way EH21 . . . . . . 123 F4
Den La ML7 . . . . 179 D6
Denny High Sch FK6 . . . . . . .57 E8
Denny Prim Sch FK6 . . . . . .57 B8
Denny Rd Denny FK4 . . . . . . .57 E6
  Larbert FK5 . . . . .38 A1
Denovan Rd FK6 . . . . .36 E4
Den Rd KY2,KY1 . . . . .17 C6
De Quincey Path EH18 . . . 172 E6
De Quincey Rd EH18 . . . . . 172 E6
Dequincey Wlk 6 EH33 . . 126 C5
Derby St EH6 . . . . .93 D6
Dervie St EH14 . . . . .79 E5
Derwent Ave FK1 . . . . .59 F4
Devlin Ct FK7 . . . . .7 B2
Devonbank FK10 . . . . .5 E3
Devon Ct FK10 . . . . .4 B2
Devon Dr FK10 . . . . .4 C1
Devon Pl Cambus FK10 . . . . .4 A1
  Edinburgh EH12 . . . . 120 F7
Devon Rd FK10 . . . . .10 C6
Devon St FK3 . . . . .61 A6
Devon Terr KY11 . . . . .29 E2
Devon Valley Dr FK10 . . . . . .5 D2
Devon Village FK10 . . . . .5 E4
Devonway FK10 . . . . .10 F5
Dewar Ave FK10 . . . . .23 E4
Dewar Pl EH3 . . . . 228 A2
Dewar Place La EH3 . . . . . 228 A2
Dewar St FK10 . . . . .14 D5
Dewar St Dunfermline KY12 . .28 F4
  Lochgelly KY5 . . . . .14 A7
Dewshill Cotts ML7 . . . . . 158 B4
Dew Way KY11 . . . . .46 D1
Dickburn Cres FK4 . . . . .57 F5
Dick Cres KY3 . . . . .33 E1
Dick Gdns EH47 . . . . 160 F6
Dickies Wells FK12 . . . . .5 C7
Dick Pl Edinburgh EH9 . . . . 121 D4
  Rosyth KY11 . . . . .46 E5
  Stoneyburn EH47 . . . . . . 162 C2
Dickson Ct
  Dunfermline KY12 . . . . . . .29 A2
  Lochgelly KY5 . . . . .14 A7
Dicksonfield EH7 . . . . .93 E2
Dickson Gr EH19 . . . . 173 B7
Dickson St
  Dunfermline KY12 . . . . . . .29 A1

Dickson St continued
  Edinburgh EH6 . . . . .93 F3
  West Calder EH55 . . . . . . 163 D2
Dick St KY12 . . . . .29 C5
Dick Terr EH26 . . . . 191 F6
Dinmont Dr EH16 . . . . 122 B2
Dirleton Ave EH39 . . . . .54 A7
Dirleton Castle EH39 . . . . . .53 B4
Dirleton Ct EH39 . . . . .53 F7
Dirleton Gdns EH39 . . . . .9 F7
Dirleton La EH39 . . . . .9 F6
Dirleton Prim Sch EH39 . . . .53 A4
Dirleton Rd Dirleton EH39 . .53 B5
  North Berwick EH39 . . . . . .53 E6
Distillery La EH11 . . . . 120 F7
Diverswell FK10 . . . . .5 D2
Dixon Ct EH47 . . . . 160 F5
Dixon Terr EH47 . . . . 161 A5
Dobbie's Rd EH18 . . . . 173 A7
Dobbie Ave Larbert FK5 . . . .59 C8
  Stenhousemuir FK5 . . . . . .38 C1
Dobson's Pl EH41 . . . . 129 F8
Dobson's View EH41 . . . . . 129 F8
Dobson's Wlk EH41 . . . . . . 129 F7
Dochart Cres FK2 . . . . .61 F2
Dochart Dr EH4 . . . . .91 C1
Dochart Path FK3 . . . . .61 D5
Dochart Pl FK1 . . . . .60 D2
Dock Pl EH6 . . . . .93 F6
Dock Rd FK3 . . . . .40 D1
Dock St Bo'ness EH51 . . . . . .64 A8
  Edinburgh EH6 . . . . .93 F6
  Falkirk FK2 . . . . .39 C2
Doctor's Pk FK10 . . . . .23 E3
Dog Well Wynd EH49 . . . . . .85 A7
Dollar Ave FK2 . . . . .60 A7
Dollar Cres KY2 . . . . .16 D7
Dollar Ct 2 KY12 . . . . .28 E5
Dollar Gdns FK2 . . . . .60 A7
Dollar Gr KY3 . . . . .33 E1
Dollar Ind Est FK1,FK2 . . . . .60 A5
Dollar Rd KY3 . . . . .33 E1
Dolphin Ave EH14 . . . . 147 F4
Dolphin Gdns E EH14 . . . . 147 F4
Dolphin Gdns W EH14 . . . . 147 E4
Dolphin Rd EH14 . . . . 147 F4
Donaldson's Coll EH12 . . . 120 F7
Donaldson Ave FK10 . . . . . . .4 C1
Donaldson Ct EH50 . . . . . . .23 E3
Donaldson Pl FK7 . . . . .6 D6
Donald St KY12 . . . . .29 C6
Don Dr EH54 . . . . 144 B5
Donibristle Gdns KY11 . . . . .48 B2
Donibristle Ho KY11 . . . . . . .48 B2
Donibristle Ind Pk KY11 . . . .48 A4
Donibristle Prim Sch
  KY11 . . . . .48 B2
Donnelly Ho FK4 . . . . .2 D6
Don Rd KY11 . . . . .29 F1
Don St FK3 . . . . .40 A1
DoO'cot Brae FK10 . . . . .10 A8
Doocot Brae EH51 . . . . .64 B7
Doocot Pl EH32 . . . . 126 A8
Doo Dells KY3 . . . . .34 F2
Doon Ave EH54 . . . . 144 A4
Doon Hill Hall EH42 . . . . . 106 F4
Doon Wlk EH54 . . . . 144 A4
Dora Ct KY4 . . . . .13 D6
Dorncoch Pl EH14 . . . . .47 C8
Dornie Wynd ML7 . . . . 180 B3
Dorrator Ct FK1 . . . . .59 E5
Dorrator Rd FK1 . . . . .59 E6
Dorset Pl EH10 . . . . 121 A5
Double Dykes EH21 . . . . . . 124 D4
Double Hedges Pk EH16 . . 122 A1
Double Hedges Rd EH16 . . 122 A1
Double Row KY11 . . . . .45 B4
Dougall Ct EH22 . . . . 174 D5
Dougall Pl EH22 . . . . 174 D5
Dougall Rd EH22 . . . . 174 D5
Dougans Sq EH48 . . . . 139 F6
Douglas Ave Airth FK2 . . . . .22 D3
  Grangemouth,Bowhouse
  FK3 . . . . .61 E6
  Grangemouth,Brightons
  FK2 . . . . .82 D8
  Linlithgow EH49 . . . . .84 E6
Douglas Cres
  Bonnyrigg and Lasswade
  EH19 . . . . 173 B7
  Edinburgh EH12 . . . . 120 F8
  Longniddry EH32 . . . . .98 E6
Douglas Dr Bo'ness EH51 . . .63 E6
  Crossford KY12 . . . . .28 A2
  Dunfermline KY12 . . . . . . .28 E5
  Stirling FK7 . . . . .7 C4
Douglas Gardens Mews 5
  EH4 . . . . 120 F8
Douglas Gdns EH4 . . . . 120 F8
Douglas Pk KY12 . . . . .28 E6
Douglas Pl Bo'ness EH51 . . .63 F6
  Linlithgow EH49 . . . . .84 E6
  Stenhousemuir FK5 . . . . . .38 F4
Douglas Rd Bo'ness EH51 . . .63 E6
  Longniddry EH32 . . . . .98 E6
  Rosyth KY11 . . . . .46 C2
Douglas Rise EH54 . . . . . . 144 A2
Douglas St Bannockburn FK7 .7 E2
  Dunfermline KY12 . . . . . . .29 A4
  Kirkcaldy KY1 . . . . .17 B3
  Stirling FK8 . . . . .2 B1
Douglas Terr Bo'ness EH51 . .63 F6
  Edinburgh EH11 . . . . 228 A2
  Stirling FK7 . . . . .6 E6
Douglas Wynd EH52 . . . . . 115 B6
Doune Cres EH55 . . . . .39 A4
Doune Pk KY11 . . . . .48 C4
Doune Terr EH3 . . . . 228 B4

Dovecot Brae EH33 . . . . . . 126 C7
Dovecot Cres KY1 . . . . .18 B8
Dovecote Pl EH54 . . . . 143 C4
Dovecot Gr EH14 . . . . 120 B1
Dovecot Loan EH14 . . . . . . 120 B1
Dovecot Pk Aberdour KY3 . . .49 B6
  Edinburgh EH14 . . . . 149 A8
  Linlithgow EH49 . . . . .85 D8
  Pencaitland EH34 . . . . . . 156 E6
Dovecot Pl
  Dunfermline KY11 . . . . . . .47 A7
  Tullibody KY10 . . . . .4 B3
Dovecot Rd
  Edinburgh EH12 . . . . 119 D5
  Tullibody FK10 . . . . .4 B3
  Westquarter FK2 . . . . .61 A2
Dovecot Way
  Dunfermline KY11 . . . . . . .47 A7
  Pencaitland EH34 . . . . . . 156 E6
Dovecot Wynd KY11 . . . . . . .46 F7
Dovehill FK10 . . . . .10 B8
Dover Dr KY11 . . . . .47 A8
Dover Rd KY11 . . . . .47 A8
Dover Pk KY11 . . . . .47 A8
Dover Way KY11 . . . . .47 A8
Dowan Pl FK7 . . . . .6 E6
Dower Cres EH51 . . . . .64 B8
Dower Pl FK2 . . . . .22 D4
Dowie's Mill La EH4 . . . . . . .90 F4
Dowie's Mill Cotts EH4 . . . .90 F4
Downfield KY4 . . . . .13 C6
Downfield Pl EH11 . . . . 120 F6
Downie Gr EH12 . . . . 119 F6
Downie Pl EH21 . . . . 124 C6
Downie Terr EH12 . . . . 119 E6
Downing Gr EH25 . . . . 172 A4
Downing Point KY11 . . . . . . .48 B2
Downs Cres FK10 . . . . .9 F6
Dr Campbell Ave FK7 . . . . . .20 D8
Dreghorn Ave EH13 . . . . . . 149 E5
Dreghorn Dr EH13 . . . . 149 E5
Dreghorn Gdns EH13 . . . . . 149 E5
Dreghorn Gr EH13 . . . . 149 E5
Dreghorn Junc EH10,
  EH13 . . . . 149 E5
Dreghorn Link EH13 . . . . . 149 F5
Dreghorn Loan EH13 . . . . . 149 E5
Dreghorn Pk EH13 . . . . 149 D6
Dreghorn Pl EH13 . . . . 149 E5
Drem Farm Cotts EH39 . . . .73 A3
Drem Sta EH39 . . . . .73 A3
Drip Rd FK9 . . . . .1 F2
Dronachy Rd KY2 . . . . .16 C4
Drossie Rd FK1 . . . . .60 A3
Drove Loan Cres FK6 . . . . . .57 F2
Drove Loan FK6 . . . . .57 F2
Drove Rd EH48 . . . . 139 F7
Droverhall Ave KY4 . . . . .31 A6
Droverhall Pl KY4 . . . . .31 A6
Drovers Rd EH51 . . . . .64 B6
Drumacre Rd EH51 . . . . .64 B6
Drum Ave EH17 . . . . 151 F5
Drum Brae Dr EH4 . . . . 119 C8
Drum Brae Cres EH4 . . . . . .91 C2
Drum Brae Dr EH4 . . . . .91 C1
Drum Brae Gdns EH12 . . . . 119 C8
Drum Brae Gr EH4 . . . . .91 C1
Drum Brae L Ctr EH4 . . . . . .91 C1
Drum Brae N EH4 . . . . .91 C2
Drum Brae Neuk EH12 . . . . 119 C8
Drum Brae Park App
  EH12 . . . . 119 C8
Drum Brae Pk EH12 . . . . . . 119 C8
Drum Brae S EH12 . . . . 119 C8
Drum Brae Terr EH4 . . . . . . .91 C1
Drum Brae Wlk EH4 . . . . . . .91 B1
Drumclair Ave FK1 . . . . 108 A6
Drum Cotts Bo'ness EH51 . . .64 C6
  Edinburgh EH17 . . . . 151 F5
Drum Cres EH17 . . . . 151 F5
Drumcross Rd EH48 . . . . . 141 B7
Drumdryan St EH3 . . . . 228 B1
Drum Farm La EH51 . . . . . . .64 C6
Drumlanrig Pl FK5 . . . . .38 F4
Drummohr Ave EH21 . . . . . 125 B5
Drummohr Gdns EH21 . . . . 125 B5
Drummond Com High Sch
  EH7 . . . . .93 D2
Drummond La FK8 . . . . .7 A6
Drummond Pk FK5 . . . . .61 C6
Drummond Pl
  Blackridge EH48 . . . . 138 C3
  Bonnybridge FK4 . . . . .58 A7
  Edinburgh FK12 . . . . .29 D5
  Edinburgh EH3 . . . . .93 D2
  Falkirk FK1 . . . . .60 A4
  Grangemouth FK3 . . . . . . .61 E8
  Stirling FK8 . . . . .7 A6
Drummond Place La FK8 . . . .7 A6
Drummond Sq
  Livingston EH54 . . . . 164 C6
  Lochgelly KY5 . . . . .14 B8
Drummond St EH8 . . . . 229 B2
Drummore Dr EH32 . . . . . . 125 E8
Drummormie Rd KY12 . . . . . .27 C1
Drumpark Ave EH51 . . . . . . .64 B6
Drumpark St FK7 . . . . .7 B3
Drum Pl
  East Whitburn EH47 . . . . . 161 E2
  Edinburgh EH17 . . . . 151 F6
Drum Rd Bo'ness EH51 . . . . .64 C6
  Dunfermline KY11 . . . . . . .47 F6

Drumsheugh Gdns EH3 . . . 228 A3
Drumsheugh Pl EH3 . . . . . 228 A2
Drumshoreland Ave
  EH53 . . . . 144 B7
Drumshoreland Cres
  EH53 . . . . 144 B7
Drumshoreland Pl EH53 . . 144 B8
Drumshoreland Rd EH53 . . 144 B7
Drumside Terr EH51 . . . . . . .64 C7
Drum Terr EH7 . . . . .94 A2
Drum View Ave EH22 . . . . . 152 B8
Drumview Gdns EH51 . . . . . .64 A5
Dryburgh Ave FK6 . . . . .36 D2
Dryburgh Way FK3 . . . . .61 F6
Dryden Ave EH20 . . . . 172 A7
Dryden Cotts EH54 . . . . . . 157 F4
Dryden Cres EH20 . . . . 172 A7
Dryden Gait EH7 . . . . .93 E3
Dryden Gdns EH7 . . . . .93 E3
Dryden Glen EH20 . . . . 171 F7
Dryden Gr EH25 . . . . 172 A4
Dryden Loan EH20 . . . . 171 F7
Dryden Pk EH20 . . . . 171 F7
Dryden Pl Edinburgh EH9 . . 121 F5
  Loanhead EH20 . . . . 171 F7
Dryden St EH7 . . . . .93 E3
Dryden Terr Edinburgh EH7 . .93 E3
  Loanhead EH20 . . . . 172 A7
Dryden Vale EH20 . . . . 171 F7
Dryden View EH20 . . . . 172 A7
Drylaw Ave EH4 . . . . .92 C2
Drylaw Cres EH4 . . . . .92 B3
Drylaw Gdns
  East Linton EH40 . . . . 103 D8
Drylaw Gn EH4 . . . . .92 B3
Drylaw Gr EH4 . . . . .92 B2
Drylaw House Gdns EH4 . . . .75 D3
Drylaw House Paddock
  EH4 . . . . .92 B3
Drylaw Terr EH40 . . . . 103 D8
Drylie Ct KY4 . . . . .13 B4
Drylie St KY4 . . . . .13 B4
Drysdale Ave EH47 . . . . . . 161 B7
Drysdale St EH10 . . . . .10 B6
Duart Cres EH4 . . . . .91 A2
Dublin St EH1 . . . . 229 A4
Dublin Street La N 2
  EH3 . . . . .93 D2
Dublin Street La S EH1 . . . 229 A4
Duchess Anne Cotts EH51 . .63 C6
Duddingston Cres
  Edinburgh EH15 . . . . 123 B6
Duddingston Terr EH52 . . . .88 A8
Duddingston Gdns N
  EH15 . . . . 122 F7
Duddingston Gdns S
  EH15 . . . . 122 F7
Duddingston Gr E EH15 . . 122 F7
Duddingston Gr W EH15 . . 122 F7
Duddingston House Ctyd
  EH15 . . . . 122 F6
Duddingston Loan EH15 . . 122 F6
Duddingston Mains Cotts
  EH15 . . . . 123 B6
Duddingston Mills EH8 . . . 122 F7
Duddingston Pk EH15 . . . . 123 A6
Duddingston Pk S EH15 . . 123 A5
Duddingston Prim Sch
  EH15 . . . . 122 F7
Duddingston Rd EH15 . . . . 122 F7
Duddingston Rd W EH16 . . 122 D5
Duddingston Rise EH15 . . 123 A6
Duddingston Row EH15 . . 122 F5
Duddingston Sq E EH15 . . 123 A7
Duddingston Sq W EH15 . . 122 F6
Duddingston View EH15 . . 123 A6
Duddingston Yds EH15 . . . 123 A5
Dudgeon Pl EH29 . . . . .89 B2
Dudley Ave EH6 . . . . .93 E6
Dudley Ave S EH6 . . . . .93 E5
Dudley Bank EH6 . . . . .93 E6
Dudley Cres EH6 . . . . .93 D6
Dudley Gdns EH6 . . . . .93 D6
Dudley Gr EH6 . . . . .93 D6
Dudley Terr EH6 . . . . .93 D6
Duff Cres FK8 . . . . .1 F2
Duff Rd EH11 . . . . 120 F6
Duff St EH11 . . . . 120 F6
Duff Street La EH11 . . . . . . 120 F6
Duffy Pl KY11 . . . . .46 D1
Dugald Stewart Ave EH51 . .64 A7
Duke's Wlk EH8 . . . . .94 B1
Duke Rd KY11 . . . . .94 A4
Duke St Alva FK12 . . . . .5 A7
  Bannockburn FK7 . . . . .7 C1
  Clackmannan FK10 . . . . . .11 B4
  Dalkeith EH22 . . . . 153 A3
  Denny FK6 . . . . .36 C2
  Dunbar EH42 . . . . .78 A2
  Edinburgh EH6 . . . . .94 A4
  Grangemouth FK3 . . . . . . .61 F8
  Rosewell EH24 . . . . 172 D1
  West Barns EH42 . . . . .77 F1
Dumbarton Rd
  Cambusbarron FK8 . . . . . . .6 E8
  Stirling FK8 . . . . .7 B7
Dumbeg Pk EH14 . . . . 148 D8
Dumbiedykes Rd EH8 . . . . 229 C2
Dumbryden Dr EH14 . . . . . 119 F1
Dumbryden Gdns EH14 . . . 119 F1
Dumbryden Gr EH14 . . . . . 119 E1

Dumbryden Ind Est EH14 119 F1
Dumbryden Rd EH14 . . . . 119 F1
Dumyat Ave FK10 . . . . 4 B2
Dumyat Dr FK11 . . . . 59 E3
Dumyat Rd Alva FK12 . . . . . 4 E6
  Menstrie FK11 . . . . 3 F6
  Stirling FK9 . . . . 2 C3
Dumyat Rise FK5 . . . . 38 C5
Dumyat St FK10 . . . . 4 F1
Dunard Gdn EH9 . . . . 121 D3
Dunavon Gdns FK6 . . . . . . 36 D4
Dunbar's Cl EH1 . . . . 229 B3
Dunbar Ave FK5 . . . . 38 F4
Dunbar Dr FK6 . . . . 38 F4
Dunbar Gram Sch EH42 . . 78 B2
Dunbar Pl KY2 . . . . 16 E5
Dunbar Prim Sch EH42 . . . 78 C2
Dunbar Rd
  Haddington EH41 . . . . 101 B1
  North Berwick EH39 . . . . . . 54 E6
Dunbar St EH3 . . . . 228 B1
Dunbar Sta EH42 . . . . 78 B1
Dunbar Town House Mus
  EH42 . . . . 78 C2
Duncairn Ave KY4 . . . . 57 F6
Duncan Ave FK2 . . . . 39 B3
Duncan Buchanan Ct FK8 . . 2 A4
Duncan Cres KY11 . . . . 29 E2
Duncan Ct EH39 . . . . 54 A6
Duncan Gdns EH33 . . . . . 126 C7
Duncan Gn EH54 . . . . 143 B7
Duncan Pl EH6 . . . . 94 A4
Duncanson Ave FK10 . . . . . 10 A8
Duncanson Dr KY3 . . . . . . 34 A1
Duncan St Bonnybridge FK4 57 F5
  Edinburgh EH9 . . . . 121 F4
  Kirkcaldy KY2 . . . . 17 A4
Duncarron Ind Est FK6 . . . 36 F1
Duncarron Pl FK6 . . . . 36 E2
Duncrahill Cotts EH34 . . 178 B8
Dunctur Rd EH31 . . . . 52 C4
Dundaff Ct FK6 . . . . 36 D1
Dundarroch St FK5 . . . . . . 38 B1
Dundas Ave
  North Berwick EH39 . . . . . . 54 C6
  Queensferry EH30 . . . . 89 C8
Dundas Cotts FK4 . . . . 57 A2
Dundas Cres
  Clackmannan FK10 . . . . . . 11 A4
  Dalkeith EH22 . . . . 152 E2
  Laurieston FK2 . . . . 61 A3
Dundas Gdns EH23 . . . . . 174 B1
Dundas Gr EH22 . . . . 152 E2
Dundas Home Farm EH30 89 B7
Dundas Pk EH19 . . . . 173 C7
Dundas Pl KY11 . . . . 29 B2
Dundas Rd Dalkeith EH22 . 152 E2
  Laurieston FK2 . . . . 61 A4
  North Berwick EH39 . . . . . . 54 D6
  Rosyth KY11 . . . . 67 D8
  Stirling FK9 . . . . 2 B2
Dundas Sta Bathgate EH48 141 A8
  Bo'ness EH51 . . . . 63 F7
Dundas St
  Grangemouth FK3 . . . . 61 C8
  Lochgelly KY5 . . . . 14 B7
  Townhill KY12 . . . . 29 C7
Dundee St EH11 . . . . 228 A1
Dundee Pl KY12 . . . . 60 A8
Dundee St EH11 . . . . 228 A1
Dundee Terr EH11 . . . . . . 120 F5
Dundonald Rd KY11 . . . . . . 46 C3
Dundonald St EH3 . . . . . . 93 C2
Dundonnell Way KY11 . . . . 30 A1
Dundrennan Cotts EH16 . 122 C2
Dunearn Bank KY3 . . . . . . 33 D1
Dunearn Dr KY2 . . . . 16 E5
Dunearn Prim Sch KY2 . . . 16 F7
Dunedin St EH7 . . . . 93 D3
Dunedin St EH16 . . . . 122 A4
Dunfermline Abbey KY12 . 28 F3
Dunfermline Bsns Ctr
  KY11 . . . . 29 B1
Dunfermline Bsns Pk
  KY11 . . . . 46 B8
Dunfermline District Mus
  KY12 . . . . 29 B2
Dunfermline High Sch
  KY11 . . . . 29 B3
Dunfermline Queen Margaret
  Sta KY12 . . . . 29 F5
Dunfermline Rd
  Crossgates KY4 . . . . 30 C6
  Limekilns KY11 . . . . 45 E4
Dunfermline Town Sta
  KY12 . . . . 29 B2
Dunfermline Wynd KY11 . . 47 A2
Dungavel La ML8 . . . . 215 B1
Dunglass Church TD13 . . 218 E4
Dunimarle Mus & Castle
  KY12 . . . . 42 B8
Dunimarle St KY12 . . . . . . 26 A2
Dunipace Cres KY12 . . . . . 29 E5
Dunipace Prim Sch FK6 . . 36 D5
Dunkeld Pl FK2 . . . . 39 C1
Dunlin Brae EH54 . . . . . . 143 C6
Dunlin Dr KY11 . . . . 30 B4
Dunlop's Ct EH1 . . . . 228 C2
Dunlop Ct EH54 . . . . 142 C5
Dunlop Sq EH54 . . . . 142 D5
Dunlop Terr EH26 . . . . . . 192 A5
Dunmar Cres FK10 . . . . 4 E1
Dunmar Dr FK10 . . . . 4 E1
Dunnet Way EH52 . . . . . . 116 A6
Dunnikier Prim Sch KY2 . . 17 B5
Dunnikier Rd KY1 . . . . 17 C5

Dunnikier Way KY1 . . . . . . 17 B8
Dunning Pl FK2 . . . . 39 C1
Dunnottar Dr FK5 . . . . 38 F4
Dunnottar Pl KY2 . . . . 16 E4
Dunn Pl EH52 . . . . 87 E2
Dunn St EH52 . . . . 115 B5
Dunn Terr KY1 . . . . 159 F6
Dunollie Ct EH12 . . . . 119 B7
Dunollie Gdns EH41 . . . . 130 C8
Dunpender Dr EH41 . . . . 100 F1
Dunpender Rd EH40 . . . . 103 C8
Dunrobin Ave FK5 . . . . . . 38 F5
Dunrobin Pl EH3 . . . . 117 E2
Dunrobin Rd KY2 . . . . 16 E4
Dunsapie Ct EH15 . . . . . . 122 D6
Dunsire St KY1 . . . . 17 E8
Dunsmuir Ct EH12 . . . . . . 119 D6
Duns Rd EH41 . . . . 220 F7
Dunster Rd FK9 . . . . 2 C3
Dunure Cres FK4 . . . . 58 A5
Dunure Pl KY2 . . . . 16 E4
Dunure St FK4 . . . . 58 A5
Dunvegan Ave
  Kirkcaldy KY2 . . . . 16 D5
  Stenhousemuir FK5 . . . . . . 38 F4
Dunvegan Ct Alloa FK10 . . 10 B6
  Crossford KY12 . . . . 28 B1
  Edinburgh EH4 . . . . 91 B4
Dunvegan Gdns EH54 . . 164 E6
Dunvegan Dr Falkirk FK2 . . 39 C1
  Stirling FK9 . . . . 2 B3
Dunvegan Pl
  Bonnybridge FK4 . . . . 57 F6
  Polmont FK2 . . . . 62 A1
Dura Rd ML2,ML7 . . . . . . 198 C5
Durar Dr FK1 . . . . 91 C1
Durham Ave
  Bathgate EH48 . . . . 140 E6
  Edinburgh EH15 . . . . 122 F7
Durham Bank EH19 . . . . . 173 C6
Durham Dr
  Bathgate EH48 . . . . 140 E6
  Edinburgh EH15 . . . . 123 A6
Durham Gdns N EH15 . . 123 A7
Durham Gdns S EH15 . . 123 A6
Durham Gr
  Bonnyrigg and Lasswade
  EH19 . . . . 173 C6
  Edinburgh EH15 . . . . 123 A6
Durham Pl EH19 . . . . 173 C6
Durham Place La EH15 . . 123 A7
Durham Pl E EH15 . . . . . . 123 A7
Durham Pl W EH15 . . . . . 122 F7
Durham Rd EH15 . . . . 123 A6
Durham Rd S EH15 . . . . . 123 A6
Durham Sq EH15 . . . . 123 A7
Durham Terr
  Newmills KY12 . . . . 26 C1
Durie's Pk EH33 . . . . 126 B1
Durie Pk KY3 . . . . 50 D8
Durie Pl KY11 . . . . 29 F4
Durward Rise EH54 . . . . . 144 A2
Durwood Gr EH16 . . . . . . 122 B2
Dyfrig St ML7 . . . . 179 E5
Dyke Brow ML7 . . . . 160 A6
Dyke Ct ML7 . . . . 160 A6
Dykehead Prim Sch ML7 179 E5
Dyke ML7 . . . . 160 A6
Dykeside Rd EH48 . . . . . 140 F8
Dykes Rd EH26 . . . . 191 E2
Dymond Gr KY11 . . . . 46 F8
Dysart Prim Sch KY1 . . . . 18 A7
Dysart Rd KY1 . . . . 17 F6

E

Eagle Brae EH54 . . . . 143 D4
Eagle Rock EH4 . . . . 91 A7
Eardley Cres KY11 . . . . . . 47 A7
Earl's Rd FK1 . . . . 60 C4
Earl Grey St EH3 . . . . 228 B2
Earl Haig Gdns EH5 . . . . . 93 B5
Earl of Mar Ct FK10 . . . . . 10 B6
Earlsburn Ave FK7 . . . . 7 A3
Earls Ct FK10 . . . . 10 B5
Earl's Gate Rdbt FK3 . . . . 61 A7
Earlshill Dr FK7 . . . . 7 F1
Earls Pl EH47 . . . . 181 E6
Earlston Pl 3 EH7 . . . . . . 94 A1
Earn Ct Alloa FK10 . . . . . . 10 C6
  Grangemouth FK3 . . . . . . 61 D5
Earn Gr KY11 . . . . 29 F4
Earn Pl FK6 . . . . 57 D6
Earn Rd KY1 . . . . 17 D8
Earn Terr ML7 . . . . 179 E6
East Adam St EH8 . . . . 229 B2
East Albert Rd KY1 . . . . . . 17 F5
East Ave KY12 . . . . 26 A7
East Baldridge Dr KY12 . . 28 E5
East Bankton Pl EH54 . . 164 F7
East Barnton Ave EH4 . . . 91 E3
East Barnton Gdns EH4 . . 91 E3
East Bay KY11 . . . . 68 C5
East Boreland Pl FK6 . . . . 36 D3
East Bridge St FK1 . . . . 60 C4
East Brighton Cres EH15 122 D6
East Broomhill Rd KY3 . . . 50 E8
East Broughton Pl 8 EH3 93 D2
East Burn Ct KY1 . . . . 17 D7
East Burn Twr EH1 . . . . . 229 B3
East Caystane Pl EH10 . . 150 A5
East Caystane Rd EH10 . 150 B5
East Calder Prim Sch
  EH53 . . . . 144 F4
East Campbell Ct EH32 . . 98 D5

East Camus Pl EH10 . . . . 150 A6
East Camus Rd EH10 . . . . 150 A6
East Castle Rd EH10 . . . . 121 A5
East Castle St FK10 . . . . . 10 B5
East Champanyie EH9 . . . 121 E3
East Clapperfield EH16 . . 122 A1
East Claremont St EH7 . . . 93 D3
East Comiston EH10 . . . . 150 A6
East Craigs Prim Sch
  EH12 . . . . 119 B8
East Craigs Rigg EH12 . . 119 A7
East Craigs Wynd EH12 . 119 A7
East Croft EH28 . . . . 117 E2
East Crosscauseway
  EH8 . . . . 229 B1
East Ct
  Edinburgh,Greendykes
  EH16 . . . . 122 E3
  8 Edinburgh,Ravelston
  EH4 . . . . 92 C1
East Dr Dunfermline KY12 . 29 B3
  Stenhousemuir FK5 . . . . . . 38 C5
East End EH55 . . . . 163 D3
East End Park (Dunfermline
  Athletic FC) KY12 . . . . 29 C4
East Fettes Ave EH4 . . . . . 92 F3
Eastfield Cotts
  Penicuik EH26 . . . . 191 F7
  Stenton EH41 . . . . 104 B1
Eastfield Dr EH26 . . . . . . 191 F7
Eastfield Farm Rd EH26 . 191 F7
Eastfield Gdns EH15 . . . . 123 E2
Eastfield Ind Est EH26 . . 191 F6
Eastfield Loan EH33 . . . . 126 D7
Eastfield Park Rd EH26 . . 191 F6
Eastfield Pl EH15 . . . . 123 E2
Eastfield Rd Carluke ML8 215 A1
  Fauldhouse EH47 . . . . . . 181 F7
  North Berwick EH39 . . . . . . 54 D6
  Ratho Station EH28 . . . . . 118 A6
Eastfield View EH47 . . . . 181 F7
East Fountainbridge
  EH3 . . . . 228 B2
East Garleton Cotts
  EH39 . . . . 100 F6
Eastgate KY3 . . . . 34 F3
East Glen Ave EH54 . . . . 142 E6
East Harbour Rd KY11 . . . 45 B3
East Hermitage Pl EH6 . . 94 A4
Easthouses Ct EH22 . . . . 174 D8
Easthouses Ind Est EH22 174 D8
Easthouses Pl EH22 . . . . 174 D8
Easthouses Rd
  Dalkeith EH22 . . . . 153 C1
  Easthouses EH22 . . . . 174 C7

Easthouses Way EH22 . . 153 C1
East Kilgate EH17 . . . . . . 151 D5
East Kilgate Rigg EH17 . 151 D5
East Kilgate Wynd
  EH17 . . . . 151 D5
East Leven St KY3 . . . . . . 50 E8
East Lillypot EH5 . . . . 93 B5
East Link Rd FK9 . . . . 2 D5
East Links Family Pk
  EH42 . . . . 77 D2
East Links Rd Dunbar EH42 77 D1
  Gullane EH31 . . . . 52 A2
East Linton Prim Sch
  EH40 . . . . 103 D7
East Linton Station Ind Site
  EH40 . . . . 103 D7
East Loan EH32 . . . . 97 A1
East London St EH7 . . . . . 93 D2
East Lorimer Pl EH32 . . . . 97 C4
East Mains FK11 . . . . 4 A6
East Mains Ind Est EH52 116 B6
East Mains of Ingliston
  (Smallholdings) EH28 . 118 A6
East Main St
  Armadale EH48 . . . . 140 A6
  Blackburn EH47 . . . . 162 D7
  Broxburn EH52 . . . . 115 F5
  Harthill ML7 . . . . 159 F5
  Uphall EH52 . . . . 115 A4
  Whitburn EH47 . . . . 161 C8
East March St KY1 . . . . . . 17 E7
East Market St EH8 . . . . . 229 B3
East Mayfield EH9 . . . . . . 121 F4
East Meikle Pinkerton Cotts
  EH42 . . . . 107 C4
East Montgomery Pl 3
  EH7 . . . . 93 F2
East Murrayfield EH12 . . . . 7 E1
East Newington Pl EH9 . 121 F5
East Norton Pl EH7 . . . . . . 93 F1
Easton Ct FK8 . . . . 2 B2
Easton Dr FK1 . . . . 81 D7
Easton Rd EH48 . . . . 140 F7
East Parkside EH16 . . . . . 229 C1
East Pier St EH51 . . . . 63 F8
East Pl Dunfermline KY12 . 29 A5
Eastpark Rd Grangemouth FK3 . 62 C5
  North Berwick EH39 . . . . . . 54 A6
East Quality St KY11 . . . . 46 D4
East Queensway EH19 . . 173 C6
East Rd Grangemouth FK3 . 62 C5
  North Berwick EH39 . . . . . . 54 A6
East Restalrig Terr EH6 . . 94 B4
East Savile Rd EH16 . . . . 122 A3
East Sciennes St 2 EH9 . 121 F5
East Scotland Street La 1
  EH3 . . . . 93 D2
East Seaside EH32 . . . . . . 96 F2
East Silvermills La EH3 . . 93 B2
East Stirling St FK12 . . . . . 5 B7
East Suffolk Rd EH16 . . . 122 A3
East Telferton EH7 . . . . . . 94 F1
East Terr EH30 . . . . 68 C1
East Toll KY3 . . . . 33 E1
East Trinity Rd EH5 . . . . . 93 C6
East Vennel FK10 . . . . 10 B6
East Vows WIk KY1 . . . . . 35 B7
East Way KY11 . . . . 48 C5
East Werberside EH4 . . . . 92 E4
East Werberside Pl EH4 . . 92 E4
East Whitefield KY12 . . . . 29 F6
Eastwood Pk
  Fauldhouse EH47 . . . . . . 181 F7
  Livingston EH54 . . . . 143 A7
Ebenezer Pl KY11 . . . . . . 81 F5
Eccles Ct FK7 . . . . 7 A4
Ecclesmachan Rd EH52 . 114 F5
Eccles Pl FK2 . . . . 83 A5
Echline EH30 . . . . 88 F8
Echline Ave EH30 . . . . 89 A8
Echline Dr EH30 . . . . 89 A7
Echline Gdns EH30 . . . . . 67 F1
Echline Gn EH30 . . . . 67 F1
Echline Gr EH30 . . . . 68 A8
Echline Pk EH30 . . . . 88 F8
Echline Rigg EH30 . . . . . . 68 A8
Echline Terr EH30 . . . . . . 89 A8
Echline View EH30 . . . . . . 89 A8
Echobank KY11 . . . . 47 B8
Eden La EH54 . . . . 144 B4
Edenhall Bank EH21 . . . . 124 E5
Edenhall Cres EH21 . . . . 124 E5
Edenhall Hospl EH21 . . . 124 D5
Edenhall Rd EH21 . . . . . . 124 E5
Eden Rd Alloa FK10 . . . . . 9 F8
  Dunfermline KY12 . . . . 29 E2
Edgar St KY12 . . . . 28 F3
Edgefield Ind Est EH20 . . 151 C1
Edgefield Pl EH20 . . . . . . 172 C8
Edgefield Rd EH20 . . . . . 151 C1
Edgehead Rd EH37 . . . . . 175 C7
Edina Pl EH7 . . . . 94 A2
Edina St EH7 . . . . 94 A2
Edinburgh Acad (Prep Sch)
  The EH3 . . . . 93 A2
Edinburgh Airport EH12 . 118 B8
Edinburgh Butterfly & Insect
  World EH18 . . . . 152 C3

Edinburgh Castle EH1 . . . 228 C2
Edinburgh Central YH
  EH2 . . . . 229 A3
Edinburgh Crystal EH26 . 191 F6
Edinburgh Park Sta
  EH11 . . . . 119 A3
Edinburgh Pk
  Edinburgh EH12 . . . . 118 F5
  Edinburgh EH12 . . . . 119 A4
Edinburgh Rd
  Bathgate EH48 . . . . 141 C5
  Carlops EH46 . . . . 206 B3
  Cockenzie & Port Seton
  EH32 . . . . 97 B3
  Dalkeith EH22 . . . . 153 A3
  Harthill ML7 . . . . 159 C5
  Linlithgow EH49 . . . . 85 B7
  Musselburgh EH21 . . . . . 124 A6
  Newbridge EH28 . . . . . . 117 A6
  Penicuik EH26 . . . . 192 A8
  South Queensferry EH30 . 68 C1
  Tranent EH33 . . . . 126 B6
  West Barns EH42 . . . . 77 F1
Edinburgh Sch of Agriculture
  EH16 . . . . 121 F1
Edinburgh West Off Pk
  EH12 . . . . 119 A4
Edinburgh Zoo (Royal
  Zoological Society of
  Scotland) EH12 . . . . . 119 F7
Edinburgh Coll of Art
  EH3 . . . . 228 C2
Edington Cottage Hospl
  EH39 . . . . 54 C7
Edington Pl KY11 . . . . 18 B8
Edmonstone Ave EH22 . . 152 B8
Edmonstone Dr EH22 . . . 152 B8
Edmonstone Rd EH22 . . . 152 B8
Edmonstone Terr EH22 . . 152 B8
Edmonton Ave EH54 . . . . 143 F4
Edward Ave
  Stenhousemuir FK5 . . . . . . 38 C4
  Stirling FK9 . . . . 2 C1
Edward Pl FK2 . . . . 39 F3
Edward Rd FK8 . . . . 2 B1
Edwards Ct FK8 . . . . 129 F8
Edward St
  Dunfermline KY12 . . . . 29 B5
  Kirkcaldy KY2 . . . . 17 B7
Edzell Way KY11 . . . . 30 A1
Eglington Dr KY12 . . . . . . 28 F6
Eglinton Cres EH12 . . . . 120 F6
Eglinton Pl KY11 . . . . 47 D2
Egypt Mews EH10 . . . . . 121 C3
Eighth St EH22 . . . . 174 B5
Eildon St EH3 . . . . 93 C3
Eildon Terr EH3 . . . . 93 C4
Eilean La KY12 . . . . 26 E1
Elam Terr EH51 . . . . 63 E7
Elbe St EH6 . . . . 94 A5
Elcho Ct EH32 . . . . 98 E5
Elcho Pl EH32 . . . . 97 C4
Elcho Rd EH32 . . . . 98 E5
Elcho Terr Aberlady EH32 . 71 C4
  Longniddry EH32 . . . . 98 E5
Elder Pl KY11 . . . . 46 E5
Elder St E EH1 . . . . 229 A4
Elderslie Dr FK2 . . . . 82 B7
Elder St Dunbar EH42 . . . 78 B1
  Edinburgh EH1 . . . . 229 A4
  Tranent EH33 . . . . 126 C7
Eldindean Ct KY12 . . . . . . 28 D6
Eldindean Pl EH19 . . . . . 173 B8
Eldindean Rd EH19 . . . . . 173 C8
Eldindean Terr EH19 . . . . 173 C8
Eldin Ind Est EH20 . . . . . 151 C2
Eldrick Ave EH47 . . . . . . 181 E5
Eldrick Cres EH47 . . . . . . 181 D5
Eldrick Dr EH47 . . . . 181 E5
Eldrick View EH47 . . . . . . 181 E5
Electra Pl EH15 . . . . 95 A1
Elgin Ct KY12 . . . . 29 A2
Elgin Dr FK7 . . . . 7 C3
Elgin Pl FK1 . . . . 60 A8
Elgin Sq KY11 . . . . 30 B1
Elgin St N EH7 . . . . 93 F2
Elgin St Dunfermline KY12 . 29 A2
  Edinburgh EH7 . . . . 93 F2
Elgin Terr FK7 . . . . 7 C3
Elgol Path ML7 . . . . 180 B3
Eliburn North Rdbt EH54 143 B6
Eliburn Rd EH54 . . . . 143 C4
Eliburn South Rd EH54 . . 143 C4
Elie Ave EH54 . . . . 142 F5
Elim Dr FK1 . . . . 81 C6
Elizabeth Ave
  Grangemouth FK3 . . . . . . 61 C8
  Stenhousemuir FK5 . . . . . . 38 C2
Elizabeth Cres FK1 . . . . . 59 B6
Elizabeth Dr EH48 . . . . . 141 F6
Elizabeth Gdns EH47 . . . 162 B2
Elizabeth La EH47 . . . . . . 141 F6
Elizabeth St
  Dunfermline KY11 . . . . 29 D2
  Stirling FK8 . . . . 7 A5
Elizafield EH6 . . . . 93 E4
Ellaleen Gr KY11 . . . . 28 B1
Ellangowan Terr EH16 . . 122 C1
Ellen's Glen Loan EH17 . 151 D7
Ellen's Glen Rd EH17 . . . 151 C7
Ellen St EH7 . . . . 161 B7
Ellersly Rd EH12 . . . . 120 C7

Elliot Gdns EH14..... 149 C8
Elliothill St KY11..... 29 B2
Elliot Pk EH14..... 149 C8
Elliot Pl EH14..... 149 C8
Elliot Rd EH14..... 149 C8
Elliot St Dunfermline KY11 ..29 B2
  Edinburgh EH7..... 93 F2
Elliot Terr FK2..... 60 A8
Ellisland Ave KY2..... 17 A7
Ellis Pl EH52..... 115 B5
Ellon Pl KY12..... 29 D6
Ellon Rd KY2..... 16 C7
Elmbank FK11..... 4 A6
Elmbank Cres FK4..... 57 D6
Elmbank Rd FK7..... 7 A8
Elmbank St FK3..... 61 C6
Elm Dr FK2..... 61 A2
Elmfield Ct EH22..... 153 A3
Elmfield Pk EH22..... 153 A3
Elmfield Rd EH22..... 153 A3
Elm Gr Alloa FK10..... 10 C5
  Blackburn EH47..... 162 E8
  Dunfermline KY11..... 46 C8
  Livingston EH54..... 144 B5
  Stenhousemuir FK5..... 38 D1
Elm Pk EH47..... 162 E8
Elm Pl Edinburgh EH6..... 94 B4
  Kirkcaldy KY2..... 16 F5
  Mayfield EH22..... 174 D6
Elm Rd EH48..... 141 E6
Elm Row
  Bonnyrigg and Lasswade
  EH18..... 152 B1
  Edinburgh EH7..... 93 E2
Elm Sq EH47..... 161 C6
Elm St Dunbar EH42..... 78 B1
  Stirling FK8..... 1 E1
Elm Terr EH47..... 162 E8
Elmwood Pk EH54..... 142 F7
Elmwood Rd ML7..... 180 B2
Elmwood Terr EH46..... 94 B3
Elphinstone Cres FK2..... 22 E4
Elphinstone Ct 2 EH33.. 126 C6
Elphinstone Prim Sch
  EH33..... 126 B1
Elphinstone Rd EH33...126 B5
Elphinstone Sq FK5..... 142 C6
Elphinstone St FK10..... 23 E4
Elphinstone Tower Farm
  Cotts HE33..... 125 F1
Elphinstone Wlk 8
  EH33..... 126 C5
Eltringham Gdns EH14...120 C4
Eltringham Gr EH14..... 120 C4
Eltringham Terr EH14...120 C4
Emily Ct EH23..... 174 C1
Emily Pl EH23..... 174 D1
Emma's Way FK4..... 57 F5
Empire Gate ML7..... 179 F4
Empire St EH47..... 161 A7
Endrick Dr FK6..... 57 E6
Endrick Pl FK7..... 7 A4
Engelen Dr FK10..... 10 B5
Engine La EH48..... 141 B6
Engine Pl 3 EH48..... 141 A6
Engine Rd
  Gorebridge EH23..... 174 B1
  Loanhead EH20..... 172 C8
Ennis Ct EH51..... 163 E4
Ennis Pk EH55..... 163 E5
Enterprise Ctr EH20....172 A7
Enterprise Way KY11..... 46 E6
Entryfoot EH48..... 137 F2
Eppiestane Rd EH47..... 161 C6
Epworth Gdns FK2..... 82 B8
Erbach Ave FK2..... 61 B4
Ercall Rd FK2..... 82 E8
Erica Gr KY11..... 46 E8
Ericht Pl ML7..... 179 E6
Eriskay Ct FK1..... 60 C2
Erngath Rd EH51..... 64 A7
Erskine Beveridge Ct
  KY11..... 29 B2
Erskine Brae KY12..... 25 D1
Erskine Gdns ML7..... 179 F5
Erskine Hill FK2..... 61 E1
Erskine Loan EH31..... 52 A3
Erskine Pl
  Clackmannan FK10..... 10 F5
  Mid Calder EH53..... 144 C6
Erskine Rd
  Broxburn EH52..... 115 C6
  Gullane EH31..... 52 A3
Erskine Sq Alloa FK10..... 10 B7
  Alva FK12..... 5 A7
  Lochgelly KY5..... 14 A6
Erskine Way
  Livingston EH54..... 143 D8
  Shotts ML7..... 179 E4
Erskine Wynd KY12..... 27 A7
Esdaile Bank EH9..... 121 D4
Esdaile Pk EH9..... 121 D4
Esk Bank Ct EH22..... 152 E2
Eskbank Rd
  Bonnyrigg and Lasswade
  EH22..... 173 D8
  Dalkeith EH22..... 152 F2
Eskbank Road Rdbt
  EH22..... 152 E1
Eskbank Terr EH22..... 152 F2
Eskdaill Ct 15 EH22..... 153 A3
Eskdaill St 11 EH22..... 153 A3
Eskdale Dr EH19..... 173 A7

Eskdale Mews EH21..... 124 C6
Eskdale Terr EH19..... 173 A7
Esk Dr EH54..... 184 B4
Eskfield Gr EH22..... 152 D2
Esk Glades EH22..... 153 B4
Eskgrove Dr EH25..... 171 E6
Eskhill EH26..... 191 F5
Eskmill Rd EH26..... 192 A5
Esk Pl EH22..... 152 F3
Eskside Ct EH22..... 152 F4
Eskside E
  Musselburgh EH21..... 124 C6
  Musselburgh EH21..... 124 C6
Eskside W EH21..... 124 C6
Eskvale Cres EH26..... 192 A5
Eskvale Ct EH26..... 192 A5
Eskvale Dr EH26..... 192 A6
Eskvale View EH26..... 192 A6
Eskview Ave EH21..... 124 B5
Eskview Cres EH21..... 124 B5
Eskview Gr Dalkeith EH22 ..152 F3
  Musselburgh EH21..... 124 B5
Eskview Rd
  Mayfield EH22..... 174 D6
  Musselburgh EH21..... 124 B5
Eskview Terr EH21..... 124 B5
Eskview Villas EH22....152 F2
Esmonde Ct KY11..... 46 E2
Esplanade Edinburgh EH1.. 228 C3
  Kirkcaldy KY1..... 17 C2
  1 Stirling FK8..... 7 A8
Esplanade Terr EH15..... 123 D8
Essendean Pl EH4..... 91 D1
Essendean Terr EH4..... 91 D1
Essex Brae EH4..... 91 A4
Essex Pk EH4..... 91 A4
Essex Rd EH4..... 91 A4
Essdemont Rd EH16..... 122 A2
Estate Ave FK1..... 60 C4
Ethel Terr EH10..... 121 A2
Etive Pl Dalgety Bay KY11 ..48 A2
  Stirling FK9..... 2 B3
Etive Way FK2..... 62 A2
Etive Wlk Livingston EH54 144 A4
  Shotts ML7..... 180 B3
Etna Ct Armadale EH48..... 140 B5
  Falkirk FK2..... 60 D7
Etna Rd FK2..... 60 D7
Etna Road Rdbt FK2..... 60 E7
Eton Terr EH4..... 228 A4
Ettrick Cres FK1..... 48 A4
Ettrickdale Pl EH3..... 93 B3
Ettrick Dr EH54..... 144 B5
Ettrick Gr EH10..... 121 A5
Ettrick Loan EH10..... 120 F4
Ettrick Rd EH10..... 120 F4
Evans Gdns EH19..... 173 D8
Evans St FK5..... 38 C3
Eva Pl EH9..... 121 E2
Everard Rise EH54..... 144 A2
Evergreen Trailer Ct FK6.. 37 A2
Evershed Ct KY11..... 29 E1
Evershed Dr KY11..... 29 E1
Ewart Ave EH48..... 140 A5
Ewart Gr EH51..... 63 F5
Eweford Cotts EH42..... 106 B8
Ewerland EH4..... 91 A4
Ewing Ave FK2..... 60 B7
Ewing Ct FK7..... 7 C3
Ewing Dr FK2..... 60 B7
Ewing Pl FK2..... 60 B7
Ewing St Cowdenbeath KY4 .13 B2
  Lochgelly KY5..... 14 A6
  Penicuik EH26..... 191 F7
Ewingston Mill Steading
  EH36..... 220 B3
Ewington Pl EH47..... 162 B2
Excise La FK10..... 23 E4
Excise St EH10..... 23 E4
Exmouth St EH54..... 144 A5
Eyre Cres EH3..... 93 C2
Eyre Pl EH3..... 93 C2
Eyre Place La EH3..... 93 C2
Eyre Terr EH3..... 93 C2

F

Fa'side Ave 3 EH33..... 126 C6
Fa'side Ave N EH21..... 125 B4
Fa'side Avenue Ct EH21..125 B4
Fa'side Ave S EH21..... 125 B4
Fa'side Bldgs EH21..... 125 B4
Fa'side Cres
  2 Tranent EH33..... 126 C5
  Wallyford EH21..... 125 A5
Fa'side Dr EH21..... 125 B4
Fa'side Gdns EH21..... 125 B4
Fa'side Gr EH33..... 126 C5
Fa'side Terr EH21..... 125 A4
Fa'side View EH33..... 126 B4
Factory Rd Bathgate EH48 140 F4
  Cowdenbeath KY4..... 13 D4
  Kirkcaldy KY1..... 17 C6
Fair-A-Far EH4..... 91 B5
Fair-A-Far Cotts EH4..... 91 B5
Fair-A-Far Shot EH4..... 91 B5
Fairbairn Gr EH4..... 143 C3
Fairbairn Rd EH54..... 143 C3
Fairbrae EH11..... 119 F3
Fairburn Rd FK1..... 33 E1
Fairfield Alloa FK10..... 5 C1
  Livingston EH54..... 143 A3
Fairfield Ave FK4..... 58 A6

Fairfield Pl FK2..... 60 C5
Fairfields FK2..... 21 E5
Fairfield Sch FK10..... 5 B1
Fairford Gdns EH16..... 122 B1
Fairgreen FK7..... 19 E8
Fairhaven Terr FK2..... 82 A8
Fairhill Rd FK7..... 7 B1
Fairinsfell EH52..... 115 B5
Fair Isle Prim Sch KY2... 16 E8
Fair Isle Rd KY2..... 16 E8
Fairley Ct KY12..... 27 D1
Fair Isle Rd KY2..... 16 E8
Fairlie St FK1..... 59 C5
Fairmile Ave EH10..... 150 B5
Fairmont Pk EH47..... 160 F6
Fairmount Dr FK10..... 5 B2
Fair Pl KY11..... 47 B3
Fairspark Terr EH51..... 63 D5
Fairview Rd EH21,EH28..117 F7
Fairway EH41..... 129 E8
Fairways KY12..... 29 B6
Fairways Ave FK2..... 82 F6
Fairways Bsns Pk EH54 . 114 D1
Fairways Pl FK4..... 58 B7
Fairway The KY1..... 17 F8
Fairyburn Rd FK10..... 9 F8
Fairy Fa' Cres KY4..... 30 F6
Fairykirk Rd KY11..... 47 A3
Faith Mission Coll The
  EH17..... 151 E6
Falahill Cotts EH38..... 214 B4
Falcon Ave EH10..... 121 B3
Falcon Brae EH54..... 143 D5
Falcon Ct EH10..... 121 B3
Falcon Dr FK5..... 38 B3
Falconer Ct FK7..... 7 C3
Falconer Rise EH54..... 144 A2
Falcon Gdns EH10..... 121 B3
Falcon Rd EH10..... 121 B3
Falcon Rd W EH10..... 121 B3
Falcons The EH31..... 52 B3
Falkirk & District Royal Infmy
  FK1..... 60 A4
Falkirk Grahamston Sta
  FK1..... 60 B5
Falkirk High Sch FK1..... 59 E4
Falkirk High Sta FK1..... 60 A3
Falkirk Rd
  Bannockburn FK7..... 19 F8
  Bonnybridge FK4..... 58 C6
  Cowie FK7..... 20 A6
  Falkirk,FK2,FK3..... 60 F6
  Falkirk,Glen Village FK1... 60 B1
  Larbert FK5..... 59 C8
  Linlithgow EH49..... 84 E7
Falkirk Stadium (Falkirk FC)
  FK2..... 60 A6
Falkland Gdns EH12..... 91 A1
Falkland Pl FK5..... 38 A3
Falla Hill Prim Sch EH47 181 D6
Fallas Pl FK7..... 181 D5
Fallhills Ct EH26..... 192 C1
Fallin Prim Sch FK7..... 8 D5
Falloden Cres KY2..... 17 A3
Falside Cres EH48..... 140 E5
Falside Dr EH48..... 140 E5
Falside Terr EH48..... 140 E5
Faraday Pl EH55..... 162 E2
Farm Ave EH18..... 172 F6
Farm Cotts EH21..... 125 C5
Farmer's Bldgs EH37....176 B5
Farm Pl EH54..... 143 A3
Farm Rd Cowdenbeath KY4..13 B3
  Cowie FK7..... 20 D8
  Crombie KY12..... 44 D6
  Fallin FK7..... 8 D4
  Roslin EH25..... 192 F6
Farm Row KY12..... 30 B6
Farm St FK2..... 39 A3
Farmstead Rd KY11..... 47 F4
Farmstead Way EH51..... 64 C6
Farne Ct KY2..... 16 F8
Farnell Way KY12..... 29 C6
Farquharson Way FK1..... 59 F1
Farquhar Sq EH48..... 138 C3
Farquhar Terr EH30..... 68 B1
Farrer Gr EH7..... 94 E1
Farrer Terr EH7..... 94 F1
Farrier Ct EH47..... 162 D7
Fauldburn EH12..... 91 B1
Fauldburn Pk EH12..... 91 B1
Fauldhouse Bsns Ctr
  EH47..... 181 E6
Fauldhouse Rd EH47..... 161 B2
Fauldhouse Sta EH47..... 181 C5
Featherhall Ave EH12..... 119 D6
Featherhall Cres N EH12 119 D6
Featherhall Cres S EH12 119 D6
Featherhall Gr EH12..... 119 D6
Featherhall Pl EH12..... 119 D6
Featherhall Rd EH12..... 119 D6
Featherhall Terr EH12..... 119 D6
Fell's Rd FK55..... 163 F5
Fendoch Rd FK3..... 61 F7
Fenton Barns Farm Cotts
  EH39..... 73 A8
Fenton St FK10..... 10 A7
Fentoun Gait EH31..... 52 C2
Feregait FK10..... 23 E4
Ferguson Ave FK4..... 143 F4
Ferguson Ct EH21..... 124 B3
Ferguson Dr Denny FK6..... 36 D1
  Falkirk FK2..... 39 A5

Ferguson Dr continued
  Musselburgh EH21..... 124 B3
Ferguson Gdns EH21..... 124 C3
Ferguson Gn EH21..... 124 B3
Ferguson Gr FK4..... 58 B6
Ferguson Pl KY3..... 33 F1
Ferguson St FK8..... 1 F2
Ferguson View EH21..... 124 B3
Ferguson Way
  Livingston EH54..... 143 D8
  Newtongrange EH22....174 B4
Fergus Pl KY11..... 29 D1
Fergusson Rd
  Broxburn EH52..... 115 E5
  Dunfermline KY11..... 47 A7
Fergus Wynd KY1..... 17 B1
Fernbank Cornton FK9..... 2 B3
  Livingston EH54..... 143 E5
Ferniehill Ave EH17..... 151 E6
Ferniehill Dr EH17..... 151 F6
Ferniehill Gdns EH17..... 151 F7
Ferniehill Gr EH17..... 151 F7
Ferniehill Pl EH17..... 151 E6
Ferniehill Rd EH17..... 151 E6
Ferniehill Sq EH17..... 151 E6
Ferniehill St EH17..... 151 E6
Ferniehill Terr EH17..... 151 E6
Ferniehill Way EH17..... 151 F7
Fernielaw Ave EH13..... 149 A5
Fernie Pl KY12..... 28 E5
Ferneside Ave EH17..... 151 E8
Ferneside Cres EH17..... 151 E7
Ferneside Dr EH17..... 151 E7
Ferneside Gdns EH17..... 151 E7
Ferneside Gr EH17..... 151 E7
Ferneside Pl EH17..... 151 E7
Fernlea EH52..... 114 F5
Fern Lea Gr FK2..... 39 C3
Ferrard Rd KY2..... 17 A4
Ferrier Cres EH48..... 140 A6
Ferris Way KY11..... 48 B4
Ferryburn Gn EH30..... 68 B6
Ferryburn Gn EH30..... 89 C8
Ferry Ct FK9..... 2 A3
Ferryfield EH5..... 93 A4
Ferry Gait Dr EH4..... 92 A4
Ferry Gait Pl EH4..... 92 A4
Ferrygate Cottages EH39..53 C6
Ferryhill Prim Sch EH4....92 C3
Ferryhill Rd
  Inverkeithing KY11..... 47 B1
  North Queensferry KY11.. 68 B7
Ferry La KY11..... 68 B6
Ferry Muir EH30..... 89 B7
Ferrymuir Gait EH30..... 89 B8
Ferrymuir La EH30..... 89 B8
Ferrymuir Rd EH30..... 89 B8
Ferry Orch FK9..... 2 D1
Ferry Rd
  Edinburgh,Drylaw EH4,
  EH5..... 92 D4
  Edinburgh,Trinity EH5..... 93 C5
  North Queensferry KY11.. 68 B6
  South Alloa FK7..... 9 D4
  Stirling FK9..... 2 D1
Ferry Road Ave EH4..... 92 C4
Ferry Road Dr EH4..... 92 D5
Ferry Road Gdns EH4..... 92 C4
Ferry Road Gr EH4..... 92 C4
Ferry Road Pl EH4..... 92 C4
Ferry Toll Pl KY11..... 46 E1
Ferry Toll Rd KY11..... 46 F2
Festival Sq EH1..... 228 B2
Festival Theatre EH8..... 229 A2
Fetteresk Cotts EH26..... 191 E4
Fettes Ave EH4..... 92 F2
Fettes Coll EH4..... 92 F3
Fettes Ct EH4..... 92 F2
Fettes Rise EH4..... 92 F3
Fettes Row EH3..... 93 C2
Fiddich Dr FK54..... 164 E5
Fidra Ave EH39..... 53 B5
Fidra Ct EH39..... 53 F7
Fidra Rd EH39..... 54 A7
Fife Coll of F & H Ed KY1..17 B4
Fife Coll (Priory Campus)
  KY1..... 17 C5
Fife Pl KY11..... 17 A3
Fifth St EH22..... 174 B5
Figgate Bank EH15..... 95 B1
Figgate La EH15..... 95 B1
Figgate St EH15..... 95 A1
Fillyside Ave EH7..... 94 E2
Fillyside Rd EH7,EH15..... 94 E3
Fillyside Terr EH7..... 94 E3
Fincastle Pl FK7..... 20 D8
Finches The EH31..... 52 B3
Findhorn Pl
  Edinburgh EH9..... 121 E4
  Falkirk FK1..... 60 D2
  Kirkcaldy KY2..... 16 E8
Findlay Ave EH7..... 94 C3
Findlay Cotts EH21..... 124 C3
Findlay Cres KY11..... 46 E4
Findlay Gdns EH7..... 94 C3
Findlay Gr EH7..... 94 C3
Findlay Medway EH7..... 94 C3
Findlay St KY1..... 46 E4
Fingal Pl EH9..... 229 A1
Fingzies Pl EH6..... 94 B4
Finistere Ave FK1..... 60 B3
Finlaggan Ct EH12..... 119 A8
Finlarig Ct FK5..... 38 F4
Finlay Ave EH53..... 144 F3
Finlay Pl EH22..... 174 D6
Finlayson Pl FK5..... 38 C5
Fintry Ave EH54..... 142 F5
Fintry Rd FK3..... 61 E5

Firbank Gr EH53..... 144 E3
Fire Mus EH3..... 228 C2
Fir Gr Dunfermline KY12.... 46 E8
  Livingston EH54..... 144 B5
  Westquarter FK2..... 61 B2
Fir La FK5..... 38 D1
Firpark Terr FK2..... 6 C5
Firrhill Cres EH13..... 149 E8
Firrhill Dr EH13..... 149 E7
Firrhill High Sch EH14 . 149 D8
Firrhill Loan EH13..... 149 E7
Firs Cres FK7..... 7 D2
Firs Entry FK7..... 7 D2
Firs Pk (East Stirlingshire
  FC) FK2..... 60 C6
Firs Rd FK10..... 4 A2
Firs St FK2..... 60 C6
First Gait EH14..... 147 E8
Firs The Bannockburn FK7...7 D2
  Dalgety Bay KY11..... 48 B2
First St EH22..... 174 B5
Firth Cres EH26..... 171 D1
Firth Rd Livingston EH54.. 143 F7
  Penicuik EH26..... 171 D1
Fir View EH20..... 171 F7
Firwood Dr FK11..... 63 D5
Fishcross Prim Sch FK10...5 D3
Fishergate Rd EH32..... 97 E3
Fishermans Wlk FK9..... 2 A3
Fishernow Ind Est EH41..124 A6
Fishers' Rd EH49..... 63 D3
Fishers Rd EH32..... 97 D4
Fishers Wynd EH21..... 124 B6
Fishmarket Sq EH6..... 93 D7
Fishwives' Cswy
  Edinburgh EH7..... 94 F1
  Edinburgh EH15..... 95 A1
Fitzgerald Pl EH48..... 111 F5
Fitzroy Sq KY1..... 18 A7
Fitzroy St KY1..... 18 A7
Five Gates EH42..... 76 B5
Fivestanks Ct EH52..... 115 A5
Fivestanks Pl EH52..... 115 A5
Flare Rd FK3..... 62 B5
Flax Mill Rd ML7..... 159 F5
Fleets Gr EH33..... 126 D4
Fleets Ind Est EH33..... 126 C4
Fleets Rd EH33..... 126 C5
Fleets View EH33..... 126 D4
Fleming Ct FK6..... 57 D8
Fleming Dr FK5..... 39 A3
Fleming Gdns EH54..... 142 F2
Fleming Pl EH48..... 138 E3
Fleming Rd EH54..... 142 F2
Fleming St EH7..... 94 B2
Flemington Gdns EH47.. 160 F6
Fleming Way KY3..... 33 E2
Fleshmarket Cl EH1..... 229 A3
Flesh Wynd 12 KY1..... 17 C6
Fletcher Gr EH26..... 191 F8
Flint Cres EH47..... 20 D8
Floors Pl KY2..... 16 E5
Floors Terr EH42..... 78 C2
Florabank Rd EH41..... 101 A1
Flora Stevenson Prim Sch
  EH4..... 92 F2
Flotterstone Visitor Ctr
  EH26..... 170 D3
Flower Pl KY4..... 12 F8
Fodbank View KY11..... 29 E4
Foleys St KY11..... 30 B5
Follyburn Pl EH54..... 143 B4
Foote St KY5..... 14 A6
Foot Pl KY11..... 14 A6
Forbes Cres FK5..... 38 C5
Forbes Ct FK2..... 60 E6
Forbeslea Gdns KY12..... 27 E7
Forbes Rd
  Edinburgh EH10..... 121 B3
  Falkirk FK1..... 60 D4
  Rosyth KY11..... 46 C2
Forbes St Alloa FK10..... 9 F6
  Edinburgh EH8..... 229 B1
Forbes Terr KY2..... 17 B5
Ford's Rd Edinburgh EH11. 120 B4
  Edinburgh EH11..... 120 B4
Fordel Cvn & Camping Pk
  EH22..... 154 A2
Fordell Gdns
  Dalgety Bay KY11..... 47 C2
  Kirkcaldy KY2..... 16 E5
Fordell Ind Est KY4..... 13 B1
Fordell Way KY11..... 47 D2
Fordel Mains Cotts
  EH22..... 154 D2
Ford Rd Bonnybridge FK4...58 A5
  Haddington EH41..... 130 C8
Ford View KY12..... 28 C2
Fordyce Gdns FK1..... 59 E4
Forebraes FK10..... 10 C3
Foredale Terr EH51..... 64 D7
Foreshot Terr EH39..... 53 B5
Forestbank EH54..... 143 E5
Forester's Lea Cres KY12..26 D6
Forester Gr EH33..... 126 D6
Forester Gr FK10..... 9 F6
Forest Kirk ML8..... 215 B1
Forest Rd KY12..... 29 D7
Forest Row KY12..... 29 D7
Forest View FK2..... 61 F1
Forfar Pl KY2..... 16 E5
Forge The KY12..... 28 C6
Forge Cres FK2..... 83 A7
Forgie St FK9..... 2 A6
Forglen Rd FK9..... 2 A6
Forker Ave KY11..... 46 D4

Forkneuk Rd EH52 . . . . . . 114 E4
Forkneuk Steadings EH52 . . . . . . 114 E4
Forman Gr KY11 . . . . . . 29 E1
Forres Dr KY2 . . . . . . 16 C7
Forres St EH3 . . . . . . 228 B4
Forrester Ct KY5 . . . . . . 14 B7
Forrester Gait FK5 . . . . . . 37 E6
Forrester High Sch EH12 . . . . . . 119 D4
Forrester Park Ave EH12 . . . . . . 119 D4
Forrester Park Dr EH12 . 119 D4
Forrester Park Gdns EH12 . . . . . . 119 D4
Forrester Park Gn EH12 . 119 D4
Forrester Park Gr EH12 . 119 D4
Forrester Park Loan EH12 . . . . . . 119 D4
Forrester Pl FK2 . . . . . . 22 D3
Forrester Rd Armadale EH48 . . . . . . 139 F7
EH12 . . . . . . 119 D7
Forrestfield Rd ML6 . . . . . 137 A5
Forrest Hill EH1 . . . . . . 229 B2
Forrest Pl Armadale EH48 140 A4
Harthill ML7 . . . . . . 159 E5
Forrest Rd Edinburgh EH1 229 A2
Forrestfield ML6 . . . . . . 137 A1
Harthill ML6,ML7 . . . . . . 158 B6
Stirling FK8 . . . . . . 2 B1
Forrest St ML7 . . . . . . 179 E5
Forrest Wlk EH52 . . . . . . 114 F3
Forteviot Ho EH17 . . . . . . 151 D8
Forteviot Royal Hospl for Sick Children EH9 . . . . 121 C4
Forth Ave Kirkcaldy KY2 . . 17 A4
Larbert FK5 . . . . . . 38 B3
Forth Ave Ind Est EH54 . . 17 A3
Forthbank Ind Est FK10 . . 10 B4
Forthbank Pl KY12 . . . . . . 25 F1
Forth Bridge Visitor Ctr KY11 . . . . . . 68 A6
Forth Cres Alloa FK10 . . . . 10 C5
Dalgety Bay KY11 . . . . . . 48 B4
High Valleyfield KY12 . . . . 26 B2
Stirling FK8 . . . . . . 7 B8
Forth Ct Cockenzie & Port Seton EH32 . . . . . . 97 C4
Dalgety Bay KY11 . . . . . . 48 B4
Dunfermline KY12 . . . . . . 29 A2
Stirling FK8 . . . . . . 2 B1
Forth Dr FK54 . . . . . . 144 B5
Forth Gdns Cockenzie & Port Seton EH32 . . . . . . 97 C4
Oakley KY12 . . . . . . 26 E7
Forth Gr EH32 . . . . . . 97 E4
Forth Ind Est EH5 . . . . . . 92 E7
Fort Ho EH6 . . . . . . 93 E6
Forth Park Dr KY2 . . . . . . 17 A5
Forth Park Gdns KY2 . . . . . 17 A5
Forth Park Maternity Hospl KY2 . . . . . . 17 A5
Forth Pk Bridge of A FK9 . 2 A5
Queensferry EH30 . . . . . . 89 E8
Stirling FK9 . . . . . . 2 A5
Forth Pl Burntisland KY3 . . 50 E8
Queensferry EH30 . . . . . . 67 F1
Stirling FK8 . . . . . . 7 B8
Forth Prim Sch ML11 . . . 201 A1
Forth Rd KY11 . . . . . . 46 B2
Forth Reach KY11 . . . . . . 47 F2
Forthside Terr KY11 . . . . . 68 C5
Forth St Cambus FK10 . . . . 9 A8
Dunfermline KY12 . . . . . . 29 A2
Edinburgh EH1 . . . . . . 93 D2
Fallin FK7 . . . . . . 8 C4
Grangemouth FK3 . . . . . . 61 D8
Kincardine FK10 . . . . . . 23 D3
North Berwick EH39 . . . . . 54 C7
Stirling FK8 . . . . . . 2 B1
Forth Street La EH54 . . . . 54 C7
Forth Terr Grangemouth FK3 . . . . . . 61 D8
Queensferry EH30 . . . . . . 89 D8
Forthvale FK11 . . . . . . 4 A6
Forthvale Ct FK9 . . . . . . 2 B2
Forth Valley Coll Clackmannan FK10 . . . . . 10 B8
Forth Valley Coll Falkirk FK2 . . . . . . 59 F5
Forth Valley Coll Hall Park (Annexe) FK10 . . . . . . 10 C8
Forth Valley Coll Stirling FK7 . . . . . . 7 E1
Forthview FK7 . . . . . . 7 E1
Forth View Dalgety Bay KY11 . . . . . . 48 B4
Inverkeithing KY11 . . . . . 47 B2
Kincardine FK10 . . . . . . 23 F3
Kirknewton EH27 . . . . . . 145 E3
Stirling FK8 . . . . . . 2 B1
West Barns EH42 . . . . . . 77 F1
Forthview Ave EH14 . . . . . 147 F4
Forth View Cotts KY12 . . . 26 A1
Forthview Cres Currie EH14 . . . . . . 147 F4
Danderhall EH22 . . . . . . 152 B7
Forthview Ct 5 Falkirk FK1 . . . . . . 59 F2
6 Tranent EH33 . . . . . . 126 D7
Forthview Dr EH21 . . . . . 125 B5

Forthview Gdns FK2 . . . . . . 82 C8
Forth View Ind Est KY12 . . 26 B1
Forthview Prim Sch EH14 . 92 D4
Forthview Rd Edinburgh EH4 . . . . . . 92 C2
Longniddry EH32 . . . . . . 98 E6
Forth View Rd EH14 . . . . 147 F4
Forthview Terr Edinburgh EH4 . . . . . . 92 B2
Grangemouth FK2 . . . . . . 82 B8
Newmills KY12 . . . . . . 26 D1
Wallyford EH21 . . . . . . 125 B4
Forthview Wlk EH33 . . . . 126 D7
Forth Wynd EH32 . . . . . . 97 D3
Forties Campus KY11 . . . . . 46 D1
Forties Rd FK3,EH51 . . . . . 62 D5
Fortingall Cres EH22 . . . . . 62 A2
Fortissat Ave ML7 . . . . . . 179 D6
Fort Kinnaird Ret Pk EH15 . . . . . . 123 C4
Fort Prim Sch EH6 . . . . . . 93 E6
Fortuna Ct FK1 . . . . . . 60 C4
Fortune Ave EH41 . . . . . . 101 A1
Foulden Pl 29 D3
Foulford Pl KY4 . . . . . . 13 B4
Foulford Prim Sch KY4 . . . 13 B5
Foulford St KY4 . . . . . . 13 B4
Foulis Cres EH14 . . . . . . 148 E6
Foulshiels Rd EH47 . . . . . 162 C2
Foundry La EH20 . . . . . . 151 D1
Foundry Loan FK5 . . . . . . 38 B2
Foundry Rd Bonnybridge FK4 . . . . . . 58 B5
Shotts ML7 . . . . . . 179 F4
Foundry St Dunfermline KY12 . . . . . . 29 A4
Falkirk FK2 . . . . . . 60 A8
Fountainbridge EH3 . . . . 229 A2
Fountain Cl EH1 . . . . . . 229 A3
Fountainhall Rd EH9 . . . . 121 E4
Fountainside Rd EH48 . . . 141 B7
Fountainpark Cres EH51 . . 64 C7
Fountain Pl Cowdenbeath KY4 . . . . . . 13 D3
Loanhead EH20 . . . . . . 172 C8
Pathhead EH37 . . . . . . 176 A5
Fountain Rd FK9 . . . . . . 2 A7
Fourth Gait EH14 . . . . . . 147 E7
Fourth St EH22 . . . . . . 174 B5
Fowler Cres Denny FK6 . . . 36 E1
Loanhead EH20 . . . . . . 172 D8
Maddiston FK2 . . . . . . 83 A5
Fowlers Ct EH32 . . . . . . 96 F2
Fowler Sq EH20 . . . . . . 172 D8
Fowler Terr EH11 . . . . . . 120 F5
Fox Covert Ave EH12 . . . . 91 E1
Fox Covert Gr EH12 . . . . . 91 E1
Fox Covert RC Prim Schs EH12 . . . . . . 91 E1
Foxdale Ave FK4 . . . . . . 58 A3
Foxdale Ct FK4 . . . . . . 58 A3
Foxdale Dr FK4 . . . . . . 58 A3
Foxdale Pl FK4 . . . . . . 58 A3
Foxglove Neuk KY12 . . . . . 29 A5
Foxknowe Pl EH54 . . . . . 143 B4
Fox Spring Cres EH10 . . . 150 A7
Fox Spring Rise EH10 . . . 150 A7
Fox St EH6 . . . . . . 94 B5
Frances Ind Pk KY1 . . . . . . 18 B8
Frances View KY1 . . . . . . 18 A8
Franchi Dr FK1 . . . . . . 60 C5
Francis La KY12 . . . . . . 28 D5
Francis St KY5 . . . . . . 14 B7
Frankfield Cres KY11 . . . . . 48 D4
Frankfield Pl KY11 . . . . . . 48 D4
Frankfield Rd KY11 . . . . . . 48 D4
Fraser Ave Edinburgh EH5 . 93 A5
Inverkeithing KY11 . . . . . 47 D2
Fraser Cres EH5 . . . . . . 93 A5
Fraser Gdns EH5 . . . . . . 93 A5
Fraser Gr EH5 . . . . . . 93 A5
Fraser of Allander Ho FK9 . 2 D6
Fraser Pl Dysart KY1 . . . . . 18 A8
Grangemouth FK3 . . . . . . 61 D6
Stirling FK9 . . . . . . 2 B4
Fraser Rd EH54 . . . . . . 142 F2
Frederick Cres KY11 . . . . . 29 B2
Frederick St EH2 . . . . . . 228 C4
Frederick Wilson Pk KY12 . 17 A7
Freeland Ave EH52 . . . . . 115 B5
Freelands Rd EH28 . . . . . 117 C3
Freeland Terr EH52 . . . . . 115 B5
Freeport Village EH51 . . . 163 A4
Fremantle St EH54 . . . . . 144 A5
Freskyn Pl EH52 . . . . . . 116 A6
Frew Ct KY11 . . . . . . 29 C5
Friar's Croft EH42 . . . . . . 78 D2
Friar's Bank Terr EH42 . . . 78 D2
Friars Brae EH49 . . . . . . 85 A6
Friars Loan EH49 . . . . . . 85 A6
Friars St FK8 . . . . . . 7 B8
Friars Way EH49 . . . . . . 85 A5
Friarton Gdns EH26 . . . . . 191 C5
Friary Ct KY11 . . . . . . 47 C2
Friendship Gdns FK2 . . . . . 39 C6
Frobisher Ave FK1 . . . . . . 59 F4
Frogston Ave EH10 . . . . . 150 B5
Frogston Brae EH17 . . . . . 150 E4
Frogston Gdns EH10 . . . . 150 C5
Frogston Gr EH10 . . . . . . 150 C5
Frogston Rd E EH17 . . . . . 150 F5
Frogston Rd W EH10 . . . . 150 C4
Frogston Terr EH10 . . . . . 150 C5
Fulfordlees Cotts TD13 . . 218 D1

Fullerton Dr FK2 . . . . . . 61 E3
Fulmar Brae EH4 . . . . . . 143 C5
Fulmar Cres FK5 . . . . . . 38 C5
Fulmar Way KY11 . . . . . . 48 B4
Furcheons Pk EH8 . . . . . . 122 E8
Furnace La EH51 . . . . . . 64 C8
Furnace Pl KY4 . . . . . . 13 E6
Furniss Ave KY11 . . . . . . 46 D5
Fyne La ML7 . . . . . . 179 E6

G

Gaberston Ave FK10 . . . . . 10 C7
Gabriel's Rd EH2 . . . . . . 229 A4
Gagarin Way KY11 . . . . . . 13 E6
Gair Cres ML8 . . . . . . 215 A3
Gairdoch Dr FK2 . . . . . . 39 C3
Gairdoch St FK2 . . . . . . 60 B8
Gairloch Cres FK2 . . . . . . 61 C2
Gair Rd ML8 . . . . . . 215 B5
Gair Wynd ML7 . . . . . . 180 B3
Galabraes Cres EH48 . . . . 141 C7
Galachlawshot EH10 . . . . 150 C6
Galachlawside EH10 . . . . 150 C5
Galadale EH22 . . . . . . 174 A6
Galadale Cres EH22 . . . . . 174 A6
Galadale Dr EH22 . . . . . . 174 A6
Gala Gn EH42 . . . . . . 78 B2
Gallacher Gn EH54 . . . . . 143 C8
Gallacher Pl KY4 . . . . . . 13 E6
Gallamuir Dr FK7 . . . . . . 20 D3
Gallamuir Rd FK7 . . . . . . 20 D5
Gallolee The EH13 . . . . . . 149 D6
Galloway Cres EH52 . . . . 115 C6
Galloway Ct FK1,FK2 . . . . . 60 B6
Galloway St FK1 . . . . . . 60 B6
Gallowsknowe EH49 . . . . . 84 D7
Gallows Loan KY12 . . . . . . 25 D2
Gallow View EH52 . . . . . . 88 A8
Gallswood Gdns EH48 . . . 140 B5
Galmeilen EH52 . . . . . . 115 C5
Galt Ave EH21 . . . . . . 125 A5
Galt Cres EH21 . . . . . . 125 A5
Galt Dr EH21 . . . . . . 125 A6
Galt Rd EH21 . . . . . . 125 A5
Galt Terr EH21 . . . . . . 125 A5
Gambeson Cres FK7 . . . . . 7 D3
Gamekeeper's Loan EH4 . . 91 B5
Gamekeeper's Pk EH4 . . . 91 B5
Gamekeeper's Rd EH4 . . . 91 B5
Garbett Rd EH54 . . . . . . 143 C1
Garden City EH47 . . . . . . 162 A1
Garden Ct KY12 . . . . . . 29 B4
Gardeners' St KY12 . . . . . . 29 B4
Gardeners Ct EH42 . . . . . . 78 C3
Gardenerswell Villas 3 EH48 . . . . . . 141 B7
Gardener's Wlk EH6 . . . . 191 C6
Gardenhead FK2 . . . . . . 61 F2
Garden La Cairneyhill KY12 . 27 C1
Clackmannan FK10 . . . . . 11 A4
Livingston EH54 . . . . . . 143 C4
Townhill KY12 . . . . . . 29 C8
Garden St FK1 . . . . . . 60 C5
Gardens The Aberlady EH32 . . . . . . 71 D5
Dirleton EH39 . . . . . . 53 B5
Garden Terr Clackmannan FK10 . . . . . 11 A4
Edinburgh EH4 . . . . . . 91 F1
Falkirk FK1 . . . . . . 60 C5
Westquarter FK2 . . . . . . 61 A2
Gardiner's Cl EH32 . . . . . . 97 C4
Gardiner's Pl EH33 . . . . . 126 C7
Gardiner Gr EH32 . . . . . . 97 B1
Gardiner Rd Cowdenbeath KY4 . . . . . . 13 B2
Newtongrange EH22 . . . 174 B6
Gardiner Terr Edinburgh EH4 . . . . . . 92 B2
Prestonpans EH32 . . . . . 126 A8
Gardner St KY5 . . . . . . 14 B7
Gardrum Gdns FK1 . . . . . . 81 D7
Gardrum Pl FK2 . . . . . . 82 F7
Gardrum Terr FK1 . . . . . . 81 F5
Gareloch Way EH47 . . . . . 161 D7
Garleton Ct EH31 . . . . . . 52 B2
Garleton Dr EH41 . . . . . . 100 F1
Garleton Pk EH41 . . . . . . 71 C4
Garngrew Rd FK4 . . . . . . 57 A3
Garrison Pl FK1 . . . . . . 60 B5
Garry Pl Falkirk FK1 . . . . . 60 D2
Garry St KY5 . . . . . . 14 B8
Garry Way ML7 . . . . . . 179 E6
Garry Wlk EH54 . . . . . . 144 B4
Garscube Terr EH12 . . . . . 120 D8
Gartclush Gdns FK7 . . . . . 19 E8
Gartcows Ave FK1 . . . . . . 60 A4
Gartcows Cres FK1 . . . . . . 60 A4
Gartcows Dr FK1 . . . . . . 60 A4
Gartcows Gdns 5 FK1 . . . 59 F4
Gartcows Pl FK1 . . . . . . 60 A4
Gartcows Rd FK1 . . . . . . 60 A4
Garten Dr ML7 . . . . . . 180 B3
Garthill Gdns FK1 . . . . . . 60 A4
Garthill La FK1 . . . . . . 60 A4

Gartmorn Dam Ctry Pk FK10 . . . . . . 11 B8
Gartmorn Rd FK10 . . . . . . 5 D1
Garvald La FK6 . . . . . . 36 C1
Garvald Rd FK6 . . . . . . 57 D7
Garvally Cres FK10 . . . . . . 10 A8
Garvock Bank KY11 . . . . . . 29 F4
Garvock Hill KY12 . . . . . . 29 A4
Garvock Terr KY12 . . . . . . 29 A4
Gascoigne Ct 8 FK2 . . . . 60 A8
Gasworks La North Berwick EH39 . . . . . 53 F6
Whitburn EH47 . . . . . . 161 B7
Gas Wynd KY1 . . . . . . 17 B2
Gateside Ave Bonnybridge FK4 . . . . . . 58 C6
Haddington EH41 . . . . . . 100 D1
Gateside Commerce Pk EH41 . . . . . . 129 D8
Gateside Ct KY4 . . . . . . 13 A3
Gateside Ind Est KY4 . . . . . 13 A3
Gateside Rd Haddington EH41 . . . . . . 129 D8
Kirkliston EH29 . . . . . . 89 A1
Stirling FK7 . . . . . . 7 A3
Whitburn EH47 . . . . . . 160 F6
Gateway Bsns Pk FK3 . . . . 61 C5
Gauger's Bush EH42 . . . . . 76 B6
Gauze Ct EH51 . . . . . . 64 A6
Gauze Pl EH51 . . . . . . 64 A6
Gauze Rd EH51 . . . . . . 64 A6
Gavald Grange Steading EH41 . . . . . . 132 D3
Gavin Pl EH54 . . . . . . 143 B5
Gavins Rd FK10 . . . . . . 4 F1
Gayfield Cl 4 EH1 . . . . . . 93 E2
Gayfield Pl 8 EH7 . . . . . . 93 E2
Gayfield Place La EH1 . . . . 93 E2
Gayfield Sq EH1 . . . . . . 93 E2
Gayfield St EH1 . . . . . . 93 E2
Gayfield Street La 6 EH1 . 93 E2
Gaynor Ave EH20 . . . . . . 172 B8
Gean Rd FK10 . . . . . . 9 F8
Geddes' Entry EH1 . . . . . 229 A3
Gelder Dr EH54 . . . . . . 164 E6
Gellatly Rd KY11 . . . . . . 29 C2
Gentiles Entry EH8 . . . . . 229 C3
George Ave EH20 . . . . . . 172 B8
George Burn Wynd KY1 . . . 17 C3
George Cres Loanhead EH20 . . . . . . 172 C8
Ormiston EH35 . . . . . . 155 D7
George Dr EH20 . . . . . . 172 C8
George Heriot's Sch EH3 . . . . . . 228 C2
George IV Bridge EH1 . . . 229 A2
George Laing Ct FK5 . . . . . 38 E2
George Pl EH48 . . . . . . 141 A6
George Sq EH8 . . . . . . 229 A1
George Square La EH8 . . . 229 A1
George Square Theatre EH8 . . . . . . 229 A1
George St Alva FK12 . . . . . 5 A6
Armadale EH48 . . . . . . 139 E6
Bathgate EH48 . . . . . . 141 A6
Bo'ness EH51 . . . . . . 63 F6
Cowdenbeath KY4 . . . . . . 13 B4
Dunfermline KY11 . . . . . . 29 B2
Edinburgh EH2 . . . . . . 228 B3
Falkirk FK1 . . . . . . 60 B5
Grangemouth FK3 . . . . . . 61 F8
Kincardine FK10 . . . . . . 23 E3
Kirkcaldy KY1 . . . . . . 60 F3
Ormiston EH35 . . . . . . 155 E7
Stenhousemuir FK5 . . . . . 38 C3
George Terr EH20 . . . . . . 172 B8
George Watson's Coll EH10 . . . . . . 120 F4
George Watson's Coll Lower Prim Sch EH10 . . . . . . 120 F4
George Watson's Coll Upper Prim Sch EH10 . . . . . . 120 F4
George Way 8 EH33 . . . 126 C5
George Wlk 4 EH33 . . . 126 C5
Georgian Ho The EH2 . . . 228 B4
Gerald Terr FK5 . . . . . . 38 E3
Gibbdun Pl FK6 . . . . . . 57 E7
Gibbs Entry EH8 . . . . . . 229 B2
Gibbshill Pl ML7 . . . . . . 159 D5
Gib Gr 11 KY11 . . . . . . 29 E1
Gibraltar Ct EH22 . . . . . . 153 B3
Gibraltar Gdns EH22 . . . . 153 A3
Gibraltar Terr EH22 . . . . . 153 A3
Gibson Dr EH22 . . . . . . 153 C4
Gibsongray St FK2 . . . . . . 60 A7
Gibson St Denny FK6 . . . . . 36 C1
Edinburgh EH7 . . . . . . 93 E4
Gibson Terr EH11 . . . . . . 228 A1
Gideon Ct EH48 . . . . . . 141 B7
Gideon St EH48 . . . . . . 141 B7
Giffordgate EH41 . . . . . . 130 C7
Gifford Pk EH8 . . . . . . 229 B1
Gifford Rd EH41 . . . . . . 130 C7
Gilbertson Rd EH15 . . . . . 123 D5
Gilbertstoun Brig EH15 . . 123 D5
Gilbertstoun Pl EH15 . . . . 123 D5
Gilbertstoun Wynd EH15 . 123 D5
Gilbert Ave EH9 . . . . . . 54 C6
Gilburn Pl Bo'ness EH51 . . 63 F7
Shotts ML7 . . . . . . 179 F4
Gilchrist Cres EH47 . . . . . 161 B6
Gilchrist Dr FK1 . . . . . . 59 E4
Giles St EH6 . . . . . . 93 F5
Gilfillan Pl FK2 . . . . . . 60 B6
Gilfillan Rd KY11 . . . . . . 29 C4

Gillespie Cres EH10 . . . . . 228 B1
Gillespie Gr KY12 . . . . . . 26 E7
Gillespie Pl Armadale EH48 . . . . . . 139 F4
Edinburgh EH11 . . . . . . 228 B1
Stirling FK7 . . . . . . 7 B1
Gillespie Rd EH13 . . . . . . 148 F6
Gillespie St EH3 . . . . . . 228 B1
Gillespie Terr FK7 . . . . . . 20 D2
Gillie Dr EH47 . . . . . . 151 D8
Gillies Ct KY11 . . . . . . 29 C2
Gillies Hill FK7 . . . . . . 6 D5
Gill Pk FK6 . . . . . . 36 E2
Gillsland Rd EH10 . . . . . . 120 F4
Gill Way KY11 . . . . . . 46 C5
Gilmerton Dykes Ave EH17 . . . . . . 151 D5
Gilmerton Dykes Cres EH17 . . . . . . 151 D5
Gilmerton Dykes Dr EH17 . . . . . . 151 D5
Gilmerton Dykes Gdns EH17 . . . . . . 151 D5
Gilmerton Dykes Gr EH17 . . . . . . 151 C6
Gilmerton Dykes Loan EH17 . . . . . . 151 D5
Gilmerton Dykes Pl EH17 . . . . . . 151 D5
Gilmerton Dykes Rd EH41 . . . . . . 151 C6
Gilmerton Dykes St EH17 . . . . . . 151 D5
Gilmerton Dykes Terr EH17 . . . . . . 151 D5
Gilmerton Dykes View EH17 . . . . . . 151 D5
Gilmerton Pl EH17 . . . . . . 151 D5
Gilmerton Prim Sch EH17 . . . . . . 151 D6
Gilmerton Rd Bonnyrigg and Lasswade EH18 . . . . . . 152 C4
Dalkeith EH22 . . . . . . 152 E3
Edinburgh EH17 . . . . . . 151 D7
Gilmerton Road Rdbt EH22 . . . . . . 152 D3
Gilmerton Station Rd EH17 . . . . . . 151 E4
Gilmore Pk EH11 . . . . . . 228 A1
Gilmore Place La EH3 . . . 228 B1
Gilmour Rd EH16 . . . . . . 121 F3
Gilmour St Cowdenbeath KY4 . . . . . . 13 C6
Edinburgh EH8 . . . . . . 229 B2
Gilsay Ct FK1 . . . . . . 60 C2
Gilsland Cvn Pk EH39 . . . . 54 C5
Gilston Cres FK2 . . . . . . 62 A1
Gipsy La KY11 . . . . . . 29 F3
Gladney Sq KY1 . . . . . . 17 B2
Gladsmuir ML11 . . . . . . 201 A1
Gladsmuir Junc EH33 . . . 128 A2
Gladstone Pl Dunfermline KY12 . . . . . . 29 A5
Edinburgh EH6 . . . . . . 94 B4
Stirling FK5 . . . . . . 7 A6
Gladstone Rd FK9 . . . . . . 38 D3
Gladstone Terr EH9 . . . . . 121 E5
Glaive Ave FK7 . . . . . . 7 D3
Glamis Gdns Dalgety Bay KY11 . . . . . . 48 B3
Polmont FK2 . . . . . . 61 F1
Glamis Rd Kinghorn KY3 . . 34 F3
Kirkcaldy KY2 . . . . . . 16 F3
Glamis Terr KY3 . . . . . . 34 F3
Glanville Pl 7 EH3 . . . . . 93 B2
Glasclune Ct EH39 . . . . . . 54 D7
Glasclune Gdns EH39 . . . . 54 D7
Glasgow Rd Bathgate EH48 . . . . . . 140 F6
Denny FK6 . . . . . . 36 E1
Edinburgh EH12 . . . . . . 119 B6
Falkirk FK1 . . . . . . 59 C6
Gogar FK1,2 . . . . . . 118 C5
Longcroft FK4 . . . . . . 57 C4
Stirling FK7 . . . . . . 7 B2
Glashkill Terr FK9 . . . . . . 191 E6
Glass Cres EH52 . . . . . . 87 F2
Glassel Park Rd EH32 . . . . 98 D4
Glasshouse Loan FK10 . . . 10 A6
Glass Pl FK52 . . . . . . 87 F2
Glass Rd EH52 . . . . . . 87 F1
Glasswork St KY1 . . . . . . 17 B3
Glebe Ave Stirling FK8 . . . . 7 A7
Uphall EH52 . . . . . . 115 A6
Glebe Cres Alva FK12 . . . . 5 B7
Athelstaneford EH39 . . . 101 F7
Stirling FK8 . . . . . . 7 A7
Glebe Ct EH47 . . . . . . 181 D6
Glebe Gdns Edinburgh EH12 . . . . . . 119 E6
4 Prestonpans EH32 . . . 96 F1
Edinburgh EH12 . . . . . . 119 D6
Glebe Pk Inverkeithing KY11 . . . . . 47 B1
Kirkcaldy KY1 . . . . . . 17 C5
Glebe Pl Bonnyrigg and Lasswade EH18 . . . . . . 151 F1
Burntisland KY3 . . . . . . 33 E1
Uphall EH52 . . . . . . 115 A4
Glebe Rd Bathgate EH48 . . 141 C6
Edinburgh EH12 . . . . . . 119 D6

Glebe Rd *continued*
Kincardine FK10 . . . . .23 E5
Uphall EH52 . . . . .115 A4
West Calder EH55 . . . . . . .163 D2
Whitburn EH47 . . . . .161 A6
Glebe St Dalkeith EH22. . .153 A3
Denny FK6. . . . . .36 E2
Falkirk FK1. . . . . .60 B5
Glebe Terr Alloa FK10. . . . .10 A6
Edinburgh EH12. . . . . .119 D6
Haddington EH41. . . . . . . .101 A1
Inverkeithing KY11. . . . . . . .47 B1
Uphall EH52. . . . . .115 A5
Glebe The Aberdour KY3. . .49 C8
Alva FK12. . . . . .5 B7
Clackmannan FK10 . . . . . . .11 A4
Dalmeny EH30. . . . . .89 E7
East Linton EH40. . . . . . . .103 E8
East Saltoun EH34. . . . . . .157 F4
Edinburgh EH4. . . . . .91 B6
Kirkliston EH29. . . . . .89 A1
Linlithgow EH49. . . . . .85 A5
Pencaitland EH34. . . . . . . .156 F7
West Calder EH55. . . . . . . .163 D2
Gledhill Ave EH51. . . . . . . .64 D5
Glenafeoch Rd ML8. . . . . .215 A1
Glen Albyn Dr KY2. . . . . . . .16 B8
Glenallan Dr EH16. . . . . . .122 B2
Glenallan Loan EH16. . . . .122 B2
Glenalmond EH47. . . . . . . .161 C5
Glenalmond Ct
Broxburn EH52. . . . . .115 B5
Whitburn EH47. . . . . .161 A6
Glenalmond Terr EH48. . . .141 B8
Glenard View EH51. . . . . . . .64 D6
Glen Artney Gr KY11. . . . . . .29 D1
Glenavon Dr KY12. . . . . .27 C1
Glen Avon Pl FK2. . . . . .82 F7
Glenavon Terr EH48. . . . . .141 B8
Glenbank FK1. . . . . .60 B5
Glenbare Ct EH48. . . . . . . .141 C6
Glen Beasdale Ct KY11. . . .29 D1
Glenbervie FK5. . . . . .38 A4
Glenbervie Ave FK5. . . . . . .38 A3
Glenbervie Cres FK5. . . . . .38 B3
Glenbervie Dr FK5. . . . . . . .38 A3
Glenbervie Gr KY11. . . . . . . .29 D1
Glenbervie Rd FK3. . . . . . . .61 F6
Glenbo Dr FK6. . . . . .57 E7
Glen Brae FK1. . . . . .60 B3
Glenbrae Ct FK1. . . . . .60 B3
Glen Bridge KY12. . . . . .28 F4
Glenbridge Ct KY12. . . . . . .28 F4
Glenbrook EH14. . . . . .167 E8
Glenbrook Rd EH14. . . . . .147 A1
Glen Bruar Pl KY2. . . . . .16 B8
Glenburn Gdns EH47. . . . .161 D6
Glenburn Gr KY12. . . . . .26 E7
Glenburn Rd Falkirk FK1. . . .60 D1
North Berwick EH39. . . . . . .54 D6
Glenburn Way EH51. . . . . . .63 D5
Glencairn Cres EH12. . . . . .120 F7
Glencairn St Falkirk FK1. . . .59 B5
Stirling FK7. . . . . .7 B3
Glencairn Terr EH48. . . . . .141 C8
Glen Clova Cres KY12. . . . . .27 C1
Glencoe EH47. . . . . .161 D6
Glencoe Rd Carluke ML8. . .215 A1
Stirling FK8. . . . . .2 A1
Glencorse Rd EH26. . . . . . .192 C8
Glencorse Prim Sch
EH26. . . . . .171 B1
Glencoul Ave KY11. . . . . . . .48 A3
Glen Cres Falkirk FK1. . . . . .60 B1
Livingston EH54. . . . . .142 E6
Glencross Gdns EH26. . . . .191 C5
Glen Ct EH54. . . . . .142 E6
Glendevon Ave EH12. . . . . .120 B6
Glendevon Dr FK5. . . . . .1 F2
Glendevon Gdns EH12. . . .120 B6
Glendevon Gr EH12. . . . . . .120 B6
Glendevon Pk
Edinburgh EH12. . . . . .120 B6
Winchburgh EH52. . . . . .87 E2
Glendevon Pl EH12. . . . . . .120 B6
Glendevon Terr EH12. . . . .120 B6
Glendinning Cres EH16. . . .151 B8
Glendinning Dr EH29. . . . . .88 F2
Glendinning Pl EH29. . . . . .88 F2
Glendinning Rd EH29. . . . . .88 F2
Glendinning Way EH29. . . . .89 A2
Gleneagles Ct EH47. . . . . .161 C5
Gleneagles Way EH54. . . . .142 E5
Glenesk Cres EH22. . . . . . .152 F2
Glenfarg Cres KY4. . . . . .13 C5
Glenfield Carnock KY12. . . . .27 C6
Livingston EH54. . . . . .143 A3
Glenfield Ave KY4. . . . . .13 C5
Glenfield Cres KY4. . . . . . . .13 C5
Glenfield Ct KY4. . . . . .13 C5
Glenfield Gdns KY4. . . . . . .13 C5
Glenfield Ind Est KY4. . . . . .13 C5
Glenfield Rd KY4. . . . . .13 C5
Glenfinlas St EH3. . . . . . . .228 B3
Glen Fruin Gr KY11. . . . . . . .29 D1
Glenfuir Ct FK1. . . . . .59 C5
Glenfuir Rd FK1. . . . . .59 C5
Glenfuir St FK1. . . . . .59 C5
Glengairn Wlk KY11. . . . . . .29 D1
Glengarry Cres FK1. . . . . . . .59 F2
Glen Gdns FK1. . . . . .60 A3
Glengyle Terr EH3. . . . . . . .228 B1
Glenisla Ct EH47. . . . . .161 D5

Glenisla Gardens La
EH9 . . . . .121 D3
Glenisla Gdns EH9. . . . . . . .121 D3
Glenisla Gr KY11. . . . . .29 D1
Glen Isla Rd KY2. . . . . .16 C8
Glen Kinchie FK10. . . . . .4 A2
Glenkinchie Distillery
EH34. . . . . .156 E2
Glenkinchie Hos EH34. . . .156 E2
Glenlee Ave EH8. . . . . .122 C8
Glenlee Gdns EH8. . . . . . . .122 C8
Glenlockhart Bank EH14 120 D1
Glenlockhart Rd EH11. . . . .120 E1
Glenlockhart Valley
EH14 . . . . .120 D2
Glen Lyon Ct FK2. . . . . .22 A2
Glenmavis Cres ML8. . . . . .215 A1
Glenmavis St ML8. . . . . . . .215 A1
Glenmavis Dr EH48. . . . . . .141 B7
Glenmore EH47. . . . . .161 C6
Glenmore Dr FK4. . . . . .57 F6
Glen More Gdns KY2. . . . . . .16 B8
Glen Moriston Dr KY12. . . . .27 C1
Glen Nevis Dr KY11. . . . . . . .29 D1
Glennie Gdns EH33. . . . . . .126 D6
Glenochil Pk FK10. . . . . .4 E4
Glenochil Rd FK10. . . . . .4 A3
Glenochil Terr FK10. . . . . . . .4 A3
Glenogle Ct EH3. . . . . .93 B2
Glen Ogle Ct FK2. . . . . .22 A2
Glenogle Ho 3 EH3. . . . . . .93 B2
Glenogle Pl 4 EH3. . . . . . . .93 B2
Glenogle Rd EH3. . . . . .93 B2
Glenogle Terr EH3. . . . . .93 B2
Glenorchy Rd EH39. . . . . . . .54 B6
Glenorchy Terr EH9. . . . . . .121 F4
Glenpeffer Ave EH32. . . . . . .71 D4
Glen Pl EH26. . . . . .191 E6
Glen Rd Armadale EH48. . .139 F5
Livingston EH54. . . . . .142 E6
Plean FK5,FK7. . . . . .37 D8
Shotts ML7. . . . . .179 F4
Torwood FK5. . . . . .37 D7
Glensburgh Rd FK3. . . . . . . .61 A8
Glenshee EH47. . . . . .161 C5
Glenshiel Gr KY11. . . . . .29 D1
Glenside Ct
Armadale EH48. . . . . .139 E6
Grangemouth FK3. . . . . .61 E6
Glenside Gdns EH48. . . . . .139 E6
Glen St EH3. . . . . .228 C1
Glen Terr Denny FK6. . . . . . .36 D1
Livingston EH54. . . . . .142 E6
Glen The Bathgate EH48. . .141 A8
Tullibody FK10. . . . . .4 C3
Glentye Gdns FK1. . . . . .59 E2
Glen Tye Rd FK7. . . . . .7 D5
Glenure Loan EH4. . . . . .92 D5
Glenvarloch Cres 1
EH16. . . . . .151 B8
Glenview Frankerton FK6. . . .36 A3
Menstrie FK11. . . . . .4 A6
Penicuik EH26. . . . . .191 E6
Glen View Bo'ness FK51. . . . .63 D4
Bonnybridge FK4. . . . . .57 D5
Glenview Cres EH47. . . . . .162 B2
Glen View Cres EH23. . . . . .195 C8
Glen View Ct EH23. . . . . . . .195 C8
Glenview Dr FK5. . . . . .59 F2
Glen View Pl EH23. . . . . . . .195 C7
Glenview Rd EH47. . . . . . . .162 B1
Glen View Rd EH23. . . . . . .174 C1
Glen View Wlk EH23. . . . . .195 C8
Glen Way 3 EH48. . . . . . . .141 B7
Glenwinnel Rd EH12. . . . . . .4 E7
Glenwood Dr EH48. . . . . . .139 D6
Glenyards Rd FK4. . . . . .57 F2
Gloag Pl EH55. . . . . .163 D3
Globe Pk EH52. . . . . .115 C5
Globe Rd KY11. . . . . .46 D2
Gloucester Gr KY12. . . . . . . .28 E5
Gloucester La EH3. . . . . . . .228 B4
Gloucester Pl EH3. . . . . . . .228 B4
Gloucester Sq EH3. . . . . . . .228 A4
Gloucester St EH3. . . . . . . .228 B4
Glover's St KY3. . . . . .35 A3
Glowrorum Dr FK6. . . . . .57 E7
Glynwed Ct FK2. . . . . .60 C7
Godfrey Ave FK6. . . . . .36 D1
Godfrey Cres FK5. . . . . .38 C1
Goff Ave FK7. . . . . .94 F1
Gogarbank Farm EH12. . . .118 C2
Gogar Bridge Rd EH12. . . .118 A7
Gogar Loan FK9. . . . . .3 D5
Gogarloch Bank EH12. . . . .119 B5
Gogarloch Haugh EH12. . . .119 B5
Gogarloch Muir EH12. . . . .119 B5
Gogarloch Rd EH12. . . . . . .119 B5
Gogarloch Syke EH12. . . . .119 C5
Gogar Mains Farm Cotts
EH12 . . . . .118 C2
Gogar Pl FK7. . . . . .7 C2
Gogar Rbdt HE12. . . . . .118 E5
Gogar Station Rd EH12. . . .118 E5
Gogarstone Rd EH12,
EH28. . . . . .118 B5
Goldenacre Terr EH3. . . . . . .93 B4
Goldenstones Ave EH42. . . .78 E1
Goldpark Pl EH54. . . . . .143 A3
Golf Course Rd
Bonnyrigg and Lasswade
EH19. . . . . .173 B8
Cowdenbeath KY4. . . . . .13 C6
Linlithgow EH49. . . . . .84 E5
Livingston EH54. . . . . .143 B8
Golf Ct EH32. . . . . .71 C4
Golf Dr EH32. . . . . .97 E4
Golfdrum St KY12. . . . . .28 E4

Golf House Rd EH42. . . . . . .78 F1
Gollet Way KY12. . . . . .43 F8
Goodall's Pl 8 EH41. . . . . .130 B8
Goodall Cres EH52. . . . . . .114 B2
Goodall Pl EH52. . . . . .114 B2
Goodman Pl FK2. . . . . .82 E7
Goodtrees Gdns EH17. . . . .151 D8
Goosecroft Rd FK8. . . . . .7 B8
Goosedubs Pl FK2. . . . . .59 F8
Goose Green Ave EH21. . . .124 D7
Goose Green Cres EH21. . .124 D7
Goose Green Pl EH21. . . . .124 D7
Goose Green Rd
Gullane EH31. . . . . .52 A2
Musselburgh EH21. . . . . . .124 D7
Gordon Ave
Bathgate EH48. . . . . .141 B5
Bonnyrigg and Lasswade
EH19. . . . . .172 F6
Gordon Cres Bridge of A FK9 2 A8
Stirling FK8. . . . . .1 F2
Gordon Ct Broxburn EH52 .115 F5
Edinburgh EH6. . . . . .94 A4
Gordon Dr FK10. . . . . .112 C8
Gordon Loan EH12. . . . . . .119 E2
Gordon Pl FK1. . . . . .59 E5
Gordon Rd
Edinburgh EH12. . . . . .119 E2
Rosyth KY11. . . . . .46 B2
Gordon St
Cowdenbeath KY4. . . . . .13 C6
Easthouses EH22. . . . . . . .174 C7
Edinburgh EH6. . . . . .94 A4
Lochgelly KY5. . . . . .14 A8
Gordon Terr
Dunfermline KY11. . . . . .29 B1
Edinburgh EH16. . . . . .122 A2
Gordon Way EH54. . . . . . . .143 D7
Gore Ave EH23. . . . . .195 D8
Gorebridge Prim Sch
EH23. . . . . .195 C8
Goremire Rd ML8. . . . . . . .215 C1
Gorgie Park Cl EH14. . . . . .120 D4
Gorgie Park Rd
Edinburgh EH11. . . . . .120 D5
Edinburgh EH14. . . . . .120 D5
Gorgie Rd EH14. . . . . .120 C4
Gorrie St Denny FK6. . . . . . .36 D2
Dunfermline KY11. . . . . .29 C2
Gorsebank EH54. . . . . .143 F5
Gorton Loan EH24. . . . . . . .172 D2
Gorton Pl EH24. . . . . .172 D2
Gorton Rd EH24. . . . . .172 D2
Gort Pl FK5. . . . . .61 C5
Goschen Pl EH52. . . . . .115 B5
Goschen Terr EH52. . . . . . .115 B5
Gosford House EH32. . . . . . .71 A2
Gosford Pl EH6. . . . . .93 D5
Gosford Rd
Cockenzie & Port Seton
EH32. . . . . .97 C4
Kirkcaldy KY2. . . . . .16 C7
Longniddry EH32. . . . . .98 E6
Gosford Wlk EH32. . . . . .97 C4
Goshen Pl FK5. . . . . .38 C6
Gote La EH30. . . . . .68 B1
Goulden Pl KY12. . . . . .28 C6
Gourlaybank EH41. . . . . . . .101 A1
Gourlay St KY2. . . . . .17 A4
Gowan Ave FK2. . . . . .60 B6
Gowanbank EH54. . . . . . . .143 D5
Gowanbrae Dr KY12. . . . . . .29 D4
Gowanbrae Pl KY12. . . . . . .29 D4
Gowanbrae Terr KY12. . . . . .29 D4
Gowanhill Farm Rd
EH14. . . . . .147 C5
Gowanhill Gdns FK8. . . . . . . .1 F1
Gowan La FK2. . . . . .60 B6
Gowanlea Dr FK6. . . . . .108 B6
Gow Cres KY1. . . . . .17 B4
Gowl Cl 7 EH47. . . . . .130 B8
Gracefield Ct EH21. . . . . . .124 B6
Gracemount Ave EH16. . . . .151 B7
Gracemount Bsns Pav
EH16. . . . . .151 C6
Gracemount Dr EH16. . . . .151 B6
Gracemount High Sch
EH16. . . . . .151 C6
Gracemount Pl EH16. . . . . .151 B6
Gracemount Prim Sch
EH16. . . . . .151 B6
Gracemount Rd EH16. . . . .151 A5
Gracemount Sq EH16. . . . .151 B6
Grace St KY5. . . . . .14 C8
Gracie's Wynd EH48. . . . . .140 B5
Gracie Cres FK7. . . . . .8 D4
Gradlon Pl FK1. . . . . .60 B3
Graeme High Sch FK1. . . . . .60 E4
Graeme Pl FK1. . . . . .59 E1
Graham's Rd FK1. . . . . .171 B1
Graham Ave Larbert FK5. . . .38 B3
Stirling FK9. . . . . .2 C4
Graham Cres EH51. . . . . . . .64 B7
Graham Ct EH47. . . . . .162 E8
Grahamsdyke Ave EH51. . . .64 B7
Grahamsdyke Cres EH51. . .64 A7
Grahamsdyke La EH51. . . . .64 B6
Grahamsdyke Rd
Bo'ness EH51. . . . . .64 C6
Bonnybridge FK4. . . . . .58 A4
Grahamsdyke St
Laurieston FK2. . . . . .60 F4
Stenhousemuir FK2. . . . . . . .61 A4
Grahamsdyke Terr EH51. . . .64 B7
Grahams Rd FK1. . . . . .60 B5
Grahams Road Rdbt FK1. . . .60 B5

Graham St Bridge of A FK9. .2 B7
Edinburgh EH6. . . . . .93 E5
Graham Terr FK2. . . . . .22 D4
Graham Way EH54. . . . . . . .143 D8
Grainger St KY5. . . . . .14 B8
Grampian Cres FK3. . . . . . . .61 B7
Grampian Ct KY11. . . . . .46 E2
Grampian Gdns KY2. . . . . . .16 F5
Grampian Pl KY11. . . . . .46 E1
Grampian Rd Rosyth KY11. .46 E2
Stirling FK7. . . . . .6 E6
Grampion Ct EH54. . . . . . . .143 E1
Granary Rd FK2. . . . . .60 A8
Granary Sq FK2. . . . . .60 B7
Granary The EH42. . . . . .78 E3
Granby Ave EH54. . . . . .143 F4
Granby Rd EH16. . . . . .121 F3
Grandfield EH6. . . . . .93 C5
Grandville EH6. . . . . .93 C6
Grange Ave FK2. . . . . .60 D6
Grange Cotts KY2. . . . . .34 F5
Grange Cres EH9. . . . . .121 D4
Grange Cres E EH32. . . . . . .96 F1
Grange Cres W EH32. . . . . .125 F8
Grange Ct
5 Edinburgh EH9. . . . . .121 E5
North Berwick EH39. . . . . . .54 C6
Grange Dr
Dunfermline KY11. . . . . .46 C8
Falkirk FK2. . . . . .60 C6
Grange Gdns EH9. . . . . .2 C7
Grange Gr EH32. . . . . .96 F1
Grange Knowe EH49. . . . . . .85 D8
Grange La FK3. . . . . .40 C1
Grangelea Ct FK3. . . . . .40 C1
Grange Loan Bo'ness EH51. .64 B7
Edinburgh EH9. . . . . .121 D4
Grange Loan Gdns EH9 .121 D4
Grangemouth Ent Ctr FK3 .61 A7
Grangemouth High Sch
FK3. . . . . .61 E5
Grangemouth Mus FK3. . . . .40 D1
Grangemouth
Bo'ness EH51. . . . . .63 B6
Falkirk FK3. . . . . .61 A4
Grangepans EH51. . . . . .64 B8
Grange Pk
Dunfermline KY11. . . . . .29 C1
Dunfermline KY11. . . . . .46 C8
Grange Pl
Grangemouth FK3. . . . . .61 D8
Redding FK2. . . . . .61 C1
Grange Prim Sch EH51. . . . .64 B7
Grange Rd Alloa FK10. . . . . .9 F6
Bridge of A FK9. . . . . .2 C8
Broxburn EH52. . . . . .115 F4
Burntisland KY3. . . . . .33 D1
Dunfermline KY11. . . . . .46 C6
Livingston EH54. . . . . .144 A7
North Berwick EH39. . . . . . .54 B6
Polmont FK3. . . . . .61 F4
Prestonpans EH32. . . . . .96 F1
Grange Terr Bo'ness EH51. .64 B7
Edinburgh EH9. . . . . .121 D3
Grange The FK2. . . . . .82 E8
Grange View
Linlithgow EH49. . . . . .85 C8
Stenhousemuir FK5. . . . . . . .38 E1
Grange Wynd KY11. . . . . . . .46 C8
Grannies Park Ind Est
EH22. . . . . .153 A4
Grannus Mews EH21. . . . . .124 D5
Grant Ave EH13. . . . . .149 A6
Granton Cres EH5. . . . . .92 F6
Granton Ctr (Mus) The
EH5. . . . . .92 D6
Granton Gdns EH5. . . . . .92 D6
Granton Gr EH5. . . . . .92 F6
Granton Harbour EH5. . . . . .92 F8
Granton Mains Ave EH4. . . .92 C6
Granton Mains Bank EH4. . .92 C6
Granton Mains Brae EH4. . .92 C6
Granton Mains Ct EH4. . . . .92 C6
Granton Mains E EH4. . . . . .92 D6
Granton Mains Gait EH4. . . .92 C6
Granton Mains Vale EH4. . . .92 C6
Granton Mains Wynd EH4 .92 C6
Granton Medway EH5. . . . . .92 D6
Granton Mill Cres EH4. . . . . .92 C6
Granton Mill Dr EH4. . . . . . . .92 C6
Granton Mill March EH4. . . .92 B5
Granton Mill Pl EH4. . . . . . . .92 C6
Granton Mill Rd EH4. . . . . . .92 B5
Granton Mill W EH4. . . . . . . .92 C6
Granton Park Ave EH5. . . . . .92 F7
Granton Pl EH5. . . . . .92 F6
Granton Prim Sch EH5. . . . .92 F6
Granton Rd EH5. . . . . .93 A6
Granton Sq EH5. . . . . .92 F7
Granton Terr EH5. . . . . .92 F6
Granton View
Dalgety Bay KY11. . . . . .47 F2
Edinburgh EH5. . . . . .92 F7
Grants Bank KY12. . . . . .29 A4
Grant St Alloa FK10. . . . . .9 F6
West Calder EH55. . . . . . . .163 D3
Grantully Pl EH9. . . . . .121 F4
Granville Terr EH10. . . . . . .121 B3
Granville Way KY11. . . . . . . .46 E3
Grassmarket EH1. . . . . .228 C2
Gray's Ct EH8. . . . . .229 B2
Gray's Loan EH10. . . . . .120 F4
Gray Buchanan Ct FK2. . . . .61 D2

Gray Pk KY4. . . . . .13 C6
Gray Pl KY11. . . . . .47 C3
Graysknowe 4 EH14. . . . . .120 B2
Graysmil Sch EH14. . . . . . .120 C1
Gray St ML7. . . . . .180 A4
Graystale Rd FK2. . . . . .7 A3
Graystonelee Rd ML7. . . . .179 D6
Great Cannon Bank EH15 .95 A1
Great Carleton Pl EH16. . . .123 A3
Great Carleton Sq EH16. . .123 A3
Great Junction St EH6. . . . .93 F5
Great King St EH3. . . . . .93 C2
Great Michael Cl EH6. . . . . .93 C7
Great Michael Rd
Rosyth KY11. . . . . .46 B1
Rosyth KY11. . . . . .67 B8
Great Michael Rise EH6. . . .93 D6
Great Michael Sq EH6. . . . . .93 D7
Great Stuart St EH3. . . . . . .228 A3
Grebe Gdns KY11. . . . . .30 A1
Greenacre EH14. . . . . .148 E2
Greenacre Ct FK7. . . . . .7 C4
Greenacre Pl
Bannockburn FK7. . . . . .7 B5
Bonnybridge FK4. . . . . .58 A3
Greenacres KY12. . . . . .12 B1
Green Apron Pk EH39. . . . . .54 B6
Greenbank Ave EH10. . . . . .121 A1
Greenbank Cres EH10. . . . .150 A8
Greenbank Ct FK1. . . . . .59 D4
Greenbank Dr
Cowdenbeath KY4. . . . . .13 A2
Edinburgh EH10. . . . . .120 F1
Edinburgh EH10. . . . . .120 F1
Greenbank Gdns EH10. . . .149 F8
Greenbank Gr EH10. . . . . . .149 F8
Greenbank La EH10. . . . . . .120 F1
Greenbank Loan EH10. . . . .121 A1
Greenbank Pk EH10. . . . . . .149 F8
Greenbank Pl
Edinburgh EH10. . . . . .121 A1
Falkirk FK1. . . . . .59 D4
Greenbank Rd
Edinburgh EH10. . . . . .120 F1
Falkirk,Greenbank FK1. . . . .59 D3
Falkirk,Summerford FK2. . . .59 D4
Greenbank Rise EH10. . . . .149 F8
Greenbank Row EH10. . . . .149 F8
Greenbank Terr EH10. . . . .121 A1
Greenburn Rd EH47. . . . . . .181 E5
Greencornhills Rdbt FK7. . .19 F8
Greencraig Ave FK4. . . . . . . .81 C6
Greendale Pk EH4. . . . . .92 A4
Greendykes Ave EH16. . . . .122 F3
Greendykes Cotts EH33. . .122 F3
Greendykes Dr EH16. . . . . .122 F3
Greendykes Gdns EH16. . .122 F3
Greendykes Ho EH16. . . . . .122 F3
Greendykes Ind Est
EH52. . . . . .115 C6
Greendykes Loan EH16. . . .122 F2
Greendykes Rd
Broxburn EH52. . . . . .115 C6
Edinburgh EH16. . . . . .122 F2
Greendykes Steadings
EH52. . . . . .115 C6
Greendykes Terr EH16. . . .122 F3
Greenend Dr EH17. . . . . . . .151 C8
Greenend Gdns EH17. . . . .151 C7
Greenend Gr EH17. . . . . . . .151 C8
Greenfield Cres EH14. . . . .168 C8
Greenfield Pk EH21. . . . . . .124 B3
Greenfield Rd EH14. . . . . . .168 C8
Greenfield St Alloa FK10. . . .10 B7
Bonnybridge FK4. . . . . .58 B6
Greenhall Rd EH23. . . . . . . .174 C1
Greenhead FK12. . . . . .5 B8
Greenheads Rd EH39. . . . . .54 C6
Greenhill Ct
Edinburgh EH10. . . . . .121 B5
Fauldhouse EH47. . . . . .181 C6
Greenhill Gdns EH10. . . . . .121 B4
Greenhill Pk
Edinburgh EH10. . . . . .121 A4
Penicuik EH26. . . . . .191 D5
Greenhill Pl EH10. . . . . .121 A4
Greenhill Rd
Blackridge EH48. . . . . .138 E3
Bonnybridge FK4. . . . . .58 A3
Greenhill Terr EH10. . . . . . .121 A4
Greenhithe Terr FK2. . . . . . .82 E7
Greenhorn's Well Ave 3
FK1. . . . . .59 E3
Greenhorn's Well Cres 1
FK1. . . . . .59 F3
Greenhorn's Well Dr 2
FK1. . . . . .59 F3
Green La
Bonnyrigg and Lasswade
EH18. . . . . .172 F8
Grangemouth FK3. . . . . .61 E8
Greenlaw Gr EH26. . . . . . . .171 A1
Greenlaw Hedge EH13. . . .149 E8
Greenlaw Rig EH13. . . . . . .149 E8
Greenloanings KY2. . . . . . . .16 D8
Greenmantle Loan 2
EH16. . . . . .122 A4
Greenmount Ave 4. . . . . . . .13 A2
Greenmount Dr
Burntisland KY3. . . . . .33 F1
Shieldhill FK1. . . . . .81 F3
Greenmount Rd N KY3. . . . .33 F2
Greenmount Rd S KY3. . . . .34 A1
Greenpark EH17. . . . . .151 C8
Greenpark Dr FK2. . . . . .60 B6

Greenrigg Cotts
Harthill ML7 . . . . .159 F5
Harthill ML7 . . . . .160 A5
Greenrigg Prim Sch ML7 159 F6
Greenshank Dr KY11 . . . .30 A2
Greenshaw EH48 . . . . . .111 F6
Greenside La EH1 . . . . .229 B4
Greenside Pl
 Edinburgh EH1 . . . . . . .229 B4
 Rosewell EH24 . . . . . . .172 D2
Greenside Row EH1 . . . .229 B4
Greenside St FK10 . . . . . .10 B6
Green St Edinburgh EH7 . .93 D2
 Townhill KY12 . . . . .29 C8
Greens The FK2 . . . . . . .82 E6
Green The Alva FK12 . . . . .5 A7
 Balerno EH14 . . . . .168 D8
 Bathgate EH48 . . . . . . .141 C7
 Edinburgh EH4 . . . . .91 F4
 Loanhead EH20 . . . . . . .151 C1
 Pencaitland EH34 . . . . .156 F6
 West Barns EH42 . . . . . . .77 F1
Green Tree La EH51 . . . . .63 D5
Greenvale Dr FK2 . . . . . . .82 E8
Greenwells Dr FK2 . . . . . .82 F8
Greenwell St EH47 . . . . .181 F6
Greenwell Terr FK2 . . . . .82 E7
Greenwood Ave EH48 . . . . .7 A8
Greenwood Pk EH54 . . . .143 D6
Greenwood St ML7 . . . . .179 E5
Gregory Rd EH14 . . . . . .164 B8
Greig Cres EH48 . . . . . .140 A5
Greig Ct KY11 . . . . .9 A2
Greig Pl KY5 . . . . .14 A7
Greig Rd KY11 . . . . .46 B2
Grendon Ct FK8 . . . . .7 A6
Grendon Gdns FK8 . . . . . .7 A6
Grenville Ct FK1 . . . . . . .59 F4
Grey Craigs KY12 . . . . . .27 D2
Greyfriar's Wlk KY11 . . . .47 C3
Greyfriars EH1 . . . . .229 A2
Greyfriars Bobby Meml
 EH1 . . . . .229 A2
Greygoran FK10 . . . . .5 C2
Grey School Cnr EH32 . . .96 F1
Grierson Ave EH5 . . . . . .93 A6
Grierson Cres
 Cambusbarron FK7 . . . . . .6 D6
 Edinburgh EH5 . . . . .93 A6
Grierson Gdns EH5 . . . . .93 A6
Grierson Rd EH5 . . . . . . .92 F6
Grierson Sq EH5 . . . . . . .93 A6
Grierson Villas EH5 . . . . .93 A6
Grieve Ct EH26 . . . . . . .191 F8
Grieve St Dunfermline KY12 .17 A6
 Kirkcaldy KY2 . . . . .17 A6
Griffith Dr EH47 . . . . . . .161 A6
Griffiths St FK1 . . . . .60 B4
Grigor Ave EH4 . . . . .92 D3
Grigor Dr EH4 . . . . .92 D3
Grigor Gdns EH4 . . . . . . .92 E3
Grigor Terr EH4 . . . . .92 D3
Grindlay St EH3 . . . . . . .228 B2
Grindlay Street Ct EH3 . .228 B2
Groathill Ave EH4 . . . . . .92 C2
Groathill Gardens E **2**
 EH4 . . . . .92 C2
Groathill Gardens W **1**
 EH4 . . . . .92 C2
Groathill Loan EH4 . . . . . .92 C3
Groathill Rd N EH4 . . . . . .92 C3
Groathill Rd S EH4 . . . . . .92 C2
Grodwell Dr FK12 . . . . . . .4 E7
Grosvenor Cres EH12 . . .120 F7
Grosvenor Gdns EH12 . . .120 F7
Grosvenor St EH12 . . . . .228 A2
Grove Cres FK2 . . . . .39 A2
Grove End EH18 . . . . . . .173 B8
Grove St Denny FK6 . . . . .36 C2
 Edinburgh EH3 . . . . . . .228 A2
 Musselburgh EH21 . . . . .124 A5
Grove The EH21 . . . . . . .124 A5
Guardie's Well Rd EH17 . .151 E6
Guardians Wood EH12 . . .120 C7
Guardwell Cres EH17 . . . .151 C7
Guildhall St KY12 . . . . . . .29 A3
Guildiehaugh Rdbt EH48 141 D5
Guildie Howes Rd EH23 . .195 F2
Guildry Gr KY12 . . . . .29 E4
Guildry The EH49 . . . . . . .65 E5
Gullan's Cl EH1 . . . . . . .229 B3
Gullane Prim Sch EH31 . . .52 B2
Gunner Rd FK3,EH51 . . . .62 C8
Gunn Rd FK3 . . . . .61 C5
Guthrie St KY12 . . . . .29 A3
Guttergates Rd KY11 . . . .30 B5
Gyle Ave EH12 . . . . .118 F5
Gylemuir Prim Sch EH12 119 C5
Gylemuir Rd EH12 . . . . . .119 A6
Gyle Park Gdns EH12 . . .119 A6
Gyle Rdbt EH12 . . . . . . .118 F5
Gylers Rd EH39 . . . . .53 A4
Gyle Sh Ctr EH12 . . . . . .119 A5

H

Haddington Inf Sch
 EH41 . . . . .130 A8
Haddington Pl
 Aberlady EH32 . . . . .71 D4
 Edinburgh EH7 . . . . .93 E2
Haddington Rd
 East Linton EH40 . . . . . .103 D7
 Musselburgh EH21 . . . . .125 B6
 North Berwick EH39 . . . . .54 C5
 Tranent EH33 . . . . .126 E6

Haddington Station Ind Est
 EH41 . . . . .129 F8
Haddon's Ct EH8 . . . . . .229 B2
Haddow Gr KY3 . . . . .50 D8
Hadfast Rd EH22 . . . . . .154 D5
Hadrian Way EH51 . . . . . .64 B6
Haig Ave Kirkcaldy KY1 . . .17 D7
 Stirling FK8 . . . . .2 A2
Haig Cres Bathgate EH48 .141 C5
 Dunfermline KY12 . . . . . .29 C5
Haig Homes EH11 . . . . . .120 A4
Haig St FK3 . . . . .61 C6
Hailes App EH13 . . . . . . .149 A7
Hailes Ave EH13 . . . . . . .149 A7
Hailes Bank EH13 . . . . . .149 A7
Hailes Castle EH41 . . . . .103 A4
Hailes Cres EH13 . . . . . .149 A7
Hailes Gdns EH13 . . . . . .149 A7
Hailes Gr EH13 . . . . .149 A7
Hailes Terr EH13 . . . . . . .149 A7
Hailesland Gdns EH14 . . .119 E1
Hailesland Gr EH14 . . . . .119 E1
Hailesland Pk EH14 . . . . .119 F1
Hailesland Pl EH14 . . . . .119 E1
Hailesland Prim Sch
 EH14 . . . . .148 E8
Hailesland Rd EH14 . . . . .119 E1
Hailes Loan HE41 . . . . . .103 B4
Hailes Pk EH13 . . . . .148 F7
Hailes Pl KY12 . . . . .29 D4
Hailes St EH3 . . . . .228 B1
Hailes Terr EH13 . . . . . . .149 A7
Hailstonegreen ML1 . . . .201 A1
Hailstones Cres EH48 . . .139 F6
Hainburn Pk EH10 . . . . . .149 F5
Haining Gr FK2 . . . . .83 B5
Haining Pl
 Grangemouth FK3 . . . . . .61 F8
 Livingston EH54 . . . . . . .143 B5
Haining Rd EH49 . . . . . . .83 F6
Haining Terr EH49 . . . . . .83 F5
Haining Valley Steadings
 EH49 . . . . .83 C6
Halbeath Dr KY11 . . . . . .29 F5
Halbeath Pl KY11 . . . . . .29 E5
Halbeath Rd
 Dunfermline KY11 . . . . . .29 D5
 Halbeath KY11 . . . . .30 A5
 Halbeath Ret Pk KY11 . . .30 A6
Halberts Cres FK7 . . . . . .7 B2
Haldane Ave Bridge of A FK9 2 A6
 Haddington EH41 . . . . . .100 F1
Haldane Gr KY12 . . . . . . .26 D7
Haldane Sq EH54 . . . . . .164 C5
Halket Cres FK2 . . . . .39 C2
Halketshall KY11 . . . . . . .45 C4
Halkett Cres KY11 . . . . . .29 D2
Halkcraigs EH27 . . . . . . .145 E3
Hall Cres EH31 . . . . .52 A2
Hallcroft Cl EH28 . . . . . .117 C2
Hallcroft Cres EH28 . . . . .117 C2
Hallcroft Gdns EH28 . . . .117 C2
Hallcroft Neuk EH28 . . . .117 C2
Hallcroft Pk EH28 . . . . . .117 C2
Hallcroft Rise EH28 . . . . .117 C2
Halley's Ct KY1 . . . . .17 B2
Hallglen Prim Sch FK1 . . .60 B1
Hallglen Rd FK1 . . . . .60 B1
Hallglen Terr FK1 . . . . . . .60 B1
Hallhead Rd EH16 . . . . . .122 A2
Hallhill EH42 . . . . .106 C8
Halliburton Terr FH39 . . . .53 A4
Hall La KY5 . . . . .14 A8
Hallows The KY1 . . . . .17 F8
Hallpark FK10 . . . . .10 C8
Hall Rd EH52 . . . . .115 E5
Hall Row KY11 . . . . .28 D8
Hall St Cowdenbeath KY4 . .13 C4
 Lochgelly KY5 . . . . .14 B8
Hall Terr FK1 . . . . .111 F5
Hallyards Cotts EH29 . . . .117 B8
Hallyards Rd
 Newbridge EH29 . . . . . . .117 B8
 Ratho Station EH28 . . . . .117 D6
Halmyre St EH6 . . . . .93 F4
Halyard Rise KY11 . . . . . .47 F2
Halyard Terr KY11 . . . . . . .15 B2
Hamburgh Pl EH6 . . . . . . .93 E6
Hamilton Ave
 Linlithgow EH49 . . . . .84 C6
 Stenhousemuir FK5 . . . . .38 C4
Hamilton Cres
 Grangemouth FK2 . . . . . .82 E6
 Gullane EH31 . . . . .52 A2
 Newtongrange EH22 . . . .174 B6
Hamilton Dr
 Edinburgh EH15 . . . . . . .122 F8
 Falkirk FK1 . . . . .60 A4
 Stirling FK9 . . . . .2 C4
Hamilton Gdns
 Armadale EH48 . . . . . . .139 F4
 Edinburgh EH15 . . . . . . .122 F7
 Edinburgh EH15 . . . . . . .122 F7
Hamilton La
 Bathgate EH48 . . . . .140 E7
 Bo'ness EH51 . . . . .63 F8
Hamilton Pk
 Edinburgh EH15 . . . . . . .122 F8
 Linlithgow EH49 . . . . .84 F6
Hamilton Pl Edinburgh EH3 .93 B2
 Linlithgow EH49 . . . . .84 F6
 Rosyth KY11 . . . . .46 E4
Hamilton Rd
 Bathgate EH48 . . . . .140 E7
 Grangemouth FK3 . . . . . .61 E6
 Gullane EH31 . . . . .52 A2
 North Berwick EH39 . . . . .54 A7

Hamilton Rd continued
 Stenhousemuir FK5 . . . . .38 D6
Hamiltons Cl EH30 . . . . . .68 C1
Hamiltons Folly Mews
 EH8 . . . . .229 B1
Hamilton Sq **5** Livingston EH51 .63 D5
 Livingston EH54 . . . . . . .164 F7
Hamilton St Falkirk FK1 . . .59 D6
 Lochgelly KY5 . . . . .14 B6
Hamilton Terr
 Edinburgh EH15 . . . . . . .123 A7
 High Valleyfield KY12 . . . .26 B2
Hamilton Way EH47 . . . . .161 E6
Hamilton Wynd EH6 . . . . .93 E6
Hammermen's Entry
 EH8 . . . . .229 B3
Hampton Pl **5** EH12 . . . .120 E7
Hampton Terr **4** EH12 . . .120 E7
Handax ML1 . . . . .201 A1
Haney's Way EH51 . . . . . .64 B8
Hanlon Gdns EH47 . . . . . .161 A6
Hannah Dr FK2 . . . . .82 E7
Hannah Prim Sch (Shotts Bon
 Accord FC) ML7 . . . . . .179 D6
Hanover Cl **4** EH48 . . . . .141 A7
Hanover Ct
 Broxburn EH52 . . . . .115 C5
 Livingston EH54 . . . . . . .143 B2
 Stirling FK9 . . . . .2 B1
Hanover Grange FK3 . . . . .61 D8
Hanover Ho EH54 . . . . . .143 B2
Hanover St EH2 . . . . .228 C4
Happy Valley Rd EH47 . . .162 E7
Harbour Ct EH42 . . . . . . .78 D3
Harbour Dr KY11 . . . . . . .47 F3
Harbour La EH30 . . . . . . .68 B1
Harbour Pl Burntisland KY3 .50 E8
 Dalgety Bay KY11 . . . . . . .47 F2
 Edinburgh EH15 . . . . .95 A1
 Inverkeithing KY11 . . . . . .47 C2
Harbour Rd Bo'ness EH51 . .64 C7
 Edinburgh EH15 . . . . .95 A1
 Kinghorn KY3 . . . . .35 A2
 Musselburgh EH21 . . . . .124 A6
Harbour View EH21 . . . . .124 B6
Harbour Way KY11 . . . . . .48 A4
Harburn Ave EH54 . . . . . .142 F6
Harburn Ct EH54 . . . . . . .142 F7
Harburn Ave W EH54 . . . .142 F7
Harburn Dr EH55 . . . . . . .163 E3
Harburn La EH55 . . . . . . .163 E3
Harburn Rd EH55 . . . . . . .163 E3
Harcourt Rd KY2 . . . . . . .17 B5
Hardengreen Bsns Ctr
 EH22 . . . . .152 E1
Hardengreen Ind Est
 EH22 . . . . .152 E1
Hardengreen Junc EH22 .173 E7
Hardengreen La EH22 . . .152 E1
Harden Pl EH11 . . . . .120 F5
Hardgate EH41 . . . . .101 B1
Hardgate Ct EH41 . . . . . .101 B1
Hardhill Dr EH48 . . . . . . .140 E6
Hardhill Pl EH48 . . . . . . .140 E6
Hardhill Rd EH48 . . . . . . .140 E6
Hardhill Road Travelling
 Peoples Site EH48 . . . .140 C5
Hardhill Terr EH48 . . . . . .140 E5
Hardie Cres FK7 . . . . .8 C4
Hardie Ct FK7 . . . . .7 C3
Hardie Rd EH54 . . . . .142 D7
Hardie Terr EH40 . . . . . . .103 D8
Hardwell Cl EH8 . . . . . . .229 B2
Hardy Gdns EH48 . . . . . .141 F5
Hareburn Ave FK1 . . . . . .110 A5
Harelaw EH22 . . . . .152 D8
Harelaw Rd EH13 . . . . . .149 B6
Hares Cl EH32 . . . . .97 C4
Hareside ML11 . . . . .217 F8
Harestanes Rd EH48 . . . .139 F3
Harewood Cres EH16 . . . .122 E4
Harewood Dr EH16 . . . . .122 E4
Harewood Rd EH16 . . . . .122 E4
Harkenburn Gdns EH26 . .191 C6
Harkness Cres EH33 . . . .126 D6
Harlands The FK10 . . . . . .9 F7
Harlaw Bank EH14 . . . . . .168 C8
Harlaw Gait EH14 . . . . . .147 D1
Harlaw Gr EH26 . . . . .191 D5
Harlaw Hill EH32 . . . . . . .96 F2
Harlawhill Gdns EH32 . . .97 A2
Harlaw House Ranger Ctr
 EH14 . . . . .169 A7
Harlaw March EH14 . . . . .168 D8
Harlaw Rd Balerno EH14 . .168 E8
 Currie EH14 . . . . .148 A2
Harley Ct FK2 . . . . .60 B8
Harley St EH11 . . . . .60 C8
Harlington Pl FK2 . . . . . . .82 E7
Harlow Ave FK2 . . . . .61 D1
Harmeny Education Trust
 EH14 . . . . .168 D8
Harmony Cres EH19 . . . . .173 D7
Harmony Ct EH19 . . . . . .173 D7
Harmony St EH19 . . . . . .173 D7
Harmony Wlk EH19 . . . . .173 D7
Harness Ct EH20 . . . . . . .172 C7
Harpenside Cres EH39 . . .53 C5
Harper's Brae EH26 . . . . .192 B6
Harperdean Cotts EH41 . .101 A3
Harperdean Terr EH41 . . .100 F1
Harriebrae Pk KY12 . . . . .28 F4
Harriet St KY1 . . . . .17 E6
Harris Ct FK10 . . . . .10 B5
Harris Dr KY2 . . . . .16 F8
Harrismith Pl EH7 . . . . . . .94 A2
Harrison Gdns EH11 . . . . .120 F5
Harrison La EH11 . . . . . . .120 F5

Harrison Pl
 Edinburgh EH11 . . . . . . .120 E4
 Falkirk FK1 . . . . .59 F5
Harrison Rd EH11 . . . . . .120 E5
Harris Pl Dunfermline KY11 .29 C1
 Grangemouth FK3 . . . . . .61 C5
Harrysmuir Cres EH53 . . .144 B3
Harrysmuir Gdns EH53 . . .144 B3
Harrysmuir N EH53 . . . . .144 B3
Harrysmuir Prim Sch
 EH54 . . . . .143 C5
Harrysmuir Rd EH53 . . . .144 B7
Harrysmuir S EH53 . . . . .144 B7
Harrysmuir Terr EH53 . . .144 B7
Hartfield Terr ML7 . . . . . .198 B8
Harthill Ind Est ML7 . . . .159 D5
Harthill Rd
 Blackridge EH48 . . . . . . .138 D2
 Fauldhouse EH47 . . . . . .181 D6
Hartington Gdns EH10 . . .121 A5
Hartington Pl EH10 . . . . .121 A5
Hartley Pl FK3 . . . . .61 B6
Hart St EH1 . . . . .93 D2
Hart Street La EH1 . . . . . .93 D2
Hartwood Gdns ML7 . . . .179 A4
Hartwoodhill Hospl ML7 . .179 C4
Hartwood Rd Shotts ML7 . .179 A3
 West Calder EH55 . . . . . .163 D2
Hart Wynd FK7 . . . . .7 F1
Harvest Dr EH28 . . . . . . .117 B5
Harvesters Way EH14 . . . .148 D8
Harvest Rd EH28 . . . . . . .117 B5
Harvest St FK9 . . . . .2 A2
Harvey Ave FK2 . . . . .61 F2
Harvey Wynd FK8 . . . . . . .2 A1
Harvie Gdns EH48 . . . . . .138 F4
Harviestoun Villas EH23 . .195 D7
Hastie Cl FK1 . . . . .229 A2
Hatfield Pl **2** EH48 . . . . .141 B7
Hatton Pl EH9 . . . . .121 D5
Haugh Gdns FK2 . . . . . . .39 B1
Haugh Park EH14 . . . . . .120 A2
Haugh Rd Burntisland KY3 . .50 D8
 North Berwick EH39 . . . . .54 F7
 Stirling FK9 . . . . .2 A2
Haughs Way FK6 . . . . . . .36 E2
Haven's Edge KY11 . . . . . .45 E3
Haven The
 Dalgety Bay KY11 . . . . . . .47 F2
 South Alloa FK7 . . . . .9 F3
Hawes Brae EH30 . . . . . .68 D1
Hawk Brae EH54 . . . . . . .143 C5
Hawkcraig Rd KY3 . . . . . .49 D7
Hawkhead Cres EH16 . . . .151 A8
Hawkhead Gr EH16 . . . . .151 A8
Hawkhill Ave EH7 . . . . . . .94 A3
Hawkhill Ct EH7 . . . . .94 A3
Hawkhill Rd Alloa FK10 . . .10 A3
 Kincardine FK10 . . . . . . .23 D5
Hawkins Terr EH26 . . . . . .192 B8
Hawk's Wynd **1** KY11 . . . .17 D6
Hawkwood Terr ML11 . . . .201 A1
Hawley Rd FK1 . . . . .60 A4
Hawthorn Bank
 Carnock KY12 . . . . .27 C6
 Cockenzie & Port Seton
  EH32 . . . . .97 B4
 Seafield EH47 . . . . .163 A8
 South Queensferry EH30 . .68 B1
Hawthornbank La EH4 . . .228 A3
Hawthornbank Pl EH6 . . .93 C5
Hawthornbank Rd EH41 . .100 F1
Hawthornbank Terr EH6 . . .93 E6
Hawthorn Cres
 Cowdenbeath KY4 . . . . . .12 F1
 Easthouses EH22 . . . . . .174 D8
 Fallin FK7 . . . . .8 B3
 Stirling FK8 . . . . .1 F2
Hawthorn Ct EH47 . . . . . .163 A8
Hawthornden Gdns
 EH19 . . . . .173 A7
Hawthornden Pl EH7 . . . . .93 E3
Hawthornden Prim Sch
 EH19 . . . . .172 F6
Hawthorn Dr Denny FK6 . . .36 D3
 Falkirk FK1 . . . . .59 E4
 Fallin FK7 . . . . .8 C4
 Harthill ML7 . . . . .159 E6
 Shotts ML7 . . . . .180 C4
Hawthorn Rd EH32 . . . . . .97 B1
Hawthorns The EH31 . . . .52 B3
Hawthorn Terr EH32 . . . . .97 B3
Hawthorn Vale EH6 . . . . .93 D6
Hay Ave EH16 . . . . .122 E4
Hay Dr EH16 . . . . .123 A4
Hayfield Edinburgh EH12 . .119 A8
 Falkirk FK2 . . . . .60 C7
Hayfield Ind Est KY2 . . . . .17 A7
Hayfield Pl KY2 . . . . .17 A7
Hayfield Rd Falkirk FK2 . . .60 C7
 Kirkcaldy KY1 . . . . .17 C7
Hayford Mills FK7 . . . . . . .6 D6
Hayford Pl FK7 . . . . .6 D6
Haygate Ave FK2 . . . . . . .82 E8

Hay Gdns EH16 . . . . .122 F5
Hay Gr KY11 . . . . .29 F1
Haymarket EH12 . . . . . . .228 A2
Haymarket EH54 . . . . . . .143 A5
Haymarket Sta EH12 . . . .228 A2
Haymarket Terr EH12 . . . .120 F7
Haymarket Yds EH12 . . . .228 A2
Haypark Bsns Ctr FK2 . . .61 E2
Haypark Rd FK6 . . . . .57 D6
Hay Pl EH16 . . . . .122 F4
Hay Rd EH16 . . . . .122 F4
Hays Com Bsns Ctr EH16 122 F4
Hay Terr EH16 . . . . .122 F4
Hayworth Ave FK2 . . . . . .61 B4
Hazel Ave KY2 . . . . .17 B6
Hazelbank Gdns FK8 . . . .2 A2
Hazelbank Terr EH11 . . . .120 E4
Hazel Cres FK4 . . . . .36 D3
Hazel Ct EH42 . . . . .78 B1
Hazeldean Ave EH51 . . . .63 D5
Hazeldean Terr EH16 . . . .122 B2
Hazel Dr EH19 . . . . .173 B6
Hazel Gr Dunfermline KY11 .46 F8
 Falkirk FK2 . . . . .60 D7
 Livingston EH54 . . . . . . .180 B4
 Shotts ML7 . . . . .180 B4
Hazelhurst FK2 . . . . .82 E8
Hazel La EH20 . . . . .171 E7
Hazel Rd FK1 . . . . .61 C6
Hazelwood Gr EH16 . . . . .122 C2
Headlesscross Rd EH47 . .180 F2
Head of Muir Prim Sch
 FK6 . . . . .57 D6
Headrigg Row EH16 . . . . .122 B1
Headrig Rd EH30 . . . . . . .88 D8
Headwell Ave KY12 . . . . .29 B5
Headwell Ct KY12 . . . . . .29 B5
Headwell Rd KY12 . . . . . .29 B5
Headwell Sch KY12 . . . . .29 B5
Heaney Ave EH53 . . . . . .144 B7
Heather Ave FK1 . . . . . . .81 C6
Heather Ct EH53 . . . . . . .144 B7
Heatherdale Gdns FK6 . . .57 E7
Heatherfield Glade EH54 164 C8
Heather Gr
 Dunfermline KY11 . . . . . .46 F8
 Maddiston FK2 . . . . .83 A5
Heather Pk EH47 . . . . . . .142 B1
Heathervale Wlk EH48 . . .140 B5
Heatherwood EH47 . . . . . .142 B1
Heatherwood Pk EH53 . . .144 B7
Heathery The KY11 . . . . . .46 F7
Heath Rd KY11 . . . . .46 F3
Hedge Row EH20 . . . . . . .171 E7
Hedges Loan FK7 . . . . . . .7 E1
Hedges The FK1 . . . . .59 E5
Heggie's Wynd KY1 . . . . .17 B1
Heights Rd EH48 . . . . . . .138 D3
Heinsberg Ho EH26 . . . . .191 E5
Helen La KY11 . . . . .68 C6
Helenslea Cotts **4** EH48 .141 A6
Helmsdale Pk KY12 . . . . .28 F2
Henderland Rd EH12 . . . .120 D7
Henderson Ave FK10 . . . .10 A8
Henderson Cres EH53 . . .115 B5
Henderson Ct EH53 . . . . .144 F3
Henderson Gdns
 Edinburgh EH6 . . . . .93 F5
 Tranent EH33 . . . . .126 D6
Henderson Pl Alva FK12 . .5 A7
 Broxburn EH52 . . . . .115 B3
 Edinburgh EH3 . . . . .93 B2
Henderson Place La EH3 . .93 B2
Henderson Row EH3 . . . . .93 B2
Henderson St
 Bridge of A FK9 . . . . .2 B7
 Edinburgh EH6 . . . . .93 F5
 Kingseat KY12 . . . . .12 B1
 Lochgelly KY5 . . . . .14 A8
Henderson Terr EH11 . . . .120 F5
Hendry's Wynd KY1 . . . . .17 B1
Hendry Cres KY2 . . . . . . .17 A6
Hendry Rd Kirkcaldy KY2 . .17 A6
 Kirkcaldy KY2 . . . . .17 A6
Henry St EH3 . . . . .60 B7
Hennings The FK10 . . . . . .5 C1
Henry Ross Pl EH30 . . . . .68 B1
Henryson Rd KY11 . . . . . .29 E4
Henry St Alva FK12 . . . . . .5 A6
 Bo'ness EH51 . . . . .64 A5
 Grangemouth FK3 . . . . . .61 E8
Hens Nest Rd EH47 . . . . .161 E6
Hepburn Dr EH22 . . . . . .153 C2
Hepburn Rd **8** EH41 . . . .101 A1
Herald Rise EH54 . . . . . .143 F2
Herbertshire St Denny FK6 .36 E2
 Denny FK6 . . . . .36 E2
Hercus Loan EH21 . . . . . .124 B6
Herd Gn EH54 . . . . .143 B7
Herdmanflatt EH41 . . . . .101 A1
Herdmanflatt Hospl
 EH41 . . . . .101 A1
Herdshill Ave FK1 . . . . . .81 C6
Herd Terr EH20 . . . . .172 A7
Heriot Bridge EH1 . . . . . .228 C2
Heriot Gdns Brightons FK2 .83 D1
 Burntisland KY3 . . . . .33 F1
Heriothill Terr EH7 . . . . . .93 C3
Heriot Pl EH3 . . . . .228 C2
Heriot Row EH3 . . . . .93 B2
Heriot St EH11 . . . . .47 C2
Heriot-Watt Univ EH14 . . .147 E8
Heriot Way FK38 . . . . . . .214 C1
Heritage Dr FK2 . . . . .39 A3
Hermand Cres EH11 . . . . .120 E4

Hermand Gdns EH55.....163 E3
Hermand Ho EH55.....163 F3
Hermand St EH11.....120 D4
Hermand Terr EH14.....120 D4
Hermiston Gait Ret Pk
 EH11.....119 A3
Hermiston House Rd EH12,
 EH14.....118 E1
Hermiston Junc EH11,
 EH12.....119 A2
Hermitage Dr EH10.....121 B1
Hermitage Gdns EH10...121 B2
Hermitage of Braid Visitor
 Ctr EH10.....121 C1
Hermitage Park EH6.....94 B3
Hermitage Park Lea EH6..94 B3
Hermitage Park Prim Sch
 EH6.....94 B3
Hermitage Pk EH6.....94 B3
Hermitage Pk S EH6......94 B3
Hermitage Pl EH6.....94 A4
Hermitage Rd FK9.....2 E6
Hermitage Terr EH10....121 B2
Hermits Croft EH8.....229 C1
Heron Ind Complex
 EH54.....142 D7
Heron Sq EH54.....142 D7
Hervey St FK10.....10 A8
Hetherington Dr FK10.....11 B4
Heugh Brae EH39.....54 E5
Heugh Rd EH39.....54 E5
Heugh St FK1.....60 A3
Heugh Study EH39.....54 E5
Heugh The
 North Berwick EH39.....54 E5
 Tranent EH33.....126 C7
Hewitt Pl KY3.....49 C7
Hie Dyke ML11.....217 E8
Higginson Loan EH22.....174 E5
High Academy Gr EH6...139 E5
High Academy St EH48..139 E5
High Beveridgewell KY12..28 F5
High Brae EH48.....111 F5
High Buckstone EH10...150 C6
Highfield Livingston EH54..143 A3
 North Berwick EH39.....54 B3
Highfield Ave EH49.....84 E7
Highfield Cres EH49.....84 E7
Highfield Rd EH49.....84 A6
High Kirk of St Giles
 EH1.....229 A3
Highland Dr FK5.....38 C3
Highland Dykes Cres FK4..58 A6
Highland Dykes Dr FK4....58 B6
Highlander Way FK10.....4 D2
Highlea Circ EH14.....168 B7
Highlea Gr EH14.....168 B8
High Mdw ML8.....215 C1
High Mill Rd ML8.....215 A2
High Park Rise EH26...191 F4
High Port EH49.....85 B7
High Rd Maddiston FK2...83 A5
 Roslin EH25.....192 F6
 Spott EH42.....106 C3
High Riggs EH3.....228 B2
High School Wynd EH1..229 B2
High School Yds EH1.....229 B2
High St Aberdour KY3.....49 B7
 Aberlady EH32.....71 C4
 Airth FK2.....22 D3
 Alloa FK10.....10 B6
 Bathgate EH48.....141 B7
 Bonnybridge FK4.....58 A5
 Bonnyrigg and Lasswade,
 Broomieknowe EH19...173 B7
 Bonnyrigg and Lasswade
 EH18.....152 A1
 Burntisland KY3.....50 E8
 Clackmannan FK10.....10 F4
 Cockenzie & Port Seton
 EH32.....97 C4
 Cowdenbeath KY4.....13 D4
 Dalkeith EH22.....153 A3
 Dunbar, Belhaven EH42...78 A2
 Dunbar EH42.....78 D2
 Dunfermline KY12.....29 A3
 Dysart KY1.....18 A7
 East Linton EH40.....103 D8
 Edinburgh EH1.....229 A3
 Falkirk FK1.....60 B4
 Gifford EH41.....220 F6
 Haddington EH41.....130 B8
 Inverkeithing KY11.....47 B2
 Kincardine FK10.....23 E4
 Kinghorn KY3.....35 C1
 Kirkcaldy KY1.....17 C3
 Kirkcaldy KY1.....17 C3
 Kirkliston EH29.....89 B1
 Linlithgow EH49.....85 A7
 Loanhead EH20.....172 C8
 Lochgelly KY5.....14 B7
 Musselburgh EH21.....124 D6
 North Berwick EH39.....54 C7
 Ormiston EH35.....155 E7
 Penicuik EH26.....191 F4
 Prestonpans EH32.....96 E1
 Shotts ML7.....179 F4
 Slamannan FK1.....108 B7
 South Queensferry EH30..68 C1
High Station EH14.....126 D6
High Station Rd FK1.....60 A3
High View Gr FK1.....81 D6
Hillary Rd KY11.....38 E1
Hillbank KY11.....47 B3

Hillcoat Loan EH15.....95 A1
Hillcoat Pl EH15.....95 A1
Hill Cres EH48.....141 B7
Hillcrest Bo'ness EH51.....63 F1
 Cowdenbeath KY4.....13 B8
Hillcrest Ave KY2.....16 E6
Hillcrest Dr FK10.....10 C6
Hillcrest Pl FK6.....57 D7
Hillcrest Rd 1 FK1.....59 F2
Hill Ct Dunfermline KY12...29 D5
 South Queensferry EH30...68 B1
Hillend Ind Pk KY11.....48 C5
Hillend Rd KY11.....47 D3
Hillfield Cres KY11.....47 B3
Hillfield Rd KY11.....47 B2
Hillfoots Rd Menstrie FK9...3 C6
 Stirling FK9.....2 E4
Hillfoot Terr ML8.....215 A1
Hill Gr KY12.....26 D7
Hillhead EH4.....92 B3
Hillhead Ave ML8.....215 A2
Hillhead Dr FK1.....59 F2
Hillhose Wynd EH27....145 F3
Hillhouse Ave EH48.....140 F8
Hillhouse Cres EH27....145 F3
Hillhouse Farm Steadings
 EH49.....145 A1
Hillhouse Rd Denny FK6...57 E7
 Edinburgh EH4.....92 B2
Hillhouseridge Rd ML7..179 D5
Hillhouse Terr EH27....145 F3
Hillock Ave FK2.....61 C2
Hill of Beath Prim Sch
 KY4.....12 F1
Hill of Kinnaird FK2.....38 E7
Hill of St Margaret KY12...29 F5
Hillpark Ave EH4.....91 F3
Hillpark Brae EH4.....91 F1
Hillpark Cres
 Bannockburn FK7.....7 C2
 Edinburgh EH4.....91 F3
Hillpark Ct EH4.....91 F3
Hillpark Dr Bannockburn FK7 7 D2
 Edinburgh EH4.....91 F3
Hillpark Gdns EH4.....91 F2
Hillpark Gn EH4.....91 F2
Hillpark Loan EH4.....92 A2
Hillpark Rd EH4.....91 F2
Hillpark Terr EH4.....91 F2
Hillpark Way EH4.....92 A2
Hillpark Wood EH4.....92 A2
Hill Pl Alloa FK10.....10 A8
 Edinburgh EH8.....229 B2
 Kirkcaldy KY1.....17 C4
 Mayfield EH22.....174 E5
 Shotts ML7.....179 E5
Hill Rd Gullane EH31.....51 F2
 Harthill ML7.....159 D5
 Pathhead EH37.....176 A5
Hillside FK10.....5 C2
Hillside Ave KY11.....48 A3
Hillside Camp Rd KY11...46 E1
Hillside Cotts
 Cousland EH22.....154 D5
 Linlithgow EH49.....85 C7
Hillside Cres EH7.....93 F2
Hillside Cres N EH23....195 B8
Hillside Cres S EH23....195 D8
Hillside Dr EH48.....138 D3
Hillside Gr EH51.....64 C6
Hillside Pl
 Blackridge EH48.....138 D3
 Longridge EH47.....161 C1
Hillside Rd EH30.....90 D4
Hillside St KY3.....49 C8
Hillside St EH7.....93 F2
Hillside Terr Alloa FK10...10 D7
 Edinburgh EH30.....90 D5
 Westquarter FK2.....61 B3
Hill Sq EH8.....229 B2
Hill St Alloa FK10.....10 B7
 Cowdenbeath KY4.....13 C4
 Dunfermline KY12.....29 A4
 Dysart KY1.....18 A7
 Inverkeithing KY11.....47 B2
 Kirkcaldy KY1.....17 B3
 Stirling FK7.....7 B3
Hill Street La N EH2.....228 C4
Hill Street La S EH2.....228 C4
Hilltop EH47.....84 D7
Hilltown Terr EH22.....123 C1
Hillview Cowdenbeath KY4..13 B8
 Edinburgh EH4.....92 B2
 Oakley KY12.....26 E7
Hillview Ave EH52.....115 F6
Hillview Cotts EH28....117 D2
Hillview Cres
 Crossgates KY4.....30 C6
 Edinburgh EH12.....119 D7
Hillview Dr Bridge of A FK9..2 A6
 Edinburgh EH12.....119 C7
Hillview Gdns EH35.....155 F7
Hillview Pl Broxburn EH52 115 F5
 Crossgates KY4.....30 C6
 Fallin FK7.....8 C4
Hillview Rd
 Bonnybridge FK4.....58 C3
 Edinburgh EH12.....119 D7
 5 Edinburgh FK2.....82 D8
 Ormiston EH35.....155 E7
Hillview Terr Alloa FK10...10 C6
 Edinburgh EH12.....119 D7
Hillwood Ave EH28.....117 C5

Hillwood Cres EH28.....117 C5
Hillwood Gdns EH28....117 C6
Hillwood Pl EH30.....68 B1
Hillwood Prim Sch EH28 117 C5
Hillwood Rd EH28.....117 C5
Hillwood Rise EH28.....117 C5
Hillwood Terr
 Ratho Station EH28.....117 C5
 Rosyth KY11.....47 A3
Hilton FK7.....20 E8
Hilton Cres FK10.....10 D7
Hilton Ct EH41.....130 A8
Hilton Farm Steadings
 KY11.....46 B3
Hilton Rd Alloa FK10.....10 D7
 Cairneyhill KY12.....27 E1
 Rosyth KY11.....46 C2
Hilton Terr FK7.....8 C4
Hilton View KY4.....13 E6
Hirst Cres FK7.....8 D4
Hirst Ct FK7.....8 D4
Hirst Gdns ML7.....179 C5
Hirst Rd ML7.....158 D3
Hoban Sq EH52.....115 F6
Hobart St EH54.....144 A5
Hodge St FK1.....60 B4
Hogarth Ave EH23.....174 C2
Hoggan Cres EH23.....29 C2
Hoggan Way FK12.....4 F6
Hoghill Ct EH53.....144 E3
Hoghill Pl EH53.....144 E3
Holborn Pl KY11.....46 F5
Holbourne Pl FK11.....4 A7
Holden Way KY11.....48 B5
Holly Ave FK5.....38 F3
Holly Bank EH22.....174 E7
Hollybank Pl EH53.....144 F2
Hollybank Terr EH11.....120 E4
Holly Cres KY11.....46 F5
Holly Gr Livingston EH54..144 B6
 Menstrie FK11.....3 F6
Hollyhock Glade EH54..164 C7
Holly Pl KY1.....17 C7
Holly Terr EH19.....173 B6
Holly Wlk EH20.....171 E7
Holmes C EH52.....115 B4
Holmes Farm La EH52...115 B4
Holmes Gdns EH52.....115 C4
Holmes Holdings EH52...115 C5
Holmes Rd EH52.....115 B4
Holmlea Ave 2 FK2.....82 D8
Holton Cotts FK10.....5 C1
Holton Cres FK10.....5 C1
Holton Ct FK10.....5 C1
Holton Sq FK10.....5 C1
Holy Cross RC Prim Sch
 EH6.....93 C5
Holy Family RC Prim Sch
 EH52.....87 E2
Holygate Pl EH52.....115 D5
Holyrood Bsns Pk EH16..122 D4
Holy Rood High Sch
 EH15.....122 D6
Holyrood Park Rd EH16..229 C1
Holyrood Pk EH8,EH15,
 EH16.....122 B7
Holyrood Pl
 Dunfermline KY12.....29 B4
 Stenhousemuir FK5.....38 E4
Holyrood Rd EH8.....229 C3
Home Farm Cotts
 Bonnybridge FK6.....57 F6
 Edinburgh EH30.....90 C7
Home Pk KY12.....49 C7
Home St EH3.....228 B1
Homesteads The FK8.....6 D7
Honeybank Cres ML8...215 A3
Honeyman Ct EH48.....139 E7
Hood Pl KY11.....46 E2
Hookney Terr FK6.....36 C2
Hopecote Gdns EH51....64 D5
Hopefield Dr EH47.....162 C8
Hopefield Pk EH19.....173 A6
Hopefield Pl
 Blackburn EH47.....162 C8
 Bonnyrigg and Lasswade
 EH19.....173 A6
Hopefield Prim Sch
 EH19.....173 A6
Hopefield Rd EH47.....162 C8
Hopefield Terr
 Bonnyrigg and Lasswade
 EH19.....173 A6
 Edinburgh EH6.....93 E6
Hope La EH15.....123 B7
Hope La N EH15.....123 B8
Hopelands Rd EH26.....190 E5
Hopepark EH48.....140 E6
Hope Park Cres
 Edinburgh EH8.....229 B1
 2 Haddington EH41....101 A1
Hope Park Gdns EH48...140 E6
Hope Park Sq EH8.....229 B1
Hopepark Terr FK4.....57 F6
Hope Park Terr EH8.....229 B1
Hope Pl EH41.....101 A1
Hope Pl
 Musselburgh EH21.....124 F6
 Tranent EH33.....126 C7
Hope St Bo'ness EH51.....63 F8
 Carluke ML8.....215 A2
 Cowdenbeath KY4.....13 C6
 Edinburgh EH2.....228 B3
 Falkirk FK1.....60 B5
 Inverkeithing KY11.....47 B1
 Queensferry EH30.....89 B8
 Stirling FK8.....1 F1
Hope Street La EH2.....228 B3

Hope Terr EH9.....121 C4
Hopetoun Cres EH7.....93 E2
Hopetoun Dr
 Bridge of A FK9.....2 A8
 Haddington EH41.....100 F1
Hopetoun House EH30....66 F2
Hopetoun La EH48.....141 B6
Hopetoun Mews 1
 EH41.....101 A1
Hopetoun Mon EH39.....100 E5
Hopetoun Pk EH31.....52 A3
Hopetoun Pl KY11.....16 C6
Hopetoun Rd EH30.....68 A1
Hopetoun St
 Bathgate EH48.....141 B6
 Edinburgh EH7.....93 E2
Hopetoun Terr
 Gullane EH31.....52 A3
 Ormiston EH35.....155 E7
Hopetoun Trout Fishery
 EH52.....88 B5
Hopetoun View KY11.....48 C4
Hopeward Ct KY11.....48 C2
Hopeward Mews KY11...48 C2
Hoprig EH33.....99 A1
Hoprig Pk TD13.....218 F3
Hoprig Rd
 Cockburnspath TD13....218 F3
 Cockburnspath TD13....218 F4
Hornbeam Cres FK2.....61 A3
Horsburgh Bank EH14...147 C3
Horsburgh Gdns EH14...147 C3
Horsburgh Gr EH14.....147 C3
Horse Wynd EH8.....229 C3
Hoseason Gdns EH4.....91 D1
Hosie Rigg EH15.....123 E8
Hospital Cross Head KY11 29 C1
Hospital Hill KY11.....29 B1
Hospital Intc EH14.....228 A1
Hospital Rd ML7.....179 E5
Hospital Rd FK11.....100 F1
Hot Pot Wynd KY1.....18 A6
Houldsworth Cres ML7..198 A8
Houldsworth St KY12.....26 A7
Houliston Ave KY11.....47 B3
House O'Hill Ave EH4.....92 A3
House O'Hill Brae EH4...92 A3
House O'Hill Cres EH4...92 A3
House O'Hill Gdns EH4...92 B3
House O'Hill Gn EH4.....92 A3
House O'Hill Gr EH4.....92 A3
House O'Hill Pl EH4.....92 A3
House O'Hill Rd EH4.....92 B2
House O'Hill Row EH4...92 B2
House O' Muir Rd ML7...158 B3
House O' Muir EH26.....172 E2
Housepark Pl EH54.....143 B3
Houston Cres EH52.....115 A1
Houston Ct 1 KY12.....28 F4
Houston Rd EH54.....115 A1
Houston Ind Est EH54...144 A8
Houston Terr EH54.....115 A1
Houstoun Gdns EH52...114 F3
Houstoun Ind Est
 Dechmont EH54.....114 E1
 Livingston EH54.....143 E7
Houstoun Intc EH54.....143 E7
Houstoun Mains Holdings
 EH52.....114 E2
Houstoun Rd
 Livingston,Eliburn EH54...143 B5
 Livingston,Ladywell EH54 143 D6
Houstoun Rd W EH54...142 C5
Howard Cres KY11.....29 C7
Howard Pl Dysart KY1.....18 A7
 Edinburgh EH3.....93 C3
Howard St Edinburgh EH3..93 C3
 Falkirk FK1.....59 F4
Howburn Cres ML7.....159 D6
Howburn Rd ML7.....159 D6
Howden East Rd EH54...143 F4
Howden Hall Cres EH16..150 F6
Howden Hall Ct EH16...150 F6
Howden Hall Gdns EH16 151 A6
Howden Hall Loan EH16..150 F5
Howden Hall Pk EH16....150 F5
Howden Hall Rd EH16...151 A5
Howden Hall Way EH16..151 A5
Howden St Andrew's RC
 Prim Sch.....
Howden South Rd EH54..143 E3
Howden St EH8.....229 B1
Howden West Rd EH54...143 D4
Howe Ness KY11.....46 D3
Howe Pk EH10.....149 F5
Howe St EH3.....228 C4
Howgate Sh Ctr 6 FK1..60 B4
Howie's Pl KY11.....46 B4
Howieson Ave EH51.....63 F5
Howieson Gn EH52.....114 F4
Howlands Rd FK7.....7 A3
Howley Ave FK54.....143 B4
Howpark Rd TD13,TD14..219 E1
Hudson Rd KY11.....46 F3
Hugh Ave KY5.....14 B8
Hugh Miller Pl EH3.....93 B2
Hugh Pl KY5.....14 B8
Hugh Russell Pl EH30....89 B8
Huly Hill Rd EH28.....117 A5
Humbie Cotts EH54.....164 B1
Humbie Prim Sch EH36..178 B2
Humbie Rd EH20.....171 A1
Humbie Smallholdings
 EH27.....145 F4
Humbie Terr KY3.....49 C8

Hume Cres FK9.....2 A6
Hume Ct FK9.....2 A6
Hummel Rd EH31.....51 F2
Hungerage Sq EH33.....126 D5
Huntburn Ave EH49.....85 C7
Hunter Cl EH22.....153 A4
Hunter Ct EH22.....153 A4
Hunter's Cl EH1.....228 C2
Hunter's La EH47.....161 A6
Hunter's Tryst Prim Sch
 EH13.....149 F7
Hunter Ave EH20.....172 D8
Hunter Ct EH20.....172 D8
Hunterfield Ct EH23.....195 C8
Hunterfield Pk EH23....174 C1
Hunterfield Rd EH23....195 C8
Hunterfield Terr EH23...174 B1
Hunter Gdns
 Bonnybridge FK4.....58 A5
 Broxburn EH52.....116 A5
 Denny FK6.....36 B2
Hunter Gr Bathgate EH48..141 E5
 Whitburn EH47.....160 F5
Hunter Pl Dunfermline KY12 28 E2
 Falkirk FK2.....39 A4
 Kirkcaldy KY1.....17 B3
 Shotts ML7.....179 E5
Hunter Rd EH54.....143 C2
Hunters Ct EH21.....124 D7
Hunters Hill EH26.....191 C6
Hunter Sq Edinburgh EH1..229 A3
 Gorebridge EH23.....195 D8
Hunter St Kirkcaldy KY1...17 B4
 Shotts ML7.....179 D5
Hunter Terr
 Bonnyrigg and Lasswade
 EH19.....173 B7
 Loanhead EH20.....172 D8
Huntingdon Pl EH7.....93 E2
Hunting Pk EH54.....114 F1
Huntly Ave EH54.....164 C6
Huntly Ave EH54.....164 C6
Huntly Cres Kirkcaldy KY2..16 C8
 Stirling FK8.....1 F2
Huntly St EH3.....93 C3
Huntly Terr ML7.....180 B3
Hunt Pl KY12.....28 B1
Huron Ave EH54.....143 F3
Hursted Ave EH22.....174 D7
Hurworth St FK1.....59 F3
Husband Pl KY1.....17 B3
Hutchison Ave EH14.....120 C3
Hutchison Cotts EH14...120 C3
Hutchison Crossway
 EH14.....120 C4
Hutchison Gdns EH14...120 C3
Hutchison Gn KY11.....29 B1
Hutchison Ho EH14.....120 D3
Hutchison Loan EH14...120 C3
Hutchison Medway
 EH14.....120 D3
Hutchison Pk EH14.....120 D3
Hutchison Terr EH14.....120 C3
Hutchison View EH14...120 C3
Hutton Pk FK10.....10 C7
Hutton Sq FK54.....164 C6
Hyndford Ho EH39.....54 A7
Hyndfords Ct EH1.....229 B3
Hyndshaw Rd ML8.....215 A3
Hyvot Ave EH17.....151 E6
Hyvot Bank Ave EH17....151 E6
Hyvot Ct EH17.....151 D5
Hyvot Gdns EH17.....151 D5
Hyvot Gn EH17.....151 D5
Hyvot Gr EH17.....151 D5
Hyvot Loan EH17.....151 D5
Hyvot Pk EH17.....151 D5
Hyvot Terr EH17.....151 D5
Hyvot View EH17.....151 D5

I

Ibris Pl EH39.....54 A7
Icehouse Brae N FK2....61 B4
Icehouse Brae S FK2....61 B4
Imex Ctr EH20.....172 A7
Implement Rd EH42.....77 E1
Imrie Pl EH26.....191 F5
Inch Ave KY3.....49 B6
Inch Colm Ave FK5.....38 C4
Inchcolm Dr KY11.....68 B6
Inchcolm Rd KY11.....29 E3
Inchcolm Terr EH30.....89 B8
Inchcorse Pl EH48.....141 C1
Inch Cres EH48.....141 D5
Inchcross EH48.....140 F3
Inchcross Dr EH48.....140 F2
Inchcross Ind Est EH48..140 F2
Inchcross Pk EH48.....140 F2
Inchcross Steadings
 EH48.....140 F2
Inches Rdbt FK5.....38 C4
Inches The
 Dalgety Bay KY11.....48 B2
 Grangemouth FK3.....61 E8
Inchgarvie Cres KY11....29 E3
Inchgarvie Pk EH30.....68 A1
Inchgarvie Rd KY2.....16 C8
Inch Garvie Terr FK5....38 C4
Inchkeith Ave KY11.....89 C8
Inchkeith Ct EH7.....29 F3
Inchkeith Dr KY11.....29 F3
Inchkeith Gr 3 EH33....126 D7
Inchkeith Pl FK1.....60 B2
Inchkeith Sch KY12.....42 C8

Inchmickery Ave KY11....48 D5
Inchmickery Rd KY11....48 C5
Inchmuir Rd EH48.....141 B2
Inchna FK11.........4 A6
Inchview EH32.......96 E1
Inch View Kinghorn KY3.34 F1
  Kirkcaldy KY1......35 B7
Inchview Cres EH31...125 C5
Inchview Gdns KY11...48 B3
Inchview N EH32.....96 E1
Inchview Rd EH21.....125 C6
Inchview Terr EH7....94 F1
Inch Wood Ave EH48..141 D4
Inchyra PI FK3......61 B5
Inchyra Rd FK3......61 E5
India PI EH3.......228 B4
India St EH3.......228 B4
Industrial Rd EH6....94 B4
Industry Homes EH6...93 E5
Industry La EH6.....93 E5
Infirmary St EH1.....229 B2
Ingleston Ave FK6....36 D4
Inglewood Gdns FK10..10 A8
Inglewood Ho FK10....4 F1
Inglewood PI 3 EH16..151 B8
Inglewood Rd EH54....9 F8
Inglewood St EH54...143 F5
Inglis Ct EH1......228 C2
Inglis Ave EH32.....97 C4
Inglis Cres KY3......34 F3
Inglis Dr FK2.......39 C2
Inglis Farm EH32.....97 C3
Inglis Green Gait 3
  EH14..........120 B2
Inglis Green Rd EH14..120 B2
Inglis Green Rigg 2
  EH14..........120 B2
Inglis La KY12......28 F5
Inglis PI FK2.......82 E8
Inglis St KY12......29 A4
Ingliston Rd EH28...117 F6
Ingram PI FK2......82 E6
Inkerman Ct EH26...192 A8
Innellan Cres ML7...179 E6
Innerpeffray Dr FK2...39 A3
Innerwick Prim Sch
  EH42..........218 A7
Innes Bldgs 1 EH33..126 C6
Innova Way KY11.....46 D1
Inn PI EH54........143 B2
Institution St KY1....17 E7
Inverallan Ct FK9.....1 F8
Inverallan Dr FK9.....1 F7
Inverallan Rd FK9....1 F7
Inveralmond Com High Sch
  EH54..........143 D5
Inveralmond Dr EH4...91 A5
Inveralmond Gdns EH4..91 A5
Inveralmond Gr EH4...91 A5
Inverary Dr FK5......38 F5
Inveravon Rd EH20...151 B1
Inveravon Rdbt EH51..62 D5
Inveravon Terr FK11..124 C5
Inveresk Brae EH21...124 D5
Inveresk Cres EH21...124 C4
Inveresk Gate EH21...124 C5
Inveresk Ind Est EH21.124 C5
Inveresk Lodge Gdn
  EH21..........124 D4
Inveresk Mills Ind Pk
  EH21..........124 B5
Inveresk Rd EH21....124 C5
Inveresk Village Rd
  EH21..........124 D4
Inverewe PI KY11.....30 A1
Inverkeithing High Sch
  KY11..........47 D3
Inverkeithing Mus KY11.47 B2
Inverkeithing Prim Sch
  KY11..........47 B3
Inverkeithing Rd
  Aberdour KY3......49 B7
  Crossgates KY4.....30 E6
Inverkeithing Sta KY11..47 C3
Inverkip Dr ML7.....179 E5
Inverleith Ave EH3....93 B4
Inverleith Ave S EH3..93 B4
Inverleith Gdns EH3...93 A4
Inverleith Gr EH3.....92 F3
Inverleith PI EH3.....93 A4
Inverleith Place La EH3.93 B4
Inverleith Row EH3...93 B4
Inverleith Terr EH3....93 B3
Inverleith Terrace La EH3.93 C3
Invertiel Bank KY1....17 B1
Invertiel Rd KY1.....35 A8
Invertiel Terr KY1....17 B1
Inzievar Ho KY12.....26 F7
Inzievar Prim Sch KY12.26 F7
Inzievar Terr KY12....26 F7
Iona PI FK1........60 B2
Iona Rd KY11.......29 E3
Iona St EH6........93 F3
Iona Terr EH5......93 E6
Ireland Ave EH47....160 F6
Irene Terr FK1......82 E2
Ironmills Rd EH22...152 F3
Irvine Cres EH48....140 F6
Irvine PI FK9.......7 A8
Irving Ct FK1.......59 E5
Islands Cres FK1.....60 B2
Islay Ct FK3.......61 C5
Islay Rd KY11.......29 E3
Ivanhoe Cres EH16...122 B1
Ivanhoe PI FK8......2 A2
Ivanhoe Rise EH54...144 A2
Ivanhoe St KY12.....61 E2
Ivy Gr KY11........46 E8

Ivy La KY1.........18 A7
Ivy Terr EH11......120 E5
Izatt Ave KY11......29 B1
Izatt St FK10.......10 B7
Izatt Terr FK10......11 A4

J

Jacklin Gn EH54.....143 B7
Jackson's CI EH11...229 A3
Jackson's Entry EH8..229 C3
Jackson Ave FK3.....61 D7
Jackson PI EH54.....143 C4
Jackson St EH26.....191 E5
Jacobite Way EH32....97 B1
Jacob PI FK1.......60 B3
Jacobs Way EH23....195 C8
Jail Wynd 6 FK8.....7 A8
Jamaica Mews EH3...228 B4
Jamaica St W EH3...228 B4
Jamaica St EH3.....228 B4
Jamaica Street N La
  EH3..........228 B4
Jamaica Street S La EH3.228 B4
James' Ct EH1......229 A3
James' Park La KY3...33 F1
James' Pk KY3......33 F1
James Bank KY12.....29 A4
James Cornwall Ct FK3.61 F6
James Craig Wk EH2..229 A4
James Croft Dr FK1...59 F1
James Ct KY4.......13 C2
James Gillespie's High Sch
  EH9..........121 C5
James Gillespie's Prim Sch
  EH9..........121 C5
James Gr KY1.......17 B2
James Hog Cres KY12..26 F6
James Lean Ave EH22.153 B3
James Leary Way EH19.173 C8
James Miller Rd KY11..46 E2
Jameson PI EH6......93 F3
James Smith Ave FK2..82 E6
James St Alva FK12....5 A6
  Armadale EH48.....139 F5
  Bannockburn FK7.....7 C1
  Cowdenbeath KY4....13 C2
  Dunfermline KY12....29 A4
  Edinburgh EH15.....123 C8
  Falkirk FK2.......60 B6
  Laurieston FK2.....60 F3
  Laurieston FK2.....61 A3
  Longcroft FK4......57 A3
  Musselburgh EH21...124 B6
  Stenhousemuir FK5...38 D2
  Stirling FK8.........2 B1
James Street La EH15..123 C8
James Watt Ave EH51..64 A7
James Wilson Dr FK2..83 A5
James Wylie PI KY10...23 F4
James Young High Sch The
  EH54..........143 E1
Jamieson Ave
  Bo'ness EH51......63 E6
  Stenhousemuir FK5...38 E3
Jamieson Gdns ML7...179 E5
Janefield EH17......151 A4
Jane St EH6........93 F4
Jane Welsh Carlyle Mus
  EH41..........130 A8
Jarnac Ct 7 EH22....153 A3
Jarvey St EH48.....141 B7
Jarvie PI 4 FK2.....60 A8
Jasper Ave FK2.....61 A4
Jawbanes Rd KY2....35 A3
Jean Armour Ave 1
  EH16..........122 A1
Jean Armour Dr EH22.153 D2
Jean Armour Gdns KY2.17 A7
Jeanette Stewart Dr
  EH22..........173 F4
Jeffrey Ave EH4.....92 B1
Jeffrey Bank EH51....63 F7
Jeffrey St EH1......229 B3
Jeffrey Terr FK2.....61 F2
Jellyholm Rd FK10....10 E8
Jenks Loan EH22....174 A5
Jennie Rennie's Rd KY11.29 B1
Jessfield PI EH51....63 C5
Jessfield Terr EH6....93 D6
Jewel & Esk Valley Coll
  Dalkeith EH22......152 F1
  Edinburgh EH15.....123 D6
Jewel The EH15.....123 B5
Jock's Hill Cres EH49..84 E7
Jock's Lodge 8 EH8...94 C1
John's La EH6......94 A5
John's PI EH6......94 A5
John Bernard Way EH20.195 C6
John Brown Ct EH41...101 B3
John Connelly Ct 3 EH12.28 E5
John Cotton Bsns Ctr
  EH7..........94 A2
John Cowane Row FK9..2 A4
John Cres EH33.....126 C6
John Davidson Dr FK6..36 C4
John Humble St EH22..174 E5
John Hunter Ct KY1...17 B4
John Knox Ho EH1...229 B3
John Knox PI EH26...191 F5
John Knox Rd EH26...98 E5
John McDouall Stuart Mus
  KY1..........18 A7
John Mason Ct EH30...89 C8
John Muir Birthplace
  EH42..........78 D2
John Muir Cres EH42.106 D8

John Muir Ctry Pk EH42..77 D4
John Muir Gdns EH42..106 D8
John Muir PI EH42...106 D8
John Muir Rd EH42...106 D8
John Murray Dr FK9....2 A8
Johnnie Cope's Rd EH33.126 A7
Johnny Moat PI EH32..96 F1
John O'Hara Ct FK1...59 D5
John Row PI KY11.....27 A7
John Rushforth PI FK8...1 F3
Johnsburn Gn EH14...147 B1
Johnsburn Haugh EH14.147 B1
Johnsburn Pk EH14...168 B8
Johnsburn Rd EH14...147 B1
John Smith Way ML7..179 D5
John St Dunfermline KY11..29 B2
  Edinburgh EH15.....123 C8
  Falkirk FK2.......60 B7
  Kincardine FK10.....23 D3
  Kirkcaldy KY2......17 B5
  Longcroft FK4......57 A3
  Penicuik EH26.....191 F6
Johnston Ave
  Stenhousemuir FK5...38 F3
  Stirling FK9.........2 B3
  Uphall EH52.......114 F3
Johnston Cres
  Dunfermline KY11....29 B1
  Lochgelly KY5......14 B7
Johnston Ct 7 Falkirk FK2.60 B8
  Uphall EH52.......114 F4
Johnstone Ct FK12.....5 A6
Johnstone La ML8....215 B3
Johnstone St Alva FK12..5 A6
  Menstrie FK11......3 F6
Johnston Pk
  Cowdenbeath KY4....13 C5
  Inverkeithing KY11...47 B2
Johnston PI Denny FK6..36 C1
  Penicuik EH26.....191 F6
Johnston St FK7......7 C1
John Street La
  Edinburgh EH15.....123 C8
  Penicuik EH26.....191 E5
John Street La E EH15..123 C8
John Street La W EH15..123 C8
John Stuart Gait KY12...26 F6
John Wood PI KY4....30 D7
Jones Ave FK5......59 C8
Jones Gn EH54......143 A7
Jones St KY12.......12 A1
Joppa Gdns EH15....123 C7
Joppa Gr EH15......123 C7
Joppa Pk EH15......123 C7
Joppa Rd EH15......123 C7
Joppa Station PI EH15..123 C7
Joppa Terr EH15.....123 C7
Jordan La EH10.....121 B3
Joseph Scott Gdns EH52.113 E4
Jubilee Ave EH54....142 F6
Jubilee Cres EH23...174 C1
Jubilee Ct KY12......29 A3
Jubilee Dr KY11......46 B1
Jubilee Rd Denny FK6..36 E3
  Ratho Station EH28..118 A7
  Whitburn EH47.....161 A6
Jubilee Way FK4.....57 F5
Junction PI 2 Alloa FK10.10 B6
  Edinburgh EH6.....93 F5
Junction Rd EH17....17 D7
Juner PI KY23......174 C1
Juniper Ave EH14....148 C5
Juniper Gdns EH14...148 C6
Juniper Gr
  Dunfermline KY11....46 D8
  Edinburgh EH14.....148 C6
  Livingston EH54....144 B6
Juniper Green Prim Sch
  EH14..........148 D6
Juniper La EH14.....148 C6
Juniperlee EH14.....148 D6
Juniper Park Rd EH14.148 C6
Juniper Terr EH14...148 D6
Jura Ct FK3.......61 C5
Jura PI FK3.......61 D5
Justinhaugh Dr EH49..84 D7
Jute PI KY11.......17 C7

K

Kaemuir Ct EH48....110 F5
Kaim Cres EH48.....141 D5
Kaimes Ave EH27....145 E5
Kaimes Cres EH27...145 E3
Kaimes Gdns EH27...145 E3
Kaimes Gr EH27.....145 E3
Kaimes Rd EH12.....120 C6
Kaimes Specl Sch EH16.151 C6
Kaimes View EH27...152 B7
Kaims Brae EH54....143 C2
Kaims Ct EH54......143 B2
Kaims Dr EH54......143 C2
Kaims Gdns EH54....143 C2
Kaims PI EH54......143 C2
Kaims PI EH54......143 B2
Kaims Terr EH54....143 B2
Kaims Wlk EH54.....143 C2
Kames PI KY12......29 D5
Kames Rd ML7......179 E6
Karries Ct FK6......57 B8
Katesmill Rd EH14...149 B8

Katherine St Kirkcaldy KY2..17 B6
  Livingston EH54....144 A5
Katrine Cres KY2.....16 C5
Katrine Ct FK10......10 C5
Katrine Dr KY12.....28 B1
Katrine PI FK6......57 D6
Katrine Rd Shotts ML7..179 E6
  Whitburn EH47.....161 D7
Kay Gdns EH32......97 C4
Kay Rd KY12........43 F8
Keavil Farm Steadings
  KY12..........45 B8
Keavil PI KY12......28 B1
Kedslie PI EH16.....150 F7
Kedslie Rd EH16.....150 F8
Keilarsbrae FK10.....10 C8
Keir Ave EH48.......2 A2
Keir Gdns FK9.......2 A7
Keirfold Ave FK10.....2 A3
Keir Hardie Dr EH22..174 E5
Keir Hardie Rd FK1....5 C7
Keir Hardie Terr KY11..29 B1
Keirsbeath Ct KY12....12 B2
Keirsbeath Rise KY12..12 B1
Keir St Bridge of A FK9...2 A7
  Cowdenbeath KY4....2 C2
  Edinburgh EH3.....228 C2
Keith Ave KY12......7 C4
Keith Cres EH4......92 B1
Keith Gdns EH52....115 C6
Keith Marischal Ct EH6.177 F5
Keith PI Dunfermline KY12..29 B1
  Inverkeithing KY11...47 C3
Keith Rd KY11.......92 D1
Keith Row EH4......92 C1
Keith St ML8........23 D3
Keith Terr EH4......92 B1
Kekewich Ave EH7....94 F2
Kelliebank FK10......9 E6
Kellie Rd EH42.....106 D8
Kelly's La ML8......215 B1
Kelly's Ct FK8.......7 A8
Kelly Dr FK6........36 E3
Kellwood Cres FK10...23 F3
Kelso Dr ML8......215 C1
Kelso St EH52......115 B5
Kelso Rd FK10......57 A6
Kelty Ave EH51......80 B4
Kelvin Sq SN54.....144 B8
Kelvin St FK3.......40 A1
Kemper Ave FK1.....60 C3
Kemp PI EH3........93 B2
Kemp's Cnr EH7.....94 C2
Kemp's End EH33...126 C4
Kempston PI EH30....89 C8
Kendieshill Ave FK2...83 A5
Kenilworth Ct FK9.....2 A7
Kenilworth Dr
  Edinburgh EH14.....151 B8
  Laurieston FK2.....60 F4
Kenilworth La FK3....61 C5
Kenilworth PI FK9.....2 A7
Kenilworth Rise EH54.143 F1
Kenilworth St EH51...61 D5
Kenmore Ave
  Livingston EH54....142 F6
  Polmont FK2.......62 A2
Kenmore Terr KY2....16 E7
Kenmuir St FK1.....59 A5
Kenmure Ave EH8....122 C8
Kenmure PI
  Dunfermline KY12....29 C5
  Stenhousemuir FK5...38 F4
Kennard Rd FK2.....82 C8
Kennard St Falkirk FK2.60 C6
  Lochgelly KY5......14 B8
Kennedie PI EH53...144 C3
Kennedy Cres
  Dunfermline KY11....29 B5
  Kirkcaldy KY2......17 B6
  Tranent EH33......126 D7
Kennedy Ct EH41....129 B7
Kennedy Way KY12...22 F3
Kennel Mus & Roman
  Fortlet EH5.......63 C6
Kennet Village FK10...11 D3
Kenningknowes Rd FK7..6 E5
Kennington Ave EH20..172 B8
Kennington Terr EH20..172 B8
Kentigern Mall EH26..191 F5
Kent St KY12.......29 C6
Keppel Rd EH39.....54 A6
Keppock PI FK1.....59 F1
Kepscaith Cres EH47..161 B5
Kepscaith Gr EH47...161 B5
Kepscaith Rd EH47...161 B5
Ker's Wynd EH21....124 D6
Kerr Ave EH22......152 B7
Kerr Cres FK4......57 A3
Kerrisk Dr KY11......29 F1
Kerr PI Denny FK6....36 D2
  Dunfermline KY11....29 F1
Kerr Rd EH33......126 C6
Kerr St EH3........93 B2
Kerr Way KY12......29 F1
Kersebonny Rd FK7....6 C7
Kerse Gdns FK2.....60 E5
Kersegreen Rd FK10...10 F5
Kershill Cres FK2.....60 C7

Kerse La FK1.......60 C4
Kerse PI FK1.......60 C5
Kerse Rd Grangemouth FK3.61 D8
  Stirling FK7.........7 C6
  Stirling,Loanhead FK7..7 E5
Kersiebank Ave FK3...61 E6
Kersie Rd FK7.......9 A3
Kersie Terr FK7.......9 B2
Kestrel Brae EH54...143 C5
Kestrel Dr FK2......82 E7
Kettil'stoun Cres EH49..84 D5
Kettil'stoun Ct EH49...84 D5
Kettil'stoun Gr EH49...84 D5
Kettil'stoun Mains EH49.84 D5
Kettilstoun Rd EH49...84 D7
Keverkae FK10.......9 F6
Kevock Rd EH18.....172 E8
Kevock Vale Cvn Pk
  EH19..........173 A8
Kew Gdns 2 EH48...141 B6
Kew Terr 3 EH11....120 E7
Kidd St KY1........17 D7
Kier Ct FK9........2 B7
Kilbagie St FK10.....23 D4
Kilbagie St FK1.......5 B2
Kilbirnie Terr FK6....36 D3
Kilbrennan Dr FK1....59 B4
Kilburn Rd KY12.....28 A2
Kilchurn Ct 1 EH12...119 A7
Kilcruik Rd KY3......34 F3
Kildean Hospl FK8.....1 F2
Kildean Sch FK8......1 F2
Kildimmery EH44....85 E6
Kildonan Pk KY12....28 F2
Kildrummy Ave FK5...38 F4
Kilduthie PI FK10....23 D6
Kilfinan Rd ML7....179 D6
Kilgour Ave KY1.....17 D7
Kilgraston Rd EH9...121 D4
Killin Ct KY12......28 F2
Killin Dr FK2.......62 A2
Killochan Way KY12...29 D5
Kilmartin Way KY12...29 C5
Kilmaurs Rd EH16...122 A4
Kilmaurs Terr EH16..122 A4
Kilmory Ct FK1.....59 C4
Kilmory Gdns ML8...215 A3
Kilmundy Dr KY3.....33 D1
Kilmun Rd KY2......16 D7
Kilncadzow Rd ML8..215 C1
Kilncraigs Ct FK10....10 C5
Kilncraigs Rd FK10...10 C6
Kilncroftside EH14...120 B2
Kilne PI EH54......143 A4
Kilngate Brae EH17..151 D5
Kilns PI FK2........59 F6
Kilns Rd FK1........60 A5
Kilpair St EH41.....130 B8
Kilpunt Gdns EH51...116 A5
Kilpunt Rdbt EH52...116 A5
Kilpunt View EH51...116 A5
Kilrie Cotts KY2......33 F7
Kilrymont ML11.....201 A1
Kilsland Terr EH51....63 D7
Kilspindie Ct EH32....71 D4
Kilsyth Rd FK4......57 A3
Kilwinning PI EH21...124 C6
Kilwinning St EH21...124 D6
Kilwinning Terr EH21..124 D6
Kinacres Gr FK10.....64 D7
Kincairne Rd FK2.....39 C3
Kincraig PI KY12.....28 F2
Kinellan Gdns EH12..120 C8
Kinellan Rd EH12....120 C7
King's Cramond EH4...91 B4
King's Ct Carluke ML8..215 A2
  Rosyth KY11.......46 E4
King's Ct EH32......98 D4
King's Dr KY3.......34 F3
King's Gr EH32......98 C4
King's Knoll Gdns EH39..54 C7
King's Mdw EH16....94 C8
King's Meadow Prim Sch
  EH41..........130 A8
King's Park Prim Sch
  EH22..........153 A2
King's Park Rd FK8....7 A7
King's Pk EH32......98 D5
King's PI KY11......46 D8
King's Rd Edinburgh EH15..95 A1
  Longniddry EH32....98 D5
  Rosyth KY11.......126 C5
King's Road Prim Sch
  KY11..........46 E4
King's Stables La EH1.228 C2
King's Stables Rd EH1.228 C2
King's Terr EH15......94 F1
King's Theatre EH3...228 B1
King Edward's Way EH29.89 A1
Kingfisher Brae EH54..143 C5
King Cres EH55.....163 D3
King Edwards Way EH29.89 A1
Kinghorn Prim Sch KY3..34 F2
Kinghorn Rd
  Burntisland KY3.....34 A1
  Kinghorn KY3......35 B7
  Kinghorn Sta KY3....34 F2
King James Dr FK10...4 C2
King James IV Rd KY11..46 C1
Kinglass Ave EH51....64 A7
Kinglass PI EH51....64 A6

248 Kin–Lei

Kinglass Dr EH51 ....64 A6
Kinglass Pk EH51 ....64 A5
King Malcolm Cl EH10 .. 150 D5
King O' Muirs Ave FK10 .... 4 E4
King O'Muirs Dr FK10 ...... 4 D4
King O' Muirs Rd FK10 ...... 4 E4
King O' Muirs Farm Steading
FK10 .... 4 F4
King Robert Ct FK8 .... 1 E1
Kingsburgh Ct EH40 .... 103 D8
Kingsburgh Gdns EH40 .. 103 D8
Kingsburgh Rd EH12 .... 120 C7
Kings Ct Alloa FK10 ....10 A7
7 Falkirk FK1 ....60 B4
Stenhousemuir FK5 ....38 D2
Kings Dr KY11 ....47 A8
Kingseat Ave FK3 ....61 D6
Kingseat Pl FK1 ....59 F3
Kingseat Rd
Dunfermline KY12 ....29 D6
Halbeath KY11, KY12 ....30 B6
Kingsfield EH49 ....85 D8
Kingsgate Ctr KY12 ....29 A4
Kings Gn EH11 ....120 E5
Kings Haugh EH16 ...... 122 C4
Kingshill Rd ML7 .... 198 A8
Kingshill View ML11 ......217 F8
Kingsinch Sch EH16 ..... 122 A2
King's Knoll EH39 ....54 B7
Kingsknowe Ave EH14 ... 120 A1
Kingsknowe Cres EH14 .. 120 A1
Kingsknowe Ct EH14 ......119 F1
Kingsknowe Dr EH14 .... 120 A1
Kingsknowe Gdns EH14 . 120 A1
Kingsknowe Gr EH14 .... 149 A8
Kingsknowe Pk EH14 ... 149 A8
Kingsknowe Pl EH14 ......119 F1
Kingsknowe Rd N EH14 . 120 A2
Kingsknowe Rd S EH14 . 120 A1
Kingsknowe Sta EH14 ... 120 A1
Kingsknowe Terr EH14 .. 120 A1
Kingslaw Ct 1 EH33 .... 126 D5
Kingslaw Farm Cotts
EH33 ....126 F6
Kingsley Ave FK5 ....38 F3
Kingsport Ave EH54 ......143 F4
King Sq EH55 .... 163 D3
Kings Rd FK3 ....61 F8
King's Rd EH47 .... 161 A6
King St Armadale EH48 ... 140 A6
Bathgate EH48 ....141 B6
Cowdenbeath KY4 ....13 B4
Edinburgh EH6 ....93 F5
Falkirk FK2 ....60 C6
Fallin FK7 ....8 C4
Inverkeithing KY11 ....47 C2
Kirkcaldy KY2 ....17 B6
Musselburgh EH21 ...... 124 D5
Shotts ML7 ....179 E4
Stenhousemuir,Antonshill
FK5 ....38 F3
Stenhousemuir FK5 ....38 D2
Stirling FK8 ....7 B7
Kingstables La 3 FK8 ...... 7 A8
Kingsthorne Pk EH54 ....114 F1
Kingston Ave EH16 ..... 122 C1
Kingston Cotts EH39 ....53 E1
Kingswell Pk FK10 ....10 C7
Kininmonth St KY1 ....17 B2
Kinleith Ind Est EH14 ....148 B4
Kinloch Pl FK3 ....61 E5
Kinloss Ct KY12 ....26 A2
Kinnaird Ave FK2 ....39 B3
Kinnaird Dr FK5 ....38 E3
Kinnaird Pl
Dunfermline KY12 ....29 D6
Kirkcaldy KY2 ....16 D4
Kinnear Rd EH3 ....93 A4
Kinneil Dr EH51 ....63 D6
Kinneil Prim Sch EH51 ....63 F6
Kinneil Rd EH51 ....63 D7
Kinneil Sta EH51 ....63 D7
Kinnell Rd KY11 ....47 B2
Kinnis Ct KY11 ....29 F1
Kinnonmonth Ave KY3 ....33 D1
Kintail Pl KY11 ....30 A4
Kintyre Pl FK1 ....59 C4
Kippielaw Dr EH22 ...... 153 C2
Kippielaw Gdns EH22 ... 153 C1
Kippielaw Medway EH22 153 C1
Kippielaw Pk EH22 ...... 174 D8
Kippielaw Rd EH22 ...... 153 C1
Kippielaw Wlk EH22 .... 153 C2
Kippilaw Steading EH22. 153 D1
Kippithill EH36 ....178 B2
Kirk Ave FK5 ....38 E2
Kirkbank Rd KY3 ....33 F1
Kirkbrae Clackmannan FK10 10 F4
Garvald EH41 .... 132 D2
Kirk Brae Edinburgh EH16 151 A8
Innerwick EH42 .... 218 A7
Kincardine FK10 ....23 E5
Longridge EH47 .... 161 C1
Kirkbride Terr FK7 ....20 C3
Kirkburn FK1 ....108 B7
Kirkcaldy High Sch KY1 ...17 B8
Kirkcaldy Mus & Art Gallery
KY1 ....17 B4
Kirkcaldy North Prim Sch
KY2 ....17 B6
Kirkcaldy Rd
Burntisland KY3 ....33 F2
Crossgates KY4 ....31 A6
Kinghorn KY3 ....35 A4
Kirkcaldy Sta KY1 ....17 A4
Kirkcaldy West Prim Sch
KY1 ....17 B2
Kirk Cramond EH4 ....91 C6
Kirkfield E EH54 ....143 B3
Kirkfield View EH54 ..... 143 C3
Kirkfield W EH54 ....143 B3
Kirkflat EH52 .... 115 A5
Kirkford Ct KY4 ....13 A4
Kirkgate Alloa FK10 ....10 B6
Burntisland KY3 ....50 E8
Currie EH14 ....148 A3
Dunfermline KY12 ....28 F3
Edinburgh EH16 .... 151 A7
Inverkeithing KY11 ....47 B4
Linlithgow EH49 ....85 A7
West Calder EH55 .... 163 D3
Kirkgate Ho EH6 ....94 A4
Kirkhall Pl FK6 ....36 E2
Kirkhill Ct Broxburn EH52. 115 C5
Fauldhouse EH47 ....181 E6
Gorebridge EH23 .... 195 C8
Kirkhill Dr EH16 .... 122 A4
Kirkhill Gdns
Edinburgh EH16 .... 122 A5
Penicuik EH26 ....191 F5
Kirkhill Pk EH52 .... 115 C5
Kirkhill Pl EH52 .... 115 D5
Kirkhill Prim Sch EH52 ...115 B6
Kirkhill Rd Broxburn EH52 115 D5
Edinburgh EH16 .... 122 A4
Penicuik EH26 ....191 F5
Kirkhill Terr
Broxburn EH52 .... 115 C5
Edinburgh EH16 .... 122 A5
Gorebridge EH23 .... 174 A1
Kirkhill Way EH26 ....191 F5
Kirk La EH54 ....143 B2
Kirkland Dr FK6 ....36 B2
Kirklands Dunfermline KY12 29 A2
Edinburgh EH12 .... 119 D4
Penicuik EH26 ....191 E5
Kirklands Park Cres EH29 . 88 F2
Kirklands Park Gdns EH29 88 F2
Kirklands Park Gr EH29 ... 88 F2
Kirklands Park Rigg EH29 88 F2
Kirklands Park St EH29 ... 88 F2
Kirkliston Prim Sch EH29 .89 A2
Kirkliston Rd EH30 ....89 B8
Kirk Loan EH12 ....119 E6
Kirknewton Ct EH27 .... 145 C3
Kirknewton Prim Sch
EH27 .... 145 D2
Kirknewton Sta EH27 ... 145 C3
Kirk Pk Dunbar EH42 ....78 B2
Edinburgh EH16 ....151 B8
Kirk Ports EH39 ....54 C7
Kirk Rd Aberlady EH32 .....71 C4
Bathgate EH48 .... 141 C5
Shotts ML7 ....179 F4
Kirkside Cres FK7 ....7 B5
Kirkslap FK6 ....36 E2
Kirk St Culross KY12 ....25 D1
Edinburgh EH6 ....93 F4
Kincardine FK10 ....23 E4
Prestonpans EH32 ....96 F2
Kirkstyle Gdns EH29 ......89 B1
Kirkton Ave EH48 .... 141 D5
Kirkton Bank EH26 ...... 191 D5
Kirkton Bsns Ctr EH54 ...143 B3
Kirkton Campus EH54 ....164 B8
Kirkton Ct EH48 .... 141 D6
Kirkton North Rd EH54 .. 143 C3
Kirkton Pl Bathgate EH48. 141 D5
Cowdenbeath KY4 ....13 B5
Falkirk FK2 ....39 C3
Kirkton Rd KY3 ....33 E1
Kirkton South Rd EH54 .. 143 C2
Kirk View EH41 .... 130 C8
Kirkway FK2 ....22 D4
Kirkwood Ave FK2 ....61 C2
Kirkwood Cres KY12 ....28 B2
Kirk Wynd
Clackmannan FK10 ....11 A5
2 Falkirk FK1 ....60 B4
Kirkcaldy KY1 ....17 C4
Stirling FK7 ....7 B4
Kisimul Ct EH12 ....119 B7
Kitchener Cres EH32 ......98 E5
Kittle Yds EH9 ....121 E4
Klondyke St EH21 ....123 E4
Knaphill KY11 ....46 F7
Knightsbridge Ho EH54 . 143 C8
Knightslaw Pl EH26 ..... 191 D5
Knightsridge Ct EH52 ... 114 C2
Knightsridge East Rd
EH54 .... 143 D8
Knightsridge Ind Est
EH54 .... 143 C7
Knightsridge Prim Sch
EH54 .... 143 D7
Knightsridge Rd EH52 ... 114 C2
Knightsridge Rdbt EH54 . 143 C7
Knightsridge West Rd
EH54 ....143 B7
Knights Way FK6 ....36 C2
Knockenhair Rd EH42 .....78 B2
Knockhill Cl KY5 ....14 B7
Knockhouse Farm Cotts
KY12 ....28 B4
Knockhouse Gdns KY12 ...28 B2
Knockhouse Rd KY12 ......28 B2
Knockhouse Terr KY12 ....28 B2
Knoll Croft Rd ML7 ..... 180 A3
Knowehead Rd
Crossford KY12 ....28 A2
Redding FK2 ....61 C2
Knowepark Ct EH47 ..... 162 A2
Knowepark Rd EH47 .... 162 A1
Knowesley Pk EH41 ..... 129 D8
Knowes Rd EH41 ....129 E8
Knowe The Alloa FK10 ...... 5 C2
Dalgety Bay KY11 ....48 C3
Knowetop EH54 .... 164 C7
Knowetop Pl EH25 ....171 F3
Knowfaulds Rd FK10 .... 4 B3
Knox Acad EH41 ....129 F8
Knox Ct EH41 .... 130 A8
Knox Pl EH41 .... 130 A8
Komarom Pl EH22 ...... 153 D3
Kyle Ave FK7 ....20 E7
Kyle Cres KY11 ....30 C1
Kyle Pl EH7 .... 229 C4
Kyles The KY1 ....17 E6

L

Labrador Ave EH54 ......143 F4
Laburnum Arch Ct 5
EH32 ....96 F1
Laburnum Ave EH32 ......97 E3
Laburnum Dr KY1 ....17 C8
Laburnum Gr
Burntisland KY3 ....33 F2
Stirling FK8 ....6 F5
Laburnum Pl EH22 ....174 E6
Laburnum Rd
Dunfermline KY11 ....29 C1
Whitburn EH47 .... 161 C6
Lade Braes KY11 ....48 B3
Lade Ct EH49 ....84 E7
Lade Dr FK5 ....59 C8
Lade Gn KY11 ....48 B3
Ladehead EH6 ....93 D4
Lade Mill FK7 ....7 C1
Lade Rd FK4 ....58 A5
Ladeside Ave EH47 ...... 162 C8
Ladeside Cres FK5 ....38 E1
Ladeside Dr EH47 ...... 162 C8
Ladeside Gdns EH47 .....162 B8
Ladeside Prim Sch FK5 ...59 C8
Ladeside Rd EH47 ...... 162 C8
Lade The EH14 .... 168 D8
Ladiemeadow EH12 ......119 E5
Lady Anne Ct KY4 ....30 E6
Lady Brae EH23 .... 195 D7
Lady Brae Pl EH23 ....195 E8
Ladyburn Pl KY3 ....35 A3
Lady Campbell's Wlk
KY12 ....29 A4
Ladycroft EH14 .... 147 C2
Lady Ct EH47 ....161 E7
Lady Emily Way EH23 ... 195 C8
Lady Hall Rd TD13 ....218 F4
Lady Helen Cotts KY5 .....15 B8
Lady Helen St KY1 ....17 B2
Lady Jane Gdns EH39 .....54 D6
Lady Jane Rd EH39 ....54 D6
Lady Lawson St EH3 .... 228 C2
Lady Menzies Pl 3 EH7 ...94 A2
Lady Nairn Ave KY1 ....17 F6
Lady Nairne Cres EH8 ... 122 D7
Lady Nairne Gr EH8 ..... 122 D7
Lady Nairne Loan EH8 .. 122 D7
Lady Nairne Pl EH8 ..... 122 D7
Lady Nairne Rd KY12 ......28 E6
Lady Pl EH54 ....143 B5
Lady Rd EH16 .... 122 A3
Lady Road Pl EH22 ....174 B6
Ladysgate Ct FK2 ....39 B3
Ladysmill FK2 ....60 D5
Ladysmill Ct KY12 ....29 A1
Ladysmill Ind Est FK1 .....60 C5
Ladysmith Rd EH9 ....121 E2
Ladysneuk Rd FK9 ....2 D2
Lady Victoria Bsns Ctr
EH22 .... 174 A4
Ladywell EH21 .... 124 C6
Ladywell Ave EH12 ...... 119 D5
Ladywell Ct
Edinburgh EH12 .... 119 D6
Larbert FK5 ....38 A3
Ladywell Dr FK10 ....4 B3
Ladywell East Rd
Livingston EH54 .... 143 D6
Livingston EH54 ....143 E5
Ladywell Gdns EH12 .... 119 D5
Ladywell Gr FK10 ....11 A4
Ladywell Pl FK10 ....4 B3
Ladywell Rd EH12 .... 119 D6
Ladywell View EH51 ....63 D5
Ladywell Way EH21 ..... 124 C6
Ladywell West Rd EH54 . 143 C6
Ladywood FK10 ....11 C4
Ladywood Pl EH54 ....143 B5
Ladywood Prim Sch
EH26 .... 192 A7
Lady Wynd EH1 .... 228 C2
Lafferty Pl FK6 ....36 F1
Lagan Rd ML8 .... 215 A1
Laggan Ave ML7 ....180 B3
Laggan Path ML7 ....179 E6
Laichfield EH14 ....120 B3
Laichpark Pl EH14 ....120 B3
Laichpark Rd EH14 ....120 B3
Laing Gdns EH52 .... 115 C6
Laing Terr
Edinburgh EH15 .... 123 C8
Penicuik EH26 ....191 F7
Laird's Entry EH37 ...... 176 C3
Laird Terr EH19 .... 173 D6
Lairox Terr FK6 ....36 D3
Lakeside Rd KY2 ....16 F4
Lamb's Cl EH8 ....229 B1
Lamb's Pend EH26 ....191 F4
Lamb Ct EH39 ....54 A7
Lambert Dr KY12 ....29 D4
Lamberton Ave FK7 ....7 C3
Lamberton Ct EH34 ......156 E6
Lambert Terr FK10 ....10 C7
Lambie St EH47 ....161 B7
Lambs Ct EH6 ....93 C7
Lamer Ct EH42 ....78 E3
Lamer St EH42 ....78 E3
Lamington Rd EH33 ..... 128 C7
Lammerlaws Rd KY3 ......50 F8
Lammermoor Gdns
EH33 ....126 B6
Lammermoor Terr
Edinburgh EH16 .... 122 C1
Tranent EH33 ....126 B6
Lammermuir Cres
Dunbar EH42 ....78 C2
Haddington EH41 .... 130 C8
Lammermuir Ct EH31 .....52 B2
Lammermuir Pl KY2 ......16 F5
Lammerview
Gladsmuir EH33 .... 128 C7
12 Tranent EH33 .... 126 C5
Lammerview Terr EH31 ....52 A2
Lamond View FK5 ....38 D1
Lamont Cres FK7 ....8 D5
Lamont Way EH54 ...... 143 D8
Lampacre Rd EH12 ....119 E5
Lanark Ave EH54 .... 143 A6
Lanark Rd
Edinburgh, Kingsknowe
EH14 ....120 B1
Edinburgh,Wester Hailes
EH14 ....148 E6
Lanark Rd W EH14 ...... 147 D3
Landale Gdns KY3 ....33 E2
Landale Pl KY3 ....33 E2
Landale St KY5 ....14 B8
Lane The EH21 ....124 E1
Langfauld Gdns EH48 ....140 E5
Langhill Farm Cotts
EH25 ....171 F6
Langhill Pl FK6 ....36 C1
Langlaw Prim Sch EH22. 174 D8
Langlaw Rd EH22 .... 174 D8
Langlees Prim Sch FK2 ...60 B8
Langlees St FK2 ....39 C1
Lang Loan
Edinburgh EH17,EH20 .... 151 C3
Loanhead EH20 ....151 B2
Langriggs EH41 ....130 B8
Langside EH40 .... 103 D8
Langside Cres EH55 ..... 164 A5
Langside Dr EH48 ....138 B3
Langside Gdns EH55 .... 164 A6
Langton Ave EH53 ....144 E4
Langton Gdns EH53 ......144 F3
Langton Rd
East Calder EH53 ....144 F3
Edinburgh EH9 ....121 E3
Westquarter FK2 ....61 A3
Langton Steadings EH53 .144 F2
Langton Terr EH53 ....144 E4
Langton View EH53 ......144 F3
Lanrigg Ave EH47 ....181 E7
Lanrigg Ct EH47 ....181 F7
Lanrigg Rd EH47 ....181 F7
Lansbury Ct 2 EH22 .... 153 A3
Lansbury St KY1 ....17 E7
Lansdowne Cres
Edinburgh EH12 .... 228 A2
Kincardine FK10 ....23 E4
Shotts ML7 ....180 B3
Lapicide Pl EH6 ....93 E5
La Porte Prec FK3 ....61 D8
Lapwing Dr KY11 ....47 B7
Larbert Ave EH54 .... 143 A6
Larbert High Sch FK5 .....38 E1
Larbert Rd FK4 ....58 B6
Larbert Sta FK5 ....38 C2
Larbert Village Prim Sch
FK5 ....38 B1
Larbourfield EH11 ...... 119 D1
Larchbank EH54 ....143 E5
Larch Cres EH22 ....174 F6
Larch Dr EH47 .... 161 C6
Larchfield EH14 .... 147 C2
Larchfield Neuk EH14 ... 147 C2
Larchfield Path ML7 ......180 B2
Larch Gr Dunfermline KY11. .46 D8
Stenhousemuir FK5 ....38 F3
Larch St FK3 ....61 C6
Largo Pl EH6 ....93 E6
Larkfield Dr EH22 ....152 E1
Larkfield Rd EH22 ....152 E2
Lasswade Bank EH17 ... 151 C5
Lasswade Ct EH18 ...... 152 A1
Lasswade Gr EH17 ...... 151 C5
Lasswade High Sch Ctr
EH19 .... 173 A7
Lasswade Prim Sch
EH19 .... 173 C8
Lasswade Rd
Bonnyrigg and Lasswade EH17,
EH20 ....151 F2
Bonnyrigg and Lasswade
EH18 .... 152 A1
Dalkeith EH22 ....152 E2
Edinburgh EH16,EH17 .... 151 C6
Loanhead EH20 .... 172 D8
Latchburn View EH47 ... 162 C7
Latch Pk EH13 .... 149 C7
Latch Rd EH42 ....78 E1
Latch The KY12 ....27 C1
Lathallan Dr FK2 ....61 E2
Lauder Coll KY11 ....30 A5
Lauderdale Cres EH42 .....78 C2
Lauderdale St EH9 ...... 121 C5
Lauder Loan EH9 ....121 E4
Lauder Lodge 14 EH22 .. 153 A3
Lauder Pl EH40 ....103 E6
Lauder Rd Dalkeith EH22 . 153 C2
Edinburgh EH9 .... 121 D4
Kirkcaldy KY2 ....17 C6
Lauder St KY12 ....29 C6
Laura Fergusson Ct EH12 .91 B1
Laurel Bank EH22 ...... 153 C2
Laurelbank Ave FK4 ....58 A3
Laurelbank Ct EH53 ......144 F2
Laurel Bank Pl EH22 .....174 E6
Laurel Bank Rd EH22 .....174 E6
Laurel Cres KY2 ....17 B7
Laurel Ct Denny FK6 ....36 D3
Falkirk FK1 ....59 C6
Laurel Gdns KY12 ....27 F6
Laurel Gr Bonnybridge FK4 ..57 F3
Westquarter FK2 ....61 A2
Laurelhill Bsns Pk FK7 .....6 F6
Laurelhill Gdns FK8 ....6 F6
Laurelhill Pl FK8 ....7 A5
Laurel Pl FK4 ....57 F3
Laurel Rd KY11 ....46 C2
Laurels The FK10 ....4 B1
Laurel Terr EH11 ....120 E5
Laurencecroft Rd FK8 ......2 B2
Laurie St EH6 ....94 A4
Laurieston Ind Est FK2 ....60 F3
Laurieston Prim Sch FK2. .61 A3
Laurieston Rd FK3 ....61 A6
Lauriston Castle EH4 ......91 E5
Lauriston Dr KY12 ....29 D5
Lauriston Farm Rd EH4 ...91 F4
Lauriston Gdns EH3 ..... 228 C1
Lauriston Pk EH3 .... 228 C1
Lauriston Pl EH3 .... 228 C2
Lauriston St EH3 .... 228 C2
Lauriston Terr EH3 ..... 228 C2
Laurmont Ct FK2 ....61 A3
Laverockbank Ave EH5 ....93 C6
Laverockbank Cres EH5 ...93 C6
Laverockbank Gdns EH5 ..93 C6
Laverockbank Gr EH5 .....93 C6
Laverockbank Rd EH5 .....93 C6
Laverockbank Terr EH5 ....93 C6
Laverockdale Cres EH13 .149 B6
Laverockdale Loan EH13 .149 B5
Laverockdale Pk EH13 ...149 B5
Laverock Dr EH26 .... 191 D6
Laverock Pk EH49 ....85 A5
Lawers Cres FK2 ....62 A1
Lawers Pl FK3 ....61 E5
Lawers Sq EH26 .... 192 A7
Lawfield Rd EH22 .... 174 D7
Lawhead Cotts EH40 ......75 F3
Lawhead Pl EH26 .... 191 C6
Lawhouse Toll EH15 ......123 B4
Lawnmarket EH1 .... 229 A3
Law Pl Denny FK6 ....36 E1
Edinburgh EH15 ....95 A1
Law Prim Sch EH39 ....54 C6
Law Rd Dunfermline KY11 ...29 F4
North Berwick EH39 ....54 C7
Lawrence Ct FK5 ....38 B5
Lawrie Dr EH26 ....191 E7
Lawrie Terr EH20 ....172 B7
Lawson Cres EH30 ....89 C8
Lawson Ct EH42 ....78 D2
Lawson Gdns KY1 ....17 E8
Lawson Glade EH54 ..... 164 C7
Lawson Pl Dunbar EH42 ....78 D2
Maddiston FK2 ....83 A5
Lawson St KY1 ....17 E8
Lawswell FK10 ....5 E3
Laxdale Dr FK6 ....57 D7
Laxford Cres KY11 ....48 A3
Leadburn Ave KY12 ....29 A7
Leadervale Rd EH16 ......150 F8
Leadervale Terr EH16 ....150 F8
Leadside Cres KY12 ....29 A7
Leamington Pl EH10 .....228 B1
Leamington Rd EH3 ..... 228 A1
Leamington Terr EH10. ..121 B5
Leapark Dr FK4 ....57 F3
Lea Rig ML11 ....217 F7
Learmonth Ave EH4 ....92 F2
Learmonth Cres
Edinburgh EH4 ....92 F2
West Calder EH55 .... 163 D3
Learmonth Ct EH4 ....92 F1
Learmonth Gardens La 1
EH4 ....92 F1
Learmonth Gdns EH4 .....92 F1
Learmonth Gr EH4 ....92 F2
Learmonth Pk 2 EH4 ......92 F2
Learmonth Pl EH4 ...... 228 A4
Learmonth St FK1 ....60 B4
Learmonth Terr EH4 .... 228 A4
Learmonth Terrace La
EH4 .... 228 A4
Learmouth Garden Mews 5
EH4 ....93 A2
Leaston Farm Cotts
EH36 .... 220 A2
Lec Ct FK2 ....60 F4
Lecropt Sch (Barnardo's)
FK1 ....59 C6
Ledi Ave FK10 ....4 B2
Ledi Pl FK1 ....81 E7
Ledi Terr EH26 .... 192 A7
Ledi View FK9 ....2 B3
Ledmore Pl FK1 ....60 E1
Lee Cres EH15 ....123 B8
Legion Ct KY2 ....17 A5
Leighton Cres EH22 ..... 174 D7
Leighton St KY12 ....26 B2
Leishman Ct EH48 ...... 138 D2

Leishman Twr FK1 . . . . .60 C4
Leith Acad EH6 . . . . .94 A3
Leith Ave KY3 . . . . .33 F2
Leithhead EH27 . . . . .166 E4
Leith Pl FK6 . . . . .57 D7
Leith Prim Sch EH6 . . . . . . .94 A4
Leith St EH1 . . . . .229 A4
Leith Walk Prim Sch EH7 .93 E2
Leith Wlk EH7 . . . . .93 F3
Lempockwells EH7 . . . . .38 D1
Lempockwells Rd EH34 .156 E6
Lendrick Ave FK1 . . . . .59 F2
Lennel Ave EH12 . . . . .120 C8
Lennie Cotts EH12 . . . . . . .118 D8
Lennox Ave FK7 . . . . .7 A4
Lennox Gdns EH49 . . . . .84 D7
Lennoxlove Acredales Cotts
 EH41 . . . . .130 B7
Lennoxlove House EH41 .130 B5
Lennox Milne Ct EH33 . . .130 B8
Lennox Rd EH41 . . . . .130 C8
Lennox Row EH5 . . . . .93 B6
Lennox St EH4 . . . . .228 A4
Lennox Street La EH4 . . .228 A4
Lennox Terr FK3 . . . . .61 F5
Lennymuir EH12 . . . . .90 B1
Leny Pl KY12 . . . . .29 B5
Lenzie Ave EH54 . . . . .143 A6
Leopold Pl ⬛ EH7 . . . . . . .93 F1
Leslie Pl EH3 . . . . .93 B2
Leslie Rd KY11 . . . . .46 F5
Leslie St KY1 . . . . .35 B8
Leslie Way EH42 . . . . .78 D1
Lesslie's Bldgs KY3 . . . . . . .33 E1
Lestrange Ave FK12 . . . . . . .5 B7
Letham Ave EH54 . . . . .144 B7
Letham Cotts FK2 . . . . .39 D8
Letham Cres EH53 . . . . . . .144 B7
Letham Dr EH41 . . . . .129 F8
Letham Gait KY11 . . . . .47 F3
Letham Gdns Dunbar EH42 .78 D2
Letham Gr EH53 . . . . .144 B7
Letham Hill Ave KY11 . . . .47 E4
Letham Holdings EH53 . . .144 C6
Letham Mains Smallholdings
 EH41 . . . . .129 C7
Letham Pk Dunbar EH42 . .78 D2
 Pumpherston EH53 . . . . . .144 B7
Letham Pl Dunbar EH42 . . .78 C3
 Pumpherston EH53 . . . . . .144 B7
Letham Prim Sch EH54 . .144 B5
Letham Rd Dunbar EH42 . . .78 C2
 Pumpherston EH53 . . . . . .144 B7
 Pumpherston EH54 . . . . . .144 A8
Letham Rise KY11 . . . . .47 F3
Letham Terr FK2 . . . . .22 C1
Letham Terrs FK2 . . . . .22 C1
Letham Way KY11 . . . . .47 F3
Leuchatsbeath Dr KY4 . . .13 B6
Leven Ct EH33 . . . . .228 B1
Leven Ct FK10 . . . . .10 C5
Leven Pl ML7 . . . . .179 E6
Levenseat Ind Est EH47 .181 F4
Leven St Edinburgh EH3 . .228 B1
 Falkirk FK2 . . . . .60 B8
Leven Terr EH3 . . . . .228 C1
Leven Wlk EH54 . . . . .144 A4
Leving Pl EH54 . . . . .143 C3
Lewis Ct Alloa FK10 . . . . . . .10 B5
 Falkirk FK1 . . . . .60 B2
Lewis Rd FK1 . . . . .61 F1
Lewis Terr EH11 . . . . .228 A2
Lewisvale Ave EH21 . . . . .124 E5
Lewisvale Ct EH21 . . . . . . .124 E5
Leyden Pk EH19 . . . . .173 B8
Leyden Pl EH19 . . . . .173 B7
Leyden Rd EH27 . . . . .166 C6
Leyland Rd EH48 . . . . .141 C3
Leys Park Rd KY12 . . . . . . .29 B4
Lighton Terr EH47 . . . . . . .162 B1
Lilac Ave EH22 . . . . .174 F6
Lilac Cres KY1 . . . . .17 C8
Lilac Gr KY1 . . . . .46 D8
Lillies La EH41 . . . . .220 F7
Lilly's La KY11 . . . . .29 B3
Lilybank Ct FK10 . . . . .5 D1
Lilyhill Terr EH8 . . . . .94 C1
Lily Terr EH11 . . . . .120 E4
Lime Ave EH30 . . . . .66 F2
Limebank Pk EH53 . . . . . . .144 F2
Limefield Pl EH47 . . . . .151 E5
Limefield Ave EH55 . . . . . .164 A5
Limefield Gdns EH55 . . . .164 A5
Limefield House Bsns Ctr
 EH55 . . . . .164 A5
Limefield La EH48 . . . . .141 D6
Limefield Pl EH48 . . . . .141 D6

Limefield Rd
 Bathgate EH48 . . . . .141 D7
 Polbeth EH55 . . . . .164 A5
 West Calder EH55 . . . . .163 E3
Lime Gr Dunfermline KY11 . .29 E1
 Livingston EH54 . . . . .144 B6
 Mayfield EH22 . . . . .174 D8
 North Berwick EH39 . . . . . . .54 F6
 Polmont FK2 . . . . .61 E2
 Stenhousemuir FK5 . . . . . . .38 D1
Limekilns EH34 . . . . .157 A6
Limekilns Gr EH53 . . . . . . .145 A3
Limekilns Prim Sch KY11 . .45 E3
Limekilns Rd KY12 . . . . .28 F1
Lime Pl EH19 . . . . .173 B6
Lime Rd FK1 . . . . .59 B4
Limerigg Prim Sch EH48 . .108 C1
Lime St EH3 . . . . .61 C6
Lime The EH16 . . . . .121 A4
Limetree Wlk EH42 . . . . . . .76 D5
Limeylands Cres EH35 . . .155 E6
Limeylands Ct EH35 . . . . . .155 D7
Limeylands Rd EH35 . . . . .155 D7
Limpet Ness KY11 . . . . .46 D3
Linay Gr KY3 . . . . .17 B5
Linburn Gr KY11 . . . . .29 F4
Linburn Pk EH27 . . . . .146 A5
Linburn Pl KY11 . . . . .29 F3
Linburn Rd
 Dunfermline KY11 . . . . .29 F3
 Wilkieston EH27 . . . . .146 B5
Lindean Pl EH6 . . . . .94 B4
Lindean Terr EH27 . . . . . . .145 F6
Linden Ave Denny FK6 . . . .36 C3
 Stirling FK7 . . . . .7 C6
Linden Pl EH54 . . . . .144 B7
Linden Pl EH20 . . . . .172 D8
Lindores Dr Kirkcaldy KY2 . .16 E8
 Tranent EH33 . . . . .126 D6
Lindsay's Wynd KY12 . . . . .26 F6
Lindsay Gdns EH48 . . . . . .141 C5
Lindsay Pl Edinburgh EH6 . .93 E5
 Lochgelly KY5 . . . . .14 A8
Lindsay Sq EH54 . . . . .142 D5
Lindsay St EH6 . . . . .93 E6
Lindsay Way EH54 . . . . . . .143 D8
Lingerwood Farm Cotts
 EH22 . . . . .174 A4
Lingerwood Rd EH22 . . . .174 B4
Lingerwood Wlk EH22 . . .174 B4
Linhouse Dr EH53 . . . . . . .144 E3
Linhouse Rd EH53 . . . . . . .144 E3
Linkfield Ct EH21 . . . . .124 E6
Linkfield Rd EH21 . . . . .124 E6
Link Rd Crombie KY12 . . . . .44 D6
 Dalgety Bay KY11 . . . . .47 F3
 Oakley KY12 . . . . .26 F7
Links Ave EH21 . . . . .124 E7
Links Ct Bo'ness EH51 . . . . .64 A8
 Cockenzie & Port Seton
 EH32 .97 D4
Links Dr KY12 . . . . .28 A2
Links Gardens La EH6 . . . . .94 B5
Links Gdns EH6 . . . . .94 B4
Links Pl Bo'ness EH51 . . . . .64 B7
 Burntisland KY3 . . . . .50 E8
 Cockenzie & Port Seton
 EH32 .97 E4
 Edinburgh EH6 . . . . .94 A5
 Longniddry EH32 . . . . .98 E5
 North Berwick EH39 . . . . . . .54 B7
Links St Kirkcaldy KY1 . . . . .17 B2
 Musselburgh EH21 . . . . . . .124 C6
Links View
 Cockenzie & Port Seton
 EH32 .97 E4
 Musselburgh EH21 . . . . . . .124 C7
Links Wlk EH32 . . . . .97 E4
Linlithgow Acad EH49 . . . . .84 E7
Linlithgow Bridge Prim Sch
 EH49 .84 D7
Linlithgow Canal Ctr
 EH49 .85 A6
Linlithgow Palace EH49 . . .85 A7
Linlithgow Pl FK5 . . . . .38 E4
Linlithgow Rd EH49 . . . . . . .63 F6
Linlithgow Rd EH51 . . . . . . .63 F6
Linlithgow Story Mus The
 EH49 .85 A7
Linlithgow Terr EH35 . . . . .155 E7
Linmill Rd FK1 . . . . .110 A5
Linn Dean Wildlife Reserve
 EH36 . . . . .224 E6
Linnet Brae EH54 . . . . .143 C5
Linnet Way KY11 . . . . .30 A2
Linn Mill
 Clackmannan FK10 . . . . .11 D6
 Queensferry EH30 . . . . .67 E2
Linn Pl Airth FK2 . . . . .22 E3
 Broxburn EH52 . . . . .115 E4
Linsay Macdonald Ct
 KY12 .29 D3
Linties Nest KY3 . . . . .34 F2
Linton Gr KY3 . . . . .35 A4
Linton La KY2 . . . . .16 E6
Linton Pl KY11 . . . . .46 E3
Lint Riggs FK1 . . . . .60 B5
Lintview FK1 . . . . .108 B5
Linty La EH26 . . . . .191 D6
Linview La EH54 . . . . .164 F4
Linwater Cvn Pk EH53 . . .145 C8
Linwell Ct KY3 . . . . .34 B1

Lionthorn Rd FK1 . . . . .59 F1
Lion Well Wynd EH49 . . . . .84 F7
Lipney FK11 . . . . .4 A6
Lismore Ave
 ⑤ Edinburgh EH8 . . . . .94 C1
 Kirkcaldy KY2 . . . . .16 F8
Lismore Cres EH8 . . . . .94 C1
Lismore Ct FK1 . . . . .60 B2
Lismore Pl KY2 . . . . .16 F7
Lismore Prim Sch EH15 . .122 F5
Lister Ct FK9 . . . . .2 A6
Lister Rd EH54 . . . . .143 B1
Listloaning Pl EH49 . . . . . . .84 D7
Listloaning Rd EH49 . . . . . .84 D7
Liston Dr EH29 . . . . .89 A2
Liston Pl EH29 . . . . .89 A1
Liston Rd EH29 . . . . .89 A1
Lithgow Pl FK1 . . . . .59 B4
Little Acre EH22 . . . . .174 D8
Little Carriden EH51 . . . . . .64 D5
Little Denny Rd FK6 . . . . . . .36 D1
Little Foothorn KY12 . . . . . .44 E6
Little France Cres EH16 . .122 E1
Little France Dr EH16 . . . .122 E1
Little France Ho EH17 . . . .151 D8
Little France Mills EH16 . .122 D1
Littlejohn Ave EH10 . . . . . .149 E8
Littlejohn Rd EH10 . . . . . . .149 E8
Littlejohn Wynd EH10 . . . .149 F8
Little King St EH1 . . . . .229 A4
Little Pinkerton Cotts
 EH42 . . . . .107 A5
Little Rd EH16 . . . . .151 B7
Little Sandhaven KY12 . . . .42 D8
Little Spott Cotts EH42 . . .105 F2
Livesay Rd KY11 . . . . .46 D1
Livesey Terr EH26 . . . . .192 A8
Livilands Ct FK8 . . . . .7 B5
Livilands Gate FK8 . . . . .7 B5
Livilands La FK8 . . . . .7 B5
Livingston Cres FK2 . . . . . .60 E5
Livingstone Dr
 Bo'ness EH51 . . . . .63 D6
 Murieston KY3 . . . . .33 F2
 Laurieston FK2 . . . . .60 F2
Livingstone E Rdbt EH54 .114 D1
Livingstone Pl EH9 . . . . . . .121 D5
Livingstone Quadrant
 ML7 .159 D4
Livingston St EH55 . . . . . . .162 E2
Livingstone Terr 61 B1
Livingstone Way FK10 . . . .11 A5
Livingston La KY3 . . . . .49 C7
Livingston North Sta
 EH54 . . . . .143 B6
Livingston Rd
 Dechmont EH52,EH54 . . . .114 D1
 Livingston EH54 . . . . .143 B1
Livingston South Sta
 EH54 . . . . .165 A7
Livingston Village Prim Sch
 EH54 . . . . .143 B3
Lixmount Ave EH5 . . . . .93 C6
Lixmount Gdns EH5 . . . . . . .93 C6
Lizzie Brice's Rdbt EH54 .144 B1
Llynallan Rd ML7 . . . . .158 F4
Loanburn EH26 . . . . .191 F5
Loanburn Ave EH26 . . . . . .191 F6
Loanfoot Cres EH52 . . . . . .115 A5
Loanfoot Gdns FK7 . . . . .20 C4
Loanfoot Rd EH52 . . . . . . .115 A4
Loanhead Ave Denny FK4 . .57 D6
 Grangemouth FK3 . . . . .61 E6
Loanhead Cotts EH29 . . . . .89 B2
Loanhead Hospl EH20 . . . .172 D8
Loanhead Pl KY2 . . . . .17 A5
Loanhead Prim Sch
 EH20 . . . . .172 C8
Loanhead Prim Sch (Annexe)
 EH20 . . . . .172 C8
Loanhead Rd EH20 . . . . . .151 A2
Loaning Cres EH7 . . . . .94 D2
Loaninghill Pk EH52 . . . . . .115 B4
Loaninghill Rd EH52 . . . . . .115 B4
Loaning Rd EH7 . . . . .94 D2
Loan Pl ML7 . . . . .159 E6
Loan The Bo'ness EH51 . . . .63 D6
 Loanhead EH20 . . . . .172 B7
 Pathhead EH37 . . . . .175 C7
 South Queensferry EH30 . . .68 B1
 Torphichen EH48 . . . . .111 F6
 Wallyford EH21 . . . . .125 B6
Lochaber KY11 . . . . .45 B4
Lochaber Cres ML7 . . . . . .180 B3
Lochaber Dr FK5 . . . . .38 E3
Lochaber Way EH47 . . . . . .161 B7
Lochbank EH54 . . . . .143 E5
Lochbrae FK10 . . . . .5 D2
Lochbridge Rd EH39 . . . . . .54 D6
Loch Earn Way EH47 . . . . .161 C7
Lochend Ave EH42 . . . . .78 E1
Lochend Castle Barns
 EH7 . . . . .94 B2
Lochend Cl EH8 . . . . .229 B3
Lochend Cres
 Dunbar EH42 . . . . .78 D1
 Edinburgh EH7 . . . . .94 C2
Lochend Dr EH7 . . . . .94 B2
Lochend Gdns
 Dunbar EH42 . . . . .78 D1
 Edinburgh EH7 . . . . .94 C2
Lochend Gr EH7 . . . . .94 C2
Lochend Ho EH7 . . . . .94 C2
Lochend Ind Est EH28 . . . .117 B5
Lochend Pk EH7 . . . . .94 B3
Lochend Quadrant EH7 . . .94 C2

Lochend Rd Dunbar EH42 . .78 E1
 Edinburgh EH7 . . . . .94 A3
 Ratho Station EH28,EH29 . .117 A7
Lochend Rd N EH21 . . . . . .124 B6
Lochend Rd S
 Edinburgh EH7 . . . . .94 B2
 Musselburgh EH21 . . . . . . .124 B6
Lochend Sq EH7 . . . . .94 B2
Loch Fyne Way EH47 . . . . .161 C7
Lochgelly Ind Pk KY5 . . . . .14 C7
Lochgelly North Prim Sch
 KY5 . . . . .14 A8
Lochgelly Rd KY4 . . . . .13 D5
Lochgelly South Prim Sch
 KY5 . . . . .14 B7
Lochgelly West Prim Sch
 KY5 . . . . .14 A7
Lochgreen Rd FK1 . . . . .59 E2
Lochgreen Rdbt FK1 . . . . . .59 F2
Lochhead Ave FK6 . . . . .36 E1
Lochhead Ct KY12 . . . . .29 A6
Lochhill Cotts EH32 . . . . . . .99 E7
Lochhouses EH42 . . . . .76 C8
Lochies Rd Burntisland KY3 .34 A1
 Clackmannan FK10 . . . . .11 A4
Lochies Sch FK10 . . . . .5 F1
Lochinvar Pl FK4 . . . . .58 C3
Lochmaben Dr FK2 . . . . .60 E5
Lochlands Ave FK5 . . . . .38 B1
Lochlands Bsns Pk FK5 . . . .59 A8
Lochlands Ind Est FK5 . . . .59 A8
Lochlands Loan FK5 . . . . . . .59 B7
Lochlea FK6 . . . . .17 A7
Lochlea Terr KY2 . . . . .17 A7
Loch Linnhe Ct EH47 . . . . .161 C7
Lochmaben Dr FK5 . . . . .38 F4
Loch Maree Way EH47 . . .161 B7
Lochpark Pl EH47 . . . . .36 E2
Loch Pl EH30 . . . . .68 B2
Loch Rd Edinburgh EH4 . . .92 A2
 South Queensferry EH30 . . .68 B1
 Tranent EH33 . . . . .126 D6
Lochridge Pl FK6 . . . . .36 D1
Lochrin Bldgs EH3 . . . . . . .228 B1
Lochrin Pl EH3 . . . . .228 B1
Lochrin Terr EH3 . . . . .228 B1
Lochshot Pl EH54 . . . . .143 A3
Lochside Ave EH12 . . . . . . .118 F4
Lochside Cotts FK1 . . . . .61 B2
Lochside Cres
 Edinburgh EH12 . . . . .118 F4
 Redding FK2 . . . . .61 B2
Lochside Ct EH12 . . . . .119 A4
Lochside Pl EH12 . . . . .119 A4
Lochside Rd FK1 . . . . .108 C1
Lochside View EH12 . . . . . .118 F5
Lochside Way EH12 . . . . . .119 A4
Loch Sq EH33 . . . . .126 D6
Loch St KY12 . . . . .29 C7
Loch Trool Way EH47 . . . . .161 B7
Lochwood Pk KY12 . . . . .12 B1
Lockerby Cotts EH16 . . . . .151 C6
Lockerby Cres EH16 . . . . . .151 C6
Lockerby Gr EH16 . . . . .151 C6
Lockharton Ave EH11 . . . .120 E2
Lockharton Cres EH11 . . . .120 E2
Lockharton Gdns EH14 . . .120 E3
Lockhart Terr EH25 . . . . . .171 F3
Lock Rd KY11 . . . . .67 B8
Lock Sixteen FK1 . . . . .59 D5
Lodge St EH22 . . . . .153 A8
Lodge St EH41 . . . . .130 A8
Loganlea Ave EH7 . . . . .94 D1
Loganlea Cres EH55 . . . . . .162 C1
Loganlea Dr EH7 . . . . .94 C2
Loganlea Gdns EH7 . . . . . . .94 C2
Loganlea Loan EH7 . . . . . . .94 C2
Loganlea Pl
 Addiewell EH55 . . . . .162 C1
 Edinburgh EH7 . . . . .94 D1
Loganlea Rd
 Addiewell EH55 . . . . .162 C1
 Edinburgh EH7 . . . . .94 D2
Loganlea Terr
 Addiewell EH55 . . . . .162 C1
 Edinburgh EH7 . . . . .94 D1
Logan Rd KY11 . . . . .46 D1
Logan St EH3 . . . . .93 C2
Logan Way EH54 . . . . .143 D8
Logie Dr FK5 . . . . .38 A3
Logie Green Loan EH7 . . . .93 C3
Logie Green Rd EH7 . . . . . . .93 C3
Logie La Bridge of A FK9 . . . .2 C7
Logie Mill EH7 . . . . .93 C3
Logie Pl KY12 . . . . .28 D5
Logie Rd FK9 . . . . .2 D4
Lomond Cres
 Dunfermline KY12 . . . . .29 F2
 Stenhousemuir FK5 . . . . . . .38 F3
 Stirling FK9 . . . . .2 D4
 Whitburn EH47 . . . . .161 A6
Lomond Ct FK10 . . . . .10 C5
Lomond Dr Bannockburn FK7 . .7 C2
 Falkirk FK2 . . . . .39 C1
Lomond Gdns KY12 . . . . . . .29 F2
Lomond Rd Edinburgh EH5 . .93 B6
 Grangemouth FK3 . . . . .61 E5
 Shotts ML7 . . . . .179 E6
Lomond St FK10 . . . . .10 C7
Lomond Vale EH26 . . . . . . .192 A7
Lomond View EH48 . . . . . .110 F4
Lomond View FK6 . . . . .57 D6
Lomond Way EH20 . . . . . . .151 C6
London Rd Dalkeith EH22 . .153 A8
 Edinburgh EH7,FH8 . . . . . . .94 B1
London St EH3 . . . . .93 D2

Loney Cres FK6 . . . . .57 E8
Longannet Cotts FK10 . . . .24 B1
Longannet Rdbt FK10 . . . .24 A2
Longbraes Gdns KY2 . . . . .16 D6
Long Byres FK2 . . . . .115 C5
Long Craig Rigg EH5 . . . . . .92 C7
Long Craigs Terr KY3 . . . . . .35 A3
Long Craig Wlk KY1 . . . . . . .35 B8
Long Cram EH41 . . . . .129 F7
Longcroft Gdns EH49 . . . . .84 E7
Longcroft Holdings FK4 . . .57 B3
Long Crook EH30 . . . . .89 A8
Longdales ML11 . . . . .217 F7
Longdales Ave FK2 . . . . .60 A8
Longdales Ct FK2 . . . . .60 A8
Longdales Pl FK2 . . . . .60 A8
Longdales Rd FK2 . . . . .60 A8
Long Dalmahoy Rd
 Currie EH14 . . . . .147 C5
 Ratho EH27 . . . . .146 C3
Longdykes Pl FK2 . . . . .39 C4
Longdykes Rd EH32 . . . . . . .97 B2
Longford ML11 . . . . .201 A1
Longformacus Rd EH16 . . .151 B7
Longhill Gdns KY11 . . . . . . .48 B3
Longnewton Cotts EH41 . .220 D3
Longniddry Farm Cotts
 EH32 .98 E5
Longniddry Prim Sch
 EH32 .98 F5
Longniddry Sta EH32 . . . . .98 F5
Longpark Pl EH54 . . . . .143 A4
Longridge Prim Sch
 EH47 . . . . .161 C2
Longridge Rd EH47 . . . . . . .161 A5
Longstone Ave
 East Linton EH40 . . . . .103 D7
 Edinburgh EH14 . . . . .120 A2
Longstone Cotts EH14 . . . .120 A2
Longstone Gdns EH11 . . . .119 F3
Longstone Gr EH14 . . . . . .120 A2
Longstone Pk EH14 . . . . . .120 A2
Longstone Prim Sch
 EH14 . . . . .120 A1
Longstone Rd EH14 . . . . . .120 A2
Longstone St EH14 . . . . . . .120 A2
Longstone Terr EH11 . . . . .119 F3
Longstone View EH14 . . . .119 F3
Longyester Farm Cotts
 EH41 . . . . .221 A4
Lonsdale Cres KY3 . . . . .33 F1
Lonsdale Terr EH3 . . . . . . .228 C1
Lookaboutye Brae FK10 . . .11 A3
Loom Rd KY2 . . . . .17 B6
Lord President Rd EH39 . . .54 A7
Loretto Ct EH21 . . . . .124 B4
Loretto Jun Sch EH21 . . . .124 C6
Loretto RC Prim Sch
 EH21 . . . . .124 D6
Loretto Schs EH21 . . . . . . .124 D6
Lorimar Pl FK2 . . . . .39 B2
Lorimer Gdns KY12 . . . . . . .29 D6
Lorimer View EH14 . . . . . .148 E6
Lorne Gr FK7 . . . . .60 F3
Lorne Gdns EH20 . . . . .151 A1
Lorne Ho KY12 . . . . .29 A4
Lorne La EH39 . . . . .54 C7
Lorne Pl EH6 . . . . .93 F3
Lorne Prim Sch EH6 . . . . . . .93 F3
Lorne Sq EH6 . . . . .93 F3
Lorne St Edinburgh EH6 . . . .93 F3
 North Berwick EH39 . . . . . . .54 C7
Lorne St Edinburgh EH6 . . . .93 F3
 Kirkcaldy KY1 . . . . .17 E7
Lorn Pl KY11 . . . . .30 C1
Lornshill Acad FK10 . . . . .4 E2
Lornshill Cres FK10 . . . . .9 F8
Losshill FK11 . . . . .4 A6
Lothian Bank EH22 . . . . . .152 F1
Lothianburn Junc EH10 . .150 B4
Lothian Coll of Nursing &
 Midwifery EH3 . . . . .228 C2
Lothian Cres Bo'ness EH51 .64 A6
 Stirling FK9 . . . . .2 C3
Lothian Ct KY11 . . . . .47 D2
Lothian Dr EH22 . . . . .174 C8
Lothian Rd Dalkeith EH22 .153 A2
 Edinburgh EH1 . . . . .228 B2
Lothian St Bathgate EH48 .141 A7
 Bo'ness EH51 . . . . .64 A6
 Bonnyrigg and Lasswade
 EH19 . . . . .173 C3
 Burntisland KY3 . . . . .50 E8
 Dalkeith EH22 . . . . .153 A3
 Edinburgh EH1 . . . . .229 A2
 Rosewell EH24 . . . . .172 D2
Lothians View KY11 . . . . . . .47 A2
Lothian Terr Kirkcaldy KY2 .17 A7
 Newtongrange EH22 . . . . . .174 B4
Louburn EH48 . . . . .138 D3
Loudens Wlk FK6 . . . . .36 D5
Loughborough Rd KY1 . . . .17 F7
Loughrigg KY11 . . . . .47 A7
Louisa Sq EH24 . . . . .172 D2
Louise St KY12 . . . . .29 C3
Louvain Gdns EH48 . . . . . .139 F4
Lovedale Ave EH14 . . . . . . .147 B1
Lovedale Cres EH14 . . . . . .147 B1
Lovedale Gdns EH14 . . . . .147 C1

Lovedale Gr EH14........147 B1
Lovedale Rd EH14........147 C1
Lovells Glen EH49.........84 C8
Lovers La EH30..........89 C8
Lovers Wlk FK8............2 B1
Low Brae EH48.........111 F5
Low Causewayside
  Culross KY12............42 D8
  Newmills KY12..........26 C1
Low Cswy Culross KY12....25 E1
  Torryburn KY12.........26 E1
Low Doors The EH27.....145 E2
Lower Alderston Rd
  EH41.................100 E1
Lower Bathville EH48....140 A5
Lower Bridge St FK8........2 A1
Lower Broomieknowe
  EH18.................173 A8
Lower Castlehill FK8.......2 A1
Lower Gilmore Pl EH3....228 B1
Lower Glebe KY3.........49 C8
Lower Granton Rd EH5....93 A7
Lower Joppa EH15.......123 C8
Lower London Rd EH7....94 A1
Lower Ridge Ct EH47....161 B2
Lower Valleyfield View
  EH26.................191 F4
Lowrie Ave EH26........191 C5
Lowry Pl KY1............46 F4
Lt. Sales Ave KY11.......47 F3
Ludgate FK10............10 A6
Luffness Ct EH32.........71 D4
Luffness Gdns EH32......71 D4
Luffness Mains Cotts
  EH32..................72 B4
Lufra Bank EH5..........93 A6
Lugton Brae EH22.......152 F4
Lugton Specl Sch EH22..152 F4
Lulach Ct KY11...........47 A8
Lumley Ct FK3...........61 D8
Lumley Pl FK3...........61 D8
Lumley St FK3...........61 D8
Lumphinnans Prim & Com
  Sch KY4..............13 C5
Lumphinnans Rd KY5....14 A7
Lumsdaine Dr KY11......48 A1
Lumsden Ct
  Broxburn EH52.........115 C5
  Ratho EH28............117 D2
Lundin Rd KY12..........28 A4
Lussielaw Rd EH9........121 F3
Lutton Court Bsns Ctr
  EH8..................229 B1
Lutton Pl EH8...........229 B1
Lyall Cres FK2...........61 E2
Lyars Rd EH32...........98 E6
Lyarthall EH52..........115 C5
Lychgate La KY11........115 D5
Lychgate Rd FK10.........4 B2
Lydgait EH41............101 A1
Lydgait Gdns EH41.......101 A1
Lyefield FK7............143 B4
Lygon Rd EH16..........121 F2
Lyle Gn EH54............143 B8
Lynburn Prim Sch KY11...29 F2
Lyndene Sq EH20........150 F1
Lynebank (Psychiatric) Hospl
  KY11..................30 A5
Lyneburn Cres KY11......30 B5
Lynedoch Pl EH3........228 A3
Lynedoch Place La EH3..228 A3
Lyne Gr KY12............28 C2
Lyne Gr KY12............28 C2
Lyne St EH7.............94 A1
Lyne Terr EH26.........192 A7
Lynn Lea Ave EH41......130 C8
Lyon Cres KY9............2 A6
Lyon Ct EH51............63 D6
Lyon Dr EH54............164 E6

M

MacAdam Pl FK1..........59 D6
McAdam Sq EH54........164 D6
McAffee Gdns EH48......139 F3
McAllister Ct FK7..........7 D1
MacAlpine Ct FK10........4 D3
MacArthur Cres FK2.......82 E6
McArthur Designer Outlet
  Ctr EH54.............143 D2
McAulay Brae FK7........20 C3
Macbeth Moir Rd EH21..125 A6
Macbeth Rd KY11.........29 E3
McCall Gdns EH40.......103 D7
McCallum Ct EH48.......135 F7
McCambridge Pl FK5.....38 C5
McCann Ave EH51........85 B5
McCathie Dr EH22.......174 B6
McClelland Cres KY11....29 B1
Mac Cormick Terr EH26.191 F4
MacDiarmid Gr EH22....174 B4
MacDonald Ave EH48....139 F6
MacDonald Dr FK7.........7 A4
MacDonald Pl FK7........93 E3
MacDonald Pl KY11.......30 B5
MacDonald Sq KY11......30 B5
McDonald St EH7.........94 A1
McDouall Stuart Pl KY11..18 A7
MacDowall Rd EH9......121 F3

Macduff Cres KY3.........34 F2
Mace Ct FK7..............7 D3
Macfarlane Cres FK1......60 B5
Macfarlane Ct EH33......126 B1
Macfarlane Pl EH11.....114 F3
McGahey Ct EH22.......174 B4
McGhee Pl FK1............59 F2
McGinley Way EH49......84 D5
McGregor Ave KY5.......14 A8
McGrigor Rd Rosyth KY11..46 D2
  Stirling FK7............7 A4
Machrie Ct FK1..........59 C4
Macindoe Cres KY1.......17 D7
McIntosh Ct KY3.........22 D8
Macintosh Pl FK1.........60 A1
Macintosh Rd
  Livingston EH54.......142 F1
  Livingston EH54.......163 F8
McKane Pl KY12.........142 C6
McKane Pl KY12..........28 F1
McKay Dr KY11...........29 F1
McKell Ct KY1............60 A3
McKinlay Cres FK10.......10 C7
McKinlay Terr EH20......172 A7
McKinnon Dr EH22......174 E5
McKinnon Rd EH47......181 F7
McLachlan Ave FK7........7 B2
MacLachlan Ave FK6......36 C1
McLachlan St FK5........38 C2
McLaren Ct FK5.........114 F3
McLaren Ave EH49.......84 A6
McLaren Ct FK5..........38 D2
McLaren Rd EH9.........122 A4
McLaren Terr
  Edinburgh EH11.......228 A2
  Stirling FK7.............7 B3
MacLaren Terr FK2.......39 A2
MacLauchlan Rise KY3....49 F5
McLauchlan Way ML7...159 F6
Maclean Cres FK12........5 C7
Maclean Ct FK7...........7 A4
Maclean Gate KY11.......46 F7
Maclean Gdns KY11......46 E7
McLean Pl
  Bonnyrigg and Lasswade
    EH18................172 A6
  Gorebridge EH23......174 D1
Maclean Pl KY11.........46 E7
McLean Prim Sch KY12...28 E5
McLean Terr EH48.......138 C3
Maclean Way KY11.......46 F7
Maclean Wlk KY11.......46 E7
McLeod Cres EH32........96 F1
McLeod St Broxburn EH52.115 E6
  Edinburgh EH11.......116 E8
McMartin Ct EH47......161 D7
Macmerry Bsns Pk EH33.127 D6
Macmerry Ind Est EH33..127 E6
Macmerry Prim Sch
  EH33................127 D6
Macmillan Rd EH54.....143 C1
McNab Gdns EH54........59 F2
Macnair Ave EH9.........54 C6
McNeil Cres EH48.......140 A6
McNeill Ave EH20.......172 B8
McNeill Path ■ EH33...126 C6
McNeill St EH11.........228 A1
McNeill Terr EH20.......172 A8
McNeill Way ■ EH33....126 C5
McNeill Wlk ■ EH33....126 C5
McPhail Sq EH33........126 D6
Macpherson Dr FK8........2 A2
Macpherson Pl ■ FK1.....59 F2
McQuade St EH19........173 D8
McRae Cres KY3.........33 F2
McRobert Gr FK9.........5 C7
McTaggart Ave FK6......36 E2
MacTaggart Loan EH27..174 B4
McVean Pl FK4...........57 B4
Madderfield Mews EH49..85 B7
Maddiston Prim Sch FK2..82 F6
Maddiston Rd FK2........82 E8
Madeira Pl EH6...........93 E5
Madeira St EH6..........93 E6
Madill Pl FK5............38 F3
Maesterton Pl EH22.....174 B4
Mag's Bank EH41........131 B1
Magdala Cres EH12.....120 F7
Magdala Mews EH12....120 F7
Magdalene Ave EH15....123 B6
Magdalene Ct EH15.....123 B6
Magdalene Dr EH15.....123 B6
Magdalene Gdns EH15...123 B6
Magdalene Loan EH15...123 B6
Magdalene Medway
  EH15................123 B6
Magdalene Pl EH15......123 B6
Maggie Wood's Loan
  Falkirk FK1............59 F4
  Falkirk FK1............59 F5
Magnus Rd EH51.........64 B6
Maidencraig Cres EH4....92 C2
Maidencraig Gr EH4......92 C2
Maidenpark Pl EH51......63 E6
Maidlands EH49...........85 C7
Maid of the Forth EH30...68 D1
Main Point EH3.........228 C2
Main Rd Charlestown KY11..45 B4
  Crombie KY12...........44 E7
  Grangemouth FK3.......62 B8

Main Rd continued
  Macmerry EH33........127 C5
  North Queensferry KY11..68 B6
Main St E FK11............4 A6
Main St W
  Dalgety Bay KY11.......47 E4
  Menstrie FK11...........3 F6
Mains Gdns EH33........126 D7
Mains Of Craigmillar
  EH16................122 D2
Mains Rd Harthill ML7...159 E5
  Linlithgow EH49........84 E6
Main St Aberdour KY3....49 C8
  Airth FK2..............22 D4
  Alloa FK10..............5 D1
  Auchtertool KY2........15 B2
  Avonbridge FK1........110 A6
  Balerno EH14..........147 C1
  Bannockburn FK7........7 D1
  Bathgate EH48........141 A7
  Blackridge EH48.......138 C3
  Bo'ness EH51...........64 A8
  Bonnybridge FK4........58 B5
  Cairneyhill KY12........27 D1
  California FK1...........81 F5
  Cambusbarron FK7.......6 D5
  Cambus FK10...........11 A4
  Carnock KY12...........27 C7
  Carrington EH23.......194 D6
  Clackmannan FK10......11 A4
  Comrie KY12............26 D7
  Cowdenbeath, Hill of Beath
    KY4..................13 A1
  Cowdenbeath, Lumphinnans
    KY4..................13 B6
  Cowie FK7..............20 D7
  Crossford KY12.........28 C2
  Crossgates KY4.........30 F6
  Dalgety Bay KY11.......47 F4
  Dalmeny EH30...........89 E7
  Dechmont EH52........114 C2
  East Calder EH53......144 E4
  East Saltoun EH34.....157 E4
  East Whitburn EH47....160 F1
  Edinburgh EH4..........91 F3
  Elphinstone EH33.......126 B1
  Falkirk,Bainsford FK2....60 B7
  Falkirk,Camelon FK1.....59 E5
  Falkirk,Carronshore FK2..39 C3
  Fallin FK7...............8 E3
  Fauldhouse EH47.......181 D6
  Forth ML11............201 B1
  Gifford EH41...........220 F7
  Gorebridge EH23.......195 C7
  Grangemouth,Brightons
    FK2..................82 D8
  Grangemouth,Rumford FK2..82 F7
  Gullane EH31...........52 B2
  Halbeath KY11..........30 B5
  High Valleyfield KY12....25 F1
  Hill Of Beath KY4.......30 B8
  Kingseat KY12...........12 B1
  Kirkliston EH29.........89 A2
  Kirknewton EH27......145 E2
  Limekilns KY11.........45 D3
  Linlithgow EH49........84 D7
  Livingston,Deans EH54..142 B6
  Livingston, Livingston Village
    EH54................143 C2
  Loanhead EH20.........171 F7
  Lochgelly KY5..........14 B7
  Longniddry EH32........98 E5
  Longridge EH47........161 C1
  Mid Calder EH53.......144 C3
  Newton EH52............88 A8
  Newtongrange EH22....174 A5
  North Queensferry KY11..68 C5
  Ormiston EH35.........155 C7
  Pathhead, Dewartown
    EH23................175 D5
  Pathhead EH37.........176 B5
  Philpstoun EH49........86 D7
  Plean FK7..............20 D3
  Polmont FK2............61 E2
  Ratho EH28............117 D2
  Redding FK2............61 C2
  Rosin EH25............172 A3
  Shieldhill FK1...........82 B7
  Shotts ML7............180 A3
  Slamannan FK1.........108 B7
  Stenhousemuir FK5......38 E2
  Stenhousemuir,Larbert FK5..38 C2
  Stirling FK7.............7 B4
  Stoneyburn,Bents EH47..162 A1
  Stoneyburn EH47......162 A1
  Torryburn KY12.........26 D1
  Townhill KY12..........29 D8
  Tullibody FK10.........11 A4
  Tyninghame EH42.......76 C3
  West Calder EH55......163 D3
  Westfield EH48.........110 F5
  Winchburgh EH52.......88 A3
Mair End EH32..........71 C4
Maitland Ave
  Bannockburn FK7........7 D1
  Musselburgh EH21.....124 A6
Maitland Cres FK7.......7 D1
Maitland Hog La EH29...89 A1
Maitland Park Rd EH21..124 A6
Maitland Rd
  Kirkliston EH29.........89 A2
  Rosyth KY11.............67 B8
Maitland St
  Dunfermline KY12.......28 F4
  Musselburgh EH21.....124 A6
Majors Loan FK1.........60 A4
Majors Pl FK1...........60 A3
Malbet Pk EH16.........151 B7

Malbet Wynd EH16......151 C7
Malcolm Ct
  Bathgate EH48........140 F5
  Dunfermline KY11.......29 B1
Malcolm Dr FK5..........38 E4
Malcolm St
  Dunfermline KY11.......29 C2
Malcolms Wynd KY1......17 C5
Mallace Ave EH48.......140 B5
Mallard Ave EH48.......140 B5
Mallard Brae KY11.......46 D2
Mallard Gr KY11.........46 D2
Mall Ave EH21..........124 C6
Mallens Brae EH48......112 A5
Malleny Ave EH14.......147 C1
Malleny Gdns EH14.....147 C1
Malleny Millgate EH14..168 D8
Mall The EH54...........144 B5
Malplaquet Ct ML8.....215 B1
Malta Gn EH3............93 B2
Malta Terr EH3..........93 B2
Maltings The
  Auchtertool KY2........15 B2
  Linlithgow EH49........84 D6
Mamre Dr FK1............81 F5
Mandela Ave FK2........60 A1
Mandora Ct ML8........215 B1
Manitoba Ave EH54.....143 F3
Mannan Dr FK10.........11 A4
Mannering Pl ■ EH16...151 B8
Mannerston Holdings
  EH49.................65 D3
Mannfield Ave FK4........57 F4
Man O' War Way EH51....64 A8
Manor Cres FK10..........4 B2
Manor Gdns EH42.........78 A2
Manor Loan FK9...........3 B5
Manor Pl EH3...........228 A3
Manor Powis Cotts FK9....3 B3
Manor Rd EH51...........60 B4
Manor Steps FK9..........3 C3
Manor Wynd FK2.........83 A5
Manse Ave
  Armadale EH48........139 E6
  Whitburn EH47.........161 A6
Manse Cres FK7..........7 B4
Manse Ct EH53.........144 F4
Mansfield
  Athelstaneford EH39....101 F7
  East Calder EH53......143 F4
Mansfield Ct
  ■ Bathgate EH48.....141 A7
  Livingston EH54.......143 C3
Mansfield Gr EH48......141 A6
Mansfield Pl EH48......141 A7
Manse Gr EH47.........162 C2
Manse La Burntisland KY3..33 E1
  Cockenzie & Port Seton
    EH32................97 C4
Mansfield Rd EH15.....123 B6
Manse Pl Aberdour KY3...49 B7
  Bannockburn FK7........7 E1
  Bathgate EH48........141 A6
  Falkirk FK1.............60 B4
  Inverkeithing KY11......47 B2
Manse Rd
  Carrington EH23.......194 D5
  Crossgates KY4.........30 E7
  Dirleton EH39..........53 A5
  Edinburgh EH12........119 B6
  Forth ML11............201 B1
  Inverkeithing KY11......47 B2
  Kincardine FK10.........23 E5
  Kinghorn KY3...........34 F3
  Kirkliston EH29.........89 A1
  Newton ML7............180 A3
  Roslin EH25............172 A3
  Shotts ML7............180 A3
  Torphichen EH48.......111 F5
  Whitburn EH47.........161 B6
Manse St Aberdour KY3...49 C7
  Edinburgh EH12........119 D6
  Forth ML11............201 A4
Manse View
  Armadale EH48........139 E6
  Innerwick EH42........107 F1
  Philpstoun EH49........86 D7
Manswood Cres EH47...161 B6
Mansfield Ave Alloa KY10..5 D1
  Musselburgh EH21.....124 C5
  Newtongrange EH22....174 A6
Mansfield Ct EH21.......124 C5
Mansfield Pl
  Edinburgh EH3..........93 D2
  Musselburgh EH21.....124 C5
  Newtongrange EH22....174 A6
Mansfield Rd
  Balerno EH14..........168 A8
  Edinburgh EH3..........93 D2
  Musselburgh EH21.....124 B5
  Newtongrange EH22....174 A6
Mansionhouse Rd
  Edinburgh EH9.........121 D5
  Falkirk FK1.............59 D5
Manson Sq EH54........142 C5
Manuel Rigg FK2.........82 E6
Manuel Terr EH49........83 F6
Maple Ave FK5...........38 F3
Maple Ct FK10...........10 B6
Maple Gr EH54.........144 B6
Maple Pl KY11...........30 B3
Maple St KY2............17 B7
Maplewood Pk EH54....142 E7
Marchbank Dr EH14......82 C8
Marchbank Gdns EH14..168 C8

Marchbank Gr EH14.....168 C8
Marchbank Pl EH14.....168 C8
Marchbank Way EH14...147 C1
Marchburn Dr EH26.....191 C5
Marches Dr EH48.......140 A5
Marches The
  ■ Armadale EH48......140 A5
  ■ Stirling FK8...........7 B7
Marchfield Gr EH4.......92 A3
Marchfield Park La EH4...91 F3
Marchfield Pk EH4.......91 F3
Marchfield Terr EH4......92 A3
March Gait EH4..........91 F2
Marchglen FK13...........5 B5
March Gr EH4............92 A2
Marchhall Cres EH16....122 A5
Marchhall Pl EH16......122 A5
Marchhall Rd EH16.....122 A5
Marchlands Ave EH51....64 A7
Marchlands La EH51......64 A7
Marchlands Terr EH51....64 A7
Marchmont Ave FK2......61 E2
Marchmont Cres EH9...121 D5
Marchmont Ct FK2.......61 F2
Marchmont Mews EH7....61 F2
Marchmont Rd EH9.....121 C5
Marchmont St EH9.....121 C5
Marchmount Rd KY2......92 A3
Marchside Ct FK10........5 C5
Marchwood Ave EH48..141 C6
Marchwood Cres EH48..141 C6
Marchwood Rd EH33....126 B1
Mardale Cres EH10......121 A4
Maree Ct FK10...........10 C6
Maree Pl ■ Crossford KY12..28 B1
  Kirkcaldy KY2...........16 E8
Maree Wlk EH54........144 A4
Margaret Ave
  Bathgate EH48........141 F6
  Longcroft FK4...........57 A3
Margaret Ct FK6.........36 E1
Margaret Dr FK4.........58 A6
Margaret Rd FK7.........7 C2
Margaret Rose Ave
  EH10................150 C5
Margaret Rose Cres
  EH10................150 C5
Margaret Rose Dr EH10.150 C5
Margaret Rose Loan
  EH10................150 C5
Margaret Rose Way
  EH10................150 C5
Margaret Rose Wlk
  EH10................150 C5
Margaret Terr FK5.......38 C4
Maria St KY1............17 C5
Marina Rd EH48........141 E6
Marine Dr EH4..........92 A6
Marine Espl EH6.........94 C5
Marine Par EH39........94 C5
Mariner Ave FK1.........59 C5
Mariner Dr FK1..........52 A3
Marine Rd Dunbar EH42...78 C3
  Gullane EH31...........52 B3
Mariner Dr FK1..........59 C5
Mariner Gdns FK1........59 C5
Mariner Rd FK1..........59 C5
Mariners St KY2..........17 B1
Mariners Wlk EH6........94 C5
Mariner Wlk KY11........47 F2
Marine Terr EH31........52 B3
Marion St FK1...........17 B2
Marionville Ave EH7......94 C1
Marionville Cres EH7.....94 C1
Marionville Dr EH7.......94 C1
Marionville Gr EH7.......94 C2
Marionville Meadway
  EH7..................94 B1
Marionville Pk EH7.......94 B1
Marionville Rd EH7.......94 B2
Marischal Pl ■ EH4......92 C1
Maritime La EH6.........94 A5
Maritime St EH6.........94 A5
Marjoribanks St EH48...141 A6
Market St ■ EH41......101 A1
Marketgate EH55........155 E7
Market La EH49..........85 A7
Market Loan EH33.......126 C7
Market Pl
  North Berwick EH39.....54 C7
  Whitburn EH47.........161 A6
Market St Bo'ness EH51...63 F8
  Dunfermline KY11.......29 A4
  Edinburgh EH1.........229 A3
  Haddington EH41......130 D8
  Mid Calder EH53......144 D4
  Musselburgh EH21.....124 B6
Market View EH33......126 C7
Market Way EH33.......126 C7
Markfield Rd KY11.......48 C4
Mark La ■ EH41........130 D8
Markle Steading EH40...103 A8
Marlborough Dr FK7......2 C4
Marlborough St EH15...125 B6
Marly Gn EH54...........84 E6
Marly Rise EH54.........84 E6
Marmion Ave EH25......171 F3
Marmion Cres
  Edinburgh EH16........122 B1
Marmion Ct ■ EH39.....54 B7
Marmion Dr
  Grangemouth FK3.......61 D5
  North Berwick FK39.....54 C7
Marmion Rd
  Bathgate EH48........141 A7
  Grangemouth FK3.......61 D5
  North Berwick EH39.....54 C7
Mar Pl Alloa FK10........10 A7
  Alloa,Sauchie FK10.......5 C7

Mar Pl *continued*
Stirling FK8 . . . . 7 A8
Marquis Dr FK10 . . . . 11 B4
Marshall Rd EH54 . . . . . . 115 A1
Marfield Terr EH54 . . . . . 115 A1
Marschal Ct FK7 . . . . 7 D3
Marshall's Ct EH1 . . . . . . 229 B4
Marshall Pl KY11 . . . . 29 E1
Marshall Rd EH29 . . . . 89 A1
Marshall St
Cockenzie & Port Seton
EH32 . . . . 97 B4
Cowdenbeath KY4 . . . . 13 D3
Edinburgh EH8 . . . . 229 A2
Grangemouth FK3 . . . . 61 D8
Marshall Terr FK3 . . . . 61 D8
Marshall Twr FK1 . . . . 60 D4
Marshill FK10 . . . . 10 A6
Mar St FK10 . . . . 10 B6
Mar Terr FK10 . . . . 11 A4
Martin Brae EH54 . . . . . . 143 C5
Martin Gr EH19 . . . . 173 D8
Martin Pl EH22 . . . . 152 E2
Maryburn Rd EH22 . . . . . 174 C8
Mary Erskine Sch EH4 . . . 92 B1
Mary Erskine & Stewart's
Melville Jun Sch EH4 . . . . 92 E1
Mayfield
2 Edinburgh,Drum EH7 . . 93 F2
Edinburgh,Portobello EH15 . 95 B1
Maryfield Dr EH51 . . . . 64 D6
Mayfield Pk EH53 . . . . . . 144 C2
Maryfield Pl
Bonnyrigg and Lasswade
EH19 . . . . 173 C7
2 Edinburgh EH7 . . . . . . 94 A2
Falkirk FK1 . . . . 59 B4
Maryflats Pl FK3 . . . . 61 E7
Maryhall St KY1 . . . . 17 C5
Mary Pl Clackmannan FK10 . 11 A5
Dunfermline KY11 . . . . 29 B2
Mary's Pl FK4 . . . . 93 A2
Mary Sq FK2 . . . . 61 A4
Mary St FK2 . . . . 60 F4
Mary Stevenson Dr FK10 . 10 A8
Mary Street Rdbt FK2 . . . . 60 F3
Marytree Ho EH17 . . . . . . 151 D8
Marywell KY1 . . . . 17 C5
Masefield Way EH12 . . . . . 90 B1
Mason Pl EH18 . . . . 172 F6
Massereene Rd KY2 . . . . . 16 F5
Masterton Rd KY11 . . . . . . 47 A7
Mathers Ave EH47 . . . . . 160 F6
Mather Terr FK2 . . . . 60 A4
Mathew Ct FK1 . . . . 61 D8
Mathieson Pl KY11 . . . . . . 29 F1
Matthews Crofts EH48 . . 138 C3
Matthews Dr EH22 . . . . . 173 F4
Matthew St KY2 . . . . 17 B6
Mauchline Ct KY4 . . . . 13 A2
Maukeshill Ct EH54 . . . . 143 C2
Maulside Rd EH52 . . . . . 115 C5
Maule Terr EH31 . . . . 52 A2
Maulsford Ave EH22 . . . . 152 B7
Maurice Ave FK7 . . . . 7 D4
Maurice Pl EH9 . . . . 121 D2
Mauricewood Ave EH26 . 191 F7
Mauricewood Bank
EH26 . . . . 191 F7
Mauricewood Gr EH26 . 191 F7
Mauricewood Pk EH26 . 191 F7
Mauricewood Prim Sch
EH26 . . . . 192 A8
Mauricewood Rd EH26 . 191 F8
Mauricewood Rise EH26 . 191 F7
Mavisbank EH20 . . . . 172 C7
Mavisbank Ave FK1 . . . . . . 81 C6
Mavisbank Pl EH18 . . . . . 172 E6
Mavishall Rd EH22 . . . . . 224 D8
Maxton Cres FK12 . . . . 5 C7
Maxton Ct EH22 . . . . 153 A3
Maxton Pl KY11 . . . . 46 E3
Maxwell Cres KY4 . . . . 13 A2
Maxwell Pl **6** FK8 . . . . 7 B8
Maxwell Rd EH39 . . . . 53 A4
Maxwell Sq EH54 . . . . . . 164 C6
Maxwell St EH10 . . . . 121 A3
Maxwell Twr FK1 . . . . 60 D3
Maybank Villas EH12 . . . 119 D7
Mayburn Ave EH20 . . . . . 151 B1
Mayburn Bank EH20 . . . 172 B8
Mayburn Cres EH20 . . . . 151 B1
Mayburn Dr EH20 . . . . . . 172 B8
Mayburn Gr EH20 . . . . . . 172 B8
Mayburn Hill EH20 . . . . . 172 B8
Mayburn Loan EH20 . . . 151 B1
Mayburn Terr EH20 . . . . 151 B1
Mayburn Vale EH20 . . . . 172 B8
Mayburn Wlk EH20 . . . . . 172 B8
Maybury Dr EH12 . . . . . . 119 A8
Maybury Rd
Edinburgh,Bughtlin EH4,
EH12 . . . . 91 A3
Edinburgh,East Craigs
EH12 . . . . 119 A8
Mayfield Rd EH21 . . . . . . 124 B3
Mayfield Cres
Clackmannan FK10 . . . . . 11 A5
Loanhead EH20 . . . . 172 C7
Musselburgh EH21 . . . . . 124 B4
Mayfield Ct
Armadale EH48 . . . . 139 F4
Loanhead EH20 . . . . 172 C8
Stirling FK7 . . . . 7 B3
Mayfield Dr
Armadale EH48 . . . . 139 F5

Mayfield Dr *continued*
Longcroft FK4 . . . . 57 B3
Mayfield Gardens La
EH9 . . . . 121 F4
Mayfield Gdns EH9 . . . . 121 F4
Mayfield Gdns La EH9 . 121 F4
Mayfield Ind Est EH22 . . 174 C5
Mayfield Mews **2** FK1 . . 59 F4
Mayfield Pk EH21 . . . . . 124 B3
Mayfield Pl
Edinburgh EH12 . . . . . . 119 D6
Edinburgh EH22 . . . . . . 174 D6
Musselburgh EH21 . . . . 124 B3
Mayfield Prim Sch EH22 174 D5
Mayfield Rd
Easthouses EH22 . . . . . . 174 D8
Edinburgh EH9 . . . . 121 F3
Redding FK2 . . . . 61 C2
Mayfield St FK7 . . . . 7 B4
Mayfield Terr EH9 . . . . . 121 F4
Mayflower St KY12 . . . . . 29 C7
Maygate **8** KY12 . . . . 29 A3
Mayne Ave FK9 . . . . 2 B6
Mayshade Rd EH20 . . . . 151 B1
May Terr EH39 . . . . 54 A7
Mayville Bank EH21 . . . . 125 A6
Mayville Gdns EH5 . . . . . 93 C6
Mayville Gdns E EH5 . . . . 93 C6
Mayville Pk EH42 . . . . . . 78 C3
Meadowbank
Edinburgh EH8 . . . . 94 B1
Livingston EH54 . . . . . . 143 E5
Ormiston EH35 . . . . 155 C6
Meadowbank Ave EH8 . 94 B1
Meadowbank Cres
Edinburgh EH8 . . . . 94 B1
Ormiston EH35 . . . . 155 D7
Meadowbank Rd
Kirknewton EH27 . . . . . 145 F3
Ormiston EH35 . . . . 155 C7
Meadowbank St FK2 . . . . 61 C1
Meadowbank Terr **5** EH8 . 94 A1
Meadowbank View EH27 145 F3
Meadow Cres EH47 . . . . 181 E5
Meadow Ct Burntisland KY3 33 E1
Carluke ML8 . . . . 215 C1
Denny FK6 . . . . 36 D4
Meadow Dr EH47 . . . . . . 162 A1
Meadowend KY12 . . . . . . 28 C2
Meadowfield
Burntisland KY3 . . . . 33 E2
Cowdenbeath KY4 . . . . . 13 C6
Dalgety Bay KY11 . . . . . . 48 C4
Meadowfield Ave EH8 . 122 E7
Meadowfield Ct EH8 . . . 122 D7
Meadowfield Dr EH8 . . . 122 D7
Meadowfield Gdns EH8 122 D6
Meadowfield Rd EH12 . . 118 C7
Meadowfield Terr EH8 . 122 D6
Meadowforth Rd FK7 . . . . 7 C7
Meadow Gn FK10 . . . . 5 B1
Meadowhead Ave EH55 . 162 E1
Meadowhead Cres EH55 162 E1
Meadowhead Gdns EH55 162 E1
Meadowhead Gr EH55 . 162 E1
Meadowhead Loan EH55 . 162 D1
Meadowhead Pl EH55 . . 162 D1
Meadowhouse Rd EH12 . 119 E6
Meadow La EH8 . . . . 229 A1
Meadowland Rd FK7 . . . . . 7 C7
Meadow Park Rd EH12 . 119 C6
Meadow Pl La EH21 . . . . 121 D5
Meadow Rd
Riccarton EH14 . . . . 147 F7
Stoneyburn EH47 . . . . . 162 A1
Meadows EH33 . . . . 126 E5
Meadowspot EH11 . . . . . 120 E2
Meadow St FK1 . . . . 60 C4
Meadows The
Falkirk,Carronshore FK2 . . 39 B2
Falkirk FK1 . . . . 60 C4
Stirling FK9 . . . . 2 B2
Meadow View
Crossford KY12 . . . . 28 B2
Halbeath KY11 . . . . 30 B6
Mearenside EH12 . . . . . . 119 A8
Medwyn Pl FK10 . . . . 9 F6
Meeks Rd FK2 . . . . 60 B5
Meetinghouse Dr EH33 . 126 C6
Meggat Pl EH23 . . . . 174 A2
Meggetland Terr EH14 . 120 E3
Meikle EH54 . . . . 143 C1
Meikleriggs Cotts EH42 . 105 A1
Meikle Sq EH54 . . . . 18 A7
Melbourne Pl EH39 . . . . . 54 D7
Melbourne Rd
Broxburn EH52 . . . . 115 F5
North Berwick EH39 . . . . 54 D7
Melbourne St EH54 . . . . 144 A5
Meldrum Cres KY3 . . . . . . 33 D1

Meldrum Ct KY11 . . . . 29 F1
Meldrum Prim Sch EH4 142 E7
Meldrum Rd KY2 . . . . 17 B5
Melford Ave ML7 . . . . . . 180 B3
Melfort Dr FK7 . . . . 7 C4
Melgund Pl EH9 . . . . 14 B8
Melgund Terr EH7 . . . . . . 93 D2
Mellerstain Rd KY2 . . . . . 16 C6
Mellock Gdns FK1 . . . . . . 59 E2
Mellor Ct KY11 . . . . 46 E4
Melrose Cres KY2 . . . . . . 17 C6
Melrose Dr FK3 . . . . 61 F6
Melrose Pl **8** FK1 . . . . 60 A4
Melville Cotts EH18 . . . . 152 C4
Melville Cres EH3 . . . . . . 228 A3
Melville Dr EH9 . . . . 229 A1
Melville Dykes Rd EH18 . 152 C1
Melville Dykes Road Rdbt
EH18 . . . . 152 D2
Melville Gate EH22 . . . . 152 D3
Melville Gate Rd EH22 . 152 E4
Melville Grange Cotts
EH18 . . . . 152 B4
Melville La **3** FK1 . . . . 60 B5
Melville Pl Bridge of A FK9 . 2 A7
Dunfermline KY12 . . . . . . 29 B4
Edinburgh EH3 . . . . 228 A2
Kirkcaldy KY2 . . . . 17 D6
Melville Rd EH22 . . . . . . 152 E2
Melville St Edinburgh EH3 228 A3
2 Falkirk FK1 . . . . 60 B5
Lochgelly KY5 . . . . 14 B8
Melville Street La EH3 . 228 A3
Melville Terr
7 Dalkeith EH22 . . . . . 152 E1
Edinburgh EH9 . . . . 229 B1
Stirling FK8 . . . . 7 B6
Melville View EH18 . . . . 173 A8
Menstrie Bsns Ctr FK11 . . 3 F6
Menstrie Castle FK11 . . . . 3 F6
Menstrie Prim Sch FK11 . . 4 A6
Menteith Ct FK10 . . . . . . 10 C6
Menteith Pl FK9 . . . . 2 F1
Menteith Rd FK9 . . . . 2 A6
Mentone Ave EH15 . . . . . 95 B1
Mentone Gdns EH9 . . . . 121 F4
Mentone Terr EH9 . . . . . 121 F4
Menzies Cres KY2 . . . . . . 16 F5
Menzies Dr FK8 . . . . 2 A2
Menzies Rd EH16 . . . . . . 141 A6
Mercat Pl FK10 . . . . 11 B4
Mercat The KY1 . . . . 17 C3
Mercat Wynd **2** FK10 . . 10 B6
Mercer Pl KY11 . . . . 29 E4
Mercer St FK10 . . . . 23 E3
Merchant St EH1 . . . . . . 229 A2
Merchants Way KY11 . . . . 47 C2
Merchiston Ave
Edinburgh EH10 . . . . . . 121 A5
Falkirk FK2 . . . . 60 A7
Merchiston Bank Ave
EH10 . . . . 121 A4
Merchiston Bank Gdns
EH10 . . . . 121 A4
Merchiston Castle Sch
EH14 . . . . 149 B7
Merchiston Cres EH10 . . 121 A4
Merchiston Gdns
Edinburgh EH10 . . . . . . 120 F3
Falkirk FK2 . . . . 60 A6
Merchiston Gr EH11 . . . . 120 E4
Merchiston Ind Est FK2 . 60 C8
Merchiston Mews EH10 . 121 A5
Merchiston Pk EH10 . . . 121 A5
Merchiston Pl EH10 . . . . 121 A5
Merchiston Pk EH10 . . . 121 A5
Merchiston Rd FK2 . . . . . 60 A6
Merchiston Terr FK2 . . . . 60 A7
Meredith Dr FK5 . . . . 38 F3
Merker Terr EH54 . . . . . . 84 E6
Merkland Cres KY11 . . . . 48 A3
Merkland Dr KY11 . . . . . . 60 E1
Merlindale ML11 . . . . . . 217 F8
Merlin Way EH54 . . . . . . 148 C5
Merlyon Way EH20 . . . . 191 D7
Merrick Rd FK3 . . . . 61 F5
Merrick Way EH33 . . . . . 126 C6
Merryfield Ave EH33 . . . 127 D5
Merrylees EH49 . . . . 65 D1
Mertoun Pl EH11 . . . . . . 120 F5
Merville Cres FK1 . . . . . . 81 F5
Merville Terr FK1 . . . . . . 81 F5
Methven Dr KY12 . . . . . . 29 B5
Methven Pl KY1 . . . . 17 B2
Methven Terr EH18 . . . . 172 F6
Meuse La EH2 . . . . 229 A3
Meylea St EH48 . . . . 141 D4
Michaelson Sq EH54 . . . 143 C1
Mid Beveridgewell KY12 . 28 F5
Mid Brae **1** KY12 . . . . 28 F5
Mid Calder Prim Sch
EH53 . . . . 144 C2
Mid Cswy KY12 . . . . 42 D8
Middlebank Holdings
KY11 . . . . 47 B6
Middlebank St KY11 . . . . 47 A4
Middleby Ct EH9 . . . . . . 121 F4
Middleby St EH9 . . . . . . 121 F4
Middlefield EH7 . . . . 93 E3
Middlefield Ind Est EH7 . 93 E4
Middle Jetty Rd KY11 . . . 67 B8
Middleknowe EH14 . . . . 148 C8
Middlemas Rd EH42 . . . 106 D8

Middlemass Ct FK2 . . . . . 60 B6
Middle Meadow Wlk
EH8 . . . . 229 A1
Middle Norton EH28 . . . 117 F5
Middlepark EH14 . . . . . . 148 C8
Middleshot EH14 . . . . . . 148 C8
Middleshot Rd EH31 . . . . 52 A3
Middleshot Sq EH32 . . . . 97 B2
Middle Street La FK3 . . . . 40 C1
Middleton FK11 . . . . 4 A5
Middleton Ave EH52 . . . 115 A4
Middleton Rd EH52 . . . . 115 A4
Middle Wlk KY12 . . . . . . 29 B3
Middlewood Pk EH54 . . 142 E7
Midfield Ho EH18 . . . . . . 172 E5
Mid Gogarloch Syke
EH12 . . . . 119 A5
Midhope Pl EH52 . . . . . . 87 F2
Mid Liberton EH16 . . . . . 122 A2
Midlothian Ski Ctr EH10 . 150 A2
Midmar Ave EH10 . . . . . 121 C2
Midmar Dr EH10 . . . . . . 121 B2
Midmar Gdns EH10 . . . . 121 B2
Mid New Cultins EH11 . . 119 B2
Mid Rd KY3 . . . . 34 F3
Mid Road Ind Est EH22 . 125 F8
Mid St Bathgate EH48 . . 141 B6
Kirkcaldy KY1 . . . . 17 D6
Livingston EH54 . . . . . . 142 E6
Lochgelly KY5 . . . . 14 B8
Mid Steil EH11 . . . . 120 E1
Midthorn Cres FK2 . . . . . 60 E5
Midtown FK1 . . . . 61 C8
Milesmark Ct KY12 . . . . . 28 C6
Milesmark Prim Sch
KY12 . . . . 28 D5
Millar Place La EH10 . . . 121 A3
Millar Pl EH33 . . . . 126 C5
Millars Wynd FK10 . . . . . 5 C2
Millbank EH14 . . . . 147 C1
Millbank Cres KY11 . . . . . 11 A5
Millbank Gr EH52 . . . . . 195 C7
Millbank Pl EH52 . . . . . . 114 F4
Millbank Sq FK7 . . . . 161 B2
Millbank Terr **4** FK2 . . . . 82 F7
Millbrae EH53 . . . . 144 C5
Millbrae Wynd **1** EH14 . 120 B2
Millbrook FK11 . . . . 3 F6
Millburn Cres EH48 . . . . 139 D6
Millburn Rd
Bathgate EH48 . . . . 141 D4
Westfield EH48 . . . . 110 F5
Millburn St FK2 . . . . 60 B5
Mill Ct Bathgate EH48 . . 141 A1
Falkirk FK2 . . . . 39 B3
Milldean Gr KY12 . . . . . . 29 D5
Millenium Ave KY1 . . . . . 14 C1
Miller Ave EH12 . . . . 26 B8
Miller Cres EH51 . . . . 64 D5
Millerfield EH49 . . . . 84 D7
Millerfield Pl EH9 . . . . . 121 D5
Millerhill Rd EH22 . . . . . 152 D7
Miller Pk EH52 . . . . 61 F1
Miller Pl Harthill ML7 . . . 159 F6
Miller Rd Dunfermline KY12 28 E5
Livingston EH55 . . . . 62 E5
Miller Row EH4 . . . . 228 A3
Millers Ct EH33 . . . . 127 D5
Millfield Harthill ML7 . . . 159 E6
Mill Farm Rd KY3 . . . . . . 49 B7
Millfield Haddington EH41 130 A7
Millfield Dr FK2 . . . . 61 E2
Millflats St FK2 . . . . 39 A1
Millgate EH52 . . . . 87 F2
Millhall Gdns KY11 . . . . . 48 A3
Millhall Rd FK7 . . . . 7 D5
Millhaugh La EH48 . . . . 141 A7
Mill Hill KY11 . . . . 47 A6
Mill Hill Ho EH48 . . . . . . 140 C7
Millhill St KY12 . . . . 28 E5
Millhill Wynd EH21 . . . . 124 D6
Millhouse **9** FK1 . . . . 60 E5
Millie St KY1 . . . . 17 D6
Mill La Edinburgh EH6 . . 93 F5
Kincardine FK10 . . . . 23 E3
Stenton EH42 . . . . 104 E5
Mill Rd Alloa FK10 . . . . . . 10 B8
Armadale EH48 . . . . 139 E6
Bathgate EH48 . . . . 141 A7
Blackburn EH47 . . . . . . 162 C4
Cambusbarron FK7 . . . . . . 6 C6
Clackmannan FK10 . . . . . 11 A5
Harthill ML7 . . . . 159 F5
Linlithgow EH49 . . . . 85 B8
Mill Rdbt EH54 . . . . 143 A3
Mill Road Ind Est EH49 . 84 C6
Millside EH8 . . . . 120 D7
Mill St Alloa FK10 . . . . 10 B8
Dunfermline KY12 . . . . . . 28 E4
Millway EH34 . . . . 157 A6

Mill Wynd
East Linton EH40 . . . . . . 103 E7
Haddington EH41 . . . . . 130 A7
Prestonpans EH32 . . . . . 96 F2
Miln-Acre EH6 . . . . 93 D4
Milne Cres KY4 . . . . 13 C3
Milne Park Rd FK7 . . . . . . 19 E8
Milne Rd Dunfermline KY11 47 A7
Rosyth KY11 . . . . 46 E1
Milnquarter Rd FK4 . . . . . 58 A3
Milrig Smallholdings
EH27 . . . . 145 C3
Milsey Ct EH39 . . . . 54 D7
Milton Cl FK6 . . . . 36 D3
Milton Cres
Bannockburn FK7 . . . . 7 C1
Edinburgh EH15 . . . . . . 123 A6
Milton Dr EH15 . . . . 123 D7
Milton Gdns FK7 . . . . 7 B1
Milton Gdns N EH15 . . . 123 A6
Milton Gdns S EH15 . . . 123 A6
Milton Glen EH15 . . . . . 123 E7
Milton Gn KY12 . . . . 29 A2
Milton Gr Bannockburn FK7 . 7 C1
Edinburgh EH15 . . . . . . 123 E7
Milton Link EH15 . . . . . . 123 E6
Milton Mill EH26 . . . . . . 171 C2
Milton Pk KY12 . . . . 15 B2
Milton Pl FK6 . . . . 36 D3
Milton Rd Bannockburn FK7 . 7 C1
Edinburgh EH15 . . . . . . 123 B6
Kirkcaldy KY1 . . . . 17 B2
Milton Rd E EH15 . . . . . 123 D7
Milton Rd W EH15 . . . . . 122 F6
Milton Row FK6 . . . . 36 E3
Milton St EH8 . . . . 94 A1
Milton Terr
Edinburgh EH15 . . . . . . 123 E7
Stirling FK7 . . . . 7 B1
Minard Rd ML7 . . . . 179 D6
Miner's Terr EH21 . . . . . 125 B5
Mine Rd FK9 . . . . 2 A8
Mingle Pl FK15 . . . . 64 A6
Minstrel Ct EH25 . . . . . . 172 A3
Minthill Pl ML7 . . . . 159 D5
Minto Ct FK12 . . . . 5 B6
Minto Gdns FK12 . . . . 5 B6
Minto Pl KY1 . . . . 17 B8
Minto St Edinburgh EH9 . 121 F4
Lochgelly KY5 . . . . 14 B8
Mission La **8** FK1 . . . . . . 60 B4
Mitchell's Cl **6** EH41 . . 130 B8
Mitchell Cres EH42 . . . . . . 9 F7
Cowdenbeath KY4 . . . . . 13 A1
Mitchellhall Brae EH41 . 130 D5
Mitchell St Falkirk FK1 . . 59 E1
2 Kirkcaldy KY1 . . . . . . 17 D6
Mitchell Way KY11 . . . . . 46 C1
Mitchell Wik Dalkeith EH22 152 F3
Edinburgh EH6 . . . . 94 A5
Mitchell Way EH33 . . . . 126 D7
Mitchell Wlk EH21 . . . . . 46 F3
Moat Dr EH14 . . . . 120 D4
Moat Ho EH14 . . . . 120 D4
Moat Pl EH14 . . . . 120 D4
Moat St EH14 . . . . 120 D4
Moat Terr EH14 . . . . 120 D4
Moat View EH25 . . . . . . 171 F3
Mochrum Dr KY2 . . . . 45 B8
Modan Rd FK7 . . . . 7 A3
Moffat Ave
Bonnyrigg and Lasswade
EH19 . . . . 173 B6
Falkirk FK2 . . . . 39 C3
Moffat Cres KY5 . . . . 14 A7
Moffat Rd EH47 . . . . 155 D6
Moidart Ave FK2 . . . . 39 D3
Moidart Rd EH47 . . . . 94 E1
Moira Pk EH7 . . . . 94 E1
Moira Terr EH7 . . . . 94 E1
Moira Terrace La EH7 . . . 94 E1
Moir Ave EH21 . . . . 125 A6
Moir Cres EH21 . . . . 125 A6
Moir Ct KY4 . . . . 12 E8
Moir Dr EH21 . . . . 125 B6
Moir Pl EH21 . . . . 125 A6
Moir St FK10 . . . . 10 B8
Moir Terr EH21 . . . . 125 A6
Mollison Ave ML7 . . . . . 159 E6
Monar Ct FK3 . . . . 61 F5
Monastery St KY12 . . . . . 29 A3
Moncks Rd FK1 . . . . 60 D4
Moncrieffe Ho EH17 . . . 151 D8
Moncrieff Terr EH9 . . . . 121 E5
Moncur St KY11 . . . . 47 A4
Moncur St KY12 . . . . 29 C7
Monkbarns Gdns **4**
EH16 . . . . 151 B8
Monkland Rd EH48 . . . . 140 F4
Monkmains Rd EH41 . . . 130 C7
Monkrigg Pl EH41 . . . . . 130 C7
Monkrigg Steading
EH41 . . . . 130 C8
Monksmuir Cvn Pk EH41 102 D5
Monksrig Rd EH26 . . . . 191 C5
Monkswood Rd EH22 . . 174 B4
Monktonhall Farm Cotts
EH21 . . . . 124 B3
Monktonhall Pl EH21 . . 124 B3
Monktonhall Terr EH21 . 124 B4
Monkwood Ct EH10 . . . . 121 B1
Monmouth Terr EH3 . . . . 93 B4
Monro St EH48 . . . . 229 B1
Montagu Terr EH3 . . . . . . 93 B4

Monteith Wlk ML7 . . . .**179** E6
Montfort Pl FK1 . . . .**60** B8
Montgomery Cres FK2 . . . . . .**39** B2
Montgomery Dr FK2 . . . .**39** B2
Montgomery Pl FK2 . . . .**39** B2
Montgomery St
  Edinburgh EH7 . . . .**93** F2
  Falkirk FK2 . . . .**60** E5
  Grangemouth FK3 . . . .**61** C6
  Kirkcaldy KY2 . . . .**17** B5
Montgomery Street La
  EH7 . . . .**93** E2
Montgomery Way FK9 . . . .**2** B3
Montgomery Well FK2 . . . .**39** B2
Montpelier EH10 . . . .**121** B5
Montpelier Pk EH10 . . . .**121** A5
Montpelier Terr EH10 . . . . . .**121** A5
Montrose Rd Polmont FK2 . .**62** A1
  Stirling FK9 . . . .**2** C4
Montrose Terr EH7 . . . .**229** C4
Montrose Way FK4 . . . .**57** D5
Monument View FK8 . . . .**2** B2
Moodie St KY12 . . . .**29** A3
Moore Cotts EH52 . . . .**115** D5
Moore House Sch EH48 . . . .**141** E5
Moorelands Gdns EH55 . . . .**162** C1
Moorelands EH55 . . . .**162** C1
Moorelands Pl EH55 . . . .**162** D1
Moorfield Cotts EH22 . . . . . .**152** C8
Moorfoot Ct EH19 . . . .**173** B7
Moorfoot Pl
  Bonnyrigg and Lasswade
    EH19 . . . .**173** B6
  Penicuik EH26 . . . .**191** E6
Moorfoot View
  Bilston EH25 . . . .**171** E5
  Bonnyrigg and Lasswade
    EH19 . . . .**173** B6
  Gorebridge EH23 . . . .**195** C7
Moorings The KY11 . . . .**47** F2
Moor Rd Fala EH37 . . . .**224** B7
  Pathhead EH37 . . . .**176** D4
  Pencaitland EH35,EH37. . . .**177** B6
Moorside St ML8 . . . .**215** A2
Morar Ct FK3 . . . .**61** D5
Morar Dr FK2 . . . .**39** C1
Morar Pl FK3 . . . .**61** D5
Morar Rd KY12 . . . .**28** B1
Moray Ct ML7. . . . .**180** B3
Moray Ct Auchtertool KY2. . .**15** B2
  Dalgety Bay KY11 . . . .**48** A3
Moray Dr EH49 . . . .**84** E6
Moray House Coll of Ed
  EH8 . . . .**229** B3
Moray Park Terr EH7 . . . .**94** A2
Moray Pk KY11 . . . .**48** A4
Moray Pl Edinburgh EH3 . . .**228** B4
  Grangemouth FK3 . . . .**61** E7
  Linlithgow EH49. . . . .**84** E6
Moray Prim Sch FK3. . . . .**61** E7
Morayvale KY3 . . . .**49** C8
Moray Way N KY11. . . . .**48** A4
Moray Way S KY11. . . . .**48** B2
Moredun Dykes Rd
  EH17 . . . .**151** D6
Moredun Ho EH17 . . . .**151** D7
Moredun Park Ct EH17 . . . .**151** D7
Moredun Park Dr EH17 . . . .**151** D7
Moredun Park Gdns
  EH17 . . . .**151** D7
Moredun Park Gn EH17. . . .**151** E7
Moredun Park Gr EH17. . . . .**151** E7
Moredun Park Loan
  EH17 . . . .**151** D7
Moredun Park Rd EH17 . . . .**151** E8
Moredun Park St EH17. . . . .**151** D7
Moredun Park View
  EH17 . . . .**151** E7
Moredun Park Way
  EH17 . . . .**151** D7
Moredun Park Wlk EH17.**151** D7
Moredunvale Bank EH17 **151** D8
Moredunvale Gn EH17. . .**151** D8
Moredunvale Gr EH17. . . .**151** D8
Moredunvale Loan EH17 **151** D8
Moredunvale Pk EH17. . .**151** D8
Moredunvale Pl EH17. . . .**151** D8
Moredunvale Rd EH17. . .**151** D8
Moredunvale View EH17.**151** D8
Moredunvale Way EH17 .**151** D8
Morgan Ct FK7 . . . .**7** C3
Morgan Way EH4 . . . .**140** A4
Morham Gait EH10. . . . .**149** E8
Morham Gdn EH10. . . . .**149** E8
Morham Lea EH10 . . . .**149** E8
Morham Pk EH10 . . . .**149** E8
Morham Village Houses
  EH41 . . . .**131** D5
Morison Gdns EH30 . . . .**68** E1
Moriston Ct FK3 . . . .**61** E4
Moriston Dr FK3 . . . .**164** F6
Morley Cres FK7. . . . .**7** A3
Morlich Cres KY11. . . . .**48** A2
Morlich Ct KY11 . . . .**48** A2
Morlich Gr KY11. . . . .**48** A2
Morlich Pk KY11 . . . .**48** A2
Morlich Pl KY11 . . . .**48** A2
Morlich Rd KY11 . . . .**48** A2
Morlich Wlk EH54 . . . .**144** A4
Mornay Way ML7 . . . .**179** E6
Morningside Ct EH10 . . . . . .**121** A2
Morningside Dr EH10 . . . . . .**121** A2
Morningside Gdns EH10. . . .**120** F2
Morningside Gr EH10 . . . . . .**120** F1
Morningside Pk EH10 . . . . . .**121** A3

Morningside Pl EH10. . . .**121** A3
Morningside Rd EH10 . . . .**121** B3
Morningside Terr EH10. . .**121** A3
Morris Ct KY11 . . . .**47** C2
Morrison Ave
  Bonnybridge FK4 . . . .**57** F6
  Tranent EH33 . . . .**126** E5
Morrison Cir EH3 . . . .**228** A2
Morrison Cres EH3 . . . .**228** A2
Morrison Dr
  Bannockburn FK7 . . . .**7** C2
  Dunfermline KY11. . . . .**46** F8
Morrison Link EH3 . . . .**228** A2
Morrison St EH3 . . . .**228** A2
Morrison Way EH54 . . . .**143** D8
Morris Rd EH22. . . . .**174** C6
Morris Sq EH54. . . . .**143** F2
Morris Terr FK8 . . . .**7** A8
Mortimer Ct KY11. . . . .**48** B2
Mortonhall Cvn Pk EH16 .**150** E6
Mortonhall Gate EH16 . . . .**150** E5
Mortonhall Park Ave
  EH17 . . . .**150** F5
Mortonhall Park Bank
  EH17 . . . .**151** A5
Mortonhall Park Cres
  EH17 . . . .**151** A5
Mortonhall Park Dr
  EH17 . . . .**151** A5
Mortonhall Park Gdns
  EH17 . . . .**150** F5
Mortonhall Park Gr
  EH17 . . . .**150** F5
Mortonhall Park Loan
  EH17 . . . .**150** F5
Mortonhall Park Pl
  EH17 . . . .**151** A5
Mortonhall Park Terr
  EH17 . . . .**151** A5
Mortonhall Park Way
  EH17 . . . .**150** F5
Mortonhall Rd EH9 . . . .**121** D3
Morton St EH15. . . . .**123** C7
Morven Ct FK1 . . . .**60** C2
Morven Dr FK2 . . . .**61** D2
Morven Gr KY12 . . . .**28** B1
Morven Pl KY11 . . . .**48** A3
Morvenside EH14 . . . .**148** C8
Morvenside Cl EH14 . . . .**148** C8
Morven St EH4 . . . .**91** C1
Mossband La ML7 . . . .**179** E6
Mossbank
  Cowdenbeath KY4 . . . .**13** B2
  Livingston EH54. . . . .**143** E5
  Rosyth KY11 . . . .**46** F5
Mossban Ave ML7. . . . .**159** D5
Mosscastle Rd FK1 . . . .**108** A7
Mossend EH55. . . . .**163** D3
Mossend Terr EH54 . . . .**143** E5
Mossgiel Ave Cowie FK7 . . . .**20** D7
  Stirling FK8 . . . .**2** A2
Mossgiel Cotts EH54 . . . . . .**142** D7
Mossgiel St FK1 . . . .**59** B5
Mossgiel Terr FK1 . . . .**61** A3
Mossgiel Wlk **3** EH16 . . . . .**122** A1
Mosshall Ind Est EH47 . . . .**162** B7
Mosshat St EH55. . . . .**202** F3
Mosshouse FK7. . . . .**6** F4
Moss-Side Rd KY4. . . . .**13** B3
Moss Way KY11. . . . .**48** B5
Moston Terr EH9 . . . .**121** F4
Motion St KY5 . . . .**14** A7
Moubray Gdns FK10 . . . .**4** B1
Moubray Gr EH30 . . . .**89** C8
Moubray Rd KY11. . . . .**48** C5
Moulin Way KY12 . . . .**29** E5
Mound Pl EH1 . . . .**228** C3
Mound The EH2 . . . .**228** C3
Mount Alvernia EH11 . . . . . .**120** F3
Mount Bartholomew FK4.**58** A4
Mountbatten Pl KY11 . . . .**46** E3
Mountbatten St FK3 . . . .**61** C5
Mountcastle Bank EH8 . . . .**122** F8
Mountcastle Cres EH8 . . . .**122** F8
Mountcastle Dr N EH8 . . . .**122** F8
Mountcastle Dr S
  Edinburgh EH15. . . . .**122** F7
  Edinburgh EH15. . . . .**123** A6
Mountcastle Gdns EH8. . . .**122** E8
Mountcastle Gn **1** EH8 . . . .**94** E1
Mountcastle Gr EH8 . . . .**122** E8
Mountcastle Loan EH8 . . . .**122** E8
Mountcastle Pk **3** EH8 . . . .**94** E1
Mountcastle Pl **2** EH8 . . . . .**94** E1
Mountcastle Terr EH8 . . . . .**122** E8
Mountfair Gdns EH33 . . . . .**127** C5
Mountfair Pl EH33 . . . .**127** C5
Mount Grange EH9 . . . .**121** C4
Mount Hooly Cres KY11 . . . .**68** C6
Mounthooly Loan EH10 . . .**150** D5
Mount Hope FK9 . . . .**2** B7
Mountjoy Ct EH21. . . . .**124** C7
Mountjoy Terr EH21. . . . . . .**124** C7
Mount Lodge Pl EH15 . . . .**123** B8
Mount Oliphant FK7. . . . .**20** D7
Mount Pleasant EH48. . . . .**141** C2
Mount Vernon Rd EH16...**151** B8
Mount William FK10 . . . .**5** E1
Mowbray Gdns KY4. . . . .**30** E6
Mowbray Rise EH54. . . . . . .**143** F1
Mowbrey Ct FK7. . . . .**7** D4

Moy Ct FK3. . . . .**61** D5
Muckle Hill Pk KY11 . . . .**47** A2
Mucklets Ave EH21 . . . .**124** A4
Mucklets Cres EH21. . . . . . .**124** A3
Mucklets Ct EH21 . . . .**124** A4
Mucklets Dr EH21 . . . .**124** A3
Mucklets Pl EH21 . . . .**124** A4
Mucklets Rd EH21. . . . .**123** F3
Mudale Ct FK1. . . . .**60** D1
Muir's Ct EH52 . . . .**114** F4
Muiralehouse Rd FK7 . . . .**19** E8
Muiravonside Ctry Pk
  EH49 . . . .**83** E4
Muir Ct KY4 . . . .**30** E6
Muirdale Terr EH4 . . . .**92** B2
Muirdyke Ave FK2 . . . .**39** C3
Muiredge and Jersy Rd
  ML7 . . . .**179** A8
Muirend Ave EH14. . . . .**148** E7
Muirend Ct EH51. . . . .**64** B6
Muirend Rd FK7 . . . .**7** B5
Muirepark Ct EH51. . . . .**64** A6
Muirfield Apartments
  EH31 . . . .**52** B2
Muirfield Cres EH31 . . . .**52** B2
Muirfield Ct EH40. . . . .**103** E7
Muirfield Dr Gullane EH31 . . .**52** B2
  Uphall EH52. . . . .**114** E4
Muirfield Gdns
  Gullane EH31. . . . .**52** B2
  Loanhead EH20 . . . .**172** C7
Muirfield Ho EH31 . . . .**52** B3
Muirfield Pk EH31 . . . .**52** B3
Muirfield Rd
  Dunbar EH42 . . . .**106** D7
  Stenhousemuir FK5. . . . .**38** E2
Muirfield Station EH31 . . . . .**52** C3
Muirfield Steading EH31. . .**52** C3
Muirfield Terr EH31 . . . .**52** B2
Muirfield Way EH54 . . . .**142** E6
Muirhall Pl FK5. . . . .**38** C3
Muirhall Rd FK5 . . . .**38** C3
Muirhead Ave EH42 . . . .**60** A8
Muirhead Pl Harthill ML7 . .**159** D4
  Penicuik EH26 . . . .**191** F8
Muirhead Rd FK5. . . . .**38** E4
Muirhouse Ave EH4. . . . .**92** B4
Muirhouse Avenue N EH4 .**92** B4
Muirhouse Bank EH4 . . . .**92** A4
Muirhouse Cl EH4 . . . .**92** A4
Muirhouse Cres EH4 . . . .**92** B5
Muirhouse Dr EH4. . . . .**92** A5
Muirhouse Gdns EH4. . . . . . .**92** A5
Muirhouse Gn EH4. . . . .**92** A5
Muirhouse Gr EH4 . . . .**92** A5
Muirhouse Loan EH4. . . . .**92** A5
Muirhouse Medway EH4 . . .**92** A5
Muirhouse Parkway EH4 . . .**92** A4
Muirhouse Pk EH4 . . . .**92** A4
Muirhouse Place E EH4 . . . .**92** B4
Muirhouse Place W EH4 . . . .**92** B4
Muirhouses Ave EH51 . . . .**64** C6
Muirhouses Cres EH51. . . . . .**64** C6
Muirhouses Sq EH51. . . . .**64** C7
Muirhouse Terr EH4 . . . .**92** A4
Muirhouse View EH4 . . . .**92** A5
Muirhouse Way EH4 . . . .**92** B4
Muirlaun ML11 . . . .**201** A1
Muirlee Rd ML8 . . . .**215** B1
Muirpark EH22 . . . .**152** E1
Muirpark Ct EH33 . . . .**126** E5
Muirpark Dr Shieldhill FK1.**81** D6
  Tranent EH33 . . . .**126** E5
Muirpark Gdns
  Tranent EH33 . . . .**126** E5
  Tullibody FK10 . . . .**4** E4
Muirpark Gn EH33 . . . .**126** E5
Muirpark Gr EH33 . . . .**126** E5
Muirpark Pl EH33 . . . .**126** E5
Muirpark Rd EH33 . . . .**126** E5
Muirpark Terr EH33 . . . .**126** E5
Muirpark Wynd EH33 . . . . .**126** E5
Muir Pl EH33 . . . .**29** D7
Muir Rd Bathgate EH48.**140** F7
  Pumpherston EH54 . . . . . .**144** A8
  Townhill KY12 . . . .**29** D7
Muirside Ave EH10 . . . .**4** C3
Muirside Ct KY12 . . . .**27** C1
Muirside Dr EH33. . . . .**126** E5
Muirside Gr KY12 . . . .**27** C1
Muirside La KY12 . . . .**44** C8
Muirside Rd
  Cairneyhill KY12 . . . .**27** C1
  Tullibody FK10 . . . .**4** C3
Muirs The FK10 . . . .**4** C4
Muirton Rdbt FK7. . . . .**7** F7
Muirton Way KY11 . . . .**48** B5
Muir Wood Cres EH14. . . . . .**148** B5
Muir Wood Dr EH14. . . . .**148** B5
Muir Wood Gr EH14. . . . .**148** B5
Muir Wood Pl EH14 . . . .**148** B5
Muir Wood Rd EH14. . . . .**148** B6
Mulberry Dr KY11. . . . .**29** E1
Mulberry Pl EH6 . . . .**93** C5
Mull Ct Alloa FK10 . . . .**10** B5
  Grangemouth FK3 . . . .**61** D6
Mulloch Ave **1** FK2. . . . .**60** A8
Multiplex Rdbt EH54 . . . . . .**143** E1
Multrees Wlk EH1 . . . .**229** A4
Mumrills Rd FK2. . . . .**61** C4
Mungalend Rd FK2 . . . .**60** B7
Mungalhead Rd FK2 . . . .**60** B7
Mungal Pl FK2. . . . .**60** B8

Mungle Pl EH55 . . . .**163** D3
Mungle St EH55 . . . .**163** D3
Mungoswells Cotts EH39. .**72** D2
Munro Ave FK2 . . . .**2** B4
Munro Dr EH13 . . . .**149** A5
Munro Gate FK9 . . . .**2** A5
Munro Gdns FK2. . . . .**60** F3
Munro Pl FK10. . . . .**9** F6
Munro Rd FK7 . . . .**7** A3
Munro St Kirkcaldy KY1 . . . . .**17** B2
  Stenhousemuir FK5. . . . .**38** E3
Munro Way EH54 . . . .**143** C8
Murano Pl EH7 . . . .**93** F2
Murderdean Rd EH22 . . . . .**174** A5
Murdoch Terr EH11 . . . .**228** A1
Murdostoun Cres ML7 . . . .**159** F6
Murieston Cres EH11 . . . . . .**120** E6
Murieston Crescent La
  EH11 . . . .**120** E6
Murieston Dr EH54 . . . .**165** A6
Murieston Gn EH54 . . . .**165** A6
Murieston East Rd EH54 . .**165** B8
Murieston Gdns EH54 . . . .**165** A7
Murieston La EH11 . . . .**120** E6
Murieston Mews EH54 . . . .**164** F5
Murieston Pk EH54 . . . .**164** F5
Murieston Pl EH11 . . . .**120** E6
Murieston Rd
  Edinburgh EH11. . . . .**120** E6
  Livingston EH54. . . . .**164** E4
Murieston Terr EH11 . . . . . .**120** E6
Murieston Vale EH54 . . . . . .**164** F5
Murieston Valley EH54 . . . .**164** F6
Murieston Way EH54 . . . . . .**165** A6
Murieston West Rd EH54 . .**164** F7
Murieston Wlk EH54 . . . . . .**164** F5
Murieston Wood EH54 . . . .**164** F5
Murnin Ct FK7 . . . .**7** C3
Murnin Rd FK4 . . . .**58** A4
Murnin Road Ind Est FK4.**58** A4
Murrayburn App EH11 . . . .**119** D1
Murrayburn Dr EH14. . . . . .**119** D1
Murrayburn Gate EH14. . . .**148** D8
Murrayburn Gdns EH14 . . .**119** E1
Murrayburn Gn EH14 . . . . .**119** D1
Murrayburn Gr EH14 . . . . . .**119** E1
Murrayburn Junc EH14. . . .**148** D8
Murrayburn Pk EH14 . . . . . .**119** E1
Murrayburn Pl EH14 . . . . . .**119** D1
Murrayburn Prim Sch
  EH11 . . . .**119** E2
Murrayburn Rd EH14. . . . . .**119** E2
Murray Cotts EH12 . . . .**119** C6
Murray Cres FK2. . . . .**83** A6
Murray St Armadale EH48 .**139** F4
  Dunbar EH42 . . . .**106** D7
Murrayfield Ave EH12 . . . . .**120** D7
Murrayfield Dr
  Blackburn EH47. . . . .**162** D8
  Edinburgh EH12. . . . .**120** C7
Murrayfield Gdns EH12 . . . .**120** C7
Murrayfield Hospl EH12. . .**120** A7
Murrayfield Pl
  Bannockburn FK7 . . . .**7** D1
  Edinburgh EH12. . . . .**120** C7
Murrayfield Prim Sch
  EH47 . . . .**141** D1
Murrayfield Rd EH12 . . . . . .**120** C7
Murrayfield Rugby Gd
  EH12 . . . .**120** C6
Murrayfield Terr
  Bannockburn FK7 . . . .**7** D1
  Blackburn EH47. . . . .**162** D8
Murray Pl Aberdour KY3. . . .**49** C8
  Cambusbarron FK7 . . . .**6** D5
  Stirling FK8 . . . .**7** B7
Murrays Brae The FK7 . . . . .**151** C4
Murraysgate Cres EH47 . . .**160** F6
Murraysgate Ind Est
  EH47 . . . .**160** F6
Murrays The EH17 . . . .**151** C4
Murray Terr KY2 . . . .**17** B5
Murray Way EH54 . . . .**143** D8
Murrell Rd KY3 . . . .**49** C8
Murrell Terr KY3. . . . .**49** C8
Museum of Communication
  KY3 . . . .**50** E8
Museum of Edinburgh
  EH8 . . . .**229** B3
Music Hall La **2** KY12 . . . . .**29** A3
Mus of Childhood EH1 . . .**229** B3
Mus of Edinburgh EH8. . .**229** B3
Musselburgh Burgh Prim Sch
  EH21 . . . .**124** C6
Musselburgh Gram Sch
  EH21 . . . .**124** C5
Musselburgh Rd
  Dalkeith EH22 . . . .**153** B4
  Edinburgh EH15. . . . .**123** B4
Musselburgh Sta EH21 . . .**124** A4
Myers Ct KY12 . . . .**29** D5
Myles Farm Cotts EH33 . .**126** A4
Myles Ho FK8 . . . .**7** A8
Mylnburn Gdns EH11. . . . . .**45** D3
Mylne Pl FK2. . . . .**39** B2
Myothill Rd FK6 . . . .**57** D7
Myot View FK6 . . . .**57** A6
Myre Cres KY3 . . . .**35** A3
Myre Dale EH19 . . . .**173** C6
Myreside EH19 . . . .**173** D5
Myreside Ct EH10 . . . .**120** F2
Myreside Rd EH10 . . . .**120** F3
Myreside View EH10 . . . . . .**120** E3
Myreton FK11 . . . .**4** A6
Myreton Dr FK7 . . . .**19** E8
Myreton Motor Mus EH32 .**72** B3

Myreton Rd FK3 . . . .**61** D6
Myreton Way FK1 . . . .**59** F3
Myretoungate FK12 . . . .**4** E6
Myrtle Cres Bilston EH25 .**171** E6
  Kirkcaldy KY2 . . . .**17** B7
Myrtle Gr EH22 . . . .**174** D7
Myrtle Terr EH11 . . . .**120** E5
Myrtle Wynd KY12 . . . .**28** F5

N

Nagle Rd KY12. . . . .**12** A1
Nailer Rd Falkirk FK1 . . . .**59** E6
  Stirling FK7 . . . .**7** B2
Nairn Ct FK1 . . . .**60** D1
Nairn Rd EH54 . . . .**142** E8
Nairn St KY1 . . . .**17** D6
Naismith Ct KY3 . . . .**40** E1
Namayo Ave FK3 . . . .**61** A5
Namur Rd EH26. . . . .**192** A8
Nantwich Dr EH7. . . . .**94** E3
Napier Ave EH48 . . . .**141** C6
Napier Cres EH54 . . . .**60** A7
Napier Loan EH10 . . . .**120** F4
Napier Pl FK2 . . . .**60** A7
Napier Rd EH10. . . . .**121** A4
Napier Sq EH54 . . . .**60** A7
Napier St KY1 . . . .**17** E8
Napier Univ EH11 . . . .**119** D2
Napier Univ (Comely Bank
  Campus) EH4 . . . .**92** E2
Napier Univ (Craighouse
  Campus) EH11 . . . .**120** E4
Napier Univ (Craiglockhart
  Campus) EH14 . . . .**120** D1
Napier Univ (Marchmont
  Campus) EH9 . . . .**121** D5
Napier Univ (Merchiston
  Campus) EH10 . . . .**121** A4
Nasmyth Ct EH54 . . . .**144** B6
Nasmyth Rd KY11. . . . .**46** B2
Nasmyth Sq EH54 . . . .**144** A6
Natal Pl KY12 . . . .**13** D3
Nat Gallery of Scotland
  EH2 . . . .**228** C3
National Flag Heritage Ctr
  EH39 . . . .**101** F7
National Lib of Scotland
  EH1 . . . .**229** A2
National Liby of Scotland
  EH3 . . . .**229** A2
National Monument EH7 .**229** B4
National Museum of Flight
  EH39 . . . .**74** B1
National Portrait Gall
  EH2 . . . .**229** A4
Nat War Mus of Scotland
  EH1 . . . .**228** C2
Navar Ct ML7. . . . .**180** A3
Nebit The FK12 . . . .**4** E6
Neidpath Ct
  2 Edinburgh EH12. . . . . . .**119** A7
  Longniddry EH32 . . . .**98** E5
Neidpath Dr FK5. . . . .**39** A4
Neidpath Pl KY12 . . . .**29** D6
Neilson Ct EH47 . . . .**162** B8
Neilson Gr KY3 . . . .**33** E1
Neilson Park Rd EH41. . . . .**130** A8
Neilson Sq EH54 . . . .**142** C5
Neilson St FK1. . . . .**60** B4
Neilston EH54 . . . .**142** F6
Nellfield EH16 . . . .**151** B8
Nelson's Monument EH7 .**229** B4
Nelson Ave EH54. . . . .**143** F3
Nelson Gdns FK3 . . . .**40** E1
Nelson Pl FK7 . . . .**7** C6
Nelson Rd EH51 . . . .**62** E6
Nelson St Edinburgh EH3 .**228** C4
  Grangemouth FK3 . . . .**61** E8
  Kirkcaldy KY2 . . . .**17** E7
  Rosyth KY11 . . . .**46** E5
Ness The KY12 . . . .**26** E1
Nether Bakehouse EH8. . .**229** C3
Netherbank EH16 . . . .**150** F6
Netherbank View EH16. . . .**150** F6
Netherbeath Rd KY4 . . . .**30** F8
Netherby Rd Airth FK2. . . . . .**22** E8
  Edinburgh EH5 . . . .**93** A6
Nether Craigour EH17. . . . .**151** B7
Nether Craigwell EH8. . . . .**229** C3
Nether Currie Cres EH14 .**148** B5
Nether Currie Pl EH14 . . . .**148** B5
Nether Currie Prim Sch
  EH14 . . . .**148** B5
Nether Currie Rd EH14. . . .**148** B5
Nether Dechmont Cotts
  EH54 . . . .**143** B7
Nether Dechmont Pl
  EH54 . . . .**143** B7
Netherfaulds Dr FK6. . . . .**36** D1
Netherfield Rd FK2 . . . .**61** D1
Nethergate KY3. . . . .**35** A2
Nethergate The FK12. . . . .**4** E6
Netherlaw EH39 . . . .**54** B6
Nether Liberton Ct EH16 .**122** A2
Nethermains Prim Sch
  FK6. . . . .**36** D1
Nethermains Rd FK6 . . . .**36** C2
Nethershot Rd EH32 . . . .**97** A2
Nether St Dysart KY1 . . . .**18** B7
  Kirkcaldy KY1. . . . .**17** C6
Netherton Gr EH47. . . . .**161** B4
Netherton Pl EH47 . . . .**161** B4
Netherton St ML7. . . . .**159** D5
Netherton Broad St
  KY12. . . . .**29** A2
Netherwood Pk EH54 . . . .**143** A7

Nettlehill Dr EH54 ....115 A1
Nettlehill Rd
  Livingston EH54 ....143 E8
  Livingston EH54 ....143 F8
  Uphall Station EH54 .....115 A1
Neuk The ML11 ....217 F8
Nevis Cres FK10 ....10 B8
Nevis Dr EH54 ....164 F6
Nevis Gdns EH26 ....192 A7
Nevis Pl Falkirk FK1 ....60 C2
  Grangemouth FK3 ....61 E5
  Shotts ML7 ....180 B3
New Arthur Pl EH8 ....229 B2
Newbattle Abbey Coll
  EH22 ....153 A1
Newbattle Abbey Cres
  EH22 ....173 F8
Newbattle Com High Sch
  EH22 ....174 C7
Newbattle Gdns EH22 ....153 A1
Newbattle Rd
  Dalkeith EH22 ....152 F2
  Newtongrange EH22 .....174 A7
Newbattle Terr EH10 .....121 B4
New Bell's Cl EH1 ....94 A5
Newbigging Cres FK10 .....4 C2
Newbigging
  Auchtertool KY2 ....15 C2
  Musselburgh EH21 ......124 D5
  Musselburgh EH21 ......124 D7
Newbigging Rd KY12 ......27 C2
Newbigging Terr KY2 ......15 C2
Newbiggin Rd FK3 ....61 E6
Newbridge Ind Est EH28 116 F5
Newbridge Junc EH28 ....117 B6
Newbridge Rd EH28 ......117 A5
New Broompark EH5 ....92 E7
Newburn Pl KY12 ....229 D3
Newbyres Ave EH23 ......174 C1
Newbyres Cres EH23 .....195 C8
Newbyres Gdns EH23 .....195 C8
Newbyth Stables EH40 .....75 D5
Newbyth Steading EH40 ...75 D5
Newcarron Ct [3] FK2 .....60 A8
New Carron Rd FK2,FK5 ...39 A3
New Century Dr ML7 .....179 E4
New Coll EH1 ....228 C3
New Cove Farm Cotts
  TD13 ....219 A4
Newcraighall Bsns Pk
  EH15 ....123 B4
Newcraighall Dr EH21 ...123 D4
Newcraighall Prim Sch
  EH21 ....123 C4
Newcraighall Rd EH15 ...123 C4
Newcraighall Sta EH21 ...123 D4
New Cut Rigg EH6 ....93 D5
Newhailes Ave EH21 .....124 A6
Newhailes Cres EH21 ....123 F5
Newhailes Rd EH21 ......123 F5
Newhall EH26 ....206 F6
New Hallglen Rd FK1 ......60 D2
Newhalls Rd EH30 ....68 C1
Newhaven Heritage Mus
  EH6 ....93 D7
Newhaven Main St EH6 ....93 D7
Newhaven Pl EH6 ....93 D7
Newhaven Rd EH6 ....93 D5
New Holygate EH52 ......115 D5
New Hos Drem EH39 ....73 A4
  East Fortune EH39 ....74 D3
  Garvald EH41 ....132 D2
Newhouse FK8 ....7 A5
Newhouse Ave EH42 ....78 E1
Newhouse Bsns Pk FK3 ....61 C7
Newhouse Dr FK1 ....59 E2
Newhouse Pl EH42 ....78 E1
Newhouse Rd FK3 ....61 D7
Newhouses Rd
  Broxburn EH52 ....116 A4
  Broxburn EH52 ....116 A4
Newhouse Terr EH42 ......78 E1
New Hunterfield EH23 ....174 B2
Newington La FK5 ....37 D6
Newington Rd EH9 ....121 E5
New John's Pl EH8 ....229 B2
New La EH6 ....93 D6
New Lairdship Pl EH11 ...119 D3
New Lairdship Yards
  EH11 ....119 D3
Newland Ave EH48 ....141 B6
Newlandrig EH23 ....175 B2
Newlands EH27 ....166 F7
Newlands Pk
  Dunfermline KY12 ....29 B5
  Edinburgh EH9 ....121 F4
Newlands Pl FK10 ....4 C8
Newlands Rd
  Bannockburn FK7 ....19 D8
  Grangemouth FK3 ....61 C6
  Polmont FK2 ....82 C8
Newlands Road Rdbt [5]
  FK2 ....82 C8
New Line Rd FK7 ....19 A7
Newliston Dr KY2 ....16 C7
New Liston Rd EH29 ......89 A1
Newmains Farm La EH29 ..89 A2
Newmains Rd EH29 ....89 A2
Newmains Smallholdings
  EH39 ....73 C2
Newmarket FK7 ....7 E1
Newmarket Ctr [5] FK1 ...60 B5
New Market Rd EH14 .....120 C3
Newmarket St [7] FK1 .....60 B5
New Mart Rd EH14 ....120 B3
New Meadowspott EH22 153 A3

Newmill and Canthill Rd
  ML7 ....179 B6
Newmills FK10 ....4 B3
Newmills Ave EH14 ......147 D3
Newmills Cres EH14 .....147 D3
Newmills Gr EH14 ....147 D3
Newmills Rd Currie EH14 147 C4
  Dalkeith EH22 ....153 B3
Newmills Terr EH22 .....153 B3
New Orchardfield EH6 .....93 F4
Newpark Cres FK7 ....7 A2
Newpark Rd
  Livingston EH54 ....164 D6
  Stirling FK7 ....7 B2
New Rd FK7 ....7 B2
New Row Dunfermline KY12 29 A3
  East Fortune EH39 ....74 B3
  Kincardine FK10 ....24 A3
  Tranent EH33 ....126 C6
New Skinners Cl EH1 ....229 B3
New St Bridge of A FK9 ....1 F8
  Cockenzie & Port Seton
  EH32 ....97 C4
  Dalkeith EH22 ....153 B3
  Musselburgh EH21 ......124 B6
  Prestonpans EH32 ....96 F1
  Slamannan FK1 ....108 B7
  Tranent EH33 ....126 C7
New Star Bank EH22 .....174 A5
New Swanston EH10 .....149 F5
Newton EH52 ....174 B5
Newton Ave KY2 ....40 A3
Newton Church Rd EH22 152 C7
Newton Cotts EH22 ......153 A8
Newton Cres EH11 ....47 A4
Newtongrange Pl EH22 174 A4
Newtongrange Prim Sch
  EH22 ....174 B5
Newtonlees Cotts EH42 106 F7
Newton Loan Ct EH23 ...174 B2
Newton of St Andrew's
  Prim Sch EH22 ....174 A3
Newton Pl KY11 ....46 F4
Newton Port EH41 ....101 B1
Newton Rd EH42 ....40 A2
Newtonshaw FK10 ....5 C1
Newton St
  Easthouses EH22 ....174 C6
  Edinburgh EH11 ....120 E5
New Tower Pl EH15 ....95 B1
Newtown EH51 ....63 F6
Newtown Cotts EH51 .....63 F6
New Well Wynd EH49 .....84 F6
Newyearfield Bsns Pk
  EH54 ....143 C5
Newyearfield Rdbt EH54 143 C5
Ney Ct KY11 ....30 A1
Nicholfield EH6 ....93 D6
Nicholson Pl EH8 ....59 F2
Nicholson Way EH54 .....143 D7
Nicklaus Gn EH54 ....143 B8
Nicol Dr KY3 ....34 A2
Nicol Pl KY11 ....115 D5
Nicol Rd EH52 ....115 D5
Nicolson St EH8 ....229 B2
Nicolson St EH8 ....229 B2
Nicolson St KY1 ....17 B3
Nicolton Ave FK2 ....82 E7
Nicolton Ct [2] FK2 ......82 F7
Nicolton Rd FK2 ....83 B8
Niddrie Cotts EH15 ......123 C4
Niddrie Farm Gr EH16 ...122 F4
Niddrie House Ave EH16 122 F3
Niddrie House Dr EH16 ..123 A3
Niddrie House Gdns
  EH16 ....122 F3
Niddrie House Pk EH16 ..122 F3
Niddrie House Sq EH16 ..122 F3
Niddrie Mains Ct EH16 ..123 A4
Niddrie Mains Dr
  Edinburgh EH16 ....122 E4
  Edinburgh EH16 ....123 A4
Niddrie Mains Rd EH16 122 E4
Niddrie Mains Terr
  Edinburgh EH16 ....122 E4
  Edinburgh EH16 ....122 F5
Niddrie Marischal Cres
  EH16 ....122 F3
Niddrie Marischal Dr
  EH16 ....122 F3
Niddrie Marischal Gdns [1]
  EH16 ....122 F3
Niddrie Marischal Gn
  EH16 ....122 F3
Niddrie Marischal Gr
  EH16 ....123 A4
Niddrie Marischal Loan [2]
  EH16 ....122 F3
Niddrie Marischal Pl
  EH16 ....122 F3
Niddrie Marischal Rd
  EH16 ....123 A3
Niddrie Marischal St [3]
  EH16 ....123 A3
Niddrie Mill Ave EH15 ..123 A4
Niddrie Mill Cres EH15 ..123 A4
Niddrie Mill Dr EH15 ....123 A4
Niddrie Mill Gr EH15 ....123 A4
Niddrie Mill Pl EH15 ....123 A4
Niddrie Mill Prim Sch
  EH15 ....123 A4
Niddrie Mill Terr EH15 123 A4
Niddry Rd EH52 ....87 F2
Niddry St S EH1 ....229 B2
Niddry St EH1 ....229 A3

Niddry View EH52 ....87 F2
Nigel Loan EH16 ....151 B8
Nigel Rise EH54 ....143 F1
Nile Gr EH10 ....121 B3
Nile St KY2 ....17 B6
Nimmo Ave EH32 ....97 A1
Ninian Rd EH51 ....62 E6
Ninth St EH22 ....174 B6
Nisbet Dr FK6 ....36 D2
Nisbet Rd EH31 ....51 F2
Nithsdale Pl KY11 ....30 C1
Nithsdale St ML7 ....179 D5
Nith St KY11 ....29 F2
Niven's Knowe Rd EH20 171 F7
Niven Rd KY11 ....47 C3
Nivensknowe Pk EH20 ..171 F7
No 7 Pit Rd KY4 ....13 C4
Nobel Pl EH25 ....171 F3
Nobel View FK2 ....82 A8
Noble Pl EH6 ....94 B4
Normand Brae KY1 ....18 A7
Normand Rd KY1 ....18 A8
Normandy Pl KY11 ....46 E2
Norman Rise EH54 ....143 F1
North Approach Rd EH12 23 E3
North Ave FK3 ....83 B7
Northbank Cotts EH48 ..141 B7
Northbank Dr EH51 ....64 A5
Northbank Pk EH51 ....63 F5
Northbank Rd KY12 ......27 D1
North Bank Rd
  Prestonpans EH32 ....96 E1
  Prestonpans EH32 ......125 E8
North Bank St EH1 ......229 A3
North Belton Cotts EH42 105 B7
North Berwick High Sch
  EH39 ....54 B7
North Berwick Sta EH39 54 B7
North Bridge EH1 ....229 A3
North Bridge St
  Bathgate EH48 ....141 A6
  Grangemouth FK3 ....40 C1
North Broomage Rdbt
  FK5 ....38 A3
North Bughtlin Bank
  EH12 ....91 B1
North Bughtlin Brae EH12 91 B1
North Bughtlinfield EH12 91 A1
North Bughtlin Gate EH12 91 A1
North Bughtlin Neuk
  EH12 ....91 B1
North Bughtlin Pl EH12 ..91 B1
North Bughtlin Rd EH12 ..91 A1
North Bughtlinrig EH12 ..91 A1
North Bughtlinside EH12 91 A1
North Cairntow EH16 ...122 D5
North Castle St Alloa FK10 10 A5
  Edinburgh EH2 ....228 B4
North Charlotte St EH2 228 B3
Northcliff KY11 ....68 B6
North Clyde Street La
  EH1 ....229 A4
Northcote St EH11 ......120 F6
North Cres EH32 ....97 C4
North East Circus Pl [6]
  EH3 ....93 B2
North East Cumberland
  Street La EH3 ....93 C2
North East Thistle Street La
  EH2 ....228 C4
North Elphinstone Farm
  Cotts EH33 ....126 B2
North Esk Rd KY11 ....46 C2
North Fed KY4 ....6 D6
Northfield
  Cowdenbeath KY4 ....13 C6
  Tranent EH33 ....126 E6
Northfield Ave
  Edinburgh EH16 ....122 D8
  Shotts ML7 ....180 B2
Northfield Broadway
  EH8 ....122 E8
Northfield Cir EH8 ......122 D8
Northfield Cres EH55 ...163 C3
Northfield Cres
  Edinburgh EH8 ....122 E8
  Longridge EH47 ....161 C1
Northfield Ct
  Prestonpans EH32 ......125 F8
  West Calder EH55 ......163 C3
Northfield Dr EH8 ....122 E7
Northfield E EH33 ....126 E6
Northfield Farm Ave
  EH8 ....122 E8
Northfield Farm Rd EH8 122 E8
Northfield Gdns
  Clackmannan FK10 ......11 B4
  Edinburgh EH8 ....122 E7
  Prestonpans EH32 ......125 F8
Northfield Mdws EH47 ..161 C1
Northfield Park Gr EH8 122 E8
Northfield Pk EH8 ......122 E8
Northfield Rd Denny FK6 36 C4
  Edinburgh EH8 ....122 D7
Northfield Sq EH8 ......122 E8
Northfield Terr
  Edinburgh EH8 ....122 D8
  Longridge EH47 ....161 C1
North Fort St EH6 ....93 E6
North Gate EH48 ....111 F6
North Grange Ave EH32 96 E1
North Grange Gr EH32 ...96 F1
North Grange Rd EH32 ...96 F1
North Green Dr FK2 ......22 D4

North Greendykes Rd
  EH52 ....115 E7
North Greens EH15 ......123 B5
North Gyle Ave EH12 ...119 B6
North Gyle Dr EH12 .....119 B7
North Gyle Farm Ct
  EH12 ....119 A6
North Gyle Farm La
  EH12 ....119 A6
North Gyle Gr EH12 .....119 A6
North Gyle Loan EH12 ..119 A7
North Gyle Pk EH12 .....119 A7
North Gyle Rd EH12 .....119 B7
North Gyle Terr EH12 ...119 A6
North High St
  Musselburgh EH21 ......124 B6
  Musselburgh EH21 ......124 C6
North Junction St EH6 ...93 E6
North Larches KY11 ......29 F4
Northlawn Ct EH4 ....91 E4
Northlawn Terr EH4 ......91 E4
North Leith Mill EH6 .....93 E6
North Leith Mill EH6 .....93 E6
North Leith Sands EH6 ...93 E6
North Loanhead KY11 ...45 E3
North Lorimer Pl EH32 ...97 B4
North Main St EH32 ......39 C3
North Meggetland EH14 120 D3
North Overgate KY3 ......34 F3
Northpark Pl EH4 ....93 A4
North Park Terr EH4 ......93 A2
North Peffer Pl EH16 ...122 D4
North Queensferry Prim Sch
  KY11 ....68 C6
North Queensferry Sta
  KY11 ....68 C6
North Rd Dunbar EH42 ...78 C3
  Fauldhouse EH47 ....181 E7
  Inverkeithing KY11 .....47 C1
North Reeves Pl EH47 ..161 B5
North Richmond St EH8 229 B2
North Roundall KY11 ....45 E3
North Row KY11 ....45 B4
North St Andrew La EH2 228 C4
North St Andrew St EH2 229 A4
North St David St EH2 ..229 A4
North Seton Pk EH32 ....97 D4
North Shore Rd FK3 ......40 E2
North St Alloa FK10 ......10 A7
  Armadale EH48 ....139 F6
  Bo'ness EH51 ....63 F8
  Clackmannan FK10 ......11 A4
  Dunbar EH42 ....78 D3
  Falkirk FK2 ....60 B8
  Lochgelly KY5 ....14 A6
  Ratho EH28 ....117 A2
  Stirling FK9 ....2 D1
Northumberland Place La
  EH3 ....228 C4
Northumberland St EH3 228 C4
Northumberland Street NW
  La EH3 ....228 C4
Northumberland Street SE La
  EH3 ....228 C4
Northumberland Street SW
  La EH3 ....228 C4
North View Burntisland KY3 50 F8
  West Calder EH55 ......163 D3
North View Cotts KY4 ...31 A8
North Werber Pk EH4 ....92 E3
North Werber Rd EH4 ....92 E4
North West Cumberland
  Street La EH3 ....93 C2
North West Thistle Street La
  EH2 ....228 C4
Northwood Pk EH14 .....142 E7
Northwood Rd FK10 ......4 D2
North Wynd EH22 ....153 A3
Norton Pk EH7 ....94 A2
Norton Pl KY11 ....29 E1
Norton St FK12 ....5 B7
Norval Pl KY11 ....46 F4
Norwood Ave Alloa FK10 9 F7
  Bonnybridge FK4 ....58 B7
  Whitburn EH47 ....161 B5
Norwood Cres FK10 ......9 F7
Norwood Ct
  Bonnybridge FK4 ....58 B7
  Whitburn EH47 ....161 B5
Norwood Pk FK10 ....9 F7
Norwood Ind Est EH47 ..161 A5
Norwood Pl FK4 ....58 B7
Nosirrom Terr EH5 ....65 E5
Novar Cres KY11 ....17 B2
Nungate Rd EH39 ....54 B4
Nunraw Abbey EH41 ....132 E1
Nursery Rd FK1 ....59 E4

O

O'Hanlon Way FK8 ....1 F7
Oak Ave EH20 ....171 F7
Oakbank EH20 ....61 A2
Oakbank Ave EH55 ......163 D6
Oakbank Cotts EH55 ....163 D6
Oakbank Park Pl EH53 ..165 C8
Oakbank Park Way EH53 165 C8
Oakbank Rd EH53 ....165 C8
Oakbank Rdbt EH53 .....165 C8
Oak Cres Mayfield EH22 174 E6
  Plean FK7 ....20 C3

Oak Dr Fallin FK7 ....8 D4
  Stenhousemuir FK5 .....38 D1
Oakfield Pl EH8 ....229 B2
Oakfield St KY4 ....17 C8
Oakfield View KY11 ......46 E8
  Livingston EH54 ....144 B6
Oakhill View FK2 ....83 B6
Oak La KY12 ....91 E1
Oaklands Specl Sch
  EH11 ....119 E3
Oakley Ind Est KY12 ....26 F7
Oak Pl EH22 ....174 F6
Oak St FK8 ....1 F5
Oaktree Ct KY1 ....17 C8
Oaktree Junc EH41 .....129 B8
Oaktree Sq KY1 ....17 C8
Oakum Bay KY12 ....26 C1
Oakville Terr EH6 ....94 B3
Oakwood Education Trust
  FK5 ....60 F2
Oatridge Ag Coll EH52 114 F8
Oberon FK2 ....9 F8
Observatory Gn EH9 ...121 E2
Observatory Rd EH9 ...121 E2
Ocean Dr EH6 ....93 E7
Ocean Terminal Sh Ctr
  EH6 ....93 F7
Ochil Ave KY2 ....16 F5
Ochil Cres FK8 ....2 B2
Ochil Ct Queensferry EH30 89 C8
  Tullibody FK10 ....4 C3
Ochil Dr Maddiston FK2 83 A5
  Stenhousemuir FK5 .....38 D3
Ochil La EH47 ....160 F6
Ochil Rd Alva FK12 ......5 B7
  Menstrie FK11 ....4 A7
Ochil Sch FK9 ....2 C4
Ochil St Alloa FK10 .....10 A7
  Grangemouth FK3 ....61 D7
  Tullibody FK10 ....4 B3
Ochil Terr
  Dunfermline KY11 ....29 E2
  Falkirk FK2 ....39 A2
Ochiltree Cres EH53 ...144 B2
Ochiltree Dr EH53 .....144 B2
Ochiltree Gdns EH16 ...122 C1
Ochiltree Terr FK1 ......59 B5
Ochilvale Terr FK10 ......5 B3
Ochilview Alva FK12 .....4 F6
  Cowie FK7 ....20 E6
Ochil View
  Cowdenbeath KY4 ....13 E6
  Denny FK6 ....57 D8
  Kincardine FK10 ....23 D4
  Shieldhill FK1 ....81 D7
Ochilview FK5 ....38 C5
Ochilview Dr KY12 .....26 B2
Ochilview Pl
  (Stenhousemuir FC)
  FK5 ....38 B5
Ochilview Rd EH51 ......63 E6
Ochilview Rd EH51 ......63 E6
Ochilview Sq EH48 .....139 F5
Ochilview Terr EH51 ...63 E6
Ochre Cres FK7 ....20 C8
Octavia St KY1 ....17 B5
Ogilface Cres EH48 ....138 C2
Ogilvie Pl FK9 ....2 A6
Ogilvie Rd FK5 ....7 A5
Ogilvie Terr EH11 ......120 E4
Ogilvie Way EH54 ......143 D7
Ogilvy Cres EH47 ......181 F6
Old Abbey Rd EH39 .....54 B7
Old Assembly Cl EH1 ..229 A2
Old Bellsdyke Rd FK5 ..38 A3
Old Bridge St [11] FK10 10 B6
Old Bridge Wynd FK1 ...2 A4
Old Broughton [9] EH3 ..93 D2
Old Burdiehouse Rd
  EH17 ....151 A3
Old Church La EH15 ...122 C6
Old College Yd EH21 ..229 A2
Old Course Gate EH11 119 A1
Old Craighall Junc EH21 124 B2
Old Craighall Rd
  EH22 ....153 E8
Old Dalkeith Colliery
  EH22 ....153 E6
Old Dalkeith Rd
  Danderhall EH16 ....152 C6
  Edinburgh EH16 ....122 C1
Old Dean Rd EH32 ......98 D4
Old Denny Rd FK5 ......38 A3
Old Drove Rd
  Cambusbarron FK7 ......6 C5
  Carlops EH46 ....205 B4
Old Eastfield St ML7 ..159 D5
Old Farm Ave EH13 ....149 C7
Old Farm EH34 ....156 C6
Old Farm Pl EH13 .....149 B7
Old Fishmarket Cl EH1 229 A3
Old Forge Gr FK10 ......4 A4
Old Glendevon Farm Cotts
  EH52 ....87 D1
Old Golf Course Rd
  EH48 ....140 B4
Old Granary FK9 ....54 C8
Old Hillview Pl KY4 ....30 E6
Old Kirk Rd EH12 ......29 C4
Old Kirk Rd
  Dunfermline KY12 ......29 D4

Old Kirk Rd continued
Edinburgh EH12 . . . . 119 C7
North Queensferry KY11 . . . 68 C6
Old Linburn Rd KY11 . . . . 29 F4
Old Liston Rd EH28 . . . . 117 A6
Old Mill Ct EH47 . . . . . . 161 F7
Old Mill Ctyd The KY11 . . 29 B2
Old Mill Gr EH47 . . . . . . 161 F7
Old Mill La
  Edinburgh EH16 . . . . . . 122 A2
  Gifford EH41 . . . . 220 F7
  Kirkcaldy KY1 . . . . 26 E6
Old Mill Rd
  Broxburn EH52 . . . . 115 F5
  Hartwood ML7 . . . . 70 A5
Old Newmills Rd EH14 . 147 D3
Old Orch The KY11 . . . . . 45 D3
Old Perth Rd KY4 . . . . . . 13 A4
Old Redding Rd FK2 . . . . 60 F3
Old Refinery Rd FK3 . . . . 62 A8
Old St Mary's La EH51 . . 64 A8
Old School Ct FK10 . . . . . . 4 B2
Old Schoolhouse The KY4 31 A6
Old Sheriffmuir Rd FK9 . . . 2 C6
Old Star Rd EH22 . . . . . 174 A5
Old Tolbooth Wynd EH8 . 229 B3
Old Town Bannockburn FK7 . . 7 D1
Oldhall Prestonpans EH32 . . 115 F5
Oldwalls Pl FK3 . . . . 61 E7
Oldwalls Rd FK3,EH51 . . . 62 C8
Old Well Rd EH44 . . . . . 141 D3
Oldwood Pl EH54 . . . . . 143 B4
Oliphant Ct FK8 . . . . 2 B1
Oliphant Gdns EH21 . . . 125 C5
Olive Bank Rd EH21 . . . . 124 A6
Olivebank Ret Pk EH21 . . 124 A6
Oliver Rd FK1 . . . . 60 D4
Ollerton Ct KY1 . . . . 17 B5
Olympia Arc KY1 . . . . 17 B3
Onich Pl ML7 . . . . 180 B3
Onslow St EH54 . . . . . . 144 A5
Orchard Bank EH4 . . . . . . 92 E1
Orchard Brae EH4 . . . . . . 92 F1
Orchard Brae Ave EH4 . . . 92 F2
Orchard Brae Gardens W
  EH4 . . . . 92 E1
Orchard Brae Gdns EH4 . . 92 F2
Orchard Brae W **1** EH4 . . 92 F2
Orchard Cres
  Edinburgh EH4 . . . . 92 D1
  Prestonpans EH32 . . . . . 115 E7
Orchardcroft **5** FK8 . . . . . . 7 B7
Orchard Ct
  East Linton EH40 . . . . . . 103 E6
  Kinghorn KY3 . . . . 35 A4
  Longniddry EH32 . . . . . . 98 D4
Orchard Dr EH4 . . . . 92 D1
Orchardfield EH49 . . . . . . 98 C7
Orchardfield Ave EH12 . 119 D6
Orchardfield Terr EH27 . 146 A6
Orchard Gdns EH4 . . . . . . 35 A4
Orchard Gr Crombie KY12 . 44 D6
  Edinburgh EH4 . . . . 92 E1
  Haddington EH41 . . . . . . 101 A1
  Kincardine FK10 . . . . 23 E3
  Polmont FK2 . . . . 61 F2
Orchardhead Loan EH16 151 A8
Orchardhead Rd EH16 . . 151 A8
Orchard House Hospl FK8 . . 2 A1
Orchard La
  Crossford KY12 . . . . 28 B2
  Dysart KY1 . . . . 18 A7
Orchard Pk EH33 . . . . . . 126 C7
Orchard Pl Dysart KY1 . . . . 18 A7
  Edinburgh EH4 . . . . 92 E1
  Livingston EH54 . . . . . . 143 B5
Orchard Rd Bridge of A FK9 . . 2 A6
  Edinburgh EH4 . . . . 92 E1
  Grangemouth FK3 . . . . . . 62 C8
  Kinghorn KY3 . . . . 34 F3
Orchard Rd S EH4 . . . . . . 92 D3
Orchard Sq KY11 . . . . 45 D3
Orchard St Falkirk FK1 . . . . 60 B5
  Grangemouth FK3 . . . . . . 61 D7
Orchard Terr
  Edinburgh EH4 . . . . 92 E1
  Kinghorn KY3 . . . . 34 F4
  Torryburn KY12 . . . . 26 F1
Orchard The
  Crossford KY12 . . . . 28 B2
  Grangemouth FK2 . . . . . . 82 D8
  Musselburgh EH21 . . . . . 124 B5
  Ormiston EH35 . . . . 155 E7
  Tranent EH33 . . . . 126 C7
  Tullibody FK10 . . . . 4 B2
Orchard Toll EH4 . . . . 92 E1
Orchard View EH22 . . . . 152 C2
Ordnance Rd KY2 . . . . 29 D1
Oriel Cres KY2 . . . . 17 A4
Oriel Rd KY2 . . . . 16 E5
Orkney Ct FK10 . . . . 10 B5
Orkney Pl Falkirk FK1 . . . . . 60 B2
  Kirkcaldy KY1 . . . . 17 E7
Orlit Cotts EH39 . . . . 74 D3
Ormelie Terr EH15 . . . . . 123 C8
Ormidale Terr EH12 . . . . 120 D7
Ormiston Ave EH33 . . . . 126 E6
Ormiston Cres E EH33 . . 126 E6
Ormiston Cres W EH33 . . 126 E6
Ormiston Cross EH35 . . 155 E7
Ormiston Dr Alloa FK10 . . . . 4 F2
  East Calder EH53 . . . . . . 145 A3
Ormiston Farm Steadings
  EH27 . . . . 145 C2
Ormiston Pk KY12 . . . . . . 29 C6

Ormiston Pl EH32 . . . . 96 E1
Ormiston Prim Sch EH35 155 E7
Ormiston Rd
  Pathhead EH37 . . . . 176 A5
  Tranent EH33 . . . . 126 E5
Ormiston Terr EH12 . . . . 119 D6
Ormond Ct FK5 . . . . 38 A3
Oronsay Ave
  Maddiston FK2 . . . . 82 F6
  Maddiston FK2 . . . . 83 A6
Orrin Gr KY11 . . . . 48 A3
Orrock Dr KY3 . . . . 33 E2
Orrok Pk EH16 . . . . 122 A2
Orr Terr ML7 . . . . 159 C4
Orwell Pl Dunfermline KY12 29 C4
  Edinburgh EH11 . . . . 120 F6
Orwell Terr EH11 . . . . . . 120 F6
Osborne Ct EH30 . . . . 97 C4
Osborne Dr FK10 . . . . 23 F4
Osborne Gdns FK1 . . . . . . 59 F3
Osborne St FK1 . . . . 59 F3
Osborne Terr
  Cockenzie & Port Seton
    EH32 . . . . 97 C4
  Edinburgh EH12 . . . . 120 E7
Ossian Dr EH54 . . . . 164 F6
Oswald Ave FK3 . . . . 61 F8
Oswald Ct EH9 . . . . 121 D3
Oswald Rd EH9 . . . . 121 D3
Oswald St FK1 . . . . 60 B4
Oswalds Wynd KY1 . . . . . . 17 C4
Oswald Terr EH12 . . . . . . 119 D6
Otterburn Pk EH4 . . . . . . 149 B8
Otterston Gr KY11 . . . . . . 48 B4
Otterston Pl KY12 . . . . 16 E8
Oudenarde Ct ML8 . . . . . 215 B1
Our Dynamic Earth EH8 . 229 C3
Our Lady's Prim Sch
  EH47 . . . . 162 B2
Our Lady of Lourdes Prim
  Sch EH47 . . . . 162 C8
Overhailes Farm Cotts
  EH41 . . . . 103 A5
Overhaven KY11 . . . . 45 E3
Overshiel Farm Cotts
  EH53 . . . . 145 B6
Overton Cres Denny FK6 . 36 D1
  East Calder EH53 . . . . . . 145 A3
  Redding FK2 . . . . 61 B1
Overton Ct
  Dunfermline KY11 . . . . . . 46 F7
  Kirkcaldy KY1 . . . . 17 E8
Overton Mains KY1 . . . . . 17 E8
Overton Rd
  Grangemouth,Bowhouse
    FK3 . . . . 61 E6
  Grangemouth,Oil Refinery
    FK3 . . . . 62 B8
  Kirkcaldy KY1 . . . . 17 D8
Overton Terr FK6 . . . . 36 C2
Owen Sq EH54 . . . . 143 F1
Owen Stone St EH48 . . . 141 D3
Oxcars Dr KY11 . . . . 48 B3
Oxcraig St EH5 . . . . 92 F7
Oxenfoord Ave EH37 . . . 176 B5
Oxenfoord Dr EH37 . . . . 176 A5
Oxford St EH8 . . . . 229 C1
Oxford Terr EH4 . . . . 228 A4
Oxgang Rd FK3 . . . . 61 E7
Oxgangs Ave EH13 . . . . . 149 F7
Oxgangs Bank EH13 . . . . 149 E6
Oxgangs Brae EH13 . . . . 149 F6
Oxgangs Broadway EH13 149 F6
Oxgangs Cres EH13 . . . . 149 F7
Oxgangs Dr
  Edinburgh EH13 . . . . 149 E7
  Edinburgh EH13 . . . . 149 F7
Oxgangs Farm Ave EH13 149 E6
Oxgangs Farm Dr EH13 . 149 E6
Oxgangs Farm Gdns
  EH13 . . . . 149 E6
Oxgangs Farm Gr EH13 . 149 E6
Oxgangs Farm Loan
  EH13 . . . . 149 E6
Oxgangs Farm Terr
  EH13 . . . . 149 E6
Oxgangs Gdns EH13 . . . . 149 E7
Oxgangs Gn EH13 . . . . . 149 F7
Oxgangs Gr EH13 . . . . . . 149 F7
Oxgangs Hill EH13 . . . . . 149 F7
Oxgangs Ho EH13 . . . . . . 149 F7
Oxgangs Loan EH13 . . . . 149 F7
Oxgangs Medway EH13 . 149 F6
Oxgangs Path EH13 . . . . 149 F6
Oxgangs Path E EH13 . . . 149 F6
Oxgangs Pl EH13 . . . . . . 149 E7
Oxgangs Prim Sch EH13 149 D7
Oxgangs Rd EH13 . . . . . . 150 A5
Oxgangs Rd N
  Edinburgh EH13 . . . . 149 E7
  Edinburgh EH14 . . . . 149 F7
Oxgangs Rise EH13 . . . . 149 F7
Oxgangs Row EH13 . . . . 149 F6
Oxgangs St EH13 . . . . . . 149 F6
Oxgangs Terr EH13 . . . . 149 E6
Oxgangs View EH13 . . . . 149 F6

P

Paddockhall Cotts EH49 . . 65 C1
Paddockholm The EH12 . 119 E6
Paddock The Dirleton EH39 53 B5
  Gullane EH31 . . . . 52 A2
  Longniddry EH32 . . . . . . 98 B3
  Musselburgh EH21 . . . . . 124 D7
  North Berwick EH39 . . . . . 54 C6

Paddock The continued
  Whitekirk EH42 . . . . 75 E8
Page St KY5 . . . . 14 B8
Paisley Ave EH8 . . . . 122 D7
Paisley Cl EH1 . . . . 229 B3
Paisley Cres EH8 . . . . . . 122 C8
Paisley Dr EH8 . . . . 122 D7
Paisley Gdns EH8 . . . . . . 122 C8
Paisley Gr EH8 . . . . 122 D7
Paisley Terr EH8 . . . . 122 C8
Palmer Ct FK3 . . . . 61 D8
Palmer Pl Currie EH14 . 147 F4
  Kingseat KY12 . . . . 12 A1
Palmer Rd EH14 . . . . 147 F4
Palmer Rise EH54 . . . . . 148 A3
Palmerston Place La
  EH12 . . . . 228 A2
Palmerston Rd EH9 . . . . . 121 D5
Panbrae Rd EH51 . . . . 64 A8
Pan Ha' KY1 . . . . 18 A6
Pankhurst Loan EH22 . . . 153 D3
Panmure Pl EH3 . . . . 228 C1
Pannie Rd KY11 . . . . 17 D7
Panstead St EH3 . . . . 61 E7
Panton Gn EH54 . . . . 143 B8
Papana Cotts EH41 . . . . . 132 D5
Papple Farm Cotts EH41 132 D5
Paradise La EH15 . . . . 61 E8
Paradykes Ave EH20 . . . . 172 B8
Paradykes Prim Sch
  EH20 . . . . 172 B8
Pardovan Cres EH49 . . . . . 86 D7
Pardovan Holdings EH49 . 86 C7
Pardovan Pl FK1 . . . . 59 F6
Paris Ave FK6 . . . . 36 C1
Paris St FK3 . . . . 61 E8
Parkandarroch Cres
  ML8 . . . . 215 A1
Park Ave Bilston EH25 . . . 171 E6
  Bonnyrigg and Lasswade
    EH19 . . . . 173 B7
  Cockenzie & Port Seton
    EH32 . . . . 97 D4
  Cowdenbeath KY4 . . . . . . 13 B3
  Dalkeith EH22 . . . . 152 F2
  Edinburgh EH16 . . . . 151 B8
  Falkirk FK2 . . . . 39 A2
  Gifford EH41 . . . . 220 F6
  Loanhead EH20 . . . . 172 B7
  Westquarter FK2 . . . . 61 A3
Park Ct Broxburn EH52 . . 115 B5
  Musselburgh EH21 . . . . . 124 E5
  Shotts ML7 . . . . 179 F4
Park Dr Bannockburn FK7 . . 7 D2
  Grangemouth FK2 . . . . . . 82 D8
  Stenhousemuir FK5 . . . . . 38 D2
  West Calder EH55 . . . . . . 164 A5
Parkdyke FK7 . . . . 6 E6
Parkend Haddington EH41 129 F3
  Penicuik EH26 . . . . 191 F4
Parkend Cres FK1 . . . . 81 C6
Parker Ave EH7 . . . . 94 E1
Parker Rd EH7 . . . . 94 E1
Parker Terr EH7 . . . . 94 E1
Parkfoot Ct FK1 . . . . 60 B3
Parkgate Alva FK12 . . . . 5 A6
  Rosyth KY11 . . . . 46 F4
Park Gdns Bannockburn FK7 . 7 D2
  Edinburgh EH16 . . . . 151 B8
  4 Grangemouth FK2 . . . 82 D8
  Tullibody FK10 . . . . 4 E5
Park Gr EH16 . . . . 151 B7
Parkgrove Ave EH4 . . . . . . 91 C2
Parkgrove Bank EH4 . . . . . 91 C2
Parkgrove Cres EH4 . . . . . 91 C2
Parkgrove Dr EH4 . . . . 91 C2
Parkgrove Gdns EH4 . . . . . 91 C2
Parkgrove Gn EH4 . . . . 91 C2
Parkgrove Loan EH4 . . . . . 91 C2
Parkgrove Neuk EH4 . . . . . 91 C2
Parkgrove Path EH4 . . . . . 91 D2
Parkgrove Pl EH4 . . . . 91 D2
Park Grove Pl EH21 . . . . . 124 E5
Parkgrove Rd EH4 . . . . 91 C2
Parkgrove Row EH4 . . . . . . 91 C2
Parkgrove St EH4 . . . . 91 D2
Parkgrove Terr EH4 . . . . . . 91 C2
Park Grove Terr EH21 . . . 124 E5
Parkgrove View EH4 . . . . . 91 C2
Parkhall Dr FK2 . . . . 83 A6
Parkhead Ave EH11 . . . . . 119 C2
Parkhead Cotts EH55 . . . 163 E2
Parkhead Cres
  Edinburgh EH11 . . . . 119 C2
  West Calder EH55 . . . . . . 163 E3
Parkhead Dr EH11 . . . . . . 119 C2
Parkhead Gdns
  Edinburgh EH11 . . . . 119 C2
  West Calder EH55 . . . . . . 163 E3
Parkhead Gr EH11 . . . . . . 119 E2
Parkhead Loan EH11 . . . . 119 E2
Parkhead Pk EH22 . . . . . 174 C8

Parkhead Pl
  Easthouses EH22 . . . . . . 174 C8
  Edinburgh EH11 . . . . 119 E2
Parkhead Prim Sch
  EH55 . . . . 163 E3
Parkhead Rd Alloa FK10 . . 10 C8
  Linlithgow EH49 . . . . 64 B1
Parkhead Smallholdings
  EH49 . . . . 64 A1
Parkhead St EH11 . . . . . . 119 E2
Parkhead Terr EH11 . . . . 119 E2
Parkhead View EH11 . . . . 119 E2
Park Hill EH22 . . . . 174 B1
Park La Aberdour KY3 . . . . 49 C7
  Bo'ness EH51 . . . . 64 B7
  Edinburgh EH15 . . . . 123 A7
  Haddington EH41 . . . . . . 129 E8
  Musselburgh EH21 . . . . . 124 E5
  Stirling FK8 . . . . 7 B8
Parkland Gr Comrie KY12 . 26 D7
  Stoneyburn EH47 . . . . . . 161 F1
Parklands EH52 . . . . 115 D4
Parklands Cres KY11 . . . . 48 A3
Park Lea KY11 . . . . 47 A5
Parkneuk Rd KY12 . . . . . . 28 D5
Park Par EH47 . . . . 181 E6
Park Pl Alloa FK10 . . . . 10 C7
  Clackmannan FK10 . . . . . 11 B4
  Cowdenbeath KY4 . . . . . . 30 F8
  Dunfermline KY12 . . . . . . 29 B4
  Edinburgh EH6 . . . . 93 C6
  Kinghorn KY3 . . . . 34 F2
  Kirkcaldy KY1 . . . . 17 B3
  Livingston EH54 . . . . 143 B5
  Stirling FK7 . . . . 6 F6
Park Rd Blackridge EH48 . 138 C3
  Bonnyrigg and Lasswade
    EH19 . . . . 173 B7
  Broxburn EH52 . . . . 115 C5
  Cockenzie & Port Seton
    EH32 . . . . 97 D4
  Cowdenbeath KY4 . . . . . . 13 B3
  Dalkeith EH22 . . . . 152 F2
  Edinburgh EH6 . . . . 93 C6
  Falkirk FK2 . . . . 39 A1
  Gifford EH41 . . . . 220 F6
  Gorebridge EH23 . . . . . . 174 C1
  Grangemouth FK3 . . . . . . 61 D8
  Harthill ML7 . . . . 160 A6
  Kirkcaldy KY1 . . . . 17 E8
  Menstrie FK11 . . . . 4 B4
  Newtongrange EH22 . . . . 174 B5
  Ormiston EH35 . . . . 155 D6
  Rosyth KY11 . . . . 46 F5
  Shotts ML7 . . . . 179 D5
Park Rd W KY11 . . . . 46 D5
Park Road Prim Sch EH47 47 A4
Parkside Ct
  10 Dalkeith EH22 . . . . . 153 A3
  Plean FK7 . . . . 20 C3
Parkside Pl EH22 . . . . . . 153 A3
Parkside Rd ML7 . . . . 179 D4
Parkside St EH8 . . . . 229 C1
Parkside Terr EH16 . . . . . 229 C1
Park St Alva FK12 . . . . 5 A7
  Bonnybridge FK4 . . . . 58 C4
  Cowdenbeath KY4 . . . . . . 13 C3
  Cowie FK7 . . . . 20 E8
  Falkirk FK1 . . . . 60 B5
  Lochgelly KY5 . . . . 14 A4
Park Terr Broxburn EH52 115 B5
  Grangemouth FK2 . . . . . . 82 D8
  Kirknewton EH27 . . . . . . 145 E2
  Newcraighall EH21 . . . . . 123 E4
  Stirling FK8 . . . . 7 A6
  Tullibody FK10 . . . . 4 E5
Parkvale Pl EH6 . . . . 94 B4
Park View Broxburn EH52 115 B5
  Fauldhouse EH47 . . . . . . 181 E7
  Grangemouth FK2 . . . . . . 82 E8
  Kirkcaldy KY2 . . . . 17 A5
  Loanhead EH20 . . . . 172 B7
Park-View EH32 . . . . 98 E5
Park View
  Musselburgh EH21 . . . . . 124 E5
  Newcraighall EH21 . . . . . 123 E4
  Prestonpans EH32 . . . . . . 97 B1
  Stoneyburn EH47 . . . . . . 162 C2
  Westfield EH48 . . . . 110 F4
  Whitburn EH47 . . . . 161 A7
Parkview Ave FK1 . . . . . . 59 F2
Park View Ct FK1 . . . . 60 B5
Park View E EH32 . . . . . . 97 D4
Park View Terr EH32 . . . . 97 D4
Park View W EH32 . . . . . . 97 D4
Parkway FK10 . . . . 10 A7
Parkway Ct FK10 . . . . 10 A7
Parkwood Cres EH52 . . . 115 D4
Parkwood Gdns EH52 . . . 115 D5
Parliament Sq EH1 . . . . . 229 A3
Parliament St EH6 . . . . . . 94 B4
Parrot Ave FK1 . . . . 193 C8
Parrotshot EH15 . . . . 123 B5
Parsonage The EH21 . . . 124 D6
Parsons Green Prim Sch
  EH8 . . . . 122 D7
Parsons Green Terr **2**
  EH8 . . . . 94 C1

Parsonspool
  Bonnyrigg and Lasswade
    EH19 . . . . 173 C5
  Dunbar EH42 . . . . 78 D2
Paterson's Ct EH52 . . . . . 115 F5
Paterson Dr FK1 . . . . 81 C6
Paterson La KY4 . . . . 13 C3
Paterson Pl
  Bonnybridge FK4 . . . . 58 C5
  Bridge of A FK9 . . . . 2 A6
Paterson Twr FK1 . . . . . . 60 D4
Paterson Way KY11 . . . . . 29 B1
Path Brae EH29 . . . . 89 A1
Pathfoot Ave FK9 . . . . 2 C7
Pathfoot Dr FK9 . . . . 2 C7
Pathfoot Rd FK9 . . . . 2 C6
Pathhead Ct **1** KY1 . . . . . 17 D6
Pathhead Prim Sch
  Kirkcaldy KY1 . . . . 17 D7
  Pathhead EH37 . . . . 176 B4
Path The Airth FK2 . . . . . . 22 D4
  Bannockburn FK7 . . . . 7 D2
  Kirkcaldy KY1 . . . . 17 D7
Pate's Rd EH14 . . . . 149 C8
Paton Ct FK10 . . . . 10 B7
Paton St Alloa FK10 . . . . . 10 A7
  Dunfermline KY12 . . . . . . 29 C6
Patrick Dr FK1 . . . . 81 E7
Patriothall **5** EH3 . . . . . . 93 B2
Patterson Gr KY12 . . . . . . 17 B6
Patterson St KY12 . . . . . . 17 B6
Pattison St EH6 . . . . 94 A5
Pattle Ct EH39 . . . . 54 A7
Paul Dr FK7 . . . . 22 E4
Paul Pl KY4 . . . . 13 D4
Paul St KY5 . . . . 14 A6
Pavilions Bsns Pk FK10 . . . 9 E7
Pavilions The FK10 . . . . . . 9 E7
Pavilion View FK10 . . . . . . 9 F8
Paxstone Cres ML7 . . . . . 159 E5
Paxstone Dr ML7 . . . . 159 E5
Paxton Cres KY5 . . . . 14 A8
Paxton Pl KY5 . . . . 14 B8
Peachdales EH41 . . . . . . 129 F8
Peacock Ave EH19 . . . . . 173 E7
Peacock Ct EH6 . . . . 93 D7
Peacock Parkway EH19 . 173 E6
Peacock Pl EH19 . . . . 173 D6
Peacocktail Cl EH15 . . . . 123 B4
Pearce Ave EH12 . . . . . . 119 C7
Pearce Gr EH12 . . . . 119 C7
Pearce Rd EH12 . . . . 119 C7
Pearson Ave FK4 . . . . 57 D5
Pearson Pl FK4 . . . . 57 D5
Peasehill Brae KY11 . . . . . 46 D3
Peasehill Fauld KY11 . . . . 46 D2
Peasehill Gait KY11 . . . . . 46 D3
Peathill Rd FK4 . . . . 58 A6
Peathill Terr FK4 . . . . 58 A5
Peatville Gdns EH14 . . . . 120 A1
Peatville Terr EH14 . . . . . 120 A1
Peddie Pl EH3 . . . . 61 E8
Peden St ML7 . . . . 159 C5
Peebles Rd EH26 . . . . . . 191 F3
Peel Ave FK5 . . . . 35 B8
Peel Ctr The EH20 . . . . . 151 A1
Peel Prim Sch EH54 . . . . 143 C4
Peel Rdbt EH54 . . . . 143 C4
Peel Terr EH9 . . . . 121 F4
Peffer's Pl EH41 . . . . 130 A8
Peffer Bank EH16 . . . . . . 122 D4
Peffer Ind Est EH16 . . . . 122 D4
Peffermill Ind Est EH16 . 122 C4
Peffermill Rd EH16 . . . . . 122 C4
Peffer Pl EH16 . . . . 122 D4
Peffer St EH16 . . . . 122 D4
Peggy's Mill Rd EH4 . . . . . 91 A4
Peirson Rd KY11 . . . . 29 F4
Pelstream Ave FK7 . . . . . . 7 B4
Pembroke Pl **7** EH12 . . . 120 E7
Pembroke St FK5 . . . . 38 C3
Pencaitland Prim Sch
  EH34 . . . . 156 E6
Pencraig Brae EH40 . . . . 103 D6
Pender Gdns FK2 . . . . 82 E7
Penders La FK1 . . . . 60 A5
Pendreich Ave EH19 . . . . 173 D8
Pendreich Dr EH19 . . . . . 173 C8
Pendreich Gr EH19 . . . . . 173 C8
Pendreich Terr EH19 . . . . 173 C8
Pendreich View EH19 . . . 173 C8
Pendreich Way FK9 . . . . . . 2 D6
Penicuik High Sch EH26 191 E5
Penicuik Rd EH25,EH26 . 171 E3
Pennelton Pl EH51 . . . . . . 63 E5
Pennyschool Pl FK10 . . . . 11 A5
Pennywell Ct EH4 . . . . . . 92 B5
Pennywell Gdns EH4 . . . . 92 B5
Pennywell Gr EH4 . . . . . . 92 B5
Pennywell Medway EH4 . 92 B5
Pennywell Pl EH4 . . . . 92 B5
Pennywell Rd EH4 . . . . . . 92 B5
Pennywell Villas EH4 . . . . 92 B6
Penston Farm Cotts
  EH33 . . . . 127 F5
Pentland Ave
  Bathgate EH48 . . . . 141 F5
  Currie EH14 . . . . 147 F4
  Edinburgh EH13 . . . . 149 A7
  Gorebridge EH23 . . . . . . 174 B3
  Penicuik EH26 . . . . 191 E6
Pentland Cres
  Edinburgh EH10 . . . . 150 A7
  Rosewell EH24 . . . . 172 D3
Pentland Ct Bilston EH25 . 171 E6
  Dalgety Bay KY11 . . . . . . 48 C4

Pentland Dr
Edinburgh EH10..........149 F6
Whitburn EH47..........161 C6
Pentlandfield Bsns Pk
EH25..........171 C5
Pentland Gait Off Pk
EH11..........119 B1
Pentland Gr EH10..........150 A7
Pentland Hills Regional Pk
FH14,EH26..........189 D7
Pentland Ind Est EH20 ..172 A7
Pentland Pk
Livingston EH54..........144 B4
Loanhead EH20..........171 F8
Pentland Pl
Cairneyhill KY12..........27 E1
Currie EH14..........147 F4
Kirkcaldy KY2..........16 F6
Pentland Rd
Bonnyrigg and Lasswade
EH19..........173 A7
Edinburgh EH13..........149 A7
Edinburgh,Old Pentland
EH20..........150 D1
Loanhead EH20..........172 A8
Pentland Rise..........48 C5
Pentlands Gdns EH10 ..150 A7
Pentlands Science Pk
EH26..........171 C3
Pentland Terr
Dunfermline KY11..........29 E2
Edinburgh EH10..........150 A8
Penicuik EH26..........191 E6
Pentland View
Currie EH14..........147 F4
Dalkeith EH22..........153 C2
East Whitburn EH47..........161 E7
Edinburgh EH10..........150 A6
Uphall EH52..........115 A5
Pentland View Cres
EH25..........171 F3
Pentland View Ct
Currie EH14..........148 A4
Livingston EH54..........143 A6
Pentland View Pl EH47..171 F3
Pentland View Rd
Kirkliston EH29..........89 A2
Roslin EH25..........171 F3
Pentland View Terr
EH25..........171 F3
Pentland Way FK3..........61 E5
Pentland Wlk EH47..........161 C6
Peoples Story Mus The
EH8..........229 B3
Peploe Rise KY11..........47 A7
Peppercraig Quarry Ind Site
EH41..........100 F2
Percival St KY2..........17 A5
Perdieus Mount KY12..........29 A2
Perdrixknowe EH14..........120 D3
Persevere Ct EH6..........93 F6
Perth Rd KY11..........13 D6
Perth's Gr EH32..........97 A2
Perth St Edinburgh EH3....93 B2
Livingston EH54..........144 A6
Petershill Gdns EH14..........5 C1
Petershill Wildlife Reserve
EH48..........141 C8
Peterswell Brae FK7..........7 E1
Petrel Way KY11..........30 A2
Pettigrew's Cl EH22.. 153 A3
Pettycur Bay KY3..........34 C1
Pettycur Bay Holiday Pk
KY3..........34 D1
Pettycur Ho KY3..........34 F1
Pettycur Rd KY3..........34 F1
Peveril Rise EH54..........164 E8
Peveril Terr EH16..........151 B8
Phantassie Cotts EH40..103 F7
Phantassie Doocot EH40.103 F7
Phantassie Sq EH40..........103 E7
Philip Ave Linlithgow
EH49..........84 E7
Philip Dr FK15..........38 D2
Philip Pl FK26..........191 E7
Philip St FK2..........60 B7
Philpingstone La EH51....64 C7
Philpingstone Rd EH51...64 C7
Phoenix Ind Est FK7..........7 D4
Phoenix La KY12..........28 F4
Picardy Pl EH1..........229 A4
Pierhead Bldgs KY11..........68 C5
Pier Pl EH6..........93 D7
Pier Rd EH51..........64 C8
Piersfield Gr EH8..........94 D1
Piersfield Pl EH8..........94 D1
Piersfield Terr EH8..........94 D1
Piershill La EH8..........94 C1
Piershill Pl 10 EH8..........94 C1
Piershill Sq E EH8..........94 C1
Piershill Sq W EH8..........94 C1
Piershill Terr 11 EH8.....94 D1
Pike Rd FK7..........7 D4
Pilgrims Hill EH49..........85 B8
Pilkham Ct KY4..........13 C3
Pilmuir St KY12..........29 A5
Pilrig Gdns EH6..........93 E3
Pilrig Glebe 3 EH6..........93 F3
Pilrig House Cl EH6..........93 E3
Pilrig Hts EH6..........93 E3
Pilrig Ind Est EH6..........93 E3
Pilrig St EH6..........93 E3
Pilton Ave EH5..........92 F5
Pilton Cres EH5..........92 F5
Pilton Dr EH5..........92 F5
Pilton Drive N EH5..........92 F5

Pilton Gdns EH5..........92 F5
Pilton Loan EH5..........92 F5
Pilton Pk EH5..........92 F5
Pilton Pl EH5..........92 F5
Pineapple The FK2..........22 B6
Pinebank EH47..........143 E5
Pine Cres FK11..........3 F6
Pinefield Glade EH54 ..164 C8
Pine Gr Alloa FK10..........10 C6
Dunfermline KY11..........46 E8
Livingston EH54..........144 B5
Westquarter FK2..........61 B2
Pinegrove Gdns EH4..........91 B2
Pines The EH42..........78 B1
Pines The EH31..........52 B3
Pine Wlk FK5..........38 D1
Pinewood Dr KY11..........48 B3
Pinewood Pk EH54..........142 E7
Pinewood Pl
Blackburn EH47..........162 E8
Mayfield EH21..........174 C6
Pinewood Rd EH22..........174 E6
Pinewood Sch EH47..........162 E8
Pinewood View EH22....174 E6
Pinkerton Pl KY11..........46 F5
Pinkhill EH12..........120 A6
Pinkie Ave EH21..........124 E5
Pinkie Dr EH21..........124 E5
Pinkie Hill Cres EH21...124 E5
Pinkie Pl EH21..........124 E5
Pinkie Rd EH21..........124 E6
Pinkie St Peter's Prim Sch
EH21..........124 E6
Pinkie Terr EH21..........124 F5
Pinkie Wlk 10 EH33..........126 C5
Pinnel Pl KY11..........48 C4
Pipe La EH15..........95 A1
Piper Cres KY3..........33 D2
Pipe St EH15..........95 A1
Pirig Cotts EH6..........93 F3
Pirleyhill Dr FK1..........81 D6
Pirleyhill Gdns FK1..........60 A2
Pirnhall Rd
Bannockburn,Chartershall
FK7..........19 A8
Bannockburn FK7..........19 D7
Bannockburn FK7..........19 E8
Pirniefield Bank EH6....94 C4
Pirniefield Gdns EH6....94 C4
Pirniefield Gr EH6..........94 C4
Pirniefield Pl EH6..........94 C4
Pirniefield Terr EH6.....94 C4
Pirnhall Prim Sch EH4 ..92 C5
Pirrie St EH6..........93 F4
Pitbauchlie Bank KY11....29 C1
Pitcairn St KY11..........29 C2
Pitcaple Gdns EH54....164 D6
Pitcorthie Dr KY11..........46 E8
Pitcorthie Prim Sch KY11..29 C1
Pitcorthie Rd KY11..........29 C1
Pitcox Cotts EH42..........105 C3
Pitdinnie Pl KY12..........27 D1
Pitdinnie Rd KY12..........27 D2
Pitfairn Rd FK10..........5 E3
Pitfirrane Pk EH21..........28 B1
Pitlour Pl KY12..........16 C7
Pitlochry Pl 4 EH7..........94 A2
Pitmedden Rd KY11..........30 A1
Pit Rd KY4..........13 E6
Pitreavie Bsns Pk KY11..46 C7
Pitreavie Cres KY11..........46 C8
Pitreavie Ct KY11..........46 D6
Pitreavie Dr KY11..........46 D6
Pitreavie Ind Est KY11 ..46 D6
Pitreavie Prim Sch KY11..46 D8
Pitsligo Rd EH10..........121 B4
Pittencrieff Ct EH21....124 F6
Pittencrieff House Mus
KY12..........28 F3
Pittencrieff Prim Sch
KY12..........28 F4
Pittencrieff St KY12..........28 F4
Pitt St EH6..........93 E5
Pitt Terr FK8..........7 B6
Pittville St EH15..........123 C8
Pittville Street La EH15..123 B8
Place Charente EH22 ....153 C2
Plane Gr KY11..........46 F8
Plane St EH42..........78 B1
Plantation St KY5..........14 B7
Player Dr KY13..........12 A1
Player Gn EH54..........143 E8
Players Rd FK7..........7 C7
Playhouse Theatre EH1..229 B4
Pleanbank Cotts FK7....20 B3
Plean Country Park Wlk
FK7..........20 B2
Plean Ind Est FK7..........20 D1
Pleasance Edinburgh EH8.229 B2
Pleasance KY11..........60 B4
Pleasance Brae KY12 ....27 D1
Pleasance Ct
12 Falkirk FK1..........60 B4
Halbeath KY12..........30 B7
Pleasance Gdns FK1..........60 B4
Pleasance Rd
Dunfermline KY12..........29 F6
Falkirk FK1..........60 B4
Halbeath KY12..........30 A6
Pleasance Row ML11....201 B3
Pleasance Sq 11 FK1....60 B4
Pleasance The EH32..........71 C4
Plewlandcroft EH30..........68 B1
Plewlands Ave EH10....120 F2
Plewlands Gdns EH10...120 F2

Plewlands Ho EH30..........68 B1
Plewlands Pl EH30..........89 B8
Plewlands Terr EH10 ....120 F2
Pleydell Pl 6 EH6..........151 B8
Plough La 2 EH33..........126 D6
Plover Brae EH14..........143 D5
Plummer Ct EH22..........153 A4
Pointgarry Rd EH39..........54 B7
Polbeth Ave EH55..........163 F5
Polbeth Cres EH55..........163 F5
Polbeth Gdns EH55..........163 F5
Polbeth Ind Est EH55....163 E4
Polbeth Rd EH55..........163 F5
Polbeth West Calder Ind Est
EH55..........163 E4
Poldrate EH41..........130 B8
Polkemmet Bsns Ctr
EH47..........160 F5
Polkemmet Ctry Pk
EH47..........160 C7
Polkemmet Dr ML7..........160 A6
Polkemmet La ML7..........159 F5
Polkemmet Prim Sch
EH47..........161 A5
Polkemmet Rd
Harthill ML7..........159 F6
Whitburn EH47..........160 E5
Pollard Glebe EH11..........120 A4
Pollock Wlk KY12..........28 C5
Polmaise Ave FK7..........7 B3
Polmaise Cres FK7..........8 C5
Polmaise Ct FK7..........7 B3
Polmaise Rd
Cambusbarron FK7..........6 E3
Stirling FK7..........7 C3
Polmont House Gdns FK2..61 E1
Polmont Pk FK2..........61 E3
Polmont Rd FK2..........61 B3
Polmont Sta FK2..........61 B3
Polson Gdns EH33..........126 B6
Polton Avenue Rd EH19..173 A6
Polton Bank EH18..........172 E6
Polton Bank Terr EH18 ..172 E6
Polton Cotts EH18..........172 D6
Polton Ct EH19..........173 B7
Polton Dr EH19..........173 A7
Polton Gdns EH18..........173 A7
Polton Pl EH19..........173 B7
Polton Rd
Bonnyrigg and Lasswade
EH18..........173 A8
Loanhead EH20..........172 C7
Polton Rd W EH18,EH19..172 F6
Polton Terr EH18..........173 A7
Polton Vale EH20..........172 C7
Polwarth Ave FK2..........82 C8
Polwarth Cres
Edinburgh EH11..........121 A5
Prestonpans EH32..........97 A1
Polwarth Gdns EH11....120 F5
Polwarth Gr EH11..........120 F5
Polwarth Ho FK9..........2 D6
Polwarth Pk EH11..........120 F5
Polwarth Pl EH11..........120 F5
Polwarth Terr
Edinburgh EH11..........120 F4
Edinburgh EH11..........120 F4
Prestonpans EH32..........97 A1
Polworth KY4..........13 D4
Pomathorn Bank EH26..191 F4
Pomathorn Rd EH26 ....191 F4
Pompee Rd FK10..........5 B1
Ponton St EH3..........228 B1
Poole Dr FK2..........61 C2
Poplar Cres KY2..........17 B7
Poplar Gdns KY2..........17 A7
Poplar Gr Dunfermline KY11..46 E8
Livingston EH54..........144 B6
Poplar La EH6..........94 B5
Poplar Pk EH32..........97 D3
Poplar St Dunbar EH42....78 B1
Grangemouth FK3..........61 C6
Mayfield EH21..........174 E6
Poplars The FK10..........4 B1
Poplar Terr EH19..........173 B6
Portal Rd FK3..........61 C5
Port Buchan EH52..........115 D5
Port Downie FK1..........59 D5
Port Edgar Water Sports Ctr
EH30..........68 B3
Porteous' Pend EH1....228 C2
Porterfield KY12..........26 E7
Porterfield Rd EH4..........92 E3
Portgower Pl EH4..........93 A2
Port Hamilton EH3..........228 B2
Port Long Wynd KY11....68 C7
Portland Gdns EH6..........93 E6
Portland Pl Edinburgh EH6..93 E6
Fauldhouse EH47..........181 D6
Portland Row EH6..........93 E6
Portland St EH6..........93 E6
Portland Terr EH6..........93 E6
Portobello High Sch
EH15..........122 F7
Portobello High St
EH15..........95 A1
Portobello Rd EH15..........123 B8
Portpatrick PK10..........4 B1
Portree Ct FK10..........5 D1
Portsburgh Sq EH1......228 C2
Post Office La KY11....68 C6
Potter's Path EH33..........126 C4

Potter Pl FK2..........39 F3
Potterrow EH8..........229 A2
Pottery St KY1..........17 E8
Pottery The
Edinburgh EH15..........95 A1
Prestonpans EH32..........96 E1
Pottishaw Ct EH47..........161 E7
Pottishaw Pl EH48..........141 C1
Pottishaw Rd EH48..........140 F1
Pottis Rd FK7..........7 D3
Povert Rd EH19,EH23 ..173 F2
Powderhall Brae EH7....93 D4
Powderhall Rd EH7..........93 D4
Powderhall Rigg EH7....93 D4
Powdrake Rd FK3..........61 F8
Powie's Path EH51..........144 D4
Pratt St KY1..........17 A1
President Kennedy Dr
FK7..........20 C3
Pressmennan Wood Forest
Trail EH42..........133 E6
Preston Ave
Linlithgow EH49..........84 F6
Prestonpans EH32..........97 B1
Preston Cres
Inverkeithing KY11..........47 C2
Linlithgow EH49..........84 F6
Prestonpans EH32..........97 B1
Preston Cross Cotts EH32..97 A1
Preston Ct Linlithgow EH49..84 F6
Prestonpans EH32..........125 F8
Prestonfield Ave EH16 ..122 B4
Prestonfield Cres EH16..122 B4
Prestonfield Gdns EH16..122 B4
Prestonfield Pk EH16 ..122 D4
Prestonfield Prim Sch
EH16..........122 B3
Prestonfield Rd EH16....122 B4
Prestonfield Terr EH16..122 A4
Preston Grange Ind Mus
EH32..........125 C8
Prestongrange Rd EH32..125 E8
Prestongrange Terr EH32..96 E1
Prestonhall Cres EH24 ..172 D2
Prestonhall Rd EH24....172 D2
Preston House Gdns
EH32..........84 E4
Prestonkirk Gdns EH40..103 E8
Preston Lodge High Sch
EH32..........97 A1
Preston Market Cross
EH32..........97 A1
Preston Mill EH40..........103 F8
Prestonpans Inf Sch EH32..96 F1
Prestonpans Prim Sch
EH32..........126 A8
Prestonpans Sta EH32..126 A8
Preston Pl EH37..........176 A4
Preston Rd
East Linton EH40..........103 E8
Linlithgow EH49..........84 F6
Prestonpans,Cuthill EH32..125 F8
Prestonpans EH32..........97 B1
Preston St
High Valleyfield KY12 ....26 A2
Rosewell EH24..........172 D2
Preston Street Prim Sch
EH8..........229 C1
Preston Terr
Inverkeithing KY11..........47 D1
Linlithgow EH49..........84 F6
Prestonpans EH32..........97 B1
Sauchie FK10..........5 D1
Preston Tower EH32..........97 A1
Preston Twr EH32..........97 A1
Pretoria Pl
Cowdenbeath KY4..........13 B4
Polmont FK2..........61 C1
Pretoria Rd FK5..........38 B1
Priest Bank EH41..........132 C2
Priestfield Ave EH16 ....122 B4
Priestfield Cres EH16....122 B4
Priestfield Gdns EH16..122 B4
Priestfield Gr EH16..........122 B5
Priestfield Rd EH16..........122 B5
Priestfield Rd N EH16....122 A5
Priesthill Pl EH16..........151 B6
Priesthill St EH16..........151 B6
Prime Gilt Box St KY2....17 B6
Primmer Pl KY4..........13 D3
Primrose Ave
Grangemouth FK3..........61 A6
Rosyth KY11..........46 D5
Primrose Avenue Ind Est
FK3..........61 B6
Primrose Bank Rd EH5..93 B6
Primrose Cres.......... 153 C2
Primrose Ct Alloa FK10 ..10 B6
Brxburn EH52..........115 E5
Rosyth KY11..........46 D5
Primrose Dr EH30..........90 D3
Primrose Gdns
Carrington EH23 ..194 D6
Queensferry EH30..........89 C8
Primrose La
Cowdenbeath KY4..........13 C5
Kincardine KY10..........23 E3
Rosyth KY11..........46 D5
Primrose Pl Alloa FK10 ..10 B6
Livingston EH54..........143 B6
Primrose Rd KY11..........46 D5
Primrose St Alloa FK10 ..10 B6
Bonnybridge FK4..........58 B6
Edinburgh EH6..........94 A4

Primrose Terr
Dalkeith EH22..........153 C2
Princes Mall EH1..........229 A3
Prince Regent St EH6....93 E6
Princess Mary Pl EH41..101 A1
Princess Mary Rd EH41..101 A1
Princess St FK4..........58 B7
Princes St California FK1..81 F5
Edinburgh EH2..........228 C3
Falkirk FK1..........60 B5
Stirling FK8..........7 B8
Priorscroft EH48..........111 F6
Priors Grange EH48..........111 F5
Priorwood Dr KY11..........30 A1
Priory Ct KY12..........29 A3
Priory Gate EH39..........54 B6
Priory Gr EH30..........89 B8
Priory La KY12..........29 A3
Priory Pl EH49..........83 F7
Priory Rd Linlithgow EH49..84 F5
Whitecross EH49..........83 F6
Priory Sq FK10..........23 F3
Priory Wlk EH41..........130 C8
Priory Wynd EH39..........54 B7
Promenade
Edinburgh EH15..........94 F3
Limekilns KY11..........45 C3
Musselburgh EH21..........124 B7
Promenade The EH42....97 D4
Prora Cotts EH39..........73 D4
Prospect Bank Cres EH6..94 B3
Prospect Bank Gdns EH6..94 A3
Prospect Bank Gr EH6....94 C4
Prospect Bank Pl EH6....94 C4
Prospect Bank Rd EH6....94 B3
Prospect Bank Sch EH6..94 B4
Prospect Bank Terr EH6..94 C4
Prospecthill Rd FK1..........60 A2
Prospect St
Cowdenbeath KY4..........13 B4
Falkirk FK1..........59 F5
Providence Brae EH51....63 F8
Provost Haugh EH14....148 C5
Provost Hunter Ave FK12..5 C7
Provost Kay Pk KY1..........17 C6
Provost Milne Gr EH30..89 B8
Provost Rd Bo'ness EH51..63 E6
Linlithgow EH49..........85 B7
Pryde Ave EH19..........173 A7
Pryde Terr EH19..........173 A7
Puir Wife's Brae EH48 ..141 D5
Pullar Ave FK9..........2 A6
Pullar Ct FK9..........2 A6
Pumpherston Prim Sch
EH53..........144 B7
Pumpherston Rd
Mid Calder EH53,EH54 ..144 C5
Pumpherston EH54..........144 A8
Uphall Station EH54..........115 A1
Pyothall Ct EH52..........115 D5
Pyothall Rd EH52..........115 D5
Pypers Wynd EH32..........96 F2

Q

Quadrant EH39..........54 D7
Quadrant La EH39..........54 D7
Quadrant The EH26....191 F6
Quakerfield FK7..........7 E1
Quality St Dysart KY11....18 A7
Edinburgh EH4..........91 F3
North Berwick EH39..........54 C7
Quality Street Junc EH4..91 F3
Quality Street La EH4....91 F3
Quarrolhall Cres FK2....39 B3
Quarrybank
Cousland EH22..........154 C5
Edinburgh EH14..........148 C8
Quarrybank Cl EH14....148 C8
Quarrybank Ct EH14....148 C8
Quarrybank End EH14...148 C8
Quarry Brae
Grangemouth FK2..........82 E8
Kirkcaldy KY1..........17 F8
Quarry Cl EH8..........229 B1
Quarry Cotts
Blackridge EH48..........138 C3
Edinburgh EH15..........123 B4
Quarry Ct KY4..........13 B4
Quarryfoot Gdns EH19..173 C7
Quarryfoot Gn EH19....173 C7
Quarryford Farm Cotts
EH41..........221 C4
Quarry Howe EH14..........147 C1
Quarry Knowe The EH51..63 E6
Quarryknowes The EH51..63 E6
Quarry Pl Alloa FK10..........10 C8
Shotts ML7..........179 D5
Quarry Rd
Cambusbarron FK7..........6 C5
Fauldhouse EH47..........181 F6
Shotts ML7..........179 D5
Quarry St Kirkcaldy KY12..28 C6
Quarry St ML7..........179 D5
Quarryview EH14..........148 C8
Quarrywood Ct EH54....143 D3
Quartermile EH3..........229 A2
Quayside Mills EH6..........93 F5
Quayside St EH6..........93 F6
Quebec Ave EH54..........143 E4
Queen's Ave Bridge of A FK9..2 B6

Queen's Ave *continued*
Edinburgh EH4 . . . . 92 B2
Queen's Ave S 3 EH4 92 C2
Queen's Bay Cres EH15 . 123 D7
Queen's Cres
Carluke ML8 . . . . 215 A2
Edinburgh EH9 . . . . 121 F4
Falkirk FK1 . . . . 59 F5
Queen's Ct FK9 . . . . 1 F7
Queen's Dr California FK1 . .81 F5
Edinburgh,Willowbrae EH8 122 C6
Pencaitland EH34 . . . . . . 156 E6
Stenhousemuir FK5 . . . . 38 C2
Queen's Gallery EH8 . . . . . 229 C3
Queen's Gdns EH4 . . . . 92 C2
Queen's La FK9 . . . . 2 A7
Queen's Park Ave EH8 . . . 94 B1
Queen's Pl EH42 . . . . 78 F1
Queen's Rd
Broxburn EH52 . . . . 115 E4
Dunbar EH42 . . . . 78 E2
Edinburgh EH4 . . . . 92 C2
Stirling FK8 . . . . 6 F7
Queen Anne Ct EH28 . . . 117 B5
Queen Anne High Sch
KY12 . . . . 28 F6
Queen Anne Pk EH28 . . . 117 B5
Queen Anne St KY12 . . . . . 29 A4
Queen Charlotte La EH6 . .94 A5
Queen Charlotte St EH6 . . .94 A5
Queen Margaret's Pl
KY11 . . . . 68 C6
Queen Margaret Cl
EH10 . . . . 150 D5
Queen Margaret Coll
EH12 . . . . 119 D8
Queen Margaret District
Hospl KY12 . . . . 29 E6
Queen Margaret Dr EH28 . .68 C1
Queen Margaret Fauld
KY12 . . . . 29 F6
Queen Margaret Gdns
KY12 . . . . 29 F6
Queen Margaret Pk KY12 . .29 F6
Queen Margaret St KY3 . . . 34 F1
Queen Margaret Univ Coll
(Leith Campus) EH6 . . . . 94 A4
Queens Ave
Broxburn EH52 . . . . 115 E4
Haddington EH41 . . . . . . 100 F1
Queens Cres KY3 . . . . 34 F1
Queens Ct FK5 . . . . 38 D3
Queen's Ct KY12 . . . . 29 A3
Queens Dr Denny FK6 . . . . . 36 E3
Falkirk FK1 . . . . 59 F5
Stenhousemuir FK5 . . . . 38 C3
Queen's Dr EH4 . . . . 229 C2
Queensferry High Sch
EH30 . . . . 89 D8
Queensferry Mus EH30 . . . 68 C1
Queensferry Prim Sch
EH30 . . . . 68 C1
Queensferry Rd
Dunfermline KY11 . . . . . . 46 D7
Edinburgh EH4 . . . . 91 C2
Edinburgh,Orchard Brae
EH4 . . . . 92 D1
Kirkliston EH29 . . . . 89 A2
Rosyth KY11 . . . . 46 E5
Queensferry St EH2 . . . . . 228 B3
Queensferry Street La
EH2 . . . . 228 B3
Queensferry Terr EH4 . . . . 92 E1
Queens Gdns
Bridge of A FK9 . . . . 1 F7
East Calder EH53 . . . . . 144 E4
Queenshaugh KY12 . . . . 27 C7
Queenshaugh Dr FK8 . . . . . 2 C1
Queen's Park Ct EH8 . . . . 128 C2
Queen St Alloa FK10 . . . . . 10 B7
Alva FK12 . . . . 5 A7
Bannockburn FK7 . . . . 7 C2
Edinburgh EH2 . . . . 228 C4
Fallin FK7 . . . . 8 C4
Grangemouth FK3 . . . . . . 61 F8
Inverkeithing KY11 . . . . . 47 B2
Stirling FK8 . . . . 7 A8
Queens Terr EH53 . . . . 144 E4
Queen's Terr FK9 . . . . 2 A7
Queenstonbank EH39 . . . . . 52 F3
Queen Street Gdns E
EH3 . . . . 228 C4
Queen Street Gdns W
EH3 . . . . 228 C4
Queensway FK10 . . . . 191 E7
Queens Way KY11 . . . . 46 B2
Queen's Wlk EH16 . . . . 122 E3
Quench FK3 . . . . 62 B5
Quentin Ct EH54 . . . . 143 E1
Quentin Rise EH54 . . . . . . 143 E1
Quidenham Ct EH39 . . . . . . 54 A6
Quilts The FH6 . . . . 93 F5
Quilts Wynd EH6 . . . . 93 E5
Quoiters Ct EH47 . . . . 162 C7

R

Race Rd EH48 . . . . 140 E7
Raeburn Cres
Kirkcaldy KY2 . . . . 17 A4
Whitburn EH47 . . . . 161 B5
Raeburn Mews EH4 . . . . . . 93 A2

Raeburn Pl EH4 . . . . 93 A2
Raeburn Rigg EH54 . . . . . 143 B6
Raeburn St EH4 . . . . 93 A2
Rae Ct FK2 . . . . 39 C3
Raes Gdns EH4 . . . . 173 C8
Rae St Cowdenbeath KY4 . .13 C2
Stenhousemuir FK5 . . . . 38 D3
Rainhill Ave FK2 . . . . 82 E6
Rainhill Ct 1 FK2 . . . . 82 F7
Raith Ave KY4 . . . . 13 C3
Raith Cres KY2 . . . . 17 A4
Raith Ctr KY4 . . . . 13 D4
Raith Dr KY2 . . . . 17 A3
Raith Gdns KY2 . . . . 17 A3
Raleigh Ct FK1 . . . . 59 E5
Ramage Rd ML8 . . . . 215 B1
Ramillies Ct Carluke ML8. 215 A1
Penicuik EH26 . . . . 192 A8
Ramsay Ave FK2 . . . . 61 A3
Ramsay Colliery EH20 . . . 172 C8
Ramsay Cres EH19 . . . . . 173 F3
Ramsay Cres
Bathgate EH48 . . . . 141 C6
Burntisland KY3 . . . . 34 A2
Mayfield EH22 . . . . 174 E5
Ramsay Ct Kincardine FK10 23 E4
Livingston EH54 . . . . 144 C5
Ramsay Gdn EH1 . . . . 228 C3
Ramsay La Edinburgh EH1 228 C3
Kincardine FK10 . . . . 23 E4
Limekilns KY11 . . . . 45 A3
Ramsay Pl Edinburgh EH15. 95 B1
Penicuik EH26 . . . . 191 C6
Stirling FK8 . . . . 2 A2
Ramsay Rd KY1 . . . . 17 B1
Ramsay Terr EH18 . . . . . . 172 F6
Ramsay Wlk EH22 . . . . . . 174 E5
Ramsey Pl KY11 . . . . 46 F3
Ramsey Tullis Dr FK10 . . . . 4 C1
Randolph Cliff EH3 . . . . . 228 A3
Randolph Cres
Bannockburn FK7 . . . . 7 C1
Dunbar EH42 . . . . 106 D8
Edinburgh EH3 . . . . 228 A3
Grangemouth FK2 . . . . . . 82 D8
Randolph Ct Kirkcaldy KY1 .18 A8
Randolph Gdns FK6 . . . . . . 36 D1
Randolph Ind Est KY1 . . . . 18 A8
Randolph La EH3 . . . . 228 B3
Randolph Pl
Bannockburn FK7 . . . . 7 C2
Edinburgh EH3 . . . . 228 B3
Kirkcaldy KY1 . . . . 17 F8
Kirkcaldy KY1 . . . . 18 A8
Randolph St
Cowdenbeath KY4 . . . . . . 13 D3
Dunfermline KY12 . . . . . . 29 A4
Randolph Terr FK7 . . . . 7 A4
Randyford Rd FK2 . . . . 60 D5
Randyford St FK2 . . . . 60 E5
Range Rd EH51 . . . . 62 D8
Rankeillor St EH8 . . . . . . 229 B1
Rankin Ave EH9 . . . . 121 F2
Rankin Cres EH4 . . . . 57 D5
Rankin Dr EH9 . . . . 121 E2
Rankin Sq EH54 . . . . 142 C5
Rankin Wynd FK10 . . . . 4 C1
Rankin Rd EH9 . . . . 121 F3
Ransome Gdns EH4 . . . . . . 91 D1
Raploch Prim Sch FK8 . . . 1 E2
Raploch Rd FK8 . . . . 1 F1
Rashiehill KY11 . . . . 201 A1
Rashiehill Cres EH55 . . . 182 F6
Rashiehill Rd FK1 . . . . . . 108 A6
Rashiehill Terr EH55 . . . 182 E6
Rashierigg EH52 . . . . 115 B5
Rashierigg Pl EH52 . . . . . 161 B2
Ratcliffe Terr EH9 . . . . . . 121 E4
Rathbone Pl EH15 . . . . 95 B1
Ratho Park Rd EH28 . . . . 117 E2
Ratho Rd EH28 . . . . 117 C6
Ratho Pl KY11 . . . . 29 C3
Ratho Prim Sch EH28 . . . 117 D2
Rattray Cres EH10 . . . . . . 149 E8
Rattray Dr EH10 . . . . 149 E8
Rattray Gdns EH54 . . . . . . 162 E7
Rattray Gr EH10 . . . . 149 E8
Rattray Loan EH10 . . . . . . 149 E8
Rattray St EH51 . . . . 64 B8
Rattray Terr KY5 . . . . 14 A7
Rattray Way EH10 . . . . . . 149 F8
Ravelrig Gait EH14 . . . . . . 147 B2
Ravelrig Hill EH14 . . . . . . 147 B3
Ravelrig Pk EH14 . . . . 147 B3
Ravelrig Rd EH14 . . . . 147 B3
Ravelrig Wynd EH14 . . . . 147 C2
Ravelston Dykes EH12. . 120 D8

Ravelston Dykes La EH4. 120 A6
Ravelston Dykes Rd EH4 .120 B8
Ravelston Gdn EH4 . . . . . . 120 C8
Ravelston Heights EH4. . 120 B8
Ravelston House Gr 10
Ravelston House Loan
EH4 . . . . 92 C1
Ravelston House Pk EH4 .92 C1
Ravelston House Rd EH4 .92 C1
Ravelston Pk EH14 . . . . . . 120 E8
Ravelston Rise EH4 . . . . . 120 C8
Ravelston Terr EH4 . . . . 92 F1
Ravelsykes Rd EH26 . . . 191 C5
Ravendean Gdns EH26 . .191 C5
Ravens Craig 11 KY1 . . . . 17 D6
Ravenscraig Castle KY1 . .17 E5
Ravenscraig Park Nature
Trail KY1 . . . . 17 F6
Ravenscroft Gdns EH17 .151 E5
Ravenscroft Pl EH17 . . . 151 E5
Ravenscroft St EH17 . . . 151 E5
Ravenshaugh Cres EH21 .125 A6
Ravenshaugh Rd EH21 . . . 125 A7
Ravenswood Ave EH16 . .122 C1
Ravenswood Rise EH4 . .164 E8
Raw Holdings EH53 . . . . . 145 B5
Recreation Pk (Alloa Athletic
FC) FK10 . . . . 10 C6
Rectory La KY1 . . . . 18 A7
Redbrae Ave EH51 . . . . 64 A5
Redbrae Rd FK1 . . . . 59 D6
Redbraes Gr EH7 . . . . 93 D4
Redbraes Pl EH7 . . . . 93 D4
Redburn Rd
Blackridge EH48 . . . . . . 138 B2
Prestonpans EH32 . . . . . 96 E1
Redburn Rd N EH32 . . . . . . 96 E1
Redburn Wynd KY1 . . . . . . 17 C4
Redcroft St EH22 . . . . 152 A8
Redcraig Rd EH53 . . . . . . 144 F2
Redcroft 1 EH47 . . . . 162 A1
Redcroft St EH22 . . . . 152 A8
Redcroft Terr EH47 . . . . 162 A1
Redding Ind Est FK2 . . . . . 61 A1
Redding Rd
Grangemouth FK2 . . . . . . 82 D8
Laurieston FK2 . . . . 60 F2
Redding FK2 . . . . 61 B1
Redding Road Rdbt FK2 . . .60 F2
Reddoch Rd
Grangemouth FK2 . . . . . . 62 A4
Grangemouth FK3 . . . . . . 61 F5
Redford Ave EH13 . . . . . . 149 C6
Redford Bank EH13 . . . . . 149 D6
Redford Cres EH13 . . . . . 149 C6
Redford Dr EH13 . . . . 149 B6
Redford Gdns EH13 . . . . . 149 D6
Redford Loan EH13 . . . . . 149 C6
Redford Neuk EH13 . . . . . 149 C6
Redford Pl EH13 . . . . 149 D6
Redford Rd EH13 . . . . 149 C6
Redford Terr EH13 . . . . . . 149 C6
Redford Wlk EH13 . . . . . . 149 C6
Red Fox Cres EH26 . . . . . 171 A1
Redgauntlet Terr EH16 .122 C1
Redhall FK7 . . . . 8 A4
Redhall Bank Rd EH14 . . 120 B2
Redhall Cres EH14 . . . . . 120 B2
Redhall Bank Rd EH14 . .120 B2
Redhall Gdns EH14 . . . . . 120 A2
Redhall Gr EH14 . . . . 120 A2
Redhall House Dr EH14 .120 B1
Redhall Pl EH14 . . . . 120 B2
Redhall Rd EH14 . . . . 120 A2
Redhall View EH14 . . . . . . 120 B1
Redhaws Rd ML7 . . . . 180 A3
Redheugh Cotts TD13 . .219 E3
Redheugh Loan EH23 . . . 174 C1
Redheughs Ave EH12 . . . 119 A4
Redheughs Rigg EH12 . . . 119 A4
Redholm Pk EH39 . . . . 54 E6
Redhouse Pk EH39 . . . . . . 54 E6
Redhouse Cotts EH49 . . . .86 F3
Redhouse Ct EH47 . . . . . . 162 E7
Redhouse Ind Est FK2 . . . 82 B8
Redhouse Rd EH47 . . . . . 163 A8
Redlands Ct EH47 . . . . . . 161 E7
Redlands Rd FK10 . . . . 4 A3
Redmill Cotts EH47 . . . . 161 E7
Redmill Ct EH47 . . . . 161 E7
Redmill View EH47 . . . . . 161 E7
Redmire Cres ML7 . . . . . . 198 B8
Redpath Dr FK7 . . . . 39 A4
Red Row Aberlady EH32 .71 C4
Limekilns KY11 . . . . 45 D3
Pathhead EH37 . . . . 176 C8
Redside EH39 . . . . 55 B1
Redwell Pl FK10 . . . . 9 F7
Redwing Brae EH54 . . . . 143 D6
Redwood Gr EH22 . . . . . . 173 F5
Redwood Wlk EH22 . . . . 149 B7
Reed Dr FK2 . . . . 174 B6
Reedlands Dr FK6 . . . . 57 D7
Regal Gr ML7 . . . . 179 E4
Regal Lodge EH19 . . . . . . 173 B7
Regent Pl EH7 . . . . 94 A2
Regent Rd EH7,EH8 . . . . . . 229 B4
Regent Sq FK7 . . . . 85 B7
Regent St Edinburgh EH15.123 B8
Kincardine FK10 . . . . 23 E3
Regent Street La EH15 .123 B8

Regents Way KY11 . . . . 48 B3
Regent Terr EH7 . . . . 229 C4
Regent Terrace Mews
EH7 . . . . 229 C4
Regis Ct EH4 . . . . 91 B4
Regent Pl EH2 . . . . 229 A4
Register St EH51 . . . . 63 F8
Reid's Ct EH8 . . . . 229 C3
Reid Ave KY4 . . . . 30 E6
Reid St Dunfermline KY12. .29 A3
Lochgelly KY5 . . . . 14 B8
Reid Terr EH3 . . . . 93 B2
Reilly Gdns FK4 . . . . 58 B3
Reilly Rd FK4 . . . . 58 B3
Relugas Gdns EH9 . . . . . . 121 E3
Relugas Pl EH9 . . . . 121 E3
Relugas Rd EH9 . . . . 121 E3
Rendall Gdns EH52 . . . . 115 F5
Rennie's Isle
Edinburgh EH6 . . . . 93 F6
Edinburgh EH6 . . . . 94 A6
Rennie Pl EH40 . . . . 103 C8
Rennie Sq EH14 . . . . 164 C6
Rennie St FK1 . . . . 60 A3
Research Ave 1 EH14 . . .147 F8
Research Ave N
Hermiston EH14 . . . . 118 F1
Riccarton EH14 . . . . 147 F8
Research Ave S EH14 . . . 147 F8
Restalrig Ave EH7 . . . . 94 D3
Restalrig Cir EH7 . . . . 94 C3
Restalrig Cres EH7 . . . . . . 94 C3
Restalrig Dr EH7 . . . . 94 C2
Restalrig Gdns EH7 . . . . . . 94 C2
Restalrig Ho EH7 . . . . 94 C2
Restalrig Pk EH7 . . . . 94 B3
Restalrig Rd EH7 . . . . 94 B3
Restalrig Rd S
Edinburgh,Jock's Lodge
EH7 . . . . 94 C1
Edinburgh,Lochend EH7 .94 C2
Restalrig Sq EH7 . . . . 94 C3
Restalrig Terr EH6 . . . . 94 A4
Restondene EH54 . . . . 142 E5
Retail Park N EH54 . . . . . 143 D1
Retail Pk Rdbt EH54 . . . 143 E1
Retreat Cres EH42 . . . . 78 D1
Retreat Gdns EH42 . . . . . . 78 D1
Reveston La EH47 . . . . 78 D1
Reynard Gdns EH49 . . . . . 84 A6
Rhodders Gr FK12 . . . . 5 B7
Rhodes Cotts EH39 . . . . . . 54 F7
Rhodes Pk EH39 . . . . 54 F6
Rhodes Smallholdings
EH39 . . . . 55 A6
Rhodes St KY1 . . . . 29 B2
Riccarton Ave EH14 . . . . . 148 A5
Riccarton Cres EH14 . . . 148 A4
Riccarton Dr EH14 . . . . . . 148 A5
Riccarton Gr EH14 . . . . . . 148 A5
Riccarton Mains Rd
EH14 . . . . 148 A6
Riccarton Prim Sch
EH14 . . . . 147 F4
Riccarton Rd EH14 . . . . . . 84 F5
Richard Quinn St FK7 . . . 20 D8
Richmond La EH8 . . . . 82 C8
Richmond La EH8 . . . . . . 229 B2
Richmond Pl
Edinburgh EH8 . . . . 229 B2
Lochgelly KY5 . . . . 14 B7
Richmond Terr
Bo'ness EH51 . . . . 63 F7
Edinburgh EH11 . . . . . . 228 A2
Riddochhill Cres EH47 .162 C7
Riddochhill Ct EH47 . . . 162 B8
Riddochhill Dr EH47 . . . 162 C8
Riddochhill Rd EH47 . . . 162 C8
Riddochhill View EH47 .162 B8
Ridge Ct EH47 . . . . 161 B2
Ridge Way KY11 . . . . 48 B5
Riding Pk EH4 . . . . 91 B4
Ridley Dr KY11 . . . . 46 F3
Riego St EH3 . . . . 228 B2
Rifle Rd EH51 . . . . 62 D8
Riggonhead Ct 4 EH32 .126 D7
Riggonhead Gdns 5
EH33 . . . . 126 D7
Rigg Pk EH42 . . . . 78 C2
Riggs View KY11 . . . . 27 D1
Rigley Terr EH32 . . . . 125 E8
Rig St FK2 . . . . 71 C4
Rig St EH22 . . . . 174 E7
Rillbank Cres EH9 . . . . . . 229 A1
Rillbank Terr EH9 . . . . 121 D5
Rimmon Cres ML7 . . . . . . 179 E6
Ring Rd FK10 . . . . 10 B2
Ringwood Pl 2 EH10 . . .151 B8
Rintoul Ave KY3 . . . . 26 A8
Rintoul Pl Blairhall KY12 . . .26 A8
Edinburgh EH3 . . . . 93 B2
Riselaw Cres EH10 . . . . . 150 A8
Riselaw Pl EH10 . . . . 150 A8
Riselaw Rd EH10 . . . . 150 A8
Riselaw Terr EH10 . . . . . . 150 A8
Ritchie Ct KY12 . . . . 29 A3
Ritchie Pl Bo'ness EH51 . . .64 A5
Grangemouth FK3 . . . . . . 61 F5
Rivaldsgreen Cres EH49 .85 A6
Riverbank View FK6 . . . . . . 2 C1
Riverbank Rd EH47 . . . . 161 F7
Riverbank View FK6 . . . . . . 2 C1
River Gore Gr EH23 . . . . 195 C8
River Gore Rd EH23 . . . . 195 C8
River Gore View EH23 . . . 195 C8
Riverside Cres EH12 . . . . 120 C7
Riverside Dr EH12 . . . . . . 120 C7

Riversdale Rd EH12 . . . . . 120 C7
Riverside
Edinburgh EH4 . . . . 91 B7
Newbridge EH28 . . . . . . 116 F6
Riverside Ct
Linlithgow EH49 . . . . 84 C7
Livingston EH54 . . . . 143 C3
Riverside Dr
Haddington EH41 . . . . . . 101 B1
Stirling FK8 . . . . 2 C1
Riverside Gdns EH21 . . . 124 B5
Riverside Lea Crofts
EH47 . . . . 162 F7
Riverside Pl EH41 . . . . . . 101 C1
Riverside Prim Sch
EH47 . . . . 144 A4
Riverside La EH54 . . . . . . 144 A4
Stirling FK8 . . . . 2 B1
Riverside Rd
Edinburgh EH3 . . . . 90 E3
Grangemouth FK3 . . . . . . 62 B5
Riverside Terr FK10 . . . . . . 23 F3
Riverside View FK10 . . . . . 10 B4
River St FK2 . . . . 39 A1
Riverview FK10 . . . . 10 A7
River View KY11 . . . . 48 B2
River Wlk KY11 . . . . 48 B2
River Wynd FK9 . . . . 2 A4
R L Stevenson's Birthplace &
Mus EH3 . . . . 62 C6
Road 4 FK3 . . . . 62 C6
Road 4a FK3 . . . . 62 C6
Road 4b FK3 . . . . 62 C6
Road 5 FK3 . . . . 62 C7
Road 6 FK3 . . . . 62 C7
Road 7 FK3 . . . . 62 C7
Road 8 FK3 . . . . 62 C7
Road 9 FK3 . . . . 62 C7
Road 10 FK3 . . . . 62 C7
Road 11 FK3 . . . . 62 C7
Road 13 FK3 . . . . 62 A6
Road 14 FK3 . . . . 62 A6
Road 17 FK3 . . . . 62 A6
Road 21 FK3 . . . . 62 A6
Road 24 FK3 . . . . 62 A6
Road 25 FK3 . . . . 62 A6
Road 27 FK3 . . . . 62 A6
Road 28 FK3 . . . . 62 A6
Road 29 FK3 . . . . 62 A6
Road 30a FK3 . . . . 62 B6
Road 30b FK3 . . . . 62 B6
Road 30c FK3 . . . . 62 B6
Road 31 FK3 . . . . 62 B6
Road 32 FK3 . . . . 62 B6
Road 33 FK3 . . . . 62 A6
Roadhead Terr FK10 . . . . . 23 E4
Roanhead Rd FK2 . . . . . . 174 C8
Robb's Loan EH14 . . . . . . 120 C4
Robb's Loan Gr EH14 . . . 120 C4
Robert Bruce Ct FK5 . . . . 38 A2
Robert Burns Dr EH16 .122 A1
Robert Burns Mews
EH22 . . . . 153 D3
Robert De Quincy Pl
EH32 . . . . 125 F8
Robert Dick Ct FK10 . . . . 4 C2
Robert Dow Ct KY5 . . . . . . 14 B8
Robert Hardie Ct FK5 . . . . 38 C2
Robert Kay Pl FK7 . . . . 38 C5
Robert Kinmond Ave FK10. .4 C2
Robert Knox Ave FK10 . . . . 4 C2
Roberts Ave FK2 . . . . 61 D2
Robert Smillie Ave EH22 .174 E5
Robert Smith Ct KY4 . . . . 13 E6
Robertson's Cl
4 Dalkeith EH22 . . . . . 153 A3
Edinburgh EH8 . . . . 229 B2
Robertson Ave
Bathgate EH48 . . . . 140 E5
Bonnybridge FK4 . . . . . . 58 B6
Edinburgh EH11 . . . . . . 120 D5
Prestonpans EH32 . . . . . 97 A2
Tranent EH33 . . . . 126 D6
Robertson Ct
Armadale EH48 . . . . 139 F4
Stenhousemuir FK5 . . . . 38 D2
Robertson Dr EH33 . . . . 126 D7
Robertson Pl FK7 . . . . 7 B3
Robertson Rd KY12 . . . . . . 29 A3
Robertsons Bank EH23. .195 C8
Robertson St KY12 . . . . . . 5 B7
Robertson Way EH54 . . . 143 D7
Robert St ML7 . . . . 179 E4
Robert St KY1 . . . . 17 E8
Robins Neuk EH33 . . . . . 127 C5
Rocheid Pk EH4 . . . . 92 F4
Rochester Terr EH10 . . . . 121 A4
Rocks Rd KY11 . . . . 45 B4
Rockville Gr EH49 . . . . 85 A6
Rockville Terr EH19 . . . . 173 B8
Roddinglaw Cotts EH12 .118 C3
Roddinglaw Rd EH12,
EH28 . . . . 118 C3
Roden Dr FK2 . . . . 61 F1
Rodger Wilson Gr KY12. .29 D8
Rodgers St FK6 . . . . 36 E1
Rodney St Edinburgh EH7 .93 C2
Grangemouth FK3 . . . . . . 61 C6
Roebuck Pl EH51 . . . . 63 D5
Roland St KY12 . . . . 29 A3
Roman Bldgs FK2 . . . . 59 D5
Roman Camp EH37 . . . . 176 B4
Roman Camp Cotts
EH52 . . . . 115 C2
Roman Camp Way EH37.176 B4
Roman Ct EH37 . . . . 176 B4
Roman Dr FK1 . . . . 59 D5
Roman Rd Bonnybridge FK4. 58 A4
Inverkeithing KY11 . . . . . 47 B2
Roman Way EH51 . . . . 63 D5
Romero Pl EH16 . . . . 121 F5

Romyn Rd KY11..........46 C1
Ronades Rd FK2.........60 A8
Ronald Cres FK5.........38 B1
Ronald Pl FK8 ....7 B8
Ronaldshay Cres FK3 ...61 E8
Ronaldson Gr KY12 .....29 D5
Roodlands Ct EH41 ....100 E1
Roodlands General Hospl
  EH41 ....104 E1
Roods Cres KY11 ....47 B3
Roods Rd KY11 ....47 B2
Roods Sq KY11 ....47 C3
Rood Well Cotts EH42...104 E1
Roomlin Gdns KY1.......17 F7
Roosevelt Rd EH27.....145 E3
Ropeway KY11...........46 B1
Rope Wlk EH32..........96 E1
Rosabelle Rd EH25....171 F3
Rosabelle St KY1.......17 E7
Rose Ave EH19 ....173 D6
Rosebank Alloa FK10 ....5 D1
  Bridgend EH49.........86 F4
  Cowdenbeath KY4 .....13 D4
  Dunfermline KY11 .....29 C2
Rosebank Ave FK1......59 F5
Rosebank Cotts EH3 ..228 A2
Rosebank Gdns Alloa FK10 10 C8
  Dunfermline KY12 .....28 D6
  Edinburgh EH5.........93 A5
  Grangemouth FK2......82 B7
  Kincardine FK10 ....23 F3
Rosebank Gr EH5.......93 A5
Rosebank Pl EH54......164 A8
Rosebank Pl FK1........59 F5
Rosebank Rd
  Edinburgh EH5.........93 A5
  Livingston EH54......164 A8
Rosebank Rdbt Falkirk FK1 59 F5
  Livingston EH54......164 B8
Rosebank Way EH54 ...164 A8
Rosebay Glade EH54 ..164 C7
Roseberry Ct EH30.....89 C8
Rosebery Ave EH30....89 C8
Rosebery Cres
  Bathgate EH48........141 B5
  Edinburgh EH12.......120 F7
  Gorebridge EH23.....195 C6
Rosebery Crescent La
  EH12 ....120 F7
Rosebery Ct
  Dalgety Bay KY11 ......47 F2
  Kirkcaldy KY1..........17 B5
Rosebery Gr KY11......47 F2
Rosebery Pl
  Dalgety Bay KY11 ......47 F2
  Gullane EH31..........52 A2
  Livingston EH54......143 B5
  Stirling FK8 ....2 B1
Rosebery Resr EH23 ..211 B6
Rosebery Terr KY1......17 B5
Rosebery View KY11....47 F2
Roseburn Ave EH12 ...120 D7
Roseburn Cliff EH12 ...120 D7
Roseburn Cres EH12 ..120 D7
Roseburn Dr EH12 .....120 D7
Roseburn Gdns EH12..120 D7
Roseburn Maltings EH12 120 E7
Roseburn Pl EH12 .....120 D7
Roseburn Prim Sch
  EH12 ....120 D6
Roseburn St EH12 .....120 D7
Roseburn Terr EH12 ...120 E7
Rosebush Cres KY11...29 C3
Rose Cotts EH19 ......173 D6
Roseneath Ct KY12.....29 A4
Rose Ct EH4............91 E4
Rosedale Ct EH24 ....193 D8
Rosedale Gr EH24......172 D1
Rosedale Neuk EH24 ..172 D1
Rosefield Ave EH15 ...123 A8
Rosefield Avenue La
  EH15 ....123 A8
Rosefield La EH15 ....123 A8
Rosefield Pl EH15 ....123 A8
Rosefield St EH15 ....123 A8
Rose Gdns
  Bonnyrigg and Lasswade
    EH19 ....173 D6
  Cairneyhill KY12 ......27 D2
Rose Gr EH19..........173 D6
Rosehall EH41..........129 F8
Rosehall Ct EH41......129 F8
Rosehall Pl EH41......129 F8
Rosehall Rd EH41......179 C3
Rosehall Terr FK1......60 B4
Rosehall Wlk EH41....129 F8
Rosehill Cres KY4.....13 B3
Rosehill Pl EH54......143 B3
Rose La Lochgelly KY5...14 B7
  South Queensferry EH30...68 B1
  Torryburn KY12 ....26 C1
Roselea Dr FK2........82 B8
Rosemaben Pl KY12...29 C4
Rosemary Ct FK6......36 D2
Rosemead Terr FK1....81 F5
Rosemill Ct KY12 .....26 C1
Rosemount EH32......96 F2
Rosemount Ave KY2...17 A8
Rosemount Bldgs EH3...228 A2
Rosemount Ct
  Bathgate EH48........141 B6
  Carluke ML8 ....215 A2
Rosemount Dr EH52...114 C4
Rosemount Gdns FK1...60 B4
Rosemount Mews EH32..96 F2
Roseneath Pl EH9 .....121 D5
Roseneath St EH9 .....121 D5

Roseneath Terr EH9 ...121 D5
Rose Neuk EH19 ......173 D6
Rose Path EH19 ......173 D6
Rose Pk
  Bonnyrigg and Lasswade
    EH19 ....173 D6
  Edinburgh EH5........93 B5
Rose Pl EH19 ....121 C7
Rose St Alloa FK10 .....4 E1
  Bonnybridge FK4......58 B6
  Burntisland KY3.......50 E8
  Cowdenbeath KY4 .....13 C3
  Dunfermline KY12 .....29 B4
  Edinburgh EH2........228 C3
  Tullibody KY10 ....4 D4
Rose Street North La
  EH2 ....228 C3
Rose Street South La
  EH2 ....228 C3
Rosetay Ct KY12........29 C4
Rose Terr
  Bonnyrigg and Lasswade
    EH19 ....173 D6
  Denny FK6.............36 D1
  Stenhousemuir FK5 ....38 E3
Rosethorn Wynd KY12 .29 C3
Rosevale Pl EH6........94 B4
Rosevale Terr EH6......94 B4
Roseville Gdns EH5 ....93 C6
Rose Way EH19 ....173 D6
Rosewell Prim Sch EH24.172 E2
Rosewell Rd EH18,EH19,..172 E2
Rosin Ct KY1...........17 C7
Roslin Glen Ctry Pk
  EH25 ....171 F1
Roslin Prim Sch EH25..171 F3
Roslin Prim Sch (Bilston
  Annexe) EH25........171 E6
Ross's Cl [12] EH41....130 B8
Ross Ave EH19 ....48 A2
Ross Cres Falkirk FK1...59 C5
  Tranent EH33.........126 D5
Ross Ct Addiewell EH55..183 C8
  Stirling FK7 ....7 B3
Rossend Terr KY3.......50 E8
Ross Gdns Edinburgh EH9 121 F3
  Kirkcaldy KY1..........17 E7
Rossglen Ct EH25 ....172 A3
Ross High Sch EH33 ..126 C6
Rosshill Terr EH30....89 D8
Rossie Pl EH7..........94 A2
Ross La KY12...........28 F4
Rossland Pl KY3........34 F2
Rosslyn Chapel EH25..172 A3
Rosslyn Cres EH6......93 E3
Rosslynlee Hospl EH25.192 F6
Rosslyn Sch KY1.......17 F8
Rosslyn Terr EH6......93 E3
Rossness Dr KY3.......34 F1
Ross Pl Edinburgh EH9 121 F3
  Kinghorn KY3..........34 F1
  Newtongrange EH22 ..174 B6
Ross Rd EH16..........122 A2
Ross St KY12...........29 B5
Ross Way EH54........143 C7
Rosyth Europarc
  North Queensferry KY11..68 A7
  Rosyth KY11...........46 D1
Rosyth Sta KY11.......46 E6
Rothesay Mews EH4 ..120 F8
Rothesay Pl
  Edinburgh EH3........228 A3
  Musselburgh EH21 ...124 D5
Rothesay Terr EH3....228 A3
Rothes Dr EH54........164 F6
Roughburn Rd FK9 .....2 A6
Roughlands Cres FK2...39 B3
Roughlands Dr FK2.....39 A3
Roull Gr EH12.........119 D5
Roull Pl EH12.........119 E5
Roull Rd EH12.........119 D5
Roundel The FK2........96 F2
Roundelwood FK10 .....5 B1
Roundhouse FK7.......20 D8
Round The KY12.......29 C3
Rowallan Ct [4] EH12...119 A7
Rowallan Dr FK7........19 F8
Rowan Cres Falkirk FK1...59 A4
  Menstrie FK11...........3 F6
  Shotts ML7 ....180 B4
Rowan Ct FK7............7 C7
Rowan Dr EH47........141 E1
Rowanfield Sch EH4 ...92 C3
Rowan Gdns EH19 ....173 B6
Rowan Gr
  Dunfermline KY11 .....29 D1
  Livingston EH54......144 B5
Rowanhill Cl EH32......97 D3
Rowanhill Dr EH32......97 D3
Rowanhill Way EH32...97 C3
Rowan Pl EH47........141 D1
Rowan Pl EH47........141 E1
Rowan St Blackburn EH47 141 D1
  Dunbar EH42..........78 B1
Rowans The Alloa FK10 ..5 C2
  Gullane EH31..........52 B3
Rowan Terr
  Blackburn EH47.......162 D8
  Cowdenbeath KY4 .....13 C3
Rowantree Ave EH14...147 E4
Rowantree Gr EH14...147 E4
Rowantree Rd EH22...174 E7
Rowantree Wlk FK5....38 B4
Roxburghe Ct EH42 ...78 F1

Roxburghe Lodge Wynd
  EH42 ....78 F1
Roxburgh Pk EH42....78 F1
Roxburghe Terr EH42...78 F1
Roxburgh Pl
  Edinburgh EH8.......229 B2
  Stenhousemuir FK5 ...38 F4
Roxburgh St
  Edinburgh EH8.......229 B2
  Grangemouth FK3.....61 F8
Royal Blind Sch The
  EH16 ....121 F3
Royal Botanic Garden
  EH3 ....93 B3
Royal Cir EH3..........93 C2
Royal Coll of Physicians
  EH2 ....228 C4
Royal Cres EH3........93 C2
Royal Cres EH26 .....191 D7
Royal (Dick) Veterinary Coll
  EH8 ....229 B1
Royal Edinburgh Hospl
  EH10 ....121 A3
Royal High Prim Sch The
  EH8 ....122 D8
Royal High Sch The EH4..91 D3
Royal Hospl for Sick Children
  EH9 ....121 D5
Royal Infirmary of Edinburgh
  EH16 ....122 E1
Royal Lyceum Theatre
  EH1 ....228 B2
Royal Mile Prim Sch
  EH8 ....229 C3
Royal Museum of Scotland
  EH1 ....229 A2
Royal Mus of Scotland
  EH1 ....229 A2
Royal Observatory EH9 121 D2
Royal Park Pl [4] EH8 ..94 B1
Royal Park Terr EH8 ..94 B1
Royal Scot Ct EH48 ..141 B6
Royal Scottish Acad EH2 228 C3
Royal Scottish Academy
  EH2 ....228 C3
Royal Scottish National
  Hospl The FK5.........37 F3
Royal Scot Way KY12 ..29 A5
Royal Terr Edinburgh EH7 229 C4
  Linlithgow EH49.......84 F6
Royal Victoria Hospl EH4 .92 E2
Royal Yacht Britannia
  EH6 ....93 F7
Roy Dr EH54...........164 F6
Royston Mains Ave EH5..92 E6
Royston Mains Cl EH5..92 E6
Royston Mains Cres EH5..92 E6
Royston Mains Gdns EH5..92 E6
Royston Mains Gn EH5..92 E6
Royston Mains Pl EH5...92 E6
Royston Mains Rd EH5..92 E6
Royston Mains St EH5..92 D6
Royston Rd EH54......142 D7
Royston Rdbt EH54 ...142 D7
Rudolf Steiner Sch EH10.120 F4
Rutley View FK6........36 C4
Rullion Green Ave EH26..191 D7
Rullion Green Cres
  EH26 ....191 D7
Rullion Green Gr EH26..191 D7
Rullion Rd EH26......191 C6
Rumblingwell KY12 ....28 D5
Rumlie The FK1.........108 A6
Run The EH51..........64 C7
Rushbank EH54.......143 E6
Ruskie Rd FK9..........2 B3
Ruskin Pl EH22........174 E5
Russel Ct KY5..........14 B8
Russell Ave EH48.....139 F7
Russell Ct KY11........29 F1
Russell Gdns EH12...120 E7
Russell Pl EH5.........93 C5
Russell Rd KY3..........33 F2
Russell Hill Ct FK5.....38 B1
Russell Pl Bonnybridge FK4 57 D5
  Edinburgh EH5........93 B6
  [1] Kirkcaldy KY1......17 C5
  Oakley KY12...........26 F7
Russell Rd EH11......120 E6
Russell St
  Cowdenbeath KY4 ....13 B4
  Lochgelly KY5........14 B8
Russel St KY12.........60 B6
Rutherford Ct
  Bridge of A FK9........2 A8
  Kirkcaldy KY1..........17 E7
Rutherford Sq EH54..164 C6
Ruthven Pl EH16......122 C3
Ruthven Rd EH9........53 A4
Rutland Court La EH3..228 B2
Rutland Sq EH1.......228 B3
Rutland St EH1........228 B3
Ryebank EH54.........143 E6
Ryehill Ave EH6........94 B3
Ryehill Gdns EH6......94 B3
Ryehill Gr EH6.........94 B3
Ryehill Pl EH6.........94 B3
Ryehill Terr EH6........94 B4
Ryalton KY1...........17 D6

Sacred Heart Prim Sch
  EH26 ....191 E5

Sacred Heart RC Prim Sch
  FK3 ....61 E6
Saddletree Loan EH16 .122 C2
Sailors' Wlk KY3........50 D8
Sainford Cres FK2......39 A1
St Alban's Rd EH9.....121 E3
St Andrew's Ct FK5....38 B3
St Andrew's Dr Armadale FK2 .22 B7
  Armadale EH48.......139 F7
  Uphall EH52...........114 F4
St Andrew's RC High Sch
  KY2....................17 D8
St Andrew's RC Prim Sch
  FK1.....................29 C2
St Andrew's Way EH54 .142 E6
St Andrew Pl EH6......94 A4
St Andrews Pl [10] FK1 ..60 B4
St Andrew Sq EH2 ....229 A4
St Andrew St
  Dalkeith EH22.........153 A3
  Dunfermline KY11 .....29 C2
  North Berwick EH39 ...54 C7
St Andrews Way Bsns Units
  EH54 ....142 E6
St Ann's Ave EH18 ....172 E6
St Ann's Path EH18 ...172 E6
St Ann's Pl EH41......130 B8
St Anne's Cres FK7 .....7 E1
St Anne's Ct FK2 .....174 A5
St Anthony's RC Prim Sch
  EH48 ....122 E6
St Anthony La EH6.....93 F5
St Anthony Pl EH6.....93 F5
St Anthony St EH6.....93 F5
St Augustine's High Sch
  EH12 ....119 C4
St Baldred's Cres EH39..54 D7
St Baldred's Rd EH39...54 D6
St Bernadette's RC Prim Sch
  FK10....................4 A2
St Bernard's Cres EH4..93 A2
St Bernard's Row [1] EH3 .93 B2
St Bride's RC Prim Sch
  KY4....................13 C3
St Bridgets Brae KY11 ..48 A4
St Brycedale Ave KY1..17 B4
St Brycedale Rd KY1...17 B4
St Catherine's Gdns
  EH12 ....120 A6
St Catherine's Pl EH9 121 E5
St Catherine's Wynd KY12 28 F3
St Catherine Pl EH9 ..121 E5
St Catherines St [4] EH22.153 A2
St Catherines Ct Nat'l [7] EH6.93 D7
St Catherine's Manor
  EH12 ....120 A6
St Catherine's RC Prim Sch
  EH16 ....151 B5
St Clair Ave EH6.......94 A3
St Clair Cres EH25 ...172 A3
St Clair Pl EH6.........94 A3
St Clair Rd EH6........94 A3
St Clairs Ct KY3.......35 A2
St Clairs Entry KY3...35 A2
St Clair St Edinburgh EH6....94 A3
  Kirkcaldy KY1..........17 E7
St Clair Terr EH10....120 F1
St Clement's Ct EH21..125 B4
St Clement's Gdns N
  EH21 ....125 B4
St Clement's Gdns S
  EH21 ....125 B4
St Clement's Terr EH21..125 B4
St Colm's Ed Ctr & Coll
  EH3 ....93 B3
St Colme Ave
  Aberdour KY3..........49 A5
  Aberdour KY3..........49 A6
St Colme Cres EH5.....94 B7
St Colme Dr KY11......48 D5
St Colme Rd KY11......48 D5
St Colme St EH3.......228 B4
St Columba's RC High Sch
  EH48 ....141 B6
St Columba's RC Prim Sch
  KY1....................29 C3
St Crispin's Pl FK1.....60 B4
St Crispin's Specl Sch
  EH16 ....121 E3
St Cuthbert's Prim Sch
  EH14 ....120 D4
St David's Bsns Pk KY11 .48 A4
St David's Ct
  Dalgety Bay KY11 .....48 A3
  Larbert FK5............38 B1
St David's Dr KY11.....48 A4
St David's RC High Sch
  EH22 ....153 D5
St David's Terr EH3 ..228 A2
St Davids EH22 ......153 C2
St Fillan's Terr EH10 .121 A1
St Fillans Cres KY3....49 C8
St Fillans Pl KY2.......16 D7
St Francis' Prim Sch
  KY1....................17 D6
St Francis Xavier's RC Prim
  Sch FK2...............60 A6
St Gabriel's RC Prim Sch
  EH32 ....95 F5
St George's Ct FK5....38 B1
St George's Sch EH12..120 E8

St Georges Sch for Girls
  EH12 ....120 D7
St Germains EH32 .....98 B2
St Germains Cnr EH33 .127 B2
St Germains Terr EH33 127 D6
St Giles Sq FK1........59 B6
St Giles St EH1.......229 A3
St Giles Way FK1.......59 B6
St Helen's Pl EH48....139 F5
Sainthill Ct EH9 ......229 A4
St James' Orch FK9....2 D1
St James' Ct KY11......29 F1
St James's Gdns EH26.191 E4
St James's View EH26..191 E4
St James Ctr EH1 ....229 A4
St James Pl Bridgend EH49 86 F4
  Kinghorn KY3..........35 A2
St James Sq EH1 ....229 A4
St John's Ave
  Edinburgh EH12.......119 E6
  Falkirk FK2............60 C6
  Linlithgow EH49.......84 F6
St John's Cres EH12 ..119 F6
St John's Ct KY11......47 D3
St John's Dr KY12.....29 C3
St John's Gate FK6.....36 C2
St John's Gdns Denny FK6 36 C2
  Edinburgh EH12.......119 E6
St John's Gr FK6.......36 C2
St John's Hill EH8 ....229 B2
St John's Hospl EH54 .143 D4
St John's Pl KY12.....29 D3
St Luke's Prim Sch FK10...9 F6
St John's RC Prim Sch
  Edinburgh EH15.......123 A7
  Rosyth KY11...........46 F3
St John's Rd
  Broxburn EH52.......115 E4
  Edinburgh EH12.......119 E6
  Falkirk FK2............60 C6
St John's Terr EH12 ..119 E6
St John's Way EH51...63 F5
St John Ogilvie RC Prim Sch
  EH54 ....142 F6
St Johns Ct EH54 ....143 E4
St Johns Ct FK54......60 C6
St John St EH8.........111 F5
St John St Edinburgh EH8 229 B3
  Spott EH42............106 C3
  Stirling FK8 ....7 A8
St John the Baptist RC Sch
  EH47 ....181 E6
St Joseph's Cotts FK33 126 D8
St Joseph's Prim Sch
  EH11 ....119 F3
St Joseph's RC Prim Sch
  Bonnybridge FK4......58 B4
  Linlithgow EH49.......84 F6
St Josephs RC Prim Sch
  EH47 ....160 F5
St Katharine's Brae
  EH16 ....151 A6
St Katharine's Cres
  EH16 ....151 A6
St Katharine's Loan
  EH16 ....151 B5
St Kentigern Rd EH26..191 D6
St Kentigerns RC Acad
  EH47 ....162 B7
St Kilda Cres KY2......16 F8
St Laurence Cres FK1..108 B6
St Lawrence EH54 ....129 E8
St Lawrence St KY11 ..29 C1
St Leonard's EH8 ....121 E5
St Leonard's Bank EH8..229 C1
St Leonard's Crag EH8..229 C1
St Leonard's Ct KY3....35 A3
St Leonard's Hill EH8 229 B1
St Leonard's Hill EH8 229 B1
St Leonard's Pl
  Dunfermline KY11 .....29 B1
  Kinghorn KY3..........34 F3
St Leonard's Prim Sch
  KY11 ....29 B1
St Leonard's St
  Dunfermline KY11 .....29 B2
  Edinburgh EH8........229 B1
St Magaret Wynd KY12..29 F6
St Magdalenes EH49...85 B7
St Margaret's Cave Mus
  KY12 ....28 F4
St Margaret's Cres KY2..61 E2
St Margaret's Dr EH48..139 E5
St Margaret's Pl EH9..121 C4
St Margaret's Prim Sch
  EH22 ....153 C3
  Loanhead EH20......151 C1
  South Queensferry EH30..68 C1
St Margaret's RC Acad
  EH54 ....143 D3
St Margaret's RC Prim Sch
  FK7.....................20 D7
St Margaret's Rd
  Edinburgh EH9........121 B4
  North Berwick EH39 ...54 C7
St Margarets Ct EH39...54 C7
St Margarets EH16....152 C4
St Margarets Gdns FK2..61 D2
St Margaret St KY12...29 A3

St Marie's RC Prim Sch
KY2...................................17 D8
St Mark's La EH15 ....123 B8
St Mark's Pl EH15 ....123 B8
St Mark's RC Prim Sch
EH14 ....149 E7
St Martin's Ct EH41 ....130 C8
St Martin's Gate EH41 ....130 B8
St Martin's Pl EH41 ....130 C7
St Martin's RC Prim Sch
EH33 ....126 D6
St Martins La EH33 ....126 E6
St Mary's Cathedral EH2 ..228 A3
St Mary's Glebe KY1 ....17 C5
St Mary's Music Sch
EH12 ....120 F7
St Mary's Pl
Bathgate EH48 ....141 C5
Edinburgh EH15 ....123 C8
Kirkcaldy KY1 ....17 C5
St Mary's Pleasance & Lady
Kitty's Garden EH41 ....130 B8
St Mary's Pl La EH15 ....123 C8
St Mary's Prim Sch EH6 ...94 B5
St Mary's RC Prim Sch
FK7 ....7 D2
Bathgate EH48 ....141 A6
Bo'ness EH51 ....64 A7
Bonnyrigg and Lasswade
EH19 ....173 B6
Edinburgh EH7 ....93 E2
Haddington EH41 ....130 A8
Polbeth EH55 ....163 F5
Stirling FK8 ....1 E2
St Mary's Rd KY1 ....17 C5
St Mary's St EH1 ....229 B3
St Mary's Wynd [8] FK8 ......7 A8
St Marys Pl FK3 ....61 E8
St Matthew's Prim Sch
EH24 ....172 E2
St Michael's Ave EH21 ....124 C5
St Michael's Hospl EH49 ...85 C6
St Michael's Wynd EH49 ...85 B7
St Michaels La EH41 ....85 B7
St Modan's High Sch FK7 ...7 A3
St Modans Ct [5] FK1 ....60 B4
St Mungo's High Sch FK2 ..60 A6
St Mungo's RC Prim Sch
FK10 ....10 C5
St Mungo's View EH26 ....191 F5
St Mungo's Wynd FK10 ....10 A6
St Nicholas RC Prim Sch
EH52 ....115 C4
St Nicholas Sch EH11 ......120 D5
St Ninian's Ave EH49 ....84 E8
St Ninian's Dr EH12 ....120 C3
St Ninian's Prim Sch
Edinburgh EH7 ....94 C2
Livingston EH54 ....144 A1
St Ninian's Rd
Edinburgh EH12 ....119 D7
Linlithgow EH49 ....84 F7
St Ninian's Row EH1 ....229 A4
St Ninian's Terr EH10 ......120 F1
St Ninian's Way EH49 ....84 F7
St Ninians Prim Sch FK7 ....7 A4
St Ninians Rd
Cambusbarron FK7 ....6 E5
Stirling FK8 ....7 B6
St Ninians Way
Blackness EH49 ....65 E4
Musselburgh EH21 ....125 A6
St Patrick's Prim Sch
ML7 ....179 F4
St Patrick's RC Prim Sch
FK6 ....36 E3
St Patrick Sq EH8 ....229 B1
St Patrick St EH8 ....229 B1
St Paul's Dr EH48 ....140 A5
St Paul's Prim Sch EH53 .144 F4
St Peter's Ct KY1 ....47 D3
St Peter's RC Sch EH10 ...121 B3
St Peter's Bldgs EH11 .....228 A1
St Peter's Pl EH11 ....228 A1
St Ronan's Terr EH10 ....121 A2
St Sarf's Pl KY1 ....118 A3
St Serf's Pl FK10 ....4 B3
St Serf's Prim Sch FK10 .....4 B3
St Serf's RC Prim Sch
KY12 ....26 A2
St Serf's Rd FK10 ....4 B3
St Serf's Sch EH12 ....120 E2
St Serf's Wlk FK12 ....4 E6
St Serfs Gr FK10 ....11 B4
St Stephen's Ct EH11 .....119 C2
St Stephen Pl EH3 ....93 B2
St Stephen St EH3 ....93 B2
St Teresa Pl EH10 ....120 F4
St Thomas's Pl FK7 ....6 E6
St Thomas's Well FK7 ....6 D7
St Thomas of Aquin's RC
High Sch EH3 ....228 C1
St Thomas Rd EH16 ....93 A5
St Triduana's Chapel EH7 .94 C1
St Valery Ct FK7 ....7 A4
St Valery Dr FK7 ....7 A4
St Vincent St EH3 ....93 B2
Salamanca Cres EH26 .....192 A8
Salamander Pl EH6 ....94 B5
Salamander St EH6 ....94 A5
Salamander Yds EH6 ....94 C5
Salen Loan ML7 ....180 B2
Salisbury Mews EH9 ....121 F5

Salisbury Pl EH9 ....121 E5
Salisbury Rd EH16 ....121 F5
Salisbury St KY2 ....17 B5
Salisbury View EH22 ....174 D6
Salmond Pl [4] EH7 ....94 A1
Salmon Dr FK1 ....59 E1
Salmon Inn Pk FK2 ....61 C2
Salmon Inn Rd FK2 ....61 C2
Saltcoats Dr FK3 ....61 E7
Saltcoats Farm Cotts
EH31 ....52 B1
Saltcoats Gdns EH54 ....164 E6
Saltcoats Rd
Grangemouth FK3 ....62 B8
Gullane EH31 ....52 A2
Salter's Rd Dalkeith EH22 .153 D4
Wallyford EH21 ....125 A4
Salters' Gr EH22 ....153 C4
Salters' Rd
Dalkeith,Woodburn
EH22 ....153 C4
Pathhead EH37 ....177 A2
Salters' Terr EH22 ....153 C4
Saltersgate Sch EH22 ......153 D5
Saltire Gdns EH31 ....101 F7
Saltoun Hall EH34 ....157 C5
Saltoun Prim Sch EH34 ...157 C5
Saltpans KY11 ....45 B4
Salt Preston Pl EH32 ....96 F1
Salvage Rd KY11 ....46 C1
Salvesen Cres EH4 ....92 A5
Salvesen Gdns EH4 ....92 B5
Salvesen Gr EH4 ....92 B6
Salvesen Terr EH4 ....92 B6
Samoa Terr EH26 ....192 A8
Samuelston East Mains Cotts
EH41 ....129 A2
Sandeman Ct FK10 ....23 E4
Sanderling Way KY11 ....30 B5
Sanderson's Gr [2] EH33 .126 D7
Sanderson's Wynd [1]
EH33 ....126 D7
Sanderson Terr KY1 ....15 B2
Sandford Gate KY1 ....17 B3
Sandford Gdns EH15 ....123 A8
Sandiland Dr EH53 ....144 B2
Sandilands KY1 ....45 D3
Sandpiper Dr KY11 ....30 C2
Sandport EH6 ....94 A6
Sandport Pl EH6 ....93 F5
Sandport St EH6 ....93 F6
Sandport Trad Est EH6 .....93 A6
Sands The EH41 ....130 B8
Sandvale Pl ML7 ....180 A3
Sandwell Cres KY1 ....35 B6
Sandyford Ave EH4 ....84 A6
Sandyhill Ave ML7 ....180 A3
Sandy La EH31 ....51 F2
Sandyloan FK2 ....61 B4
Sandy Loan EH31 ....52 A2
Sandyloan Cres FK2 ....61 B3
Sandy Rd KY3 ....32 C5
Sang Pl KY1 ....17 B4
Sang Rd KY1 ....17 B4
Sarazen Ct EH54 ....143 B8
Sarazen Gn EH54 ....143 B8
Sauchenbush Rd KY2 ....16 F5
Sauchenford Smallholdings
FK7 ....20 A5
Sauchiebank EH11 ....120 E6
Sauchie Ct FK7 ....7 F1
Sauchie Hospl FK10 ....10 C8
Sauchie St FK7 ....7 A2
Saughbank EH52 ....115 B5
Saughland Cotts EH37 ....197 F7
Saughs The EH22 ....174 A4
Saughton Ave EH11 ....120 C4
Saughton Cres EH12 ....120 B5
Saughton Gdns EH12 ....120 B6
Saughton Gr EH12 ....120 B6
Saughton Mains Ave
EH11 ....119 F3
Saughton Mains Bank
EH11 ....120 A4
Saughton Mains Dr
EH11 ....119 F3
Saughton Mains Gdns
EH11 ....119 F3
Saughton Mains Loan
EH11 ....119 F3
Saughton Mains Pk
EH11 ....119 F4
Saughton Mains Pl EH11 .119 F3
Saughton Mains St EH11 .120 A4
Saughton Mains Terr
EH11 ....119 F4
Saughton Rd EH11 ....119 E4
Saughton Rd N EH12 ....119 E5
Saunders Ct KY1 ....17 B2
Saunders St
Edinburgh EH3 ....228 A4
Kirkcaldy KY1 ....17 B2
Savile Pl EH9 ....121 F3
Savile Terr EH9 ....121 F3

Sawers Ave FK6 ....36 A3
Saxe Coburg Pl EH3 ....93 B2
Saxe Coburg St EH3 ....93 B2
Scarlett Pk EH21 ....125 B5
Schaw Ct FK10 ....5 D1
Schawpark Ave FK10 ....5 D1
Schaw Rd EH32 ....97 B1
Schilton Way FK7 ....7 D3
Scholars' Brae KY3 ....50 E8
School Brae Bo'ness EH51 ..63 F8
Bonnyrigg and Lasswade
EH18 ....152 A1
Dysart KY1 ....18 A7
Edinburgh EH4 ....91 B6
West Barns EH42 ....105 F8
School Gn
Bonnyrigg and Lasswade
EH18 ....152 A1
Longniddry EH32 ....98 E5
Schoolhouse Ind Est
EH55 ....162 E2
School La Allanton ML7 ....198 B8
Bathgate EH48 ....141 B6
Cockenzie & Port Seton
EH32 ....97 C4
Dalgety Bay KY11 ....47 F4
Menstrie FK11 ....4 A7
Mid Calder EH53 ....144 D4
School Mews FK11 ....4 A7
School Pl EH52 ....114 F4
School Rd Aberlady EH32 ...71 C4
Broxburn EH52 ....115 D5
East Linton EH40 ....103 E7
Laurieston FK2 ....61 A3
Longridge EH47 ....161 C2
North Berwick EH39 ....54 D7
Redding FK2 ....61 B2
Tullibody FK10 ....4 B2
School Row KY12 ....28 C6
School St
Cowdenbeath KY4 ....13 D3
Shotts ML7 ....179 F4
School View Bo'ness EH51 .64 A7
Redding FK2 ....61 C1
School Wlk FK5 ....38 D3
Schoolyard Ct EH25 ....172 A3
Sciennes EH9 ....121 E5
Sciennes Gdns EH9 ....121 E5
Sciennes Hill Pl [2] EH9 ..121 E5
Sciennes House Pl [3]
EH9 ....121 E5
Sciennes Pl [1] EH9 ....121 E5
Sciennes Prim Sch EH9 ...121 D5
Sciennes Rd EH9 ....121 D5
Scion Ho FK9 ....2 D5
Sclandersburn Rd FK6 ....57 C8
Scobie Pl KY12 ....29 F8
Scollon Ave EH10 ....173 C8
Scone Gdns EH8 ....94 C1
Scotch Whisky Heritage Ctr
The EH1 ....228 C2
Scotia Pl FK2 ....60 C5
Scotland Dr KY12 ....29 E4
Scotlands Cl EH51 ....63 F8
Scotland St EH3 ....93 C3
Scotmill Way KY12 ....97 C3
Scots Mill Pl KY11 ....47 E4
Scotstoun Ave EH30 ....89 C7
Scotstoun Gdns EH30 ....89 B8
Scotstoun Gn EH30 ....89 C7
Scotstoun Pk EH30 ....89 C7
Scotstoun Rd FK7 ....20 E7
Scott Ave FK2 ....61 E2
Scott Cres EH10 ....10 B5
Scott Ct Alva FK12 ....5 B6
Livingston EH54 ....144 C5
Scottish Ag Science Agency
EH12 ....119 A8
Scottish Korean War
Memorial EH48 ....112 D6
Scottish Mining Mus
EH22 ....174 A4
Scottish Nat Gall of Mod Art
EH4 ....120 C6
Scottish Parliament The
EH8 ....229 C3
Scottish Pol Coll FK10 ....23 F5
Scottish Prison Service Coll
FK2 ....82 C8
Scottish Railway Exhibition
EH51 ....64 A8
Scottish Seabird Ctr EH39 ..54 C8
Scott Mon EH2 ....229 A3
Scott Pl EH47 ....181 F6
Scott Rd EH26 ....191 E7
Scott St Dunfermline KY12 .28 E5
Grangemouth FK3 ....61 D5
Kirkcaldy KY1 ....17 B2
Stirling FK8 ....2 A2
Scott Terr Bathgate EH48 .141 C5
Falkirk FK2 ....39 B1
Scoughall Cotts EH39 ....56 D3
Seabegs Cres FK4 ....58 A4
Seabegs Pl FK4 ....57 F4
Seabegs Rd FK4 ....57 F4
Seabegs Wood Antonine
Wall FK4 ....57 E3
Seacliff EH39 ....56 A5
Seacot EH6 ....94 C4
Seafield Ave EH6 ....94 C4
Seafield Cres
Bilston EH25 ....171 E6
Dunbar EH42 ....78 A1
Kirkcaldy KY1 ....35 B8
Seafield Ct [3] EH6 ....59 F2
Seafield Gdns KY1 ....35 B8
Seafield Moor Rd EH10,
EH25 ....171 C6

Seafield Pl
Dalgety Bay KY11 ....48 A2
Edinburgh EH6 ....94 C4
Seafield Prim Sch EH47 ...142 B1
Blackburn EH47 ....162 F8
Edinburgh EH6 ....94 D4
Kirkcaldy KY1 ....35 B8
Seafield Rd E EH15 ....94 F3
Seafield Rows EH47 ....142 B1
Seafield St EH6 ....94 D4
Seafield View
Kinghorn KY3 ....35 A3
Kirkcaldy KY1 ....35 B8
West Barns EH42 ....94 E3
Seaforth Dr EH4 ....92 C2
Seaforth Pl
Burntisland KY3 ....50 D8
Kirkcaldy KY1 ....17 F8
Seaforth Rd FK2 ....39 C1
Seaforth Terr
Bonnyrigg and Lasswade
EH19 ....172 F6
Edinburgh EH4 ....92 C2
Sealcar St EH5 ....92 E7
Sealock Ct KY2 ....61 D5
Sealstrand KY11 ....48 C4
Seaport St EH6 ....94 A5
Sea Rd EH42 ....77 F1
Seaside Pl KY3 ....69 C7
Seaton Dr FK1 ....60 D4
Seaview Cres EH15 ....123 E7
Seaview Pl EH51 ....63 F8
Seaview Terr
Edinburgh EH15 ....123 E7
Maddiston FK2 ....82 F6
Sea Wynd EH32 ....71 D5
Second Gait EH14 ....147 E8
Second St EH22 ....174 B5
Seco Pl KY4 ....13 D4
Sedgebank EH54 ....143 E6
Segal Pl KY12 ....28 F4
Seggarsdean Cres EH41 ...130 D7
Seggarsdean Ct EH41 ......130 D8
Seggarsdean Pk EH41 ......130 D8
Seggarsdean Terr EH41 ...130 D8
Selkirk Ave KY4 ....13 C2
Selkirk Rd KY11 ....67 B8
Selm Pk EH54 ....144 A3
Selvage Pl KY11 ....47 A3
Selvage St KY11 ....47 A3
Semple St EH3 ....228 B2
Seton Chapel EH32 ....97 F3
Seton Ct
Cockenzie & Port Seton
EH32 ....97 E4
[6] Tranent EH33 ....126 C5
Seton Dr FK7 ....7 C4
Seton Mains Cotts EH32 ....98 B3
Seton Pl
Cockenzie & Port Seton
EH32 ....97 D4
Dalgety Bay KY11 ....48 D5
Edinburgh EH9 ....121 E5
Kirkcaldy KY2 ....16 D7
Seton Rd EH32 ....98 E5
Seton Sands Cvn Pk EH32 .97 F4
Seton Steading EH32 ....98 B3
Seton Terr EH51 ....64 B7
Seton View EH32 ....97 E3
Seton Wynd EH32 ....97 E4
Seventh St EH22 ....174 B5
Shadepark Cres EH22 ....153 B4
Shadepark Dr EH22 ....153 B4
Shadepark Gdns EH22 .....153 B4
Shaftesbury Pl KY11 ....120 E4
Shaftesbury St KY10 ....120 A7
Shafto Pl EH51 ....63 F5
Shamrock St KY12 ....29 B5
Shandon Cres EH11 ....120 E4
Shandon Pl EH11 ....120 E4
Shandon Rd EH11 ....120 E4
Shandon St EH11 ....120 E4
Shandon Terr EH11 ....120 E4
Shandwick Pl EH2 ....228 B3
Shanks Ave FK6 ....57 E8
Shanks Rd EH47 ....161 B7
Shannon Dr FK1 ....59 F4
Shanter Way [2] KY11 ....122 A1
Sharpdale Loan EH16 ....122 B3
Sharp Terr FK3 ....61 C6
Shaw's Cres EH26 ....171 A1
Shaw Ave EH48 ....139 F6
Shaw Cres KY5 ....14 B7
Shawfair Farm Cotts
EH22 ....123 D2
Shaw Pl Armadale EH48 ...139 F6
Grangemouth FK3 ....61 C5
Mayfield EH22 ....174 D8
Shaws Ct EH26 ....171 B1
Shaw's Pl EH7 ....93 E3
Shaw's Sq EH7 ....93 E3
Shaw's St EH7 ....93 E3
Shaw St KY11 ....29 D2
Shaw's Terr EH7 ....93 E3
Shearer Sq KY11 ....47 A3
Sheephousehill EH47 ....181 F6
Sheelings The FK10 ....4 B1
Shepherd Cres KY3 ....50 D8
Shepherdlands Gr KY12 ....26 D7
Sherbrooke Rd KY11 ....46 D3
Sheriff Bank EH6 ....93 F5
Sheriff Brae EH6 ....93 F5
Sheriffhall Junc EH22 ....152 D5
Sheriffhall Mains Cotts
EH22 ....152 E6
Sheriffmuirlands FK9 ....2 C3
Sheriffmuir Rd FK9 ....2 D7

Sheriff Pk EH6 ....93 F5
Sheriffs Pk EH49 ....85 E8
Sherriff Hall Cotts EH54 ...74 E8
Sherriff La FK5 ....38 F3
Sherwood Ave EH19 ....173 C6
Sherwood Cres EH19 ....173 C6
Sherwood Ct EH19 ....173 C6
Sherwood Dr EH19 ....173 C6
Sherwood Gr EH19 ....173 C6
Sherwood Ind Est EH19 ...173 C7
Sherwood Loan EH19 ....173 C6
Sherwood Pk EH19 ....173 C6
Sherwood Pl EH19 ....173 C6
Sherwood Terr EH19 ....173 C6
Sherwood View EH19 ....173 C6
Sherwood Way EH19 ....173 C6
Sherwood Wlk EH19 ....173 D5
Shetland Ct FK10 ....10 B5
Shetland Pl KY1 ....17 E7
Shiel Ct FK3 ....61 A6
Shieldhill Prim Sch FK1 ....81 D6
Shieldhill Rd FK2 ....82 A8
Shields Ct EH52 ....115 C5
Shields Pl EH47 ....29 B3
Shiel Gdns Falkirk FK2 ......39 C1
Shotts ML7 ....180 A3
Shiel Ho EH54 ....144 A5
Shieling The KY12 ....27 E1
Shiel Wlk EH54 ....144 A5
Shierlaw Gdns FK2 ....22 D4
Shillinghill KY10 ....10 B6
Shinwell Pl KY11 ....46 A4
Shiphaugh Pl FK8 ....2 C1
Shire Way FK10 ....9 F6
Shirra's Brae Rd FK7 ....7 B8
Shoestanes Rd EH38 ....214 C3
Shoestanes Terr EH38 .....214 C2
Shore Edinburgh EH6 ....93 F5
Edinburgh EH6 ....94 A6
Shore Pl EH6 ....94 A5
Shore Rd Aberdour KY3 .....49 C7
Airth FK2 ....22 D4
Dysart KY1 ....18 A6
South Queensferry EH30 ....68 B1
Stirling FK8 ....7 C8
Shore St EH42 ....78 E3
Shore The FK10 ....10 A5
Shorthope St EH21 ....124 C6
Shottsburn Rd ML7 ....158 A3
Shottskirk Rd ML7 ....179 C6
Shotts Rd
Fauldhouse EH47 ....181 C4
Harthill ML7 ....158 A2
Shotts Sta ML7 ....179 E4
Shrub Mount EH15 ....95 A4
Shrub Place La EH7 ....93 E3
Sibbald Pl EH54 ....143 B5
Sibbalds Brae EH48 ....140 D5
Sidegate EH41 ....130 B8
Sidegate Mews EH41 ....130 B8
Sidehead Rd ML7 ....159 E5
Sidlaw Pl FK3 ....61 E5
Sidlaw St KY2 ....16 F7
Sienna Gdns EH9 ....121 E5
Sighthill Ave EH11 ....119 E2
Sighthill Bank EH11 ....119 D2
Sighthill Cres EH11 ....119 D1
Sighthill Ct EH11 ....119 D2
Sighthill Dr EH11 ....119 D1
Sighthill Gdns EH11 ....119 D2
Sighthill Gn EH11 ....119 D2
Sighthill Gr EH11 ....119 D2
Sighthill Ind Est EH11 ......119 B3
Sighthill Loan EH11 ....119 D2
Sighthill Neuk EH11 ....119 D2
Sighthill Pk EH11 ....119 D2
Sighthill Pl EH11 ....119 D2
Sighthill Prim Sch EH11 ...119 C1
Sighthill Rd EH11 ....119 D1
Sighthill Rise EH11 ....119 D1
Sighthill St EH11 ....119 D1
Sighthill Terr EH11 ....119 D1
Sighthill View EH11 ....119 D1
Sighthill Wynd EH11 ....119 D1
Signal Station KY11 ....68 C5
Silk Ho [1] FK1 ....60 B5
Silverbarton Terr KY3 ....33 D1
Silverbirch Glade EH54 ...164 C7
Silverburn Dr EH26 ....191 C6
Silverburn Gdns FK12 ....5 C7
Silverdale Rd FK2 ....82 E8
Silverknowes Ave EH4 ....91 F4
Silverknowes Bank EH4 .....91 F4
Silverknowes Brae EH4 .....92 A4
Silverknowes Ct EH4 ....91 F4
Silverknowes Dell EH4 ......91 F4
Silverknowes Eastway
EH4 ....91 F4
Silverknowes Gdns EH4 ....92 A4
Silverknowes Gn EH4 ....92 A3
Silverknowes Gr EH4 ....91 F5
Silverknowes Hill EH4 ....91 F4
Silverknowes Loan EH4 .....91 F4
Silverknowes Midway
EH4 ....92 A4
Silverknowes Neuk EH4 ....92 A3
Silverknowes Parkway
EH4 ....91 F5
Silverknowes Rd EH4 ....91 F5
Silverknowes Rd E EH4 .....92 A4
Silverknowes Rd S EH4 .....91 F3
Silverknowes Southway
EH4 ....92 A4
Silverknowes Terr EH4 ......91 F4

Silverknowes View EH4 . . . .92 A4
Silversands Nature Reserve KY3 . . . . .49 D7
Silver St Dunbar EH42. . . . .78 D2
Kincardine FK10 . . . . .23 E3
Simon Sq EH8 . . . . .229 B2
Simpson Cres EH48 . . . . . .141 C5
Simpson Dr
Simpson Parkway EH54 . . .143 B2
Simpson Rd EH52. . . . . . . .116 B6
Simpson St FK1 . . . . .59 E6
Simpson Wlk KY11 . . . . .29 F1
Sinclair Cl EH11 . . . . .120 E4
Sinclair Cres FK6 . . . . .36 D1
Sinclair Ct Aberlady EH32 . .71 D4
Bannockburn FK7 . . . . .7 E1
Sinclair Dr
Cowdenbeath KY4 . . . . . . .13 B2
Fallin FK7 . . . . .8 D4
Sinclair Gdns
Dunfermline KY12 . . . . . . .29 B4
Edinburgh EH11 . . . . .120 E5
Sinclair Pl
Edinburgh EH11 . . . . .120 E5
Falkirk FK2. . . . . .39 A1
Sinclairtown Prim Sch KY1. . . . .17 F7
Sinclair Way EH54 . . . . . . .143 D6
Sir George Bruce Rd KY12. . . . .26 F7
Sir Harry Lauder Rd EH15. . . . .123 B8
Sir James Black Gait KY5 . .14 A8
Sir John Brown Pl KY11 . . . .46 F7
Sir John Graham Ct FK5 . . .38 B1
Sir Robert Maule Pl FK10 . .23 E4
Sir Walter Scott Pend EH32 . . . . .96 F2
Sir William Fraser Homes EH15. . . . .38 B3
Sir William Wallace Ct FK5. . . . .38 B3
Sirewright Ct FK10 . . . . . . .23 E4
Sixth St EH22 . . . . .174 B5
Skaithmuir Ave FK2. . . . . . .39 B3
Skaithmuir Cres FK2 . . . . . .39 B3
Skedsbush Cotts EH41 . . . .220 D5
Skelmorlie Pl FK5 . . . . .38 F4
Skeltiemuir Ave EH19 . . . .173 A5
Skeltiemuir Ct EH19 . . . . .173 A5
Skeltiemuir Gr EH19 . . . . .173 B5
Skene St FK4 . . . . .58 A6
Skibo Ct KY12 . . . . .29 A3
Skibo Pl KY7 . . . . .16 D5
Skivo Wynd EH54 . . . . . . .164 E4
Skye Ct FK3 . . . . .61 D6
Skye Dr FK2. . . . . .61 F1
Skye Rd KY11. . . . . .29 E2
Skylaw Terr ML11 . . . . .201 A1
Skythorn Way FK1 . . . . .59 D5
Slaeside EH14 . . . . .147 C1
Slamannan Prim Sch FK1. . . . .108 A7
Slamannan Rd
Avonbridge FK1 . . . . .109 F6
Falkirk FK1. . . . . .60 A2
Limerigg FK1. . . . . .108 B2
Slateford Gn EH14 . . . . . . .120 D4
Slateford Rd EH14 . . . . . . .120 D4
Slateford Sta EH14. . . . . . .120 C3
Sleigh Dr EH7 . . . . .94 C2
Sleigh Gdns EH7. . . . . .94 C2
Sligo St KY12. . . . . .26 F7
Sloan St EH6 . . . . .93 F3
Smallburn Pl FK3 . . . . .61 E6
Small St KY5 . . . . .9 A2
Smart Village Bsns Campus EH10 . . . . . .9 E7
Smeaton Farm Cotts EH22. . . . .153 E8
Smeaton Gdns KY2 . . . . . . .17 C6
Smeaton Gr EH21. . . . . . . .124 D3
Smeaton Ind Site KY1. . . . .17 C7
Smeaton Rd KY1 . . . . .17 D6
Smiddy Brae FK2 . . . . .61 F4
Smiddy View KY7 . . . . .6 D6
Smiddy Wynd Alva FK12 . . . .5 A6
East Linton EH40. . . . . . . .103 E7
Newmills KY12. . . . . .26 C1
Smileyknowes Ct EH39. . . . .54 A6
Smith's Pl EH6 . . . . .93 F4
Smith's Terr 3 KY1 . . . . . . .17 C5
Smith Art Gallery & Mus 7 A8
Smith Ave KY4 . . . . .13 B3
Smithfield Loan FK10 . . . . . .9 E6
Smithfield Mdws FK10 . . . . . .9 E6
Smithfield St EH11 . . . . . . .120 D5
Smith Pl FK6 . . . . .36 D1
Smith St FK2 . . . . .60 B7
Smithy Brae EH27 . . . . .145 E4
Smithy Green Ave EH22 . . .152 B7
Smithy Row EH39 . . . . .74 A3
Snab Brae EH51. . . . . .63 D6
Snab La EH51. . . . . .63 D7
Snowden Sch FK4 . . . . .7 A6
Snowdon Pl FK8. . . . . .7 A6
Snowdon Place La FK8 . . . . .7 A6
Society La EH55 . . . . .163 D3
Society Pl EH55. . . . . .163 D3
Society Rd EH30. . . . . .68 D7
Solway Dr FK6. . . . . .57 D7
Somerset Pl EH6 . . . . .94 A4
Somers Pk 11 EH33 . . . . . .126 C5
Somerville Ave KY12 . . . . . .28 E4
Somerville Rd KY11. . . . . . . .46 C2
Somerville Sq KY3 . . . . .50 E8
Somerville St KY3 . . . . .50 E8

Sommers Pk EH53 . . . . . . .144 C2
Somerville Gdns EH30. . . .89 D7
Somerfield Ave EH41 . . . . .129 E8
Somerfield Cres EH41 . . . .129 F8
Somerfield Ct EH41. . . . . .129 F8
Somerfield Dr EH41. . . . . .129 E8
Somerfield Pk EH41 . . . . . .129 E8
Souillac Dr FK6. . . . . .36 C1
Souter Way FK5 . . . . .38 C4
South Acres KY12. . . . . . . .27 D1
South Approach Rd
Airth FK2. . . . . .23 B2
Skinflats FK2 . . . . .39 F8
South Ave Blairhall KY12 . .26 A7
Maddiston FK2. . . . . .83 B7
Southbank EH4 . . . . .91 E4
South Bank Ct EH4 . . . . . . .91 E4
South Bantaskine Dr FK1 .60 A3
South Bantaskine Rd FK1 .60 A3
South Barnton Ave EH4 . . .91 E3
South Beechwood E12. . . .120 A6
South Belton Farm Cotts EH42. . . . .105 E7
South Brae FK2. . . . . .83 A5
South Bridge EH1. . . . . . . .229 A3
South Bridge St
Bathgate EH48. . . . . .141 A6
Grangemouth FK3 . . . . . . .40 C1
South Broomage Ave FK5 .38 C1
South Castle Dr KY11 . . . . .46 F6
South Charlotte St EH2 . .228 B3
South Clerk St EH8 . . . . . .229 B1
South College St EH8 . . . .229 A2
South Craigs Rd FK2. . . . . .82 E7
South Cres
East Saltoun EH34. . . . . .157 F4
Prestonpans EH32. . . . . . .97 A1
Southcroft FK12 . . . . .4 F6
South Dewar St KY12 . . . . .28 E4
South Doors EH32. . . . . . . .97 C4
South Dr KY12. . . . . .29 B3
South East Circus Pl EH3 . . . .228 B4
South East Cumberland Street La EH3 . . . .93 C2
South East Longridge Crofts EH47. . . . .161 E2
South East Thistle Street La EH2 . . . .228 C4
South Elixa Pl EH8 . . . . . . .122 C3
Southerton Cres KY2. . . . .16 F3
Southerton Gdns KY2 . . . . .16 F3
Southerton Rd KY2 . . . . . . .16 F3
South Ettrick Rd EH10 . . . .120 F4
South Fergus Pl KY1. . . . . . .17 B3
Southfield Ave ML7 . . . . . .180 A4
Southfield Cres
Shotts ML7. . . . . .180 B4
Stirling FK8 . . . . .7 A6
Southfield Ct EH42. . . . . . .78 B2
Southfield Dr FK1. . . . . . . .108 A6
South Farm Gr EH15. . . . .122 E7
Southfield Gdns E EH15. . .122 F7
Southfield Gdns W EH15. . .122 F6
Southfield Loan EH15. . . . .122 F6
Southfield Pl EH15 . . . . . . .122 F7
Southfield Rd
Cousland EH22. . . . . .154 D5
Shotts ML7. . . . . .180 B4
Southfield Rd E EH15. . . . .122 F6
Southfield Rd W EH15. . . . .122 F6
Southfield Sq EH15. . . . . . .122 F6
Southfield Terr EH15. . . . . .122 F6
South Fort St EH6 . . . . .93 F5
South Gait EH39. . . . . .53 F7
South Gayfield La 3 EH7 .93 E2
South Gillsland Rd EH10 .120 F3
South Grange Ave EH32. . .96 F1
South Gray's Cl EH1 . . . . .229 B3
South Gray St EH9. . . . . . .121 F4
South Green Dr FK2. . . . . . .22 E3
South Groathill Ave EH4 . .92 C2
South Gyle Access EH12 . .119 C4
South Gyle Broadway EH12. . . .119 B4
South Gyle Cres EH12. . . . .119 B4
South Gyle Crescent La EH12. . . .119 B4
South Gyle Gdns EH12. . . .119 C5
South Gyle Ind Est EH12. .119 B4
South Gyle Mains EH12 . . .119 C5
South Gyle Pk
Edinburgh EH12. . . . . .119 B4
South Gyle Rd EH12. . . . . .119 B4
South Gyle Sta EH12. . . . . .119 B5
South Gyle Wynd EH12. . . .119 C4
South Hamilton St 11 EH39. . . . .54 A7
South Hill St KY3 . . . . .50 E8
South Hirst Rd ML7. . . . . . .158 D3
Southhouse Ave EH17. . . . .151 B5
Southhouse Brae EH17. . . .151 C5
Southhouse Broadway EH17. . . .151 B4
Southhouse Cres EH17. . . .151 C4
Southhouse Gdns EH17. . . .151 C4
Southhouse Gr EH17. . . . . .151 B4
Southhouse Loan EH17. . . .151 C4
Southhouse Rd EH17. . . . . .151 C5
Southhouse Terr EH17. . . . .151 C5

Southhouse Wlk EH17. . . . .151 B5
South Kersebonny Steading FK8. . . . .6 C7
South Knowe KY11. . . . . . . .29 E3
South Larch Rd KY11 . . . . . .29 F4
South Lauder Rd EH9 . . . . .121 E4
South Laverockbank Ave EH5. . . . .93 C6
Southlawn Ct EH4 . . . . .91 E4
South Learmonth Ave 4 EH4 . . . .92 F1
South Learmonth Gdns 2 EH4 . . . .92 F1
South Loanhead EH11. . . . .45 E3
South Loch Pk EH48 . . . . . .141 A6
South Lodge Ave EH53 . . . .144 C2
South Lorimer Pl EH32. . . .97 C3
South Lorne Pl 1 EH6 . . . . .93 F3
South Lumley St FK3. . . . . .61 D8
South Mains FK7 . . . . .9 B1
South Marshall St FK3. . . . .61 D7
South Maybury EH12 . . . . .118 A6
South Mellis Pk EH8. . . . . .122 E8
South Melville La 4 FK7. . .6 F7
South Mid St EH48. . . . . . . .141 B6
South Morningside Prim Sch EH10 . . . .121 A2
South Morton St EH15 . . . .123 C7
South Oswald Rd EH9 . . . .121 E3
South Overgate KY1. . . . . . .35 A3
South Oxford St EH8 . . . . .121 F5
South Parrotshot EH15 . . .123 B5
South Philpingstone La EH51. . . . .64 C7
South Pilmuir Rd EH11. . . . .11 A4
South Pk Armadale EH48 . .139 F4
Edinburgh EH6. . . . . .93 D6
South Pleasance Ave FK1 .60 A3
South Rd
Fauldhouse EH47. . . . . . .181 E7
Grangemouth FK3 . . . . . . .62 B5
South Roundall KY11. . . . . .45 E3
South Row
Charlestown KY11. . . . . . .45 B4
Kirkcaldy KY1. . . . . .17 E8
South St Andrew St 2 EH2 229 A4
South St David St EH2. . . .228 C4
South Scotstoun EH30. . . .89 C7
South Seton Pk EH32 . . . . .97 D4
South Shore Rd FK3 . . . . . .41 B2
South Sloan St EH6. . . . . . .93 F3
South St Armadale EH48. . .139 F5
Bo'ness EH51. . . . . .63 F8
Cambus FK10 . . . . .9 B8
Cowdenbeath KY4 . . . . . . .13 D4
Dalkeith EH22 . . . . .153 A3
Dunbar EH42 . . . . .78 B2
Lochgelly KY5 . . . . .14 A4
Musselburgh EH21 . . . . . .124 B6
Stirling FK9 . . . . .2 D1
South Steil EH11. . . . . .120 E1
South Trinity Rd EH5. . . . . .93 B5
South View Burntisland KY3 .50 F8
Prestonpans EH32. . . . . . .97 A1
South Village EH53. . . . . . .144 C4
South West Cumberland Street La EH3 . . . .93 C2
South West Thistle Street La EH2 . . . .228 C4
Soutra Aisle EH37 . . . . . . .224 D5
Sovereign Ct EH48 . . . . . . .140 B5
Spalding Cres EH53 . . . . . .153 B3
Spa Pl EH15 . . . . .95 B1
Speedwell Ave EH42 . . . . .152 A8
Spey Ave KY3 . . . . .33 F2
Spey Ct EH54 . . . . .144 B4
Spey Dr EH54 . . . . .144 B4
Spey St EH7 . . . . .93 E3
Spey Street La EH7 . . . . . . .93 E3
Spey Terr EH7 . . . . .93 E3
Spier's Pl EH6 . . . . .93 F5
Spilmersford View EH34. . .157 A6
Spinks Ind Est KY7 . . . . .6 F2
Spinnaker Way KY11 . . . . . .47 F2
Spinner's Ct KY12 . . . . .26 C3
Spinneys The KY11. . . . . . . .48 C3
Spinney The KY11. . . . . .48 C3
Spittalfield Cres
Edinburgh EH8. . . . . .229 B1
Inverkeithing KY11. . . . . . .47 C2
Spittalfield Rd KY11. . . . . . .47 C2
Spittal Hill FK9 . . . . .2 C4
Spittal St Edinburgh EH3. .228 B2
Stirling FK8 . . . . .7 A8
Spott Ave EH42. . . . . .106 C3
Spottiswoode Gdns EH53. . . . .144 C2
Spottiswoode Rd EH9. . . . .121 C5
Spottiswoode St EH9 . . . . .121 C5
Spott End FK2 . . . . .78 E1
Spott Road Ind Est EH42 . .78 E1
Sprig Way ML7 . . . . .179 D6
Springbank Gdns Pk. 60 C5
Springbank Rd
Shotts ML7. . . . . .179 D6
Stirling FK7 . . . . .7 D5
Springbank Terr KY12 . . . . .29 A6

Springfield EH6. . . . . .93 F4
Springfield Cres
8 North Berwick EH39. . . .54 A7
Queensferry EH30. . . . . . .67 F1
Springfield Ct EH49. . . . . . .85 D8
Springfield Dr FK1. . . . . . . .59 F5
Springfield Gdns 2 EH39 . .54 A7
Springfield La EH6. . . . . . . .93 F4
Springfield Lea EH30. . . . . .67 F1
Springfield Pl
Gorebridge EH23. . . . . . .195 D7
Queensferry EH30. . . . . . .67 F1
Roslin EH25 . . . . .172 A4
Springfield Prim Sch EH30 . . . .85 D8
Springfield Rd Alloa FK10. .10 C7
Denny FK6. . . . . .36 F2
Linlithgow EH49 . . . . .85 C7
Penicuik EH26 . . . . .208 E6
Queensferry EH30. . . . . . .67 F1
Stirling FK7 . . . . .7 C5
Springfield St EH6 . . . . . . .93 F4
Springfield Terr
Dunbar EH42 . . . . .77 F7
West Barns EH42 . . . . .77 D7
Springfield View EH30. . . . .68 A1
Spring Gdns EH8 . . . . .94 A1
Springhead Rd ML7. . . . . . .198 A8
Springhill Brae KY12 . . . . . .46 B8
Springhill & Leadloch Rd ML7, EH47. . . . .180 E2
Springhill Rd ML7. . . . . . . .180 B3
Springhill View ML7. . . . . . .180 B3
Springkerse Bsns Pk FK7. . .7 E7
Springkerse Ind Est FK7 . . .7 D6
Springkerse Rdbt FK7. . . . . .7 D6
Springkerse Ret Pk FK7. . . .7 E6
Springvalley Gdns EH10. . .121 A4
Springvalley Terr EH10. . . .121 A3
Springwell Pl EH11 . . . . . . .120 F6
Springwood
Dunfermline KY11. . . . . . . .47 A7
Stirling FK7 . . . . .6 F5
Springwood Ave FK8. . . . . . .6 F5
Springwood Pk EH16. . . . . .151 B8
Sprinty Ave EH35 . . . . .155 D7
Sprinty Dr EH35 . . . . .155 D7
Sprotwell Terr FK10 . . . . . . .5 D1
Spruce Gr KY11 . . . . .47 F1
Spruce Gr
Dunfermline KY11. . . . . . . .46 D8
Livingston EH54. . . . . . . .144 B5
Spylaw Ave EH13 . . . . .148 F7
Spylaw Bank Rd EH13 . . . .149 A7
Spylaw Ho EH13 . . . . .149 A6
Spylaw Pk EH13 . . . . .148 F7
Spylaw Rd EH10 . . . . .120 F4
Spylaw St EH13 . . . . .149 B7
Square The
Cockburnspath TD13 . . . .218 F4
Danderhall EH22. . . . . . . .152 B8
East Linton EH40. . . . . . . .103 E7
Fallin FK7. . . . . .8 D4
Gifford EH41 . . . . .220 F7
Newtongrange EH22 . . . . .174 A5
Penicuik EH26 . . . . .191 F4
Spott EH42. . . . . .106 C3
Torphichen EH48 . . . . . . .126 B7
Sraehouse Wynd ML8. . . . .215 B1
Stable Ct EH42 . . . . .78 E2
Stable La EH10 . . . . .121 A4
Stable Rd ML7 . . . . .180 A4
Stables Rd KY11 . . . . .46 C1
Stables The
Newtongrange EH22 . . . . .174 A8
Pathhead EH37 . . . . .175 E8
Stadium House Bsns Ctr EH54 . . . .143 D2
Staffa EH12 . . . . .142 E5
Staffa Pl FK1 . . . . .60 B2
Stafford St EH3 . . . . .228 A3
Stair Pk Edinburgh EH12 . .120 D6
North Berwick EH39 . . . . . .54 B6
Tranent EH33. . . . . .126 B7
Standalane FK10. . . . . .23 E3
Standhill Ct EH48 . . . . .140 F4
Standhill Rd EH48 . . . . .140 F3
Standingstane Rd EH30 . . . .89 E5
Standing Stone Wlk KY11 . .47 D6
Standrigg Ave FK2. . . . . . . .82 C7
Standrigg Gdns FK2 . . . . . . .82 C6
Standrigg Rd FK2. . . . . .82 B6
Stanedykehead EH16. . . . .150 F6
Stane Gr ML7 . . . . .180 A3
Stane Prim Sch ML7. . . . . .180 A4
Stane Rd ML7 . . . . .180 A3
Stanhope Pl EH12 . . . . .120 F6
Stanhope St EH12 . . . . .120 F6
Stankards Rd EH52 . . . . . .114 F3
Stanley Ave EH25 . . . . .171 E6
Stanley Dr Bridge of A FK9 . .2 B7
Harthill ML7 . . . . .160 A6
Stanley Pk FK2. . . . . .17 B5
Stanley Pl Dunbar EH42 . . .78 C3
Edinburgh EH7 . . . . .94 A1
Stanley Rd Edinburgh EH6 . .93 D6
Gullane EH31. . . . . .52 B2
Harthill ML7. . . . . .160 A6
Stanley St EH15. . . . . .123 A7
Stanley St Alva FK12 . . . . . .5 A6
Oakley KY12. . . . . .27 A6
Stanton Ave FK10 . . . . .9 F6
Stanwell St EH6 . . . . .93 E4

Stapeley Ave EH4 . . . . .94 E2
Starbank Rd EH5 . . . . .93 C6
Starch Mill EH41. . . . . .130 C8
Stark's Brae EH51 . . . . .64 A7
Stark's Park (Raith Rovers FC) KY1. . . . .17 A1
Stark Ave FK1 . . . . .59 D5
Starlaw Ave EH48 . . . . .141 E5
Starlaw Bsns Pk EH54. . . . .142 D4
Starlaw Cres EH48 . . . . . . .141 F5
Starlaw Gdns EH48 . . . . . . .141 F5
Starlaw Rd EH54 . . . . .142 C3
Starlaw Terr EH48 . . . . .141 E5
Starlaw West Rdbt EH54. . .142 A3
Starlaw Wlk EH48 . . . . .141 F5
Starley Hall Sch KY3 . . . . . .50 A8
Starryshaw Rd ML7 . . . . . . .179 E6
Station Ave EH41 . . . . .129 F8
Station Brae
Edinburgh EH15. . . . . . . .123 A7
Kinghorn KY3 . . . . .34 F2
Station Ct Addiewell EH55 .162 E2
Haddington EH41 . . . . . . .130 B6
North Berwick EH39 . . . . . .54 B7
Station Hill EH39 . . . . .54 B7
Station Loan EH14 . . . . . . .147 C3
Station Pl KY3. . . . . .49 C7
Station Rd
Addiewell EH55 . . . . .162 E2
Armadale EH48 . . . . .139 F3
Bannockburn FK7 . . . . .7 E1
Blackridge EH48 . . . . .138 D2
Bridge of A FK9 . . . . .1 F8
Brightons FK2. . . . . .61 E1
Broxburn EH52. . . . . .115 E5
Cambus FK10. . . . . .4 B1
Cowdenbeath KY4 . . . . . . .13 D4
Cowie FK7 . . . . .20 D2
Dalkeith EH22 . . . . .152 E2
Dirleton EH39 . . . . .53 D3
Dunbar EH42 . . . . .78 E2
Dysart KY1. . . . . .18 A7
East Linton EH40. . . . . . . .103 E7
Edinburgh EH12. . . . . . . .119 E6
Gifford EH41 . . . . .220 F7
Gorebridge EH23. . . . . . .195 D7
Grangemouth FK3 . . . . . . .40 D1
Gullane EH31. . . . . .52 B2
Haddington EH41 . . . . . . .130 A8
Kincardine FK10 . . . . .23 D4
Kirkliston EH29 . . . . .89 B1
Kirknewton EH27 . . . . . . .145 D3
Linlithgow EH49. . . . . .85 A7
Loanhead EH20 . . . . .172 C8
Lochgelly KY5 . . . . .14 A4
Longcroft FK4 . . . . .57 B4
Musselburgh EH21 . . . . . .124 C5
Newtongrange EH22 . . . . .174 A5
North Berwick EH39 . . . . . .54 B7
Oakley KY12. . . . . .26 F6
Prestonpans EH32. . . . . . .126 A8
Ratho Station EH28 . . . . .117 C5
Roslin EH25 . . . . .179 E4
Slamannan FK1 . . . . .108 B6
South Queensferry EH30. . .68 C1
Stirling FK8 . . . . .7 B8
Uphall EH52,EH54 . . . . . .114 F3
Whitecross EH49 . . . . .83 F6
Winchburgh EH52 . . . . . . .88 A3
Station Row
Macmerry EH33 . . . . .127 C5
Plean FK7. . . . . .20 B3
Station Terr EH29 . . . . .89 B1
Station View EH30 . . . . .89 D8
Station Yd KY3 . . . . .35 A2
Staunton Rise EH54 . . . . . .164 D8
Stead's Pl EH6. . . . . .93 F4
Steadings Cres EH42. . . . . .106 D8
Steadings The Airth FK2 . . .21 E5
Fallin FK7. . . . . .8 A4
Whitecross EH49 . . . . .84 B8
Steading The
Longniddry EH32 . . . . .98 C2
Mid Calder EH53 . . . . . . .144 B3
Steel's Pl EH10 . . . . .121 B3
Steel Cres FK6 . . . . .36 F1
Steele Ave EH22 . . . . .174 F6
Steel Gr FK5 . . . . .38 C4
Steelyard The 4 EH48 . . . .141 A6
Steeple Cres KY11. . . . . . . .48 A3
Steils The EH11. . . . . .120 E1
Stein's Pl KY4 . . . . .13 C3
Stein Sq FK7 . . . . .7 F1
Stenhouse Ave EH11 . . . . .120 A4
Stenhouse Ave W EH11. . . .120 A4
Stenhouse Cotts EH11. . . . .120 A3
Stenhouse Cres EH11. . . . .120 A4
Stenhouse Cross EH11. . . .120 A4
Stenhouse Dr
Burntisland KY3 . . . . .33 C1
Edinburgh EH11 . . . . .120 A3
Stenhouse Gdns EH11. . . . .120 A4
Stenhouse Gdns N EH11 . .120 A4
Stenhouse Mill Cres EH11. . . . .120 B3
Stenhouse Mill La EH11. . . . .120 B3
Stenhouse Mill Wynd EH11. . . . .120 B3
Stenhousemuir Prim Sch FK5. . . . .38 D3
Stenhouse Pl E EH11. . . . .120 A4
Stenhouse Pl W EH11. . . . .120 A4

Stenhouse Prim Sch
EH11 . . . . 120 A4
Stenhouse Rd
Edinburgh EH11 . . . . 120 A3
Stenhousemuir FK2 . . . . . . 38 F2
Stenhouse St E EH11 . . . . 120 A4
Stenhouse St W EH11 . . . 119 F4
Stenhouse St KY4 . . . . 13 B4
Stennis Gdns EH17 . . . . . . 151 C7
Stenton Loan EH42 . . . . . . 133 E8
Stenton Rd Dysart EH42 . 104 E1
Stenton Rd EH11 . . . . 105 F8
Stephen's Dr KY11 . . . . 47 C3
Stephen Pl KY5 . . . . 14 B8
Stephens Croft FK2 . . . . . . 59 FB
Steps St FK5 . . . . 38 E3
Steuart Rd FK9 . . . . 1 F7
Stevenlaw's Cl EH1 . . . . . 229 A3
Stevenson Ave
Edinburgh EH11 . . . . 120 C5
Polmont FK2 . . . . 61 D1
Stevenson Coll EH11 . . . . 119 C3
Stevenson Ct
Bridge of A FK9 . . . . 2 A5
Falkirk FK2 . . . . 39 B1
Livingston EH54 . . . . 144 C5
Longniddry EH32 . . . . 98 D4
Stevenson Dr EH11 . . . . . 120 B4
Stevenson Gr EH11 . . . . . 120 C5
Stevenson La EH22 . . . . . 174 B4
Stevenson Pk EH32 . . . . . . 98 D4
Stevenson Pl EH18 . . . . . 172 D6
Stevenson Rd
Edinburgh EH11 . . . . 120 C5
Penicuik EH26 . . . . 171 B1
Stevenson St FK3 . . . . 61 D5
Stevenson Terr
Bathgate EH48 . . . . 141 C5
Edinburgh EH11 . . . . 120 C5
Stevenson Way EH32 . . . . . 98 D4
Stewart's Melville Coll
EH4 . . . . 92 F1
Stewart Ave Bo'ness EH51 . 63 F8
Currie EH14 . . . . 147 E3
Linlithgow EH49 . . . . 84 E6
Stenhousemuir FK2 . . . . . . 39 A2
Stewart Clark Ave EH30 . . 89 C8
Stewart Cres Currie EH14 147 E4
Lochgelly KY5 . . . . 14 A8
Stewart Ct EH55 . . . . 163 D2
Stewart Dr EH47 . . . . 160 F7
Stewartfield EH6 . . . . 93 D4
Stewartfield Cres EH52 . . 115 F5
Stewartfield Rd EH52 . . . 115 F6
Stewart Gdns EH14 . . . . . 147 E4
Stewart Gr
Danderhall EH22 . . . . 152 A8
Harthill ML7 . . . . 159 F5
Stewart Pk EH22 . . . . 154 D5
Stewart Pl Currie EH14 . . 147 E3
Kirkliston EH29 . . . . 89 B2
Stewart Rd Currie EH14 . 147 E3
Falkirk FK2 . . . . 60 C5
Stewart Sq FK8 . . . . 2 A3
Stewart St Bonnybridge FK4 57 F5
Cambusbarron FK7 . . . . 6 D6
Dysart KY1 . . . . 18 B8
Townhill KY12 . . . . 29 C7
West Calder EH55 . . . . . . 163 D3
Stewart Terr
Edinburgh EH11 . . . . 120 E5
South Queensferry EH30 . . 68 B1
Stewart Way EH54 . . . . . . 143 C6
Stiel Gr EH33 . . . . 126 D5
Stirling Br EH3 . . . . 2 B2
Stirling Bsns Ctr FK8 . . . . . 7 B6
Stirling Castle FK8 . . . . 7 A8
Stirling Ent Pk FK7 . . . . 7 C7
Stirling High Sch FK8 . . . . 7 A5
Stirling Pl FK7 . . . . 20 C3
Stirling Rd FK2 . . . . 8 C4
Alva FK12 . . . . 4 F7
Edinburgh EH5 . . . . 93 B6
Fallin FK7 . . . . 8 C4
Kirkliston EH29 . . . . 89 A2
Larbert,North Broomage
FK5 . . . . 38 A3
Larbert,South Broomage FK2,
FK5 . . . . 59 C8
Torwood FK5 . . . . 37 E5
Tullibody FK10 . . . . 4 C5
Stirling Royal Infmy FK8 . 7 B5
Stirling St Alva FK12 . . . . . . 5 A7
Denny,Dunipace FK6 . . . . 36 D4
Denny FK6 . . . . 36 E1
Stirling Sta FK8 . . . . 7 B8
Stobhill Prim Sch EH23 195 D8
Stobhill Rd EH23 . . . . 174 B3
Stobie Pl KY12 . . . . 26 F7
Stobs Pl KY3 . . . . 16 C7
Stockbridge Prim sch
EH3 . . . . 93 B2
Stone Ave EH22 . . . . 174 D6
Stonebank EH54 . . . . 143 E6
Stone Cres EH22 . . . . 174 D6
Stonedyke Cres ML8 . . . . 215 A3
Stonedyke Rd ML8 . . . . . . 215 B3
Stoneheap Crofts EH47 . 182 E8
Stonelaws Cotts EH40 . . . 75 A6
Stone Pl EH22 . . . . 174 D6
Stoneybank Ave EH21 . . . 124 B4
Stoneybank Cres EH21 . . 124 B4
Stoneybank Ct EH21 . . . . 124 A5
Stoneybank Dr EH21 . . . . 124 A5

Stoneybank Gdns EH21 . 124 A5
Stoneybank Gdns N
EH21 . . . . 124 A5
Stoneybank Gdns S
EH21 . . . . 124 B5
Stoneybank Gr EH21 . . . . 124 B4
Stoneybank Pl EH21 . . . . 124 B4
Stoneybank Rd EH21 . . . 124 B4
Stoneybank Terr EH21 . . 124 B4
Stoneyburn Prim Sch
EH47 . . . . 162 C3
Stoneycroft Rd EH30 . . . . . 68 C1
Stoneyflatts EH30 . . . . 89 A8
Stoneyflatts Cres EH30 . . 89 A8
Stoneyflatts Pk EH30 . . . . 89 A8
Stonyhill Ave EH21 . . . . . 124 A5
Stonyhill Cres EH21 . . . . 124 A5
Stonyhill Ct EH21 . . . . . . 124 A5
Stonyhill Dr EH21 . . . . . . 124 A5
Stonyhill Farm Rd
EH21 . . . . 124 B5
Stonyhill Gdns **3** EH21 124 A5
Stonyhill Pl EH21 . . . . 124 A5
Stonyhill Prim Sch
EH21 . . . . 124 A5
Stonyhill Rd EH21 . . . . . . 124 A5
Stonyhill Rise EH21 . . . . . 124 A5
Stonyhill Steadings
. . . . 124 A5
Stonyhill Terr EH21 . . . . . 124 A5
Stonyhill Wynd **1**
EH21 . . . . 124 A5
Stonypath Cotts EH41 . . . 133 C3
Stoneywood Pk FK6 . . . . . . 36 B2
Stony Brae FK4 . . . . 24 C2
Stories Pk EH40 . . . . 103 E7
Strachan Ct EH51 . . . . 63 D7
Strachan Gdns EH4 . . . . . . 92 A2
Strachan Rd EH4 . . . . 92 A2
Strachan St FK1 . . . . 59 E4
Straiton Mains EH20 . . . . 151 A2
Straiton Park Cvn Site
EH20 . . . . 150 F1
Straiton Park Way EH20 . 150 F1
Straiton Pk EH20 . . . . 151 A2
Straiton Pl EH15 . . . . 123 B8
Strand Dr EH48 . . . . 140 F1
Strang's Pl FK1 . . . . 81 F5
Strathallan Dr FK9 . . . . 2 A6
Strathallan St KY2 . . . . 16 E5
Strathallan Rd EH21 . . . . . 2 A6
Strathalmond Ct EH4 . . . . 90 F3
Strathalmond Gn EH4 . . . 90 F3
Strathalmond Pk EH4 . . . . 90 F3
Strathalmond Rd EH4 . . . . 90 F3
Strathavon Terr EH48 . . . 170 F5
Strathbeg Dr KY11 . . . . . . 47 F3
Strathbrock Pl
Broxburn EH52 . . . . 115 E5
Uphall EH52 . . . . 114 F4
Strathearn Ct
Grangemouth FK3 . . . . . . 61 E8
West Barns EH42 . . . . 77 F1
Strathearn Pl EH9 . . . . . . 121 B4
Strathearn Rd
Edinburgh EH9 . . . . 121 C4
Kirkcaldy KY2 . . . . 17 C2
North Berwick EH39 . . . . 53 F7
Strathesk Gr EH26 . . . . . . 192 A6
Strathesk Pl EH26 . . . . . . 192 A6
Strathesk Rd EH26 . . . . . 192 A6
Strathfillan Rd EH9 . . . . . 121 C4
Strathkinnes Rd KY2 . . . . 17 A4
Strathlachlan Ave ML8 . . 215 A1
Strathlogie EH48 . . . . 110 F5
Strathmiglo Pl FK5 . . . . . . 38 F4
Strathmore Cres FK9 . . . . . 2 A3
Strathmore Dr
Dunfermline KY12 . . . . . . 29 D5
Stirling FK9 . . . . 2 A3
Strathmore St KY3 . . . . . . 34 F3
Strathyre Dr EH47 . . . . . . 162 C2
Strathyre Pl EH47 . . . . . . 162 C2
Strawberry Bank
Dalkeith EH22 . . . . 152 E1
Linlithgow EH49 . . . . 85 A6
Streets Pl KY12 . . . . 29 D7
Stripehead **3** FK10 . . . 10 B6
Striven Dr FK2 . . . . 39 C1
Striven Pl KY2 . . . . 16 E8
Stromness Gdns EH54 . . 146 D6
Strowan Rd FK3 . . . . 61 F7
Strowan Sq FK3 . . . . 61 F7
Struan Dr KY11 . . . . 47 B3
Struan House Sch FK10 . . 10 A7
Struan Pl KY11 . . . . 47 B3
Strude Howe FK12 . . . . 5 B7
Strude Mill FK12 . . . . 5 B7
Strude St FK12 . . . . 5 B7
Stuart Cres EH12 . . . . 119 B8
Stuart Ct Bathgate EH48 . 141 C7
Edinburgh EH12 . . . . 119 B8
Stuart Gn EH12 . . . . 119 B8
Stuart Gr FK3 . . . . 61 B6
Stuart Pk EH12 . . . . 119 B8
Stuart Pl KY4 . . . . 13 D5
Stuart Rd KY11 . . . . 46 C2
Stuart Sq EH12 . . . . 119 B8
Stuart Terr EH48 . . . . 141 B5
Stuart Wynd EH12 . . . . . . 119 B8
Styles Pl KY1 . . . . 59 F2
Succoth Ave EH12 . . . . . . 120 D8
Succoth Ct EH12 . . . . 120 D8
Succoth Gdns EH12 . . . . 120 D8

Succoth Pk EH12 . . . . 120 D8
Succoth Pl EH12 . . . . 120 D8
Suffolk Rd EH16 . . . . 121 F3
Suffolk Rd La EH16 . . . . . 122 A3
Suffolk Road La EH16 . . . 121 F3
Sugarhouse Cl EH8 . . . . . 229 B3
Suilven Hts FK2 . . . . 22 A6
Sultery Bldg KY11 . . . . . . 45 B4
Summer Bank EH3 . . . . . . 93 C2
Summer Pl EH3 . . . . 93 C2
Summerfield Gdns EH6 . . 94 B4
Summerfield Pk EH42 . . . 77 C3
Summerfield Pl EH6 . . . . . 94 B4
Summerfield Rd EH42 . . . 78 C1
Summerford EH9 . . . . 59 D4
Summerford Gdns FK1 . . 59 D4
Summerford Rd FK1 . . . . . 59 D4
Summerhall EH9 . . . . 229 B1
Summerhall Cres EH9 . . . 229 B1
Summerhall Pl EH9 . . . . . 229 B1
Summerhall Sq EH9 . . . . 229 B1
Summerlee EH32 . . . . 96 E1
Summer Pl EH3 . . . . 93 C2
Summerside Pl EH6 . . . . . 93 D5
Summerside St EH6 . . . . . 93 D5
Summertrees Ct EH16 . . 122 B1
Summerville St EH54 . . . 144 A8
Suna Path ML7 . . . . 180 B3
Sunbury Mews **4** EH4 . 120 F8
Sunbury Pl EH4 . . . . 120 F8
Sunbury St EH4 . . . . 120 F8
Sundew Glade EH54 . . . . 164 C8
Sunningdale La KY12 . . . . 28 D6
Sunnybank ML7 . . . . 179 F6
Sunnybank Pl **3** EH7 . . 94 B1
Sunnybank Terr **2** EH7 94 B1
Sunnybrae EH54 . . . . 144 A8
Sunnybrae Terr FK2 . . . . . 82 F6
Sunnydale Dr EH48 . . . . . 138 E3
Sunnydale Rd EH48 . . . . . 138 E3
Sunnylaw Pl FK1 . . . . 59 F3
Sunnylaw Rd FK9 . . . . 2 A3
Sunnyside Edinburgh EH7 . 94 A2
Stirling FK7 . . . . 7 A4
Stoneyburn EH47 . . . . 162 B2
Sunnyside Ave
Bathgate EH48 . . . . 141 C7
Grangemouth FK2 . . . . . . 82 C7
Sunnyside Cotts
East Linton EH41 . . . . 103 E4
Grangemouth FK2 . . . . . . 82 D7
Sunnyside Ct Alloa FK10 . 10 B7
Cowdenbeath KY4 . . . . . . 13 D4
Grangemouth FK2 . . . . . . 82 C8
Sunnyside Pl Lochgelly KY5 14 A6
Stirling FK7 . . . . 7 A4
Sunnyside Prim Sch FK10 10 B7
Sunnyside Rd Alloa FK10 . 10 B7
Falkirk FK1 . . . . 59 F6
Grangemouth FK2 . . . . . . 82 D7
Sunnyside St FK1 . . . . 59 E6
Surcoat Loan FK7 . . . . 7 E3
Sutherland Ave Alloa FK10 10 C7
Falkirk FK1 . . . . 59 E6
Sutherland Cres EH48 . . 141 A5
Sutherland Dr FK1 . . . . . . 60 D5
Sutherland Ho **2** EH4 . . 93 C2
Sutherland Pl KY1 . . . . . . 17 F7
Sutherland St EH12 . . . . 120 F7
Sutherland Way EH54 . . 143 C6
Suttieslaw Cres EH22 . . . 174 C6
Suttieslaw Dr EH22 . . . . . 174 C6
Suttieslaw Pl EH22 . . . . . 174 C6
Suttieslaw Rd EH22 . . . . . 174 C6
Suttieslaw Wlk EH22 . . . 174 C6
Suttie Way FK9 . . . . 1 B8
Sutton Park Cres FK5 . . . . 38 E3
Sutton Pl FK2 . . . . 60 D5
Swallow Brae EH54 . . . . . 143 D6
Swallow Craig KY11 . . . . . 48 B1
Swallowdrum Rd KY12 . . 28 E6
Swanfield EH6 . . . . 93 F5
Swan Pl FK3 . . . . 61 D5
Swan Rd Kirkcaldy KY1 . . 17 B3
Tranent EH33 . . . . 126 D7
Swan Spring Ave EH10 . . 150 A7
Swanston Ave EH10 . . . . 150 A5
Swanston Cres EH10 . . . 150 A5
Swanston Dr EH10 . . . . . 150 B4
Swanston Gdns EH10 . . . 150 A5
Swanston Gn EH10 . . . . . 150 A5
Swanston Loan EH10 . . . 150 A5
Swanston Muir EH10 . . . 149 E5
Swanston Pl EH10 . . . . . . 150 A4
Swanston Rd EH10 . . . . . 150 A4
Swanston Row EH10 . . . . 150 A5
Swanston Terr EH10 . . . . 150 B4
Swanston View EH10 . . . 150 A5
Swanston Way EH10 . . . . 150 A4
Swift Brae EH54 . . . . 143 D6
Swinburne Dr FK10 . . . . . . 5 B2
Swintons Pl KY4 . . . . 12 F1
Sword's Way FK2 . . . . 39 A1
Sycamore Ave
Bo'ness EH51 . . . . 63 D5
Cockenzie & Port Seton
EH32 . . . . 97 D3
Kirkcaldy KY1 . . . . 17 C8
Sycamore Cres KY4 . . . . . 13 C6
Sycamore Dr EH47 . . . . . 161 C6
Sycamore Gdns EH12 . . 119 E6
Sycamore Glade EH54 . . 164 D8

Sycamore Gr
Dunfermline KY11 . . . . . . 46 C8
Winchburgh EH52 . . . . . . 87 F2
Sycamore Pl FK8 . . . . 6 F5
Sycamore Rd EH22 . . . . . 174 E6
Sycamores The FK10 . . . . 4 B1
Sycamore Terr **3** EH12 119 E6
Sycamore Wlk EH47 . . . . 162 D8
Sydney Pk EH7 . . . . 94 E2
Sydney Pl EH7 . . . . 94 E2
Sydney St EH54 . . . . 144 A5
Sydney Terr EH7 . . . . 94 E2
Sylvan Gr EH51 . . . . 63 C5
Sylvan Pl EH9 . . . . 121 D5
Sylvan Way EH48 . . . . . . 140 F5
Syme Cres EH10 . . . . 149 E8
Syme Pl Edinburgh EH10 . 149 E8
Rosyth KY11 . . . . 46 C5
Syme Rigg EH10 . . . . 149 E8
Symington Pl FK2 . . . . 39 B3
Symon Twr FK1 . . . . 60 D4

T

Tailend Ind Pk EH54 . . . . 142 D4
Tailend Rdbt EH54 . . . . . . 142 D3
Tait Dr Larbert FK5 . . . . . . 59 C8
Penicuik EH26 . . . . 191 F5
Tait St **3** EH22 . . . . 153 A3
Talbot St FK3 . . . . 61 D8
Talisker FK10 . . . . 4 B2
Talisman Pl EH16 . . . . . . 122 B1
Talisman Rise EH54 . . . . 164 D8
Talman Gdns FK2 . . . . 61 E3
Tamfourhill Ave FK1 . . . . . 59 C4
Tamfourhill Ind Est FK1 . 59 C4
Tamfourhill Rd FK1 . . . . . . 59 C4
Tam O'shanter Dr FK7 . . . 20 D7
Tanderlane Cotts EH41 . . 132 C3
Tanera Ct FK1 . . . . 60 B2
Tanfield EH3 . . . . 93 C3
Tanhouse Brae KY12 . . . . 42 D8
Tanners Rd FK1 . . . . 60 A4
Tannery La FK8 . . . . 2 A1
Tantallon Castle EH39 . . . 55 F7
Tantallon Dr FK2 . . . . 39 A3
Tantallon Gdns EH54 . . . 164 E6
Tantallon Pl EH9 . . . . 121 D5
Tantallon Rd EH39 . . . . . . 54 F6
Tantallon Terr EH39 . . . . . 55 A6
Tapitlaw Gr KY12 . . . . 26 D7
Tappoch Pl FK5 . . . . 38 A3
Taransay Dr FK2 . . . . 61 F1
Tarbert Ct EH54 . . . . 164 F7
Tarbert Pl Carluke ML8 . . 215 A1
Polmont FK2 . . . . 61 F1
Tarbert Terr FK10 . . . . 23 F3
Tarbolton St KY2 . . . . 17 A7
Tarbrax Path ML7 . . . . . . 188 C2
Tarbrax Rd EH55 . . . . 203 E2
Tarduff Pl FK2 . . . . 83 A5
Tarduff Pl FK6 . . . . 36 B2
Targate Rd KY12 . . . . 28 C5
Target Rd FK3 . . . . 62 C8
Targe Wynd FK7 . . . . 7 E3
Tarrareoch Ct EH48 . . . . 140 B4
Tartraven Pl EH52 . . . . . . 116 A5
Tarvit St EH3 . . . . 228 C1
Tashieburn Rd ML11 . . . . 201 E2
Tavern Cotts KY4 . . . . 30 F8
Ta-Verne La KY11 . . . . 29 D1
Taxi Way KY11 . . . . 48 C5
Tay Ct FK10 . . . . 10 C6
Taylor Ave KY5 . . . . 14 B4
Taylor Ct Falkirk FK2 . . . . 60 C7
Grangemouth FK3 . . . . . . 40 E1
Taylor Gdns EH6 . . . . 93 F5
Taylor Gn EH54 . . . . 143 C8
Taylor Pl Dalkeith EH22 . 153 C2
8 Edinburgh EH7 . . . . . 94 A1
Taylor Rd EH47 . . . . 160 F6
Taymouth Rd FK2 . . . . 83 A4
Tay Pl ML7 . . . . 179 E6
Tay St Edinburgh EH11 . . 120 F5
Falkirk FK3 . . . . 39 C1
Grangemouth FK3 . . . . . . 40 A1
Tay Terr KY11 . . . . 29 E2
Tay Wlk EH54 . . . . 144 A4
Teal Pl KY11 . . . . 30 A1
Tedder St KY3 . . . . 61 C5
Telferton EH7 . . . . 94 F1
Telford Coll (North Campus)
EH5 . . . . 92 F6
Telford Coll (South Campus)
EH4 . . . . 92 E4
Telford Dr EH4 . . . . 92 D3
Telford Dr EH4 . . . . 92 D3
Telford Pl Edinburgh EH4 . 92 D3
Linlithgow EH49 . . . . 84 C8
Telford Rd EH4 . . . . 92 D3
Telford Sq Falkirk FK1 . . . 59 E6
Livingston EH54 . . . . 143 F8
Telford View EH49 . . . . . . 84 C6
Telny Pl KY3 . . . . 49 C7
Templar's Cramond EH4 . 91 A4
Templar La EH31 . . . . 52 A2
Templar Pl EH31 . . . . 52 A2
Templar Rise EH54 . . . . . 164 D8
Templars Cres KY3 . . . . . . 34 F3
Temple Ave EH48 . . . . . . 140 A5
Templedean Pk EH41 . . . 101 A1
Temple Denny Rd FK6 . . 36 D2
Templehall Ave KY2 . . . . . 16 F7
Templeland Gr EH12 . . . . 119 D7
Templeland Rd EH12 . . . . 119 D7

Temple Park Cres EH11 . 120 F5
Temple Pk EH23 . . . . 194 C6
Temple Prim Sch EH23 . 194 D2
Ten Acres EH10 . . . . 5 B1
Tenacres Pl FK3 . . . . 61 E6
Tenacres Rd FK3 . . . . 62 B7
Tenant's March EH55 . . . 163 C3
Tennant St EH6 . . . . 93 F4
Tennent Pk EH53 . . . . . . 144 C2
Tenterfield Dr EH41 . . . . 101 B1
Tenterfield Ho EH41 . . . . 101 B1
Tenth St EH22 . . . . 174 B6
Tern Brae EH54 . . . . 143 C6
Tern Rd KY11 . . . . 30 A1
Terrace Rdbt EH54 . . . . . 143 E1
Terrars St KY1 . . . . 18 A7
Terrars Croft EH8 . . . . . . 229 C2
Terregles EH26 . . . . 191 D6
Terris Pl KY3 . . . . 13 D3
Teviotdale Pl EH3 . . . . 93 B2
Teviot Dr EH54 . . . . 165 A7
Teviot Gr EH26 . . . . 191 F7
Teviot Pl EH1 . . . . 229 A2
Teviot St FK1 . . . . 59 F4
Thane Pl KY11 . . . . 29 F1
Thimblehall Dr KY12 . . . . 29 D4
Thimblehall Pl KY12 . . . . 29 D4
Thimblehall Rd KY12 . . . . 29 D4
Third Gait EH14 . . . . 147 E7
Third St EH22 . . . . 174 B5
Thirlestane EH51 . . . . 64 B8
Thirlestane La EH9 . . . . . 121 C4
Thirlestane Pl FK1 . . . . . . 64 B8
Thirlestane Rd EH9 . . . . . 121 C5
Thirlfield Wynd EH54 . . . 142 F2
Thistle Ave Denny FK6 . . . 36 D3
Grangemouth FK3 . . . . . . 61 B5
Thistle Chambers **4** FK8 . 7 B7
Thistle Ct KY4 . . . . 30 E5
Thistle St FK7 . . . . 7 B7
Thistle Ind Est
Broxburn EH52 . . . . 116 A5
Cowdenbeath KY4 . . . . . . 13 E4
Stirling FK7 . . . . 7 C6
Thistle Pl Edinburgh EH11 228 A1
Stirling FK8 . . . . 2 A1
Thistle St Alloa FK10 . . . . 10 C6
Burntisland KY3 . . . . 50 E8
Cowdenbeath KY4 . . . . . . 13 D3
Dunfermline KY12 . . . . . . 29 B5
Edinburgh EH2 . . . . 228 C4
Falkirk FK2 . . . . 60 C6
Kirkcaldy KY1 . . . . 17 C3
Thistly Cross EH42 . . . . . 105 E8
Thistly Cross Rdbt EH42 . 105 E7
Thompson's Ct EH11 . . . 228 C2
Thomson Cres
Cockenzie & Port Seton
EH32 . . . . 97 D4
Currie EH14 . . . . 148 B5
Falkirk FK1 . . . . 59 F4
Thomson Ct EH52 . . . . . . 114 F4
Thomson Dr EH14 . . . . . . 148 C5
Thomson Gn EH54 . . . . . 143 B8
Thomson Gr Currie EH14. 148 B5
Uphall EH52 . . . . 114 F4
Thomson Pl
Cambusbarron FK7 . . . . . . 6 D5
Limerigg FK1 . . . . 108 B3
Rosyth KY11 . . . . 46 F3
Thomson Rd EH14 . . . . . . 148 B5
Thomson Terr ML7 . . . . . 179 D6
Thorburn Gr EH13 . . . . . . 149 C6
Thorburn Rd EH13 . . . . . 149 B6
Thorburn Terr EH26 . . . . 191 F4
Thornbridge Gdns FK2 . . 60 E8
Thornbridge Rd FK2 . . . . 60 E5
Thornbridge Sq FK2 . . . . 60 E5
Thorndale Gdns FK4 . . . . 57 B2
Thorndene Ct **2** EH22 . 59 F2
Thorndene Terr FK1 . . . . 108 B3
Thorne Ct EH39 . . . . 54 A7
Thorne Rd FK10 . . . . 4 E1
Thorn Gr KY11 . . . . 46 C6
Thornhill Ct FK2 . . . . 60 C6
Thornhill Dr KY2 . . . . 17 B6
Thornhill Rd Falkirk FK2 . 60 C6
Kirkcaldy KY2 . . . . 17 B6
Thornton Ave FK4 . . . . . . 58 B6
Thornton Cres FK4 . . . . . 58 B6
Thornton Glen Cvn Site
EH42 . . . . 218 D7
Thorntonloch Holdings
EH42 . . . . 218 B6
Thornton Pl EH47 . . . . . . 181 D5
Thornton Rd EH24 . . . . . 172 D1
Thorntree Cres EH32 . . . 97 B1
Thorn Tree Pl KY12 . . . . . 26 F6
Thorntreeside Ind Est
EH6 . . . . 94 A3
Thornton St EH6 . . . . 94 A3
Thornville Terr EH6 . . . . . 94 A3
Thorny Bank EH22 . . . . . 153 C4
Thornybauk EH3 . . . . 228 B1
Thornycroft Terr FK7 . . . . 20 E3
Thornyhall EH22 . . . . 153 C4
Threave Loan KY11 . . . . . 30 A1
Three Bridges Rbt FK1 . . 81 A6
Threipmuir Ave EH14 . . . 168 C8
Threipmuir Gdns EH14 . . 168 C8
Threipmuir Pl EH14 . . . . 168 C8
Thrums The FK1 . . . . 61 A4
Thurston Pl EH16 . . . . . . 122 B1
Thymebank EH54 . . . . . . 143 E6
Tibbies Loan FK7 . . . . 20 D5
Timber Bush EH6 . . . . 94 A6

Timmeryetts EH52 ...... 115 C6
Timmons La KY5 ...... 14 A8
Timmons Pl FK6 ...... 36 D1
Tinian Cres KY12 ...... 26 D1
Tinto Dr FK3 ...... 61 E5
Tinto Pl Dunfermline KY11 .29 F2
  Edinburgh EH6 ...... 93 E4
Tipperary Pl FK5 ...... 38 E2
Tipperlinn Rd EH10 ...... 121 A3
Tippethill House Hospl
  EH48 ...... 140 B1
Tippet Knowes Ct EH52 ..87 E3
Tippet Knowes Pk EH52 ..87 E3
Tippet Knowes Rd EH52 ..87 E2
Tiree Cres EH52 ...... 61 D2
Tiree Pl Falkirk FK1 ...... 60 B1
  Kirkcaldy KY2 ...... 16 F8
Tirran Dr KY11 ...... 30 B1
Titania FK10 ...... 10 A8
Toddricks Wynd EH1 .... 229 B3
Toddshill Rd EH29 ...... 89 A1
Todd Sq EH54 ...... 114 E1
Tolbooth St **3** Falkirk FK1 .60 B4
  Kirkcaldy KY1 ...... 17 C3
Tolbooth Wynd EH6 ...... 94 A5
Tollbraes Rd EH48 ...... 141 D4
Tollcross EH3 ...... 228 B1
Tollcross Prim Sch EH3 228 B1
Tollgate KY11 ...... 29 B2
Toll Rd FK10 ...... 23 F3
Toll Rdbt EH54 ...... 142 E3
Toll View TD13 ...... 218 F4
Tolmount Cres KY12 ...... 29 C3
Tolmount Dr KY12 ...... 29 C3
Tolsta Cres FK1 ...... 61 F1
Tophill Entry FK1 ...... 59 F5
Toravon Dr FK2 ...... 83 A6
Torbain KY2 ...... 16 D8
Torbain Prim Sch KY2 ...16 D8
Torbain Rd KY2 ...... 16 B6
Torbane Ave EH47 ...... 161 E2
Torbane Dr EH47 ...... 161 E7
Torbeith Gdns
  Cowdenbeath KY4 ...... 12 F1
  Hill Of Beath KY4 ...... 13 A1
Torbothie Rd ML7 ...... 180 B4
Torbrex Farm Rd FK7 ...... 7 A4
Torbrex La FK7,FK8 ...... 7 A5
Torbrex Rd FK7 ...... 6 F4
Torburn Ave FK7 ...... 20 D3
Torduff Rd EH13 ...... 148 F4
Torlea Pl FK5 ...... 38 B3
Toronto Ave EH54 ...... 143 E4
Toronto Pl EH54 ...... 143 E3
Torosay Ave FK2 ...... 82 F6
Torphichen Ave EH53 .... 144 B2
Torphichen Pl EH3 ...... 228 A2
Torphichen Preceptory
  EH48 ...... 111 F6
Torphichen Prim Sch
  EH48 ...... 141 B8
Torphichen Rd EH48 .... 141 B8
Torphichen St
  Bathgate EH48 ...... 141 B7
  Edinburgh EH3 ...... 228 A2
Torphin Bank EH13 ...... 148 F5
Torphin Rd EH13 ...... 148 F5
Torrance Pk EH4 ...... 91 C1
Torridon Ave FK2 ...... 39 C1
Torridon Ct FK10 ...... 10 C5
Torridon Dr KY11 ...... 46 B2
Torridon La KY11 ...... 46 E2
Torridon Pl Kirkcaldy KY2 ..16 E8
  Rosyth KY11 ...... 46 E2
Torridon Rd EH47 ...... 161 C7
Torridon Wlk EH54 ...... 144 B4
Torrin Gdns ML7 ...... 180 B3
Torrin Prim Sch KY12 ..26 E1
Torry Dr FK12 ...... 4 F7
Torsonce Rd EH22 ...... 152 F2
Torvean Pl KY11 ...... 29 C2
Torwood Ave
  Grangemouth FK3 ...... 61 E6
  Larbert FK5 ...... 38 B2
Torwood Pl KY12 ...... 29 D5
Torwood Sch FK5 ...... 37 C6
Tory Bay Ct KY12 ...... 26 C1
Toscana Ct EH22 ...... 152 A8
Touchhill Cres FK7 ...... 20 C3
Touch Prim Sch KY11 ...29 E4
Touch Rd FK7,FK8 ...... 6 B6
Touch Wards KY12 ...... 29 E4
Tovey Rd KY11 ...... 46 D2
Toward Ct **3** EH42 ...... 119 A7
Towerbank Prim Sch
  EH15 ...... 95 B1
Tower Gdns The EH51 ...64 C7
Tower Pl Clackmannan FK10 10 F5
  Edinburgh EH6 ...... 94 A6
Towers Ct FK2 ...... 60 B6
Towers Pl FK9 ...... 2 C4
Tower Sq FK10 ...... 10 B5
Tower St Alloa FK10 ...... 10 A4
  Edinburgh EH6 ...... 94 A6
Tower Terr KY11 ...... 5 E1
Tower View FK10 ...... 3 F2
Tower Wynd EH6 ...... 94 A6
Town Burn FK7 ...... 6 F4
Town Ctr Rdbt EH54 .... 143 F2
Townhall St KY11 ...... 47 C2
Townhead Dysart KY1 ...18 A7
  Kinghorn KY3 ...... 35 B1
Townhead Apartments **9**
  ...... 10 B6
Townhead Gdns EH47 .. 161 C6
Town Head Mus KY12 ...42 D8
Townhill Ctry Pk KY12 ...29 D8

Townhill Prim Sch KY12 ..29 D8
Townhill Rd KY12 ...... 29 B5
Town House St FK6 ...... 36 E2
Townsend Cres KY1 ...... 17 C4
Townsend Pl KY1 ...... 17 C4
Town Sq EH54 ...... 143 E2
Trafalgar La EH6 ...... 93 E5
Trafalgar St EH6 ...... 93 E5
Trainers Brae EH39 ...... 54 F6
Train Terr KY11 ...... 46 C5
Tranent Inf Sch EH33 .. 126 D7
Tranent Prim Sch EH33 . 126 D7
Tranent Rd EH33 ...... 126 B1
Transy Gr KY12 ...... 29 C4
Transy Pl KY12 ...... 29 C4
Tranter Cres EH32 ...... 71 C4
Tranter Rd EH32 ...... 71 C4
Traprain Cotts HE41 .... 103 E4
Traprain Cres EH48 .... 140 F7
Traprain Terr
  Haddington EH41 ...... 101 B1
  Loanhead EH20 ...... 172 C7
Traquair Pl E EH12 .... 119 F6
Traquair Pk W EH12 .... 119 F6
Trelawney Terr EH26 ...192 A8
Tremayne Pl KY12 ...... 28 F6
Trenchard Pl KY12 ...... 28 F5
Trench Knowe EH10 .... 150 A5
Tressilian Gdns **1** EH16 ..122 B1
Trevelyan Cres EH4 .... 156 E6
Trevelyan Pl EH34 .... 156 E6
Trinity Acad EH5 ...... 93 C6
Trinity Cres EH5 ...... 93 B6
Trinity Ct EH5 ...... 93 B5
Trinity Gr EH5 ...... 93 B5
Trinity Mains EH5 ...... 93 B5
Trinity Prim Sch EH6 ...93 D6
Trinity Rd EH5 ...... 93 B6
Trinity Way EH5 ...... 93 B5
Tron Ct FK10 ...... 4 B2
Trondheim Parkway KY11 .29 F2
Trondheim Pl KY11 ...... 29 F2
Trongate KY3 ...... 35 A3
Tron Kirk Centre EH1 .. 229 A3
Tron Sq EH1 ...... 229 A3
Trotter Haugh EH9 .... 121 D3
Troup Ct FK3 ...... 61 D8
Tryst Pk Edinburgh EH10 .149 F5
  Stenhousemuir FK5 ...... 38 C5
Tryst Rd FK5 ...... 38 D3
Tudor Ct FK2 ...... 61 C2
Tuke St KY12 ...... 29 A5
Tulliallan Pl FK5 ...... 39 A4
Tulliallan Prim Sch FK10 .23 E4
Tulliallan Terr FK10 ...... 23 E5
Tullibody Rd FK10 ...... 9 F8
Tulligarth Pk KY10 ...... 10 A7
Tulloch Ct KY4 ...... 13 C5
Tulloch Rd ML7 ...... 180 B3
Tummel Dr KY12 ...... 16 D8
Tummel Pl
  Grangemouth FK3 ...... 61 E4
  Stenhousemuir FK5 ...... 38 E3
Turf Pl FK47 ...... 162 D7
Turnbull Gr KY11 ...... 29 F1
Turnbull Way EH54 .... 143 D6
Turner Ave EH14 ...... 147 C3
Turner Pk EH14 ...... 147 C3
Turner St EH48 ...... 141 A7
Turnhigh Rd EH47 ...... 161 A4
Turnhouse Farm Rd EH12 .118 D8
Turnstone Rd KY11 ...... 30 B1
Turret Ct FK10 ...... 10 C6
Turret Dr FK2 ...... 62 A2
Turret Gdns EH32 ...... 125 F8
Turret Rd FK3 ...... 61 D5
Turriff Pl KY12 ...... 16 E8
Twain Ave FK5 ...... 39 A3
Tweed Ave KY1 ...... 17 E8
Tweeddale Ave EH41 ...220 F7
Tweeddale Cres EH41 ...220 F7
Tweeddale Ct EH1 .... 229 B3
Tweeddale Dr KY11 ...... 29 E1
Tweeddale Gr EH41 .... 220 F6
Tweed Dr EH54 ...... 144 B4
Tweed St Dunfermline KY11 .29 F2
  Grangemouth FK3 ...... 40 A1
Tygershaugh Ct FK6 ...... 36 D4
Tyler's Acre Ave EH12 .. 119 E5
Tyler's Acre Gdns EH12 .119 E5
Tyler's Acre Rd EH12 .. 119 E5
Tyndrum Pl KY2 ...... 16 E7
Tynebank Rd EH41 ...... 130 A7
Tynecastle High Sch
  EH11 ...... 120 E6
Tynecastle La EH11 .... 120 E6
Tynecastle Pk (Heart of
  Midlothian FC) EH11 ..120 E5
Tynecastle Terr EH11 .. 120 E5
Tyne Cl East Linton EH40 .103 E7
  Haddington EH41 ...... 130 B8
Tyne Ct EH41 ...... 130 B8
Tynefield Cotts EH41 ...105 A8
Tyne Ho EH41 ...... 130 B7
Tynemount Cotts EH34 .156 E6
Tynemount Ave EH35 ...155 D6
Tynemount Rd EH35 ...155 D7
Tynepark Sch EH41 .... 130 B8
Tyne Pk EH34 ...... 157 A6
Tyneview EH35 ...... 155 C7
Tyrie Ave KY1 ...... 35 B7
Tyrie Ct KY1 ...... 35 B7
Tyrie Gr KY1 ...... 35 B7
Tyrie Pl KY1 ...... 35 B7
Tywhitt Pl KY11 ...... 46 F3
Tytler Ct EH8 ...... 94 A1
Tytler Gdns EH8 ...... 94 A1

U

Ugston Cotts EH41 .... 100 C2
Uig Way ML7 ...... 180 A3
Ulster Cres EH8 ...... 122 D8
Ulster Dr EH8 ...... 122 D8
Ulster Gdns EH8 ...... 122 D7
Ulster Gr EH8 ...... 122 D7
Ulster Terr EH8 ...... 122 D7
Underwood Cotts FK7 ...6 D5
Underwood Rd FK7 ...... 6 D5
Union Ct EH51 ...... 64 A8
Union Dr EH47 ...... 161 B6
Union Gdns EH11 ...... 59 D5
Union Pk EH19 ...... 173 B6
Union Pl Brightons FK2 ...61 D1
  Edinburgh EH1 ...... 229 A4
  Larbert FK5 ...... 38 B1
Union Rd Bathgate EH48 .141 B6
  Broxburn EH52 ...... 115 D5
  Falkirk FK1 ...... 59 D5
  Grangemouth FK3 ...... 40 D1
  Linlithgow EH49 ...... 84 F6
  Whitburn EH47 ...... 161 B6
Union Sq EH55 ...... 163 D3
Union St **4** Alloa FK10 ...10 B6
  Bo'ness EH51 ...... 63 F8
  Bo'ness EH51 ...... 64 A8
  Bridge of A FK9 ...... 2 A3
  Burntisland KY3 ...... 50 E8
  Cowdenbeath KY4 ...... 13 C4
  Edinburgh EH1 ...... 93 E2
  Falkirk FK2 ...... 60 C7
  Kirkcaldy KY1 ...... 17 F7
  Lochgelly KY5 ...... 14 B8
  Shotts ML7 ...... 179 D5
  Stenhousemuir FK5 ...... 38 E3
  Stirling FK8 ...... 2 B1
Unity Pk ML7 ...... 179 D4
Universal Rd FK2 ...... 60 E7
University of Stirling FK9 .2 D6
University Rd W FK9 ...... 2 C6
Univ of Dundee Sch of
  Nursing & Midwifery Fife
  Campus KY2 ...... 17 A2
Univ of Edinburgh EH8 . 229 A2
Univ of Edinburgh (King's
  Buildings Campus)
  EH9 ...... 121 F2
Uphall Prim Sch EH52 . 115 A5
Uphall Sta EH54 ...... 115 A2
Uphall Station Rd EH53 .144 B7
Upper Bathville EH48 .. 139 F4
Upper Bow EH1 ...... 229 A3
Upper Bridge St FK8 ...... 2 A1
Upper Broomieknowe
  EH18 ...... 173 A8
Upper Castlehill **2** FK8 ...7 A8
Upper Coltbridge Terr
  EH12 ...... 120 E8
Upper Craigour EH17 .. 151 E8
Upper Craigour Way
  EH17 ...... 122 D1
Upper Cramond Ct **4** EH4 .91 A4
Upper Dalhousie Cotts
  EH19 ...... 173 C3
Upper Damside **1** EH4 ..120 F8
Upper Dean Terr EH4 ...228 A4
Upper Gilmore Pl EH3 ..228 B1
Upper Gilmore Terr EH3 .228 B1
Upper Gray St EH9 ...... 121 E5
Upper Grove Pl EH3 .... 228 A1
Upper Hermitage EH6 ...94 A4
Upper Keith EH36 ...... 178 B2
Upper Millhill St EH7 ...60 B5
Upper Newmarket St **6**
  FK1 ...... 60 B5
Upper Wellheads KY11 ...45 E3
Ure Cres EH48 ...... 58 A6
Ure Ct KY12 ...... 16 D5
Urquhart Cres KY12 ...... 28 E3
Urquhart St KY12 ...... 16 D5
Urquhart Cut KY12 ...... 28 E3
Urquhart Farm Cotts
  KY12 ...... 28 D2
Usher Hall EH1 ...... 228 B2

V

Vale Gr FK9 ...... 1 F5
Vale Of Bonny View FK4 ..57 F5
Vale Pl FK6 ...... 36 E3
Valeview FK5 ...... 38 D2
Valley Field KY4 ...... 13 C5
Valleyfield Pl
  Cowdenbeath KY4 ...... 13 D5
  Stirling FK7 ...... 7 A5
Valleyfield Rd EH26 .... 191 F4
Valleyfield St EH3 ...... 228 C1
Valleyfield View EH26 .. 191 F4
Valleyfield Woodland Pk ...26 B3
Valley Gdns KY2 ...... 16 F6
Valley Gdns S KY2 ...... 16 F6
Valley Prim Sch KY2 ...17 A7
Valley View FK2 ...... 61 C4
Valleyview Dr FK2 ...... 60 A8
Valleyview Pl FK2 ...... 60 A8
Vanburgh Pl EH6 ...... 94 A4
Vancouver Ave FK5 ...... 38 A3
Vandeleur Ave EH7 ...... 94 E2
Vandeleur Gr EH7 ...... 94 F1
Vandeleur Pl EH7 ...... 94 E1
Vardon Gn EH54 ...... 143 C4
Vardon Rd EH31 ...... 52 B3

Vaucluse Pl EH26 ...... 191 E4
Veere Pk KY12 ...... 25 E1
Veitch's Sq **2** EH3 ...... 93 B2
Vellore Rd FK2 ...... 83 A6
Vennachar St ML7 ...... 179 E6
Vennel The Denny FK6 ...36 E2
  Dunbar EH42 ...... 78 E2
  Linlithgow EH49 ...... 85 A7
  South Queensferry EH30 ..68 C1
Ventnor Pl EH9 ...... 122 A4
Ventnor Terr EH9 ...... 121 F4
Venturefair Ave KY12 ...29 A5
Veronica Cres KY1 ...... 17 C8
Vetch Pk EH41 ...... 101 A1
Veterane Cotts EH48 ...141 C6
Vexhim Pk EH15 ...... 123 B5
Vicar St FK1 ...... 60 B5
Viceroy St KY2 ...... 17 B6
Victoria Gdns
  Kirkcaldy KY1 ...... 17 B4
  Newtongrange EH22 ...173 F6
Victoria Hospl KY2 ...... 17 B7
Victoria Mills Ind Est
  EH51 ...... 64 C8
Victoria Pk
  Fauldhouse EH47 ...... 181 F7
  Haddington EH41 ...... 101 A1
Victoria Pl Bo'ness EH51 ..64 B7
  Brightons FK2 ...... 61 D1
  Dunbar EH42 ...... 78 D3
  Stirling FK8 ...... 7 A7
Victoria Prim Sch
  Edinburgh EH6 ...... 93 D7
  Falkirk FK1 ...... 60 D6
Victoria Rd Falkirk FK2 ...60 C6
  Fauldhouse EH47 ...... 181 F7
  Grangemouth FK3 ...... 61 E8
  Haddington EH41 ...... 130 A8
  Harthill ML7 ...... 159 E5
  Kirkcaldy KY1 ...... 17 C5
  Larbert FK5 ...... 38 B1
  Newtongrange EH22 ...173 F5
  North Berwick EH39 ...54 C7
  Stirling FK8 ...... 7 A7
Victoria Sq FK8 ...... 7 A7
Victoria St Alloa FK10 ...10 A7
  Dunbar EH42 ...... 78 D3
  Dysart KY1 ...... 18 A7
  Edinburgh EH1 ...... 229 A3
  Gorebridge EH23 ...... 174 B1
  Harthill ML7 ...... 159 E5
  Kirkcaldy KY1 ...... 17 C5
  Livingston EH54 ...... 144 A4
  Rosewell EH24 ...... 172 D2
Victoria Terr
  Dunfermline KY11 ...... 29 A5
  Edinburgh EH1 ...... 229 A5
  Haddington EH41 ...... 130 B8
  Menstrie FK11 ...... 4 B7
  Musselburgh EH21 ...... 124 E6
Victor Park Terr EH12 .. 119 D7
Viewbank Dr EH19 ...... 173 C8
Viewbank Rd EH19 ...... 173 B8
Viewbank View EH19 ...173 C8
Viewcraig Gdns EH8 .... 229 B2
Viewcraig St EH8 ...... 229 B2
Viewfield Ave EH19 .... 173 D8
Viewfield Dr FK2 ...... 4 F6
Viewfield Ho KY12 ...... 29 B3
Viewfield Pl Harthill ML7 .159 F6
  8 Stirling FK8 ...... 7 B8
Viewfield Rd
  Edinburgh EH14 ...... 148 E2
  Tarbrax EH55 ...... 203 F3
Viewfield Terr
  Cowdenbeath KY4 ...... 13 F6
  Dunfermline KY11 ...... 29 B3
Vieworth Bo'ness EH51 ...64 A7
  Cockenzie & Port Seton
  EH32 ...... 97 D4
  Dunbar EH42 ...... 78 C3
  Edinburgh EH10 ...... 121 A5
  North Berwick EH39 ...54 C7
Viewforth FK3 ...... 61 E8
Viewforth Ct KY3 ...... 34 F2
Viewforth Dr FK2 ...... 61 B4
Viewforth Gdns
  Edinburgh EH10 ...... 121 B5
  Kirkcaldy KY1 ...... 17 F7
  Tranent EH33 ...... 126 C6
Viewforth High Sch KY1 ..34 F2
Viewforth Pl Kinghorn KY3 .34 F2
  Queensferry EH30 ...... 89 B8
Viewforth Rd EH30 ...... 89 B8
Viewforth Sq EH10 ...... 121 A5
Viewforth St KY1 ...... 17 F7
Viewforth Terr
  Edinburgh EH10 ...... 121 A5
  Kirkcaldy KY1 ...... 17 F7
  Tranent EH33 ...... 126 C6
Viewpark Gdns EH19 ...173 B8
Viking Way KY11 ...... 46 D2
Villabank EH52 ...... 36 E2
Village La EH54 ...... 143 B3
Villa Pl FK10 ...... 11 A5
Villa Rd EH30 ...... 68 B1
Vinefields EH34 ...... 156 F6
Vineyard Bsns Ctr EH27 .108 C2
Violet Bank **5** EH48 ...141 B6
Violet Terr FK11 ...... 120 E5
Vivian Terr EH4 ...... 92 C3
Vogrie Cres S EH23 .... 195 D8
Vogrie Ctry Pk EH23 ...175 D3

Vogrie Pl EH23 ...... 195 D3
Vogrie Rd EH23 ...... 195 D7
Voil Rd FK9 ...... 2 A3
Volunteer's Gn KY1 ...... 17 C3
Vorlich Cres EH52 ...... 192 A7
Vorlich Dr FK1 ...... 81 E7
Vorlich Pl FK9 ...... 2 A3
Vorlich Way KY11 ...... 30 B1

W

Waddell St FK2 ...... 39 C2
Wadingburn La EH18 .... 151 F1
Wadingburn Rd EH18 ...172 E8
Waggon Rd Bo'ness EH51 .63 E8
  Crossford KY11 ...... 45 C7
  Falkirk FK2 ...... 60 B7
  Grangemouth FK2 ...... 82 C8
  Inverkeithing KY11 ...... 47 C2
Wakefield Ave EH7 ...... 94 F2
Walden Dr EH41 ...... 220 F7
Walden Pl EH41 ...... 220 F6
Walden Terr EH41 ...... 220 F6
Waldie Ave EH49 ...... 85 A5
Walker Cres EH22 ...... 152 D1
Walker Dr Bonnybridge FK4 .57 D5
  South Queensferry EH30 ..68 A1
Walker Pl
  Bonnyrigg and Lasswade
  EH18 ...... 172 E6
  Dunfermline KY11 ...... 29 E2
Walker Rd EH47 ...... 161 D5
Walkers Ct EH14 ...... 119 E1
Walkers Rigg EH11 .... 119 E1
Walker St
  Cowdenbeath KY4 ...... 13 B3
  Edinburgh EH3 ...... 228 A3
  Kincardine FK10 ...... 23 E3
  Kirkcaldy KY2 ...... 17 B6
  Lochgelly KY5 ...... 14 A6
Walkers Wynd EH14 .... 119 E1
Walker Terr
  East Linton EH40 ...... 103 D7
  Edinburgh EH11 ...... 228 A2
Walk The Alloa FK10 ...... 10 A5
  Dysart KY1 ...... 18 B7
Wallace Bldgs FK2 ...... 60 B6
Wallace Brae Ave FK2 ...82 C8
Wallace Brae Bank FK2 ..82 C8
Wallace Brae Ct **1** FK2 ...82 C8
Wallace Brae Dr FK2 ...... 82 C8
Wallace Brae Gdns **4**
  FK2 ...... 82 C8
Wallace Brae Gr **2** FK2 ...82 C8
Wallace Brae Pl **3** FK2 ...82 C8
Wallace Brae Rise FK2 ...82 C8
Wallace Cres Denny FK6 ..36 C2
  Plean FK7 ...... 20 D3
  Roslin EH25 ...... 172 A3
Wallace Ct
  Grangemouth FK3 ...... 61 D8
  Stirling FK8 ...... 2 B1
Wallace Gate FK9 ...... 7 B8
Wallace High Sch FK9 ...2 E4
Wallacelea FK2 ...... 82 F7
Wallace Mill Gdns EH53 .144 C4
Wallace Monument FK9 ...2 E4
Wallace View
  Bo'ness EH51 ...... 63 D5
  Shieldhill FK1 ...... 81 D7
  Tullibody FK10 ...... 4 D3
Wallace Wlk EH47 ...... 162 A1
Wall Gdns FK1 ...... 59 C5
Wallsend Ct EH21 ...... 28 D5
Walls Pl KY11 ...... 29 E1
Wall St KY1 ...... 59 C5
Wallstale Rd FK7 ...... 7 A3
Wallyford Ind Est EH21 .125 B4
Wallyford Prim Sch
  EH21 ...... 125 B5
Wallyford Sta EH21 ...... 125 B5
Wallyford Toll EH21 .... 125 C6
Walmer Dr KY12 ...... 29 A3
Walnut Gr KY11 ...... 46 D8
Walter Hay Ct KY11 ...... 46 F3
Walter Scott Ave EH16 .122 B1
Wanless Ct EH21 ...... 124 D6
Ward Ave FK2 ...... 61 C2
Wardie Ave EH5 ...... 93 A5
Wardieburn Place E EH5 .92 F6
Wardieburn Place N EH5 .92 F6
Wardieburn Place W EH5 .92 F6
Wardieburn Rd EH5 ...... 92 F6

Wardieburn St E EH5 . . . . .92 F6
Wardieburn St W EH5 . . . . . .92 E6
Wardieburn Terr EH5 . . . . .92 F6
Wardie Cres EH5 . . . . .93 A6
Wardie Dell EH5 . . . . .93 A6
Wardiefield EH5 . . . . .92 F6
Wardie Gr EH5 . . . . .92 F6
Wardie House La EH5 . . . . .93 A6
Wardie Pk EH5 . . . . .93 A5
Wardie Prim Sch EH5 . . . . .93 A6
Wardie Rd EH5 . . . . .93 A5
Wardie Sq EH5 . . . . .93 A6
Wardie Steps EH5 . . . . .93 A6
Wardlaw Cres
  Dunfermline KY11 . . . . .29 D1
  Oakley KY12 . . . . .26 F7
Wardlaw Pl
  Edinburgh EH11 . . . . .120 E5
  Falkirk FK2 . . . . .39 C2
Wardlaw St
  Cowdenbeath KY4 . . . . .13 C3
  Edinburgh EH11 . . . . .120 E5
Wardlaw Terr EH11 . . . . .120 E5
Wardlaw Way KY12 . . . . .26 F7
Ward Pl EH54 . . . . .143 C5
Wardrop Cres EH48 . . . . .139 E5
Ward St FK10 . . . . .10 A5
Ware Rd Dirleton EH39 . . . . . . .53 C6
  North Berwick EH39 . . . . .54 A7
Warrender Cres EH42 . . . . .78 E1
Warrender Ct EH39 . . . . .54 A6
Warrender Park Cres
  EH9 . . . . .121 C5
Warrender Park Rd EH9 . 121 C5
Warrender Park Terr
  EH9 . . . . .121 C5
Warren Hill EH31 . . . . .51 F2
Warriston Ave EH3 . . . . .93 C4
Warriston Cres EH3 . . . . .93 C3
Warriston Dr EH3 . . . . .93 C3
Warriston Farm Rd
  EH14 . . . . .147 C6
Warriston Gdns EH3 . . . . .93 C4
Warriston Gr EH3 . . . . .93 B4
Warriston Pl EH3 . . . . .93 C3
Warriston Rd EH7 . . . . .93 C4
Warriston Terr EH3 . . . . .93 A4
Washington La 3 EH11 . .120 F6
Waterfall Wlk EH22 . . . . .153 B2
Waterfront Ave EH5 . . . . .92 D7
Waterfront Broadway
  EH5 .92 D6
Waterfront Way FK9 . . . . .2 A3
Waterfurs Dr FK2 . . . . .60 A8
Waterlands Gdns ML8 . . .215 A3
Waterloo Bank EH26 . . . . . .191 F4
Waterloo Pl
  Edinburgh EH1 . . . . .229 A4
  Elphinstone EH33 . . . . .126 B2
Water Of Leith Visitor Ctr
  EH14 . . . . .120 C2
Water of Leith Walkway
  EH14 . . . . .147 D2
Waters' Cl EH6 . . . . .94 A5
Waters End FK2 . . . . .39 A2
Waterside
  9 Haddington EH41 . . . . . .130 B8
  Linlithgow EH49 . . . . .84 C7
Water Ski Ctr KY12 . . . . .29 C7
Water St EH6 . . . . .94 A5
Watertoun Rd EH9 . . . . .121 E3
Watt Yett EH49 . . . . .84 F7
Watling Ave FK1 . . . . .59 C5
Watling Dr FK1 . . . . .59 D5
Watling Gdns FK1 . . . . .59 D6
Watling St FK1 . . . . .59 C5
Watson Cres EH11 . . . . .120 F5
Watson Gn EH54 . . . . .143 C8
Watson Pl Armadale EH48 .140 A6
  Dunfermline KY12 . . . . .29 B6
  Longcroft FK4 . . . . .57 C4
Watson St
  Cowdenbeath KY4 . . . . .13 D3
  Falkirk FK2 . . . . .60 B5
  Penicuik EH26 . . . . .191 F5
Watt's Cl EH21 . . . . .124 B6
Watt Ave EH48 . . . . .140 A5
Watters Cres KY5 . . . . .14 B6
Watt Gdns FK1 . . . . .59 E6
Watt Gr EH22 . . . . .174 D6
Watt Pk EH22 . . . . .174 B4
Watt St KY1 . . . . .18 A7
Wauchope Ave EH16 . . . . . . .122 E4
Wauchope Cres EH16 . . . . . .122 F4
Wauchope Ho EH16 . . . . .122 F3
Wauchope Pl EH16 . . . . .122 F4
Wauchope Rd EH16 . . . . .122 E4
Wauchope Sq EH16 . . . . .122 F4
Wauchope Terr EH16 . . . . . . .122 F4
Waugh Path EH19 . . . . .173 D8
Waughton Cotts EH40 . . . .74 F5
Waughton Steading EH40 .74 F5
Waulker Ave FK8 . . . . .1 F2
Waulkmill Dr EH26 . . . . .192 A5
Waulkmill Loan EH14 . . . .147 E3
Waulkmill Rd EH26 . . . . .192 A5
Waulkmill View EH26 . . . . . .191 F5
Wavell St FK3 . . . . .61 C5
Waverley Bridge EH1 . . .229 A3
Waverley Cres
  Bonnyrigg FK4 . . . . .58 B3
  Bonnyrigg and Lasswade
  EH19 . . . . .173 C7
  Grangemouth FK3 . . . . .61 D5

Waverley Cres *continued*
  Livingston EH54 . . . . .143 B6
  Stirling FK8 . . . . .2 C1
Waverley Ct EH19 . . . . .173 C7
Waverley Dr EH19 . . . . .173 C7
Waverley Ho N EH31 . . . . .52 A2
Waverley Ho S EH31 . . . . .52 A2
Waverley Park Terr EH8 . .94 A1
Waverley Pk
  Bonnyrigg and Lasswade
  EH19 . . . . .173 C7
  Edinburgh EH8 . . . . .94 A1
  Mayfield EH22 . . . . .174 D6
  Redding FK2 . . . . .61 B1
Waverley Pl
  2 Bathgate EH48 . . . . .141 A7
  Edinburgh EH7 . . . . .94 A2
Waverley Rd
  Bonnyrigg and Lasswade
  EH19 . . . . .173 C7
  Dalkeith EH22 . . . . .152 F2
  Stenhousemuir FK5 . . . . .38 C2
Waverley St
  Bathgate EH48 . . . . .141 A7
  Falkirk FK2 . . . . .60 B8
  Mayfield EH22 . . . . .174 D6
Waverley Sta EH1 . . . . .229 A3
Waverley Steps EH2 . . . . . .229 A3
Waverley Street Ind Units 1
  EH48 . . . . .141 A7
Waverley Terr
  Bonnyrigg and Lasswade
  EH19 . . . . .173 C7
  Mayfield EH22 . . . . .174 D6
  Stenhousemuir FK5 . . . . .38 C2
Wayfarers Dr KY11 . . . . .47 F3
Wayfarers Pl KY11 . . . . .47 F3
Wayfarers Way KY11 . . . . . . .47 F3
Weaver's Knowe Cres
  EH14 . . . . .147 F5
Weaver Pl EH48 . . . . .141 B7
Weaver Row FK7 . . . . .7 A4
Weavers Cres KY2 . . . . .17 B6
Weavers La EH47 . . . . .161 A6
Weaver's Terr KY12 . . . . .27 D1
Weavers Wlk KY12 . . . . .29 A2
Webster's Land EH1 . . . . . .228 C2
Webster Ave FK2 . . . . .39 B3
Webster Ct EH52 . . . . .115 E5
Webster Pl KY11 . . . . .46 C5
Wedderburn Cres KY11 . .29 E1
Wedderburn Ct EH21 . . . . . .124 D3
Wedderburn Ho EH21 . . . . . .124 D3
Wedderburn Pl KY11 . . . . . . .29 D2
Wedderburn Rd KY1 . . . . .16 C7
Wedderburn St KY11 . . . . . . .29 D2
Wedderburn Terr EH21 . .124 D4
Wee Brae EH18 . . . . .152 A1
Wee Cswy KY12 . . . . .42 D8
Wee Row FK2 . . . . .60 B6
Weir Ave KY11 . . . . .13 B2
Weir Cres EH22 . . . . .152 E2
Weir Ct EH22 . . . . .152 E2
Weir Dr FK7 . . . . .8 D4
Weir St Falkirk FK1 . . . . .60 C5
  Stirling FK8 . . . . .1 F2
Wellbank EH22 . . . . .61 B2
Well Ct EH3 . . . . .228 A3
Wellflats Rd EH29 . . . . .89 B1
Wellgate Dr FK2 . . . . .2 C7
Wellington La 11 FK8 . . . . . . .2 C2
Wellgreen Pl FK8 . . . . .7 B6
Wellgreen Rd FK8 . . . . .7 B6
Wellhead Cl EH30 . . . . .89 D8
Wellheads The KY11 . . . . . . .45 D3
Wellington Pl EH6 . . . . .94 A5
Wellington Sch EH26 . . . . .208 F6
Wellington St EH7 . . . . .93 F2
Wellpark Ho EH10 . . . . .11 A3
Wellpark EH52 . . . . .114 F8
Wellpark Cres FK7 . . . . .6 F4
Wellpark Terr FK4. . . . . .58 A5
Well Rd Bridge of A FK9 . . . . . .2 A8
  Falkirk FK1. . . . . .59 F3
  Lochgelly KY5 . . . . .14 B7
Wellside EH1 . . . . .129 F8
Wellside Cl FK1 . . . . .60 A5
Wellside Pl FK1 . . . . .60 A5
Wellview La EH54 . . . . .164 F5
Wellwood Prim Sch KY12 .29 A7
Well Wynd EH33 . . . . .126 D6
Welsh Cl FK6 . . . . .36 E1
Welsh Gdns FK9 . . . . .2 A8
Welsh Rd EH47 . . . . .160 F6
Wemyss Ct KY11 . . . . .46 E5
Wemyssfield KY1 . . . . .17 B3
Wemyss Gdns EH21 . . . . . .125 C5
Wemyss Pl
  Cockenzie & Port Seton
  EH32 . . . . .97 C4
  Edinburgh EH3 . . . . .228 A4
  Haddington EH41 . . . . .130 A8
  Longniddry EH32 . . . . .98 E6
Wemyss Place Mews
  EH3 . . . . .228 A4
Wemyss Rd EH32 . . . . .97 C4
Wemyss St
  Cowdenbeath KY4 . . . . .13 D3
  Rosyth KY11 . . . . .46 F5
Wemyss Terr EH32 . . . . .98 F5
Werberside Mews EH4 . . .92 E4
Wesley Cres EH19 . . . . .173 D7
Wesley Pl FK2 . . . . .82 B8
West Adam St EH8 . . . . . . .229 B2
West Adniston Cotts
  EH33 . . . . .127 C6
West Albert Rd KY1 . . . . .17 B4
West Annandale St EH7 .93 D3

West Approach Rd
  Edinburgh,Dalry EH11 . . . . .120 E6
  Edinburgh,Fountainbridge EH3,
  EH11 . . . . .228 A2
West Baldridge Rd KY12 .28 E5
Westbank Ct EH33 . . . . .127 D5
Westbank Gdns EH33 . . . . .127 D5
Westbank Loan EH15 . . . . . .95 A1
Westbank Pl EH15 . . . . .95 A1
Westbank Rd EH33 . . . . .127 C5
Westbank St EH15 . . . . .95 A1
Westbank Terr EH33 . . . . . . .127 C5
West Bankton Pl EH54 . .164 F7
West Barns Prim Sch
  EH42 . . . . .77 F1
West Bay Ct EH39 . . . . .54 B7
West Bay Rd EH39 . . . . .54 B7
West Benhar Rd ML7 . . . . . .159 B3
West Boreland Rd FK6 . . . . .36 D2
West Bow EH1 . . . . .229 A2
West Bowling Green St
  EH6 .93 E5
West Bridge St FK1 . . . . .60 A5
West Brighton Cres
  EH15 . . . . .123 A8
West Broomhill Rd KY3 . .50 E8
West Bryson Rd EH11 . . . . .120 F5
Westburn Ave
  Cowdenbeath KY4 . . . . .13 B2
  Edinburgh EH14 . . . . .148 C8
Westburn Gr EH14 . . . . .148 C8
Westburn Middlefield
  EH14 . . . . .148 C8
Westburn Pk EH14 . . . . .148 D8
Westburn Prim Sch
  EH11 . . . . .119 D1
West Burnside EH52 . . . . . .115 E5
West Cairn Cres EH26 . . . .191 E6
West Caiystane Rd EH10 .150 A5
West Calder High Sch
  EH55 . . . . .164 B5
West Calder Sta EH55 . . . . .163 D3
West Calder Workspace
  EH55 . . . . .163 C3
West Camus Rd EH10 . . . . . .150 A5
West Carmuirs Loan FK5. .58 F6
West Carnethy Ave EH13 .149 A5
West Castle Rd EH10 . . . . . .121 A5
West Catherine Pl EH12 .120 E7
West Cherrybank EH6 . . . . . .93 C6
West Church Dr FK3 . . . . .40 B1
Westcliffe Ct FK3 . . . . .61 F6
West Clifton Farm Cotts
  EH53 . . . . .145 D8
West Coates EH12 . . . . .120 E7
West Colinton Ho EH13 . .149 A6
West College St EH1 . . . . . .229 A2
West Craigs Ave EH12 . . . .119 A6
West Craigs Cres EH12. . .119 A6
West Craigs Ind Est
  EH12 . . . . .118 F7
Westcraigs Pk EH48 . . . . . .138 C3
Westcraigs Rd
  Blackridge EH48 . . . . .138 D2
  Harthill ML7 . . . . .159 F6
West Cres EH34. . . . . .157 E4
West Croft EH28 . . . . .117 E2
West Cromwell St EH6 . . . . . .93 F6
West Crosscauseway
  EH8 . . . . .229 B1
West Ct
  Edinburgh,Niddrie Mains
  EH16 . . . . .122 E3
  Edinburgh,Ravelston EH4 . . . .92 B3
West Dr Dunfermline KY12 . .29 B3
  Stenhousemuir FK5 . . . . .38 C1
West End
  Cockburnspath TD13 . . . . . .218 F4
  West Calder EH55 . . . . .163 C2
West End Gdns FK10 . . . . . . .10 A6
Westend Pl EH11 . . . . .39 B7
West End Pl EH11 . . . . .120 F6
Wester Bankton EH54 . . .165 A7
Wester Bogie Rd KY2 . . . . . .16 B7
Wester Broom Ave EH12 .119 C5
Wester Broom Dr EH12 . .119 C5
Wester Broom Gdns
  EH12 . . . . .119 C5
Wester Broom Gr EH12. . .119 C5
Wester Broom Pl EH12 . . .119 C5
Wester Broom Terr
  EH12 . . . . .119 C5
Wester Coates Ave EH12 .120 E7
Wester Coates Gdns
  EH12 . . . . .120 E7
Wester Coates Pl EH12 . . .120 E7
Wester Coates Rd EH12 . .120 E7
Wester Coates Terr
  EH12 . . . . .120 E7
Wester Cowden Cotts
  EH22 . . . . .153 E3
Wester Dalmeny Steading
  EH30 . . . . .89 E8
Wester Drylaw Ave EH4 . . . .92 B3
Wester Drylaw Dr EH4 . . . . .92 B3
Wester Drylaw Pk EH4 . . . . .92 C3
Wester Drylaw Pl EH4 . . . . .92 B3
Wester Drylaw Row EH4 . .92 C2
Westerdunes Ct EH39 . . . . . .53 E7
Westerdunes Pk EH39 . . . . . .53 D7
Westerfield Dr KY12 . . . . .26 F5
Westerglen Rd FK1 . . . . .60 A2
Wester Hailes Ed Ctr
  EH11 . . . . .119 C1

Wester Hailes Pk EH14. . .148 E8
Wester Hailes Rd EH14. . .148 D7
Wester Hailes Sta EH14 .148 D8
Wester Hill 149 E8
Wester Inch Rdbt EH48. .141 D4
Westerlands Dr FK8. . . . . .7 B5
Westerlea Ct FK9 . . . . .2 A5
Westerlea Dr FK9 . . . . .2 A5
Westerlea Sch EH12 . . . . . .120 C7
Westermains EH48 . . . . .139 E5
Western Ave
  Crossford KY12 . . . . .28 B1
  Falkirk FK2 . . . . .60 B6
Western Cnr EH12 . . . . .120 B7
Western Gdns EH12 . . . . . . .120 C7
Western General Hospl
  EH4 .92 D3
Western Harbour Breakwater
  EH6 .93 D8
Western Harbour Dr EH6. .93 D8
Western Harbour Pl EH6 .93 D8
Western Harbour Terr
  EH6 .93 D8
Western Pl EH12. . . . . .120 C7
Western Terr EH12 . . . . .120 C7
Wester Row EH14 . . . . .118 E1
Wester Steil EH10 . . . . .120 E1
Westerton FK7. . . . . .20 D8
Westerton Dr FK9. . . . . .2 A7
Westerton Rd
  Broxburn EH52 . . . . .116 B5
  Grangemouth FK3 . . . . .61 F7
Westerton Terr FK2 . . . . .39 C3
West Fairbrae Cres
  EH11 . . . . .119 E3
West Fairbrae Dr EH11. . .119 E3
West Fenton Cotts EH39 . .72 E8
West Fenton Ct EH39 . . . . . .72 D8
West Fenton Gait EH31. . . .52 C2
West Fergus Pl KY1 . . . . .17 B3
West Ferryfield EH5. . . . . .92 F5
Westfield FK10 . . . . .24 B3
Westfield Ave EH11 . . . . . . .120 C5
Westfield Bank 6 EH22 . .152 E1
Westfield Ct EH41 . . . . .129 D3
Westfield Dr 4 EH22 . . . . .152 E1
Westfield Gr
  Crossgates KY4 . . . . .30 E6
  Dalkeith EH22 . . . . .152 E1
Westfield Pk EH14 . . . . .120 C4
Westfield Pl EH22 . . . . .152 E1
Westfield Prim Sch
  EH14 . . . . .110 F4
Westfield Rd EH11 . . . . .120 D5
Westfield Rdbt FK2 . . . . .60 F6
Westfield Specl Sch
  EH22 . . . . .152 F4
Westfield St
  Edinburgh EH11 . . . . .120 D5
  Falkirk FK2 . . . . .60 C5
Westfield Trad Est FK6 . .36 E1
West Fountain Pl EH11. . .120 F6
West Garleton Holdings
  EH41 . . . . .100 A4
Westgarth Ave EH13 . . . . . .149 B6
Westgate Dunbar EH42 . . . . .78 D3
  Mid Calder EH53 . . . . .144 B3
  North Berwick EH39 . . . . . . .54 B7
Westgate Ct 2 EH54 . . . . . .62 A8
West Gate Rd FK3 . . . . .62 A8
West Glen Ave EH54 . . . . . .142 E6
West Gorgie Pk EH14 . . . . . .120 C4
West Gorgie Pl EH14 . . . . . .120 C3
West Grange Gdns EH9 .121 D3
West Granton Access
  EH5 .92 D5
West Granton Rd EH5. . . . . .92 D6
Westhall Cres KY12 . . . . .27 D1
Westhall Gdns
  Edinburgh EH11 . . . . .121 B5
  Uphall EH52 . . . . .115 A4
West Hall Rd EH52 . . . . .115 E4
West Harbour Rd
  Charlestown KY11 . . . . .45 A4
  Cockenzie & Port Seton
  EH32 . . . . .97 B4
  Edinburgh EH5 . . . . .92 F7
West Harwood Crofts
  EH55 . . . . .184 C6
Westhaugh Cvn Site FK10 . .5 A4
Westhaugh Rd FK9 . . . . .1 F4
West Holmes Gdns EH21 .124 B6
West Holmes Pl EH52 . . . . .115 B4
West Holmes Rd EH52 . . . .115 B4
Westhouses Ave EH22 . . . .174 E5
Westhouses Dr EH22 . . . . . .174 E5
Westhouses Rd EH22 . . . . .174 E5
Westhouses St EH22 . . . . . .174 E5
West James St FK12 . . . . . . .5 A6
West Johnstone St FK12 . .5 A6
West La KY4 . . . . .13 B2
Westland Cotts EH17 . . . . .151 E5
West Leven St KY3 . . . . .50 E8
West Link Rd FK9 . . . . .2 D5
West Links Rd EH39 . . . . .54 B8
West Loan EH32 . . . . .96 F1
West Loan Ct EH32 . . . . . . .125 F8
West Lodge Gdns FK10 . . . .9 F8
West Lorimer Pl EH32. . . . . .97 B3
West Lothian Coll EH54 .143 D1
West Lothian Council
  Museum Service EH41 .162 C8
Westmains Cotts EH41 . .132 A5
West Mains Cotts EH55 .183 F8
West Mains Ind Est
  Falkirk FK3. . . . . .60 F7
  Grangemouth FK3 . . . . .61 A7

West Mains Rd
  Edinburgh EH9. . . . . .121 F2
  Falkirk FK3. . . . . .60 F7
West Main St
  Aberlady EH17 . . . . .71 C4
  Armadale EH48 . . . . .139 E5
  Blackburn EH47 . . . . .162 C7
  Broxburn EH52 . . . . .115 D5
  Harthill ML7 . . . . .159 E5
  Uphall EH52 . . . . .114 F4
  Whitburn EH47 . . . . .160 F6
West Maitland St EH12 . .228 A2
West March St KY1 . . . . .17 C7
West Mayfield EH9 . . . . .121 F4
West Meikle Pinkerton Cotts
  EH42 . . . . .107 C4
West Mill Bank EH13 . . . . .149 A6
West Mill La EH4 . . . . .228 A3
West Mill Rd EH13 . . . . .173 A8
West Mill Rd EH13 . . . . .148 F5
Westmill Wynd EH18 . . . . . .173 A8
Westminster Pl FK5 . . . . .38 C4
West Montgomery Pl 4
  EH7 .93 F2
Westmost Cl EH6 . . . . .93 C7
Westmuir Rd EH55 . . . . .163 D2
West Murrayfield FK7. . . . . . .7 C1
West Nethertown St KY12 .29 A3
West Newington Pl 7
  EH9 . . . . .121 E5
West Nicolson St EH8 . . . .229 B2
West Norton Pl EH7. . . . . . .229 C4
West Park Gr EH52 . . . . .115 B5
West Park Pl EH11. . . . . .120 F6
West Pilton Ave EH4 . . . . .92 C4
West Pilton Bank EH4 . . . . . .92 C4
West Pilton Brae EH4 . . . . . . .92 C5
West Pilton Cres EH4 . . . . . . .92 B5
West Pilton Crossway
  EH4 .92 C5
West Pilton Dr EH4 . . . . .92 C5
West Pilton Gdns EH4 . . . . . .92 C5
West Pilton Gn EH4 . . . . .92 C5
West Pilton Gr EH4 . . . . .92 C5
West Pilton Lea EH4 . . . . .92 C5
West Pilton March EH4 . . . . .92 C5
West Pilton Pk EH4 . . . . .92 C5
West Pilton Pl EH4 . . . . .92 C5
West Pilton Rd EH4 . . . . .92 C5
West Pilton Rise EH4 . . . . . . .92 C5
West Pilton Terr EH4 . . . . .92 C5
West Pilton View EH4 . . . . . . .92 C4
West Pilton Way EH4 . . . . . . .92 C5
West Pk Carnock KY12 . . . . .27 C6
  Lochgelly KY5 . . . . .14 A7
Westpoint Dunbar EH42 . . . .78 C2
  Garvald EH41 . . . . .132 D2
West Port Dunbar EH42. . . .78 C2
  Dysart KY1 . . . . .18 A7
  Edinburgh EH1 . . . . .228 C2
  Linlithgow EH49 . . . . .84 F7
West Port Pl EH49 . . . . .84 F6
West Powburn EH9 . . . . .121 E3
West Preston St EH8 . . . . .121 E5
West Quality St KY11 . . . . . . .18 A7
Westquarter Ave FK2 . . . . . .61 B2
Westquarter Dovecot FK2 .61 A2
Westquarter Prim Sch
  FK2 .61 A2
Westray Terr FK1 . . . . .60 C2
West Rd Charlestown KY11 . .45 A4
  Haddington EH41 . . . . .129 E8
  Whitekirk EH42 . . . . .75 E7
West Register St EH2 . . . . .229 A4
West Register Street La
  EH2 . . . . .229 A4
West Relugas Rd EH9 . . . .121 D3
Westrecon Ho
  Bridge of A FK9 . . . . .2 A8
  Stirling FK9 . . . . .2 A7
West Richmond St EH8 .229 B2
West Saltoun EH34. . . . . . . .157 C3
West Sands KY5 . . . . .68 C6
West Savile Gdns EH9 . . .121 E3
West Savile Rd EH16 . . . . .121 F3
West Savile Terr EH9 . . . . .121 E3
West Scotland Street La 1
  EH3 .93 C2
West Seaside EH32 . . . . .96 F1
West Shore Bsns Ctr EH5 .92 C7
West Shore Rd EH5 . . . . .92 C7
West Shore Road Trad Est
  EH5 .92 C7
Westside Plaza Sh Ctr
  EH14 . . . . .148 D8
West Silvermills La EH3 . .93 B2
West St EH26 . . . . .191 E4
West Stanhope Pl 6
  EH12 . . . . .120 F7
West Stirling St FK12 . . . . . . .4 F7
West Telferton EH7 . . . . .94 D3
West Terr Blackness EH49. . .65 D5
  South Queensferry EH30 . . . .68 B1
West Tollcross EH3 . . . . .228 C1
West Torbain KY2 . . . . .16 D8
West Vennel 6 FK10 . . . . .10 B6
Westview EH41 . . . . .84 C7
Westview Cres FK10 . . . . .4 C2
West Vows Wlk KY1 . . . . .35 B6
Westwater St KY5 . . . . .14 B7
West Way KY11 . . . . .48 B5
West Werberside EH4. . . . . . .92 E4
West Windygoul Gdns
  EH33 . . . . .126 C5
West Windygoul Gdns
  EH33 . . . . .126 C4

West Winnelstrae EH5 ....92 F4
Westwood Ave KY1 ....17 E8
Westwood Pk EH54 ....142 F7
Westwood Pl KY11........29 E4
West Woods EH4 ....92 D3
Westwood View EH55 ... 163 D3
West Wynd 13 KY1.......17 D6
Whale Brae EH6 ....93 D6
Wharry Rd FK12 ....4 E7
Whauphill KY1.............217 F8
Whauphill Cres ML11 ....217 F8
Wheatfield Gr EH20 ....212 A4
Wheatfield Loan EH20 ...151 B1
Wheatfield Pl EH11 ... 120 D5
Wheatfield Rd
 Bo'ness EH51 ....64 C6
 Edinburgh EH11.........120 D5
Wheatfield St EH11 ......120 D5
Wheatfield Terr EH11 ...120 D5
Wheatfield Wlk EH20 ...172 B8
Wheatlands Ave EH4 ....58 A6
Wheatsheaf La EH22 ....153 A3
Whimbrel Pl KY11 ....30 C4
Whim Rd EH31 ....51 F2
Whinbank EH54............143 E6
Whinhill KY11 ....29 C3
Whinneyknowe KY11.....68 C6
Whinniehill Terr KY12 ...27 C6
Whinnyburn Pl KY15 ......46 D5
Whinny Hill Cres KY11 ...47 A1
Whinny View EH32 ....71 C4
Whin Pk EH32 ....97 B3
Whinrig EH52..............115 D6
Whins of Milton Sch FK7...7 B1
Whins Pl EH15.............95 A1
Whins Rd Alloa FK10.......10 C7
 Stirling FK7 ....7 B2
Whinwell Rd FK8 ....2 A1
Whirlbut Cres KY11 .....29 B2
Whirlbut St KY11.........29 B2
Whitburn Mains Cotts
 EH37.................176 D4
Whitburn Acad EH47....161 C7
Whitburn Rd
 Bathgate EH48...........140 E3
 Livingston EH54 ....143 C3
Whitdale then Sch EH47 161 C6
White's Cl 5 EH22.......153 A3
White Castle Fort EH14 ..222 B7
Whitecraig Ave EH21....124 C1
Whitecraig Cres EH21...124 C1
Whitecraig Gdns EH21...124 C1
Whitecraig Gdns E EH21.124 C1
Whitecraig Prim Sch
 EH21.................124 C1
Whitecraig Rd EH21 ....124 C1
Whitecraig Terr EH21 ...124 C1
Whitecross Ind Pk EH49...83 E7
Whitecross Prim Sch
 EH49.................83 F6
Whitedalehead Rd EH47..161 C6
Whitedales EH10 ....150 C5
Whitefield Neuk KY12 ...29 F6
Whitefield Rd KY12 ....29 E6
Whitefield St KY11 ....59 C4
Whitegates Pl KY1.......59 C4
White Hart St 12 EH22 ..153 A3
Whitehead Gr EH30 ....89 D8
Whitehill EH22............153 F2
Whitehill Ave EH21 ...124 A4
Whitehill Bsns Ctr EH22..153 E2
Whitehill Dr
 Blackburn EH47.........162 C8
 Dalkeith EH22 ....153 D2
Whitehill Farm Rd EH22 124 A4
Whitehill Gdns EH21 ...124 A4
Whitehill Gr EH22.......153 D2
Whitehill Ind Est EH48...141 C2
Whitehill Pl
 Rosewell EH24.........172 D2
 Stirling FK8 ....7 A5
Whitehill Rd
 Blackburn EH47.........141 C1
 Edinburgh EH15.........123 D3
 Rosewell EH24.........172 E1
Whitehill St EH21.......123 E4
Whitehill View EH47....162 C8
White Horse Cl EH8......229 C3
Whitehouse Loan EH9 ...121 C5
Whitehouse Rd
 Edinburgh EH4..........91 A4
 Stirling FK7 ....7 D7
Whitehouse Terr EH9 ...121 C4
Whitelaw Cres KY11 .....29 D2
Whitelaw Dr EH48 ....141 E6
Whitelaw Pl KY11 ....29 D2
Whitelaw Rd KY11 ....29 D2
Whitelaw St EH48........138 D1
Whitelea Cres EH14 ....168 C8
Whitelea Rd EH14 ......168 C8
Whiteloch Ct EH33......127 C5
Whiteloch Rd EH33......127 C5
Whitemoss La EH27.....145 E2
Whitemoss Rd EH27.....145 E2
Whitemyre Ct KY12......28 D5
White Pk EH11 ....120 E5
Whitequarries Ind Est
 EH52.................87 C7
Whitesands Geology Trail
 EH42.................107 F7
Whiteside EH48..........140 F4
Whiteside Cotts EH48...140 F4
Whiteside Ct EH48 ......140 F4
Whitesideloan FK2.......82 E8
Whites Quay KY11 ....47 F2
White St EH47..........161 A6
Whitestone Pl EH48.....141 C1

Whiteyetts Cres FK10 .....5 D2
Whiteyetts Dr FK10 ......5 D2
Whiteyetts Pl FK10 ....5 D2
Whitingford EH6...........93 D5
Whitson Cres EH11 ......120 B5
Whitson Gr EH11 ....120 B5
Whitson Pl E EH11........120 B5
Whitson Pl W EH11.......120 B5
Whitson Rd EH11.........120 B5
Whitson Terr EH11 ......120 B5
Whitson Way EH11.......120 B5
Whitson Wlk EH11.......120 A5
Whitten La EH49..........84 F7
Whittingehame Dr EH41 130 C8
Whittret Knowe
 Forth ML11 ....217 E8
 Forth ML11 ....217 F7
Wholeflats Rd FK2,FK3 ..62 A4
Wholeflats Rdbt FK3.....61 F2
Wholequarter Ave FK2 ..61 B2
Whytehouse Ave KY1 ....17 B3
Whyteman's Brae KY1 ...17 C8
Whytemans Brae Hospl
 KY1..................17 B7
Whyte Melville Rd KY2...17 A4
Whyte Pl 7 EH7..........94 A1
Whytescauseway KY1 ...17 B3
Whyte St Harthill ML7...159 F4
 Lochgelly KY5 ....1 B8
Whyte Wlk KY11 ....29 F4
Widows Row EH42........76 B3
Wilderness Rdbt EH54 ..164 C6
Wilderness The FK2......22 D4
Wilfrid Terr 6 EH8......94 C1
Wilkieston Rd EH28 ....117 C2
William Black Pl EH30 ..89 C8
William Booth Pl FK7 ....7 A4
Williamfield Ave FK7.....7 A4
Williamfield Sq 2 EH6..123 A8
William Jameson Pl EH15 95 A1
William Sharp Pl KY4 ...13 D4
Williamson's Quay KY1 .17 B4
Williamson La EH22......39 A1
Williamson Pl KY2.......60 C7
Williamson St FK1.......60 B4
William St
 Dunfermline KY12 ......28 E4
 Edinburgh EH3 ....228 A3
 Kirkcaldy KY1...........17 B2
Williamstone Ct EH4.....54 A6
Williamston Intc EH54 ..144 A1
Williamston Prim Sch
 EH54.................164 F8
William Street NE La
 EH3 ....228 A3
William Street NW La
 EH3 ....228 A3
William Street SE La
 EH3 ....228 A3
William Street SW La
 EH3 ....228 A2
Willow Ave
 Bonnyrigg and Lasswade
  EH19 ....173 B6
 Fauldhouse EH47.......181 F5
Willowbank EH54 ....143 E6
Willowbank Row EH6 ....93 D6
Willowbrae FK2...........82 D8
Willow Brae
 Fauldhouse EH47.......181 F5
 Plean FK7 ....20 C3
Willowbrae Ave EH8 ...122 C8
Willowbrae Gdns EH8 ..122 D8
Willowbrae Rd EH8 .....122 C8
Willowdean EH49........86 C4
Willow Dell EH51.........63 D5
Willow Dr KY1............17 B8
Willow Gr
 Dunfermline KY11......46 E8
 Fauldhouse EH47.......181 F5
 Livingston EH54........144 B5
 Menstrie KY11 ....3 E6
Willow Grange FK2......61 C1
Willowpark Sch EH11...120 D5
Willow Rd EH47..........181 F5
Willow Rd EH22 ....174 E6
Willows The
 Cairneyhill KY12 ....27 D1
 Tullibody FK10 ....4 B1
Willow Tree Pl EH14....147 D3
Willowtree Ave EH47....181 F5
Wilson's Cl 1 KY12.....29 A3
Wilson's Cl EH1 ....229 B3
Wilson's Pk EH15 ....95 B1
Wilson Ave Dalkeith EH22.153 C3
 Denny FK6 ....36 C2
 Falkirk FK1...........59 C6
 Kirkcaldy KY2 ....17 B6
 Polmont FK2...........61 F2
 Prestonpans EH32.....96 F1
Wilson Bruce Ct KY5...14 C8
Wilson Ct ML11..........217 F7
Wilson Dr Bannockburn FK7..7 C2
 Falkirk FK1............59 C5
Wilson Gdns FK1 ....59 C6
Wilson Pl Bannockburn FK7.7 C2
 Dunbar EH42...........106 E8
Wilson Rd Allanton ML7..198 A8
 Dunbar EH42...........106 D8
 Falkirk FK1...........59 C6
 Gorebridge EH23......174 D1
 Livingston EH54.......142 E3
Wilson's Cl 15 FK1.....60 B4
Wilson St Blairhall KY12..26 A8
 Cowdenbeath KY4 .....13 C4
 Kirkcaldy KY1..........17 B2
 Penicuik EH26 ....191 E5
 Townhill KY12..........29 D8

Wilson Terr
 Broxburn EH52.........115 B5
 Stoneyburn EH47.......162 A2
Wilsontown Rd ML11...201 C2
Wilson Way KY11 ....46 D2
Wilson Wlk 5 EH33....126 C5
Wilton Rd Carluke ML8...215 B1
 Edinburgh EH16........121 F3
Winchburgh Cotts EH52..87 F2
Winchburgh Prim Sch
 EH52.................87 E2
Winchester Ave EH6 .....36 E3
Winchester Avenue Ind Est
 FK6..................36 F3
Winchester Ct FK6.......36 F3
Winchester Dr FK6.......36 F3
Windlebrook KY11 ....47 A7
Windmill Cl EH8 ....229 B1
Windmill Gr KY1.........17 F8
Windmill Knowe KY4.....30 E6
Windmill La EH8.........229 B1
Windmill Pl
 Edinburgh EH8.........229 B1
 Kirkcaldy KY1..........18 A8
Windmill Rd KY1 ....17 F8
Windmill St EH8 ....229 A1
Windmill View FK10.......5 D2
Windsor Ave KY1 ....59 E4
Windsor Cres Falkirk FK1..59 E4
 Maddiston FK2.........83 A4
 Penicuik EH26 ....192 A6
Windsor Dr Denny FK6...36 D3
 Penicuik EH26 ....192 A6
Windsor Gdns Alloa FK10..9 F8
 3 Falkirk FK1..........59 F4
 Musselburgh EH21.....124 E6
Windsor Park Dr EH21 ..124 E6
Windsor Park Pl EH21...124 F6
Windsor Park Sch FK1...59 E4
Windsor Park Terr EH21..124 E6
Windsor Pk EH21 ....124 E6
Windsor Pl
 Edinburgh EH15........123 B8
 Shotts ML7 ....179 E5
 Stirling FK8 ....7 A7
Windsor Rd Falkirk FK1...59 E4
 Penicuik EH26 ....192 A6
Windsor Sq EH26 ....192 A6
Windsor St Edinburgh EH7..93 E2
 Menstrie FK11 ....3 F6
 Shotts ML7 ....179 E5
Windsor Terr EH26 .....192 A6
Windygate KY1...........16 F1
Windygates Rd EH39 ....54 B6
Windygoul Cres EH33 ..126 E5
Windyhall Ave EH48 .....23 D6
Windyknowe Cres EH48..140 E6
Windyknowe Pk EH48...140 E6
Windyknowe Prim Sch
 EH48.................140 D6
Windy Mains Farm Cotts
 EH36.................177 D5
Wingate Cres EH42 ......78 C2
Winifred Cres KY2 ....17 A6
Winifred St KY2 ....17 A6
Winterfield Mains EH42..78 A2
Winterfield Pl EH42......78 A2
Winterthur La KY12.....29 A4
Winton Cl EH33..........126 E4
Winton Ct
 Cockenzie & Port Seton
  EH32 ....97 C4
 New Winton EH33 .....127 B3
 Tranent EH33 ....126 E4
Winton Dr EH10 ....150 C4
Winton Gdns EH10 .....150 C4
Winton Gr
 Edinburgh EH10........150 C4
 Tranent EH33..........126 E4
Wintonhill Cotts EH34...127 D7
Winton Ho EH33.........156 D7
Winton Loan
 Edinburgh EH10........150 C4
 Macmerry EH33........127 A6
Winton Pk
 Cockenzie & Port Seton
  EH32 ....97 C3
 Edinburgh EH10........150 B4
Winton Pl EH33..........126 D6
Winton Terr
 Edinburgh EH10........150 C4
 New Winton EH33 .....127 B3
Winton Way EH33........126 D4
Wishart Ave
 Bonnyrigg and Lasswade
  EH19 ....173 D8
 North Berwick EH39 ...54 C6
Wishart Dr FK7 ....7 D3
Wishart Pl Dalkeith EH22..152 E2
 Kirkcaldy KY1..........17 B2
Wishaw Terr EH7.........94 B1
Wisp Gn EH15 ....123 B4
Wisp The Dalkeith EH22..123 B1
 Edinburgh EH15,EH16..123 B3
Witchbrae KY2 ....29 B4
Witholm EH22............153 E2
Wolfe Rd EH11...........60 D4
Wolfstar Farm Cotts
 EH35.................155 F6
Wolrige Rd EH16........151 A8
Wolseley Cres EH8 .....94 C1
Wolseley Pl EH8.........94 C1
Wolseley Terr 8 EH8...94 C1
Wolsey Ave EH19 ......173 C6
Wood's Ct EH19 ....173 B7

Woodbank KY4 ....13 B2
Woodbank Crofts EH48...110 F2
Woodbank Gr KY11 ....26 D7
Woodbine Gdns 1 EH32..96 F1
Woodbine Terr EH6 ......94 A3
Woodburn Ave
 Dalkeith EH22 ....153 C2
 Redding FK2............61 B2
Woodburn Bank EH22...153 C3
Woodburn Cres
 Bonnyrigge FK4 ....57 F3
 Oakley KY12...........26 F7
 Redding FK2...........61 B2
Woodburn Dr Alloa FK10...4 F1
 Dalkeith EH22 ....153 B3
Woodburn Gdns
 Dalkeith EH22 ....153 C3
 Falkirk FK2.............60 E5
Woodburn Gr EH22 ....153 C2
Woodburn Loan EH22 ..153 C3
Woodburn Medway
 EH22 ....153 C2
Woodburn Pk EH22 ....153 C2
Woodburn Pl EH22......153 C2
Woodburn Prim Sch
 EH22 ....153 C3
Woodburn Rd
 Dalkeith EH22 ....153 C2
 Falkirk FK2.............60 D5
Woodburn St
 Dalkeith EH22 ....153 C3
 Falkirk FK2.............60 E5
Woodburn Terr
 Dalkeith EH22 ....153 C2
 Edinburgh EH10........121 B3
Woodburn View EH22 ..153 C3
Woodburn Way FK12 .....5 A6
Woodbush EH42 ....78 E2
Woodbush Brae EH42 ...78 E2
Woodbush Ct EH42 ......78 E2
Woodbush Pl EH42 ......78 E2
Wood Dr EH47............160 F6
Woodend Gdns KY11....47 F5
Woodend Ind Est KY4....29 A3
Woodend Pk EH26 .....171 F3
Woodend Pl KY4 ....13 B1
Woodend Rd ML8........215 A2
Woodend Wlk EH48....139 E6
Woodfield Ave EH13 ....148 F6
Woodfield Pk
 Bilston EH25 ....171 D6
 Edinburgh EH13........148 F6
Woodhall Ave EH14 ....148 D6
Woodhall Bank EH13...148 F5
Woodhall Cotts EH47 ...135 F6
Woodhall Dr EH14 ......148 D6
Woodhall Gr EH13 ......148 F5
Woodhall Millbrae EH14.148 E6
Woodhall Pl EH34.......156 E6
Woodhall Rd
 Edinburgh EH13........148 F5
 Pencaitland EH34 .....156 D6
Woodhall Terr EH14 ...148 D6
Woodhead Farm Rd KY12.25 F2
Woodhead Gr EH48 .....139 D5
Woodhead Pl EH48 .....140 E6
Woodhead Rd KY12.....26 A2
Woodhill Cl KY13 ....61 D6
Woodhill Gr KY12.......28 B2
Woodhill Pl KY11........29 A3
Woodhill Rd KY11........29 B3
Woodhill St KY11........29 B3
Woodhill Terr KY11.......29 B3
Woodmuir Pl EH55.......182 E6
Woodmuir Prim Sch
 EH55.................182 E6
Woodmuir Rd
 Breich EH55...........182 E6
 Whitburn EH47 ....161 G6
Wood Pl Livingston EH54.143 C4
 Rosyth KY11 ....46 E5
Wood Rd KY11...........46 C2
Woodrow EH21 ....174 C1
Woodruff Gait KY12.....28 F5
Woodrush Glade EH54...13 C3
Woodside Ave KY11......46 D6
Woodside Ct
 Cambusbarron FK7......6 D5
 Falkirk FK1.............60 B3

Woodside Dr EH26......191 F5
Woodside Gdns
 Grangemouth FK2......82 E8
 Musselburgh EH21 ....124 E6
Woodside Gr FK5 ....59 D8
Woodside Pl
 Bridgend EH49.........86 C4
 Fallin FK7..............8 C4
Woodside Rd Alloa FK10...4 F1
 Forrestfield ML6 ......137 A3
 Stirling FK8 ....2 A3
 Tullibody FK10 ....4 A1
Woodside St KY11 ....46 F5
Woodside Terr
 Bridgend EH49.........86 C4
 Clackmannan FK10 .....10 F4
 Edinburgh EH15........123 D7
 Falkirk FK1.............60 B3
 Tarbrax EH55..........203 F3
Wood St FK3.............61 C7
Woodstock Pl EH16......122 B1
Wood Terr EH48 ....140 A6
Woodville Ct EH52 .....115 D4
Woodville Terr EH6......94 A3
Wooer St 4 FK1..........60 B4
Woodcarders Ct FK7.....6 D6
Woolfords Cotts EH55...203 A7
Woolmet Cres EH22.....152 B8
Wordie Rd FK7 ....6 F4
World's End Cl EH1 .....229 B3
Wotherspoon Cres EH48 .139 F3
Wotherspoon Dr EH51...63 D6
W Parliament Sq EH1 ...229 A3
Wright Pl Kirkcaldy KY1 ..17 D7
 Lochgelly KY5 ....14 A3
Wright St FK2 ....60 B6
Writer's Mus EH1........229 A3
Writers Ct EH42 ....78 D3
Wycklieffe KY12..........28 C6
Wymet Ct KY12..........29 A3
Wymet Ho KY12..........29 A3
Wyndford Ave EH52....115 A5
Wyndford Brae EH49 ....86 E7
Wyndford Pl EH52.......115 A5
Wynd The Alva FK12 .....5 A7
 Dalgety Bay KY11......48 C3
 Gifford EH41 ....220 F6
 Ormiston EH35 ....155 F7
Wyre Hayes Cotts KY4 ..30 F8
Wyvern Pk EH9..........121 D4
Wyvis Pl EH26............192 A7
Wyvis Pl ML7 ....180 B3

Y
Yardheads EH6 ....93 F5
Yardley Pl FK2 ....39 A1
Yarrow Ct EH26 ....192 A7
Yarrow Pl FK3 ....29 A3
Yeaman La EH11 ....120 F6
Yeaman Pl EH11 ....120 F5
Yellowcraig Trail EH39 ...53 B8
Yester Mains Cotts EH41.220 F1
Yester Pl EH41,EH22....100 F1
Yester Prim Sch EH41...220 F6
Yetholm Pk KY12........28 F2
Yetts The FK7............6 C5
Yew Gr EH54 ....148 B5
Yewlands Cres EH16....151 B7
Yewlands Gdns EH16...151 B7
Yew Terr FK2 ....61 A2
Yieldshields Rd ML8 ...216 D3
York Arc FK3 ....40 D1
York Bldgs EH1 ....229 A3
York Dr FK2 ....40 D6
York La Edinburgh EH1 ..229 A4
 Grangemouth FK3......40 D1
York Pl Dunfermline KY12..29 A4
 Edinburgh EH1.........229 A4
 Kirkcaldy KY1..........17 F8
York Rd Edinburgh EH5...93 C6
 North Berwick EH39 ...54 A7
York Sq FK3.............40 D1
York St Edinburgh EH5 ..93 C6
Young's Terr 2 KY1.....17 C5
Young Ave EH33 ....126 D5
Young Cres EH48 ....140 F5
Young Ct KY4 ....13 C3
Young Sq EH54 ....164 B6
Youngs Rd EH52 ....116 A6
Young St Edinburgh FK2..228 B3
Young Street La N EH2..228 B3
Young Street La S EH2..228 B3
Young Terr KY4 ....13 B3
Yule Pl EH47............141 C1
Yule Terr EH47 ....162 C8

Z
Zealandia Rd KY11......46 B1
Zetland Dr
 Grangemouth FK3......61 A8
 Laurieston FK2.........61 A4
Zetland Pl Edinburgh EH5..93 B6
 Lochgelly KY5 ....14 A7
 Skinflats FK3 ....39 F3
Zetland St FK10 ....11 B4
Zetland Terr FK2.........61 F2

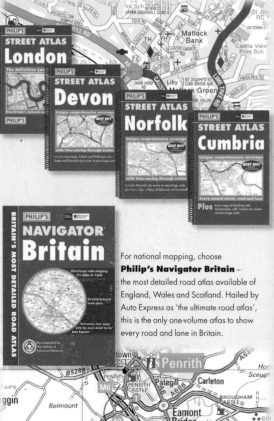